Illinois Real Estate Law
for Paralegals

Illinois Real Estate Law for Paralegals

Transactions and Landlord-Tenant Law

Thomas Wendt

CAROLINA ACADEMIC PRESS

Durham, North Carolina

ISBN 978-1-53100-025-7
eISBN 978-1-53100-169-8
LCCN 2017938481

Carolina Academic Press, LLC
700 Kent Street
Durham, North Carolina 27701
Telephone (919) 489-7486
Fax (919) 493-5668
www.cap-press.com

Printed in the United States of America

Contents

Author's Notes and Acknowledgments

The author wishes to acknowledge the following people and organizations for their assistance in the assembly of this material.

Illinois Real Estate Lawyers Association (IRELA). The Multi-Board Residential Real Estate Contract 6.0 is the property of the IRELA.
American Land Title Association
Illinois Legal Aid Online
Truman College, one of the City Colleges of Chicago
Wright College, one of the City Colleges of Chicago

Please note: This text is intended for informational and instructional use only. Nothing in this text is intended to be taken as legal advice and nothing in this text is intended as a substitute of the advice of an attorney. If an attorney is required for representation, it is recommended to contact the local bar association or the IRELA website for referrals to an experienced real estate attorney.

Illinois Real Estate Law
for Paralegals

Chapter 1

Introduction to Real Estate Transactions

Learning Objectives

After studying Chapter 1, you will be able to:

- Identify the primary forms of real estate law
- Categorize the various forms of property
- Differentiate between the various methods of owning and conveying property

Chapter Summary

Topics covered:

- Introduction to Real Estate Law
- Forms of Ownership
- Participants in Real Estate Transactions and Their Roles

This chapter introduces basic concepts of residential real estate transactions in Illinois. The chapter begins with a brief discussion about why a real estate attorney is necessary in a residential real estate transaction. The chapter then discusses the different forms of property. The chapter looks at how paralegals are utilized within a real estate law office. The chapter concludes with various ways to own property and with a relatively new concept in Illinois real estate law, the Transfer on Death Instrument.

1. Introduction

Real estate law affects almost everyone. Almost everyone leases, rents, or owns/purchases an apartment or house at some point or another. Buying a house or condominium is the most significant financial decision most people make in their lifetime, and the real estate attorney is an integral part of the transaction. The practice of real estate transactional law is not glamorous; the popular conception of what a lawyer does usually does not include transactional work. Unfortunately, this perception has led to a diminution in the role of the attorney in the transaction, and lawyers have only themselves to blame for this misconception. However, real estate law is an important area of law and real estate attorneys play, and should continue to play, a vital role in the real estate transaction.

This text covers the basics of residential real estate law, with an emphasis on the residential real estate transaction. In addition, leasing and landlord-tenant law will be addressed. Each chapter will have a section on the law and a section on the role of the paralegal. By the end of this text, the student should have the requisite knowledge and understanding of the legal concepts of real estate law to work in the real estate law field.

There are six primary forms of real estate law:

1) **Residential Real Estate Transaction.** Residential real estate transactions are the process of buying and selling residential properties. This is the primary focus of this text.

2) **Commercial Real Estate Transaction.** Commercial real estate transactions involve the acquisition and dispossession of commercial real estate. Included in commercial real estate are office buildings and office leasing, retail property and retail leasing, residential apartment buildings, and other commercial spaces.

3) **Leasing and Rental.** Included in leasing and rental are tenancies, leaseholds, and evictions. This is what is often referred to as landlord-tenant law.

4) **Commercial Leasing.** Included in commercial leasing are letters of inquiry, commercial leases, covenants, and subordination agreements.

5) **Real Estate Litigation.** Real estate litigation involves court litigation in regards to real estate, including breach of contract, quiet title, ownership disputes, claims for property damage, adverse possession claims, and other forms of litigation. There are a variety of issues involved in the litigation and litigation may involve acquisitions, sales, financing, brokerage, zoning, leasing, land use matters, and building code/municipal code violations. Real estate litigation may also include real estate foreclosure, tax sales, and redemption actions.

6) **Real Estate Taxation.** Real estate taxation involves the valuation of properties and contesting real estate taxation. It also involves situations where the property has been sold for "unpaid taxes" and the owner attempts to "redeem" the property taxes.

2. The Lawyer's Role in Real Estate Transactions in General

There has been controversy in the past over the need for counsel in real estate transactions (see *Chicago Bar Ass'n. v. Quinlan & Tyson, Inc.*, 34 Ill. 2d 116 (1966) in Chapter 2). It is important to remember that only real estate attorneys can adequately protect the interests of the Buyer or Seller. In many states, lawyers are not involved in real estate transactions. In the Chicago area, and in most of Illinois, the Buyer and Seller generally will have representation in real estate transactions. However, even in Chicago, parties (especially Buyers) sometimes do not have representation in real estate transactions. The reason for this lack of representation is the perception that the lawyer's services are unnecessary and costly.

As will be explained throughout this text, this can be a very dangerous idea. The attorney plays a vital role navigating the real estate transaction from start to finish, drafting the requisite documents, and advocating for, and protecting the interests of, the client. In some states, real estate document preparers and escrow companies prepare the Closing documents and close the transaction, so lawyers may not be as involved in the transaction. However, a lawyer is recommended even under those circumstances.

3. Why Is an Attorney Needed in Real Estate Transactions?

As will be demonstrated throughout this text, an attorney is absolutely necessary in a real estate transaction. An individual Buyer or Seller has an unfettered right to represent themselves in a transaction, just as an individual has a right to represent themselves in almost any case. However, as in any other legal matter, the unrepresented individual, who is acting *pro se*, takes tremendous risks.

There are several reasons why Buyers and Sellers should hire a private attorney to represent them in the transaction.

1. Only an attorney can provide legal counsel and legal advice to a client. Real estate brokers, mortgage companies, title officers, and governmental agencies all play a role in the real estate transaction, but the attorney, and *only* the attorney, may provide much needed legal advice and advocacy. Any other professional who provides legal advice is committing the unauthorized practice of law, which, under the Illinois Attorney Act 705 ILCS 205/1 (see below), is illegal in Illinois.

2. Many specific issues require the advice of an attorney.

3. Although real estate contracts have been standardized, they are complex, and although there is no requirement that they be drafted by an attorney, there are serious ramifications if they are not drafted correctly. Only attorneys (not real estate brokers) are allowed to make substantive changes to the contracts through the attorney approval clause.

4. The trained attorney can objectively review financing documents and advise clients on the documents. When representing the Buyer, only the real estate attorney has the interest of the Buyer at heart, without conflicts. The other parties to the transaction, the Buyer's real estate broker, the mortgage broker (or lender), and the title company, all have a vested interested in the Buyer paying as high of a price for the property as possible, since their relative incomes are based upon the sales price of

the property that the Buyer pays. Buyers' brokers will say that the price the Buyer pays is never a factor in determining their representation of the Buyer (and, in fact, it is an ethical violation for them to put their interests over the interests of the client), but the fact remains that they do have a vested interest in the Buyer paying the maximum purchase price for any property.

5. Title insurance issues arise. Only an attorney can adequately address these issues in conjunction with the title company.

6. Finally, the real estate transaction attorney is one of the greatest bargains, not only in law, but in all of business. The service that the attorney provides is a tremendous value, considering the amounts that a real estate attorney charges, which average approximately $450–$600 per transaction.

> 705 ILCS 205/1

> Any person practicing, charging or receiving fees for legal services or advertising or holding himself or herself out to provide legal services within this State, either directly or indirectly, without being licensed to practice as herein required, is guilty of contempt of court and shall be punished accordingly, upon complaint being filed in any Circuit Court of this State. The remedies available include, but are not limited to: (i) appropriate equitable relief; (ii) a civil penalty not to exceed $5,000, which shall be paid to the Illinois Equal Justice Foundation; and (iii) actual damages. Such proceedings shall be conducted in the Courts of the respective counties where the alleged contempt has been committed in the same manner as in cases of indirect contempt and with the right of review by the parties thereto.

> The provisions of this Act shall be in addition to other remedies permitted by law and shall not be construed to deprive courts of this State of their inherent right to punish for contempt or to restrain the unauthorized practice of law.

4. Definition of "Property"

There are two primary "forms" of property—real property and personal property. In a real estate transaction, the form of property is very important, as it may influence how (or even if) the property is conveyed to the Buyer in the transaction.

Real property is land and all things that are permanently attached to land. Houses, garages, trees, in-ground swimming pools, and sheds on a concrete foundation are all part of real property. In addition, property that may have been personal property (see below), but has become affixed to real property (called "fixtures") is treated as real property for purposes of the real estate transaction. In general, when owning "real property" the owner owns the land, everything located on the land, the minerals below the surface, and the rights to the air above the surface.

Personal property is all property that is not real property. Things that can be possessed, moved (without damaging real property), and conveyed are personal property. There are two primary forms of personal property—tangible and intangible personal property.

Tangible personal property is that property where the value of the property is the thing itself. This textbook, a pen, and a car are all tangible personal property. The value of the property is the book itself. If you buy this textbook and destroy it in frustration (and it is hoped you do not do that, but if you do, wait until after the final exam), you are out the textbook and its value. The value of the textbook was the price you paid for it and, while the knowledge contained has a value, it is the physical book that you purchased.

Intangible personal property is that property that either does not have a physical presence or, more likely, that the physical thing is representative of some other value. For example — copyrights, shares of stock, and checks are intangible personal property.

If you write a check for $200.00 and present it to your professor so you will receive an "A" in the class (not that this is recommended) and your professor tears up the check (since bribing a professor is just wrong), are you out the $200.00? No, you are not. The check was representative of the fact that you had $200.00 (or more) in your account and that you were conveying that $200.00 to your professor. You could simply write another check if needed.

Some items can be both tangible and intangible personal property. An original work of art is both tangible (it exists in the real world and has a physical presence on its own), and is intangible in that the value of the work of art is representative of the artist's skill, technique, and reputation. You go to the art museum and you look at an original Picasso. Then you go to the museum book store and see a lithograph or student-painted copy of that painting. The original Picasso is valued in the millions of dollars, while the lithograph or copy is $60.00.

What is the difference between the two? They are both the "same" artwork, correct? They are both a combination of paper/canvas, paint/ink, time, and technique. They may look almost exactly alike. The original is worth millions of dollars as it *represents* the work, experience, and reputation of Picasso, as well as its rarity (since it is a "unique" piece of art and Picasso is dead and cannot paint any additional pictures). The value is also that it is the actual work of Picasso, while the lithograph is simply a "copy" of the original. For these reasons, it is intangible personal property.

However, it is also tangible personal property. If you were at the museum and destroyed the original (again, do not that!), the museum would be out the millions of dollars paid for that painting (and you would likely go to jail). Unlike the check, which could be replaced with another check at the same value, the painting would be forever destroyed. Simply hanging the copy would not suffice, as the copy has almost no value, beyond the combination of materials that went into making it.

What about currency, good old cash? Is that tangible or intangible personal property? Well, it is both, really. It is tangible personal property as a $10.00 bill can be exchanged for $10.00 worth of goods or services and if you destroy the $10.00 bill (not that this is recommended), you are out the $10.00. However, it is also intangible personal property in that the *value* of the money is beyond the "paper" (although currency is made primarily of linen and cotton) and the ink that went into making it. What gives money value? Many people think it is gold or silver. Historically, this was true, but it is no longer the case. There is not enough gold in the world to support the US currency. The US abandoned the gold standard as of June 6, 1933, when it was declared against public policy for anyone to demand to be paid in gold, as opposed to currency (with subsequent laws in 1934 and later). In 1971, President Nixon declared that US currency would no longer be convertible into gold.

So, if gold is not supporting our currency, what does? The US dollar is a "fiat" currency, and it is therefore not backed by any tangible commodity, but rather the "full faith and credit of the United States," as is printed on every Federal Reserve note. The bill states "In God We Trust," but really it should be "In US, We Trust." It is the collective belief of our creditors, our manufacturers, and our consumers that gives money its value. It is our collective belief that money has value that gives it value.

Cash is intangible, since the value of a dollar is representative of the collective "full faith and credit" of the United States. However, it is also tangible, since if you burn a $10.00 bill, you are out the $10.00.

Fixtures. A fixture is an item of tangible personal property that has been "affixed" to real property in such a way as to become part of the real property. For example, a stove is tangible personal property. A built-in stove and oven, that is part of the structure of the kitchen, is a fixture. A washing machine sitting in the basement is tangible personal property. A built-in washer/dryer is a fixture.

What determines if something is a fixture is important. If there is a dispute about whether an item is "personal property" or a "fixture," there are several factors to be taken into consideration. The determining factors include: (1) the extent to which the item is "affixed" to the real property; (2) how the item and the real property were adapted to "affix" the item; (3) the intent of the owner of the real property to affix the personal property; and (4) most importantly, the existence of any agreement between the parties to the transaction.

For example, if the owner buys a set of shelves, that would be tangible personal property. The owner assembles the shelving unit and leans the unit against the wall. It is still personal property. The owner notices that the unit is unstable, so the owner uses a small L-shaped bracket (supplied by the manufacturer) to "stabilize" the unit. The owner does this by screwing the bracket to the shelving unit and to the wall.

What is the status of the shelving unit—personal property or a fixture? It depends on the criteria described above. The item is only "affixed" by two screws, could be removed without really damaging the real property (other than leaving a small screw hole in the wall), and the owner's intent was only to "stabilize" the unit and not to make it part of the real property, like a "built-in" bookcase would be. However, the Buyer of the property could argue that, by screwing it to the wall, the owner had made it part of the real property and, thus, it is a fixture. During a real estate transaction, this can be a major source of controversy. It is important (see Chapter 2) that items of personal property and fixtures are clearly delineated *in the contract*, to document the intent of the parties.

Of course, the best way to resolve a controversy of this type is to avoid the controversy. If the Seller wants to make sure that the set of shelves are not considered a fixture by the Buyer, the Seller could simply unscrew the shelves from the wall prior to listing the house for sale. That way, there would be no question as to whether the shelves were personal property or a fixture.

Conveyance of Property

Property can be conveyed in a number of ways. The most common include gift, inheritance, and sale. How the property is conveyed may have tax and other implications.

Gift. A gift is a conveyance of property without an expectation of return. The conveyor is called the "donor" and the recipient is called the "donee." Once a gift is conveyed ("given" to the recipient) it is complete and the donor loses all right to return. A gift must be unconditional to be considered a gift. If the gift has "strings attached" (called "conditions") it is not really a gift. It is the donor, and not the donee, who pays any taxes on the gift. There is an annual exemption of the "gift tax" and certain gifts (such as gifts between spouses, gifts of school payments made directly to the school, gifts of medical expenses given directly to the healthcare provider, and certain political gifts) are excluded from the gift tax.

Inheritance. In order to inherit property, there must be a relationship between the decedent and the recipient (often called an "heir"). Traditionally, leaving real property in a will was called a "devise" and the person who inherited was called a "devisee" (for personal property it was called a "bequest" and "bequestee"), although those terms are rather archaic now. Another way that a property may be inherited is through "**intestate succession.**" In Illinois, the Intestate Succession Act may be found at 755 ILCS 5/2-1. The Intestate Succession Act specifies who inherits a decedent's estate if there is no will, based on a strict hierarchy of relation.

Sale. For a sale, there must be a contract (see Chapter 2). To form a contract, there must be a "meeting of the minds" between the Grantor (Seller) and Grantee (Buyer). Both parties must have capacity (the legal ability to enter into the contract), the contract must be for a legal purpose, there must be "consideration" (an exchange of one thing for another, sometimes called a "promise for a promise") and many contracts must be in writing in order to be enforceable. The types of contracts that must be in writing include:

Contracts in contemplation of	Marriage
Contracts that cannot be completed within a	Year
Contracts for the sale of	Land
Contracts (such as wills) for	Estates
Contracts (over $500) for the sale of	Goods
Contracts to act for another, to be a	Surety

The mnemonic MY LEGS covers the basic contracts that must be in writing. Please note, there are variety of laws involved, including the Frauds Act ("Statute of Frauds") (740 ILCS 80/2), the Uniform Commercial Code (810 ILCS 5), the Uniform Premarital Agreement Act (750 ILCS 10/1), and the Illinois Wills Act (755 ILCS 5/4).

810 ILCS 5/2-201

Sec. 2-201. Formal requirements; statute of frauds.

(1) Except as otherwise provided in this Section a contract for the sale of goods for the price of $500 or more is not enforceable by way of action or defense unless there is some writing sufficient to indicate that a contract for sale has been made between the parties and signed by the party against whom enforcement is sought or by his authorized agent or broker. A writing is not insufficient because it omits or incorrectly states a term agreed upon but the contract is not enforceable under this paragraph beyond the quantity of goods shown in such writing.

(2) Between merchants if within a reasonable time a writing in confirmation of the contract and sufficient against the sender is received and the party receiving it has reason to know its contents, it satisfies the requirements of subsection (1) against such party unless written notice of objection to its contents is given within 10 days after it is received.

(3) A contract which does not satisfy the requirements of subsection (1) but which is valid in other respects is enforceable

(a) if the goods are to be specially manufactured for the buyer and are not suitable for sale to others in the ordinary course of the seller's business and the seller, before notice of repudiation is received and under circumstances which reasonably indicate that the goods are for the buyer, has made either a substantial beginning of their manufacture or commitments for their procurement; or

(b) if the party against whom enforcement is sought admits in his pleading, testimony or otherwise in court that a contract for sale was made, but the contract is not enforceable under this provision beyond the quantity of goods admitted; or

(c) with respect to goods for which payment has been made and accepted or which have been received and accepted (Section 2-606).

740 ILCS 80/) Frauds Act.

Sec. 0.01. Short title. This Act may be cited as the Frauds Act.

(740 ILCS 80/2) (from Ch. 59, par. 2)

Sec. 2. No action shall be brought to charge any person upon any contract for the sale of lands, tenements or hereditaments or any interest in or concerning them, for a longer term than one year, unless such contract or some memorandum or note thereof shall be in writing, and signed by the party to be charged therewith, or some other person thereunto by him lawfully authorized in writing, signed by such party. This section shall not apply to sales for the enforcement of a judgment for the payment of money or sales by any officer or person pursuant to a judgment or order of any court in this State.

(740 ILCS 80/3) (from Ch. 59, par. 3)

Sec. 3. The consideration of any such promise or agreement need not be set forth or expressed in the writing, but may be proved or disproved by parol or other legal evidence.

(740 ILCS 80/8) (from Ch. 59, par. 8)

Sec. 8. This act shall not extend to any estate or interest in any lands, goods or chattels, or any rents, common or profit, out of the same, which shall be upon good consideration, and bona fide lawfully conveyed or assured to any person, bodies politic or corporate.

(740 ILCS 80/9) (from Ch. 59, par. 9)

Sec. 9. All declarations or creations of trusts or confidences of any lands, tenements or hereditaments, shall be manifested and proved by some writing signed by the party who is by law enabled to declare such trust, or by his last will in writing; or else they shall be utterly void and of no effect: Provided, that resulting trust or trusts created by construction, implication or operation of law, need not be in writing, and the same may be proved by parol.

(750 ILCS 10/1) Sec. 1. This Article shall be known and may be cited as the Illinois Uniform Premarital Agreement Act.

(750 ILCS 10/3)

Sec. 3. Formalities. A premarital agreement must be in writing and signed by both parties. It is enforceable without consideration.

(755 ILCS 5/) Wills Act

(755 ILCS 5/4-3)

Sec. 4-3. Signing and attestation.

(a) Every will shall be in writing, signed by the testator or by some person in his presence and by his direction and attested in the presence of the testator by 2 or more credible witnesses.

(b) A will that qualifies as an international will under the Uniform International Wills Act is considered to meet all the requirements of subsection (a).

It is important to remember that the parties to the contract must have the capacity to enter into the contract. If a party lacks the ability to contract, called "**contract capacity**" (due to age, illness, incapacity, or disability), that person cannot execute a contract and have that contract be enforceable. If the owner of the property has lost the capacity to enter into the contract, a third party decision-maker may be able to step in sign the contract on behalf of the incapacitated individual. For instance, if the owner executed a **Power of Attorney for Property**, naming someone as an agent (also called an "attorney-in-fact" or, colloquially, a POA), that agent could enter into the contract on behalf of the incapacitated owner. In order to execute the Power of Attorney for Property, the individual (called the "Principal") must have capacity at the time of signing the document. Powers of Attorney are called "Advance Directives" as they allow a person with capacity to appoint an agent, to be used in the future if the Principal is unable or unavailable to make decisions.

Powers of Attorney also may be used when someone is buying or selling a piece of property and will not be present at the Closing of the transaction. That person appoints an agent under a Power of Attorney for Property to appear on the Principal's behalf. This is common in sales of investment property, where the Seller will not be present, so the Seller appoints (through a Power of Attorney) the lawyer to sign the final conveyance documents (see Chapter 9). Also, when a couple is purchasing a piece of property and one spouse will not be available to attend the Closing, one spouse may appoint the other spouse as agent to sign the necessary Closing documents.

Another possibility for an incapacitated owner, who has not executed a valid Power of Attorney for Property, is a **guardianship of the estate**. A guardianship is a court proceeding that occurs when someone has lost the ability to make decisions and a third party, often a family member, (called the"**petitioner**") goes to court (generally the Probate Court in Illinois) and "petitions" the court to have the incapacitated individual declared "disabled under law" and requests the court to appoint the petitioner guardian over the incapacitated individual. Guardianships are long, drawn-out court procedures that may take a significant amount of time and money to complete. However, once completed, the "**guardian of the estate**" would have the right and responsibility to properly oversee the estate, property, and money of the incapacitated individual (called the "**ward**" after the guardianship has been established), including the right to contract, sell, and convey real property.

5. What Does a Real Estate Paralegal Do?

Paralegals are very heavily involved in all aspects of the real estate transaction. Many real estate law firms' work depend on their real estate paralegals. Client intakes, correspondences, drafting documents, and attending Closings are all handled by real estate paralegals, under the guidance and supervision of the attorney. In addition, paralegals are often employed by title companies, real estate companies, and governmental agencies involved in real estate transactions.

Paralegals might:

- Meet with clients or potential clients.
- Review contracts for critical dates and monitor calendars for deadlines.
- Draft contracts, addenda, and modifications.
- Draft the preliminary review of contracts.
- Conduct title searches or order title searches.
- Draft legal descriptions to be used for the deed and other Closing documents.
- Review surveys and condominium plats.
- Obtain Closing figures from the bank.
- Prepare deeds or other Closing documents.
- Research and prepare municipal documents.
- Prorate real estate taxes.

- Draft Closing statements and arrange Closing dates.
- Arrange for payment and release of the mortgage.
- Notify the parties involved of the Closing time and location.
- Assist attorneys at Closing.
- Notarize documents for clients.
- Follow up on post-Closing items, including drafting Closing letters and closing out files.
- Draft leases.
- Analyze and abstract leases and other agreements.
- Draft eviction notices and complaints in eviction cases.

Ethics Alert:

It is important to note that, in Illinois, paralegals may not provide service directly to the public.

Paralegals must work under the supervision of a licensed attorney and ultimately the attorney remains responsible for all work undertaken by paralegals.

Throughout this text, we will discuss the role of the paralegal in the real estate transaction. Examples of the documents involved in the real estate transaction will be provided and written exercises will be assigned.

6. Forms of Ownership

The *highest* form of property ownership that a person can have is a grant in **Fee Simple** (sometimes referred to as "Fee Simple Absolute"). A Fee Simple grants ownership of the real estate from someone (the "**Grantor**") to a person (the "**Grantee**") unconditionally and absolutely. There may be a sole owner of the property or multiple owners in Fee Simple. However, regardless of the number of owners, the owner or owners have sole control of the property.

Fee Simple Defeasible

A Fee Simple may be unconditional or conditions may be placed upon the ownership. If there are conditions placed upon the ownership, it is called a **Fee Simple Defeasible**. If the condition is violated or there is a condition that is not met, then the property will either go back to the original Grantor or a specified third party. Please note, these are extremely rare and generally only occur in gratuitous situations (like a rich landowner donating land to a school) or under very unusual circumstances. They are generally not part of a typical real estate transaction.

Types of Fee Simple Defeasible

There are three types of Fee Simple Defeasible transactions. Two confer future property interests back to the Grantor. In the third, the future interest goes to a specified third party.

1. Fee Simple Determinable

A Fee Simple Determinable automatically ends the interest in the property when a condition is violated or not met. The Grantor retains a "possibility of reverter," meaning that if the condition is violated the property will automatically shift back to the Grantor without any additional action.

In order to create a Fee Simple Determinable, the words of conveyance must be durational (e.g., as long as, so long as, during, while, or until).

Example: A to B so long as the property is used as a school. B would have a Fee Simple interest in the property so long as the property is used as a school. If, however, the property is no longer used as a school, then the property will automatically go back to A.

2. Fee Simple Subject to Condition Subsequent

A Fee Simple Subject to a Condition Subsequent is very similar to the Fee Simple Determinable except that the violation of the condition would give the Grantor the option to take back the property. The property does not automatically shift to the Grantor. Instead, upon violation of the condition, the Grantor has the option to reassert his right to the property. This option is called a "right of reentry."

In order to convey a Fee Simple Subject to a Condition Subsequent, the words of conveyance must state that the Grantor can reenter and retake the property if the condition is violated.

Example: A to B, but if the property is used for commercial purposes, then A has a right of reentry. Again, B has a Fee Simple interest in the property so long as the property is not used for commercial purposes. If, however, the property is used for commercial purposes, then A can retake the property.

3. Fee Simple Subject to Executory Limitation

A Fee Simple Subject to Executory Limitation is the same as a Fee Simple Determinable, except that it confers a future property interest in a third party, and not the Grantor.

In order to create a Fee Simple Subject to Executory Limitation, the Grantor uses either durational or conditional words that establish a condition and names a third party to whom the property would go if the condition is not met or is violated. Like a Fee Simple Determinable, the property shifts automatically and does not require the third party to take any action.

The third party interest is called a "**remainder**" interest.

Example: A to B only if the property is used as a place of residence; if not used as a place of residence, then to C. Thus, B has a Fee Simple interest in the property. If, however, the property is used as something other than a place of residence, then the property will automatically shift to C.

It is important to note that A, the Grantor, no longer has an interest in the property.

Adverse Possession

Adverse possession is a way to acquire legal title to property that was not legally acquired. Essentially, a person who is not legally entitled to the property possesses the property for a certain period of time. Normally, this would be considered a **trespass**, the intentional and unauthorized entry onto the land of another. Trespass is a **tort** (a civil wrong for which a remedy may be available) and may also be a crime. However, if the occupier of the property (called a "**Disseisor**") occupies the property for a certain period of time, the Disseisor may be able to stake a legal claim to the property, thus dispossessing the original owner.

There are five (5) primary requirements to raise an adverse possession claim. The Disseisor must be in:

- **Actual Possession**
- **Without the Permission of the Legal Owner**
- The Possession must be **Open and Notorious**
- The Possession must be **Continuous**
- **The Possession must be for the** Statutory Period of Time

In Illinois, adverse possession is a Statute of Limitations, as defined in 735 ILCS 5/13. Typically, it is a 20-year statute of limitations (735 ILCS 5/13-101), unless the Disseisor is paying the real estate taxes, in which case the limit is reduced to seven years (735 ILCS 5/13-109).

(735 ILCS 5/13-101) (from Ch. 110, par. 13-101)

Sec. 13-101. Twenty years—Recovery of land. No person shall commence an action for the recovery of lands, nor make an entry thereon, unless within 20 years after the right to bring such action or make such entry first accrued, or within 20 years after he, she or those from, by, or under whom he or she claims, have acquired title or possession of the premises, except as provided in Sections 13-102 through 13-122 of this Act.

(735 ILCS 5/13-102) (from Ch. 110, par. 13-102)

Sec. 13-102. Breach of condition subsequent. No person shall commence an action for the recovery of lands, nor make an entry thereon, by reason of the breach of a condition subsequent, unless within 7 years after the time that condition is first broken. Continuing, successive or recurring breaches shall not extend the time for commencing the action or making the entry. Possession shall be deemed to be adverse and hostile from and after the first breach of a condition subsequent, notwithstanding the occurrence of successive or recurrent breaches.

(735 ILCS 5/13-103) (from Ch. 110, par. 13-103)

Sec. 13-103. Termination of estate upon limitation. No person shall commence an action for the recovery of lands, nor make an entry thereon, by reason of the termination of an estate upon limitation or of an estate upon conditional limitation, unless within 7 years after the termination.

(735 ILCS 5/13-104) (from Ch. 110, par. 13-104)

Sec. 13-104. Under mortgage or lease. Nothing in Sections 13-102 and 13-103 of this Act affects the time for the enforcement of any right under or by virtue of a mortgage or lease.

(735 ILCS 5/13-105) (from Ch. 110, par. 13-105)

Sec. 13-105. Twenty years—Computation. If such right or title first accrued to an ancestor or predecessor of the person who brings the action or makes the entry, or to any person from, by, or under whom he or she claims, the 20 years shall be computed from the time when the right or title so first accrued.

(735 ILCS 5/13-106) (from Ch. 110, par. 13-106)

Sec. 13-106. Accrual of right of entry or to bring action. The right to make an entry or bring an action to recover land shall be deemed to have first accrued at the times respectively hereinafter provided:

(a) When any person is wrongfully ousted from possession, his or her right of entry or of action shall be deemed to have accrued at the time of such wrongful ouster.

(b) When he or she claims as heir or legatee of an owner in possession who died, his or her right shall be deemed to have accrued at the time of such death, unless there is an estate intervening after the death of such ancestor or testator; in which case his or her right shall be deemed to accrue when such intermediate estate expires, or when it would have expired by its own limitations.

(c) When there is such an intermediate estate, and in all other cases when the party claims by force of any remainder or reversion, his or her right, so far as it is affected by the limitation herein prescribed, shall be deemed to accrue when the intermediate or precedent estate would have expired by its own limitation, notwithstanding any forfeiture thereof for which he or she might have entered at an earlier time.

(d) Paragraph (c) of this Section shall not prevent a person from entering when entitled to do so by reason of any forfeiture or breach of condition; but if he or she claims under such a title, his or her right shall be deemed to have accrued when the forfeiture was incurred or the condition was broken.

(e) In all cases not otherwise specially provided for, the right shall be deemed to have accrued when the claimant, or the person under whom he or she claims, first became entitled to the possession of the premises under the title upon which the entry or the action is founded.

(735 ILCS 5/13-107) (from Ch. 110, par. 13-107)

Sec. 13-107. Seven years with possession and record title. Actions brought for the recovery of any lands, tenements or hereditaments of which any person may be possessed by actual residence thereon for 7 successive years, having a connected title, deductible of record, from this State or the United States, or from any public officer or other person authorized by the laws of this State to sell such land for the non-payment of taxes, or from any sheriff, marshal, or other person authorized to sell such land for the enforcement of a judgment or under any order or judgment of any court shall be brought within 7 years next after possession is taken, but when the possessor acquires such title after taking such possession, the limitation shall begin to run from the time of acquiring title.

(735 ILCS 5/13-108) (from Ch. 110, par. 13-108)

Sec. 13-108. Right extended to heirs. The heirs, legatees and assigns of the person having such title and possession, shall have the same benefit of the preceding Section as the person from whom the possession is derived.

(735 ILCS 5/13-109) (from Ch. 110, par. 13-109)

Sec. 13-109. Payment of taxes with color of title. Every person in the actual possession of lands or tenements, under claim and color of title, made in good faith, and who for 7 successive years continues in such possession, and also, during such time, pays all taxes legally assessed on such lands or tenements, shall be held and adjudged to be the legal owner of such lands or tenements, to the extent and according to the purport of his or her paper title. All persons holding under such possession, by purchase, legacy or descent, before such 7 years have expired, and who continue such possession, and continue to pay the taxes as above set forth so as to complete the possession and payment of taxes for the term above set forth, are entitled to the benefit of this Section.

(735 ILCS 5/13-110) (from Ch. 110, par. 13-110)

Sec. 13-110. Vacant land—Payment of taxes with color of title. Whenever a person having color of title, made in good faith, to vacant and unoccupied land, pays all taxes legally assessed thereon for 7 successive years, he or she shall be deemed and adjudged to be the legal owner of such vacant and unoccupied land, to the extent and according to the purport of his or her paper title. All persons holding under such taxpayer, by purchase, legacy or descent, before such 7 years expired, and who continue to pay the taxes, as above set out, so as to complete the payment of taxes for such term, are entitled to the benefit of this Section. However, if any person, having a better paper title to such vacant and unoccupied land, during the term of 7 years, pays the taxes assessed on such land for any one or more years of the term of 7 years, then such taxpayer, his or her heirs, legatees or assigns, shall not be entitled to the benefit of this Section. (Source: P.A. 83-707.)

(735 ILCS 5/13-111) (from Ch. 110, par. 13-111)

Sec. 13-111. State and United States. Sections 13-109 and 13-110 of this Act shall not extend to lands or tenements owned by the United States or of this State, nor to school and seminary lands, nor to lands held for the use of religious societies, nor to lands held for any public purpose. Nor shall they extend to lands or tenements when there is an adverse title to such lands or tenements, and the holder of such adverse title is a minor, person under legal disability, imprisoned, out of the limits of the United States, and in the employment of the United States or of this State. Such person shall commence an action to recover such lands or tenements so possessed, as above set out, within 3 years after the several disabilities herein enumerated cease to exist, and shall prosecute such action to judgment, or in case of vacant and unoccupied land, shall, within the time last set out, pay to the person or persons who have paid the same, all the taxes, with interest thereon, at the rate of 12% per annum, that have been paid on such vacant and unimproved land.

The exceptions provided in this Section shall not apply to the provisions of Sections 13-118 through 13-121 of this Act.

Legal Forms of Ownership

Anything bought, inherited, or received as a gift is owned under one of seven different legal forms of ownership. This includes everything, not just the more valuable assets such as houses, automobiles, investments, watercrafts, accounts, stocks, bonds, other real estate, etc.

The form of ownership is established when the person purchases an item, purchases a piece of property, sets up a bank account, or acquires ownership of the property. For certain items, particularly items of substantial value, the form of ownership may be stated on the documents of ownership, such as a car title, a deed to property, a bank account document, or other documentation.

Please note, that various forms of ownership have different rights and responsibilities and choosing the "correct" method to take title to property may affect many aspects of the ownership. There may be tax implications to one type of ownership over another. There may be restrictions on conveyance depending on the form of ownership. As shall be demonstrated throughout this text, the form of ownership plays a significant role in the decision-making process.

There are many forms of ownership. This text will only look at seven of the most common forms of ownership. Not all forms of ownership are available in all jurisdictions.

Sole

There is one owner and only one owner of the asset. This is, by far, the most common form of property ownership. The sole owner can do with the property as he/she sees fit, within the confines of the law. The owner has the right to possess, sell, convey, will, or otherwise dispose of the property. If the sole owner dies intestate (that is, dies without a will), the property will go to the sole owner's heirs, according to Illinois' Intestate Succession Act (see above).

Tenancy in Common

The asset is owned by two or more people together. Each owner has an "undivided ownership interest" in the property. There is an equal right to use the property, even though the actual percentages of ownership may not be equal.

There is no right of survivorship for tenants-in-common if one of the owners dies. Each tenant-in-common interest may be separately sold, mortgaged, given away, transferred, or willed to another person. If an owner dies, the property must go through probate and is left to the heirs of that tenant-in-common. Of course, if a tenant-in-common wishes to leave his/her interest to the other tenants-in-common, he/she may do so, but that must be done through a will or other estate planning documents. Intestate law does not provide an automatic right to inherit for the other tenants-in-common.

Joint Tenancy

Like tenancy in common, the asset is owned by two or more other people. Each joint tenant has an "undivided ownership interest" in the property. There is an equal right to use the property.

The major difference with joint tenants is that each joint tenant has the right of survivorship. Upon the death of one joint tenant, full title in the property is transferred to the surviving joint tenant(s) without going through probate.

To create a joint tenancy with right of survivorship, the ownership must satisfy the "**four unities**" of **time** (all tenants must take title at the same time), **title** (all tenants must take title by the same document, i.e., same deed), **interest** (all tenants must have an equal interest in the property), and **possession** (all tenants must have an equal and undivided right to possession). The default ownership in Illinois is tenancy in common, unless joint tenancy is specifically stated in the conveyance document (the deed or other conveyance document). The conveyance must state "in joint tenancy" or "as joint tenants" for a joint tenancy to be created.

The right of survivorship for joint tenancy even supersedes a will. If one of the joint tenants wills his or her interest in the property to a third party, that section of the will generally will not be valid, and the property will pass to the remaining joint tenants.

A joint tenancy is broken if one joint tenant conveys his/her interest to a third party. The remaining joint tenants become tenants-in-common with the outside party, while remaining joint tenants with one another. A joint tenancy may also be dissolved by agreement of the parties.

Another way to break a joint tenancy is through a partition suit, in which a court can break a joint tenancy and create a tenancy in common. In a partition suit, the court orders a division of the joint tenancy and can either force one joint tenant to buy out the other joint tenant(s) or order that the property be sold at auction.

If a third party wants to buy into a property that is currently owned in joint tenancy, all of the joint tenant owners must convey their interest to all of the new joint tenant owners.

Example: A, B, and C own the property as joint tenants. D wants to become joint tenant owner with A, B, and C. The conveyance would be: A, B, and C to A, B, C, and D in joint tenancy. This is creating a new deed (title), at once (time), equally (interest) and all four would have the right to use the property (possession), thus the four unities of title are created, and a new joint tenancy is established.

If they simply add "D" onto the title, D would be a tenant-in-common owner with A, B, and C. However, A, B, and C would remain joint tenants with each other.

Tenancy by the Entirety

Tenancy by the entirety is limited to married spouses' (or couples in a valid civil union) principal place of residence. Tenancy by the entirety must have the "four unities" of joint tenancy, but adds a fifth unity, "marriage," as only married couples may own property in tenancy by the entirety.

In Illinois, there is a sixth unity, as well—only the principal place of residence (also called the "homestead" see 765 ILCS 1005/1c, below) can be owned by a married couple in tenancy by the entirety (not investment property, second homes, personal property, etc.). The asset is owned by the spouses as tenants by the entirety. Like joint tenants, there is a right of survivorship upon the death of one of the spouses. Upon the death of one spouse, the property transfers to the surviving spouse without going through probate.

Tenancy by the entirety also protects the asset against collection for the debt owed by only one of the spouses. That is, if one spouse has specific debts attributable to that spouse only, the house may not be sold to satisfy the debt. However, if the debts are joint debts, this protection is not available.

The rationale for tenancy by the entirety is that the husband does not own a one-half interest and the wife does not own a one-half interest, but that the married couple owns the asset in its entirety.

Additionally, the property may not be transferred to a third party, nor may any interest in the property be transferred by one spouse, without the express consent of both spouses. Any attempt to effect such a transfer without the consent of the other spouse will generally be invalid. The legal fiction is that the house is owned by the "entirety" (the marriage) and not one-half for each spouse. As such, one spouse lacks the power to convey his/her interest to a third party.

In Illinois, tenancy by the entirety is the preferred method of taking title for a married couple's place of residence. Please note, however, that married couples taking title by tenancy by the entirety must elect to take title by tenancy by the entirety, and it is not a "default" method of taking title. Illinois courts have determined that there must be specific language in the conveyance document (the "deed") that states the couple is taking title by tenancy by the entirety. The deed should indicate that the parties are married and use specific words to create the tenancy. Typically, a Grantee clause in a deed would state: ".... to John Doe and Jane Doe, a married couple, not as tenants in common, nor as joint tenants with the right of survivorship, but as TENANTS BY THE ENTIRETY" (or in "TENANCY BY THE ENTIRETY").

Tenancy by the entirety may be terminated by selling the property, by the death of one spouse, satisfaction of a joint debt, through the divorce of the spouses, or by agreement between spouses.

Note, unmarried couples may never take title by tenancy by the entirety, no matter how long the couple has been together and no matter that it is the couple's principal place of residence. Same sex couples in Illinois may hold property through tenancy by the entirety, if they are in a valid civil union (through the Illinois Religious Freedom Protection and Civil Union Act, 750 ILCS 75) or in a valid marriage, and it is important to note that recent changes to the amendment to the Illinois Marriage and Dissolution of Marriage Act, 750 ILCS 5, (as well as the *Obergefell v. Hodges*, 576 U.S. ___, 135 S. Ct. 2584 (2015)) extend marriage to same sex couples.

750 ILCS 75/20.

A party to a civil union is entitled to the same legal obligations, responsibilities, protections, and benefits as are afforded or recognized by the law of Illinois to spouses, whether they derive from statute, administrative rule, policy, common law, or any other source of civil or criminal law.

In Illinois, joint tenancy and tenancy by the entirety ownership of property is governed by the Illinois Joint Tenancy Act.

765 ILCS 1005/0.01

Sec. 0.01. Short title. This Act may be cited as the Joint Tenancy Act.

765 ILCS 1005/1

Sec. 1. No estate in joint tenancy in any lands, tenements or hereditaments, or in any parts thereof or interest therein, shall be held or claimed under any grant, legacy or conveyance whatsoever heretofore or hereafter made, other than to executors and trustees, unless the premises therein mentioned shall expressly be thereby declared to pass not in tenancy in common but in joint tenancy; and every such estate other than to executors and trustees (unless otherwise expressly declared as aforesaid, or unless, as to a devise or conveyance of homestead property, expressly declared to pass to a husband and wife as tenants by the entirety in the manner provided by Section 1c), shall be deemed to be in tenancy in common and all conveyances heretofore made, or which hereafter may be made, wherein the premises therein mentioned were or shall be expressly declared to pass not in tenancy in common but in joint tenancy, are hereby declared to have created an estate in joint tenancy with the accompanying right of survivorship the same as it existed prior to the passage of "An Act to amend Section 1 of an Act entitled: 'An Act to revise the law in relation to joint rights and obligations,' approved February 25, 1874, in force July 1, 1874," approved June 26, 1917.

765 ILCS 1005/1a

Sec. 1a. Whenever any contract for the purchase of real estate hereafter entered into shows that the title is to be taken by the vendees as joint tenants and not as tenants in common, and one or more of such vendees die before the delivery of the deed to such vendees, then in such case no heir, legatee or legal representative of such deceased vendees shall have or take any right, title or interest under the contract or in such real estate, but the obligation of the vendor or vendors under the contract (upon the performance thereof) shall be to convey such real estate to such surviving vendee or vendees, and if all such vendees die before such delivery then to the heirs or legatees of the last survivor; but nothing herein contained shall operate to change the effect of any assignment by any of the above stated vendees.

765 ILCS 1005/1b

Sec. 1b. Whenever a grant or conveyance of lands, tenements, or hereditaments shall be made where the instrument of grant or conveyance does not create an estate in tenancy by the entirety in the manner provided by Section 1c but declares that the estate created be not in tenancy in common but with right of survivorship, or where such instrument of grant or conveyance does not create an estate in tenancy by the entirety in the manner provided by Section 1c but declares that the estate created be not in tenancy in common but in joint tenancy, the estate so created shall be an estate with right of survivorship notwithstanding the fact that the grantor is or the grantors are also named as a grantee or as grantees in said instrument of grant or conveyance. Said estate with right of survivorship, so created, shall have all of the effects of a common law joint tenancy estate.

This section shall not apply to nor operate to change the effect of any grant or conveyance made prior to the effective date of this amendatory Act.

765 ILCS 1005/1c

Sec. 1c. Whenever a devise, conveyance, assignment, or other transfer of property, including a beneficial interest in a land trust, maintained or intended for maintenance as a homestead by both husband and wife together during coverture shall be made and the instrument of devise, conveyance, assignment, or transfer expressly declares that the devise or conveyance is made to tenants by the entirety, or if the beneficial interest in a land trust is to be held as tenants by the entirety, the estate created shall be deemed to be in tenancy by the entirety. Where the homestead is held in the name or names of a trustee or trustees of a revocable inter vivos trust or of revocable inter vivos trusts made by the settlors of such trust or trusts who are husband and wife, and the husband and wife are the primary beneficiaries of one or both of the trusts so created, and the deed or deeds conveying title to the homestead to the trustee or trustees of the trust or trusts specifically state that the interests of the husband and wife to the homestead property are to be held as tenants by the entirety, the estate created shall be deemed to be a tenancy by the entirety. Subject to the provisions of paragraph (d) of Section 2 and unless otherwise assented to in writing by both tenants by the entirety, the estate in tenancy by the entirety so created shall exist only if, and as long as, the tenants are and remain married to each other, and upon the death of either such tenant the survivor shall retain the entire estate; provided that, upon a judgment of dissolution of marriage or of declaration of invalidity of marriage, the estate shall, by operation of law, become a tenancy in common until and unless the court directs otherwise; provided further that the estate shall, by operation of law, become a joint tenancy upon the creation and maintenance by both spouses together of other property as a homestead. A devise, conveyance, assignment, or other transfer to 2 grantees who are not in fact husband and wife that purports to create an estate by the entirety shall be construed as having created an estate in joint tenancy. An estate in tenancy by the entirety may be created notwithstanding the fact that a grantor is or the grantors are also named as a grantee or the grantees in a deed. No deed, contract for deed, mortgage, or lease of homestead property held in tenancy by the entirety shall be effective unless signed by both tenants. This Section shall not apply to nor operate to change the effect of any devise or conveyance.

This amendatory Act of 1995 is declarative of existing law.

765 ILCS 1005/2

Sec. 2. Except as to executors and trustees, and except also where by will or other instrument in writing expressing an intention to create a joint tenancy in personal property with the right of survivorship, the right or incident of survivorship as between joint tenants or owners of personal property is hereby abolished, and all such joint tenancies or ownerships shall, to all intents and purposes, be deemed tenancies in common. However, the foregoing shall not be deemed to impair or affect the rights, privileges and immunities set forth in the following paragraphs (a), (b), (c), (d) and (e):

(a) When a deposit in any bank or trust company transacting business in this State has been made or shall hereafter be made in the names of 2 or more persons payable to them when the account is opened or thereafter, the deposit or any part thereof or any interest or dividend thereon may be paid to any one of those persons whether the other or others be living or not, and when an agreement permitting such payment is signed by all those persons at the time the account is opened or thereafter the receipt or acquittance of the person so paid shall be valid and sufficient discharge from all parties to the bank for any payments so made.

(b) When shares of stock, bonds or other evidences of indebtedness or of interest are or have been issued or registered by any corporation, association or other entity in the names of 2 or more persons as joint tenants with the right of survivorship, the corporation, association or other entity and their respective transfer agents may, upon the death of any one of the registered owners, transfer those shares of stock, bonds, or other evidences of indebtedness or of interest to or upon the order of the survivor or survivors of the registered owners, without inquiry into the existence, validity or effect of any will or other instrument in writing or the right of the survivor or survivors to receive the property, and without liability to any other person who might claim an interest in or a right to receive all or a portion of the property so transferred.

(c) When shares of stock, bonds, or other evidences of indebtedness or of interest are or have been issued in the joint names of 2 or more persons or their survivors by corporations, including state chartered savings and loan associations, federal savings and loan associations, and state and federal credit unions, authorized to do business in this State, all payments on account thereof made then or thereafter, redemption, repurchase or withdrawal value or price, accumulations thereon, credits to, profits, dividends, or other rights thereon or accruing thereto may be paid or delivered in whole or in part to any of those persons whether the other person or persons be living or not, and when an agreement permitting such payment or delivery is signed by all those persons at the time when the shares of stock, bonds or evidences of indebtedness or of interest were issued or thereafter, the payment or delivery to any such person, or a receipt or acquittance signed by any such person, to whom any such payment or any such delivery of rights is made, shall be a valid and sufficient release and discharge of any such corporation for the payment or delivery so made.

(d) When the title to real property is held in joint tenancy by 2 or more persons or in tenancy by the entirety, and payment of compensation is made to any county treasurer for the taking or damaging of that real property in the manner provided for the exercise of the right of eminent domain under the Eminent Domain Act, or pursuant to any Act of the General Assembly now or hereafter enacted for the exercise of the sovereign power of eminent domain, the right of survivorship to the title in and to that real property shall be transferred to the money so paid to and in the hands of the county treasurer. However, upon application to the county treasurer holding the money by any joint tenant for his proportionate share thereof, or by any tenant by the entirety for a one half share thereof, he shall receive the same from the county treasurer without the consent or approval of any other joint tenant, and the person making the application shall have no survivorship rights in the balance remaining in the hands of the county treasurer after deducting therefrom his proportionate share.

(e) When the property owned in joint tenancy is a motor vehicle which is the subject of a title issued by the Secretary of State, the owners shown on the certificate of title shall enjoy the benefits of right of survivorship unless they elect otherwise. A certificate of title which shows more than one name as owner shall give rise to a presumption of ownership in joint tenancy with right of survivorship.

Furthermore, any non transferable United States Savings Bond, debenture, note or other obligation of the United States of America therein named shall, upon the death of the designated person, if the bond or other obligation is now or hereafter issued made payable to a designated person and upon his death to another person then outstanding, become the property of and be payable to the other person therein named. If any such non transferable bond, debenture, note or other obligation of the United States of America be made payable to 2 persons, in the alternative, the bond or other obligation shall, upon the death of either person, if the bond or other obligation is then outstanding, become the property of and be payable to the survivor of them.

765 ILCS 1005/2.1

Sec. 2.1. Whenever a transfer of tangible or intangible personal property shall be made in which the estate or interest created shall be declared to be an estate or interest not in tenancy in common, but in joint tenancy with right of survivorship, notwithstanding the fact that the transferor is or the transferors are also named as a transferee or as transferees, the estate or interest so created shall have all of the effects of a common law joint tenancy estate.

This section shall not apply to nor operate to change the effect of any transfer made prior to the effective date of this amendatory Act.

765 ILCS 1005/3

Sec. 3. Except as otherwise provided in this Act, all joint obligations and covenants shall be taken and held to be joint and several obligations and covenants.

765 ILCS 1005/4

Sec. 4. If any person shall assume and exercise exclusive ownership over, or take away, destroy, lessen in value, or otherwise injure or abuse any property held in joint tenancy or tenancy in common, the party aggrieved shall have his civil action for the injury in the same manner as he would have if such joint tenancy or tenancy in common did not exist.

765 ILCS 1005/4a

Sec. 4a. When one or more joint tenants, tenants in common or co partners in real estate, or any interest therein, shall take and use the profits or benefits thereof, in greater proportion than his or their interest, such person or persons, his or their executors and administrators, shall account therefor to his or their cotenants jointly or severally.

765 ILCS 1005/5

Sec. 5. Real estate; real property. As used in this Act, "real estate" and "real property" include a manufactured home as defined in subdivision (53) of Section 9-102 of the

Uniform Commercial Code that is real property as defined in the Conveyance and En-cumbrance of Manufactured Homes as Real Property and Severance Act.

Community Property

In certain states (Arizona, California, Idaho, Louisiana, Nevada, New Mexico, Texas, Washington, and Wisconsin), property owned or received by a husband and wife during their marriage is considered **community property.** Each spouse owns an undivided one-half interest in the property. Upon a break-up of a marriage, if the spouses cannot agree otherwise, all community property is divided equally between the spouses, regardless of fault. In most community property states, if one spouse passes away, all community property will transfer directly to the surviving spouse.

Inheritances, specific gifts to one of the spouses, certain awards of money and property, and profits clearly traceable to property owned before marriage, are con-sidered separate property and are not community property.

❋ Note, Illinois is *not* a community property state. Illinois is an "equitable property" state; if a couple cannot agree on the division of property, a court can decide the di-vision based upon what is equitable under the specific circumstances of the case.

Trusts

There are many types of trusts, and two that involve property are "**inter vivos**" (during life) trusts (including real estate trusts) and **testamentary** trusts. In a real estate trust, legal ownership is conveyed from the transferor to a trust set up specifically for the purpose of receiving and administering the property. This property is no longer legally owned by the transferor.

The person setting up the trust, who owns the property at the time of formation, is called the "**settlor**" (or "**trustor**"). The person who controls the trust, and makes decisions about the property, is called the "**trustee**." The person for whom the trust is established is called the "**beneficiary**." The property itself is called the "**res**" (also called the "property," "fund," "body," or "estate") of the trust.

A land trust is a method of asset protection in that the property is protected from creditors. Also, when the beneficiary passes away, the beneficial interest passes to any other beneficiaries (or contingent beneficiaries). The property is not part of the estate of the decedent or subject to the probate process.

The owner of the property prior to conveying the property into the trust is often a beneficiary of the trust. What is important with a land trust is that the Grantor (the person who owned the property prior to creating the trust) is no longer the legal owner of the property. The trust is the legal owner. If the property is sold, it is the trust that is the legal title holder of the property and the trustee must sign a trustee's deed (discussed in Chapter 6).

Also, it is important that real estate trusts are carefully drafted to make sure that the intent of the trustor is being followed. Since the trustor is no longer the owner of the property, there may be restrictions on how the property may be conveyed or financed through a land trust. For instance, if the trustor conveys the house to the trust and names himself and his two children as the beneficiaries (as opposed to the trustor as the main beneficiary and the children as successor beneficiaries), the trustee must take into account the interests of all three beneficiaries before agreeing to sell the property. This is something that trustor may not have considered at the time of setting up the real estate trust.

A second type of trust is a testamentary trust. In a testamentary trust, the testator (the individual who signs the will) states in the will that property (of any type — land, money, other personal property, etc.) will go into a trust upon the death of the testator. The property is then conveyed into the trust and the trust instrument will state who will be the trustee and the beneficiaries.

Life Estate

If the owner of the property transfers ownership of property to someone else, but through a life estate, the transferor continues to enjoy full use of the property for the rest of the transferor's life. Often a life estate is retained by a parent who transfers ownership of a property (typically a home) to a child or other relative, so the parent can still live in the property. *Example*: Parent has conveyed the property to Child (who is now the legal title holder), but Parent continues to live in the property for the duration of Parent's life.

A second form of life estate occurs when the transferor creates a life estate in a property the transferor owns. *Example*: Son owns a condominium that he was renting. He then decides to allow Mom to live in the condo for the rest of her life, regardless of what happens to him. He conveys a life estate in the condo to Mom (recording the conveyance), for Mom's life. Son is still the owner of the property, but mom has the legal right to live there for the rest of her life. Even if Son passes away or conveys the property, Mom still has the right to possess the property. When Mom passes, the life estate is extinguished and Son can do with the property as he sees fit.

A third form of life estate occurs when someone creates a life estate and the life being used for the life estate is a third party. That is a called a life estate *pur autre vie* ("for another life"). *Example*: Mom owns a home and has two children, Joan, who is very ill, and Mary. Mom does not want to own the home anymore, but is living in the home with Joan. Mom conveys the home to Mary, but retains a life estate for the life of Joan. This way, Joan can live in the house for the rest of her life, regardless of what happens to Mom. If Joan dies first, Mom plans to move, and Mary can do with the house as she pleases. If Mom dies first, Joan will still have a place to live for the rest of her life.

Life estates are a way for someone to avoid the responsibilities of home ownership, but still live in the house. They also keep the property out of the estate of the life tenant upon the death of the life tenant, as it has already been conveyed.

Ethics Alert:

Please note, all 7 forms of ownership may not be available in all states.

It is important to understand which forms of ownership are legal (or available) in your state. However, paralegals should never choose which form of ownership should be pursued, as doing so would be considered giving legal advice, which is prohibited for non-lawyers and would constitute the Unauthorized Practice of Law.

Transfer on Death Instrument (TODI)

A residential real estate Transfer on Death Instrument (TODI) is a document that allows residential property to be kept out of probate. If a person has a valid TODI that has been recorded with the Recorder of Deeds Office in the county where the property is located, the title to the property will pass to the beneficiary named in the TODI at the time of death, and upon acceptance by the named beneficiary. The TODI is a relatively new conveyance in Illinois (enacted in 2012), and provides the same avoidance of probate as a real estate trust, but is easier to set up and does not have any of the restrictions on ownership or the costs to maintain as a real estate trust.

Property can be left to beneficiaries in a will, but a TODI allows the property to be transferred more easily to the designated beneficiary. Essentially, it removes the property from the owner's probate estate. Additionally, if an estate is under $100,000, and there is no real property in the estate and no unknown or unpaid debt, the executor of a will (or a beneficiary if there is no will) can file a Small Estate Affidavit, which is an easier and less costly way to distribute property after death.

The owner of the property who executes a TODI must record the TODI with the Recorder of Deeds office in the county where the property is located. The TODI is not effective unless it is recorded before death.

Upon the death of the owner of the property, the beneficiary must record a Notice of Death Affidavit and Acceptance of Transfer on Death Instrument ("Acceptance"). The Acceptance is usually drafted at the same time as the TODI and retained until the death of the owner.

Examples of the TODI and Acceptance are included in Chapter 6.

(755 ILCS 27/) Illinois Residential Real Property Transfer on Death Instrument Act.

(755 ILCS 27/1)

Sec. 1. Short title. This Act may be cited as the Illinois Residential Real Property Transfer on Death Instrument Act.

(755 ILCS 27/5)

Sec. 5. Definitions. In this Act:

"Beneficiary" means a person that receives residential real estate under a transfer on death instrument.

"Designated beneficiary" means a person designated to receive residential real estate in a transfer on death instrument.

"Joint owner" means an individual who owns residential real estate concurrently with one or more other individuals with a right of survivorship. The term includes a joint tenant or a tenant by the entirety. The term does not include a tenant in common.

"Owner" means an individual who makes a transfer on death instrument.

"Person" means an individual, corporation, business trust, land trust, estate, inter-vivos revocable or irrevocable trust, testamentary trust, partnership, limited liability company, association, joint venture, public corporation, government or governmental subdivision, agency, or instrumentality, or any other legal or commercial entity.

"Residential real estate" means real property improved with not less than one nor more than 4 residential dwelling units, units in residential cooperatives; or, condominium units, including the limited common elements allocated to the exclusive use thereof that form an integral part of the condominium unit; or a single tract of agriculture real estate consisting of 40 acres or less which is improved with a single family residence.

"Transfer on death instrument" means an instrument authorized under this Act.

(755 ILCS 27/10)

Sec. 10. Applicability. This Act applies to only a transfer of residential real estate as defined in this Act by means of a transfer on death instrument made before, on, or after the effective date of this Act, by an owner dying on or after the effective date of this Act.

(755 ILCS 27/20)

Sec. 20. Transfer on death instrument authorized. An owner may transfer residential real estate by a transfer on death instrument to one or more beneficiaries as owners, concurrently or successively, and upon any contingency, effective at the owner's death.

(755 ILCS 27/25)

Sec. 25. Transfer on death instrument revocable. A transfer on death instrument is revocable even if the instrument or another instrument contains a contrary provision.

(755 ILCS 27/30)

Sec. 30. Transfer on death instrument nontestamentary. A transfer on death instrument is a nontestamentary instrument and is subject to all other laws governing or affecting nontestamentary instruments.

(755 ILCS 27/35)

Sec. 35. Capacity of owner and agent's authority. The capacity required to make or revoke a transfer on death instrument is the same as the capacity required to make a will. Unless expressly authorized by the owner under a power of attorney or similar instrument creating an agency, an agent for an owner does not have the authority to create or revoke a transfer on death instrument.

(755 ILCS 27/40)

Sec. 40. Requirements.

(a) A transfer on death instrument:

(1) must contain the essential elements and formalities of a properly recordable inter vivos deed; and must be executed, witnessed, and acknowledged in compliance with Section 45;

(2) must state that the transfer to the designated beneficiary is to occur at the owner's death; and

(3) must be recorded before the owner's death in the public records in the office of the recorder of the county or counties in which any part of the residential real estate is located.

(b) The failure to comply with any of the requirements of subsection (a) will render the transfer on death instrument void and ineffective to transfer title to the residential real estate at the owner's death.

(755 ILCS 27/45)

Sec. 45. Signing, attestation, and acknowledgement. Every transfer on death instrument shall be signed by the owner or by some person in his or her presence and by his or her direction, and shall be attested in writing by 2 or more credible witnesses, whose signatures along with the owner's signature shall be acknowledged by a notary public. The witnesses shall attest in writing that on the date thereof the owner executed the transfer on death instrument in their presence as his or her own free and voluntary act, and that at the time of the execution the witnesses believed the owner to be of sound mind and memory.

(755 ILCS 27/50)

Sec. 50. Notice, delivery, or consideration not required. A transfer on death instrument is effective without:

(1) notice or delivery to the designated beneficiary during the owner's life; or

(2) consideration.

(755 ILCS 27/55)

Sec. 55. Revocation by recorded instrument authorized; revocation by act or unrecorded instrument, not authorized.

(a) An instrument is effective to revoke a recorded transfer on death instrument, or any part of it, only if:

(1) it is:

(A) another transfer on death instrument that revokes the instrument or part of the instrument expressly or by inconsistency; or

(B) an instrument of revocation that expressly revokes the instrument or part of the instrument; and

(2) it is:

(A) executed, witnessed, and acknowledged in the same manner as is required by Section 45 on a date that is after the date of the acknowledgment of the instrument being revoked; and

(B) recorded before the owner's death in the public records in the office of the recorder of the county or counties where the prior transfer on death instrument is recorded.

revoke -ødvsorac

(b) A transfer on death instrument executed and recorded in accordance with this Act may not be revoked by a revocatory act on the instrument, by an unrecorded instrument, or by a provision in a will.

(755 ILCS 27/60)

Sec. 60. Effect of transfer on death instrument during owner's life.

(a) During an owner's life, a transfer on death instrument does not:

(1) affect the right of the owner, any other owner, or an agent for the owner to sell or encumber the residential real estate;

(2) affect an interest or right of a transferee, lienholder, mortgagee, option holder or grantee even if the transferee, lienholder, mortgagee, option holder or grantee has actual or constructive notice of the instrument;

(3) affect an interest or right of a secured or unsecured creditor or future creditor of the owner, even if the creditor has actual or constructive notice of the instrument;

(4) affect the owner's or designated beneficiary's eligibility for any form of public assistance;

(5) create a legal or equitable interest in favor of the designated beneficiary; or

(6) subject the residential real estate to claims or process of a creditor of the designated beneficiary.

(b) If after recording a transfer on death instrument, the owner makes a contract for the sale or transfer of the residential real estate or some part thereof that is the subject of the transfer on death instrument and the whole or any part of the contract remains executory at the owner's death, the disposition of the residential real estate by the contract does not revoke the transfer on death instrument but the residential real estate passes to the designated beneficiary or beneficiary subject to the contract.

(755 ILCS 27/65)

Sec. 65. Effect of transfer on death instrument at owner's death.

(a) Except as otherwise provided in the transfer on death instrument, in this Section, or in the Probate Act of 1975 or any other Act applicable to nontestamentary instruments, on the death of the owner, the following rules apply to residential real estate that is the subject of a transfer on death instrument and owned by the owner at death:

(1) Subject to the beneficiary's right to disclaim or refuse to accept the transfer, the interest in the residential real estate is transferred to the beneficiary in accordance with the instrument.

(2) If a designated beneficiary fails to survive the owner or is not in existence on the date of the owner's death, then except as provided in paragraph (3) the residential real estate shall pass to the owner's estate.

(3) Unless the owner provides otherwise, if the designated beneficiary is a descendant of the owner who dies before the owner, the descendants of the deceased designated beneficiary living at the time of the owner's death shall take the residential real estate per stirpes. If the designated beneficiary is one of a class of designated beneficiaries, and any member of the class dies before the owner, the members of the class living when the owner dies shall

take the share or shares which the deceased member would have taken if he or she were then living, except that if the deceased member of the class is a descendant of the owner, the descendants of the deceased member then living shall take per stirpes the share or shares which the deceased member would have taken if he or she were then living.

(b) Subject to the Probate Act of 1975 and the Conveyances Act, a beneficiary takes the residential real estate subject to all conveyances, encumbrances, assignments, contracts, options, mortgages, liens, and other interests to which the residential real estate is subject at the owner's death.

(c) A transfer on death instrument transfers residential real estate without covenant or warranty of title even if the instrument contains a contrary provision.

(d) If there is no sufficient evidence of the order of the owner and designated beneficiary's deaths, otherwise than simultaneously, and there is no other provision in the transfer on death instrument, for purposes of this Section, the designated beneficiary shall be deemed to have predeceased the owner.

(755 ILCS 27/70)

Sec. 70. Joint owners.

(a) One or more joint owners may execute a transfer on death instrument.

(b) If all of the joint owners execute a transfer on death instrument, then an instrument of joint owners is revoked only if it is revoked by all of the then living joint owners. A transfer on death instrument is revocable by the last surviving joint owner notwithstanding any contract or agreement between the joint owners to the contrary.

(c) If less than all of the joint owners execute a transfer on death instrument, the transfer on death instrument will be governed by the designation of the joint owner who is the last to die of all the joint owners. If the last to die joint owner did not execute a transfer on death instrument, the designation of any prior deceased joint owner is ineffective.

(d) A transfer on death instrument shall not sever a joint tenancy or tenancy by the entirety.

(755 ILCS 27/75)

Sec. 75. Notice of death affidavit, acceptance and effective date of transfer. A transfer on death instrument is effective as of the owner's death upon the filing of a notice of death affidavit and acceptance by the beneficiary or beneficiaries in the office of the recorder in the county or counties where the residential real estate is located. The notice of death affidavit and acceptance shall contain the name and address of each beneficiary who shall take under the transfer on death instrument, a legal description of the property, the street address, and parcel identification number of the residential real estate, the name of the deceased owner, and the date of death. The notice of death affidavit and acceptance shall be signed by each beneficiary or by the beneficiary's authorized representative. If a notice of death affidavit and acceptance has not been filed by at least one beneficiary or by a beneficiary's authorized representative in the office of the recorder in the county or counties where the residential real estate is located within 30 days after the owner's death, the personal representative of the owner's estate, if any, may take possession of the residential real estate in accordance with Section 20-1 of the Probate Act of 1975, and shall be entitled to a lien for all reasonable costs and expenses incurred in the management and care thereof provided that a reasonable attempt to notify the beneficiary or beneficiaries has been made. If a notice of death affidavit and acceptance has not been filed by at least one beneficiary or by the beneficiary's authorized representative in the office of the recorder in the county or counties where the residential real estate is located within 2 years after the owner's death, the transfer on death instrument shall be void and ineffective and the residential real estate shall pass to the owner's estate as provided in paragraph (2) of subsection (a) of Section 65 to be administered and distributed in accordance with the terms thereof.

(755 ILCS 27/80)

Sec. 80. Disclaimer. A beneficiary may disclaim all or part of the beneficiary's interest as provided by the Disclaimer Under Nontestamentary Instrument Act.

(755 ILCS 27/85)

Sec. 85. Rights of creditors and statutory claimants. A beneficiary of a transfer on death instrument is subject to the claims of creditors and statutory claimants to the same extent as a beneficiary of any nontestamentary transfer.

(755 ILCS 27/90)

Sec. 90. Limitations. An action to set aside or contest the validity of a transfer on death instrument shall be commenced within the earlier of 2 years after the date of the owner's death or 6 months from the date that letters of office are issued.

(755 ILCS 27/95)

Sec. 95. Preparation of a transfer on death instrument or its revocation. A transfer on death instrument or its revocation shall be prepared only by an Illinois licensed attorney. Nothing in this Section, however, shall prohibit an owner from preparing his or her own transfer on death instrument or revocation.

Key Terms

Real Property
Personal Property
Tangible Personal Property
Intangible Personal Property
Fixtures
Intestate Succession
Fee Simple
Fee Simple Defeasible
Fee Simple Determinable
Fee Simple Subject to Condition Subsequent
Fee Simple Subject to Executory Limitation
Guardianship of the Estate
Guardian of the Estate
Petitioner
Ward
Contract Capacity
Power of Attorney for Property

Attorney-in-Fact
Remainder
Adverse Possession
Disseisor
Tenancy in Common
Joint Tenancy
Four Unities
Tenancy by the Entirety
Homestead
Community Property
Land Trust
Inter Vivos Trust
Testamentary Trust
Settlor
Trustor
Trustee
Beneficiary
pur autre vie
Life Estate
Transfer on Death Instrument ("TODI")

Review Questions

1. What contracts must be in writing?

2. What is the difference between real and personal property?

3. Who are the Grantor and Grantee?

4. What is adverse possession?

5. What are four ways multiple people may own property together?

Materials included in the following chapter appendix include:

- Common Forms of Multiple Ownership Chart

- Illinois Statutory Short Form Power of Attorney for Property

- *Robert Butler v. Mark Harris*, 13 N.E.3d 380 (2014)

Chapter 1 Appendix

Common Forms of Multiple Ownership	Tenancy in Common	Joint Tenancy	Tenants by the Entirety	Community Property
Parties	Any number of persons (can be husband and wife).	Any number of persons (can be husband and wife).	Only husband and wife (or couple in valid civil union) for their principal place of residence.	Only husband and wife and only in the states that allow Community Property.
Division	Ownership can be divided and may be equal or unequal.	Ownership interests are equal and undivided.	Ownership interests are equal and undivided.	Ownership interests are equal and undivided.
Title	Each co-owner has a separate legal title to interests and may be unequal.	There is only one title to the whole property, and each tenant is "joined" to the others.	Title is in the name of both spouses, "not as tenants in common, nor joint tenants, but as Tenants by the Entirety."	Title is by the "community" of the spouses.
Possession	Equal right of possession	Equal right of possession	Equal right of possession	Equal right of possession
Conveyance	Each tenant in common's interest may be conveyed separately by the tenant in common owner.	Conveyance by one co-owner without the others breaks the joint tenancy with the third party.	Both co-owners must join in conveyance of property. Separate interests cannot be conveyed.	Both co-owners must join in conveyance of property. Separate interests cannot be conveyed.
Purchasers Status	Purchaser is a tenant in common with the other tenants in common.	Purchaser is a tenant in common with the other owners, who remain joint tenants, unless all joint owners convey to the new purchaser (and remaining joint tenants).	Purchaser can only acquire full title of the property. Purchaser cannot acquire part of property from one spouse only or it is a void transaction.	Purchaser can only acquire full title of community. Purchaser cannot acquire part of property from one spouse only.

Death	On co-owner's death, interest passes by will or succession to heirs. No survivorship right in other tenants.	Right of survivorship. Title passes to surviving tenants without going through probate. Interest cannot be willed. Survivor owns the property outright.	Right of survivorship. Title passes directly to other spouse without going through probate. Interest cannot be willed to third person. Surviving spouse becomes owner outright.	Right of survivorship. On co-owner's death, one-half of interest goes to surviving spouse. Up to one-half may go by will or succession to people other than the surviving spouse.
Successors Status	Beneficiaries become tenants in common with one another and with other tenants in common.	Final survivor owns the property outright and can convey the property accordingly.	Surviving spouse owns the property outright and can convey the property accordingly.	Surviving spouse owns the property outright and can convey the property accordingly.
Creditors	Tenant in common owner's interest may be sold by creditor to satisfy a debt. Creditor would be a tenant in common with other tenants.	Joint tenant owner's interest may be sold to satisfy debt. Joint tenancy is broken. Creditor would be a tenant in common with any remaining joint tenants.	The property cannot be seized and sold to satisfy the individual debt of one spouse. Property may be seized to satisfy a joint debt.	Property may be seized and sold to satisfy debts of one spouse under certain circumstances.
Presumption in Illinois	Default ownership in Illinois.	Joint tenancy must be expressly stated in the conveyance document, through the use of joint tenancy language.	Preferred method in Illinois for married couples to hold title to their principal place of residence. Must be expressly stated in the conveyance document.	Not valid in Illinois.

NOTICE TO THE INDIVIDUAL SIGNING THE ILLINOIS
STATUTORY SHORT FORM POWER OF ATTORNEY FOR PROPERTY

PLEASE READ THIS NOTICE CAREFULLY. The form that you will be signing is a legal document. It is governed by the Illinois Power of Attorney Act. If there is anything about this form that you do not understand, you should ask a lawyer to explain it to you.

The purpose of this Power of Attorney is to give your designated "agent" broad powers to handle your financial affairs, which may include the power to pledge, sell, or dispose of any of your real or personal property, even without your consent or any advance notice to you. When using the Statutory Short Form, you may name successor agents, but you may not name co-agents.

This form does not impose a duty upon your agent to handle your financial affairs, so it is important that you select an agent who will agree to do this for you. It is also important to select an agent whom you trust, since you are giving that agent control over your financial assets and property. Any agent who does act for you has a duty to act in good faith for your benefit and to use due care, competence, and diligence. He or she must also act in accordance with the law and with the directions in this form. Your agent must keep a record of all receipts, disbursements, and significant actions taken as your agent.

Unless you specifically limit the period of time that this Power of Attorney will be in effect, your agent may exercise the powers given to him or her throughout your lifetime, both before and after you become incapacitated. A court, however, can take away the powers of your agent if it finds that the agent is not acting properly. You may also revoke this Power of Attorney if you wish.

This Power of Attorney does not authorize your agent to appear in court for you as an attorney-at-law or otherwise to engage in the practice of law unless he or she is a licensed attorney who is authorized to practice law in Illinois.

The powers you give your agent are explained more fully in Section 3-4 of the Illinois Power of Attorney Act. This form is a part of that law. The "NOTE" paragraphs throughout this form are instructions.

You are not required to sign this Power of Attorney, but it will not take effect without your signature. You should not sign this Power of Attorney if you do not understand everything in it, and what your agent will be able to do if you do sign it.

Please place your initials on the following line indicating that you have read this Notice:

_____Initials

ILLINOIS STATUTORY SHORT FORM
POWER OF ATTORNEY FOR PROPERTY

1. I, _____

_____

hereby revoke all prior powers of attorney for property executed by me and appoint:

(NOTE: You may not name co-agents using this form.)

_____

as my attorney-in-fact (my "agent") to act for me and in my name (in any way I could act in person) with respect to the following powers, as defined in Section 3-4 of the "Statutory Short Form Power of Attorney for Property Law" (including all amendments), but subject to any limitations on or additions to the specified powers inserted in paragraph 2 or 3 below:

(NOTE: You must strike out any one or more of the following categories of powers you do not want your agent to have. Failure to strike the title of any category will cause the powers described in that category to be granted to the agent. To strike out a category you must draw a line through the title of that category. You should initial next to the line drawn through the title of any category stricken out.)

    (a) Real estate transactions.
    (b) Financial institution transactions.
    (c) Stock and bond transactions.
    (d) Tangible personal property transactions.
    (e) Safe deposit box transactions.
    (f) Insurance and annuity transactions.
    (g) Retirement plan transactions.
    (h) Social Security, unemployment and military service benefits.
    (i) Tax matters.
    (j) Claims and litigation.
    (k) Commodity and option transactions.
    (l) Business operations.
    (m) Borrowing transactions.
    (n) Estate transactions.
    (o) All other property transactions.

(NOTE: Limitations on and additions to the agent's powers may be included in this power of attorney if they are specifically described below.)

2. The powers granted above shall not include the following powers or shall be modified or limited in the following particulars:

(NOTE: Here you may include any specific limitations you deem appropriate, such as a prohibition or conditions on the sale of particular stock or real estate or special rules on borrowing by the agent.)

_____

_____

3. In addition to the powers granted above, I grant my agent the following powers:

(NOTE: Here you may add any other delegable powers including, without limitation, power to make gifts, exercise powers of appointment, name or change beneficiaries or joint tenants or revoke or amend any trust specifically referred to below.)

(NOTE: Your agent will have authority to employ other persons as necessary to enable the agent to properly exercise the powers granted in this form, but your agent will have to make all discretionary decisions. If you want to give your agent the right to delegate discretionary decision-making powers to others, you should keep paragraph 4, otherwise it should be struck out.)

4. My agent shall have the right by written instrument to delegate any or all of the foregoing powers involving discretionary decision-making to any person or persons whom my agent may select, but such delegation may be amended or revoked by any agent (including any successor) named by me who is acting under this power of attorney at the time of reference.

(NOTE: Your agent will be entitled to reimbursement for all reasonable expenses incurred in acting under this power of attorney. Strike out paragraph 5 if you do not want your agent to also be entitled to reasonable compensation for services as agent.)

5. My agent shall be entitled to reasonable compensation for services rendered as agent under this power of attorney.

(NOTE: This power of attorney may be amended or revoked by you at any time and in any manner. Absent amendment or revocation, the authority granted in this power of attorney will become effective at the time this power is signed and will continue until your death, unless a limitation on the beginning date or duration is made by initialing and completing one or both of paragraphs 6 and 7.)

6. (___) This power of attorney shall become effective on _____.

(NOTE: Insert a future date or event during your lifetime, such as a court determination of your disability or a written determination by your physician that you are incapacitated, when you want this power to first take effect.)

7. (___) This power of attorney shall terminate on _____.

(NOTE: Insert a future date or event, such as a court determination that you are not under a legal disability or a written determination by your physician that you are not incapacitated, if you want this power to terminate prior to your death.)

(NOTE: If you wish to name one or more successor agents, insert the name and address of each successor agent in paragraph 8.)

8. If any agent named by me shall die, become incompetent, resign or refuse to accept the office of agent, I name the following (each to act alone and successively, in the order named) as successor(s) to such agent:

For purposes of this paragraph 8, a person shall be considered to be incompetent if and while the person is a minor or an adjudicated incompetent or disabled person or the person is unable to give prompt and intelligent consideration to business matters, as certified by a licensed physician.

(NOTE: If you wish to, you may name your agent as guardian of your estate if a court decides that one should be appointed. To do this, retain paragraph 9, and the court will appoint your agent if the court finds that this appointment will serve your best interests and welfare. Strike out paragraph 9 if you do not want your agent to act as guardian.)

9. If a guardian of my estate (my property) is to be appointed, I nominate the agent acting under this power of attorney as such guardian, to serve without bond or security.

10. I am fully informed as to all the contents of this form and understand the full import of this grant of powers to my agent.

(NOTE: This form does not authorize your agent to appear in court for you as an attorney-at-law or otherwise to engage in the practice of law unless he or she is a licensed attorney who is authorized to practice law in Illinois.)

11. The Notice to Agent is incorporated by reference and included as part of this form.

Dated: _____

Signed _____

            (principal)

(NOTE: This power of attorney will not be effective unless it is signed by at least one witness and your signature is notarized, using the form below. The notary may not also sign as a witness.)

The undersigned witnesses certify that _____, known to me to be the same person whose name is subscribed as principal to the foregoing power of attorney, appeared before me and the notary public and acknowledged signing and delivering the instrument as the free and voluntary act of the principal, for the uses and purposes therein set forth. I believe him or her to be of sound mind and memory. The undersigned witness also certifies that the witness is not: (a) the attending physician or mental health service provider or a relative of the physician or provider; (b) an owner, operator, or relative of an owner or operator of a health-care facility in which the principal is a patient or resident; (c) a parent, sibling, descendant, or any spouse of such parent, sibling, or descendant of either the principal or any agent or successor agent under the foregoing power of attorney, whether such relationship is by blood, marriage, or adoption; or (d) an agent or successor agent under the foregoing power of attorney.

Dated: _____

Printed Name:_____

Signed _____

(Witness)

Dated: _____

Printed Name:_____

Signed _____

(Second Witness)

(NOTE: Illinois requires only one witness, but other jurisdictions may require more than one witness.)

State of Illinois)

) SS.

County of _____)

    The undersigned, a notary public in and for the above county and state, certifies that_____, known to me to be the same person whose name is subscribed as principal to the foregoing power of attorney, appeared before me and the witness(es) _____ (and _____) in person and acknowledged signing and delivering the instrument as the free and voluntary act of the principal, for the uses and purposes therein set forth, (and certified to the correctness of the signature(s) of the agent(s)).

Dated: _____

_____

Notary Public

My commission expires _____

(NOTE: You may, but are not required to, request your agent and successor agents to provide specimen signatures below. If you include specimen signatures in this power of attorney, you must complete the certification opposite the signatures of the agents.)

Specimen signatures of agent
(and successors).

I certify that the signatures of my
agent (and successors) are correct.

_____	_____
(agent)	(principal)
_____	_____
(successor agent)	(principal)
_____	_____
(successor agent)	(principal)

(NOTE: The name, address, and phone number of the person preparing this form or who assisted the principal in completing this form should be inserted below.)

This document was prepared by:

NOTICE TO AGENT

When you accept the authority granted under this power of attorney a special legal relationship, known as agency, is created between you and the principal. Agency imposes upon you duties that continue until you resign or the power of attorney is terminated or revoked.

As agent you must:

(1) do what you know the principal reasonably expects you to do with the principal's property;

(2) act in good faith for the best interest of the principal, using due care, competence, and diligence;

(3) keep a complete and detailed record of all receipts, disbursements, and significant actions conducted for the principal;

(4) attempt to preserve the principal's estate plan, to the extent actually known by the agent, if preserving the plan is consistent with the principal's best interest; and

(5) cooperate with a person who has authority to make health-care decisions for the principal to carry out the principal's reasonable expectations to the extent actually in the principal's best interest.

As agent you must not do any of the following:

(1) act so as to create a conflict of interest that is inconsistent with the other principles in this Notice to Agent;

(2) do any act beyond the authority granted in this power of attorney;

(3) commingle the principal's funds with your funds;

(4) borrow funds or other property from the principal, unless otherwise authorized;

(5) continue acting on behalf of the principal if you learn of any event that terminates this power of attorney or your authority under this power of attorney, such as the death of the principal, your legal separation from the principal, or the dissolution of your marriage to the principal.

If you have special skills or expertise, you must use those special skills and expertise when acting for the principal. You must disclose your identity as an agent whenever you act for the principal by writing or printing the name of the principal and signing your own name "as Agent" in the following manner:

"(Principal's Name) by (Your Name) as Agent"

The meaning of the powers granted to you is contained in Section 3-4 of the Illinois Power of Attorney Act, which is incorporated by reference into the body of the power of attorney for property document.

If you violate your duties as agent or act outside the authority granted to you, you may be liable for any damages, including attorney's fees and costs, caused by your violation.

If there is anything about this document or your duties that you do not understand, you should seek legal advice from an attorney.

AGENT'S CERTIFICATION AND ACCEPTANCE OF AUTHORITY

I, _____ (insert name of agent), certify that the attached is a true copy of a power of attorney naming the undersigned as agent or successor agent for _____ (insert name of principal).

I certify that to the best of my knowledge the principal had the capacity to execute the power of attorney, is alive, and has not revoked the power of attorney; that my powers as agent have not been altered or terminated; and that the power of attorney remains in full force and effect.

I accept appointment as agent under this power of attorney.

This certification and acceptance is made under penalty of perjury.*

Dated: _____

_____

(Agent's Signature)

_____

(Print Agent's Name)

_____

(Agent's Address)

*(NOTE: Perjury is defined in Section 32-2 of the Criminal Code of 2012, and is a Class 3 felony.)

Robert Butler v. Mark Harris, 13 N.E.3d 380 (2014)

13 N.E.3d 380 (2014)

Robert BUTLER and Elizabeth Butler, Plaintiffs-Appellees and Cross-Appellants,

v.

Mark HARRIS, Defendant-Appellant and Cross-Appellee (Lisa Harris, n/k/a Lisa Bohnenstiehl, Defendant).

No. 5-13-0163.

Appellate Court of Illinois, Fifth District.

June 27, 2014.

OPINION

Justice GOLDENHERSH delivered the judgment of the court, with opinion.

Plaintiffs, Robert and Elizabeth Butler, filed a two-count complaint against defendants, Mark Harris and Lisa Harris (now Lisa Bohnenstiehl due to defendants' divorce), to recover between $3,200 and $4,000 in septic system repairs and over $32,000 in attorney fees. Count I alleged common law fraud, and count II alleged a violation of the Residential Real Property Disclosure Act (Disclosure Act) (765 ILCS 77/1 et seq. (West 2008)). After a bench trial in the circuit court of Madison County, the trial court entered judgment in favor of defendants on count I and a judgment in favor of plaintiffs on count II in the amount of $12,000. Mark Harris filed a timely notice of appeal, raising the following two issues: (1) whether the trial court erred in finding that the standard of proof in a case based upon the Disclosure Act is preponderance of the evidence, and (2) whether the trial court erred in finding defendants violated the Disclosure Act. Plaintiffs filed a cross-appeal in which they raise the following issues: (1) whether the trial court erred in refusing to find defendants committed fraud, and (2) whether the trial court erred in failing to award them all of their damages and attorney fees. We affirm in part and reverse in part on the basis that plaintiffs failed to meet their burden of proof on either count and remand with directions that each party pay his or her own attorney fees. We note that Lisa Bohnenstiehl has not participated in this appeal.

BACKGROUND

On October 30, 2008, plaintiffs purchased a house located at 20 Creekwoods Trail in Highland from defendants. Approximately six months after moving into the home, plaintiffs received notice from Madison County that the septic system was not in compliance with its codes and ordinances and that the county had received complaints regarding drainage on plaintiffs' property. As a result, on October 30, 2009, plaintiffs filed a two-count small claims complaint against defendants in which they alleged that defendants fraudulently misrepresented the condition of the property with the intent to induce plaintiffs to complete the purchase and failed to disclose the septic system defects and prior drainage problems on the residential real property disclosure report form (disclosure report form) required by the Disclosure Act (765 ILCS 77/35 (West 2008)). Plaintiffs alleged that as of the date of filing the complaint their damages exceeded $5,000, but were less than $10,000.

...

A bench trial was conducted on January 29 and 30, 2013, during which the following evidence was adduced. Plaintiffs and defendants entered into negotiations for the purchase of property. Plaintiffs received a disclosure report form before they made an offer on the property. The form was signed by both defendants, but at different times due to the fact they were separated at the time. On the form, defendants checked "No" to the question, "I am aware of material defects in the septic, sanitary, sewer, or other disposal system." However, defendants made a notation on the form in which they specifically stated: "In the past, the ejector pump has backed up twice. Replaced GFI[-] has not happened since."

Defendants' original asking price was $242,000. Elizabeth Butler testified that she and her husband were not willing to pay that much, so they originally ruled out the home. However, a few months later she noticed the price was lowered to $185,000, so they called the realtor and went to look at the home. Before making an offer, Robert Butler prepared a sheet outlining problems with the property and the estimated costs of repairs. This sheet was submitted along with plaintiffs' offer to purchase the home and was entered into evidence as exhibit 11 by defendants. The sheet that outlines the home's problems specifically lists flooring, roof, furnace, central air, and septic system as items which need to be repaired. The sheet also contains an estimated repair value on all of these items, except the septic system repair. The sheet specifically states that the costs of such repairs are "unknown."

On August 21, 2008, plaintiffs offered to purchase the home for $162,375. Along with the offer, they submitted the sheet on which Robert Butler set forth problems with the home in the hope that they could justify their low offer. Defendants accepted the offer, and closing was scheduled for September 21, 2008. An addendum was later added as more time was needed to complete the sale because the sale of the property was a "short sale" and the bank needed more time to decide whether to accept the offer. Closing was extended to November 7, 2008. An addendum to the original contract specifically provided, "Property is being sold in an 'as is' condition."

Elizabeth Butler testified that prior to closing, plaintiffs hired both a home inspector to do an inspection of the property and Frank's Septic Company to do a more thorough inspection of the septic system. Frank's report specifically states:

> "Pump out [and] inspect tank—precast aeration tank—Jet tank aprox 1500 Gal—Tank looks ok—Inlet line open water level good—motor working media looks good—Needs rock in back filter vaults by chlorinator—needs chlorine in tube—Discharge open—Discharge area may need new rock at some point."

Elizabeth Butler testified she first noticed problems with the septic system "around that January/February mark as things start to kind of thaw outside [sic]." The actual closing on the home took place on October 30, 2008.

According to Elizabeth Butler, water would come into the basement when she ran the dishwasher or did too many loads of laundry. She said the problems were worse when it rained heavily.

Robert Butler testified that he first noticed water problems on the property in the spring of 2009 when there were heavy rains. Eventually, he selected Phillip McDowell of D-N-P Plumbing to correct the septic problem at a cost of $3,275. On one occasion, he came home to find that Deborah Toennies placed clay mud on the common road leading to the neighborhood tennis courts and covered it with straw. Robert Butler removed the clay and straw because he said it was aggravating drainage problems on his property. In removing these layers, he found a drainage pipe on his property that was covered with dirt and impacted with mud. Robert Butler confirmed that he put river rock in this area in May 2009. Robert Butler denied adding to the aeration pipe on his property.

Andrew Butler, plaintiffs' son, age 28, testified that he lived in the basement of the home in question. He said within months of moving into the house, he and his dad stopped water intrusion by making necessary repairs.

Mark Harris testified that he bought the home in 2002 and lived there until July 2007, when he and his wife separated. Defendants were not the original owners of the property. He testified that he did not have any trouble with water in the basement or with the septic system while he lived there, except for the time the ejector pump failed, which he disclosed prior to closing. He said his divorce was contentious and during divorce proceedings he was ordered to pay the mortgage on the house to his wife, but his wife failed to pay the mortgage with that money, so the home went into foreclosure. He testified that after he moved out of the home, his ex-wife never complained to him about any issues with the septic system. He said he never had any complaints from any of his neighbors about a water problem similar to the complaints alleged in the lawsuit filed by plaintiffs. He testified Jet Precast performed routine maintenance on the septic system every two years while he lived there, with the last maintenance done in 2006. Jet Precast never indicated there was any type of problem with the system.

Lisa Bohnenstiehl testified that there were no problems with the septic system while she lived in the house, except for the ejector pump failure. When she lived in the property, she did not experience any of the problems with the dishwasher and the washing machine or water in the basement as experienced by plaintiffs.

Jeffrey Hurst, an inspector for Madison County Planning and Development, testified that he went out to inspect the property on May 5, 2009, after Deborah Toennies called to complain about effluent (water that comes out of the system after it is treated) running onto her property from plaintiffs' property. This was after plaintiffs did work on the common road and placed river rock on the road. Hurst sent defendants a letter on May 7, 2009, outlining the problems he discovered during his inspection, including the fact that the discharge pipe for the aeration system was not 10 feet from plaintiffs' property line as required, there was no sample port, there was effluent draining onto neighboring property creating a nuisance, there was no perforated cover at the end of the discharge, and the discharge pipe did not allow a free flow.

At trial, Hurst testified the discharge pipe did not allow a free flow because it was buried in rock. He said this would allow fecal bacteria to grow and cause an odor.

In order to be in compliance with the code, effluent from an aeration system should not leave a property and the discharge pipe should be 10 feet back from the property line. Hurst confirmed he never received complaints from anyone else prior to the complaint lodged in the spring of 2009.

Deborah Toennies testified that she built her home in 1996 and moved in that year. She moved out of the neighborhood two years prior to trial. During the time she lived there, three different people owned the neighboring property, including the original owners, defendants, and, finally, plaintiffs. Prior to plaintiffs' arrival, she always took care of what was known as tennis court road, which was dirt and then a top layer of rock. She treated it as if it were her own yard. However, when plaintiffs moved in, they "dug out the tennis court road where it dips down, the lowest point, dug all the dirt out and filled it in with rock and disturbing the flow of everything that came down, the rain, water, everything. It just disturbed everything because it did not absorb anymore."

Deborah talked to the neighborhood association and learned plaintiffs did not get permission from the association to do what they did, so she called the county inspector. The inspector told her plaintiffs added more pipe to their aeration system and were now in violation of the code because it was running right up to the road. Deborah testified she never had a problem with drainage prior to plaintiffs making changes to the road. Deborah explained that her property was the lowest lying in the subdivision and she and her husband put in an elaborate drainage system in order to ensure they did not have problems even during heavy rains. However, after plaintiffs moved in and "dug out the tennis court road because of where their aeration system is, it would drain by the walkout basement door." Deborah further explained that after plaintiffs "removed all that dirt out of the road and put rock in, then it all filtered into [her] front yard to the point that [her] riding mower would get stuck in [her] front yard." Deborah said plaintiffs came over to her house and spoke to her and her husband about the problem and she and her husband asked plaintiffs to undo what they did to the road, but plaintiffs refused.

Deborah insisted she never had any of these water or drainage issues with the original owners of the property or with defendants. She admitted that sometimes it was wet at tennis court road because of where the aeration discharge was located, but she never had any problems with the previous two owners. She also said that sometimes there was flooding on her property, but it had nothing to do with defendants. Instead it was due to the low-lying nature of her property, of which she and her husband were cognizant and the reason why they put in an elaborate drainage system.

Phillip McDowell of D-N-P Plumbing testified that he corrected the code violations involving the septic system in August 2009 after he was called by plaintiffs to correct the discharge pipe covered by rock. He recommended that the discharge be moved and a rock pit installed. The repairs cost $3,275. McDowell testified he could smell the system when he went out to inspect it and the previous owners should have known about the septic system issues because the rock was built up, the water was running out, and there was an odor. According to McDowell, this type of situation does not occur overnight. Plaintiffs also hired Leroy Dawson, an architect, to inspect their home on September 7, 2010, after the lawsuit was filed. Plaintiffs paid Dawson $250 for an inspection. Dawson did not prepare a written report.

    . . .

    . . .

On March 5, 2013, the trial court entered judgment in favor of defendants on count I, the fraud count, but found in favor of plaintiffs on count II, violation of the Disclosure Act. The trial court awarded plaintiffs $12,000, without itemizing the award. The trial court's order specifically states:

> "After review of the relevant law, and taking all the relevant facts and circumstances into consideration, the court finds the proper award, arising from the Disclosure Act case, and including reasonable attorneys fess [sic], and cost of suit, is in the amount of [$12,000]." Mark Harris filed a timely notice of appeal. Plaintiffs filed a cross-appeal.

ANALYSIS

The first issue we are asked to address is whether the trial court applied the proper standard of proof in determining whether defendants violated the Disclosure Act. The trial court applied the preponderance of the evidence standard to plaintiffs' claim under the Disclosure Act, but defendant Mark Harris insists the proper standard of proof is clear and convincing. We agree with defendant.

We review the question of whether the proper standard of proof was applied de novo because the question requires interpretation of the Disclosure Act and is, therefore, a question of law. *Hogan v. Adams*, 333 Ill.App.3d 141, 146, 266 Ill.Dec. 655, 775 N.E.2d 217, 221 (2002). The Disclosure Act does not provide an express provision regarding the standard of proof to be applied for a violation. However, according to established rules of statutory construction, a statute is construed as changing common law "only to the extent that the terms thereof warrant, or as necessarily implied from what is expressed." *Hawkins v. Hawkins*, 102 Ill. App.3d 1037, 1039, 58 Ill.Dec. 620, 430 N.E.2d 652, 654 (1981). An inference that the common law is repealed is not favored. *Hawkins*, 102 Ill.App.3d at 1039, 58 Ill. Dec. 620, 430 N.E.2d at 654. Common law requires that fraud be proven by clear and convincing evidence. *Brown Specialty Co. v. Allphin*, 75 Ill.App.3d 845, 850–51, 31 Ill.Dec. 457, 394 N.E.2d 659, 663 (1979).

Here, the trial court applied the preponderance standard on the basis that it is the standard of proof to be applied in cases brought pursuant to the Consumer Fraud and Deceptive Business Practices Act (Consumer Fraud Act) (815 ILCS 505/1 et seq. (West 2008)). See *Fox v. Heimann*, 375 Ill.App.3d 35, 48, 313 Ill.Dec. 366, 872 N.E.2d 126, 139 (2007). However, we decline to analogize the Disclosure Act to the Consumer Fraud Act because "an individual who casually sells his or her own single-family home is not subject to liability under the Consumer Fraud Act." *Provenzale v. Forister*, 318 Ill.App.3d 869, 877, 252 Ill.Dec. 808, 743 N.E.2d 676, 682 (2001). Moreover, while our General Assembly specifically states that the Consumer Fraud Act "shall be liberally construed to effect the purposes thereof" (815 ILCS 505/11a (West 2008)), there is no such provision for liberal construction in the Disclosure Act. Accordingly, we believe the trial court improperly applied the preponderance of the evidence standard and that the proper standard of proof is actually clear and convincing.

The second issue raised by defendant is whether the trial court erred in finding defendants violated the Disclosure Act. Defendant contends there is no need to remand the case for further review because the trial court already considered the facts of this case as to defendants' knowledge under the clear and convincing standard with respect to the common law fraud claim.

. . .

Moreover, even assuming arguendo that the preponderance of the evidence standard is the proper standard to be applied, we believe the trial court erred in finding that under the evidence presented at trial, plaintiffs proved their case under the Disclosure Act. The Disclosure Act provides a seller is not liable for error, inaccuracy, or omission of any information delivered pursuant to the Act if the seller had no knowledge of such error, inaccuracy, or omission based upon a reasonable belief that a material defect had been corrected. 765 ILCS 77/25(a) (West 2010). The Disclosure Act also requires that a violation be done knowingly. 765 ILCS 77/55 (West 2010); *Woods v. Pence*, 303 Ill.App.3d 573, 576, 236 Ill.Dec. 977, 708 N.E.2d 563, 565 (1999). Here, the evidence as to defendants' knowledge was insufficient to meet either the clear and convincing standard or a preponderance of the evidence standard for the following reasons.

First, on the disclosure report form required by the Disclosure Act, defendants specifically identified the septic system as a potential problem by noting that in the past the ejector pump backed up twice. Second, prior to closing, plaintiffs hired not only a home inspector to do a complete inspection on the property, but also a separate septic system inspector to inspect the septic system. The home inspector did not notice any problems with the system, and Frank's Septic Company found only minor issues that might necessitate the need for future repairs, but ultimately found that the system looked good. Third, during negotiations, plaintiffs submitted a document in which they identified problems with the house in an effort to negotiate a lower price. Included on the list of potential problems was the septic system.

We acknowledge that plaintiffs' best evidence came from Phillip McDowell of D-N-P Plumbing who was hired by plaintiffs to correct the code violations involving the septic system. McDowell testified he could smell the system when he went out to inspect it and that the previous owners should have known about the septic system issues because it was not the type of situation which would occur overnight. Leroy Dawson, who was also hired by plaintiffs, testified that while he did not smell any foul odors, defendants nevertheless should have known about the septic system problems. However, we also note that Dawson's real concern seemed to be with the home inspector who failed to notice the problem with the septic system.

Given the fact that neither the home inspector nor Frank's Septic Company, both of whom were hired by plaintiffs prior to their purchase of the property, noticed the septic system problems, we cannot say defendants had actual knowledge of the problems in question. Finally, our review of the record indicates that no one actually testified that the repairs made to the septic system constituted a "material" defect which should have been known when the home was sold, which is required by the Disclosure Act (765 ILCS 77/25(a) (West 2010)).

In reviewing a judgment entered after a bench trial, the trial court's findings will not be disturbed on appeal unless they are against the manifest weight of the evidence. *Eychaner v. Gross*, 202 Ill.2d 228, 251, 269 Ill.Dec. 80, 779 N.E.2d 1115, 1130 (2002). A judgment is against the manifest weight of the evidence where the opposite conclusion is apparent or where findings appear to be arbitrary, unreasonable, or not based upon the evidence. *Corral v. Mervis Industries, Inc.*, 217 Ill.2d 144, 155, 298 Ill.Dec. 201, 839 N.E.2d 524, 531 (2005). *Eychaner*, 202 Ill.2d at 252, 269 Ill.Dec. 80, 779 N.E.2d at 1130. Here, we find the trial court's decision against defendants with regard to count II was against the manifest weight of the evidence under either standard of proof.

The only remaining issue is the award of damages and attorney fees. In the instant case, the trial court did not itemize the damages awarded. The judgment order merely awards plaintiffs $12,000, which includes both attorney fees and the cost of the suit. From this award, it is impossible for us to know how much was allocated toward septic repairs, which were alleged to be $3,275, attorney fees, which are identified in the trial court's order as "almost thirty-five thousand dollars," or costs. What is clear is that the trial court reduced the demand for attorney fees, but the trial court failed to provide any analysis of how it arrived at that figure. In any event, because a buyer seeking attorney fees under the Disclosure Act is required to establish knowing misconduct on the part of the seller in order to recover attorney fees, the award must be reversed in its entirety. Plaintiffs failed to prove that defendants knowingly failed to disclose problems with the septic system.

We point out that the Disclosure Act specifically provides for an award of attorney fees to the "prevailing party":

> "A person who knowingly violates or fails to perform any duty prescribed by any provision of this Act or who discloses any information on the [disclosure report form] that he knows to be false shall be liable in the amount of actual damages and court costs, and the court may award reasonable attorney fees incurred by the prevailing party." 765 ILCS 77/55 (West 2008).

The sentence allowing for the grant of attorney fees does not specify a specific party to a transaction. It also uses the term "prevailing party" when addressing the award of attorney fees.

Because the Disclosure Act does not limit the award of attorney fees to a specific party, "either plaintiffs or defendants, in appropriate circumstances, may recover fees under the [Disclosure] Act." *Miller v. Bizzell*, 311 Ill.App.3d 971, 975, 244 Ill.Dec. 579, 726 N.E.2d 175, 178 (2000). However, attorney fees would only be appropriate for a prevailing seller if the buyer filed a "meritless claim." See *Miller*, 311 Ill.App.3d at 974, 244 Ill.Dec. 579, 726 N.E.2d at 178. In the instant case, we cannot say plaintiffs' claims were meritless in light of the fact that Phillip McDowell and Leroy Dawson testified that defendants should have been aware of the problems with the septic system.

We agree with the trial court that this case presents a "pretty simple real estate disclosure case." It is unfortunate that this small claims case escalated from something simple to something much larger and that the attorney fees and costs got out of hand. It is time to end this litigation.

The facts clearly show that plaintiffs were aware of potential problems with the septic system before they purchased the property. Plaintiffs signed an "as is" contract. "Generally, a sale of property 'as is' means that the property is sold in its existing condition, and use of the phrase *as is* relieves the seller from liability for defects in that condition." (Emphasis in original.) *Black's Law Dictionary* 129–30 (9th ed. 2009). Furthermore, plaintiffs even negotiated a lower price based on their own enumerated deficiencies, including the septic system. Accordingly, we find that plaintiffs are not entitled to recovery under either count I or count II. However, because we do not find plaintiffs' suit meritless, we believe each party should pay his or her own attorney fees.

For the foregoing reasons, we hereby affirm the judgment of the circuit court of Madison County in favor of defendants on count I, reverse the judgment of the circuit court in favor of plaintiffs on count II, and remand with directions that each party is required to pay his or her own costs and attorney fees.

Affirmed in part and reversed in part; cause remanded with directions.

Presiding Justice WELCH and Justice CATES concurred in the judgment and opinion.

Chapter 2

Commencement of the Transaction

Learning Objectives

After studying Chapter 2, you will be able to:

- Identify the various actors involved in a real estate transaction
- Explain the provisions in a standard real estate contract
- Analyze a real estate contract

Chapter Summary

Topics covered:

- The Participants in a Real Estate Transaction
- Engagement Letters
- "Do We Have a (Binding) Deal?"
- Contract Review
- Attorney Review

This chapter begins to look at the transaction that will form the basis of the course. It discusses the process of listing a property with a real estate broker and how properties are negotiated. The chapter then moves to the various participants who may be involved in a typical real estate transaction. The subject of engagement letters is discussed. The bulk of the chapter involves a breakdown of a standard real estate contract. The chapter concludes with the attorney review component of a real estate transaction. The contract for the hypothetical transaction is included at the end of the chapter.

Hypothetical:

Please note, this hypothetical will form the core of the entire course. We will follow this transaction noted below throughout its development from contract formation to Closing. We will build upon the facts listed in this hypothetical, adding information as time progresses. We will be looking at this transaction from both the prospective of the Buyer and the Seller, so it is important to remain aware of who is who in the transaction.

Roberta Buyer Purchase from Jonathan Seller Hypothetical (Part I)

Paralegal Dina Raven is working for Ms. Eileen Dover, a solo practitioner in real estate law. Roberta Buyer calls, stating that she recently signed a contract to purchase a piece of property located at 4802 W. Wellington, Chicago, IL 60641. Dina asks the caller how she heard about the firm and Roberta states that her real estate broker, Janet Coldheart of Buywell Real Estate Brokers, referred her. Dina knows that Ms. Coldheart has made several referrals to the firm in the past and that Ms. Dover and Ms. Coldheart have worked closely on many transactions. Dina tells Ms. Buyer that someone from the firm will contact Ms. Coldheart for a copy of the contract and that Ms. Dover will contact Ms. Buyer within the next day.

On the same day, paralegal Timothy Sparrow, working for the law firm of Gohing, Gohing and Gone, a three-attorney real estate firm located in Chicago, receives a fax from real estate broker John Attack of Sales Max Real Estate. The contract is in the name of Jonathan Seller, for a property located at 4802 W. Wellington, Chicago, IL 60641. Tim calls the Sales Max office to confirm receipt of the contract and also speaks with Irwin M. Gone, a partner in the firm. Mr. Gone states that they need to contact the potential client prior to proceeding.

Mr. Gone calls Mr. Seller and confirms that Mr. Seller would like the firm to represent him in the sale of the property.

Ethics Alert:

According to the *ABA Model Guidelines for the Utilization of Paralegal Services*, there are three things which an attorney may not delegate to a paralegal, and which constitute the Unauthorized Practice of Law:

(1) Responsibility for establishing an attorney-client relationship,
(2) Responsibility for establishing the amount of a fee to be charged for a legal service,
(3) Responsibility for a legal opinion rendered to a client.

A fourth prohibition is representing someone in court, as set by Illinois statute (705 ILCS 205/11).

Question for Discussion

According to the above definition, do you think either Ms. Raven or Mr. Sparrow did anything that could rise to the "unauthorized practice of law"? Why or why not?

A copy of the contract is included at the end of this chapter.

1. "Do We Have a (Binding) Deal?"

Every real estate transaction begins with an agreement between the **Buyer** and **Seller**. In a transaction, there is a Seller looking to convey a property and a Buyer looking to purchase a property. This is, of course, the core of all contracts.

Much of the negotiations take place prior to formation. Often a Buyer will engage a real estate broker to assist the Buyer in searching for a property. The Buyer's broker will conduct searches for properties based upon the criteria desired by the Buyer, using the Multi-Listing Service (the "MLS," www.mls.com), Zillow.com, realtor.org, or other websites.

The Seller will engage a real estate broker to market a property for sale. This service includes conducting a property analysis (in order to adequately price the property), creating a "Listing Sheet" for the property (which describes the various attributes of the property), often creating a webpage for the property (allowing access to the property, generally including photographs or a "virtual tour" of the property), and actively attempting to market the property to potential Buyers.

Traditionally, real estate salespersons (so-called "real estate agents") had to be licensed and must have worked for a broker (Real Estate License Act of 2000, 225 ILCS 454/). However, a recent change in the law eliminated the real estate "salesperson" in Illinois. All salespeople must now be "brokers" in Illinois.

225 ILCS 454/5-46

Sec. 5-46. Transition from salesperson's license to broker's license.

No new salesperson licenses shall be issued by the Department after April 30, 2011, and existing salesperson licenses shall end as of 11:59 p.m. on April 30, 2012. The following transition rules shall apply to individuals holding a salesperson's license as of April 30, 2011, and seeking to obtain a broker's license. The individual must:

(1) provide evidence of having completed 30 hours of post-license education in courses approved by the Advisory Council and having passed a written examination approved by the Department and administered by a licensed pre-license school; or

(2) provide evidence of passing a Department-approved proficiency examination administered by a licensed pre-license school, which proficiency examination may only be taken one time by any one individual salesperson; and

(3) present a valid application for a broker's license no later than April 30, 2012, accompanied by a sponsor card and the fees specified by rule.

(b) The education requirements specified in clause (1) of subsection (a) of this Section do not apply to applicants who are currently admitted to practice law by the Supreme Court of Illinois and are currently in active standing.

(c) No applicant may engage in any of the activities covered by this Act until a valid sponsor card has been issued to such applicant. The sponsor card shall be valid for a maximum period of 45 days after the date of issuance unless extended for good cause as provided by rule.

A real estate **broker** is defined as:

225 ILCS 454 1/10

"Broker" means an individual, partnership, limited liability company, corporation, or registered limited liability partnership other than a real estate salesperson or leasing agent who for another and for compensation, or with the intention or expectation of receiving compensation, either directly or indirectly:

(1) Sells, exchanges, purchases, rents, or leases real estate.

(2) Offers to sell, exchange, purchase, rent, or lease real estate.

(3) Negotiates, offers, attempts, or agrees to negotiate the sale, exchange, purchase, rental, or leasing of real estate.

(4) Lists, offers, attempts, or agrees to list real estate for sale, lease, or exchange.

(5) Buys, sells, offers to buy or sell, or otherwise deals in options on real estate or improvements thereon.

(6) Supervises the collection, offer, attempt, or agreement to collect rent for the use of real estate.

(7) Advertises or represents himself or herself as being engaged in the business of buying, selling, exchanging, renting, or leasing real estate.

(8) Assists or directs in procuring or referring of prospects, intended to result in the sale, exchange, lease, or rental of real estate.

(9) Assists or directs in the negotiation of any transaction intended to result in the sale, exchange, lease, or rental of real estate.

(10) Opens real estate to the public for marketing purposes.

(11) Sells, leases, or offers for sale or lease real estate at auction.

The Buyer and the Buyer's broker will review listing sheets and websites of properties matching the Buyer's criteria and, should the Buyer desire to see a property in person, the Buyer's broker will contact the Seller's broker to set up a "showing." This can be set up through an "Open House" (where the Seller's broker sets up a time, usually on a weekend afternoon, when the property is open for viewing by multiple potential Buyers) or through a private showing.

When the Buyer decides on a property of his/her liking, the Buyer may place an offer on the property. This offer frequently comes in the form of a "contract" (see "Contract" at the end of this chapter). It is then reviewed by the Seller and the Seller's broker.

Under the Illinois "Statute of Frauds" (740 ILCS 80) (see Chapter 1), contracts for the sale of real property must be in writing to be effective. In addition, under the Illinois Uniform Commercial Code (810 ILCS 5/2201), all contracts for goods over $500.00 must be in writing.

A real estate broker may not draft a real estate contract. A famous Illinois Supreme Court case ruled that the drafting of contracts and Closing documents in a real estate transaction is considered the practice of law (*Chicago Bar Ass'n. v. Quinlan & Tyson, Inc.*, 34 Ill. 2d 116 (1966). Only the Buyer or Seller directly or an attorney may draft a contract, although this rarely occurs. A real estate broker is allowed to complete a preprinted contract or, in the words of the Court, brokers are "permitted to fill in the blanks of customary offer forms and contract forms as a necessary incident to its business" (*CBA.*, 34 Ill. 2d at 118). The text of this seminal decision is included at the end of this chapter.

This is fundamentally important because the contracts are often completed prior to the attorney becoming involved in the transaction. As in the hypothetical above, the contract was sent to the Buyer's attorney and the Seller's attorney after it had been signed already by both parties.

If this is the case, when does the contract become valid or enforceable? As with other written contracts, the answer is when it was executed by the party against whom the contract is being enforced. In real estate law, that is generally when the contract is accepted and signed by the Seller. As explained above, the Buyer and Buyer's broker ← fill out a preprinted contract, the Buyer signs it and submits it to the Seller (through the Seller's broker). Once the Seller has reviewed it and signs it, it becomes an enforceable contract. The date that the Seller executes the contract is very important, as that is the date that sets "the clock ticking" on the transaction. One thing paralegals often do when the firm first receives the contract is to find the date of execution to create a "tickler" on the firm's calendar to note the important dates that stem from the date of execution.

Often, the contract (normally because of the price or some other provision) is rejected by the Seller. A typical transaction goes something like this:

1. Our property was listed by Mr. Seller for $299,900.00 (Seller does not want a potential Buyer to think the property is being listed for $300,000.00; the house is not worth "that much").

2. Ms. Buyer and her broker complete an offer, in the form of a contract, and enter a price of $270,000.00 on the contract. The broker sends the offer Mr. Seller's broker.

3. Mr. Seller (or his broker) scratches out $270,000.00 and writes in $295,000.00 on the contract. The broker then sends the changed document back to Ms. Buyer's broker.

4. Ms. Buyer (or her broker), scratches out the $295,000.00 and writes in $275,000.00. She sends it to Mr. Seller's broker.

And so it goes, they send the contract back and forth until a price of $285,000.00 is agreed upon by both parties. The contract is then considered enforceable. — *nykonalny*

First, a note about contract formation must be stated. The original price was the **offer** of $270,000.00. That was the contract price, as stated by Ms. Buyer. In this hypothetical, Ms. Buyer is the **offeror** (the person making the offer) and Mr. Seller is the **offeree** (the one to whom the offer is made).

Mr. Seller changing the price to $295,000.00 was a **rejection** of the contract and a **counter-offer**. Mr. Seller (or Mr. Seller's broker) really should not simply scratch out the price, but should present an entirely new contract. The reason for this is because it a new offer (Mr. Seller is now the offeror), and Seller may wish to change other provisions of the offer. Ms. Buyer is now the offeree.

In addition, the form (Ms. Buyer's offer) has already been signed by Ms. Buyer. It was Ms. Buyer's offer. If Mr. Seller rejects, but changes the price and sends it back, Mr. Seller usually does not sign the form at that time. In reality, however, it is now Mr. Seller's offer, not Ms. Buyer's offer. It should be signed by the Seller at that point. Any change, such as the change in the price, should be initialed by all parties to the contract.

It is a better idea to provide a new form at that point. This, unfortunately, is almost never done. Ms. Buyer's broker and Mr. Seller's broker simply scratch out prices, have the changes initialed and fax/email the document back and forth, each time degrading the legibility of the document until it becomes almost unreadable.

If Ms. Buyer rejects the new price, Mr. Seller has no right to accept the earlier offer. Mr. Seller's objection to the price is a rejection of the offer. Mr. Seller providing a new price is a new offer (as mentioned above, Mr. Seller is now the offeree).

rejecting an offer

Under contract law, a rejection of an offer renders the offer unacceptable. If Ms. Buyer walks at that point, Mr. Seller cannot state to the Buyer "Okay, I was only negotiating. I accept the $270,000.00." The "accepting" of the $270,000.00, is *not* an acceptance of the Buyer's offer; *it is an entirely new offer.* Remember, the Seller *cannot* retroactively accept the offer, as it has been rejected. *It is an offer to sell at $270,000.00.* The Buyer is now the offeree and has the right to accept or reject the offer.

This is a critical point and something that neither Mr. Buyer nor Ms. Seller normally understands. If the Seller "accepted" the $270,000.00 (which, again, is really a new offer), and Ms. Buyer did not respond, a contract has *not* been formed, for the reasons discussed. If Mr. Seller attempted to enforce the contract at that point, it would not be enforceable.

Returning to the hypothetical, Ms. Buyer and Mr. Seller agreed upon $285,000.00, the contract has been signed, and it became enforceable at that moment. Hopefully, this raises at least a couple of flags for paralegal students. For instance, if the broker can fill in the blanks, but not draft the contract, what purpose does the attorney serve in the contract formation? That question will be addressed as the text proceeds through the transaction.

One final point about contract formation is commercial real estate transactions. Unlike residential real estate contracts (the primary subject of this text), in commercial real estate contracts, the Buyer's real estate attorney generally drafts the sales contract for each transaction. This is because every commercial real estate deal is unique and often has very specific terms and requirements. Commercial real estate attorneys have "boiler plate" forms that they use, but the contracts are tailored to the transaction based upon the requirements of the Buyer and Seller, and may be very complex documents and the result of weeks or months of negotiations.

In contrast, with residential real estate, although each property is considered "unique" (this concept of uniqueness of real property will be addressed again later in the text, during the discussion of breach of contract and remedies for breach), the transactions are similar enough to avoid the need for the drafting of specific contract forms. In addition, there are certain contingencies that allow real estate attorneys an opportunity to review and revise the contract.

2. Actors in the Transaction

Most transactions have a variety of players involved in the deal, all of whom play keys roles throughout the transaction. As described in Chapter 1, the real estate lawyer plays a vital role in the transaction.

Buyer's Side:
- Buyer
- Buyer's Broker
- Buyer's Attorney
- Home Inspector
- Loan Officer
- Insurance Agent

Seller's Side
- Seller
- Seller's Broker
- Seller's Attorney
- Surveyor
- Seller's Current Lender
- Property Association (if the property is subject to a homeowner's or condominium association)

In addition to the people listed above, there are a variety of third parties who play an important part in the transaction. Title company personnel and local, county, and state governmental officials all have integral roles in the real estate transaction.

3. Engagement Letters

Roberta Buyer Purchase from Jonathan Seller Hypothetical (Part II)

After hanging up the telephone with Ms. Buyer, paralegal Dina Raven goes into Ms. Dover's office to discuss Ms. Buyer's call regarding the contract to purchase the property located at 4802 W. Wellington, Chicago, IL 60641. Ms. Dover instructs Dina to draft an **engagement letter** for Ms. Dover's review. A copy of the letter is at the end of this chapter.

The **engagement letter** spells out the scope of the representation to the client. Somewhat surprisingly, the Illinois Rules of Professional Conduct (RPC) do not require written engagement letters in real estate transactions. Rule 1.5(b) only requires that the "scope of the representation and the basis or rate of the fee and expenses for which the client will be responsible shall be communicated to the client, preferably in writing, before or within a reasonable time after commencing the representation" (RPC 1.5(b)). Of course, it is always better to put such statements in writing, to avoid confusion later. In addition, any disputes between an oral representation and written statement (or contract) will usually be decided in favor of the written statement.

The engagement letter is really a separate contract, a contract between the attorney and the client. Many attorneys have the client sign the engagement letter (often referred to as an Engagement Agreement or Representation Agreement) prior to beginning the representation, providing the attorney with evidence that the client has read it and understands the scope of the representation.

The engagement letter should clarify the scope of the representation. Almost all firms have a "boilerplate" engagement letter, which is adapted and revised for individual clients. Often, a firm will have a variety of engagement letters to serve as templates, as different types of transactions (single family home, condominium, new construction, investment property, etc.) will have different requirements.

Nonengagement Letter. A nonengagement letter is utilized when an attorney has declined the representation. There can be many reasons why an attorney may decline representation, including:

- The attorney does not have the time to fully represent the client;
- There is an actual or apparent conflict of interest; or
- If the client declines to further engage the attorney (for instance, the client and attorney do not agree on a fee).

The nonengagement letter is intended to demonstrate that there is no attorney-client relationship and no further action will be taken by the attorney on behalf of the client. The nonengagement letter should state the reason for the nonengagement and should also inform the recipient of any deadlines (such as attorney review clauses in the contract), statute of limitations issues, and that they should seek counsel (if the recipient desires) as soon as possible. It should be sent to the recipient immediately upon making the decision not to represent.

Ethics Alert:

Conflicts of Interest (RPC 1.7)

A lawyer shall not represent a client if the representation involves a concurrent conflict of interest. A concurrent conflict of interest exists if:

(1) the representation of one client will be directly adverse to another client; or

(2) there is a significant risk that the representation of one or more clients will be materially limited by the lawyer's responsibilities to another client, a former client, or a third person or by a personal interest of the lawyer.

(b) Notwithstanding the existence of a concurrent conflict of interest under paragraph (a), a lawyer may represent a client if:

(1) the lawyer reasonably believes that the lawyer will be able to provide competent and diligent representation to each affected client;

(2) the representation is not prohibited by law;

(3) the representation does not involve the assertion of a claim by one client against another client represented by the lawyer in the same litigation or other proceeding before a tribunal; and

(4) each affected client gives informed consent.

Question for Discussion

According to the above rule, can a lawyer represent both the Buyer and Seller in a real estate transaction?

Why or why not?

4. Contract Review

The real estate attorney faces a dilemma with each real estate contract. The contract is completed and signed (and is, therefore, binding) on the clients *prior* to the attorney even having a chance to see the contract. The attorney cannot negotiate a contract that has been agreed to prior to the attorney having an opportunity to examine the document.

As described previously, real estate brokers are not permitted to draft contracts, as that is considered the practice of law. To resolve this problem, real estate professionals use "form contracts" and fill in the blank spaces on the form. There are many, many "form" contracts that are utilized in real estate law. The current standard form is the Illinois Real Estate Lawyers Association ("IRELA") Form 6.0 and 6.1 (the "contract"). However, almost all real estate firms have standard forms and there are other commercially available forms, either from stationary stores, from form books, or from the Internet. Due to the varying reliability of these standard forms, this text will focus on IRELA Form 6.0.

Almost all standard real estate contracts have a provision for contract review. These provisions may vary and it is imperative that the real estate attorney receive the contract as soon as possible to preserve the client's right to have the attorney review and modify the contract. Some contracts have attorney review provisions with as little as five (5) calendar days, although five (5) or seven (7) business days is standard.

When is 7 days not *7 days*? Seven (7) calendar days is just as it states, seven (7) days. Seven (7) business days means weekdays without holidays. *Example*: the contract is signed on Thursday, December 31, 2015. If a contract states that attorney review is "seven calendar days after execution," when does attorney review expire? The answer is January 7, 2016. Generally, if the contract states "seven calendar days *after* execution," most attorneys begin counting with the next day. However, some attorneys include the date of execution, so if there is a question, it must be raised and resolved immediately.

Compare the example immediately above with a contract that states attorney review is "seven *business* days after execution." Again, the date of execution is December 31, 2015. Seven *business* days would include one holiday (New Year's Day) and two weekends. The expiration of attorney review would be January 12, 2016. New Year's Day does not count; neither do the weekends. December 31, 2015, does not count as it is the date of execution and the contract says seven business days *after* execution. January 1, 2016, does not count (not a business day); January 2 and 3 do not count (as they are weekend days); January 4–8, count; (Monday–Friday); January 9 and 10 do not count (weekend); January 11 and 12 count (Monday and Tuesday). The final day for attorney review would be January 12, 2016.

It is easy to see how important a careful review of the contract can make a significant difference to clients. Occasionally, the contract will simply state "x days after execution." It is important that the attorneys and their clients come to agreement over the meaning of the term in the contract. Many deals are lost over such issues. An attorney misinterpreting such a term could be liable for malpractice.

Provisions of the IRELA Multi-Board Residential Real Estate Contract 6.0

Paragraph 1: Name—It is important that the name of the parties be complete and correct. Many Sellers will simply list the Seller as "O.O.R." or "Owner of Record." This is done because the Seller listing the property and signing the contract may not be the sole owner or the person on title to the property and the "legal" owner of the property may not be known until the title report is produced. For example, the Seller could be a corporation or LLC (limited liability company) or the property could be in a trust. If the Seller is listed as "O.O.R." it is incumbent upon the Seller's attorney to disclose the true owner of record as soon as possible, including providing any additional documents or signatures that may be required. It is also incumbent upon the Buyer's attorney to request the disclosure of the Seller as soon as practicable.

Paragraph 2: This information needs to be correct. If there are errors, such as it states there is deeded parking when there is only a numbered parking spot or the P.I.N. (Parcel Identification Number, Property Identification Number or Permanent Index Number) is incorrect, it must be corrected during Attorney Modification. Failure to do so could bring a breach of contract claim.

Paragraph 3: The attorney may *not* adjust the price of the property. It is very important that all parties have the same price on the contract. It may seem self-evident, but, as described above, often the brokers will send the contract back and forth to each other (which, of course, are really offers and counter-offers), scratching out the price and (hopefully, at least) having the parties initial each change. It is important to confirm the price so everyone is on the same page.

Paragraph 4: Also, it is important to confirm that the earnest has been paid. If there is an increase in earnest money, it is important to confirm that any increase has taken place at the appropriate time in the transaction.

Paragraph 5: As described in Chapter 1, a "fixture" is an item that is permanently attached to the property (i.e., fireplaces, furnaces, built-in shelving, etc.). Items of "personal property" include items that are not permanently affixed to the property (movable appliances, rugs, grandfather clocks, etc.). There is often confusion about what the Seller intends to convey to the Buyer and what the Buyer believes he/she is buying. For this reason, Paragraph 5 spells out the items that are intended to be conveyed with the premises. It is very important that the attorneys (and paralegals) confirm with their clients that the list of items checked is accurate. Frequently, disputes arise at Closing over items missing from the list or misinterpretations of items in the list. Any ambiguities should be addressed during attorney review.

Paragraph 6: There must be sufficient time for each side to complete the necessary preparations. Usually, the Seller's Attorney chooses the exact location for the Closing, with the agreement of the Buyer's attorney.

Paragraph 8: The Buyer must have time to obtain a loan/mortgage. If the Buyer is not able to obtain a "Clear to Close" (basically, that means that all of the necessary paperwork has been completed and the lender is ready to fund the loan and close the transaction) by the specified date, either party can cancel the contract or allow the Buyer more time to obtain the necessary commitment from the lender.

Paragraph 10: Real estate tax proration is a very mysterious part of the real estate transaction and often causes consternation for clients, real estate brokers and, even real estate attorneys. In attorney review, it is important to confirm the proration percentage. Real estate taxes and how they are computed will be discussed in Chapter 7.

Paragraph 11: As described above, the time period of attorney review is vitally important. Note, in this contract it clearly states "Five (5) Business Days after the Date of Acceptance." When is the date of acceptance? Per line 515 of the contract, it is the date the Seller signs and dates the contract.

Paragraph 12: Buyers have a right to have a home inspection performed (at their expense) and to have a reasonable amount of time to obtain financing. Please note, it specifically states the inspection was intended only "cover only major components of the Real Estate." However, in reality, Buyer's attorneys will often attempt to raise issues regarding everything. Inspections will be discussed in detail in Chapter 3.

Paragraph 15: The Seller must comply with the rules and laws associated with selling a condominium. Condominiums will be discussed in detail in Chapter 5.

Paragraph 16: The Seller is required in the contract to provide a Warranty Deed to the property. Deeds will be discussed in detail in Chapter 6.

Paragraph 18: The Seller is required to provide adequate Title Insurance to the property. Title Insurance will be discussed in detail in Chapter 4.

Paragraph 19: The Seller is required to provide a survey to the property (unless the property is a condominium, a cooperative or if there has been some other agreement). Surveys will be discussed in detail in Chapter 4.

Paragraph 20: This paragraph deals with the risk of loss should something happen to the property (fire, flood, earthquake, etc.) prior to Closing. Surprisingly, the former rule was that risk of loss passed to the Buyer at the time of contracting. Now, the risk of loss only passes at the time of Closing. The Seller must maintain adequate insurance protection over the property until the Closing and the conveyance of title to the Buyer.

Chapter 21: The Seller is to leave the property in substantially the same condition at the time of Closing as it is at the time of contract formation. That is, the Seller will be responsible for any damage that occurs to the property prior to Closing and must leave the property in "broom clean" condition upon vacating the property.

Paragraph 22: The Seller is required to declare if there is a pending special assessment or if the property is located in a Special Service Area.

Paragraph 41: This is the so-called "As-Is" clause. There are few clauses in real estate contracts that cause as much concern as the As-Is clause. If the As-Is clause is checked the Buyer may have a home inspection performed, but may not negotiate deficiencies discovered as a result of the home inspection. The concept is to speed up the transaction by not bogging down the transaction with home inspection issues. What people do not understand is, if the Buyer discovers any deficiencies as a result of the home inspection, the Buyer may still cancel the contract and receive a return of the earnest money. The "As-Is" clause will be discussed in detail in Chapter 3.

Attorney Review

One of the most important tasks for a paralegal in a real estate practice is reviewing contracts with the attorneys. Part of this review is the attorney modification letter. In the Attorney Modification Letter, the attorney carefully scrutinizes the contract and drafts a letter of recommended alterations.

Per Paragraph 11 of the contract, each attorney has the right to "a) Approve this Contract, b) Disapprove of this Contract, c) Propose modifications except for the purchase price, or d) Propose suggested changes to this Contract." The attorney need not provide a reason for the disavowal of the contract. However, there should be a reason for the any disavowal of the contract, especially if the other side suspects the contract is being cancelled due to the price of the property. The attorney cannot cancel the contract because of the price or modify the purchase price of the property.

There are examples of attorney review letters at the end of this chapter.

Key Terms

Broker
Offer
Offeror
Offeree
Counter-offer
Buyer
Buyer's Broker
Buyer's Attorney
Home Inspector
Loan Officer
Insurance Agent
Seller
Seller's Broker
Seller's Attorney
Surveyor
Seller's Current Lender
Property Association
Engagement Letter
Nonengagement Letter

Review Questions

1.   Name five people on the Seller's side of the transaction.

2.   What is an engagement letter?

3.   Why is it important for the attorney (and paralegal) to know the date of execution for a contract?

4.   What is attorney review?

5.   Why is the *CBA v. Quinlan & Tyson* decision important?

Materials included in the following chapter appendix include:

*   *Chicago Bar Association v. Quinlan and Tyson, Inc.*, Ill. 2d 116; 214 N.E.2d 771 (1966)

*   Multi-Board Residential Real Estate Contract 6.0

*   Engagement letter

*   Sample Attorney Modifications Letters

Chapter 2 Appendix

CBA v. Quinlan Decision

THE CHICAGO BAR ASSOCIATION et al., Appellees, v. QUINLAN AND TYSON, INC., Appellant No. 39131 Supreme Court of Illinois

Ill. 2d 116; 214 N.E.2d 771; 1966 Ill. LEXIS 390

JUDGES:

Mr. Justice UNDERWOOD, dissenting.

OPINION BY: PER CURIAM

Rehearing Denied March 23, 1966.

OPINION:

The Chicago Bar Association filed a complaint in the circuit court of Cook County to enjoin a real-estate brokerage firm, Quinlan and Tyson, Inc., from engaging in the unauthorized practice of law. After a lengthy hearing before a master in chancery it was found that the activities in question, performed in connection with negotiating purchases and sales of real estate for customers, constitute the practice of law. A decree was entered as prayed, except that the defendant was permitted to fill in the blanks of customary offer forms and contract forms as a necessary incident to its business. Upon review in the appellate court that part of the decree was reversed which allowed the filling in of forms, the court holding that none of the challenged services could be performed by persons not licensed to practice law. (*Chicago Bar Association v. Quinlan and Tyson*, 53 Ill. App. 2d 388.) We have granted leave to appeal. The Illinois State Bar Association, the Chicago Real Estate Board and others have appeared and filed briefs as amici curiae.

The defendant is a corporation employing some fifty or sixty persons of which three are licensed real-estate brokers and twenty-three are licensed real-estate salesmen. In conducting its business defendant prepares offers to purchase real estate, draws contracts of purchase and sale, prepares deeds and other instruments necessary to clear or transfer title, and supervises the closing of the transaction. No separate fee is charged for these services, the defendant's compensation consisting solely of brokerage commissions.

The documents ordinarily used—consisting of the contract of sale, the deed, bill of sale for personalty, escrow agreement, application for a mortgage and affidavits waiving possible objections to title—come in standardized forms which defendant's brokers, real-estate salesmen and office personnel fill out for the parties involved. The forms are completed by inserting pertinent factual information and by deleting or striking out portions which do not apply. The forms themselves have been drawn or composed by lawyers.

Defendant contends such services do not amount to the practice of law because their performance by real-estate men has become an established custom and no harm is shown to have resulted. It is argued that they are a necessary incident of the real-estate business and that the filling in of these forms is a simple matter, for which ordinary business intelligence is sufficient. Relied upon also is the assertion that no compensation is charged for the service. Cited and discussed, State by State, are decisions from other jurisdictions tending to support the position taken by the defendant.

We have considered the authorities referred to but find it unnecessary to discuss them at length. The question is not one of first impression in this State. It was settled by our decision in *People ex rel. Illinois State Bar Association v. Schafer*, 404 Ill. 45, where a licensed real-estate broker was held in contempt of court for preparing contracts, deeds, notes and mortgages in transactions for which he received a broker's commission. This court found unacceptable the contention that the drawing of such instruments was proper because done in connection with his real-estate business. Rejected also was the argument which considers those acts to be more or less mechanical and routine, requiring no legal knowledge or skill. We pointed out (at p. 54) that "Those who prepare instruments which affect titles to real estate have many points to consider. A transaction which at first seems simple may upon investigation be found to be quite involved. One who merely fills in certain blanks when other pertinent information should be elicited and considered is rendering little service but is acting in a manner calculated to produce trouble."

Except for the matter of filling in blanks on the customary preliminary contract-of-sale form, which we shall hereinafter discuss, we agree with the appellate court that the *Schafer* case is not distinguishable from the case at bar. The fact that other kinds of unauthorized practice were also involved in that case does not affect the holding. Nor are we convinced from defendant's arguments that this authority should be overruled. It is not decisive that defendant is compensated only by its commission, making no special charge for the services in question; nor is it relevant that the services are customarily provided by real-estate men and that no identifiable harm is proved to have ensued. As the appellate court pointed out, it is the character of the acts themselves that determines the issue. If by their nature they require a lawyer's training for their proper performance it does not matter that there may have been a widespread disregard of the requirement or that considerations of business expediency would be better served by a different rule.

We think, however, that in one respect the prohibition in the appellate court's opinion is too broad. In the *Schafer* case this court did not in so many words discuss the preliminary or earnest money contract form, nor did we specifically condemn the mere filling in of the blanks on such forms. The decree of the trial court in the case at bar, permitting real-estate brokers to fill in the blanks of whatever form of such contract is customarily used in the community and to make appropriate deletions from such contract to conform to the facts, is approved. In the usual situation where the broker is employed to find a purchaser he performs this service when he produces a prospect ready, willing and able to buy upon the terms proposed by the seller. (See

Fox v. Ryan, 240 Ill. 391.) The execution of an offer or preliminary contract is an evidencing or recording of this service in bringing together the buyer and seller. It coincides with the job the broker was employed to perform and which he is licensed to perform, and in practice it marks the point at which he becomes entitled to his commission. It seems reasonable therefore that he be authorized to draft this offer or preliminary contract, where this involves merely the filling in of blank forms. *Keys Co. v. Dade County Bar Ass'n*, (Fla. 1950,) 46 So. 2d 605.

In *Gustafson v. V. C. Taylor & Sons*, 138 Ohio St. 392, 35 N.E.2d 435, a real-estate broker followed the practice of filling in the blanks of a printed "offer to purchase" form which, like those involved in the case at bar, had been prepared by a regularly admitted attorney-at-law. In a suit to enjoin this as unauthorized practice of law the court held that where the broker did nothing more than fill in simple factual material such as the date, price, name of the purchaser, location of the property, date of giving possession and duration of the offer he was not engaging in the practice of law. It was pointed out that such services require no more than ordinary business intelligence and do not require the skill peculiar to one trained and experienced in the law. The *Gustafson* case was cited and fully stated in the opinion of this court in the *Schafer* case, where we proceeded to say that if a particular service performed by the broker "requires legal skill or knowledge, or more than ordinary business intelligence, it constitutes the practice of law" but that "when filling in blanks as directed he may not by that simple act be practicing law, * * *." We think, therefore, that the broker may properly fill in the usual form of earnest money contract or offer to purchase where this involves merely the supplying of simple factual data.

But when the broker has secured the signatures on the usual form of preliminary contract or offer to purchase, completed by the insertion of necessary factual data, he has fully performed his obligation as broker. The drawing or filling in of blanks on deeds, mortgages and other legal instruments subsequently executed requires the peculiar skill of a lawyer and constitutes the practice of law. Such instruments are often muniments of title and become matters of permanent record. They are not ordinarily executed and delivered until after title has been examined and approved by the attorney for the purchaser. Their preparation is not incidental to the performance of brokerage services but falls outside the scope of the broker's function. *Commonwealth v. Jones & Robins*, 186 Va. 30, 41 S.E.2d 720; *Washington State Bar Ass'n v. Washington Ass'n of Realtors*, 41 Wash. 2d 697, 251 P.2d 619.

The defendant and the real-estate board amici argue that all the forms in question are so standardized that only ordinary business intelligence is required to complete them. If the question were merely one of skill in filling out forms the argument would be persuasive. But more is involved than this simple operation and the question cannot realistically be viewed in such isolation. The legal problems involved often depend upon the context in which the instrument is placed, and only a lawyer's training gives assurance that they will be identified or pointed out. The mere completion of a form can readily be done by a stenographer. But it requires a lawyer's advice to determine whether it will accomplish the desired result under all the circumstances.

As this court emphasized in the *Schafer* case, (at p. 52) quoting from a Missouri decision: " 'Any one who wants to pay the price may purchase a set of form books and read and copy them. He may use them in his own business if he so desires. But when he advises others for a consideration, that this or that is the law, or that this form or that is the proper form to be used in a certain transaction, then he is doing all that a lawyer does when a client seeks his advice.' "

Drafting and attending to the execution of instruments relating to real-estate titles are within the practice of law, and neither corporations nor any other persons unlicensed to practice the profession may engage therein. (*People ex rel. Illinois State Bar Association v. Peoples Stock Yards State Bank*, 344 Ill. 462.) Nor does the fact that standardized forms are usually employed make these services an incident of the real-estate broker business. Many aspects of law practice are conducted through the use of forms, and not all of the matters handled require extensive investigation of the law. But by his training the lawyer is equipped to recognize when this is and when it is not the case. Neither counsel nor amici have suggested any practicable way in which an exception to the general rule can be made where only the use of forms is involved, or where the transaction is a "simple" one. Mere simplicity cannot be the basis for drawing boundaries to the practice of a profession. A pharmacist, for example might be competent to prescribe for many of the simpler ailments, but it takes a medical background to recognize when the ailment is simple. Protection of the public requires that only licensed physicians may prescribe or treat for any ailment, regardless of complexity or simplicity. And protection of the public requires a similar approach when the practice of law is involved.

The judgment of the appellate court is affirmed except insofar as it reversed in part the judgment of the circuit court. In that respect it is reversed. The decree of the circuit court is affirmed.

Appellate court affirmed in part and reversed in part; circuit court affirmed.

DISSENT

Mr. JUSTICE UNDERWOOD, dissenting:

In resolving the very difficult questions presented in this case this court has compromised the differing positions of the parties in a result with which I cannot agree. Most of the reasons compelling my dissent are adequately treated in the well considered opinion of the appellate court (53 Ill. App. 2d 388), and it would add little for me to restate them here. There is, however, one undiscussed facet of the many serious questions requiring informed consideration by the parties to every real-estate transaction before a contract is signed.

Increasingly apparent in recent years is the fact that every real-estate purchase and sale involves far-reaching tax consequences of a character partially or wholly unknown to the ordinary buyer and seller. As to such property the dollar amount of estate, inheritance and income tax liabilities of the parties will be determined largely by the manner in which the transaction is consummated. The year in which it occurs, the manner in which title is taken, whether it is a cash or installment sale or an exchange of properties will all substantially affect tax liability, not only of the parties but of their estates and heirs. As a result, such tax obligations may be increased, diminished or completely eliminated, depending on the decisions made by the parties as to the terms of their contract.

The opinion of this court permits real-estate brokers to prepare contracts for the purchase and sale of real estate by "filling the blanks" in, and making "appropriate deletions" from form contracts customarily used in the community and to secure the signatures of the parties thereon. It prohibits explanation by the brokers of the provisions of the contract and bars them from preparing any other documents subsequent to the contract. Actually, the contract between the parties is the fundamental instrument in a real-estate transaction and determines their future rights and obligations. It seems to me somewhat anomalous to permit the broker to prepare the controlling agreement but not those which it controls. Be that as it may, the practical result of this decision will be a binding contract executed by the parties without informed consideration of the serious questions involved except in those instances where the buyer or seller is aware of the inherent hazards and consults his attorney before signing the contract.

The desired objective here is neither the preservation of business for lawyers nor commissions for brokers—it is the protection of the public. In my opinion this is best accomplished by entrusting the preparation of real-estate contracts to those trained to recognize the substantial questions involved and competent to advise the parties regarding what, in many instances, is the most important investment they will ever make.

For these reasons, as well as those set forth in the appellate court opinion, the judgment of that court should be affirmed.

Roberta Buyer Purchase from Jonathan Seller Hypothetical (Part II)

 MULTI-BOARD RESIDENTIAL REAL ESTATE CONTRACT 6.0

1   **1. THE PARTIES:** Buyer and Seller are hereinafter referred to as the "Parties".
2   Buyer Name(s) *[please print]* **Roberta Buyer** _____
3   Seller Name(s) *[please print]* **O.O.R.** _____
4   **If Dual Agency Applies, Complete Optional Paragraph 31.**
5   **2. THE REAL ESTATE:** Real Estate shall be defined as the property, all improvements, the fixtures and Personal
6   Property included therein. Seller agrees to convey to Buyer or to Buyer's designated grantee, the Real Estate
7   with approximate lot size or acreage of **32x125** _____ commonly known as:
8   **4802 W. Wellington**   **Chicago**   **IL**   **60641**
9   Address   City   State   Zip
10 **Cook**   **13-29-212-029-0000**
11 County   Unit # (If applicable)   Permanent Index Number(s) of Real Estate
12 **If Condo/Coop/Townhome Parking is Included:** # of spaces(s) _____; identified as Space(s) # _____;
13 *[check type]* ❏ deeded space, PIN: _____ ❏ limited common element ❏ assigned space.
14 **3. PURCHASE PRICE:** The Purchase Price shall be $ **285,000** _____. After the payment of
15 Earnest Money as provided below, the balance of the Purchase Price, as adjusted by prorations, shall be paid at
16 Closing in "Good Funds" as defined by law.
17 **4. EARNEST MONEY:** Earnest Money shall be held in trust for the mutual benefit of the Parties by *[check one]*:
18 ☒ Seller's Brokerage; ❏ Buyer's Brokerage; ❏ As otherwise agreed by the Parties, as "Escrowee".
19 Initial Earnest Money of $ **5,000** _____ shall be tendered to Escrowee on or before **0** day(s) after Date
20 of Acceptance. Additional Earnest Money of $ _____ shall be tendered by _____, 20 __.
21 **5. FIXTURES AND PERSONAL PROPERTY AT NO ADDITIONAL COST:** All of the fixtures and included Personal
22 Property are owned by Seller and to Seller's knowledge are in operating condition on the Date of Acceptance,
23 unless otherwise stated herein. Seller agrees to transfer to Buyer all fixtures, all heating, electrical, plumbing,
24 and well systems together with the following items of Personal Property at no additional cost by Bill of Sale at
25 Closing *[Check or enumerate applicable items]*:

✔ Refrigerator	✔ Central Air Conditioning	✔ Central Humidifier	✔ Light Fixtures, as they exist
__ Oven/Range/Stove	__ Window Air Conditioner(s)	__ Water Softener (owned)	✔ Built-in or attached shelving
__ Microwave	__ Ceiling Fan(s)	__ Sump Pump(s)	✔ All Window Treatments & Hardware
__ Dishwasher	__ Intercom System	__ Electronic or Media Air Filter(s)	__ Existing Storms and Screens
__ Garbage Disposal	__ Backup Generator System	__ Central Vac & Equipment	__ Fireplace Screens/Doors/Grates
__ Trash Compactor	✔ Satellite Dish	__ Security System(s) (owned)	__ Fireplace Gas Log(s)
✔ Washer	__ Outdoor Shed	✔ Garage Door Opener(s)	__ Invisible Fence System, Collar & Box
✔ Dryer	✔ Planted Vegetation	with all Transmitters	✔ Smoke Detectors
__ Attached Gas Grill	__ Outdoor Play Set(s)	✔ All Tacked Down Carpeting	✔ Carbon Monoxide Detectors

35 **Other Items Included at No Additional Cost: Semi-built in Hutch in Kitchen** _____
36 _____
37 **Items Not Included: 4 rose bushes on west side of house** _____
38 _____
39 Seller warrants to Buyer that all fixtures, systems and Personal Property included in this Contract shall be in
40 operating condition at Possession except: _____ .
41 A system or item shall be deemed to be in operating condition if it performs the function for which it is
42 intended, regardless of age, and does not constitute a threat to health or safety.
43 **If Home Warranty will be provided, complete Optional Paragraph 34.**

Buyer Initial _____ *Buyer Initial* _____   *Seller Initial* _____ *Seller Initial* _____
Address: **4802 W. Wellington**   **Chicago**   **IL**   **60641** *v6.0*
Page 1 of 13

Escrow - przechowanie, depozyt

44   **6. CLOSING:** Closing shall be on **July 23**_____, 20 **15**___ or at such time as mutually agreed by the
45   Parties in writing. Closing shall take place at the escrow office of the title company (or its issuing agent) that will
46   issue the Owner's Policy of Title Insurance, situated nearest the Real Estate or as shall be agreed mutually by the Parties.

47   **7. POSSESSION:** Unless otherwise provided in Paragraph 40, Seller shall deliver possession to Buyer at Closing.
48   Possession shall be deemed to have been delivered when Seller has vacated the Real Estate and delivered keys
49   to the Real Estate to Buyer or to the office of the Seller's Brokerage.

50   **8. MORTGAGE CONTINGENCY:** If this transaction is NOT CONTINGENT ON FINANCING, Optional Paragraph 36 a) OR
51   Paragraph 36 b) MUST BE USED. If any portion of Paragraph 36 is used, the provisions of this Paragraph 8 are NOT APPLICABLE.
52   This Contract is contingent upon Buyer obtaining a *[check one]* ☑ fixed; ☐ adjustable; *[check one]* ☑ conventional;
53   ☐ FHA/VA (if FHA/VA is chosen, complete Paragraph 37); ☐ other _____ loan for **7**___ %
54   of the Purchase Price, plus private mortgage insurance (PMI), if required, with an interest rate (initial rate if an
55   adjustable rate mortgage used) not to exceed _____% per annum, amortized over not less than **30**___ years.
56   Buyer shall pay loan origination fee and/or discount points not to exceed **2**_____ % of the loan amount. Buyer
57   shall pay the cost of application, usual and customary processing fees and closing costs charged by lender.
58   (Complete Paragraph 35 if closing cost credits apply). Buyer shall make written loan application within five (5)
59   Business Days after the Date of Acceptance and shall cause an appraisal of Real Estate to be ordered by the
60   lender no later than ten (10) Business Days after the Date of Acceptance; **failure to do either shall constitute an**
61   **act of Default under this Contract.**

62   If Buyer, having applied for the loan specified above *[complete both a) and b)]*:

63   a) is unable to provide written evidence that the loan application has been submitted for underwriting
64   approval by Buyer's lender on or before **July 10**_____, 20 **15**___, (if no date is inserted, the date shall
65   be thirty (30) days after the Date of Acceptance) either Buyer or Seller shall have the option of declaring this
66   Contract terminated by giving Notice to the other Party not later than two (2) Business Days after the date
67   specified herein or any extension date agreed to by the Parties in writing.

68   b) is unable to obtain a written "Clear to Close" from Buyer's lender on or before **July 15**_____, 20 **15**___,
69   (if no date is inserted, the date shall be forty-five (45) days after the Date of Acceptance) either Buyer or
70   Seller shall have the option of declaring this Contract terminated by giving Notice to the other Party not later
71   than two (2) Business Days after the date specified herein or any extension date agreed to by the Parties in writing.

72   **A Party causing delay in the loan approval process shall not have the right to terminate under either of the**
73   **preceding paragraphs. In the event neither Party elects to declare this Contract null and void as of the latter**
74   **of the dates specified above (as may be amended from time to time), then this Contract shall continue in full**
75   **force and effect without any loan contingencies.**

76   **Unless otherwise provided in Paragraph 32, this Contract shall not be contingent upon the sale and/or**
77   **closing of Buyer's existing real estate.** Buyer shall be deemed to have satisfied the financing conditions of this
78   paragraph if Buyer obtains a loan commitment in accordance with the terms of this paragraph even though the
79   loan is conditioned on the sale and/or closing of Buyer's existing real estate.

80   **9. STATUTORY DISCLOSURES:** If applicable, prior to signing this Contract, Buyer:
81   *[check one]* ☑ has ☐ has not received a completed Illinois Residential Real Property Disclosure;
82   *[check one]* ☑ has ☐ has not received the EPA Pamphlet, "Protect Your Family From Lead In Your Home";
83   *[check one]* ☑ has ☐ has not received a Lead-Based Paint Disclosure;
84   *[check one]* ☑ has ☐ has not received the IEMA, "Radon Testing Guidelines for Real Estate Transactions";
85   *[check one]* ☑ has ☐ has not received the Disclosure of Information on Radon Hazards.

Buyer Initial _____ *Buyer Initial* _____   *Seller Initial* _____ *Seller Initial* _____
Address: **4802 W. Wellington**_____   **Chicago**   **IL**   **60641** *v6.0*
Page 2 of 13

86 **10. PRORATIONS:** Proratable items shall include without limitation, rents and deposits (if any) from tenants;
87 Special Service Area or Special Assessment Area tax for the year of Closing only; utilities, water and sewer; and
88 Homeowner or Condominium Association fees (and Master/Umbrella Association fees, if applicable).
89 Accumulated reserves of a Homeowner/Condominium Association(s) are not a proratable item. Seller
90 represents that as of the Date of Acceptance Homeowner/Condominium Association(s) fees are $ **N/A**_____
91 per _____ (and, if applicable Master/Umbrella Association fees are $ _____ per _____).
92 Seller agrees to pay prior to or at Closing any special assessments (by any association or governmental entity)
93 confirmed prior to the Date of Acceptance. Special Assessment Area or Special Service Area installments due
94 after the year of Closing shall not be proratable items and shall be paid by Buyer. The general Real Estate taxes
95 shall be prorated as of the date of Closing based on **110** % of the most recent ascertainable full year tax bill. All
96 prorations shall be final as of Closing, except as provided in Paragraph 22. If the amount of the most recent
97 ascertainable full year tax bill reflects a homeowner, senior citizen or other exemption, a senior freeze or senior
98 deferral, then Seller has submitted or will submit in a timely manner all necessary documentation to the
99 appropriate governmental entity, before or after Closing, to preserve said exemption(s). The requirements of
100 this Paragraph shall survive the Closing.

101 **11. ATTORNEY REVIEW:** Within five (5) Business Days after Date of Acceptance, the attorneys for the respective
102 Parties, by Notice, may:

103 a) Approve this Contract; or

104 b) Disapprove this Contract, which disapproval shall not be based solely upon the Purchase Price; or

105 c) Propose modifications except for the Purchase Price. If within ten (10) Business Days after the Date of
106   Acceptance written agreement is not reached by the Parties with respect to resolution of the proposed
107   modifications, then either Party may terminate this Contract by serving Notice, whereupon this Contract
108   shall be null and void; or

109 d) Propose suggested changes to this Contract. If such suggestions are not agreed upon, neither Party may
110   declare this Contract null and void and this Contract shall remain in full force and effect.

111 **Unless otherwise specified, all Notices shall be deemed made pursuant to Paragraph 11 c). If Notice is not**
112 **served within the time specified herein, the provisions of this paragraph shall be deemed waived by the**
113 **Parties and this Contract shall remain in full force and effect.**

114 **12. PROFESSIONAL INSPECTIONS AND INSPECTION NOTICES:** Buyer may conduct at Buyer's expense (unless
115 otherwise provided by governmental regulations) any or all of the following inspections of the Real Estate by
116 one or more licensed or certified inspection services: home, radon, environmental, lead-based paint, lead-based
117 paint hazards or wood-destroying insect infestation.

118 a) Buyer agrees that minor repairs and routine maintenance items of the Real Estate do not constitute defects
119   and are not a part of this contingency. **The fact that a functioning major component may be at the end of**
120   **its useful life shall not render such component defective for purposes of this paragraph.** Buyer shall
121   indemnify Seller and hold Seller harmless from and against any loss or damage caused by the acts of
122   negligence of Buyer or any person performing any inspection. The home inspection shall cover only the
123   major components of the Real Estate, including but not limited to central heating system(s), central cooling
124   system(s), plumbing and well system, electrical system, roof, walls, windows, doors, ceilings, floors,
125   appliances and foundation. A major component shall be deemed to be in operating condition if it performs
126   the function for which it is intended, regardless of age, and does not constitute a threat to health or safety. If
127   radon mitigation is performed, Seller shall pay for any retest.

128 b) Buyer shall serve Notice upon Seller or Seller's attorney of any defects disclosed by any inspection for which
129   Buyer requests resolution by Seller, together with a copy of the pertinent pages of the inspection reports

Buyer Initial _____ *Buyer Initial* _____   *Seller Initial* _____ *Seller Initial* _____
Address: **4802 W. Wellington**_____   **Chicago**_____ **IL**_____ **60641** *v6.0*
Page 3 of 13

130 within five (5) Business Days (ten (10) calendar days for a lead-based paint or lead-based paint hazard
131 inspection) after the Date of Acceptance. If within ten (10) Business Days after the Date of Acceptance
132 written agreement is not reached by the Parties with respect to resolution of all inspection issues, then either
133 Party may terminate this Contract by serving Notice to the other Party, whereupon this Contract shall be
134 null and void.

135 c) Notwithstanding anything to the contrary set forth above in this paragraph, in the event the inspection
136 reveals that the condition of the Real Estate is unacceptable to Buyer and Buyer serves Notice to Seller
137 within five (5) Business Days after the Date of Acceptance, this Contract shall be null and void. Said Notice
138 shall not include any portion of the inspection reports unless requested by Seller.

139 **d) Failure of Buyer to conduct said inspection(s) and notify Seller within the time specified operates as a**
140 **waiver of Buyer's rights to terminate this Contract under this Paragraph 12 and this Contract shall remain**
141 **in full force and effect.**

142 **13. HOMEOWNER INSURANCE:** This Contract is contingent upon Buyer obtaining evidence of insurability for an
143 Insurance Service Organization HO-3 or equivalent policy at standard premium rates within ten (10) Business
144 Days after the Date of Acceptance. **If Buyer is unable to obtain evidence of insurability and serves Notice**
145 **with proof of same to Seller within time specified, this Contract shall be null and void. If Notice is not**
146 **served within the time specified, Buyer shall be deemed to have waived this contingency and this Contract**
147 **shall remain in full force and effect.**

148 **14. FLOOD INSURANCE:** Buyer shall have the option to declare this Contract null and void if the Real Estate is
149 located in a special flood hazard area. **If Notice of the option to declare contract null and void is not given to**
150 **Seller within ten (10) Business Days after the Date of Acceptance or by the date specified in Paragraph 8 a),**
151 **whichever is later, Buyer shall be deemed to have waived such option and this Contract shall remain in full**
152 **force and effect.** Nothing herein shall be deemed to affect any rights afforded by the Residential Real Property
153 Disclosure Act.

154 **15. CONDOMINIUM/COMMON INTEREST ASSOCIATIONS:** (If applicable) The Parties agree that the terms
155 contained in this paragraph, which may be contrary to other terms of this Contract, shall supersede any
156 conflicting terms.

157 a) Title when conveyed shall be good and merchantable, subject to terms, provisions, covenants and conditions
158 of the Declaration of Condominium/Covenants, Conditions and Restrictions ("Declaration/CCRs") and all
159 amendments; public and utility easements including any easements established by or implied from the
160 Declaration/CCRs or amendments thereto; party wall rights and agreements; limitations and conditions
161 imposed by the Condominium Property Act; installments due after the date of Closing of general
162 assessments established pursuant to the Declaration/CCRs.

163 b) Seller shall be responsible for payment of all regular assessments due and levied prior to Closing and for all
164 special assessments confirmed prior to the Date of Acceptance.

165 c) Seller shall notify Buyer of any proposed special assessment or increase in any regular assessment between
166 the Date of Acceptance and Closing. The Parties shall have three (3) Business Days to reach agreement
167 relative to payment thereof. Absent such agreement either Party may declare the Contract null and void.

168 d) Seller shall, within five (5) Business Days from the Date of Acceptance, apply for those items of disclosure
169 upon sale as described in the Illinois Condominium Property Act, and provide same in a timely manner, but
170 no later than the time period provided for by law. This Contract is subject to the condition that Seller be able
171 to procure and provide to Buyer a release or waiver of any right of first refusal or other pre-emptive rights to
172 purchase created by the Declaration/CCRs. In the event the Condominium Association requires the personal
173 appearance of Buyer or additional documentation, Buyer agrees to comply with same.

174   e) In the event the documents and information provided by Seller to Buyer disclose that the existing
175   improvements are in violation of existing rules, regulations or other restrictions or that the terms and
176   conditions contained within the documents would unreasonably restrict Buyer's use of the premises or
177   would result in financial obligations unacceptable to Buyer in connection with owning the Real Estate, then
178   Buyer may declare this Contract null and void by giving Seller Notice within five (5) Business Days after the
179   receipt of the documents and information required by this Paragraph, listing those deficiencies which are
180   unacceptable to Buyer. If Notice is not served within the time specified, Buyer shall be deemed to have
181   waived this contingency, and this Contract shall remain in full force and effect.

182   f) Seller shall not be obligated to provide a condominium survey.

183   g) Seller shall provide a certificate of insurance showing Buyer and Buyer's mortgagee, if any, as an insured.

184   **16. THE DEED:** Seller shall convey or cause to be conveyed to Buyer or Buyer's Designated grantee good and
185   merchantable title to the Real Estate by recordable Warranty Deed, with release of homestead rights, (or the
186   appropriate deed if title is in trust or in an estate), and with real estate transfer stamps to be paid by Seller
187   (unless otherwise designated by local ordinance). Title when conveyed will be good and merchantable, subject
188   only to: covenants, conditions and restrictions of record and building lines and easements, if any, provided they
189   do not interfere with the current use and enjoyment of the Real Estate; and general real estate taxes not due and
190   payable at the time of Closing.

191   **17. MUNICIPAL ORDINANCE, TRANSFER TAX, AND GOVERNMENTAL COMPLIANCE:**

192   a) The Parties are cautioned that the Real Estate may be situated in a municipality that has adopted a pre-
193   closing inspection requirement, municipal Transfer Tax or other similar ordinances. Transfer taxes required
194   by municipal ordinance shall be paid by the Party designated in such ordinance.

195   b) The Parties agree to comply with the reporting requirements of the applicable sections of the Internal
196   Revenue Code and the Real Estate Settlement Procedures Act of 1974, as amended.

197   **18. TITLE:** At Seller's expense, Seller will deliver or cause to be delivered to Buyer or Buyer's attorney within
198   customary time limitations and sufficiently in advance of Closing, as evidence of title in Seller or Grantor, a title
199   commitment for an ALTA title insurance policy in the amount of the Purchase Price with extended coverage by
200   a title company licensed to operate in the State of Illinois, issued on or subsequent to the Date of Acceptance,
201   subject only to items listed in Paragraph 16. The requirement to provide extended coverage shall not apply if the
202   Real Estate is vacant land. The commitment for title insurance furnished by Seller will be presumptive evidence
203   of good and merchantable title as therein shown, subject only to the exceptions therein stated. **If the title**
204   **commitment discloses any unpermitted exceptions or if the Plat of Survey shows any encroachments or other**
205   **survey matters that are not acceptable to Buyer, then Seller shall have said exceptions, survey matters or**
206   **encroachments removed, or have the title insurer commit to either insure against loss or damage that may**
207   **result from such exceptions or survey matters or insure against any court-ordered removal of the**
208   **encroachments.** If Seller fails to have such exceptions waived or insured over prior to Closing, Buyer may elect
209   to take title as it then is with the right to deduct from the Purchase Price prior encumbrances of a definite or
210   ascertainable amount. Seller shall furnish Buyer at Closing an Affidavit of Title covering the date of Closing, and
211   shall sign any other customary forms required for issuance of an ALTA Insurance Policy.

212   **19. PLAT OF SURVEY:** Not less than one (1) Business Day prior to Closing, except where the Real Estate is a
213   condominium (see Paragraph 15) Seller shall, at Seller's expense, furnish to Buyer or Buyer's attorney a Plat of
214   Survey that conforms to the current Minimum Standard of Practice for boundary surveys, is dated not more
215   than six (6) months prior to the date of Closing, and is prepared by a professional land surveyor licensed to
216   practice land surveying under the laws of the State of Illinois. The Plat of Survey shall show visible evidence of
217   improvements, rights of way, easements, use and measurements of all parcel lines. The land surveyor shall set

Buyer Initial _____ *Buyer Initial* _____   *Seller Initial* _____ *Seller Initial* _____
Address: **4802 W. Wellington** _____   **Chicago**   **IL**   **60641** *v6.0*
Page 5 of 13

218 monuments or witness corners at all accessible corners of the land. All such corners shall also be visibly staked
219 or flagged. The Plat of Survey shall include the following statement placed near the professional land surveyor's
220 seal and signature: "This professional service conforms to the current Illinois Minimum Standards for a
221 boundary survey." A Mortgage Inspection, as defined, is not a boundary survey and is not acceptable.

222 **20. DAMAGE TO REAL ESTATE OR CONDEMNATION PRIOR TO CLOSING:** If prior to delivery of the deed the
223 Real Estate shall be destroyed or materially damaged by fire or other casualty, or the Real Estate is taken by
224 condemnation, then Buyer shall have the option of either terminating this Contract (and receiving a refund of
225 earnest money) or accepting the Real Estate as damaged or destroyed, together with the proceeds of the
226 condemnation award or any insurance payable as a result of the destruction or damage, which gross proceeds
227 Seller agrees to assign to Buyer and deliver to Buyer at Closing. Seller shall not be obligated to repair or replace
228 damaged improvements. The provisions of the Uniform Vendor and Purchaser Risk Act of the State of Illinois
229 shall be applicable to this Contract, except as modified by this paragraph.

230 **21. CONDITION OF REAL ESTATE AND INSPECTION:** Seller agrees to leave the Real Estate in broom clean
231 condition. All refuse and personal property that is not to be conveyed to Buyer shall be removed from the Real
232 Estate at Seller's expense prior to delivery of Possession. Buyer shall have the right to inspect the Real Estate,
233 fixtures and included Personal Property prior to Possession to verify that the Real Estate improvements and
234 included Personal Property are in substantially the same condition as of the Date of Acceptance, normal wear
235 and tear excepted.

236 **22. REAL ESTATE TAX ESCROW:** In the event the Real Estate is improved, but has not been previously taxed for
237 the entire year as currently improved, the sum of three percent (3%) of the Purchase Price shall be deposited in
238 escrow with the title company with the cost of the escrow to be divided equally by Buyer and Seller and paid at
239 Closing. When the exact amount of the taxes to be prorated under this Contract can be ascertained, the taxes
240 shall be prorated by Seller's attorney at the request of either Party and Seller's share of such tax liability after
241 proration shall be paid to Buyer from the escrow funds and the balance, if any, shall be paid to Seller. If Seller's
242 obligation after such proration exceeds the amount of the escrow funds, Seller agrees to pay such excess
243 promptly upon demand.

244 **23. SELLER REPRESENTATIONS:** Seller's representations contained in this paragraph shall survive the Closing.
245 Seller represents that with respect to the Real Estate Seller has no knowledge of nor has Seller received any
246 written notice from any association or governmental entity regarding:
247 a) zoning, building, fire or health code violations that have not been corrected;
248 b) any pending rezoning;
249 c) boundary line disputes;
250 d) any pending condemnation or Eminent Domain proceeding;
251 e) easements or claims of easements not shown on the public records;
252 f) any hazardous waste on the Real Estate;
253 g) any improvements to the Real Estate for which the required initial and final permits were not obtained;
254 h) any improvements to the Real Estate which are not included in full in the determination of the most recent tax assessment; or
255 i) any improvements to the Real Estate which are eligible for the home improvement tax exemption.
256 Seller further represents that:
257 *[Initials]* ____ ____ ____ ____ There *[check one]* ❑ is ☑ is not a pending or unconfirmed special assessment
258 affecting the Real Estate by any association or governmental entity payable by Buyer after the date of Closing.
259 ____ ____ ____ ____ The Real Estate *[check one]* ❑ is ☑ is not located within a Special Assessment Area or
260 Special Service Area, payments for which will not be the obligation of Seller after the year in which the Closing occurs.

Buyer Initial _____ *Buyer Initial* _____   *Seller Initial* _____ *Seller Initial* _____
Address: **4802 W. Wellington** _____   **Chicago**   **IL**   **60641** *v6.0*
Page 6 of 13

261 All Seller representations shall be deemed re-made as of Closing. If prior to Closing Seller becomes aware of
262 matters that require modification of the representations previously made in this Paragraph 23, Seller shall
263 promptly notify Buyer. If the matters specified in such Notice are not resolved prior to Closing, Buyer may
264 terminate this Contract by Notice to Seller and this Contract shall be null and void.

265 **24. BUSINESS DAYS/HOURS:** Business Days are defined as Monday through Friday, excluding Federal
266 holidays. Business Hours are defined as 8:00 A.M. to 6:00 P.M. Chicago time.

267 **25. FACSIMILE OR DIGITAL SIGNATURES:** Facsimile or digital signatures shall be sufficient for purposes of
268 executing, negotiating, and finalizing this Contract, and delivery thereof by one of the following methods shall
269 be deemed delivery of this Contract containing original signature(s). An acceptable facsimile signature may be
270 produced by scanning an original, hand-signed document and transmitting same by facsimile. An acceptable
271 digital signature may be produced by use of a qualified, established electronic security procedure mutually
272 agreed upon by the Parties. Transmissions of a digitally signed copy hereof shall be by an established, mutually
273 acceptable electronic method, such as creating a PDF ("Portable Document Format") document incorporating
274 the digital signature and sending same by electronic mail.

275 **26. DIRECTION TO ESCROWEE:** In every instance where this Contract shall be deemed null and void or if this
276 Contract may be terminated by either Party, the following shall be deemed incorporated: "and Earnest Money
277 refunded upon the joint written direction by the Parties to Escrowee or upon an entry of an order by a court of
278 competent jurisdiction."

279 In the event either Party has declared the Contract null and void or the transaction has failed to close as
280 provided for in this Contract and if Escrowee has not received joint written direction by the Parties or such court
281 order, the Escrowee may elect to proceed as follows:

282 a) Escrowee shall give written Notice to the Parties as provided for in this Contract at least fourteen (14) days
283 prior to the date of intended disbursement of Earnest Money indicating the manner in which Escrowee
284 intends to disburse in the absence of any written objection. If no written objection is received by the date
285 indicated in the Notice then Escrowee shall distribute the Earnest Money as indicated in the written Notice
286 to the Parties. **If any Party objects in writing** to the intended disbursement of Earnest Money then Earnest
287 Money shall be held until receipt of joint written direction from all Parties or until receipt of an order of a
288 court of competent jurisdiction.

289 b) Escrowee may file a Suit for Interpleader and deposit any funds held into the Court for distribution after
290 resolution of the dispute between Seller and Buyer by the Court. Escrowee may retain from the funds
291 deposited with the Court the amount necessary to reimburse Escrowee for court costs and reasonable
292 attorney's fees incurred due to the filing of the Interpleader. If the amount held in escrow is inadequate to
293 reimburse Escrowee for the costs and attorney's fees, Buyer and Seller shall jointly and severally indemnify
294 Escrowee for additional costs and fees incurred in filing the Interpleader action.

295 **27. NOTICE:** Except as provided in Paragraph 32 c) 2) regarding the manner of service for "kick-out" Notices, all
296 Notices shall be in writing and shall be served by one Party or attorney to the other Party or attorney. Notice to
297 any one of the multiple person Party shall be sufficient Notice to all. Notice shall be given in the following manner:

298 a) By personal delivery; or

299 b) By mailing to the addresses recited herein by regular mail and by certified mail, return receipt requested. Except
300 as otherwise provided herein, Notice served by certified mail shall be effective on the date of mailing; or

301 c) By facsimile transmission. Notice shall be effective as of date and time of the transmission, provided that the
302 Notice transmitted shall be sent on Business Days during Business Hours. In the event Notice is transmitted

303   during non-business hours, the effective date and time of Notice is the first hour of the next Business Day after
304   transmission; or
305   d) By e-mail transmission if an e-mail address has been furnished by the recipient Party or the recipient Party's
306   attorney to the sending Party or is shown in this Contract. Notice shall be effective as of date and time of e-mail
307   transmission, provided that, in the event e-mail Notice is transmitted during non-business hours, the effective
308   date and time of Notice is the first hour of the next Business Day after transmission. An attorney or Party may
309   opt out of future e-mail Notice by any form of Notice provided by this Contract; or
310   e) By commercial overnight delivery (e.g., FedEx). Such Notice shall be effective on the next Business Day
311   following deposit with the overnight delivery company.

312   **28. PERFORMANCE: Time is of the essence of this Contract.** In any action with respect to this Contract, the Parties
313   are free to pursue any legal remedies at law or in equity and the prevailing party in litigation shall be entitled to
314   collect reasonable attorney fees and costs from the non-prevailing party as ordered by a court of competent jurisdiction.

315   **29. CHOICE OF LAW AND GOOD FAITH:** All terms and provisions of this Contract including but not limited to the
316   Attorney Review and Professional Inspection paragraphs shall be governed by the laws of the State of Illinois and
317   are subject to the covenant of good faith and fair dealing implied in all Illinois contracts.

318   **30. OTHER PROVISIONS:** This Contract is also subject to those OPTIONAL PROVISIONS initialed by the Parties
319   and the following additional attachments, if any: **N/A**_____
320   _____.

321   **OPTIONAL PROVISIONS (Applicable ONLY if initialed by all Parties)**

322   *[Initials]* ____ ____ ____ ____ **31. CONFIRMATION OF DUAL AGENCY:** The Parties confirm that they have previously
323   consented to _____ (Licensee) acting as a Dual Agent in providing
324   brokerage services on their behalf and specifically consent to Licensee acting as a Dual Agent with regard to the
325   transaction referred to in this Contract.

326   ____ ____ ____ ____ **32. SALE OF BUYER'S REAL ESTATE:**
327   a) **REPRESENTATIONS ABOUT BUYER'S REAL ESTATE:** Buyer represents to Seller as follows:
328   1) Buyer owns real estate (hereinafter referred to as "Buyer's real estate") with the address of:
329   _____
330   Address   City   State   Zip
331   2) Buyer *[check one]* ❑ has ❑ has not entered into a contract to sell Buyer's real estate.
332   If Buyer has entered into a contract to sell Buyer's real estate, that contract:
333   a) *[check one]* ❑ is ❑ is not subject to a mortgage contingency.
334   b) *[check one]* ❑ is ❑ is not subject to a real estate sale contingency.
335   c) *[check one]* ❑ is ❑ is not subject to a real estate closing contingency.
336   3) Buyer *[check one]* ❑ has ❑ has not listed Buyer's real estate for sale with a licensed real estate broker and
337   in a local multiple listing service.
338   4) If Buyer's real estate is not listed for sale with a licensed real estate broker and in a local multiple listing
339   service, Buyer *[check one]*:
340   a) ❑ Shall list real estate for sale with a licensed real estate broker who will place it in a local multiple
341   listing service within five (5) Business Days after Date of Acceptance.
342   *[For information only]* Broker: _____
343   Broker's Address: _____ Phone: _____
344   b) ❑ Does not intend to list said real estate for sale.

Buyer Initial _____ *Buyer Initial* _____   *Seller Initial* _____ *Seller Initial* _____
Address: **4802 W. Wellington**_____ **Chicago**_____ **IL**_____ **60641**____ *v6.0*
Page 8 of 13

345 **b) CONTINGENCIES BASED UPON SALE AND/OR CLOSING OF REAL ESTATE:**
346   1) This Contract is contingent upon Buyer having entered into a contract for the sale of Buyer's real estate that
347   is in full force and effect as of _____, 20 ____. Such contract should provide for a closing
348   date not later than the Closing Date set forth in this Contract. **If Notice is served on or before the date set**
349   **forth in this subparagraph that Buyer has not procured a contract for the sale of Buyer's real estate, this**
350   **Contract shall be null and void. If Notice that Buyer has not procured a contract for the sale of Buyer's**
351   **real estate is not served on or before the close of business on the date set forth in this subparagraph,**
352   **Buyer shall be deemed to have waived all contingencies contained in this Paragraph 32, and this**
353   **Contract shall remain in full force and effect.** (If this paragraph is used, then the following paragraph **must**
354   be completed.)
355   2) In the event Buyer has entered into a contract for the sale of Buyer's real estate as set forth in Paragraph 32
356   b) 1) and that contract is in full force and effect, or has entered into a contract for the sale of Buyer's real
357   estate prior to the execution of this Contract, this Contract is contingent upon Buyer closing the sale of
358   Buyer's real estate on or before _____, 20 ____. **If Notice that Buyer has not closed the sale**
359   **of Buyer's real estate is served before the close of business on the next Business Day after the date set**
360   **forth in the preceding sentence, this Contract shall be null and void. If Notice is not served as described**
361   **in the preceding sentence, Buyer shall have deemed to have waived all contingencies contained in this**
362   **Paragraph 32, and this Contract shall remain in full force and effect.**
363   3) If the contract for the sale of Buyer's real estate is terminated for any reason after the date set forth in
364   Paragraph 32 b) 1) (or after the date of this Contract if no date is set forth in Paragraph 32 b) 1)), Buyer shall,
365   within three (3) Business Days of such termination, notify Seller of said termination. **Unless Buyer, as part**
366   **of said Notice, waives all contingencies in Paragraph 32 and complies with Paragraph 32 d), this Contract**
367   **shall be null and void as of the date of Notice. If Notice as required by this subparagraph is not served**
368   **within the time specified, Buyer shall be in default under the terms of this Contract.**
369 **c) SELLER'S RIGHT TO CONTINUE TO OFFER REAL ESTATE FOR SALE:** During the time of this contingency,
370   Seller has the right to continue to show the Real Estate and offer it for sale subject to the following:
371   1) If Seller accepts another bona fide offer to purchase the Real Estate while contingencies expressed in
372   Paragraph 32 b) are in effect, Seller shall notify Buyer in writing of same. Buyer shall then have _____
373   hours after Seller gives such Notice to waive the contingencies set forth in Paragraph 32 b), subject to
374   Paragraph 32 d).
375   2) Seller's Notice to Buyer (commonly referred to as a 'kick-out' Notice) shall be in writing and shall be served
376   on Buyer, not Buyer's attorney or Buyer's real estate agent. Courtesy copies of such 'kick-out' Notice should
377   be sent to Buyer's attorney and Buyer's real estate agent, if known. Failure to provide such courtesy copies
378   shall not render Notice invalid. Notice to any one of a multiple-person Buyer shall be sufficient Notice to all
379   Buyers. Notice for the purpose of this subparagraph only shall be served upon Buyer in the following manner:
380   a) By personal delivery effective at the time and date of personal delivery; or
381   b) By mailing to the address recited herein for Buyer by regular mail and by certified mail. Notice shall be
382   effective at 10:00 A.M. on the morning of the second day following deposit of Notice in the U.S. Mail; or
383   c) By commercial delivery overnight (e.g., FedEx). Notice shall be effective upon delivery or at 4:00 P.M.
384   Chicago time on the next delivery day following deposit with the overnight delivery company,
385   whichever first occurs.
386   3) If Buyer complies with the provisions of Paragraph 32 d) then this Contract shall remain in full force and effect.
387   4) If the contingencies set forth in Paragraph 32 b) are NOT waived in writing, within said time period by
388   Buyer, this Contract shall be null and void.

Buyer Initial _____ *Buyer Initial* _____   *Seller Initial* _____ *Seller Initial* _____
Address: **4802 W. Wellington**   **Chicago**   **IL**   **60641** *v6.0*
Page 9 of 13

389   5) Except as provided in Paragraph 32 c) 2) above, all Notices shall be made in the manner provided by
390   Paragraph 27 of this Contract.
391   6) Buyer waives any ethical objection to the delivery of Notice under this paragraph by Seller's attorney or
392   representative.
393 **d) WAIVER OF PARAGRAPH 32 CONTINGENCIES:** Buyer shall be deemed to have waived the contingencies in
394   Paragraph 32 b) when Buyer has delivered written waiver and deposited with the Escrowee additional earnest
395   money in the amount of $ _____ in the form of a cashier's or certified check within the time
396   specified. **If Buyer fails to deposit the additional earnest money within the time specified, the waiver shall be**
397   **deemed ineffective and this Contract shall be null and void.**
398 **e) BUYER COOPERATION REQUIRED:** Buyer authorizes Seller or Seller's agent to verify representations contained
399   in Paragraph 32 at any time, and Buyer agrees to cooperate in providing relevant information.
400 ___ ___ ___ ___ **33. CANCELLATION OF PRIOR REAL ESTATE CONTRACT:** In the event either Party has entered
401 into a prior real estate contract, this Contract shall be subject to written cancellation of the prior contract on or before
402 _____, 20 ____. **In the event the prior contract is not cancelled within the time specified, this**
403 **Contract shall be null and void.** Seller's notice to the purchaser under the prior contract should not be served
404 **until after Attorney Review and Professional Inspections provisions of this Contract have expired, been**
405 **satisfied or waived.**
406 ___ ___ ___ ___ **34. HOME WARRANTY:** Seller shall provide at no expense to Buyer a Home Warranty at a cost
407 of $ _____. Evidence of a fully pre-paid policy shall be delivered at Closing.
408 ___ ___ ___ ___ **35. CREDIT AT CLOSING:** Provided Buyer's lender permits such credit to show on the HUD-1
409 Settlement Statement or Closing Disclosure, **and if not, such lesser amount as the lender permits,** Seller agrees to
410 credit $ _____ to Buyer at Closing to be applied to prepaid expenses, closing costs or both.
411 ___ ___ ___ ___ **36. TRANSACTIONS NOT CONTINGENT ON FINANCING: IF EITHER OF THE FOLLOWING**
412 **ALTERNATIVE OPTIONS IS SELECTED, THE PROVISIONS OF THE MORTGAGE CONTINGENCY PARAGRAPH 8**
413 **SHALL NOT APPLY [*CHOOSE ONLY ONE*]:**
414 a) ___ ___ ___ ___ **Transaction With No Mortgage (All Cash):** If this selection is made, Buyer will pay at closing,
415   in the form of "Good Funds" the difference (plus or minus prorations) between the Purchase Price and the
416   amount of the Earnest Money deposited pursuant to Paragraph 4 above. Buyer represents to Seller, as of the
417   Date of Offer, that Buyer has sufficient funds available to satisfy the provisions of this paragraph. Buyer agrees
418   to verify the above representation upon the reasonable request of Seller and to authorize the disclosure of such
419   financial information to Seller, Seller's attorney or Seller's broker that may be reasonably necessary to provide
420   the availability of sufficient funds to close. Buyer understands and agrees that, so long as Seller has fully
421   complied with Seller's obligations under this Contract, any act or omission outside of the control of Seller,
422   whether intentional or not, that prevents Buyer from satisfying the balance due from Buyer at closing, shall
423   constitute a material breach of this Contract by Buyer. The Parties shall share the title company escrow closing
424   fee equally. **Unless otherwise provided in Paragraph 32, this Contract shall not be contingent upon the sale**
425   **and/or closing of Buyer's existing real estate.**
426 b) ___ ___ ___ ___ **Transaction, Mortgage Allowed:** If this selection is made, Buyer will pay at closing, in the
427   form of "Good Funds" the difference (plus or minus prorations) between the Purchase Price and the amount of
428   the Earnest Money deposited pursuant to Paragraph 4 above. Buyer represents to Seller, as of the Date of Offer,
429   that Buyer has sufficient funds available to satisfy the provisions of this paragraph. Buyer agrees to verify the
430   above representation upon the reasonable request of Seller and to authorize the disclosure of such financial
431   information to Seller, Seller's attorney or Seller's broker that may be reasonably necessary to prove the
432   availability of sufficient funds to close. Notwithstanding such representation, Seller agrees to reasonably and

Buyer Initial _____ *Buyer Initial* _____   *Seller Initial* _____ *Seller Initial* _____
Address: **4802 W. Wellington**   **Chicago**   **IL**   **60641** *v6.0*
Page 10 of 13

promptly cooperate with Buyer so that Buyer may apply for and obtain a mortgage loan or loans including but not limited to providing access to the Real Estate to satisfy Buyer's obligations to pay the balance due (plus or minus prorations) to close this transaction. Such cooperation shall include the performance in a timely manner of all of Seller's pre-closing obligations under this Contract. **This Contract shall NOT be contingent upon Buyer obtaining a commitment for financing.** Buyer understands and agrees that, so long as Seller has fully complied with Seller's obligations under this Contract, any act or omission outside of the control of Seller, whether intentional or not, that prevents Buyer from satisfying the balance due from Buyer at Closing shall constitute a material breach of this Contract by Buyer. Buyer shall pay the title company escrow closing fee. **Unless otherwise provided in Paragraph 32, this Contract shall not be contingent upon the sale and/or closing of Buyer's existing real estate.**

____ ____ ____ ____ **37. VA OR FHA FINANCING:** If Buyer is seeking VA or FHA financing, **required FHA or VA amendments and disclosures shall be attached to this Contract.** If VA, the Funding Fee, or if FHA, the Mortgage Insurance Premium (MIP) shall be paid by Buyer and *[check one]* ❏ shall ❏ shall not be added to the mortgage loan amount.

____ ____ ____ ____ **38. WELL OR SANITARY SYSTEM INSPECTIONS:** Seller shall obtain at Seller's expense a well water test stating that the well delivers not less than five (5) gallons of water per minute and including a bacteria and nitrate test and/or a septic report from the applicable County Health Department, a Licensed Environmental Health Practitioner, or a licensed well and septic inspector, each dated not more than ninety (90) days prior to Closing, stating that the well and water supply and the private sanitary system are in operating condition with no defects noted. Seller shall remedy any defect or deficiency disclosed by said report(s) prior to Closing, provided that if the cost of remedying a defect or deficiency and the cost of landscaping together exceed $3,000.00, and if the Parties cannot reach agreement regarding payment of such additional cost, this Contract may be terminated by either Party. Additional testing recommended by the report shall be obtained at the Seller's expense. If the report recommends additional testing after Closing, the Parties shall have the option of establishing an escrow with a mutual cost allocation for necessary repairs or replacements, or either Party may terminate this Contract prior to Closing. Seller shall deliver a copy of such evaluation(s) to Buyer not less than one (1) Business Day prior to Closing.

____ ____ ____ ____ **39. WOOD DESTROYING INFESTATION:** Notwithstanding the provisions of Paragraph 12, within ten (10) Business Days after the Date of Acceptance, Seller at Seller's expense shall deliver to Buyer a written report, dated not more than six (6) months prior to the Date of Closing, by a licensed inspector certified by the appropriate state regulatory authority in the subcategory of termites, stating that there is no visible evidence of active infestation by termites or other wood destroying insects. Unless otherwise agreed between the Parties, if the report discloses evidence of active infestation or structural damage, Buyer has the option within five (5) Business Days of receipt of the report to proceed with the purchase or to declare this Contract null and void.

____ ____ ____ ____ **40. POST CLOSING POSSESSION:** Possession shall be delivered no later than 11:59 P.M. on the date that is _____ days after the date of Closing ("the Possession Date"). Seller shall be responsible for all utilities, contents and liability insurance, and home maintenance expenses until delivery of possession. Seller shall deposit in escrow at Closing with _____, *[check one]* ❏ one percent (1%) of the Purchase Price or ❏ the sum of $ _____ to be paid by Escrowee as follows:

a) The sum of $ _____ per day for use and occupancy from and including the day after Closing to and including the day of delivery of Possession, if on or before the Possession Date;

b) The amount per day equal to three (3) times the daily amount set forth herein shall be paid for each day after the Possession Date specified in this paragraph that Seller remains in possession of the Real Estate; and

474   c) The balance, if any, to Seller after delivery of Possession and provided that the terms of Paragraph 21 have been
475   satisfied. Seller's liability under this paragraph shall not be limited to the amount of the possession escrow
476   deposit referred to above. Nothing herein shall be deemed to create a Landlord/Tenant relationship between the Parties.

477   ___ ___ ___ ___ **41. "AS IS" CONDITION:** This Contract is for the sale and purchase of the Real Estate in its "As
478   Is" condition as of the Date of Offer. Buyer acknowledges that no representations, warranties or guarantees with
479   respect to the condition of the Real Estate have been made by Seller or Seller's Designated Agent other than those
480   known defects, if any, disclosed by Seller. Buyer may conduct an inspection at Buyer's expense. In that event, Seller
481   shall make the Real Estate available to Buyer's inspector at reasonable times. Buyer shall indemnify Seller and hold
482   Seller harmless from and against any loss or damage caused by the acts of negligence of Buyer or any person
483   performing any inspection. **In the event the inspection reveals that the condition of the Real Estate is**
484   **unacceptable to Buyer and Buyer so notifies Seller within five (5) Business Days after the Date of Acceptance,**
485   **this Contract shall be null and void. Buyer's notice SHALL NOT include a copy of the inspection report, and**
486   **Buyer shall not be obligated to send the inspection report to Seller absent Seller's written request for same.**
487   **Failure of Buyer to notify Seller or to conduct said inspection operates as a waiver of Buyer's right to terminate**
488   **this Contract under this paragraph and this Contract shall remain in full force and effect.** Buyer acknowledges
489   that the provisions of Paragraph 12 and the warranty provisions of Paragraph 5 do not apply to this Contract.

490   ___ ___ ___ ___ **42. SPECIFIED PARTY APPROVAL:** This Contract is contingent upon the approval of the Real
491   Estate by _____
492   Buyer's Specified Party, within five (5) Business Days after the Date of Acceptance. In the event Buyer's Specified
493   Party does not approve of the Real Estate and Notice is given to Seller within the time specified, this Contract shall
494   be null and void. If Notice is not served within the time specified, this provision shall be deemed waived by the
495   Parties and this Contract shall remain in full force and effect.

496   ___ ___ ___ ___ **43. INTEREST BEARING ACCOUNT:** Earnest money (with a completed W-9 and other
497   required forms), shall be held in a federally insured interest bearing account at a financial institution designated
498   by Escrowee. All interest earned on the earnest money shall accrue to the benefit of and be paid to Buyer. **Buyer**
499   **shall be responsible for any administrative fee (not to exceed $100) charged for setting up the account.** In
500   anticipation of Closing, the Parties direct Escrowee to close the account no sooner than ten (10) Business Days
501   prior to the anticipated Closing date.

502   ___ ___ ___ ___ **44. MISCELLANEOUS PROVISIONS:** Buyer's and Seller's obligations are contingent upon the
503   Parties entering into a separate written agreement consistent with the terms and conditions set forth herein, and
504   with such additional terms as either Party may deem necessary, providing for one or more of the following *[check applicable boxes]*:
505   ❑ Articles of Agreement for Deed   ❑ Assumption of Seller's Mortgage   ❑ Commercial/Investment
506   or Purchase Money Mortgage   ❑ Cooperative Apartment   ❑ New Construction
507   ❑ Short Sale   ❑ Tax-Deferred Exchange   ❑ Vacant Land

508   *[LINES 508-511 LEFT INTENTIONALLY BLANK]*
509
510
511

Buyer Initial _____ Buyer Initial _____   Seller Initial _____ Seller Initial _____
Address: **4802 W. Wellington** _____ **Chicago** _____ **IL** _____ **60641** *v6.0*
Page 12 of 13

512 THIS DOCUMENT WILL BECOME A LEGALLY BINDING CONTRACT WHEN SIGNED BY ALL PARTIES AND DELIVERED TO THE PARTIES OR THEIR AGENTS.

513 THE PARTIES REPRESENT THAT THE TEXT OF THIS COPYRIGHTED FORM HAS NOT BEEN ALTERED AND IS IDENTICAL TO THE OFFICIAL
514 MULTI-BOARD RESIDENTIAL REAL ESTATE CONTRACT 6.0.

515	July 1, 2015			July 2, 2015		
516	Date of Offer			DATE OF ACCEPTANCE		
517						
518	Buyer Signature			Seller Signature		
519						
520	Buyer Signature			Seller Signature		
521	**Roberta Buyer**			**O.O.R.**		
522	Print Buyer(s) Name(s) *[Required]*			Print Seller(s) Name(s) *[Required]*		
523	**8741 W. Cicero**			**4802 W. Wellington**		
524	Address			Address		
525	**Chicago**	**IL**	**60659**	**Chicago**	**IL**	**60641**
526	City	State	Zip	City	State	Zip
527	**872-555-9874**	**roberta666@umail.com**		**312-555-2587**	**jseller@2mail.com**	
528	Phone	E-mail		Phone	E-mail	

FOR INFORMATION ONLY

529						
530	**Caldwell Real Estate Brokers**		**987654**	**ReMix Real Estate**		**147258**
531	Buyer's Brokerage		MLS #	Seller's Brokerage		MLS #
532						
533	Address	City	Zip	Address	City	Zip
534	**Janet Coldheart**		**98765432**	**John Attack**		**14725836**
535	Buyer's Designated Agent		MLS #	Seller's Designated Agent		MLS #
536	**773-555-5894**		**773-555-5899**	**312-555-9630**		**312-555-9631**
537	Phone		Fax	Phone		Fax
538	**jcoldheart@caldwell.com**			**jattack@remix.com**		
539	E-mail			E-mail		
540	**Eileen Dover**		**edover@dover.com**	**Irwin M. Gone**		**imgone@ggg.com**
541	Buyer's Attorney		E-mail	Seller's Attorney		E-mail
542		**Chicago**	**60659**		**Chicago**	**60603**
543	Address	City	Zip	Address	City	Zip
544	**312-555-4125**		**312-555-4126**	**773-555-1047**		**773-555-1048**
545	Phone		Fax	Phone		Fax
546	**Hi-Interest Mortgage**		**312-555-2540**			
547	Mortgage Company		Phone	Homeowner's/Condo Association (if any) Phone		
548	**Penelope Miller**		**312-555-2541**			
549	Loan Officer		Phone/Fax	Management Co./Other Contact		Phone
550	**penelope@hiinterest.com**					
551	Loan Officer E-mail			Management Co./Other Contact E-mail		

552 Illinois Real Estate License Law requires all offers be presented in a timely manner; Buyer requests verification that this offer was presented.

553 Seller rejection: This offer was presented to Seller on _____, 20 ____ at ___:___ A.M./P.M. and rejected on _____

554 _____, 20 ____ at ___:___ A.M./P.M. ____ ____ *[Seller Initials]*

Buyer Initial _____ Buyer Initial _____   Seller Initial _____ Seller Initial _____

Address: **4802 W. Wellington**   **Chicago**   **IL**   **60641** *v6.0*

Page 13 of 13

RESIDENTIAL REAL PROPERTY DISCLOSURE REPORT

NOTICE: THE PURPOSE OF THIS REPORT IS TO PROVIDE PROSPECTIVE BUYERS WITH INFORMATION ABOUT MATERIAL DEFECTS IN THE RESIDENTIAL REAL PROPERTY. THIS REPORT DOES NOT LIMIT THE PARTIES' RIGHT TO CONTRACT FOR THE SALE OF RESIDENTIAL REAL PROPERTY IN "AS IS" CONDITION. UNDER COMMON LAW, SELLERS WHO DISCLOSE MATERIAL DEFECTS MAY BE UNDER A CONTINUING OBLIGATION TO ADVISE THE PROSPECTIVE BUYERS ABOUT THE CONDITION OF THE RESIDENTIAL REAL PROPERTY EVEN AFTER THE REPORT IS DELIVERED TO THE PROSPECTIVE BUYER. COMPLETION OF THIS REPORT BY THE SELLER CREATES LEGAL OBLIGATIONS ON THE SELLER; THEREFORE, THE SELLER MAY WISH TO CONSULT AN ATTORNEY PRIOR TO COMPLETION OF THIS REPORT.

Property Address: <u>4802 W. Wellington</u>

City, State & Zip Code: <u>Chicago, IL 60641</u>

Seller's Name: <u>Jonathan Seller</u>

This Report is a disclosure of certain conditions of the residential real property listed above in compliance with the Residential Real Property Disclosure Act. This information is provided as of <u>July 1, 2015</u>, and does not reflect any changes made or occurring after that date or information that becomes known to the seller after that date. The disclosures herein shall not be deemed warranties of any kind by the seller or any person representing any party in this transaction.

In this form, "am aware" means to have actual notice or actual knowledge without any specific investigation or inquiry. In this form, "material defect" means a condition that would have a substantial adverse effect on the value of the residential real property or that would significantly impair the health or safety of future occupants of the residential real property unless the seller reasonably believes that the condition has been corrected.

The seller discloses the following information with the knowledge that even though the statements herein are not deemed to be warranties, prospective buyers may choose to rely on this information in deciding whether or not and on what terms to purchase the residential real property.

The seller represents that to the best of his or her actual knowledge, the following statements have been accurately noted as "yes" (correct), "no" (incorrect), or "not applicable" to the property being sold. If the seller indicates that the response to any statement, except number 1, is yes or not applicable, the seller shall provide an explanation, in the additional information area of this form.

YES NO N/A

1. ☑☐☐ Seller has occupied the property within the last 12 months. (No explanation is needed.)

2. ☐☑☐ I am aware of flooding or recurring leakage problems in the crawl space or basement.

3. ☐☑☐ I am aware that the property is located in a flood plain or that I currently have flood hazard insurance on the property.

4. ☐☑☐ I am aware of material defects in the basement or foundation (including cracks and bulges).

5. ☐☑☐ I am aware of leaks or material defects in the roof, ceilings, or chimney.

6. ☐☑☐ I am aware of material defects in the walls or floors.

7. ☐☑☐ I am aware of material defects in the electrical system.

8. ☐☑☐ I am aware of material defects in the plumbing system (includes such things as water heater, sump pump, water treatment system, sprinkler system, and swimming pool).

9. ☐☑☐ I am aware of material defects in the well or well equipment.

10. ☐☑☐ I am aware of unsafe conditions in the drinking water.

11. ☐☑☐ I am aware of material defects in the heating, air conditioning, or ventilating systems.

12. ☐☑☐ I am aware of material defects in the fireplace or woodburning stove.

13. ☐☑☐ I am aware of material defects in the septic, sanitary sewer, or other disposal system.

14. ☐☑☐ I am aware of unsafe concentrations of radon on the premises.

15. ☐☑☐ I am aware of unsafe concentrations of or unsafe conditions relating to asbestos on the premises.

16. ☐☑☐ I am aware of unsafe concentrations of or unsafe conditions relating to lead paint, lead water pipes, lead plumbing pipes or lead in the soil on the premises.

17. ☐☑☐ I am aware of mine subsidence, underground pits, settlement, sliding, upheaval, or other earth stability defects on the premises.

18. ☐☑☐ I am aware of current infestations of termites or other wood boring insects.

19. ☐☑☐ I am aware of a structural defect caused by previous infestations of termites or other wood boring insects.

20. ☐☑☐ I am aware of underground fuel storage tanks on the property.

21. ☐☑☐ I am aware of boundary or lot line disputes.

22. ☐☑☐ I have received notice of violation of local, state or federal laws or regulations relating to this property, which violation has not been corrected.

23. ☐☑☐ I am aware that this property has been used for the manufacture of methamphetamine as defined in Section 10 of the Methamphetamine Control and Community Protection Act.

Note: These disclosures are not intended to cover the common elements of a condominium, but only the actual residential real property including limited common elements allocated to the exclusive use thereof that form an integral part of the condominium unit.

Note: These disclosures are intended to reflect the current condition of the premises and do not include previous problems, if any, that the seller reasonably believes have been corrected.

If any of the above are marked "not applicable" or "yes," please explain here or use additional pages, if necessary:

Check here if additional pages used: ☐

Seller certifies that seller has prepared this statement and certifies that the information provided is based on the actual notice or actual knowledge of the seller without any specific investigation or inquiry on the part of the seller. The seller hereby authorizes any person representing any principal in this transaction to provide a copy of this report, and to disclose any information in the report, to any person in connection with any actual or anticipated sale of the property.

Seller: _____ Date: _____

Seller: _____ Date: _____

THE PROSPECTIVE BUYER IS AWARE THAT THE PARTIES MAY CHOOSE TO NEGOTIATE AN AGREEMENT FOR THE SALE OF THE PROPERTY SUBJECT TO ANY OR ALL MATERIAL DEFECTS DISCLOSED IN THIS REPORT ("AS IS"). THIS DISCLOSURE IS NOT A SUBSTITUTE FOR ANY INSPECTIONS OR WARRANTIES THAT THE PROSPECTIVE BUYER OR SELLER MAY WISH TO OBTAIN OR NEGOTIATE. THE FACT THAT THE SELLER IS NOT AWARE OF A PARTICULAR CONDITION OR PROBLEM IS NO GUARANTEE THAT IT DOES NOT EXIST. THE PROSPECTIVE BUYER IS AWARE THAT HE MAY REQUEST AN INSPECTION OF THE PREMISES PERFORMED BY A QUALIFIED PROFESSIONAL.

Prospective Buyer: _____ Date: _____ Time: _____

Prospective Buyer: _____ Date: _____ Time: _____

(765 ILCS 77/Art. 1 **heading**)

ARTICLE 1

SHORT TITLE

(765 ILCS 77/1)

Sec. 1. Short title. This Act may be cited as the Residential Real Property Disclosure Act.

(765 ILCS 77/Art. 2 heading)

ARTICLE 2

DISCLOSURES

(765 ILCS 77/5)

Sec. 5. Definitions. As used in this Act, unless the context otherwise requires the following terms have the meaning given in this Section.

"Residential real property" means real property improved with not less than one nor more than 4 residential dwelling units; units in residential cooperatives; or, condominium units, including the limited common elements allocated to the exclusive use thereof that form an integral part of the condominium unit.

"Seller" means every person or entity who is an owner, beneficiary of a trust, contract purchaser or lessee of a ground lease, who has an interest (legal or equitable) in residential real property. However, "seller" shall not include any person who has both (i) never occupied the residential real property and (ii) never had the management responsibility for the residential real property nor delegated such responsibility for the residential real property to another person or entity.

"Prospective buyer" means any person or entity negotiating or offering to become an owner or lessee of residential real property by means of a transfer for value to which this Act applies.

(765 ILCS 77/10)

Sec. 10. Except as provided in Section 15, this Act applies to any transfer by sale, exchange, installment land sale contract, assignment of beneficial interest, lease with an option to purchase, ground lease, or assignment of ground lease of residential real property.

(765 ILCS 77/15)

Sec. 15. The provisions of this Act do not apply to the following:

(1) Transfers pursuant to court order, including, but not limited to, transfers ordered by a probate court in administration of an estate, transfers between spouses resulting from a judgment of dissolution of marriage or legal separation, transfers pursuant to an order to the following:

(2) Transfers pursuant to court order, including, of possession, transfers by a trustee in bankruptcy, transfers by eminent domain, and transfers resulting from a decree for specific performance.

(3) Transfers from a mortgagor to a mortgagee by deed in lieu of foreclosure or consent judgment, transfer by judicial deed issued pursuant to a foreclosure sale to the successful bidder or the assignee of a certificate of sale, transfer by

a collateral assignment of a beneficial interest of a land trust, or a transfer by a mortgagee or a successor in interest to the mortgagee's secured position or a beneficiary under a deed in trust who has acquired the real property by deed in lieu of foreclosure, consent judgment or judicial deed issued pursuant to a foreclosure sale.

(4) Transfers by a fiduciary in the course of the administration of a decedent's estate, guardianship, conservatorship, or trust.

(5) Transfers from one co?owner to one or more other co?owners.

(6) Transfers pursuant to testate or intestate succession.

(7) Transfers made to a spouse, or to a person or persons in the lineal line of consanguinity of one or more of the sellers.

(8) Transfers from an entity that has taken title to residential real property from a seller for the purpose of assisting in the relocation of the seller, so long as the entity makes available to all prospective buyers a copy of the disclosure form furnished to the entity by the seller.

(9) Transfers to or from any governmental entity.

(10) Transfers of newly constructed residential real property that has not been occupied.

(765 ILCS 77/20)

Sec. 20. A seller of residential real property shall complete all applicable items in the disclosure document described in Section 35 of this Act. The seller shall deliver to the prospective buyer the written disclosure statement required by this Act before the signing of a written agreement by the seller and prospective buyer that would, subject to the satisfaction of any negotiated contingencies, require the prospective buyer to accept a transfer of the residential real property.

(765 ILCS 77/25)

Sec. 25. Liability of seller.

(a) The seller is not liable for any error, inaccuracy, or omission of any information delivered pursuant to this Act if (i) the seller had no knowledge of the error, inaccuracy, or omission, (ii) the error, inaccuracy, or omission was based on a reasonable belief that a material defect or other matter not disclosed had been corrected, or (iii) the error, inaccuracy, or omission was based on information provided by a public agency or by a licensed engineer, land surveyor, structural pest control operator, or by a contractor about matters within the scope of the contractor's occupation and the seller had no knowledge of the error, inaccuracy, or omission.

(b) The seller shall disclose material defects of which the seller has actual knowledge.

(c) The seller is not obligated by this Act to make any specific investigation or inquiry in an effort to complete the disclosure statement.

(765 ILCS 77/30)

Sec. 30. Disclosure supplement. If, prior to closing, any seller has actual knowledge of an error, inaccuracy, or omission in any prior disclosure document after delivery of that disclosure document to a prospective buyer, that seller shall supplement the prior disclosure document with a written supplemental disclosure.

(765 ILCS 77/40)

Sec. 40. Material defect. If a material defect is disclosed in the Residential Real Property Disclosure Report, after acceptance by the prospective buyer of an offer or counter?offer made by a seller or after the execution of an offer made by a prospective buyer that is accepted by the seller for the conveyance of the residential real property, then the prospective buyer may, within 3 business days after receipt of that report by the prospective buyer, terminate the contract or other agreement without any liability or recourse except for the return to prospective buyer of all earnest money deposits or down payments paid by prospective buyer in the transaction. If a material defect is disclosed in a supplement to this disclosure document, the prospective buyer shall not have a right to terminate unless the material defect results from an error, inaccuracy, or omission of which the seller had actual knowledge at the time the prior disclosure document was completed and signed by the seller. The right to terminate the contract, however, shall no longer exist after the conveyance of the residential real property. For purposes of this Act the termination shall be deemed to be made when written notice of termination is personally delivered to at least one of the sellers identified in the contract or other agreement or when deposited, certified or registered mail, with the United States Postal Service, addressed to one of the sellers at the address indicated in the contract or agreement, or, if there is not an address contained therein, then at the address indicated for the residential real property on the report.

(765 ILCS 77/45)

Sec. 45. This Act is not intended to limit or modify any obligation to disclose created by any other statute or that may exist in common law in order to avoid fraud, misrepresentation, or deceit in the transaction.

(765 ILCS 77/50)

Sec. 50. Delivery of the Residential Real Property Disclosure Report provided by this Act shall be by:

(1) personal or facsimile delivery to the prospective buyer;

(2) depositing the report with the United States Postal Service, postage prepaid, first class mail, addressed to the prospective buyer at the address provided by the prospective buyer or indicated on the contract or other agreement; or

(3) depositing the report with an alternative delivery service such as Federal Express, UPS, or Airborne, delivery charges prepaid, addressed to the prospective buyer at the address provided by the prospective buyer or indicated on the contract or other agreement.

For purposes of this Act, delivery to one prospective buyer is deemed delivery to all prospective buyers. Delivery to an authorized individual acting on behalf of a prospective buyer constitutes delivery to all prospective buyers. Delivery of the report is effective upon receipt by the prospective buyer. Receipt may be acknowledged on the report, acknowledged in an agreement for the conveyance of the residential real property, or shown in any other verifiable manner.

(765 ILCS 77/55)

Sec. 55. Violations and damages. If the seller fails or refuses to provide the disclosure document prior to the conveyance of the residential real property, the buyer shall have the right to terminate the contract. A person who knowingly violates or fails to perform any duty prescribed by any provision of this Act or who discloses any information on the Residential Real Property Disclosure Report that he knows to be false shall be liable in the amount of actual damages and court costs, and the court may award reasonable attorney fees incurred by the prevailing party.

(765 ILCS 77/60)

Sec. 60. No action for violation of this Act may be commenced later than one year from the earlier of the date of possession, date of occupancy, or date of recording of an instrument of conveyance of the residential real property.

(765 ILCS 77/65)

Sec. 65. A copy of this Act, excluding Section 35, must be printed on or as a part of the Residential Real Property Disclosure Report form.

Engagement Letter

Eileen Dover

Attorney at Law

5446 Northeast Highway   Phone: (312) 352-4125
Suite 203   Fax: (773) 987-5432
Chicago, Illinois 60644   dover@law.com

ENGAGEMENT AGREEMENT PURCHASE OF PROPERTY

On the 2 day <u>July</u>, <u>2015</u>, the undersigned, <u>Roberta Buyer</u> (Client), retains <u>Eileen Dover</u> (Attorney) to represent Client for a <u>Residential Real Estate Closing</u> ("Transaction") and Attorney accepts this employment. The address of the Subject property is <u>4802 W. Wellington Chicago, IL 60641</u>. Transaction is scheduled to close ("Close" or "Closing") on or about <u>July 23, 2015</u>.

ADVANCE FEE: Client agrees to pay Attorney an initial deposit of <u>$0.00</u>. Client understands that no work will be performed until both Attorney and Client have signed this engagement agreement **and** Attorney has received the full deposit, if required.

RATE: Attorney will charge at the flat rate of <u>$450.00</u>, to be paid at or after Closing, for all work up to and including Closing, including: meeting with Client, review of contract, drafting letters as appropriate, communicating with Client's real estate and lending professionals, communicating with opposing counsel, review of lending documents, and representation at Closing. In addition to fees, Client will pay any court costs, process server fees, copy charges, and all other reasonable costs, as may be applicable. Any additional services would be at Attorney's regular rate of <u>$150.00</u> per hour. In the event that Transaction fails to Close through no fault of Attorney, Client will be responsible for a fee of <u>$100.00</u> if the transaction terminates prior to expiration of the Attorney Review period and a fee of <u>$200.00</u> if the transaction terminates prior to or at Closing.

DISCHARGE AND WITHDRAWAL: Client may discharge Attorney at any time, although no refund shall be given of fees paid, unless required by law. Attorney may withdraw with Client's consent for good cause or if there is any other good reason within the meaning of the Illinois Supreme Court Rules of Professional Conduct for Attorney to withdraw and cease handling the file. If Attorney withdraws, Attorney shall refund to Client within 10 days any fees not earned, based upon work actually completed and the hourly rate quoted herein.

CONCLUSION OF SERVICES: When Attorney's services conclude, all unpaid charges shall become immediately due and payable. After Attorney's services conclude, Attorney will, upon Client's request, deliver Client's file to Client, along with any Client funds or property in Attorney's possession.

DISCLAIMER OF GUARANTEE: Nothing in this Agreement and nothing in Attorney's statements to Client will be construed as a promise or guarantee about the outcome of Client's matter. Attorney makes no such promises or guarantees. Attorney's comments about the outcome of Client's matter are expressions of opinion only.

RELEASE OF CLIENT'S PAPERS: At the termination of services under this Agreement, Attorney will release promptly to Client upon request, all of Client's papers and property, including correspondence, legal documents, and other items reasonably necessary to Client's representation. Attorney is free to dispose of any such items if not requested by Client after a period of seven years of the termination of services.

EFFECTIVE DATE: This Agreement will take effect when Client has performed the conditions stated in Paragraph 1, but its effective date will be retroactive to the date Attorney first provided services. The date at the beginning of this Agreement is for reference only. Even if this Agreement does not take effect, Client will be obligated to pay Attorney the reasonable value of any services Attorney may have performed for Client.

QUALITY OF SERVICES: Attorney will competently represent the interests of Client as set forth in this Agreement.

CONFIDENTIALITY: Client understands that Client's contacts with Attorney are protected by a duty of confidentiality and Attorney-Client Privilege, which means that if Client gives Attorney information in confidence, Attorney cannot disclose this information to someone else without permission or unless a court orders Attorney to reveal such information. However, Client understands that Attorney has an affirmative duty to reveal information of any attempt by Client to commit an act that would result in death or serious bodily harm. Client further understands that Attorney may be permitted to disclose information relating to the representation should there be a dispute between Attorney and Client regarding fees and/or the adequacy of the Attorneys' work on Client's behalf.

Client hereby authorizes Attorney to discuss matters related to the Transaction, including the disclosure of information normally considered to be protected under the Attorney-Client Privilege with Client's real estate and lending professionals.

E-Mail — E-mail is a convenient, fast method of communication. It is, however, not always secure and communications between attorney and client could be seen by others. Nevertheless, Client may wish to utilize this method of communication. If Client wishes to do so and waive any possible breach of confidentiality, please enter e-mail address below.

ATTORNEY	CLIENT
Address:	_____
	_____
Phone:	_____
Email:	_____
Dated:	_____

Attorney Review Letters

Attorney Review Letter from the Buyer's Perspective

Please note: This letter may not refer to the same contract as the contract in the hypothetical. As such, it is extremely important to that the individual contract being reviewed is analyzed on its own, as many of the provisions vary from contract to contract.

Paul Pitch
Attorney at Law

111 N. Jackson
Suite 452
Waukegan, IL 60085

(847) 354-9872
Fax: (847) 354-4869

18 July, 2012

Mr. William Jonestown, Esq.
111 S. Waller Dr. Suite 2620
Libertyville, IL 60048
(847) 592-8118
Fax: (847) 592-9001

SENT VIA FACSIMILE

RE: O'Neill ("Seller") Sale to Ocwen ("Buyer")
       41 E. Normandy, Grayslake, IL 60030 ("Property")

Dear Mr. Jonestown:

Please be informed that I represent the Buyer of the above-referenced property ("Property"). Pursuant to the Attorney Modification provision in Paragraph 10 of the Real Estate Contract ("Contract"), please review the following:

Paragraph 4. Please confirm that the Mortgage Contingency is August 15, 2012. The Buyer is in the process of applying for her loan and the lender is Concordeon Mortgage and the Loan Officer is Lauren Marx. She may be contacted at (847) 400-5121.

Paragraph 6. Please confirm that that there are no special assessments currently pending on the Property or within the Association and confirm that, to the best of Seller's knowledge, no special assessments are scheduled to be assessed. Please confirm that there is no right of first refusal or that any such has been waived in writing. In addition, please provide copies of all declaration, bylaws, certificates of insurance, and paid assessment letters not previously provided by Seller or Seller's broker.

Paragraph 7. Please confirm that the Closing is set per the Contract for August 24, 2012, at a location to be determined. Please inform us of the location and time that you wish the Closing to take place. We request a copy of the Preliminary Title Report as soon as is practicable.

Paragraph 8. Please confirm there will be no Post-Closing Possession and that Possession will be tendered at Closing.

Paragraph 9. Please confirm that the current taxes and that the prorations are going to be based upon the most recent tax bill. In addition, please confirm that the taxes are not subject to any homeowners, senior citizen, or other exemptions and that there are no SSA or special, regular, or extraordinary governmental taxes or assessments which have not been previously disclosed.

Paragraph 12. The Buyers had a Home Inspection on July 12, 2012. A copy of the Condensed Home Inspection is attached to this letter. The Home Inspection uncovered several deficiencies in the Property. Please find those certain items in the attached letter that the Buyer's require to be addressed per the Home Inspection.

Paragraph 16. Please provide a copy of the title commitment to me for review as soon as it is available (an electronic copy of the title commitment provided to this office by email would be acceptable).

Paragraph 18. As email is an acceptable form of notice, please provide your email address to facilitate communication. My email address is ppitch@law.com.

Paragraph 19. Please confirm that all systems associated with the Property are in working order and shall so remain as of the time of Closing. If any systems are not or do not remain in working order, we request notification immediately upon discovery by the Seller or his broker.

Paragraph 22. Please confirm that there are no Code Violations currently pending against the Property and that Seller has not received information regarding any Code Violations, if applicable.

Until resolution of these items is achieved, the Buyer's consider the Attorney Review provision, Paragraph 11 of the Contract, pending and not waived. We await your response to these reasonable requests and look forward to working towards closing on August 24, 2012.

With Regards,
Paul Pitch
Buyer's Attorney

Enc.
CC: Ms. Kate Ocwen, via email
Mr. Joe Halter, Sales Max Signature South, via email

David Helmsley and Associates

Attorneys at Law

412 W. Broad Ave.   (618) 762-3336
Centralia, IL 62801   Fax: (618) 762-3390

dhelmsleylaw@kmail.com

29 February, 2013

Anthony Jones,
Jones, Schoenfield, Swartsman,
303 North Elm,
Centralia, Illinois 62801
Tel: 618.943.1915
Fax: 618.651.0322
JSSlawyer@aol.com

SENT VIA FACSIMILE

RE: OOR ("Seller") Sale to Janek ("Buyer")
        1131 W. Belwell, Centralia, IL 62801 ("Property")

Dear Mr. Jones:

Please be informed that I represent the Buyer of the above-referenced property ("Property"). Pursuant to the Attorney Modification provision in Paragraph 11 of the Real Estate Contract ("Contract"), please review the following:

Paragraph 1, Line 1. Please provide the full name(s) and correct spelling of the Seller(s).

Paragraph 1, Line 4. Please confirm that there are two assigned parking spaces. Please confirm whether these spaces are located on the outside pad or if they are in the garage (if there is a garage). Please inform us whether the spaces are deeded or not.

Paragraph 2. The purchase price is set for $151,000.00. Since there are two units being conveyed, the Lender requires separate valuations for each property. We request that you stipulate that the unit referred to in the Contract as "GW" (the "west" unit) is valued at $90,000.00 and that the unit referred to in the Contract as "GE" (the "east" unit) is valued at $61,000.00 ("Stipulated Values"). The appraisal is being completed and the Contract is hereby contingent upon each unit appraisal for the Stipulated Values.

Paragraph 3. Since the Contract was not accepted until February 15, 2013, and the automatic "cancellation" date was February 14, 2013, we are hereby informing you that we are not cancelling the Contract per that clause as of this date.

Paragraph 4. The Mortgage Contingency was originally set for February 21, 2013. However, since the Contract was not accepted until February 15, 2013, and since we are still in Attorney Modification, I request that the Mortgage Contingency be extended to March 10, 2013. The Buyer is in the process of applying for her loan and the lender is Lincolnside Mortgage and the Loan Officer is Charles Eckle. His contact number is (618) 555-8484.

The Contract is hereby amended that item (1) of Paragraph 4 is deleted in its entirety and replaced with the following: "If Buyer is unable to obtain the Required Commitment by the Commitment Date, Buyer shall so notify Seller (or Seller's broker or attorney) in writing on or before that Date."

The Contract is hereby amended by removing the words "nor Seller" in Paragraph 4, Line 35 of the Contract.

Paragraph 6. Please confirm that that there are no special assessments currently pending on the Property or within the Association and confirm that, to the best of Seller's knowledge, no special assessments are scheduled to be assessed. In addition, please confirm the current taxes, provide the current taxes for each unit, and confirm that all taxes now due and owing have been paid.

Please confirm that there is no right of first refusal or that any such has been waived in writing. In addition, please provide copies of all declaration, bylaws, certificates of insurance, and paid assessment letters, which have not previously provided by Seller or Seller's broker.

Paragraph 6: Please confirm that the proration is going to be based upon 110% the most recent tax bill. In addition, please confirm that the taxes are not subject to any homeowners, senior citizen, or other exemptions and that there are no SSA or special, regular, or extraordinary governmental taxes or assessments which have not been previously disclosed.

Paragraph 6: Please note, per Paragraph 11 of the Contract, the Association's Rules and Regulations, Declarations and By-Laws and previously approved Renovation Plans are required to be delivered to the Buyer during Attorney Approval and, furthermore, Attorney Approval remains open until said documents are delivered to the Buyer. We make this request because the Buyer intends on renting the units and wishes to make certain that rentals are allowed by the Association.

Paragraph 7. As the original Closing date was set per the Contract for February 28, 2013, yet Attorney Approval has not been satisfied, we hereby request that the Closing be set for April 2, 2013, at a location to be determined. Please inform us of the location and time that you wish the Closing to take place. We request a copy of the Preliminary Title Report as soon as is practicable.

Paragraph 8. Please confirm that there will be no Post-Closing Possession and that Possession will be tendered at Closing.

Paragraph 10: Please confirm that Christina Cruss, Braid and Wartner, is acting as "Dual Agent" and that there are no other agents or brokers connected with this transaction.

Paragraph 11: The Attorney Approval of the Contract is contingent upon delivery to Buyer of the Association's Rules and Regulations, Declarations and Bylaws and previously approved Renovation Plans and, furthermore, Attorney Approval maintains open until said documents are delivered to the Buyer. As mentioned above, we make this request because the Buyer intends on renting the units and wishes to make certain that rentals are allowed by the Association.

Paragraph 12. The Buyer is purchasing the Property "As-Is" and will not have a Home Inspection.

Paragraph 14. Please provide a copy of the title commitment for review as soon as it is available (an electronic copy of the title commitment provided by email would be acceptable).

Paragraph 18. As email is an acceptable form of notice, please provide your email address to facilitate communication. My email address is dhelmsleylaw@kmail.com.

Paragraph 22. Please confirm that all systems associated with the Property are in working order and shall so remain as of the time of Closing. If any systems are not or do not remain in working order, we request notification immediately upon discovery by the Seller or his broker.

Paragraph 24. Please confirm that there are no Code Violations currently pending against the Property and that Seller has not received information regarding any previous Code Violations, if applicable.

Until resolution of these items is achieved, the Buyer's consider the Attorney Review provision, Paragraph 11 of the Contract, pending and not waived.

We await your response to these reasonable requests and look forward to working towards closing on April 2, 2013.

With Regards,

David Helmsley

CC: Mr. Michael Janek, via email
Ms. Christinia Cross, Braid and Wartner, via email

Attorney Review Letter from the Seller's Perspective

Please note: The following letters may not review the same contract as the contract listed above. As such, it is extremely important to that the individual contract being reviewed is analyzed on its own, as many of the provisions vary from contract to contract.

Robert Ranier

Attorney at Law

876 W. Laramie Ave.

Jacksonville, IL 62650

Phone: (217) 776-4096   Fax: (217) 776-7470

rob@rranierrealestate.com

January 3, 2013

SENT VIA FACSIMILE ONLY

Mr. John Leeson

David B. Stowelman & Associates, Inc.

70 W. Highway 82, Suite 205

Berlin, IL 62670

(217) 238-8485

FAX: (217) 238-8490

> RE: Grig ("Sellers") Sale to Spall ("Buyer")
>
> 626 W. Sheridan Rd, Unit 251, Jacksonville, IL 62650 ("Property")

Dear Mr. Leeson:

Please be reminded that I represent the Sellers of the above-referenced Property. Pursuant to the attorney modification provision in Paragraph 9 of the Contract, and your extension request dated December 28, 2012, please review the following:

Paragraph 4. Per the Contract the Buyer was required to deposit additional earnest money in the amount of $4,000.00 (increasing the earnest money to a total of $5,000.00) by December 30, 2012. I have yet to receive confirmation that this has taken place. Please confirm that the Buyer has deposited the additional earnest money.

Paragraph 5. Please confirm that the Closing is set per the Contract for February 26, 2013, at a location to be determined. Please note that the Property is in Chicago and, as such, we would prefer the Closing to take place in Cook County. However, we will strive to find a location that is mutually acceptable.

Paragraph 9. We approved your request for an extension to the Attorney Review provision until January 3, 2013. We have yet to receive any Attorney Review or Modification letter and the expiration of this extension in January 3, 2013.

Paragraph 10. Please confirm that the Buyer has had the home inspection performed. I have received no notification of the Home Inspection and the Home Inspection contingency contained in Paragraph 10, and the subsequent extension request dated and agreed to on December 28, 2012, expires on January 3, 2013.

Paragraph 11. Please confirm that the Mortgage Contingency is January 19, 2013. Per the pre-approval letter sent as an attachment to the Contract, the Buyer is obtaining a mortgage through Chicago Funding, Inc. and the Loan Officer is Dominic Noia. Please confirm this information and, if incorrect, please provide the correct loan information.

Paragraph 14. I shall be contacting the Condominium Association/management company within the next few days and will provide confirmation of any actions that may be required of the Buyer. I have not been informed of any Special Assessments, but I will request confirmation when I contact the Association.

Paragraph 16. I shall be ordering title next week and will inform you of the title company at that time. I will provide a copy of the title commitment as soon as I receive it.

Paragraph 17 shall be amended to state that, as this property is legally defined as a condominium, no survey shall be provided.

Paragraph 27. As email is an acceptable form of Notice, please provide an email address, if available, as no email address is listed on your letter dated December 28, 2012.

Please inform me as soon as is practicable, the correct spelling of the Buyer's name and how the Buyer is taking title so we may prepare the Deed properly.

Please call me if you have any questions.

With regards,

Robert Ranier

CC: Steven Malhone, Sidler Realty via fax 217-728-9807

LAW OFFICE OF RANDALL PETHERS

4824 W. Colfax Ave.   (773) 985-2968
Suite 7777   FAX: (773) 985-0554
Chicago, IL 60641   rpeters@laws.com
November 21, 2014

SENT VIA FACSIMILE ONLY

Mr. Sherwood Zwirinsky
ATTORNEY AT LAW
9101 Evanston Blvd.
Suite 114
Skokie, IL 60362
(847) 950-8081
FAX: (847) 950-6015
zwirlaw@aol.com

RE: Carney Sale to Flay
5101 Carrion Way, Unit 310 B, Flat Meadow, IL

Dear Mr. Zwirinsky:

Please be informed that I represent the Sellers of the above-referenced property. Pursuant to the attorney modification provision in Paragraph 12 of the contract, please review the following:

Paragraph 5 be confirmed that the Closing shall is set per the contract for December 9th, 2014, at a location to be determined.

Paragraph 10 be amended to confirm that Buyer's waive their right to a home inspection and the home inspection contingency is therefore waived.

Paragraph 11 be confirmed that the Mortgage Contingency is December 2nd, 2014. Per the contract, the Buyer is obtaining a mortgage through Association Financial Services and the Loan Officer is Darla Smelter. Please confirm this information and, if incorrect, please provide the correct loan information.

Paragraph 12 be amended to state that the Attorney Approval date shall be November 22, 2014. The contract states seven (7) business days from the date of execution.

Paragraph 13 be amended to state that, as this property is legally defined as a condominium, no survey shall be provided.

I shall be ordering title this week and will inform you of the title company at that time.

Please inform me as soon as is practicable, the correct spelling of the Buyer's name and how the Buyer is taking title so we may prepare the Deed properly.

Please be informed that I have contacted the Management Company, Vinguard Management, and have been informed that there is a $100 move-in fee that the Buyer is responsible to pay. The "Move-In Form" and additional forms shall be forthcoming. I have been informed by the Seller that the Declarations and Bylaws for the Association are presently located in the Condominium.

Please call me if you have any questions.

With regards,
Randall Pethers

Linda Rakes and Associates

Attorneys at Law

7824 W. Norridge Ave.   Norridge, IL 60641   (708) 722-9896   fax: (708) 722-9899

26 March, 2014

Mr. Stanley Kelsey, Esq.
3295 W. Arlington Heights Rd, Suite 786
Palatine, IL 60001-1586
(847) 218-3333
Fax: (847) 218-3337

SENT VIA FACSIMILE

RE: LaSille Bank National Association ("Seller") Sale to Paul Saturn ("Buyer")
2706 W. Nevergreen, Unit #3 Chicago, IL 60622 ("Property")

Dear Mr. Kelsey:

Please be reminded that I represent the Buyer of the above-referenced Property. As I am sure you are aware, the Buyer has not received signed copies of the Contract or the various Addenda to the Contract. In addition, on March 19, 2014, the Buyer requested an extension of the Attorney Review and Home Inspection contingencies through March 27, 2014. We received no response to our request.

After careful review of the Contract and the Addenda, and in light of the fact as there apparently has been no acceptance to the Buyer's offer, I have advised my client not to pursue this transaction. Please consider this letter as notice of Termination of the Contract pursuant to Paragraph 12 of the Contract.

Please execute this letter where indicated below. We expect the immediate return of any earnest money deposited. If you have any questions, please feel free to contact me.

With Regards,
Linda Rakes

Accepted, this ___ day of March, 2014

_____

Seller/Attorney/Broker

CC: Paul Saturn, via fax (773) 762-5531
Anita Drogba, Sales Max Exterior, via fax (773) 765-1100
Michael S. Olson, Areawide Realty Co., via fax (708) 111-4444

MEMORANDUM

To: Student

From: Attorney

Re: Writing Assignment I

Date: Today's Date

As has been explained in class, one of the most important tasks for a paralegal in a real estate practice is reviewing contracts with the attorneys. For this writing assignment, you will use the completed real estate contract (Version 6.0) located earlier in this chapter and draft an attorney modification letter.

Please note that you will be writing the letter as if you were a paralegal working for one of the attorneys listed (you may be working either for the Seller's attorney, Irwin M. Gone, or the Buyer's attorney, Eileen Dover, unless informed otherwise by the instructor). Also, you will normally not see a contract this clean; there are not the usual scratch-outs in order to keep the contract (and the assignment) as straightforward as possible.

For the background of the transaction, you may assume that the contract has been signed by both parties on the dates of the contract. The Seller owns the property outright and has the right to convey. Also, the Buyer is married to Brett Buyer, but please note that only the wife has signed the contract (you may decide whether the Buyer and her spouse are going to live in the property as their permanent residence—remember, it may affect how they can take title), if you are working for the Seller's attorney, you should ask how the Buyer intends to take title.

You should use the letters that we have reviewed in class and also the letters from the textbook as a guide. Among the points to clue into are the dates (Hint: there is a holiday during the attorney and inspection review period). Also, there a few blanks in the contract that need clarification.

The Buyer has not had an inspection done yet. Due to the busy holiday season, she will have the inspection done on the Wednesday after the holiday on July 8, 2015, by Home Wright Inspection, owned by Willie Wright.

Good Luck

Chapter 3

Contract Contingencies

Learning Objectives

After studying Chapter 3, you will be able to:

- Summarize the home inspection contingency of a real estate contract
- Locate and interpret the financing contingency of a real estate contract
- Draft a home inspection letter

Chapter Summary

Topics covered:

- Home Inspection
- Financing Extension

This chapter discusses to important contingencies in a real estate transaction: the home inspection and the financing contingency. The chapter discusses what the home inspection contingency is, what is covered, and what is excluded. The topic of the "As-Is" clause is covered. The chapter concludes with a brief introduction to notes and mortgages and ends with a discussion of the financing contingency of the contract. A sample home inspection for the hypothetical is included at the end of the chapter.

1. Home Inspection Contingency

As described in the contract dissected in Chapter 2, Buyers of a property always have a right to have the property inspected (unless specifically waived in the contract) at their own expense. This is referred to as the Home Inspection Contingency and is a very important contingency in real estate transactions.

The purpose of the home inspection is to allow a professional inspector to look at the house and to determine if there are any significant deficiencies in the property. In particular, the inspector will investigate to see if there are any deficiencies that would not be readily apparent to the Buyer. If there are things that the Buyer saw as part of the initial viewing of the house, the Buyer would generally take that into consideration when determining the price that the Buyer would want to pay for the property.

The first major issue is what is to be included in the home inspection. The contract is quite clear that the Buyer may secure a "home, radon, environmental, lead-based paint and/or lead-based paint hazards ... and/or wood destroying insect infestation inspection(s) of the Real Estate by one or more licensed or certified inspection service(s)." This implies that only if the inspection(s) is performed by a licensed home inspector will the Buyer have negotiating power. While this is technically true, the parties are often motivated to consummate the transaction, so they may be willing to negotiate even if the inspector is not licensed. The problem with unlicensed inspectors (such as general contractors and "handymen") is that these people may be trained in construction, but not in home inspection and they have somewhat different skills. Second, and more importantly, the handyman generally will not produce a report that can be utilized by the Buyer and Buyer's attorney to substantiate any home inspection requests.

Paragraph 12 of the contract further states that only "major components of the Real Estate" are subject to home inspection and

> The home inspection shall cover only major components of the Real Estate, including but not limited to, central heating system(s), central cooling system(s), plumbing and well system, electrical system, roof, walls, windows, ceilings, floors, appliances and foundation. A major component shall be deemed to be in operating condition if it performs the function for which it is intended, regardless of age, and does not constitute a threat to health or safety. The fact that a functioning component may be at the end of its useful life shall not render such component defective for the purpose of this paragraph.

This implies that minor issues, such as maintenance and routine repairs, are not to be included in the home inspection. In fact, the contract goes so far as to state: "Buyer agrees minor repairs and routine maintenance items are not a part of this contingency." But this clause causes many disputes between Buyers and Sellers.

Buyers' attorneys will often attempt to raise issues regarding everything and anything disclosed in an inspection report. Buyers' attorneys will ask for things listed on an inspection report which would not ordinarily be included. There have been cases where the Buyers' attorney simply faxed the inspection report and stated that the Buyer wants "everything" on the report to be fixed or an appropriate credit provided. This violates the spirit of the Home Inspection Contingency.

Some Buyers' attorneys fight for every penny for their clients, in the (somewhat) mistaken idea that they are "zealously" representing their clients. Many attorneys believe that this is the very essence of representation and they have to do everything in their power to make sure that their clients receive the "best" deal possible, even at the risk of terminating the contract. In reality, they may be doing a disservice to their clients, as they may destroy the deal by being too contentious. There is a fine balance between being overly aggressive and being just assertive enough to protect the client's interests.

It is important for the legal professionals to keep in mind what it is that the Buyer is really looking to accomplish with the home inspection. Typically, Buyers want assurances that the property is free from major defects, such as structural damage or defects in the major systems of the property. The home inspector will attempt to find any defects and note them on the home inspection report. Copies of a Home Inspection Report and Home Inspection Letter are included at the end of this chapter.

The Seller has the right to review the inspection report and may choose to address any requests made by the Buyer. Paragraph 12 states the Buyer must conduct the home inspection and inform the Seller of any defects shortly after acceptance of the contract by the Seller.

> Buyer shall serve written notice upon Seller or Seller's attorney of any defects disclosed by any inspection for which Buyer requests by the seller, together with a copy of the pertinent page(s) of the report(s) within five (5) Business Days (ten (10) calendar days for a lead-based paint and/or lead-based paint hazard inspection) after Date of Acceptance. If within ten (10) Business Days after the Date of Acceptance written agreement is not reached by the Parties with respect to resolution of all inspection issues, then either Party may terminate this Contract by Serving Notice to the other Party, whereupon this Contract shall be null and void. Notwithstanding anything to the contrary set forth above in the paragraph, in the event the inspection reveals that the condition of the Real Estate is unacceptable to Buyer and Buyer serves Notice to Seller within five (5) Business Days after the Date of Acceptance, this Contract shall be null and void. Said Notice shall not include any portion of the inspection reports unless requested by Seller. **Failure of Buyer to conduct said inspection(s) and notify Seller within the time specified operates as a waiver of Buyer's rights to terminate this Contract under this Paragraph 12 and this Contract shall remain in full force and effect.**

Although the contract puts a rather draconian ten business day deadline on resolution of the home inspection issues or the contract becomes "null and void," the parties may, of course, continue to negotiate past the ten day point, and they often negotiate home inspection issues until final resolution. The deadline allows either party an opportunity to void the contract if they feel that resolution is impracticable.

What Is Radon?

According to the Environmental Protection Agency publication *A Citizen's Guide to Radon*:

> Radon is a radioactive gas. It comes from the natural decay of uranium that is found in nearly all soils. It typically moves up through the ground to the air above and into your home through cracks and other holes in the foundation. Your home traps radon inside, where it can build up. Any home may have a radon problem. This means new and old homes, well-sealed and drafty homes, and homes with or without basements. Radon from soil gas is the main cause of radon problems. Sometimes radon enters the home through well water. In a small number of homes, the building materials can give off radon, too. However, building materials rarely cause radon problems by themselves.

Nearly 1 out of every 15 homes in the U.S. is estimated to have elevated radon levels. Elevated levels of radon gas have been found in homes in your state. Contact your state radon office (www.epa.gov/radon/whereyoulive.html) for general information about radon in your area. While radon problems may be more common in some areas, any home may have a problem. The only way to know about your home is to test. (May, 2012, pg. 4, available at http://www.epa.gov/radon)

Radon can be easily detected through testing. Radon testing is standard in western suburban homes, especially in Kane and DeKalb counties, but not as common in Chicago. Radon is common in the western suburbs as many properties on built on ground which often contains elevated amounts of radon. (available at http://www.epa.gov/radon/states/illinois.html, last viewed July 25, 2013)

If a Buyer orders a radon test and the test finds radon levels higher than 4.0 p/cL (parts per cubic litre), radon abatement may be required, at the Seller's expense. Many Sellers try to cancel the contract to avoid the expense of a radon abatement system. The problem is that the Seller will be required to disclose the radon test results to any future potential Buyer, since it is now a known defect. The Seller then risks losing a second transaction due to the disclosure. The prudent course of action is usually to pay to have the abatement system installed.

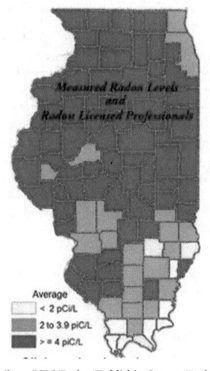

https://www.illinois.gov/iema/NRS/Radon/PublishingImages/RadonStateMap.jpg

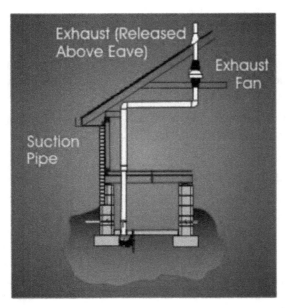

http://www.dep.pa.gov/Business/RadiationProtection/RadonDivision/Pages/default.aspx#.V0SHVf
krKM8

Radon Abatement System

(420 ILCS 46/) Illinois Radon Awareness Act.

(420 ILCS 46/1)

Sec. 1. Short title. This Act may be cited as the Illinois Radon Awareness Act.

(420 ILCS 46/5)

Sec. 5. Definitions. As used in this Act, unless the context otherwise requires:

(a) "Agent" means a licensed real estate "broker" or "salesperson," as those terms are defined in Section 1-10 of the Real Estate License Act of 2000, acting on behalf of a seller or buyer of residential real property.

(b) "Buyer" means any individual, partnership, corporation, or trustee entering into an agreement to purchase any estate or interest in real property.

(c) "Final settlement" means the time at which the parties have signed and delivered all papers and consideration to convey title to the estate or interest in the residential real property being conveyed.

(d) "IEMA" means the Illinois Emergency Management Agency Division of Nuclear Safety.

(e) "Mitigation" means measures designed to permanently reduce indoor radon concentrations according to procedures described in 32 Illinois Administrative Code Part 422.

(f) "Radon hazard" means exposure to indoor radon concentrations at or in excess of the United States Environmental Protection Agency's, or IEMA's recommended Radon Action Level.

(g) "Radon test" means a measurement of indoor radon concentrations in accordance with 32 Illinois Administrative Code Part 422 for performing radon measurements within the context of a residential real property transaction.

(h) "Residential real property" means any estate or interest in a manufactured housing lot or a parcel of real property, improved with not less than one nor more than 4 residential dwelling units.

(i) "Seller" means any individual, partnership, corporation, or trustee transferring residential real property in return for consideration.

(420 ILCS 46/10)

Sec. 10. Radon testing and disclosure.

(a) Except as excluded by Section 20 of this Act, the seller shall provide to the buyer of any interest in residential real property the IEMA pamphlet entitled "Radon Testing Guidelines for Real Estate Transactions" (or an equivalent pamphlet approved for use by IEMA) and the Illinois Disclosure of Information on Radon Hazards, which is set forth in subsection (b) of this Section, stating that the property may present the potential for exposure to radon before the buyer is obligated under any contract to purchase residential real property. Nothing in this Section is intended to or shall be construed to imply an obligation on the seller to conduct any radon testing or mitigation activities.

(b) The following shall be the form of Disclosure of Information on Radon Hazards to be provided to a buyer of residential real property as required by this Section:

DISCLOSURE OF INFORMATION ON RADON HAZARDS

(For Residential Real Property Sales or Purchases)

Radon Warning Statement

Every buyer of any interest in residential real property is notified that the property may present exposure to dangerous levels of indoor radon gas that may place the occupants at risk of developing radon-induced lung cancer. Radon, a Class-A human carcinogen, is the leading cause of lung cancer in non-smokers and the second leading cause overall. The seller of any interest in residential real property is required to provide the buyer with any information on radon test results of the dwelling showing elevated levels of radon in the seller's possession.

The Illinois Emergency Management Agency (IEMA) strongly recommends ALL homebuyers have an indoor radon test performed prior to purchase or taking occupancy, and mitigated if elevated levels are found. Elevated radon concentrations can easily be reduced by a qualified, licensed radon mitigator.

Seller's Disclosure (initial each of the following which applies)

(a) . . . . Elevated radon concentrations (above EPA or IEMA recommended Radon Action Level) are known to be present within the dwelling. (Explain)

(b) . . . . Seller has provided the purchaser with the most current records and reports pertaining to elevated radon concentrations within the dwelling.

(c) ....Seller either has no knowledge of elevated radon concentrations in the dwelling or prior elevated radon concentrations have been mitigated or remediated.

(d) ....Seller has no records or reports pertaining to elevated radon concentrations within the dwelling.

Purchaser's Acknowledgment (initial each of the following which applies)

(e) ....Purchaser has received copies of all information listed above.

(f) ....Purchaser has received the IEMA approved Radon Disclosure Pamphlet.

Agent's Acknowledgment (initial) (if applicable)

(g) ....Agent has informed the seller of the seller's obligations under Illinois law.

Certification of Accuracy

The following parties have reviewed the information above and each party certifies, to the best of his or her knowledge, that the information he or she provided is true and accurate.

Seller	Date	Seller	Date
Purchaser	Date	Purchaser	Date
Agent	Date	Agent	Date

(c) If any of the disclosures required by this Section occurs after the buyer has made an offer to purchase the residential real property, the seller shall complete the required disclosure activities prior to accepting the buyer's offer and allow the buyer an opportunity to review the information and possibly amend the offer.

(420 ILCS 46/15)

Sec. 15. Applicability. This Act shall apply only to leased properties to the extent specified in Section 25 of this Act and to transfers by sale of residential real property.

(420 ILCS 46/20)

Sec. 20. Exclusions. The provisions of this Act do not apply to the following:

(1) Transfers pursuant to court order, including, but not limited to, transfers ordered by a probate court in administration of an estate, transfers between spouses resulting from a judgment of dissolution of marriage or legal separation, transfers pursuant to an order of possession, transfers by a trustee in bankruptcy, transfers by eminent domain, and transfers resulting from a decree for specific performance.

(2) Transfers from a mortgagor to a mortgagee by deed in lieu of foreclosure or consent judgment, transfer by judicial deed issued pursuant to a foreclosure sale to the successful bidder or the assignee of a certificate of sale, transfer by a collateral assignment of a beneficial interest of a land trust, or a transfer by a mortgagee or a successor in interest to the mortgagee's secured position or a beneficiary under a deed in trust who has acquired the real property by deed in lieu of foreclosure, consent judgment or judicial deed issued pursuant to a foreclosure sale.

(3) Transfers by a fiduciary in the course of the administration of a decedent's estate, guardianship, conservatorship, or trust.

(4) Transfers from one co-owner to one or more other co-owners.

(5) Transfers pursuant to testate or intestate succession.

(6) Transfers made to a spouse, or to a person or persons in the lineal line of consanguinity of one or more of the sellers.

(7) Transfers from an entity that has taken title to residential real property from a seller for the purpose of assisting in the relocation of the seller, so long as the entity makes available to all prospective buyers a copy of the disclosure form furnished to the entity by the seller.

(8) Transfers to or from any governmental entity.

(9) Transfers of any residential dwelling unit located on the third story or higher above ground level of any structure or building, including, but not limited to, condominium units and dwelling units in a residential cooperative.

(420 ILCS 46/25)

Sec. 25. Disclosure of Radon hazard to current and prospective tenants.

(a) A lessor of a dwelling unit shall disclose to lessees the existence of a radon hazard consistent with the provisions of this Section. For the purposes of this Section, "dwelling unit" means a room or suite of rooms used for human habitation and for which a lessor and a lessee have a written lease agreement.

(b) The provisions of this Section apply only to dwelling units located below the third story above ground level.

(c) If a current lessee has provided in writing to the lessor the results of a radon test that indicate that a radon hazard exists in a dwelling unit covered by this Section, then the lessor shall disclose in writing to any individual seeking to enter into a lease of that dwelling unit that a radon test has indicated that a radon hazard may exist in the dwelling unit. After receiving a notification of a radon test that indicates a radon hazard, the lessor may choose to conduct a radon test in the dwelling unit. If the lessor's radon test indicates that a radon hazard does not exist on the premises, the lessor shall not be required to disclose that a radon hazard exists in the dwelling unit.

(d) If a lessor conducts a radon test in a dwelling unit and the radon test indicates that a radon hazard exists in the dwelling unit, the lessor shall disclose in writing to the current lessee, and any individual seeking to enter into a lease of that dwelling unit, the existence of a radon hazard in the dwelling unit.

(e) If a lessor has undertaken mitigation activities and a subsequent radon test indicates that a radon hazard does not exist in the dwelling unit, then the lessor is not required to provide the disclosure required by this Section.

(f) Nothing in this Section shall be construed to require a lessor to conduct radon testing.

(420 ILCS 46/99)

Sec. 99. Effective date. This Act takes effect January 1, 2008.

As-Is Clause

Paragraph 41 of the contract contains an "As-Is" Clause. This clause is often used when a Buyer is purchasing the property with the intention of remodeling or rebuilding the property. In typical residential purchases, some Buyers believe that they will receive a better price for the property if they accept the property As-Is. This is because it is assumed that the Seller will not have to make any concessions during the home inspection period.

Paragraph 41 of the contract states as follows:

> This Contract is for the sale and purchase of the Real Estate and personal property in its "As Is" condition as of the Date of Offer. Buyer acknowledges that no representations, warranties or guarantees with respect to the condition of the Real Estate and personal property have been made by Seller or Seller's Designated Agent other than those known defects, if any, disclosed by Seller. Buyer may conduct an inspection at Buyer's expense. In that event, Seller shall make the property available to Buyer's inspector at reasonable times. Buyer shall indemnify Seller and hold Seller harmless from and against any loss or damage caused by the acts or negligence of Buyer or any person performing any inspection(s). **In the event the inspection reveals that the condition of the improvements, fixtures or personal property to be conveyed or transferred is unacceptable to Buyer and Buyer so notifies Seller within five (5) Business Days after the Date of Acceptance, this Contract shall be null and void. Failure of Buyer to notify Seller or to conduct said inspection operates as a waiver of Buyer's right to terminate this Contract under this paragraph and this Contract shall remain in full force and effect.** Buyer acknowledges the provisions of Paragraph 12 and the warranty provisions of Paragraph 5 do not apply to this Contract.

Reading this paragraph, it is clear that a Buyer **retains** the right to have a home inspection performed. Should the home inspection raise any deficiencies in the property, the Buyer, however, only has two choices:

(1) Accept the property with the deficiencies (that is, accepting the property as it is); or

(2) Declare the contract null and void.

The Buyer does not have the right to negotiate with Seller to have repairs made or credits offered by Seller for deficiencies discovered during the home inspection. This, in theory, will speed up the transaction.

Unfortunately, many unscrupulous real estate brokers will encourage the Buyer to enter contacts "As-Is" without understanding the potential ramifications of the designation. What frequently happens in these transactions is that the home inspection will uncover certain deficiencies and the broker will want the Buyer's attorney to negotiate with Seller's attorney regarding the deficiencies.

As described above, the As-Is clause does not provide a provision for negotiating deficiencies raised by the home inspection. It is important when reviewing a contract to look to see if the As-Is clause has been initialed. If so, the attorney should explain the ramifications of this clause to the client immediately so that the client fully understands the potential risks.

Most properties that are purchased from foreclosure sales, auctions, or governmental agencies will be purchased "As-Is" and no negotiations will be allowed. In
fact, the contracts for many properties purchased at auction or from governmental
agencies will not have a home inspection clause in them at all. Purchasing a property
that has been foreclosed upon and then repurchased by the lender at the auction
(often called "Real Estate Owned" or REO), will generally still be "As-Is," but will frequently have a home inspection clause in the contract to allow the Buyer to have the
property inspected prior to purchasing. This depends on the company or organization
selling the property and the location of the property.

Some Definitions

Prior to discussing the various aspects of financial contingencies, a few definitions
will be helpful.

Note: A note is a promise to pay. A note can be **secured** (that is, backed up by
some asset "securing" the note) or **unsecured** (that is, the promise to pay is not backed
up by any asset, but it is up to the borrower to pay based upon the promise).

Home loans and auto loans are generally secured notes. The lender of the funds
for the property or the automobile generally retains an interest in the item purchased
and can reclaim the item, either through repossession (for an automobile) or foreclosure (for real property).

Credit cards are unsecured. If someone buys an item with a credit card and fails
to pay, the credit card company has no interest in the item purchased and cannot reclaim the item for the borrower's failure to pay. The credit card company's only recourse is to sue for money damages, not to reclaim the item.

Mortgage: The mortgage is *not* the loan on the property; it is the lender's security
for a debt. The mortgage is a lien that is recorded against the property. It transfers a
potential interest in the property as a security for the debt. The Borrower (or obligor)
is the Mortgagor and the Lender (or obligee) is the Mortgagee.

Fixed Rate Loan: A loan where the interest rate stays constant throughout the life
of the loan.

Adjustable Rate Loan: A loan where the interest rate adjusts at regular intervals,
as defined in the note and mortgage.

Private Mortgage Insurance: Insurance that a borrower obtains to insure the lender
in the case of default on the loan. "PMI" as it is called is generally required when a
borrower has less than a standard percentage (usually 20%) of the acquisition cost
as a down payment. This insurance allows the lender to be "made whole" if the property goes into foreclosure and the property sells at auction for less than the outstanding
balance of the foreclosure judgment (see Chapter 7).

2. Financing Contingencies

It is rare indeed when a Buyer can enter into a transaction and pay cash for a property. Paragraph 8 of the contract provides for the Buyer to have the opportunity to obtain financing for the property. The Mortgage Contingency is broken down into two parts.

The first section of Paragraph 8 of the contract states as follows:

8. MORTGAGE CONTINGENCY: If this transaction is NOT CONTINGENT ON FINANCING, Optional Paragraph 36a or 36b MUST BE USED. If any portion of Paragraph 36 is used, the provisions of Paragraph 8 ARE NOT APPLICABLE. This Contract is contingent upon Buyer obtaining a *[check one]* ☐ fixed ☐ adjustable; *[check one]* ☐ conventional ☐ FHA/VA (if FHA/VA is chosen, complete Paragraph 27); ☐ other _____ loan for ____% of the Purchase Price, plus private mortgage insurance (PMI), if required, with an interest rate (initial rate if an adjustable rate mortgage used) not to exceed _____% per annum, amortized over not less than _____ years. Buyer shall pay loan origination fee and/or discount points not to exceed ____% of the loan amount. Buyer shall pay the cost of application, usual and customary processing fees and closing costs charged by the lender. (Complete Paragraph 35 if closed cost credits apply). Buyer shall make written loan application within five (5) Business Days after the Date of Acceptance and shall cause an appraisal of Real Estate to be ordered by the lender no later than ten (10) Business Days after the Date of Acceptance; **failure to do either shall constitute an act of Default under this Contract.**

This establishes the amount of the loan that the Buyer is required to obtain. The Buyer is required to apply for the loan by the date specified, for no more than the amount and interest rate stated in the contract.

The second section of Paragraph 8 states:

If Buyer, having applied for the loan specified above *[complete both a) and b)]*:

a)   is unable to provide written evidence that the loan application has been submitted for underwriting

approval by Buyer's lender on or before _____, 20 ____, (if no date is inserted, the date shall be thirty (30) days after Date of Acceptance) either Buyer or Seller shall have the option of declaring this Contract terminated by giving Notice to the other Party not later than two (2) Business Days after the date Specified herein or any extension date agree to by the Parties in writing.

b)   Is unable to obtain a "Clear to Close" from Buyer's lender on or before _____, 20____, (if no date is inserted, the date shall be forty-five (45) days after the Date of Acceptance) either Buyer or Seller shall have the option of declaring this Contract terminated by giving Notice to the other Party not later than two (2) Business Days after the date specified herein or any extension date agreed to by the Parties in writing.

A party causing delay in the loan approval process shall not have the right to terminate under either of the Preceding paragraphs. In the event neither Party elects to declare this Contract null and void as of the latter of the dates specified above (as may be amended from time to time), then this Contract shall continue in full force and effect with any loan contingency.

Ethics Alert:

Remember: Paralegal can draft documents and letters such as:

- Attorney Modification letters,
- Home Inspection letters, and
- Financing Extensions.

But they must be drafted under the attorney's supervision. Paralegals cannot draft and send them on their own. To do so might constitute the unauthorized practice of law.

If the Buyer fails to obtain a loan by the time specified, a "Clear to Close" from the lender, and fails to cancel the contract, either the Buyer or Seller may cancel the contract. If neither does so, the Buyer may be forced to go through with the transaction or be declared in breach of contract. This does not mean the Buyer could not still obtain the loan, and ideally the Buyer would still obtain the loan. But the clause waives the Buyer's ability to cancel the contract for failure to obtain financing.

The Buyer's attorney may request an extension if the Buyer is attempting to obtain financing, but unable to do so within the time specified. This request, called a **financing extension letter**, must be received by the Seller's attorney prior to the expiration of the Financing Contingency. Sellers may or may not accept an extension request, and the Seller has the option to deny the request. If the Seller denies the extension request, the Buyer may proceed on the contract (effectively "waiving" the contingency and taking a chance that the financing will be approved) or may cancel the contract.

A sample financing extension letter is included at the end of this chapter.

Key Terms

Home Inspection
Radon
As-Is Clause
Mortgage Contingency
Note
Secured
Unsecured
Mortgage
Adjustable Rate Mortgage (ARM)
Fixed Rate Loan
Private Mortgage Insurance (PMI)
Financing Extension Letter

Review Questions

1.   What is the purpose of the home inspection contingency of a real estate contract?

2.   What is radon?

3.   What are the options available when buying a property "As-Is"?

4.   What are a "note" and "mortgage"?

5.   What is the purpose of the financing contingency?

Materials included in the following chapter appendix include:

- Sample Home Inspection Report
- Sample Home Inspection Letters
- Sample Financing Extension Letter
- *Harry S. Posner et al. v. Sander A. Davis, et al.*, 76 Ill. App.3d 638, 395 N.E.2d 133(1979)

Chapter 3 Appendix

Sample Home Inspection

Inspection Report
Roberta Buyer
Property Address:
4802 W. Wellington, Chicago, Illinois
Home Wright Home Inspection, Inc.

Inspection Report for Property at: 4802 W. Wellington, Chicago, IL

Private Home Inspection for: Roberta Buyer

Date: July 8, 2015

Customer's Home Phone Number: xxx-xxx-xxxx

This report reflects the inspection Willie Wright ("Inspector") completed on July 8, 2015, on the above-referenced property. This report is based solely on the visual inspection of accessible areas of the property and does not constitute a report on those areas of the above-referenced property not personally inspected by the Inspector. This inspection conforms to the current Standards of Practice of the American Society of Home Inspectors and the State of Illinois Office of Professional Regulations. This report concerns only those items personally inspected and specifically reported.

The Inspector does NOT test the following: sprinkler systems, security systems, and smoke/carbon dioxide detectors. The Inspector may make reference to these systems, but has NOT inspected the same. This report and any comments as to these systems should be not construed as the above-referenced property containing these systems. Any such safety systems, to the extent that they may exist, should be examined and checked regularly by the homeowner.

PLEASE NOTE: This report is not, and should not be construed as, a warranty or guarantee as to the condition of any of the items included in this report. The comments made are the professional opinion of the Inspector and are not meant to imply any guarantee to as to the condition of the premises. This report, and any comments made with respect to radon, insect damage, mold, and environmental condition are meant for reference only and are not to be considered as part of this report.

The information contained herein constitutes the entire report of the inspection of the premises and supersedes any oral discussions, comments, or opinions made in connection therewith. This report is not intended to be used for remodeling, construction, or other purposes. This report is intended for the recipient's sole use and should not be distributed, relied upon, or otherwise utilized except by the recipient of this report. This report is specifically not to be used by any third party and no decisions should be made by third parties based upon this report.

You should be aware that any structure built prior to 1978 has the potential of containing lead based paint. Lead based paint poses a potential health hazard. This inspection did not include any investigation for lead based paint and no part of this report should be construed as a substitute for a lead based paint inspection. If lead based paint is a concern, it is suggested and recommended that the recipient have the property tested accordingly.

Please refer to the Home Inspection Contract Agreement document for details as to what items are excluded from this inspection. In addition, please note that there is no warranty as to the accuracy of the opinions contained herein.

It is hoped that this report serves the needs of the recipient.

Willie Wright, President, Home Wright Home Inspection, Inc.

Illinois License # 3500984325

1—General Information

Name of Inspector: Willie Wright

Client's Broker:

Name:	Jane Coldheart
Company:	Buywell Real Estate Brokers
Phone:	(xxx) xxx-xxxx

Seller's Broker:

Name:	John Attack
Company:	Sales Max Real Estate Agency
Phone:	(xxx) xxx-xxxx

Payment:

Paid by Check:	Check #: 9854
Amount:	$350.00

Start time of inspection: 9:00 am Finish time: 12:10 pm

Present at Inspection:

Buyer

Buyer's Broker

Seller's Broker

Is the home occupied: Yes

Direction front entry is facing: east

Recent rain, snow, sleet: none

Estimated outdoor temperature: 83 degrees Fahrenheit

Skies: cloudy

Style of home: 2 story

Age of home: 40–50 years

2—Roof

Roof style: Gable

Roof seen from: Ladder

Number of Layers of roofing: 1 (estimate)

Estimated age of roof: 9–10 years

Estimated remaining life of roof: 6–11 years

Roofing material: 240 lb (estimate) Fiberglass/Asphalt Shingles

Comments: There are several broken/wind damaged shingles on south side of roof. These should be replaced.

Flashing and Joint material: Galvanized steel/tin or aluminum

Comments: There is evidence of moderate roof leakage at roof to wall interface above north bedroom. Drip edge flashing at edge of roof to soffit interface is non-existent.

Gutters and Downspouts: Aluminum

Comments: The gutter system appeared to be clogged at the time of inspection. This should be cleaned.

*Recommend adding gutters and downspouts to areas without them to improve the perimeter drainage. Keep gutters clean and seams sealed to allow proper control of run-off. Recommend extending downspouts 3–5 feet away from home to improve drainage.

Chimney material: Chimney is brick. Keep the chimney cap screened well sealed to exclude birds & moisture.

Soffits and Fascia: Wood and aluminum. There are several sections of the soffit that have large gaps and without screens. This may harbor birds and other animals. There is evidence of birds nesting in front area of home.

General roof comments: Visible and accessible components only. No comment can be made regarding underlying damage to the roof, soffit, or chimney.

3—Exterior

Siding: Brick and wood

Comments: Sections of the wood siding are in contact with the soil. This could lead to insect infestation or deterioration. Sections of the wood in front (NE) are rotting at the base. There is chipped and missing mortar on the north side of the house.

Window material: wood

Comments: Kella & Weather Shield

Window Type: Double Hung and casements

Window Glazing: Double pane

Window screens: yes

Exterior Door material: wood and metal

Comments: The exterior doors appeared serviceable at the time of inspection.

Walks, Driveway, Stairs, and Railing:

Comments: Appear functional

Trim material: Wood & aluminum

Comments: Appears sound

Garage door opener:

Comments: One of the garage door springs is broken and should be replaced for safety. The concrete floor of garage is cracked and damaged.

General Exterior Comments: Sections of the wood decking on the balcony are rotted and should be replaced as needed for safety.

4—Foundation & Structure

Foundation material: Concrete Basement Floor: Concrete

Structural wall material: Wood studs

Structural floor framing: 2 x 10 x 16 o.c.

Structural beam material: wood Structural column material: wood

Foundation Comments: Settling cracks in foundations occur as a result of past movement in the walls and/or footing and are very common. Comments made in this report regarding foundation cracks are based solely on observations made at the time of this inspection and are not based on any engineering evaluations. Future movement of the foundation can occur with changes in soil conditions or foundation loads, which cannot be foreseen. If you have continuing concerns about the foundation, we recommend you seek the counsel of a professional engineer.

Basement Drainage System: sump pump. The sump pump discharge is run with a garden house. This should be routed with a proper size pipe to the outside.

Site Drainage: Slopes away

Basement Ventilation System: Windows. The basement window is covered with dirt. Recommend a proper window well be installed.

General Foundation and Structural Notes: Sections of the home foundation are of poured concrete slab on concrete footings. No evidence of any structural instability was observed. There is a shallow space below the sub floor of the bedroom wing. There is evidence of prior seepage in sections of the basement. Recommend discussing any past seepage problems with Seller.

Limits of Inspection: 80% of the basement is finished. The foundation inspection is limited to only accessible and visible areas of the foundation walls & components.

5 — Electrical

Wiring type: Conduit, NM & BX Wiring: Copper

Main Panel: Volts—240V, Amps—200 amp

Location: MBR closet and laundry closets (2 sub panels)

Circuit protection: circuit breakers

Room for expansion: yes

Exterior service and meter: 3 conductors underground

Interior light fixtures: OK

Outlets: Outside (NE) outlets are not grounded properly. These should be corrected for safety. The outside GFCI outlet at back patio door would not reset and should be replaced.

GFCI Receptacles: Ground fault receptacles in kitchen, bathrooms, and outside test OK. Retest each month. Recommend converting outlets in garage to GFCI for added protection.

Electrical Comments: Some basement circuits are wired with type NM wiring. This may not be in strict compliance with local electrical code requirements. Missing switch plates and/or receptacle covers were noted in the basement. These should be installed for safety.

Limitations of Inspection: Visible and accessible components only.

6 — Plumbing

Water Supply: City Sewer Supply: City

Main water line material: Copper Supply water line material: Copper

Comments: The main supply comes under ground from the city.

Main shutoff valve: Meter

Interior water pressure: Water pressure was adequate throughout the home.

Interior waste lines: Cast iron, PVC

Comments: Appears functional

Type of Water Heater: Gas 50 gallon. Manufactured 2005

Comments: Rhame

Limitations of Inspection: Visible and accessible components only. This is a sealed water heater.

7 — Heating

Type of system: Gas Forced Air. Borg & Cartier

Estimated age of units: 10–15 years

Estimated remaining life of units: 0–10 years

System capacity: 1 @ 85,000 BTU, regular efficiency

Number of Zones: 2.

Filters: 12 x 20 x 1—Change filter elements regularly.

Thermostats: 1 Mechanical & 3 Electronic

Comments: The MBR furnace is a higher efficiency type equipped with induced draft and electronic ignition. The attic ducting had a significant amount of rust and carbon buildup on the draft hood. Gas leaks were detected at elbow on attic furnace & shut off valve on furnace. These should be sealed for safety. There is evidence of birds entering the flue pipes of basement furnaces. There does not appear to be adequate fresh air to attic furnace. There is a buildup of scale and corrosion on humidifier components. These units should be serviced and repaired as needed to insure proper operation.

Recommend having the furnaces checked by a professional heating contractor and repaired or replaced as needed to insure safe & proper operation.

*Consider having the furnace duct work professionally cleaned.

It is recommended that a thorough cleaning and inspection of the heating systems be made each year.

Limits of Inspection: Most of the heat exchangers are not visible and are not represented in this inspection report.

8—Air Conditioning

Equipment: Electric powered, central. Carria

Age of units: 9–19 years

Estimated remaining life of system: 0–6 years

Comments: The AC system started up and cooled down properly at the time of inspection.

9—Bathroom(s)

Second Floor Bathroom: OK

Hall Bathroom: The toilet is not secure at the base. This should be repaired.

Master Bathroom: Caulking around bathtub is peeling. It is recommended that is be replaced.

General Comments: All fixtures are functional.

10—Interior

Flooring: Tile and wood. There is a damaged section of sub floor in NE bedroom. This should be repaired as needed. Sections of the wood floor need refinishing.

Wall material: Drywall

Ceiling material: Drywall. There is water damage to north bedroom ceiling.

Doors and Trim: Wood

Handrails: Wood. The rail at the top of 2nd floor stairway is loose.

Comments: The interior of the home appears to be in adequate condition.

11 — Insulation/Attic

Type of Insulation: Walls: 3.5 inch fiberglass = R-11 (according to the paper backing)

Attic: 5–8 inches fiberglass = R-17 (according to the paper backing)

Attic Framing: 2 x 6 x 16 on center

Attic Ventilation System: one aluminum vent

Comments: Recommend adding 8" more fiberglass or cellulose insulation to attic areas where possible. There is evidence of recent rodent activity in the attic, although no rodents were viewed.

Limitations of Inspection: Sections of the attic space are inaccessible.

Visible and accessible components only.

12 — Kitchen and Appliances

Oven/Range: Electric. The left rear burner did not heat up quickly. The fan is noisy.

Dishwasher: Appears functional.

Sink: The fixture drips at the stem of fixture.

Garbage Disposal: Appears functional.

Counters: Appear functional

Refrigerator: Appears functional.

Laundry: Laundry area has hookup for gas or electric dryer. The dryer vent empties into the attic and should be routed outside.

Comments: All appliances, counters, and cabinets appear to be adequate.

13 — Summary

Smoke/fire detectors were not tested as part of this inspection. Check these prior to occupancy and twice a year thereafter.

Recommend at least one functional Carbon Monoxide (CO) detector be installed in the home for safety.

Comment: Carbon Monoxide detectors are required by City of Chicago Code.

The sprinkler system and the security system were not checked as part of this inspection. Recommend having Seller or installer demonstrate proper operation and maintenance.

Home Inspection Letter

Paul Pitch
Attorney at Law

111 N. Jackson
Suite 452
Waukegan, IL 60085

(847) 354-9872
Fax: (847) 354-4869

18 July, 2012

Mr. William Jonestown, Esq.
111 S. Waller Dr. Suite 2620
Libertyville, IL 60048
(847) 592-8118
Fax: (847) 592-9001

SENT VIA FACSIMILE

RE: O'Neill ("Seller") Sale to Ocwen ("Buyer")
41 E. Normandy, Grayslake, IL 60030 ("Property")

Dear Mr. Jonestown:

Please be reminded that I represent the Buyer of the above-referenced property ("Property"). Pursuant to the Home Inspection provision in Paragraph 11 of the Real Estate Contract ("Contract"), please review the following:

The Home Inspection was performed on July 12, 2012. As the entire inspection report is 28 pages, I am attaching the Condensed Version of the Report. The entire report may be supplied upon request. The Inspector found many items determined to be "Marginal" and "Defective." The Buyers wish only to raise those certain substantial deficiencies in the Property listed below.

Exterior

Window screen missing. As there is a missing screen in the master bathroom window, Buyer requests a $100 credit at Closing for purchase and installation of a new screen.

Paint maintenance. The exterior wood door requires scraping, priming, and re-painting. Buyer requests a $200 credit at Closing to cover the cost of scraping, priming, and repainting.

Interior

Bathroom. The vanity lighting in the second floor half bath is not operational. Please confirm that the light is operational or fix/replace as needed. In addition, the Buyer stated that the light on the first floor bath is not operating. Please confirm that the light is operational or fix/replace as needed.

Kitchen. The kitchen disposal leaks. Buyer requests a $100 credit at Closing to have the disposal repaired.

Interior Findings.

Bedroom. Third floor northwest bedroom has a plaster patch that requires finishing and painting and Buyer requests a $200 credit at Closing to have the bedroom finished and painted.

The drywall is not flush with the wall. Buyer requests a $500 credit at Closing to have the drywall properly repaired.

Fireplace. The fireplace contained debris from fires.

Carpet Cleaning. The carpets show evidence of wear and requires cleaning.

Buyer requests a credit of $450 at Closing in order to have the fireplace, floors, and carpets professionally cleaned.

To facilitate your discussions with the Sellers, please find a copy of the Condensed Home Inspection Report ("Report") attached to this letter.

All repairs, or appropriate credits, must be performed or agreed upon prior to Closing, with receipts provided. The Home Inspection provision, Paragraph 11 of the Contract, is considered open and pending until all repairs or appropriate credits have been agreed upon and completed.

We await your response to these reasonable requests and look forward to working towards closing on August 24, 2012.

With Regards,
Paul Pitch
Buyer's Attorney

Enc.
CC: Ms. Kate Ocwen, via email
Mr. Joe Halter, Sales Max Signature South, via email

David Helmsley and Associates
Attorneys at Law

412 W. Broad Ave.   (618) 762-3336
Centralia, IL 62801   Fax: (618) 762-3390

dhelmsleylaw@kmail.com

04 March, 2013

Anthony Jones,
Jones, Schoenfield, Swartsman
303 North Elm,
Centralia, Illinois 62801
Tel: 618.943.1915
Fax: 618.651.0322
JSSlawyer@aol.com

SENT VIA FACSIMILE

RE: OOR ("Seller") Sale to Janek ("Buyer")
        1131 W. Belwell, Centralia, IL 62801 ("Property")

Dear Mr. Jones:

Please be informed that I represent the Buyer of the above-referenced property ("Property"). Pursuant to the Home Inspection provision in Paragraph 12 of the Real Estate Contract ("Contract"), please review the following. The Inspection was completed on March 3, 2013. A copy of the report is attached to this letter. The Buyer is only requesting those issues marked a "marginal" be addressed.

Laundry:

Dryer vent is flimsy. Buyer requests that the vent be replaced or a $100 credit offered.

A lack of drain pan on the washing machine. Buyer requests that the pan be installed or a $50 credit offered.

Kitchen:

Faucet does not switch from spray to stream. Buyer requests that the faucet be repaired or replaced or a $200 credit offered.

The counter top needs to be resealed. Buyer requests that the counter top be properly sealed or a $100 credit offered.

Flooring:

The floors need refinishing. Buyer requests that the hardwood floors be refinished or a $350 credit offered.

The carpet needs to be "stretched" to remove creases for the safety of the inhabitants. Buyer requests that the carpeting be smoothed or a $100 credit offered.

Buyer hereby requests that the above items are repaired/replaced by Seller, with receipts provided or that the requested credits by provided, at or before Closing.

We await your response to these reasonable requests and look forward to working towards closing on April 2, 2013.

With Regards,
David Helmsley

CC: Mr. Michael Janek, via email
Ms. Christinia Cross, Braid and Wartner, via email

Home Inspection Response Letter

William Jonestown, Esq.

Mr. William Jonestown, Esq.
111 S. Waller Dr. Suite 2620
Libertyville, IL 60048
(847) 592-8118
Fax: (847) 592-9001

22 July, 2012

Mr. Paul Pitch
111 N. Jackson
Suite 452
Waukegan, IL 60085
(847) 354-9872
Fax: (847) 354-4869

SENT VIA FACSIMILE

RE: O'Neill ("Seller") Sale to Ocwen ("Buyer")
41 E. Normandy, Grayslake, IL 60030 ("Property")

Dear Mr. Pitch:

I am in receipt of your letter dated July 18, 2012. I have reviewed your letter and have consulted with my client. In response to your letter please review the following:

Exterior

Window screen missing in master bedroom. Seller has the screen and has placed the screen in the Property in the master bedroom closet.

Paint maintenance. The exterior wood door is an exterior door and subject to the weather. Buyer is purchasing the property subject to condition of the door. No credit will be offered.

Interior

Bathroom. Seller confirms that the vanity lighting in the second floor half bath is operational. In addition, the light on the first floor bath is operational. The light bulbs in both fixtures have been replaced.

Kitchen. The Seller states that he had no knowledge of leak in the kitchen disposal. However, Seller will provide a $100 credit at Closing to have the disposal repaired.

Interior Findings.

Bedroom. Seller agrees to have the plaster patch finished and painted in the third floor northwest bedroom.

The Seller does not agree that the drywall is not flush with the wall. However, Seller will provide a $100 credit at Closing.

Fireplace. The Seller states that the fireplace was used in the Spring. The Seller will remove the debris from the fireplace.

Carpet Cleaning. The carpets are not new and would show evidence of wear.

Per Paragraph 18 of the Contract, Seller is required to leave the Property in "broom clean condition." Seller is under no obligation to provide a credit to Buyer to have the fireplace, floors, and carpets professionally cleaned.

Please accept the Seller's generous offer of a total credit of $200 (for the kitchen disposal and drywall) in order to satisfy the Home Inspection. We look forward to closing on August 24, 2012.

With Regards,
William Jonestown

Enc.
CC: Mr. James O'Neill, via email
Mr. William Yeats, Realty World, via email

Sample Financing Extension Letter

Paul Pitch
Attorney at Law

111 N. Jackson
Suite 452
Waukegan, IL 60085

(847) 354-9872
Fax: (847) 354-4869

22 July, 2012

Mr. William Jonestown, Esq.
111 S. Waller Dr. Suite 2620
Libertyville, IL 60048
(847) 592-8118
Fax: (847) 592-9001

SENT VIA FACSIMILE

RE: O'Neill ("Seller") Sale to Ocwen ("Buyer")
     41 E. Normandy, Grayslake, IL 60030 ("Property")

Dear Mr. Jonestown:

Pursuant to the Mortgage Contingency, Paragraph 5 of the Contract, I have yet to receive an unconditional Mortgage Commitment. I did receive the attached Loan Commitment [Editor's Note: not attached], which is contingent upon the property appraising for the purchase price. As you can see from the Commitment, there are very few conditions outstanding and, although we are very confident that the property will appraise for the purchase price, we request time for the appraisal be completed and reviewed prior to allowing the Mortgage Contingency to expire. I spoke with the Lender, Patrick Kim at FES Home Loans, and he stated that the appraisal was ordered today. The appraisal should be completed by Tuesday or Wednesday, with approval to follow shortly thereafter.

We therefore request an extension to the Mortgage Contingency until **Friday, August 10, 2012**. Please consult with your client and execute this letter where indicated below. If this extension is not accepted, we reserve the right to withdraw this request. We look forward to moving towards closing as scheduled.

With Regards,
Paul Pitch
Buyer's Attorney

I hereby agree to the extension above:

_____

       Seller/Attorney/Broker

Enc.

CC: Ms. Kate Ocwen, via email

Mr. Joe Halter, Sales Max Signature South, via email

MEMORANDUM

To: Student

From: Attorney

Re: Writing Assignment II

Date: Today's Date

As has been explained in class, the next step in the real estate transaction is the home inspection and the home inspection contingency. For this writing assignment, you will use the completed home inspection located earlier in this chapter and the draft home inspection letter.

The Buyer had the inspection done on July 8, 2015, by Home Wright Inspection, owned by Willie Wright. You should review the home inspection and draft the letter, using the sample letters provided as your template.

Please note that you will be writing the letter as if you were a paralegal working for the attorney for whom you wrote the attorney modification letter. If you are writing on behalf of the Buyer, you may ask for any deficiencies you wish, but please pay close attention to the home inspection contingency in the contract and any limitations the contract places on what may be negotiated in the home inspection letter.

If you are working for the Seller, you should draft a response letter to the home inspection letter provided to you. DO NOT SHARE THE HOME INSPECTION LETTER WITH STUDENTS "WORKING" FOR THE BUYER.

Good Luck

76 Ill. App.3d 638 (1979) 395 N.E.2d 133

HARRY S. POSNER et al., Plaintiffs-Appellees,

v.

SANDER A. DAVIS et al., Defendants-Appellants.

No. 78-1833.

Illinois Appellate Court — First District (1st Division).

Opinion filed September 17, 1979.

Affirmed in part, and reversed in part and remanded.

Mr. JUSTICE O'CONNOR delivered the opinion of the court:

Harry S. Posner and Diane M. Posner, plaintiffs, sued Sander A. Davis and Pearl E. Davis, defendants, for fraudulently concealing certain defects in a house in Evanston, which plaintiffs purchased from defendants in 1973. The alleged defects included basement flooding, rotted basement stairs, roof leakage and water-soaked and rotted plaster. After a bench trial, defendants were found guilty of fraud and judgment was entered for plaintiffs for $3,500. Defendants appeal, arguing that (1) plaintiffs failed to prove fraud and (2) the evidence did not support the award of $3,500.

Sander Davis testified that during the eight to 10 years prior to the sale the basement had flooded whenever there was a heavy rain, the flooding sometimes reaching three inches. After the water receded, defendants would have to wash and mop the basement. He also testified that approximately one year to 18 months before the house was sold to plaintiffs, he hired a roofer to deal with a leakage problem in the main roof. Sander Davis admitted that at the time of the sale this leakage had caused part of a third-floor bedroom wall to rot. In addition, he testified that the porch roof had leaked prior to the sale. He stated that he had never told plaintiffs about any of these defects.

Plaintiffs testified that after purchasing the house from defendants they owned it for approximately 10 months before selling it in May 1974. During that time, the basement flooded on at least six occasions, and in a few instances the water contained fecal matter. The water would usually take a day to a day and one-half to recede, after which plaintiffs had to mop and clean the basement. Plaintiffs also found that the bottom basement stair had rotted due to flooding.

Plaintiffs further testified that the main roof leaked, causing part of a third-floor bedroom wall to rot. This leakage also caused part of the bedroom's ceiling to fall after plaintiffs had begun occupying the house. In addition, plaintiffs stated that the porch roof leaked and that water seeped into the ceiling of the dining room, which was adjacent to the porch.

Defendants contend that plaintiffs failed to prove fraud by clear and convincing evidence. (See *Ray v. Winter* (1977), 67 Ill.2d 296, 367 N.E.2d 678.) On June 8, 1973, plaintiffs entered into a contract to purchase defendants' home in Evanston. The sale was closed on July 25, 1973. Plaintiffs testified that the only statement either defendant made to them concerning any of the defects in the house took place on June 13, 1973, when Sander Davis allegedly told Harry Posner that defendants had never had a basement flooding problem. Defendants maintain that this alleged statement by Sander Davis, which at trial he denied having made, was plaintiffs' only evidence of fraud and that plaintiffs could not have relied on it when they entered into the real estate sales contract on June 8, 1973, because plaintiffs concede the statement was not made until five days later. Thus, defendants argue, plaintiffs failed to prove that when they purchased the house they detrimentally relied on a fraudulent statement or act by defendants concerning any of the defects, and that the judgment against them was against the manifest weight of the evidence, because detrimental reliance is an essential element of fraud. Defendants also argue that it is unlikely plaintiffs believed they had been defrauded, because plaintiffs did not file their complaint in this action until January 2, 1975, approximately 17 months after plaintiffs had begun occupying the house and eight months after plaintiffs had sold it.

Plaintiffs contend that, if the seller of a house at any time prior to closing misrepresents its condition, that misrepresentation may be the basis for a fraud action by a buyer who relied on it when closing the sale; that Sander Davis' alleged misrepresentation concerning basement flooding was made on June 13, 1973; that the closing was not until July 25, 1973, and that plaintiffs detrimentally relied on Sander Davis' misrepresentation when they closed the sale. Because of the conclusion we have reached, we need not consider this contention.

Plaintiffs argue that in addition to the misrepresentation by Sander Davis, there was clear and convincing evidence that defendants actively concealed the defects from plaintiffs prior to entering into the sales contract and that this constitutes fraud.

We agree.

Both plaintiffs and defendants testified that defendants never told plaintiffs about the basement flooding problem. Plaintiffs also testified that the real estate broker did not inform them of the flooding. Furthermore, Sander Davis admitted he never advised the broker about the flooding or instructed the broker to inform prospective buyers of this condition.

In addition, plaintiffs and defendant Pearl Davis testified that plaintiffs made two visits to the house on a day shortly before June 8, 1973, the date of the sales contract. Harry Posner stated that on the first visit plaintiffs inspected the entire house, and Pearl Davis testified that Harry Posner examined the basement on this visit. Sander Davis testified that the main room in the basement had a tile floor and that flooding had, in part, caused some of the tiles there to flake and crack. He admitted he had removed many of these flaked and cracked tiles and had placed a large rug over the area where the tiles had been removed. This rug covered the entire floor of the main room in the basement, except for an approximately one foot border of intact tile extending around the room between the rug and the walls. Whenever the basement had flooded, defendants had taken the rug outside to dry, but Sander Davis admitted that the rug was never drying outside when plaintiffs visited the house. Moreover, Sander Davis admitted he never told plaintiffs that tiles under the basement rug were flaking and cracking, or that he had removed some of the tiles because of this damage.

Sander Davis also testified that no watermarks were visible on the basement walls, and that the basement stairs were completely carpeted.

Harry Posner testified that on one occasion when the basement flooded after plaintiffs had moved into the house, he had to lift the carpet covering the bottom basement step in order to discover that the step had rotted and that water was seeping through there into the basement. In addition, Diane Posner stated that the flooding problem prompted plaintiffs to sell the house.

Sander Davis also testified that when the main roof leakage had caused plaster in part of the third-floor bedroom wall to rot, he had covered the damaged area with a vinyl fabric which was "maintainable and aesthetically acceptable." Also, Harry Posner testified that when he visited the house, both prior to and after entering into the contract, he saw nothing to indicate there was any problem with roof leakage. He further testified that it was not until sometime after plaintiffs had occupied the house that he placed his hand against the vinyl covering on the third-floor bedroom wall and discovered that main roof leakage had caused a substantial amount of plaster underneath to become wet and crumble. In addition, plaintiffs testified that defendants and the broker never told them about the roof leakage, and Sander Davis admitted he never said anything to plaintiffs about this problem.

Finally, Harry Posner testified that when plaintiffs purchased the house, they relied on the fact defendants did not disclose anything about basement flooding or roof leakage. He also testified plaintiffs would not have bought the house if they had known about these conditions.

In *Russow v. Bobola* (1972), 2 Ill. App.3d 837, 841, 277 N.E.2d 769, a suit involving active concealment of basement flooding in a house, the court stated:

> "* * * Silence accompanied by deceptive conduct or suppression of material facts results in active concealment, and it then becomes the duty of a person to speak. In such case, if a party to a contract of sale does not disclose the whole truth, having the requisite intent to deceive, this amounts to fraud equally with an affirmative falsehood. * * *"

The evidence here is clear and convincing that when plaintiffs entered the contract to purchase defendants' home, they relied to their detriment on silence and conduct by defendants which resulted in active concealment of both the fact that there had been basement flooding which had caused the floor tiles to flake and crack and which had caused the bottom basement step to rot, and also the fact that there had been main-roof leakage which had damaged the plaster wall of the third-floor bedroom. Defendants testified that they did not intend to conceal these conditions from plaintiffs by silence or by the rug they had placed on the basement floor or by the vinyl with which they had covered the bedroom wall. However, their silence so resulted. A party is considered to intend the necessary consequences of his own acts or conduct. 37 Am.Jur.2d, Fraud and Deceit § 158 (1968).

Defendants argue that Sander Davis' alleged misrepresentation was the only evidence on which the trial court relied in finding fraud. We disagree, because the record discloses that the court also stated that the evidence showed defendants had a "duty to speak." This can be construed to be a finding of active concealment as to the basement flooding and main roof leakage. In addition, in a bench trial as here, "[n]o special findings of fact or propositions of law are necessary to support the judgment or as a basis for review in a non-jury case [citation]; and the appellee is permitted to endeavor to sustain the judgment of the trial court by any argument, for any reason, and upon any basis in the record showing that the judgment was proper." (*Long v. Arthur Rubloff & Co.* (1975), 27 Ill. App.3d 1013, 1022, 327 N.E.2d 346. See Ill. Rev. Stat. 1977, ch. 110A, par. 366(b)(3)(i).) The evidence here sustains the finding of fraud. The fact that plaintiffs did not file suit until January 2, 1975, does not militate against the finding of fraud.

Plaintiffs also argue that, although silence alone, absent the existence of a confidential relationship, generally does not amount to fraud (see *Shockley v. Ryder Truck Rental, Inc.* (1979), 74 Ill. App.3d 89, 392 N.E.2d 675), and that the rule that liability for fraud ordinarily cannot be based on silence alone has been a corollary to the traditional doctrine of caveat emptor, the modern trend in the law regarding the sale of a home is away from strict adherence to the doctrine of caveat emptor. In *Petersen v. Hubschman Construction Co.* (1979), 76 Ill.2d 31, 389 N.E.2d 1154, for example, our supreme court held that there is an implied warranty of fitness with the sale of a new house by a builder-vendor, and stated that the existence of such a warranty helped avoid "the harshness of caveat emptor." 76 Ill.2d 31, 38.

The amelioration of the doctrine of caveat emptor in a number of other jurisdictions has resulted in a used-home seller being liable for failing to disclose material defects of which he was aware at the time of sale. This view is succinctly expressed in *Lingsch v. Savage* (1963), 213 Cal. App.2d 729, 735, 29 Cal. Rptr. 201, 204:

> "It is now settled in California that where the seller knows of facts materially affecting the value or desirability of the property which are known or accessible only to him and also knows that such facts are not known to, or within the reach of the diligent attention and observation of the buyer, the seller is under a duty to disclose them to the buyer."

(See also *Lawson v. Citizens & Southern National Bank* (1972), 259 S.C. 477, 193 S.E.2d 124; *Obde v. Schlemeyer* (1960), 56 Wash.2d 449, 353 P.2d 672.) We are of the opinion, in view of our supreme court's amelioration of the doctrine of caveat emptor in *Petersen*, that this should also be the law in Illinois with reference to the sale of used homes.

The evidence clearly shows defendants knew of and failed to disclose that there had been problems with basement flooding and with main and porch roof leakage, and Harry Posner testified that plaintiffs would not have bought the house if they had known about the basement flooding or roof leakage. The finding of fraud on the part of defendants was correct.

Defendants' second contention is that plaintiffs' evidence did not support the award of $3,500 as damages. We agree.

A defrauded purchaser is entitled to damages which will give him the "benefit of his bargain." Thus, the measure of damages for fraudulently concealing defects in property is the value the property would have had at the time of sale if the defects did not exist, less the value the property actually had at the time of sale due to the defects. See *Ginsburg v. Bartlett* (1931), 262 Ill. App. 14; 19 Ill. L. & Prac. Fraud §53 (1956).

Much of plaintiffs' evidence on damages dealt with either the value the house had at the time when plaintiffs sold it, or with the amount of profit they would have made if the defects in the house had not existed. This particular evidence was not relevant to the question of plaintiffs' damages. Instead, the actual value of the house and the value it would have had without the defects should have been determined as of the date plaintiffs purchased the house from defendants. Plaintiffs did state that they purchased the house for $130,000. This may have been sufficient evidence of the value the house would have had when it was sold to plaintiffs if the defects had not existed. (37 Am.Jur.2d Fraud and Deceit §353 (1968).) However, no evidence was presented concerning the value the house actually had with the defects at the time plaintiffs purchased it.

An alternative measure of damages for fraudulent concealment is the cost of fixing the property to make it conform to the condition it would have had without the defects. (37 Am.Jur.2d Fraud and Deceit §357 (1968).) Such evidence may also be probative of the value the property actually had at the time of sale. (37 Am.Jur.2d Fraud and Deceit §357 (1968).) Plaintiffs did submit as evidence certain repair bills which they paid to have the defects fixed, and also testified that they themselves had to spend time cleaning the basement after it had flooded. However, the record is somewhat confusing concerning the amount plaintiffs paid to correct the defects, because plaintiffs also submitted evidence of expenditures they made for repairs and improvements to the house which had nothing to do with the complained-of defects. The record also shows that no attempt was made to place a value on the time plaintiffs themselves spent in dealing with the defects.

Absolute certainty concerning the amount of damage is not necessary to justify a recovery where the existence of damage is established; the evidence need only tend to show a basis for the computation of damages with a fair degree of probability. (*DeKoven Drug Co. v. First National Bank* (1975), 27 Ill. App.3d 798, 327 N.E.2d 378.) However, "damages may not be predicated on mere speculation, hypothesis, conjecture or whim." *DeKoven Drug Co. v. First National Bank* (1975), 27 Ill. App.3d 798, 802, 327 N.E.2d 378.

The record does not indicate any basis for the trial court's assessment of $3,500 damages. Plaintiffs' evidence concerning damages was confusing and much of it was based on an incorrect assumption concerning the proper measure of relief for fraudulent concealment. The award of $3,500 is reversed and the cause is remanded for an evidentiary hearing on damages.

The judgment of the circuit court of Cook County is affirmed as to defendants' liability and reversed and remanded for a new trial as to damages.

Affirmed in part and reversed and remanded in part.

GOLDBERG, P.J., and McGLOON, J., concur.

618 N.E.2d 1013 (1993) 248 Ill. App.3d 1000 188 Ill. Dec. 443

Michael L. MITCHELL and Renee Mehlinger Mitchell, Plaintiffs-Appellants,

v.

John and Luba SKUBIAK, Defendants-Appellees (Home Inspection Consultants of Greater Chicago, Inc., Defendant).

No. 1-89-3514.

Appellate Court of Illinois, First District, Third Division.

June 30, 1993.

Presiding Justice TULLY delivered the opinion of the court:

This cause arises out of the purchase of a residential home in Oak Park, Illinois, by plaintiffs, Michael and Renee Mitchell, from defendants, John and Luba Skubiak. Subsequent to purchase, plaintiffs discovered various defects and damage to the property which were not obvious or were concealed during plaintiffs' inspection of the property. The same defects were also not discovered by a third-party professional inspection firm, employed by plaintiffs to inspect the property prior to closing. Plaintiffs filed a complaint alleging fraudulent misrepresentation, concealment and non-disclosure by the defendant-sellers as well as negligence by the inspection company. The trial court dismissed plaintiff's complaint against the defendant-sellers, finding as a matter of law that plaintiffs could not have reasonably relied upon the representations or actions of the sellers, since plaintiffs employed their own expert home inspector. Plaintiffs appeal from the dismissal of their complaint.

On May 9, 1987, plaintiffs and defendants signed a contract for the purchase of defendants' residence in Oak Park. An addendum to the contract allowed plaintiffs four days to retain an expert to inspect the residence for defects. Plaintiffs were given the option, based upon the inspector's report, to either rescind the contract or negotiate for a reduction in price. Plaintiffs then engaged defendant, Home Inspection Consultants of Greater Chicago, Inc. (Home Inspection Consultants), to perform the inspection. Following examination of the premises, Home Inspection Consultants sent a written report to plaintiffs, listing various defects which were discovered and on the basis of this report, the parties mutually agreed to adjust the purchase price.

Pursuant to the contract of sale, plaintiffs were permitted a final walk-through inspection of the property, prior to closing. This final inspection took place on May 20, 1987, although the closing did not occur until July 15, 1987.

During the walk-through inspection, plaintiffs discovered new cracks in the walls and ceiling of the master bedroom. Defendants represented to plaintiffs that these were due to the differences in humidity between the attic and the bedroom and further stated that the cracks were not due to any other cause. While inspecting the garage, defendants stated that "from time to time a little rain water collected on the roof of the garage and would require sweeping the water off." While inspecting the porch, plaintiffs did not notice any structural defects to the door or area leading under the porch, although they subsequently discovered that a damaged doorway area had been covered with carpeting.

Count I of plaintiffs' complaint alleges that defendants knew that the roof of the main residence contained serious structural defects affecting value; that defendants affirmatively misrepresented the roof's condition and the reason for the cracks in the master bedroom; that such statements were made with the intention of inducing plaintiffs' reliance thereon; and that plaintiffs justifiably relied upon the representations of defendants, resulting in substantial damage to plaintiffs.

Count II of the complaint alleges essentially the same elements of misrepresentation found in count I, except the facts concerned the representation that the garage roof had to be swept from time to time after a rainfall. According to the complaint, this statement was a "halftruth," creating an impression that the garage roof was not defective and misrepresenting the roof's true condition.

Count III alleges that defendant knew of serious structural defects in the front porch and the doorway leading to the area beneath the front porch; that as a result of these defects, water was allowed to accumulate in the basement after each rain; that prior to any inspection by either plaintiffs or Home Inspection Consultants, the Skubiaks concealed the alleged defects by permanently gluing carpeting in place and placing furniture and other objects in front of the damaged doorway; that these acts of concealment amounted to affirmative misrepresentations that the porch was in good condition; that the acts were done with the intent of inducing reliance by plaintiffs and Home Inspection Consultants on the outward appearance of the porch and to discourage further investigation.

Count IV of the complaint alleges that defendants knew of the various defects described in the other counts; knew that such defects were not easily discoverable upon inspection; knew that plaintiffs and their inspector would be misled by the nondisclosure of such defects; knew that these defects would be material to plaintiffs' decision in purchasing their home; and that defendants possessed an affirmative duty as vendors of real estate to disclose the existence of these defects to the plaintiffs as purchasers. Furthermore, plaintiffs allege that they reasonably relied on the silence of defendants in purchasing their home and as a result of this reliance they incurred damages.

After hearing arguments on defendants' motion to dismiss, the trial court concluded the following:

> "Gentlemen, I conclude here there was not reasonable reliance. There may have been reliance, but it was not reasonable when you had an inspector, your clients had an inspector to go out and inspect the property. You have an action against the inspector. That is why I asked you if you were charging collusion between the owners and the inspector.
>
> * * * * * *
>
> That failing, you have an independent inspector to go out, then there was no — it was not reasonable for your clients to rely on the sellers. And in fact they didn't rely on them because they got their own inspector to go out.

* * * * * *

I will grant the motion."

The trial court dismissed plaintiffs' complaint, finding as a matter of law: (1) plaintiffs did not actually rely upon the acts or omissions of defendants because they hired a third-party inspection company, upon whose opinion they relied; and (2) even if plaintiffs could show actual reliance on the sellers' representations, such reliance was unreasonable because they hired a professional inspector.

On appeal, plaintiffs contend: (1) by actively concealing defects from the buyers as well as the home inspector, defendants can be held liable for fraud; (2) examination by an independent home inspector does not, as a matter of law, preclude buyers from relying upon the representations of sellers; (3) plaintiffs' action against the home inspector does not defeat a claim against the vendors of the property, even if the pleadings are inconsistent.

On appeal, the appropriate standard for considering a motion to dismiss is de novo. That is, this court must examine the complaint and consider, in light of all factual and legal circumstances, whether or not there exists any set of facts, if proven, which would support a cause of action under the laws of Illinois. (*Ostendorf v. International Harvester Co.* (1982), 89 Ill.2d 273, 60 Ill. Dec. 456, 433 N.E.2d 253.) All sufficiently plead facts must be accepted as true and any reasonable inferences to be drawn must be construed in a light most favorable to the plaintiff. (*Towne v. Cole* (1985), 133 Ill.App.3d 380, 88 Ill. Dec. 404, 478 N.E.2d 895.) A complaint should only be dismissed where there appears absolutely no set of facts which would permit recovery. *Neuman v. City of Chicago* (1982), 110 Ill.App.3d 907, 66 Ill. Dec. 700, 443 N.E.2d 626.

We initially consider whether plaintiffs' complaint sufficiently states a cause of action for fraudulent misrepresentation and fraudulent nondisclosure in the purchase and sale of a residential home.

The requisite elements of a common law fraud cause of action are: (1) a false statement of material fact, intentionally made; (2) the party to whom the statement was made had a right to rely on it; (3) the statement was made for the purpose of inducing reliance thereon; and (4) the reliance by the person to whom the statement was made led to his injury. (*Redarowicz v. Ohlendorf* (1982), 92 Ill.2d 171, 65 Ill. Dec. 411, 441 N.E.2d 324.) While silence in a business transaction does not generally amount to fraud, mere silence is quite different from concealment. Silence accompanied by deceptive conduct or suppression of material facts results in active concealment and it then becomes the duty of a person to speak. Under such circumstances, if a party to a contract of sale fails to disclose the whole truth, having the requisite intent to deceive, this amounts to fraud, equivalent to an affirmative falsehood. *Russow v. Bobola* (1972), 2 Ill. App.3d 837, 277 N.E.2d 769.

While traditionally, sellers of real estate were not liable for undisclosed defects under the doctrine of caveat emptor, the modern trend among courts is to impose a duty upon the sellers for failure to disclose defects which could not be discovered upon a reasonable and diligent inspection. (See, *Petersen v. Hubschman Construction*

Co. (1979), 76 Ill.2d 31, 27 Ill. Dec. 746, 389 N.E.2d 1154; *Zimmerman v. Northfield Real Estate, Inc.* (1986), 156 Ill.App.3d 154, 109 Ill. Dec. 541, 510 N.E.2d 409; *Posner v. Davis* (1979), 76 Ill.App.3d 638, 32 Ill. Dec. 186, 395 N.E.2d 133.) However, a seller's silence in not disclosing defects, standing alone, does not give rise to a cause of action for misrepresentation. Silence must be combined with active concealment. (*Dee v. Peters* (1992), 227 Ill. App.3d 1030, 169 Ill. Dec. 235, 591 N.E.2d 115.) Moreover, liability will not be imposed where the buyer was aware of the defects prior to purchase or could have discovered them through diligent inspection. *Fleisher v. Lettvin* (1990), 199 Ill. App.3d 504, 145 Ill. Dec. 613, 557 N.E.2d 383.

Turning to the facts in this case, during their final walk-through inspection, plaintiffs observed cracks in the master bedroom. Count I of the complaint alleges that defendants "explained away new cracks within the ceiling plaster of one bedroom as a condition due to the natural variances in the temperature and humidity between the attic and the bedroom, thus concealing the defects and discouraging further investigation by the plaintiffs."

The complaint further alleges that defendants knew of structural defects in the roof of the main residence, including "cracked, broken and insufficiently repaired rafters resulting in a condition of chronic leakage of rain water into two upstairs bedrooms within the residence." Plaintiffs further allege that defendants knew of the defects and the faulty repair work and knew that they were not apparent or readily discoverable upon inspection.

Count II alleges essentially the same cause of action for misrepresentation, except the allegations concern defects in the roof of the garage. During the walk-through inspection, defendant, John Skubiak, stated that from time to time, rain water would collect on the roof and would require sweeping.

Considering the facts and surrounding circumstances contained in count I, we find that plaintiffs have presented facts which, if proven, could sufficiently support a finding of fraud. It is alleged that faulty repair work on the roof caused large amounts of water to leak into two of the upstairs bedrooms. It is further alleged that defendants knew of this faulty repair work and not only did they fail to disclose it, but they actively misled plaintiffs, by explaining a crack in the upstairs bedroom to be caused by temperature and humidity variances. There were no apparent water marks or wet areas which would have indicated a defective roof as the source of the cracks. Upon plaintiffs' inquiring about the source of the crack, a duty to speak arose on behalf of the defendants. Their failure to speak, or rather to disclose the entire truth of the matter, sufficiently states a cause of action for fraudulent misrepresentation.

Whether or not defendants' actions were intentional and whether or not plaintiffs' reliance was reasonable are questions of fact to be properly decided by the trier of fact. In determining whether reliance was reasonable, all of the facts available to the buyer as well as those he could have discovered with ordinary prudence, must be taken into account. (*Central States Joint Board v. Continental Assurance Co.* (1983), 117 Ill.App.3d 600, 73 Ill. Dec. 107, 453 N.E.2d 932.) We cannot find, as a matter of law, that plaintiffs' belief in and reliance upon the representation that the cracked ceiling was caused by temperature variances was unreasonable.

Count II, however, presents a different set of facts. Plaintiffs were informed that water collects on the roof of the garage and that it has to be swept off. Plaintiffs claim that defendants had a duty to inform them that this water, if not swept off, would cause damage to the inside walls of the garage. This presents an easier case of shifting the duty of inspection to the buyer. Defendants fully disclosed the water problem and the fact that "it had to be swept off." A little old-fashioned common sense on the part of the purchasers would have lead them to the conclusion that if they did not sweep the water off the garage roof, it would probably drain into the garage, since obviously the water was collecting due to a faulty or non-existent drainage system. Under these facts, we conclude that count II was properly dismissed for failing to state a cause of action.

Count III alleges that the front porch of the residence contained serious structural defects which were knowingly concealed by defendants, such that the plaintiffs and home inspector would not discover their true condition. Allegedly, defendants covered the porch and steps with indoor-outdoor carpeting, permanently affixed with glue, and further concealed a damaged door and doorway leading to the basement underneath the porch by placing furniture and other items in front of the door and doorway during inspections by plaintiffs and Home Inspection Consultants.

In the seminal case of *Posner v. Davis* (1979), 76 Ill.App.3d 638, 32 Ill. Dec. 186, 395 N.E.2d 133, the defendant-sellers misrepresented to the buyers that there had never been a basement flooding problem in their home. They later admitted that they had concealed the flooding problem by removing damaged basement floor tiles and covering the area with a large rug. The owners also covered water-damaged walls in a bedroom with vinyl wall-covering. The court found that the sellers' silence accompanied by such acts of concealment were sufficient to support a finding of fraud. Citing *Russow v. Bobola* (1972), 2 Ill. App.3d 837, 277 N.E.2d 769.

Again, count III alleges actions by defendants, which, if proven, amount to an active concealment of defects. Plaintiffs must still prove, as in any action for fraud, scienter or intent to defraud by the defendants. Moreover, there must be sufficient evidence that defendants knew about the alleged defects and knew that plaintiffs would not discover them upon reasonable inspection. Plaintiffs must also prove that the undisclosed information was material to their decision in purchasing or negotiating the price of the home.

Count IV encompasses all of the factual allegations contained in the prior three counts, but states a cause of action for fraudulent nondisclosure as opposed to misrepresentation. As heretofore discussed, the allegations contained in counts I and III of the complaint sufficiently created a situation in which the defendant home owners owed plaintiffs a duty to disclose the true nature of the cracked ceiling in the bedroom and the porch door and doorway which had been concealed with carpeting. However, regarding the garage roof, plaintiffs have not stated a cause of action for concealment, as they were informed by defendants of the drainage problem and did not further investigate. A prospective home buyer may not shut his eyes to the obvious and then charge that he has been deceived, particularly where there was ample opportunity to further investigate and ascertain the true condition of the garage roof. (See, e.g., *Fleisher v. Lettvin* (1990), 199 Ill.App.3d 504, 145 Ill. Dec. 613, 557 N.E.2d 383; *Seefeldt v. Milikin National Bank* (1987), 154 Ill.App.3d 715, 107 Ill. Dec. 161, 506 N.E.2d 1052; *Carter v. Mueller* (1983), 120 Ill.App.3d 314, 75 Ill. Dec. 776, 457 N.E.2d 1335.) Therefore, count IV sufficiently states a cause of action for nondisclosure as to the roof of the main residence and the porch area. However, the factual allegations regarding the garage roof must be stricken.

We next consider whether the hiring of an independent professional home inspector precludes plaintiffs' cause of action as a matter of law. Defendants argue that any condition or defect which should have been discovered upon diligent inspection by Home Inspection Consultants was imputed to the buyers. It is further contended that a buyer cannot circumvent his or her duty to examine a house by employing a third-party professional home inspector.

We agree. While purchasers are free to seek expert advice as to the quality of a prospective home, they cannot subrogate their common law duty to inspect the premises to a third party and then later claim they had no knowledge of a defect which could have been discovered with reasonable diligence. In the same way, sellers are not relieved of their duty to disclose hidden or concealed defects, simply because the buyer has interposed a third-party to conduct the inspection. A duty to speak or disclose defects to a professional inspector arises under the same conditions as when a home is inspected by the buyer personally. We need not address whether or not this duty runs directly to the buyer or exists only as between the seller and the inspector company, since in this case, the alleged misrepresentation and concealment were practiced against the third-party inspector as well as the plaintiff buyers.

In an analogous case, the seller misrepresented the true nature of a basement flooding problem in the presence of both the buyer and the home inspector. Because the home inspector did not attempt to explain the basement's evidence of flooding, but instead, allowed the seller to explain water marks in the basement, the trial court upheld a cause of action in fraud as against the seller. *Connor v. Merrill Lynch* (1991), 220 Ill.App.3d 522, 163 Ill. Dec. 245, 581 N.E.2d 196.

Turning to the instant case, plaintiffs' inspector knew about the drainage problem on the garage roof and informed them of this. As previously set forth, plaintiffs were also informed of the problem by the sellers personally. Therefore, plaintiffs would have no cause of action based upon the defective garage roof, even if they had not hired a professional inspector.

Home Inspection Consultants did inspect the rafters in the attic, but failed to note their condition in its written report. Plaintiffs allege in their complaint that the attic rafters had been repaired but that the repair work was faulty and that defendant-sellers were aware of this since there had been water draining into the upstairs bedrooms. During plaintiffs' walk-through inspection, defendants explained away a crack in the master bedroom as due to temperature variances. The complaint further alleges that defendants stated or implied that there was no other cause for the crack. While plaintiffs may have a viable claim against defendant, Home Inspection Consultants, this does not exonerate the sellers, who allegedly made a misrepresentation about the cracked ceiling directly to plaintiffs. Arguably, plaintiffs were relying upon the written report of the inspector as well as the statements of the sellers in concluding that the roof was not defective. Under this set of facts, there is sufficient evidence to support a cause of action against the defendant-sellers, notwithstanding the employment of a third-party home inspector.

Likewise, the active concealment of the porch door and door way may have prevented plaintiffs from discovering the damage beneath. While the defendant-inspectors may have acted negligently in failing to discover the defective porch, the concealment was also practiced upon plaintiffs who justifiably relied upon defendants' silence during the walk-through inspection. This is not a case where a rug could have been simply moved or picked up in order to inspect beneath. Rather, defendants permanently affixed the carpeting with glue, requiring it to be pryed [sic] from the area. Again, the employment of the home inspector in this instance did not serve to intervene in the alleged act of concealment as between the sellers and buyers in this case.

In this case, sufficient facts have been alleged to support the notion that the plaintiff buyers relied upon the representations of both the sellers and the home inspector. Whether plaintiffs' reliance upon either party was material to their purchase decision and to what extent reliance was placed upon the sellers versus the home inspector are issues to be resolved by the trier of fact. As the late Dean Prosser poignantly wrote:

> "Each of two liars may play a significant part in leading [the plaintiff] to his final conclusion; and the mere fact that he has made inquiries, or obtained additional information from other sources, does not necessarily mean that he had disregarded what defendant told him. An independent investigation which fails to discover the truth may not be enough to preclude reliance upon the defendant's statement. Thus, inspection of the property by a purchaser will not always prevent his reliance upon an assurance of latent defects. The question becomes one of fact, as to whether substantial weight was given to the [defendant's] representation, and it usually is one for the jury."

Prosser, Law of Torts at p. 715 (4th ed. 1971).

Finally, we consider whether inconsistent allegations against each of two defendants precludes a cause of action against the Skubiaks in this case. It is well settled in Illinois that inconsistent pleadings are permitted against the same party in separate counts. (Ill.Rev.Stat. 1987, ch. 110, par. 2-613.) Clearly, in this case, the existence of inconsistent allegations against two different defendants in separate counts does not require the dismissal of the complaint.

In summation, we affirm the trial court's dismissal of count II of the complaint and reverse the dismissal of counts I, III and IV. However, the allegations in count IV regarding latent defects in the garage roof and drainage system must be stricken.

Affirmed in part; reversed in part and remanded with instructions.

CERDA and GREIMAN, JJ., concur

Chapter 4

Title Insurance Surveys

Learning Objectives

After studying Chapter 4, you will be able to:

- Explain what title is and what is contained in a title report
- Interpret a basic real estate survey
- Identify and distinguish the various forms of easement

Chapter Summary

Topics covered:

- Title Insurance
- Surveys

This chapter introduces the concept of title and survey, two very important considerations in most real estate transactions. The chapter introduces what it means to have title to something. The chapter then moves to what a title policy is and the different forms of title policies. The concept of marketable title is addressed. The basics of a title search are addressed. The chapter then moves to the survey. Surveys, and what may be contained in a survey, are defined. Easements are discussed and examples of easements are provided. The final topic in the chapter is a brief description of encroachments. The sample title policy and survey for the hypothetical are included at the end of the chapter. The chapter concludes with a breakdown of a legal description.

1. Title Insurance

To have "**Title**" to something means to have both ownership of and the right to use the property. When a person purchases a vehicle, that person is said to have title to the vehicle. The title is registered with the state and presented to the owner of the vehicle. Similarly, title for real property is ownership of the property. The title to a piece of real property is in the form of a "deed" to the property (see Chapter 6). Title to real property is an insurable interest in the property.

Title insurance is a form of indemnity insurance which insures against financial loss from defects in title to real property, as well as protection from the invalidity or unenforceability of mortgage liens. Indemnity means a protection against a financial burden or loss. Title insurance is designed to protect an owner's and/or a lender's financial interest in real property against loss due to title defects, liens, or other encumbrances. It is primarily used when a property is being conveyed, in order to provide the Buyer (and, often, the Buyer's lender) with assurances that the Seller is legally entitled to convey the property, and serves as a protection against any defects in title. The title insurance company will defend against lawsuits attacking the title, or reimburse the insured for the actual monetary loss incurred, up to the dollar amount of insurance provided by the policy. There are two primary forms of title insurance policies: Owner's policy and Lender's policy.

A **title insurance policy** serves two purposes. First, title insurance policies provide a search of the legal records of the property and disclose the rightful owner of the property (who is authorized to sell the property), if liens are recorded against the property, and what title exceptions, if any, exist. Second, it provides insurance against risk of loss due to unforeseen problems that might arise.

A title insurance policy is a contract between the title holder and the title insurance company that the title insurance company will defend against and pay losses arising from any claim covered by the policy's terms. Lenders usually require buyers to obtain title insurance that protects the lender. This is known as a mortgage title policy, also known as a "lender's title policy" (or "loan policy"). Lenders require title insurance to protect their interest in loans secured by real estate.

Note: many, if not most, real estate attorneys in Illinois are agents of title companies. Some attorneys actually own the title companies. The work that a paralegal may do in a real estate office where the attorney is an agent or owner of the title company can vary, and may include conducting preliminary title searches and ordering the underlying documents that form the basis of the title commitment and title policy.

Owner's Policy

The owner's policy is purchased by the Seller and assures the Buyer that the Seller is the legal owner of the property, that the Seller may convey the property, that title to the property will be vested in that Buyer, and that title is free from defects, liens, and encumbrances (except those which are listed as exceptions in the policy or are excluded from the scope of the policy's coverage). This is very important as it provides assurances to the Buyer that the Seller can convey the property to the Buyer.

Title insurance also covers losses and damages suffered if the title is unmarketable. The policy also provides coverage for loss if there is no right of access to the land.

The liability limit of the owner's policy is typically the purchase price paid for the property. The Seller of the property is responsible for paying the costs of the owner's policy and it is only paid for once, generally at Closing. There are no annual premiums, as in other forms of insurance. When an owner wishes to sell the property, they are required to purchase a new owner's policy to cover the new Buyer. Additional coverage may be added or terminated with additional insurance called "an endorsement." There are many forms of standard endorsements to cover a variety of common issues. For instance, there can be endorsements for Zoning (Endorsement 3), Condominiums (Endorsement 4), Planned Unit Developments (Endorsement 5), and Environmental (Endorsement 8). These endorsements provide additional protection against specific title defects.

Lender's Policy

A Lender's (or loan) policy is issued to mortgage lenders. It provides assurances to the lender that the title is free from defects and follows the assignment of a mortgage loan, meaning that the policy benefits the purchaser of the loan if the loan is sold. For this reason, these policies greatly facilitate the sale of mortgages onto the secondary market.

The Lender's policy is generally purchased by the Buyer and is paid at Closing. Like an owner's policy, there are no annual premiums. The policy limit is generally the mortgage amount (not the purchase price of the property). It is designed to protect the lender's interest in the property. It does not provide any protection for the Buyer of the property.

2. Marketable Title

To be **marketable**, the property must be conveyed reasonably free of encumbrances. An encumbrance is something that is an impediment or hindrance. In real estate, an encumbrance on title might be a lien, such as a mechanic's lien, a mortgage, an easement, a contract on property, a judgment, etc. In title policy parlance, it is called a "cloud" on title. Generally speaking, when selling real estate there is an "implied warranty" of marketability of title (except with so-called "quit claim" deeds, discussed in Chapter 6). An **unmarketable** title is one that has a defect in title or has unreasonable or incurable encumbrances on it. For instance, someone who is not the legal title holder of the property cannot convey that property (because title was lost to a foreclosure, see Chapter 7). One of the advantages of title insurance is that the title company will work to ensure that title is marketable before insuring the title to the property.

There are other concerns that could render title unmarketable. For instance, the deed could have the wrong name on it. That will render the title unmarketable, as the Seller could not demonstrate that the Seller owns the property and has the right to convey the property. This actually happens more often than one might think. If the owner is married and subsequently divorces (called a "dissolution of the marriage" in Illinois), the title to the property may still be the owner's married name, but the owner has changed names. Another example is when people inherit property. The owner passes and the interest in the property is conveyed (by will or intestate succession) to a beneficiary. Until the property is properly titled in the name of the beneficiary, the beneficiary may not be able to sell, mortgage, convey, or otherwise dispose of or encumber the property.

Lack of capacity of the owner may render title unmarketable. If the owner has advanced dementia and is unable to make decisions, that person cannot contract for the sale of, or sign the deed to, the property. If there is a legally authorized decision maker for that person (an agent through a properly executed Power of Attorney for Property or a court-appointed Guardian of the Estate), that authorized person will be able to contract for, and convey the property on behalf of, the incapacitated owner.

3. Contract Provisions

Paragraph 18 of the contract covers the Title Provision.

> **18. TITLE:** At Seller's expense, Seller will deliver or cause to be delivered to Buyer or Buyer's attorney within customary time limitations and sufficiently in advance of Closing, as evidence of the title in Seller or Grantor, a title commitment for an ALTA title insurance policy in the amount of the Purchase Price with extended coverage by a title company licensed to operate in the State of Illinois, issued on or subsequent to the Date of Acceptance, subject only to items listed in Paragraph 16. The requirement to provide extended coverage shall not apply if the Real Estate is vacant land. The commitment for title insurance furnished by Seller will be presumptive evidence of good and merchantable title as therein shown, subject only to the exceptions therein stated. **If the title commitment discloses any unpermitted exceptions or if the Plat of Survey shows any encroachments or other survey matters that are not acceptable to Buyer, then Seller shall have said exceptions, survey matters or encroachments removed, or have the title insurer commit to either insure against loss or damage that may result from such exceptions or survey matters or insure against any court-ordered removal of the encroachments.** If Seller fails to have such exceptions waived or insured over prior to Closing, Buyer may elect to take title as it then is with the right to deduct from the Purchase Price prior encumbrances of a definitive or ascertainable amount. Seller shall furnish Buyer at Closing an Affidavit of Title covering the date of Closing, and shall sign any other customary forms required for issuance of an ALTA Insurance Policy.

In general, the contract requires that the Seller provide the title policy ensuring that the title will be marketable. In addition, it requires that any issue must be resolved before the Closing of the property. If the Seller is not able to provide a title policy, that would be a breach of contract. The Buyer would then be able to cancel the contract, sue for breach of contract, or both.

4. Preliminary Title Insurance Policy

Paralegals are often asked to order title policies. Every title company has its own order form. It is imperative that all of the information on the order form be filled out completely and accurately. A sample Title Policy Order Form is included at the end of this chapter.

The preliminary title policy is produced by the title company. After the Title Policy Order is placed, the title company begins the process of **title examination.**

The examiner then runs a chain of title at the county recorder's office. In order for a "**chain of title**" to begin, the title examiner creates, in reverse chronological order, the names of all the persons who have owned the land or had an interest in the property for a specific period of time (usually 24 or 36 months). The examiner investigates this historical record in order to determine what documents have been recorded against the property. This investigation will establish: the owner of the property; how the property is titled; in whose name the property is titled; the location of the property; and whether liens have been filed against the property. When running a chain of title, the examiner will check if there are any "out of conveyances" and will have to look at those to determine ownership and uncover flaws.

A title examiner usually then examines the records at the county tax assessor's office. Here the examiner can check the status of the real estate taxes, verify the name of the taxpayer (to make sure the Seller is listed as the taxpayer), verify whether taxes were paid and whether the taxes have been sold for failure to pay. Often, if a homeowner has not paid the property taxes on the property, the property may be sold by the county for "back taxes." The tax buyer may then pay the taxes during the pendency of the redemption period, and ultimately become the owner of the property. When the title examiner investigates the county tax assessor records, they will discover if a tax sale has taken place.

After the examiner has determined the chain of title, the examiner should note any outstanding recordings pertaining the subject property including, but not limited to: mortgages, liens, easements, restrictions, and rights of way. After the examiner reviews the chain of title (and, if applicable, out of conveyances), the examiner searches other public records such as civil judgments and, often, UCC Financing Statements.

The preliminary title report (**Title Commitment**) is produced by the title company and provided to the Seller's attorney. The Seller's attorney then provides a copy to the Buyer's attorney. The attorneys for each party review the title commitment. The Seller's attorney generally provides a copy to the survey company. Any issues with title that the attorneys find should be addressed prior to Closing. In general, the title company will not allow the transaction to close without any of the parties addressing any outstanding title issues.

A title company will not insure a property that it reasonably believes will have a cloud on title. It is often said, that the title company will only insure properties that do not need insurance. This is not correct, of course, but the title company will do everything possible to make sure that the title is marketable and that the property can close. The title insurance covers certain unforeseen problems that were not discovered during the title examination.

At Closing, the title officer or Seller's attorney (if the attorney is an agent of the title company) reviews the title policy again and notes on the title commitment any material that is to be removed from the title policy prior to the production of the final policy. This is known as "**waiving**" the title commitment. The items that are frequently waived include the Seller's mortgage (the loan is typically paid in full at Closing and the mortgage will then be released), any taxes that will be paid at Closing, and any liens or judgments that will be satisfied at Closing.

In addition, every owner's title policy contains five standard exceptions, also called "general exceptions." The five **General Exceptions** that should be waived at Closing include:

1. Rights or claims of parties in possession not shown by the public records.

2. Encroachments, overlaps, boundary line disputes, or other matters which would be disclosed by an accurate survey and inspection of the premises.

3. Easements, or claims of easements, not shown by public record.

4. Any lien, or right to a lien, for services, labor, or material heretofore or hereafter furnished, imposed by law, and not shown by public records.

5. Taxes or special assessments which are not shown as existing liens by public records.

As stated below (in the section about surveys) the title company is frequently provided with a copy of the plat of survey and other necessary documentation. If the survey and additional documentation reveal no adverse interests, the title company can waive these five standard exceptions from the owner's title policy. This is called providing "extended coverage" to the policy and policyholder.

Title insurance is an important protection for the Buyer of the property and is really a necessity when purchasing a property. Without title insurance, the Buyer may have no ability to adequately determine that the Seller has the legal right to convey the property! The lender will almost always require the Buyer to purchase a title policy to provide assurances for the lender that its interests will be protected.

A sample title policy is included at the end of this chapter.

5. Surveys

A "plat of survey" is a two-dimensional drawing of a piece of property. The survey depicts the physical limits of the land, placement of buildings, improvements, fences, sidewalks, driveways, and other improvements located on the property.

Surveys, also known as "plats of survey" are prepared by Illinois professional land surveyors, who are licensed by the State of Illinois (Illinois Professional Land Surveyor Act of 1989, 225 ILCS 330/1 and the Permanent Survey Act, 765 ILCS 215/0.01). The survey itself is in the form of a drawing and consists of the opinion of the surveyor.

Paragraph 19 of the contract describes the requirements of the survey. Paragraph 17 states as follows:

19. PLAT OF SURVEY: Not less than one (1) Business Day prior to Closing, except where the Real Estate is a condominium (see Paragraph 15) Seller shall, at Seller's expense, furnish to Buyer or Buyer's attorney a Plat of Survey that conforms to the current Minimum Standard of Practice for boundary surveys, is dated not more than six (6) months prior to the date of Closing, and is prepared by a professional land surveyor licensed to practice land surveying under the laws of the State of Illinois. The Plat of Survey shall show visible evidence of improvements, rights of way, easements, use and measurements of all parcel lines. The land surveyor shall set monuments or witness corners at all accessible corners of the land. All such corners shall also be visibly staked or flagged. The Plat of Survey shall include the following statement placed near the professional land surveyor's seal and signature: "This professional service conforms to the current Illinois Minimum Standards for a boundary survey." A Mortgage Inspection, as defined, is not a boundary survey, and is not acceptable.

As stated, the survey is generally ordered by the Seller at the Seller's expense. The Seller's attorney generally orders the survey and will review the survey upon receipt. A copy of the survey is often provided to the title company for review as well, preferably prior to Closing, but often a copy of the survey is provided to the title company at Closing. As described above, the title company will examine the title in order to determine if encroachments or other potential concerns exist that must be resolved. If there are encroachments or other concerns, the title company can work with the Seller's attorney to resolve those issues. An **encroachment** is something on the property that intrudes over the boundaries listed on the survey (such as a portion of a building that crosses a building line).

The survey can be no more than six (6) months old. If the survey is more than six (6) months old, the Seller must obtain an updated survey or sign an **affidavit of no new improvements**. An affidavit of no new improvements is a statement in which the Seller swears that no improvements have been performed on the property that would alter the survey. Typically, affidavits of no new improvement are acceptable for a survey between six (6) and twelve (12) months old, when no work has been performed on the property. Transactions where the survey is older than one (1) year will generally need an updated survey. Surveys generally cost between $300.00 and $600.00.

A copy of an affidavit of no new improvements is included at the end of this chapter.

Most law firms have a relationship with one or more survey companies. Paralegals often order the surveys. It is suggested that the survey is ordered as soon as the preliminary title policy is produced. As stated in Paragraph 19 of the contract, the Seller is required to provide the survey at least one day prior to Closing. Ideally, the survey should be provided well in advance in order for the Seller's attorney, Buyer's attorney, and title company to have sufficient time to review the survey prior to Closing.

When reviewing a survey in the law office, the paralegal should look for building lines, easements, permanent structures, ingress and egress, and fences. Typically, the survey will display the property lines as thick black lines. The survey will display the building line(s) (if any) as long dashed lines. Easements are displayed as dashed lines.

Buildings and permanent structures are displayed as two dimensional drawings. Concrete is generally delineated by thin black lines, often with a speckled appearance.

A sample survey is included at the end of the chapter.

A **Property Line** is the edge of the property as delineated on the survey. The property line is where one's property ends and the neighbor's property begins. Any part of one's property that extends into the property of another is considered an "encroachment" onto the other's property.

A **Building Line** is a specific line on the property which no part of the building may cross. Building lines are designed to provide a certain level of conformity to the neighborhood. In many parts of Illinois, building lines are used extensively and are often written into the recorded plat of the neighborhood that was drafted at the time of subdivision. They are often used to keep a neighborhood's appearance homogenous.

An **Easement** is a portion of the property that is owned by the owner of the property, but has been set aside for a specific purpose, such as for utility lines. Easements are determined by recording a document stating the purpose of the easement, what properties are covered, and what portion of the properties are to be set aside as easements. Generally speaking, no permanent structure may intrude into an easement.

Utility Easement. The purpose for utility easements is to allow a utility company or other agency to have access to and use of the property if required for a specific purpose, such as installing or maintaining utility lines. The idea is that utilities cross boundaries and that utility companies need to have access to multiple properties to conduct maintenance or for another purpose. By setting aside a section of each property, the utility companies do not need to receive the permission of each property owner prior to commencing any work in the easement. Utility easements will be disclosed on the survey.

Private Easements. There can also be private easements which allow a non-owner certain rights to use or possess the land of the owner. The person requesting the access is called the "dominant tenement" and the property upon which the easement is being requested is called the "servient tenement." For instance, A and B own adjacent pieces of property by a lake. A has access to the lake, but B does not have access to the lake. B can ask for access to the lake through an easement.

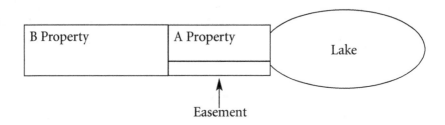

In the example above, B would have access to cross A's property to have access to the lake. An easement may be created by agreement between two parties (**express easement**), which is recorded and "runs with the land" (that is, subsequent buyers of the servient tenement would take "subject to" the easement as long as the agreement was in force).

In addition, an easement may be **implied**, when it is created without an express agreement, but by the conduct of the parties. In addition, an easement may be created by "**necessity**," when access may be required by the dominant tenement. Easements by necessity are generally implied easements and are limited to fairly extreme cases.

Express easements may have a specific **termination date** in the agreement. Easements may also terminate if the easement is *no longer necessary*, if the dominant tenement "abandons" the easement (that is, no longer uses the servient tenement) or if the interests of the two parties combine, thus making the easement no longer necessary (called the **doctrine of merger**).

In our hypothetical above, A and B could have an agreement that says that B can have access across A's land for 5 years. They record an agreement to that effect. At the end of the five years, the easement expires and they record a **release**.

Second, B simply stops using the easement for three years. **Abandonment** of an easement is when a party with a right to easements fails to use the easement. After a certain period of non-use, it is said that the dominant tenement has abandoned. B is said to have abandoned the easement. A can attempt to record a release, hopefully with B's agreement.

Third, B buys another parcel of land with lake access and no longer needs the easement over A's land. B and A can record a release.

Finally, B buys A's land and creates a single parcel of land. Since B now has access to the lake (by virtue of owning the whole area), the doctrine of merger applies and the easement is no longer necessary.

The other option for B to obtain access to the lake would be through a **license**. A license is a revocable permission to do something. With a license, B would simply ask A if he could traverse A's property to go fishing. If so, A would issue B a license to do so. The license could be oral (that is, A gives oral permission for B to go onto the land for the specific purpose), or A could (and should) draft and issue B a license to go onto A's land to go fishing. A license is a permission, not a right. A could always revoke B's permission if A no longer wanted to permit B to go onto A's land. The license could be for a specific period of time or at will (that is, for as long as A wanted to permit B enter the property).

Encroachments are improvements, buildings, or obstructions that intrude upon, or trespass upon, the property of another. The term is also used to describe improvements that "encroach" into easements or over building lines. Encroachments will be disclosed on the survey.

Encroachments pose particular problems when it comes to improvements on the property. An encroachment will be an encroachment when it is a "permanent" or immobile improvement to the property. A concrete patio or a garage that extends over into an easement or property line is an example of an encroachment. Due to the permanence of the material used to construct the improvement, the improvement "encroaches" into the easement or onto the neighbor's property. Should the utility company or neighbor ever demand that the encroachment be removed, the owner of the encroaching property must remove the encroachment at that person's expense. If the concrete patio extends onto the neighbor's property, the neighbor may demand that the owner remove that part of the patio that extends across the property line. The owner would then have to comply or risk being subject to a lawsuit.

If the encroachment is not too severe (especially for encroachments into easements), the title company may "insure over" the encroachment on the title insurance policy, usually for an extra fee. If the title company insures over the encroachment, the Seller would pay for the additional insurance. If the encroached party attempted to assert its rights regarding the encroachment (i.e., removes or demands the removal of the encroachment), the new owner of the property would file a claim with the title insurance company and the title insurance company would be pay the costs associated with the encroachment. Alternatively, the Buyer may elect to take the property "subject to" the encroachment. In this case, if the Seller refuses to pay for an endorsement, or if the title company refuses to provide an endorsement (more likely), the Buyer may elect to take the property anyway. If the Buyer takes subject to the encroachment, the Buyer would be responsible for any costs associated with curing or otherwise dealing with the encroachment.

A second way the encroachment may be handled is by agreement between the owner and the neighbor. The parties may enter into a written agreement stating that they agree to allow this invasion on the property. This agreement is then signed by all parties and recorded with the Recorder of Deeds. This agreement may be for a specific period of time or may "run with the land," that is, it will be enforceable against future owners of either property. If the agreement is recorded, the agreement will be reflected on the title commitment. If the parties agree to do this, they (or their devisees, heirs, or future owners) would have to all agree to rescind the agreement. If this happens another agreement is recorded rescinding the first agreement, which is a form of release.

If the encroaching item is not a permanent part of the property, it is not considered an encroachment. For example, if the patio in the example above was not concrete, but concrete pavers, which were set onto a sand base, that would not be an encroachment, as the pavers are considered movable. It may take some effort to move them, but they could be moved without damaging the surrounding property.

Another example is a shed which extends over a property line. If the shed is affixed to a concrete foundation, it is an encroachment. If it has a wood or metal floor, or set on bricks or pavers which are set in sand, it is considered movable and is not an encroachment.

In general, the Seller will pay for the survey. However, when buying property from an auction, foreclosure, or related "distressed" property, the Seller will not provide a survey. If the lender and the title company require a survey, the Buyer will have to pay the cost of the survey.

Surveys are not required for condominium transactions, but generally are required for townhouses, row houses, and other attached structures. When conducting a transaction for a property that is an attached property, make sure to check the legal form of ownership. Often, people will say they own a condominium when they in fact own a townhouse. Condominiums will be discussed in detail in Chapter 5.

Key Terms

Title
Title Insurance Policy
Marketable Title
Unmarketable Title
Owner's Policy
Lender's Policy
Title Examination
Title Commitment
Waiving
General Exceptions
Survey
Property Line
Building Line
Affidavit of No New Improvements
Easement
Express Easement
Implied Easement
Necessity
Termination Date
Encumbrance
Encroachment
Doctrine of Merger
Release
Abandonment
License
Legal Description
Chain of Title

Review Questions

1.   What does it mean to have title to something?
2.   What is a title insurance policy?
3.   What is a title examination?
4.   What is generally contained in a real estate survey?
5.   What is an easement?

Materials included in the following chapter appendix include:

- General Title Policy Order Form

- Sample Title Insurance Policy

- Affidavit of No New Improvements

- Sample Survey

- *Joel P. Perry and Laura A. Perry v. Fidelity National Title Insurance Company*, 2015 IL App (2d) 150168 (2015)

Chapter 4 Appendix

GENERAL TITLE POLICY ORDER INFORMATION

DATE:_____

Owner's Policy $_____

      Lender: _____

Loan Policy $_____ Lender Ph. _____
          With Exceptions or Without Exceptions

SELLER:_____

Seller(s) Current Address:_____

Seller(s) Phone Number:_____ Email Address_____

Seller(s) Address after Sale:_____

Marital Status of Seller:_____ Spouse's Name:_____

BUYER/BORROWER:_____

Buyer(s) Current Address:_____

Buyer(s) Phone Number:_____ Email Address_____

How are Buyer(s) taking Title?:_____

Will this property be the PRINCIPAL RESIDENCE of Buyer? _____

Legal
Description:_____

_____

Street Address of Property:_____

Parcel Identification Number:_____

Any Prior Title Insurance or Abstract:_____

Closing
Date:_____

Place:_____

Sales Price: $_____ Earnest Money: $_____

Additional Information:_____

DISCLOSURE STATEMENT CONTROLLED BUSINESS ARRANGEMENT
(By a Producer of Title Insurance Business or Associate thereof)

This Disclosure is made to: (Check one or both)   Seller/Owner_____   Buyer_____
      Seller(s)/Owner(s) _____
          [Print Name(s)] _____
      Buyer(s) _____
          [Print Name(s)] _____
Regarding the Property located at: _____
                             Street   City   State   Zip Code

For Title Insurance Company, Title Insurance Agent, and/or Escrow Agent:
(Print Company Name) _____

In connection with the property described above, the undersigned has recommended, or is about to recommend, the above named title insurance company, title agent, and/or escrow agent to the above named party(ies) to provide title insurance and/or escrow services.

The undersigned producer has a financial interest in the above named company/business, or is an associate of the party or entity which has said financial interest and therefore, makes, or has made, the following estimate of the fees and charges that are known and which will be made in connection with the recommended title and/or escrow services.

Only those charges which may be paid by the party(ies) to whom this disclosure is made, are (were) disclosed herein. If there are additional parties who choose to utilize services from the above named company/business, there may be additional charges for those services.
      * Owner's Title Policy: $_____
      * Mortgage Title Policy: _____
      Escrow or Closing Fee: _____
      Other Fees: _____
      Total Estimated Charges: $_____
*These estimated figures include all charges/ services such as title search, title examination, title insurance premiums, and final issuance of Policy(ies). These estimates may be revised if any unusual circumstances occur, unusual risks are "insured over", and/or lenders require special endorsements which extends their coverage.

You are not required to use _____(name of provider) as a condition for, settlement of your loan on, or purchase, sale, or refinance of, the subject property. There are frequently other settlement service providers available with similar services. You are free to shop around to determine that you are receiving the best services and the best rate for these services. The undersigned does hereby certify that the above disclosure was made to the above named party(ies) on
Signature of Producer: _____Date:_____

ACKNOWLEDGMENT
I/we have read this disclosure form and understand that _____ (referring party) is referring me/us to purchase the above described settlement services from
_____(provider receiving referral) and may receive a
financial or other benefit as a result of this referral.
Seller/Owner: _____   Date: _____
Buyer: _____   Date: _____
(NOTE: PURSUANT TO SECTION 18.(b) OF THE TITLE INSURANCE ACT, THE TITLE INSURANCE COMPANY, INDEPENDENT ESCROWEE, OR TITLE INSURANCE AGENT SHALL MAINTAIN THIS DISCLOSURE FORM FOR A PERIOD OF 3 YEARS.)

Sample Title Policy

CHICAGO INTERNATIONAL TITLE INSURANCE COMPANY
COMMITMENT FOR TITLE INSURANCE

ALTA COMMITMENT
SCHEDULE A

REFERENCE AND TITLE POLICY NUMBER: 15-65432

EFFECTIVE DATE: JULY 8, 2015

1. POLICY TO BE ISSUED:
   OWNER'S POLICY   ALTA OWNERS
   AMOUNT: $285,000.00
   PROPOSED INSURED   ROBERTA BUYER

   LOAN POLICY   ALTA LOAN
   AMOUNT: $240,000.00
   PROPOSED INSURED: ILLINOIS NINTH STATE BANK MORTGAGE

2. THE ESTATE OR INTEREST IN THE LAND DESCRIBED OR REFERRED TO IN THIS COMMITMENT AND COVERED HEREIN IS A FEE SIMPLE UNLESS OTHERWISE NOTED.

3. TITLE TO SAID ESTATE OR INTEREST IN SAID LAND IS AT THE EFFECTIVE DATE VESTED IN:
   JONATHAN SELLER

4. MORTGAGE OR TRUST DEED TO BE INSURED:
   ILLINOIS NINTH STATE BANK MORTGAGE

5. THE LAND REFERRED TO IN THIS COMMITMENT IS DESCRIBED AS FOLLOWS:

   LOT 2 IN ONOFRIO'S RESUBDIVISION OF LOT 11 IN FALCONERS SUBDIVISION OF BLOCK 4 OF FALCONERS ADDITION TO CHICAGO, IN THE NORTH ½ OF THE NORTHEAST ¼ OF SECTION 28, TOWNSHIP 40 NORTH, RANGE 13 EAST OF THE THIRD PRINCIPAL MERIDIAN, IN COOK COUNTY, ILLINOIS

6. THE LAND REFERRED TO IN THIS COMMITMENT IS:
   4802 W. WELLINGTON
   CHICAGO, IL 60641

THIS COMMITMENT IS VALID ONLY IF SCHEDULE B IS ATTACHED

ALTA COMMITMENT

SCHEDULE B

TITLE POLICY NUMBER: 15-65432

Schedule B of the policy or policies to be issued will contain the exceptions shown on inside front cover of this Commitment and the following exceptions, unless same are disposed of to the satisfaction of the Company:

If any document herein contains a covenant, condition or restriction of 42 UCS 3604(c), such covenant, condition or restriction to the extent of such violation is hereby deleted.

1. General taxes for the year 2015 and subsequent years which are not yet due and payable.

2. 2014 taxes:

    1st Installment in the amount of $1,380.17 has been PAID
    2nd Installment in the amount of $2,151.22 is due on September 10, 2015
    Property Tax Identification No.: 13-28-212-229-0000

3. Mortgage recorded January 24, 2004, as document 0434938490 made by Jonathan Seller (Grantor) to State Bank of Nowhere (Grantee), to secure a note in the originally stated principal amount of $205,000.00, and the terms and conditions thereof.

4. Note, if Closing takes place at a CHICAGO INTERNATIONAL TITLE INSURANCE COMPANY Office and if the above mortgage(s) are equity lines of credit loans, the payoff letter(s) presented at Closing must state that the account is now closed and the amount stated is sufficient to secure a release.

5. The spouse of the party in title should join in any conveyance for the purpose of releasing their homestead interest, if any.

6. It appears that the land described herein lies within the municipal boundaries of Chicago. Please contact the municipality for any requirements which must be complied with prior to Closing. The property may be subject to a Real Estate Transfer Tax in the amount of $3.75 per $500.00 and a Real Estate Transfer Tax in the amount of $1.50 per $500.00. The tax stamps must be affixed prior to Closing.

7. The Standard Exceptions 1 through 5 will be deleted from our policy upon review and acceptance of a properly executed ALTA Extended Coverage Statement.

END OF SCHEDULE B

The terms, conditions, requirements and standard exceptions contained in the CHICAGO INTERNATIONAL TITLE INSURANCE COMPANY jacket are incorporated herein by reference and together with the foregoing ALTA Commitment Schedules A and B for the entire Commitment.

ENDORSEMENT

ISSUED BY

CHICAGO INTERNATIONAL TITLE INSURANCE COMPANY

ATTACHED TO COMMITMENT ORDER NUMBER: 15-65432

CHAIN OF TITLE

The Company insures the proposed insured under this commitment against loss or damage arising from any inaccuracy in the following assurances:

A search of the public record reflects the following deeds conveying the land as described in Schedule A in the 24 months prior to July 8, 2015:

> Deed recorded January 24, 1998, as document number 983498761 from Richard Butler (Grantor) to Jonathan Seller (Grantee).
>
> Mortgage recorded January 25, 1998, as document number 983498764 from Jonathan Seller (Grantor) to Last Chance Lending and Loan (Grantee).
>
> Assignment of Mortgage recorded March 4, 2002, as document 028642157 from Last Chance Lending and Loan (Grantor) to Bank of Illinois (Grantee).
>
> Mortgage recorded January 24, 2004, as document 0434938490 made by Jonathan Seller (Grantor) to State Bank of Nowhere (Grantee).
>
> Release of Mortgage recorded February 7, 2004, as document 0450158743 from Bank of Illinois (Grantor) to Jonathan Seller (Grantee).

No other deeds of conveyance appear in public record other than those stated herein for the 24-month period ending July 8, 2015.

This endorsement is made a part of the commitment and is subject to all of the terms and provisions thereof and of any prior endorsements thereto. Except to the extent expressly stated, it neither modifies any of the terms and provisions of the commitment and any prior endorsements, nor does it extend the effective date of the commitment and any other prior endorsements, nor does it increase the face amount thereof.

CHICAGO INTERNATIONAL TITLE INSURANCE COMPANY

DATED: 12 July, 2015

CONDITIONS AND STIPULATIONS

1. **The term mortgage, when used herein, shall include deed of trust, trust deed, or other security instrument.**

2. **If the proposed Insured has or acquired actual knowledge of any defect, lien, encumbrance, adverse claim or other matter affecting the estate or interest or mortgage thereon covered by this Commitment other than those shown in Schedule B hereof, and shall fail to disclose such knowledge to the Company in writing, the Company shall be relieved from liability for any loss or damage resulting from any act of reliance hereon to the extent the Company is prejudiced by failure to so disclose such knowledge. If the proposed Insured shall disclose such knowledge to the Company, or if the Company otherwise acquires actual knowledge of any such defect, lien, encumbrance, adverse claim or other matter, the Company at its option may amend Schedule B of this Commitment accordingly, but such amendment shall not relieve the Company from liability previously incurred pursuant to paragraph 3 of these Conditions and Stipulations.**

3. Liability of the Company under this Commitment shall be only to the named proposed Insured and such parties included under the definition of Insured in the form of policy or policies committed for and only for actual loss incurred in reliance hereon in undertaking in good faith (a) to comply with the requirements hereof, or (b) to eliminate exceptions shown in Schedule B, or (c) to acquire or create the estate or interest or mortgage thereon covered by this Commitment. In no event shall such liability exceed the amount stated in Schedule A for the policy or policies committed for and such liability is subject to the insuring provisions and Conditions and Stipulations and the Exclusions from Coverage of the form of policy or policies committed for in favor of the proposed Insured which are hereby incorporated by reference and are made a part of this Commitment except as expressly modified herein.

4. Any action or actions or rights of action that the proposed Insured may have or may bring against the Company arising out of the status of the title to the estate or interest or the status of the mortgage thereon covered by this Commitment must be based on and are subject to the provisions of this Commitment.

CHICAGO INTERNATIONAL TITLE INSURANCE COMPANY
INVOICE FOR TITLE SERVICES

Owner's Policy	$1,250.00 (Paid by Seller)
Lender's Coverage	$750.00 (Paid by Buyer)
Settlement Closing Fee	$550.00 (Paid by Buyer)
Recording Service Fee	$80.00 (Paid by Buyer)
Mortgage Release Fee	$60.00 (paid by Seller)
Later Date Fee:	$65.00 (Paid by Buyer)
Package Fee:	$20.00 (Paid by Buyer)
State of Illinois Fee:	$3.00 (each to Buyer and Seller)

AFFIDAVIT OF NO NEW IMPROVEMENTS

Dated: _____, 20_____

Title Order No. _____

The undersigned, being first duly sworn, depose[s] and say[s]: That [I] [we], being the owner[s] of record and Seller[s] described in the above-numbered commitment for title insurance, have not made or caused to be made any structural improvements or structural additions to existing improvements on the premises described in the above-referenced title insurance commitment except for:

[Describe]

Affiant[s] further state[s] that the plat of survey made by _____, dated _____, 20_____, number _____, is a correct and complete representation of all improvements now located on the premises described in the above-referenced title insurance commitment except for:

[Describe]

This affidavit is given to _____ Title Insurance Company as an inducement to issue extended coverage over matters of survey and unrecorded easements to its owner's title insurance policy.

_____

_____

Subscribed and sworn to before me this

_____ day of _____, 20_____.

_____

Notary Public

PLAT of SURVEY

By

JOHN M. HENRIKSEN

OF

LOT 4 IN ONOFRIO'S RESUBDIVISION OF LOT II IN FALCONERS SUBDIVISION OF BLOCK 4 OF FALCONERS ADDITION TO CHICAGO, IN THE NORTH 1/2 OF THE NORTHEAST 1/4 OF SECTION 28, TOWNSHIP 40 NORTH, RANGE 13 EAST OF THE THIRD PRINCIPAL MERIDIAN, IN COOK COUNTY, ILLINOIS.

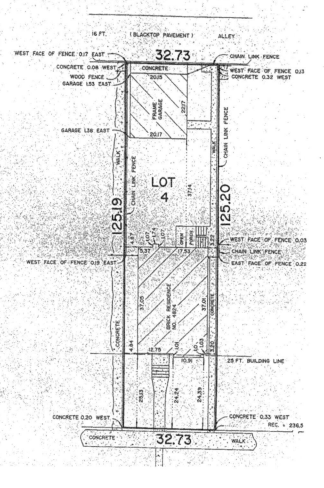

Map of the Principal Meridian and Base Lines

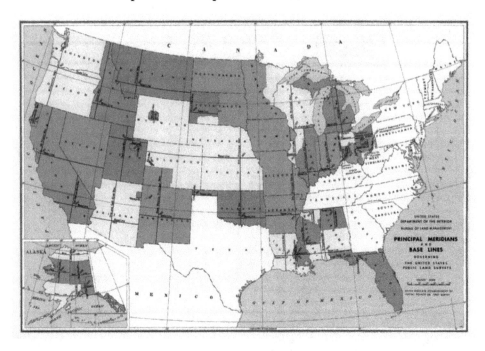

Sections of a Township   Divisions of a Section

6	5	4	3	2	1
7	8	9	10	11	12
18	17	16	15	14	13
19	20	21	22	23	24
30	29	28	27	26	25
31	32	33	34	35	36

NW ¼ of NW ¼	NE ¼ of NW ¼	NE ¼	
SW ¼ of NW ¼	SE ¼ of NW ¼		
N ½ of SW ¼		NW ¼ of SE ¼	NE ¼ of SE ¼
S ½ of SW ¼		SW ¼ of SE ¼	SE ¼ of SE ¼

A **Township** is a square of land 6 miles by 6 miles and is divided into 36 sections of 1 square mile (640 acres). A section may then be divided into smaller and smaller sections. Legal descriptions in areas of the state that utilize the township method will generally be read from the smallest unit into ever increasing units. Often it will be lot, then division, then section, then township location, then range (in relation to the third principal meridian) and then county and state.

The legal description for the hypothetical would is:

LOT 2 IN ONOFRIO'S RESUBDIVISION OF LOT 11 IN FALCONERS SUBDIVISION OF BLOCK 4 OF FALCONERS ADDITION TO CHICAGO, IN THE NORTH ½ OF THE NORTHEAST ¼ OF SECTION 28, TOWNSHIP 40 NORTH, RANGE 13 EAST OF THE THIRD PRINCIPAL MERIDIAN, IN COOK COUNTY, ILLINOIS

To break that down a little:

LOT 2 IN ONOFRIO'S RESUBDIVISION OF LOT 11 IN FALCONERS SUBDIVISION OF BLOCK 4 OF FALCONERS ADDITION TO CHICAGO

This means that there was an addition to Chicago at some point in the past. That addition, called "Falconers" was then subdivided in at least 4 blocks. Those blocks were then subdivided into at least 11 Lots. Those lots were then divided at least in half.

IN THE NORTH ½ OF THE NORTHEAST ¼ OF SECTION 28

This "block" is located in Section 28 (second to last row, third from left) of the township. That Section is divided into 4 and it is the North ½ of the Northeast ¼ of that section.

TOWNSHIP 40 NORTH, RANGE 13 EAST OF THE THIRD PRINCIPAL MERIDIAN, IN COOK COUNTY, ILLINOIS

This means that property is the 40th township north (240 miles) of the baseline. It is the 13th Range east (96 miles) of the third Principal Meridian (which runs through Western Illinois). It is in Cook County, Illinois.

Basically, if you ever want to tell someone your address and never have that person find you ... give them the legal description.

Ethics Alert:

When drafting a legal description for a deed (Chapter 6), TODI, or other document, the legal description **MUST** be *exactly* correct. Spelling counts, punctuation counts. If Section 27 is typed instead of Section 28, a property one mile away is being conveyed. This can have serious legal and economic ramifications. These errors are very common and must be avoided.

It is best to have someone else check the legal description against a previous deed or title commitment.

MEMORANDUM

Course title: REAL ESTATE for PARALEGALS
Instructor:
Instructor's Email:
RE: Writing Assignment III

This extra credit assignment is worth a maximum of 25 points. You are to pick an address in Chicago (it can be any real address). You are to conduct a preliminary title search by searching the public records. Please note: This can be accomplished for any property in Cook County (except for the Building Code section).

For other counties, you would need to start with the county property look up.
For instance: DuPage County, start with DuPage County Property Search (https://www.dupageco.org/PropertyInfo/PropertyLookup.aspx).
Sangamon County, start with Sangamon County Property Tax, Search for Properties (http://tax.co.sangamon.il.us/SangamonCountyWeb/app/searchByParcelNumber.action).
Will County, start with Will Count Property Search (http://www.willcountysoa.com/search_address.aspx).

For Chicago:

First: Go to the Cook County Assessor's Office (http://www.cookcountyassessor.com) and do a search by address. You should then be able to recover the PIN for the property. Print that page out (and the picture of the property if you wish).

Second: Go to the Cook County Treasurer's Office http://www.cookcountytreasurer.com/default.aspx) and do a payment search to discover the status of the taxes. You should print that page.
Or, for steps 1 & 2, go to Cook County Property Tax Portal (www.cookcountypropertyinfo.com).

Third: Go to the Cook County Recorder of Deed Office (http://www.ccrd.info/CCRD/controller) and do a search of the documents recorded against the property. You should do this through a PIN search. You should print that page.

Fourth: Go to the Cook County Clerk of Court Office (http://www.cookcountyclerkofcourt.org). Click "Online Case Info" to see if any litigation is pending against the homeowner. You should search (Plaintiff and Defendant ... Defendant is more important) for Civil, Law and Chancery divisions. Print out the relevant pages (even if no records are found).

Fifth: Do a Delinquent Tax Search (http://www.cookcountyclerk.com/tsd/delinquenttaxsearch/Pages/DelinquentTaxSearch.aspx)

Sixth: Go to the City of Chicago and look up the building code violations. You should click on "I Want to Check the Status of" and look for Building Code Violations.
You should print the relevant page (even if no violations are found).

You can also find the tax information by going to the Cook County Property Tax Portal: http://www.cookcountypropertyinfo.com/Pages/pin-search.aspx, although you cannot find the Building Code Information outside of the City of Chicago.

2015 IL App (2d) 150168

JOEL P. PERRY and LAURA A. PERRY, Plaintiffs-Appellants,

v.

FIDELITY NATIONAL TITLE INSURANCE COMPANY, Defendant-Appellee.

No. 2-15-0168.

Appellate Court of Illinois, Second District.

Opinion filed November 6, 2015.

PRESIDING JUSTICE SCHOSTOK delivered the judgment of the court, with opinion.

Justices Burke and Spence concurred in the judgment and opinion.

OPINION

Plaintiffs, Joel P. and Laura A. Perry, sued defendant, Fidelity National Title Insurance Company, seeking a declaration that it was obligated to defend them in an underlying action brought by plaintiffs' neighbors. That suit sought to prevent plaintiffs from placing improvements on an easement for access to their property. The trial court granted defendant judgment on the pleadings. Plaintiffs appeal, contending that the trial court erred in holding that the neighbors' suit did not trigger defendant's duty to defend. We reverse and remand.

On March 1, 2010, defendant issued plaintiffs a title insurance policy. The policy covered property that plaintiffs owned at 1450 S. Snipe Hollow Road in Elizabeth (designated Parcel 1), as well as a 30-foot easement (designated Parcel 2) for ingress and egress across an adjacent parcel. The policy covered, among other risks, loss or damage caused by "Unmarketable Title," defined as "Title affected by an alleged or apparent matter that would permit a prospective purchaser or lessee of the Title or lender on the Title to be released from the obligation to purchase, lease, or lend if there is a contractual condition requiring the delivery of marketable title." However, the policy specifically excluded coverage for "[t]erms and provisions of the easement described as Parcel 2 herein, as contained in the document creating said basement."

On July 2, 2010, the owners of the servient parcel, David and Dana Hundrieser, sued plaintiffs to enjoin them from paving and otherwise improving the access strip. The Hundriesers' complaint alleged as follows. The Hundriesers used the area burdened with the easement as pasture for their cattle, and paving the easement would interfere with this use. Moreover, the area was part of a conservation zone and, when the easement was created, the parties had an unwritten understanding that the area would not be improved. The complaint further alleged that plaintiffs would continue to have access to their property without the improvements.

Plaintiffs filed a counterclaim, in which they alleged that the subdivision of the property left their parcel landlocked and that, accordingly, their deed included an easement for ingress and egress and defined a specific path across the Hundriesers' parcel. Without a driveway between their parcel and Snipe Hollow Road, they were effectively denied the easement granted in the deed, and their parcel's value was markedly diminished.

Plaintiffs tendered defense of the action to defendant. Defendant refused, stating that the Hundriesers' lawsuit did not implicate any covered risks under the policy. Defendant argued that the Hundriesers' suit did not dispute plaintiffs' title to the easement, but merely disputed how they could use it.

In the meantime, the trial court ruled for plaintiffs in the underlying action. This court affirmed in part, reversed in part, and remanded. *Hundrieser v. Perry*, 2013 IL App (2d) 121321-U. While the appeal was pending, plaintiffs moved for summary judgment in this case. Plaintiffs asserted that the underlying action raised at least the possibility of coverage under the policy in that the inability to improve the easement would render title to the main property unmarketable. They claimed that the dirt trail across the easement became muddy and often impassible during wet weather, leaving the main parcel essentially landlocked. In response, defendant continued to maintain that the Hundrieser suit did not dispute plaintiffs' title to the easement and that, because coverage under the policy was not implicated, defendant had no duty to defend plaintiffs in that case. At the hearing on the motion, defendant argued that coverage under the policy "just isn't" broad enough to encompass the allegations of the underlying complaint.

Following a hearing, the trial court denied plaintiffs' summary-judgment motion. The court essentially agreed with defendant that there was no duty to defend under the policy because the underlying action did not dispute plaintiffs' title to the easement. Defendant then orally moved for judgment on the pleadings. The trial court granted the motion and plaintiffs appeal.

Plaintiffs contend that the trial court erroneously held that defendant had no duty to defend. They argue that the underlying suit at least potentially implicated coverage under the policy because the policy protects against loss caused by unmarketable title and the underlying suit had the potential to make plaintiffs' title unmarketable by eliminating access to their property as granted in the deed. In response, defendant renews its contention that the policy simply does not cover allegations that do not directly contest plaintiffs' title to the easement.

A motion for judgment on the pleadings is like a motion for summary judgment that is limited to the pleadings. *Employers Insurance of Wausau v. Ehlco Liquidating Trust*, 186 Ill. 2d 127, 138 (1999). Judgment on the pleadings is proper if the pleadings disclose no genuine issue of material fact and that the movant is entitled to judgment as a matter of law. *M.A.K. v. Rush-Presbyterian-St. Luke's Medical Center*, 198 Ill. 2d 249, 255 (2001). "For purposes of resolving the motion, the court must consider as admitted all well-pleaded facts set forth in the pleadings of the nonmoving party, and the fair inferences drawn therefrom." *Employers Insurance of Wausau*, 186 Ill. 2d at 138. We review the grant of judgment on the pleadings de novo. *Gillen v. State Farm Mutual Automobile Insurance Co.*, 215 Ill. 2d 381, 385 (2005). Additionally, the construction of an insurance policy is a question of law, which we review de novo. *Pekin Insurance Co. v. Wilson*, 237 Ill. 2d 446, 455 (2010).

An insurance policy is a contract, and the primary object of contract construction is to ascertain and give effect to the parties' intentions as expressed in their agreement. *American States Insurance Co. v. Koloms*, 177 Ill. 2d 473, 479 (1997). If an insurance policy is clear and unambiguous, we must give the language its plain meaning. Id.; *American Family Mutual Insurance Co. v. Jeris*, 376 Ill. App. 3d 1070, 1073 (2007).

The purpose of title insurance is to protect a transferee of real estate from the possibilities of loss through defects that cloud title. *First National Bank of Northbrook, N.A. v. Stewart Title Guaranty Co.*, 279 Ill. App. 3d 188, 192 (1996). The policy insures against defects in the title to the land, not the land itself. Id. Title insurance policies, like other insurance policies, should receive a practical, reasonable, and fair construction consistent with the apparent object and intent of the parties, viewed in light of their purpose. Id. at 193. Where doubts or ambiguities in a policy do exist, they should be liberally construed in favor of the insured. *Rackouski v. Dobson*, 261 Ill. App. 3d 315, 317 (1994).

The trial court held that defendant had no duty to defend plaintiffs in the underlying action. In deciding whether an insurer has a duty to defend its insured, the court must look to the allegations in the underlying complaint and compare these allegations to the policy's relevant coverage provisions. *Crum & Forster Managers Corp. v. Resolution Trust Corp.*, 156 Ill. 2d 384, 393 (1993); *Sabatino v. First American Title Insurance Co.*, 308 Ill. App. 3d 819, 822 (1999). If the facts alleged in the underlying complaint fall within, or potentially within, the policy's coverage, then the insurer has a duty to defend its insured in the underlying action. *Crum & Forster*, 156 Ill. 2d at 393. We read the underlying complaint liberally in deciding an insurer's duty to defend. *State Farm Mutual Automobile Insurance Co. v. Pfiel*, 304 Ill. App. 3d 831, 834 (1999). Thus, an insurer is required to defend its insured whenever the alleged conduct is potentially within the policy's coverage, even if the insurer discovers that the allegations are groundless, false, or fraudulent. Id. Moreover, a court may look beyond the allegations of the underlying complaint in determining the existence of a duty to defend. *Metzger v. Country Mutual Insurance Co.*, 2013 IL App (2d) 120133, ¶ 26. "The insurer's duty to defend is much broader than its duty to indemnify its insured." *Crum & Forster*, 156 Ill. 2d at 393–94.

We agree that plaintiffs raised at least the possibility of coverage under the policy, thus triggering defendant's duty to defend. The failure to provide ingress and egress to a property can render title unmarketable. *Melcer v. Zuck*, 245 A.2d 61, 64 (N.J. Super. Ct. App. Div. 1968). In *Melcer*, for example, the sellers of a parcel guaranteed ingress and egress to it but failed to take any steps to create an easement for that purpose, thus allowing the purchasers to terminate the contract. Id.

Here, likewise, the Hundrieser complaint raised the possibility that plaintiffs would be effectively denied the easement granted in the deed. Plaintiffs' deed included a specifically defined easement for ingress and egress. Plaintiffs asserted, however, that without improvements the easement could not consistently allow ingress and egress. Thus, while defendant is correct that the underlying suit did not dispute the validity of plaintiffs' title to the easement, the suit did place at issue whether the easement could actually be conveyed. That is, it placed at issue the marketability of plaintiffs' title. See id.

Plaintiffs here seek only reimbursement for defense costs (having at least partially prevailed in the underlying suit), and the duty to defend is broader than the duty to indemnify. *Crum & Forster*, 156 Ill. 2d at 393–94. Because the underlying suit was at least potentially within the policy's coverage, defendant had a duty to defend plaintiffs in that litigation.

In response, defendant essentially renews its argument that the policy's coverage "just isn't" broad enough to cover this situation. However, defendant cites no case suggesting that the "Unmarketable Title" provision is not broad enough to encompass this situation. *First National Bank of Northbrook*, on which defendant principally relies, is clearly distinguishable. There, the title company issued to a bank a location note endorsement containing a mistaken description of the land. However, it was undisputed that the bank did not see the mistaken document until after its borrower had defaulted on a note. Thus, the bank did not rely on the endorsement in making the loan, so its loss did not result from the mistaken endorsement. *First National Bank of Northbrook*, 279 Ill. App. 3d at 194–95.

Defendant observes that plaintiffs' "claim could have also been denied by [defendant] under Schedule B, Special Exception Number 2" of the policy.

However, defendant does not even quote that provision, much less develop an argument that it excludes coverage here, thus forfeiting such an argument. See Ill. S. Ct. R. 341(h)(7) (eff. Feb. 6, 2013). In any event, the special exception mentioned excludes coverage for loss by virtue of the "[t]erms and provisions of the easement described as Parcel 2 herein, as contained in the document creating said easement." At most, this provision, purporting to exclude coverage for anything related to the terms and provisions of the easement, conflicts with the portion of the policy covering losses caused by unmarketable title. This creates an ambiguity, which we must resolve in favor of the insured. See *Rackouski*, 261 Ill. App. 3d at 317.

The judgment of the circuit court of Jo Daviess County is reversed, and the cause is remanded.

Reversed and remanded.

Chapter 5

Condominiums and Cooperatives

Learning Objectives

After studying Chapter 5, you will be able to:

- Define condominium
- Summarize the requirements of in a condominium real estate transaction
- Differentiate between a condominium and a cooperative

Chapter Summary

Topics covered:

- Condominiums
- Cooperatives

This chapter provides an introduction to the concept of condominiums and co-operatives. Condominiums are defined and the differences between condominium ownership and owning a single-family house are addressed. The chapter looks at condominium associations and the statutory power provided to condominium associations`. The chapter describes the condominium board and the powers of the board. Condominium assessments (and special assessments) are discussed. The condominium section of the chapter concludes with a look at the contract provisions and the special requirements that are needed in a real estate transaction concerning a condominium. The chapter concludes with a brief introduction to cooperatives and how cooperatives differ from condominiums.

1. Condominium Overview

A **condominium**, or **condo**, is a form of property ownership where a specified unit of a parcel of real estate is owned individually by the unit owner in Fee Simple, while ownership, access, and use of common facilities in the property (including the exterior structure, common spaces, hallways, HVAC, parking, elevators, etc.) is controlled by the **Condominium Association** (the "Condo Association" or "Association") that represents ownership of the whole property. Each unit is owned in Fee Simple by the individual unit owners. In addition, each **unit owner** is a tenant in common

177

owner of a small piece of the entire complex and a member of the Association. The Association is responsible for maintaining the common areas and administering management and controlling matters under the purview of the Association. Typically, such properties are either purposely constructed properties or converted apartment buildings or other structures (so-called "**condo conversions**").

The condominium building (or condominium project) is the collection of individual home units, along with the physical structure and parcel of land. Individual home ownership within a condominium is construed as ownership of only the unit itself and the contents contained within the unit. The entire parcel and the units are determined by a legal document known as a Declaration of Condominium, filed with the local governing authority (in Cook County, Illinois, it is filed with the Cook County Recorder of Deeds Office). Typically, the outer structure of the building (including exterior walls, windows, and balconies of each unit) is owned collectively by the unit owners through the Association. These boundaries generally include the interior spaces and interior walls within a unit. This allows a homeowner to make certain modifications to the unit, but not to the physical structure of the unit. Associations have strict rules about what modifications may be made to the unit.

Anything outside of the individual units is held in an undivided ownership interest as tenants in common by the unit owners, and is represented by a corporation established at the time of the condominium's creation. The corporation does not have ownership itself, but generally holds the property in trust on behalf of the unitowners as a group. Each unit owner owns a percentage of the whole, generally based upon the unit owner's percentage of the entire building or development.

One of the reasons that people purchase condominiums is that people think that they are more affordable than single-family housing, at least in upfront acquisition costs. This may be the case, and in some urban areas, condominium ownership may be the only viable alternative for people who wish to own property. In some parts of Chicago, particularly along the lakefront of Lake Michigan, condominiums are the only option for most people who wish to own property. There are simply no single-family houses, or if they do exist, they are prohibitively expensive. However, as will be discussed, it is important to understand the total cost of ownership when considering a condominium. It is more than purchasing the unit; the Buyer must take into account the assessments, special assessments, taxes, etc. when deciding whether to purchase the condominium.

Condominiums also allow for more housing units in the same physical area. By building multi-unit, and, generally, multi-story structures, many housing units can be located on one parcel of land. In addition, the maintenance of the property is controlled by the Association, relieving individual unit owners of maintenance of common areas. The Association maintains control over the property and attempts to maintain the value of the units. Often, real estate taxes and insurance rates on condominiums are less than on a single-family house, since the Association pays the real estate taxes on the land and the physical structures.

Condominium Association

A condominium association, consisting of all the members, manages the condominium through a Board of Directors elected by the membership. The restrictions for condominium usage are established in a document commonly called a **Declaration of Condominium**. The Declaration is recorded with the Recorder of Deeds Office in the county where the property is located. There is a set of **Bylaws** that govern the actions of the Association and also the unit owners. Finally, the Association (or, in some cases, the developer) develops a set of **Rules and Regulations** providing specific details of restrictions and conduct are established by the board.

Typical rules include:

- Association fees,
- Mandatory maintenance fees,
- Restrictions on use of the units,
- Pet restrictions,
- Restrictions on use of common areas, and
- Restrictions on conveyances of individual units.

In Illinois, condominiums are governed under the Illinois Condominium Property Act (765 ILCS 605) (the "Condominium Act"), as well as local ordinances. The Condominium Act provides condo associations broad powers to self-govern the association.

(765 ILCS 605/2) (from Ch. 30, par. 302)

Sec. 2. Definitions. As used in this Act, unless the context otherwise requires:

(a) "Declaration" means the instrument by which the property is submitted to the provisions of this Act, as hereinafter provided, and such declaration as from time to time amended.

(b) "Parcel" means the lot or lots, tract or tracts of land, described in the declaration, submitted to the provisions of this Act.

(c) "Property" means all the land, property and space comprising the parcel, all improvements and structures erected, constructed or contained therein or thereon, including the building and all easements, rights and appurtenances belonging thereto, and all fixtures and equipment intended for the mutual use, benefit or enjoyment of the unit owners, submitted to the provisions of this Act.

(d) "Unit" means a part of the property designed and intended for any type of independent use.

(e) "Common Elements" means all portions of the property except the units, including limited common elements unless otherwise specified.

(f) "Person" means a natural individual, corporation, partnership, trustee or other legal entity capable of holding title to real property.

(g) "Unit Owner" means the person or persons whose estates or interests, individually or collectively, aggregate fee simple absolute ownership of a unit, or, in the case of a leasehold condominium, the lessee or lessees of a unit whose leasehold ownership of the unit expires simultaneously with the lease described in item (x) of this Section.

(h) "Majority" or "majority of the unit owners" means the owners of more than 50% in the aggregate in interest of the undivided ownership of the common elements. Any specified percentage of the unit owners means such percentage in the aggregate in interest of such undivided ownership. "Majority" or "majority of the members of the board of managers" means more than 50% of the total number of persons constituting such board pursuant to the bylaws. Any specified percentage of the members of the board of managers means that percentage of the total number of persons constituting such board pursuant to the bylaws.

(i) "Plat" means a plat or plats of survey of the parcel and of all units in the property submitted to the provisions of this Act, which may consist of a three-dimensional horizontal and vertical delineation of all such units.

(j) "Record" means to record in the office of the recorder or, whenever required, to file in the office of the Registrar of Titles of the county wherein the property is located.

(k) "Conversion Condominium" means a property which contains structures, excepting those newly constructed and intended for condominium ownership, which are, or have previously been, wholly or partially occupied before recording of condominium instruments by persons other than those who have contracted for the purchase of condominiums.

(l) "Condominium Instruments" means all documents and authorized amendments thereto recorded pursuant to the provisions of the Act, including the declaration, bylaws and plat.

(m) "Common Expenses" means the proposed or actual expenses affecting the property, including reserves, if any, lawfully assessed by the Board of Managers of the Unit Owner's Association.

(n) "Reserves" means those sums paid by unit owners which are separately maintained by the board of managers for purposes specified by the board of managers or the condominium instruments.

(o) "Unit Owners' Association" or "Association" means the Association of all the unit owners, acting pursuant to bylaws through its duly elected board of managers.

(p) "Purchaser" means any person or persons other than the Developer who purchase a unit in a bona fide transaction for value.

(q) "Developer" means any person who submits property legally or equitably owned in fee simple by the developer, or leased to the developer under a lease described in item (x) of this Section, to the provisions of this Act, or any person who offers units legally or equitably owned in fee simple by the developer, or leased to the developer under a lease described in item (x) of this Section, for sale in the ordinary course of such person's business, including any successor or successors to such developers' entire interest in the property other than the purchaser of an individual unit.

(r) "Add-on Condominium" means a property to which additional property may be added in accordance with condominium instruments and this Act.

(s) "Limited Common Elements" means a portion of the common elements so designated in the declaration as being reserved for the use of a certain unit or units to the exclusion of other units, including but not limited to balconies, terraces, patios and parking spaces or facilities.

(t) "Building" means all structures, attached or unattached, containing one or more units.

(u) "Master Association" means an organization described in Section 18.5 whether or not it is also an Association described in Section 18.3.

(v) "Developer Control" means such control at a time prior to the election of the Board of Managers provided for in Section 18.2(b) of this Act.

(w) "Meeting of Board of Managers or Board of Master Association" means any gathering of a quorum of the members of the Board of Managers or Board of the Master Association held for the purpose of conducting board business.

(x) "Leasehold Condominium" means a property submitted to the provisions of this Act which is subject to a lease, the expiration or termination of which would terminate the condominium and the lessor of which is (i) exempt from taxation under Section 501(c)(3) of the Internal Revenue Code of 1986, as amended, (ii) a limited liability company whose sole member is exempt from taxation under Section 501 (c)(3) of the Internal Revenue Code of 1986, as amended, or (iii) a Public Housing Authority created pursuant to the Housing Authorities Act that is located in a municipality having a population in excess of 1,000,000 inhabitants.

2. Administration of the Condominium Property

As stated above, the unit owner owns the individual unit and a collective percentage of the whole property. The property is controlled by an Association, made up of unit owners and/or their delegates. Section 18.3 of the Condominium Act specifies how the Association is governed.

(765 ILCS 605/18.3)

> Sec. 18.3. Unit Owners' Association. The unit owners' Association is responsible for the overall administration of the property through its duly elected board of managers. Each unit owner shall be a member of the Association. The Association, whether or not it is incorporated, shall have those powers and responsibilities specified in the General Not For Profit Corporation Act of 1986 that are not inconsistent with this Act or the condominium instruments, including but not limited to the power to acquire and hold title to land. Such land is not part of the common elements unless and until it has been added by an amendment of the condominium instruments, properly executed and placed of record as required by this Act. The Association shall have and exercise all powers necessary or convenient to effect any or all of the purposes for which the Association is organized, and to do every other act not inconsistent with law which may be appropriate to promote and attain the purposes set forth in this Act or in the condominium instruments.

The Association is responsible for the governance of the property. In general, the Association will be a non-profit corporation and will be treated as such. The Association has broad powers to govern the property, and those powers are defined by the Bylaws and Rules and Regulations. These powers are generally enforced by the

Board of Managers, also called the "Condo Board," who are generally elected by all of the Association members.

(765 ILCS 605/18.4) (from Ch. 30, par. 318.4)

Sec. 18.4. Powers and Duties of Board of Managers. The board of managers shall exercise for the Association all powers, duties and authority vested in the Association by law or the condominium instruments except for such powers, duties and authority reserved by law to the members of the Association. The powers and duties of the board of managers shall include, but shall not be limited to, the following:

(a) To provide for the operation, care, upkeep, maintenance, replacement and improvement of the common elements. Nothing in this subsection (a) shall be deemed to invalidate any provision in a condominium instrument placing limits on expenditures for the common elements, provided, that such limits shall not be applicable to expenditures for repair, replacement, or restoration of existing portions of the common elements. The term "repair, replacement or restoration" means expenditures to deteriorated or damaged portions of the property related to the existing decorating, facilities, or structural or mechanical components, interior or exterior surfaces, or energy systems and equipment with the functional equivalent of the original portions of such areas. Replacement of the common elements may result in an improvement over the original quality of such elements or facilities; provided that, unless the improvement is mandated by law or is an emergency as defined in item (iv) of subparagraph (8) of paragraph (a) of Section 18, if the improvement results in a proposed expenditure exceeding 5% of the annual budget, the board of managers, upon written petition by unit owners with 20% of the votes of the Association delivered to the board within 14 days of the board action to approve the expenditure, shall call a meeting of the unit owners within 30 days of the date of delivery of the petition to consider the expenditure. Unless a majority of the total votes of the unit owners are cast at the meeting to reject the expenditure, it is ratified.

(b) To prepare, adopt and distribute the annual budget for the property.

(c) To levy and expend assessments.

(d) To collect assessments from unit owners.

(e) To provide for the employment and dismissal of the personnel necessary or advisable for the maintenance and operation of the common elements.

(f) To obtain adequate and appropriate kinds of insurance.

(g) To own, convey, encumber, lease, & otherwise deal with units conveyed to or purchased by it.

(h) To adopt and amend rules and regulations covering the details of the operation and use of the property, after a meeting of the unit owners called for the specific purpose of discussing the proposed rules and regulations. Notice of the meeting shall contain the full text of the proposed rules and regulations, and the meeting shall conform to the requirements of Section 18(b) of this Act, except that no quorum is required at the meeting of the unit owners unless the declaration, bylaws or other condominium instrument expressly provides to the contrary. However, no rule or regulation may impair any rights guaranteed by the First Amendment to the Constitution of the United States or Section 4 of Article I of the Illinois Constitution including, but not limited to, the free exercise of religion, nor may any rules or regulations conflict with the provisions of this Act or the condominium instruments. No rule or regulation shall prohibit any reasonable accommodation for religious practices, including the attachment of religiously mandated objects to the front-door area of a condominium unit.

(i) To keep detailed, accurate records of the receipts and expenditures affecting the use and operation of the property.

(j) To have access to each unit from time to time as may be necessary for the maintenance, repair or replacement of any common elements or for making emergency repairs necessary to prevent damage to the common elements or to other units.

(k) To pay real property taxes, special assessments, and any other special taxes or charges of the State of Illinois or of any political subdivision thereof, or other lawful taxing or assessing body, which are authorized by law to be assessed and levied upon the real property of the condominium.

(l) To impose charges for late payment of a unit owner's proportionate share of the common expenses, or any other expenses lawfully agreed upon, and after notice and an opportunity to be heard, to levy reasonable fines for violation of the declaration, by-laws, and rules and regulations of the Association.

(m) Unless the condominium instruments expressly provide to the contrary, by a majority vote of the entire board of managers, to assign the right of the Association to future income from common expenses or other sources, and to mortgage or pledge substantially all of the remaining assets of the Association.

(n) To record the dedication of a portion of the common elements to a public body for use as, or in connection with, a street or utility where authorized by the unit owners under the provisions of Section 14.2.

(o) To record the granting of an easement for the laying of cable television cable where authorized by the unit owners under the provisions of Section 14.3; to obtain, if available and determined by the board to be in the best interests of the Association, cable television service for all of the units of the condominium on a bulk identical service and equal cost per unit basis; and to assess and recover the expense as a common expense and, if so determined by the board, to assess each and every unit on the same equal cost per unit basis.

(p) To seek relief on behalf of all unit owners when authorized pursuant to subsection (c) of Section 10 from or in connection with the assessment or levying of real property taxes, special assessments, and any other special taxes or changes of the State of Illinois or of any political subdivision thereof or of any lawful taxing or assessing body.

(q) To reasonably accommodate the needs of a handicapped unit owner as required by the federal Civil Rights Act of 1968, the Human Rights Act and any applicable local ordinances in the exercise of its powers with respect to the use of common elements or approval of modifications in an individual unit.

(r) To accept service of a notice of claim for purposes of the Mechanics Lien Act on behalf of each respective member of the Unit Owners' Association with respect to improvements performed pursuant to any contract entered into by the Board of Managers or any contract entered into prior to the recording of the condominium declaration pursuant to this Act, for a property containing more than 8 units, and to distribute the notice to the unit owners within 7 days of the acceptance of the service by the Board of Managers. The service shall be effective as if each individual unit owner had been served individually with notice.

In the performance of their duties, the officers and members of the board, whether appointed by the developer or elected by the unit owners, shall exercise the care required of a fiduciary of the unit owners.

The collection of assessments from unit owners by an Association, board of managers or their duly authorized agents shall not be considered acts constituting a collection agency for purposes of the Collection Agency Act.

The provisions of this Section are applicable to all condominium instruments recorded under this Act. Any portion of a condominium instrument which contains provisions contrary to these provisions shall be void as against public policy and ineffective. Any such instrument that fails to contain the provisions required by this Section shall be deemed to incorporate such provisions by operation of law.

As can be seen, the powers of the Board of Managers are quite extensive. A couple of points to stress are the assessment (section c and d), insurance (section f), and real estate tax (section k) provisions of the statute. Condominiums are taxed to both the Association and the unit owner.

The individual unit owner is required to pay **assessments** to the Association. Typically, these assessments are paid monthly and reflect the unit owner's percentage share of the costs for maintenance, taxes, insurance, and other expenses of the Association. It is a breach of the Association's Rules and Regulations to fail to pay assessments. The Association may bring a suit for eviction against a unit owner for failure to pay the assessments. In addition, it is often a breach of a unit owner's mortgage to fail to pay one's assessments.

The Association may also impose **special assessments** on the unit owners to build up the reserve fund or for extraordinary expenses, such as a new roof or windows. When there is an extraordinary expense, the financial reserves of the Association may not be sufficient to pay for the expense. As a result, the Association has the right to collect additional fees to help pay these expenses. These assessments are proposed, discussed, and voted upon by the Association and they are enforced and collected by the Board of Managers. When a property is being sold, it is required that the Seller disclose any special assessments imposed or contemplated as part of the Seller's disclosure (see below).

The entire property (the Condominium Development) is assessed **real estate taxes** based upon the value of the entire property. The Board of Managers is responsible to pay those fees and they are then passed on to the unit owners as part of the assessment. The condominium unit is taxed based upon the value of the individual unit. The unit owner is required to pay his/her own taxes and it is generally a breach of both the unit owner's mortgage (if there is a note and mortgage) and also the Rules and Regulations to fail to pay the unit owner's individual real estate taxes.

Associations exert great control over the use of the unit and unit owners. The purpose of Association restrictions is to prevent degradation to the property's appearance and maintain the value of the property. Associations are often criticized for having restrictive Rules and Regulations on how unit owners conduct themselves and use their property.

For instance, the Bylaws may state whether or not the units may be rented to others by unit owners. The Rules and Regulations may determine whether a business may be operated by the unit owner (such as a home-based business) or whether the units are for residential purposes only. Associations may control certain aspects of unit ownership, including decorating, satellite dishes, whether pets are allowed, and other limits on the rights of the unit owners. Before buying a condo, it is important to review the Association's restrictions carefully.

Ethics Alert:

Often, Buyers will request that the attorney review the Declarations and Bylaws. It is important to check with the attorney to see if the attorney provides that service, and, if so, if there are extra charges for this service. Many lawyers will not review the Declarations and Bylaws or Rules and Regulations as part of the attorney's regular "flat" fee for the transaction. The reason for this is that the attorney cannot determine how extensive the documents are until actually seeing the documents. The entire Condo Document package (consisting of the Declarations and Bylaws, as well as the Rules and Regulations) may be only fifty (50) pages long, for a small Association, or may be several hundred pages long, for an established Association.

Remember, paralegals are not allowed to set fees for legal services, so it is important to check with the attorney about the policy of the firm about condo documents.

As described in 18.4(k) of the Condominium Act, the Board of Managers is required to make sure that the property is properly insured. Unlike a free-standing home, the primary insurance liability is the responsibility of the Association. The Association holds the primary liability insurance policy. The unit owner is generally only required to provide insurance for their contents. Some Associations do not require that the unit owners insure the contents. Conversely, some Associations require unit owners to purchase separate liability insurance to cover the contents of the unit, the negligence of the unit owner, and any guests of the unit owner. The Rules and Regulations generally will define the insurance requirements.

When the property is being conveyed, the Buyer's lender will require proof of the property's insurance and also will require that the lender be an additional insured under the property's liability insurance. The lender will generally provide a **mortgagee clause**, stating exactly how the lender is to be referred to in the insurance coverage. A mortgagee clause is a provision in a hazard insurance contract stipulating that in the event of a loss, proceeds will be paid to a secured party, such as the mortgage company. A typical mortgagee clause will state: *Lender's Full Name ISAOA/ATIMA and address*. **ISAOA** means "Its Successors And/Or Assigns." **ATIMA** means "As Their Interests May Appear." It is very important that the mortgagee clause be exactly correct, as it is used by the lender and insurance company to ensure that the lender is correctly identified. Normally, the lender will provide its mortgagee clause prior to Closing (and in the Closing instructions provided to the title company). Errors or incomplete mortgagee clauses can cause substantial delays at Closing. For many lending institutions, there may be many, many entities that are subsidiaries of the institution. It is very important to name the exact, correct entity.

3. Condominium Associations in Real Estate Closings

During the transaction of a condominium, both the Buyer's attorney and Seller's attorney will generally have to work with the Association or their management company. The Seller is required to disclose whether there is an Association, the name of the Association, and other relevant information. It is important to begin working with the Association early in the transaction in order to make sure that all requests are complied with and that all contingencies are satisfied. Associations may have very different rules from one another, and it is imperative that the individual requirements of the Association be satisfied. This is especially true for Associations that work with a management company for the day-to-day operations of the Association and the condominium. Since there are several requests for documentation required, it is important to make the requests to the correct entities. When a management is involved, many requests are directed to the management company and others are directed to the Association directly. Making a request to the wrong entity can create delays and slow the process.

The most common issues that are experienced when dealing with the Association include ordering the Declarations, Bylaws, and Rules and Regulations (if the Seller does not currently possess a copy), requesting the minutes of the Association meetings, and ordering a **Paid Assessment Letter.** The paid assessment letter is a statement by the Association that the Seller's current assessments are paid in full, that there is no right of first refusal (or if there is, that it has been waived) on behalf of the Association (see below). Section 18(i) of the Condominium Act requires a condominium Association to issue a statement of the unit owner's account upon a certain notice (often, 10–15 days) and payment of a "reasonable" fee; many Associations (or their managing agents) charge for this statement, sometimes as much as $100 for the letter, as well as a "premium" for expedited service (if the letter is ordered less than seven (7) days prior to Closing).

The Seller's attorney should request the paid assessment letter early in the transaction, although never more than one month prior to Closing. The request should always be in writing and should reference § 18(i) of the Condominium Act. Many Associations have their own forms and those forms should be used to expedite the delivery of the letter. As stated previously, many larger Associations have management companies that handle the day-to-day management of the condominium development. Some management companies have automated the service and allow the Seller's attorney to order the paid assessment letter online, often with electronic delivery. This obviously speeds up the process and it is recommended to use online resources where available.

A copy of a paid assessment letter request is included at the end of this chapter.

Many Associations and management companies require the Seller and/or the Buyer to pay certain fees prior to or at Closing. For instance, many management companies charge a "move-out" or "move-in" fee or "elevator" fee (a fee for reserving the elevator for purposes of moving in or out). Some companies require a pet deposit or damage deposit for damage to common areas when moving in or out of the unit. If there is a common area "party room," many Associations will require a contract and a fee to use the party room. Some Associations require the Buyer to submit an "owner's information form" (detailing who will be living in the unit, their contact information, their employer, the names and ages of children, the make of their vehicle, etc.). Most Associations will withhold issuance of the paid assessment letter until these forms and fees are completed.

A **right of first refusal** is a provision in the Declarations that allows the Association the right of first refusal in the sale of the unit. Should a unit owner wish to sell the unit on the open market, the unit owner must notify the Association. The Association may then invoke its right to purchase the property from the unit owner. The Association must pay the fair value for the property. The Association may then decide what to do with the property. It is intended to allow the Association the ability to control the transfer of the property, but there are concerns that it could be (and in the past, was) used for discriminatory purposes. The paid assessment letter should state whether there is a right of first refusal and, if there is, that it has been waived. It is very important that, if the Association has a first refusal, that the right of first refusal is waived, either in the paid assessment letter or through a separate letter waiving the right.

As described above, the Association wields broad power and control over the unit owners. When living communally, it is important to remember that certain freedoms may be restricted. In addition to the pet policies and other restrictions listed above, the unit owners (and their tenants, if they rent the unit to others) must abide by the Bylaws and all of the Rules and Regulations. It is very important to take this into consideration, since there is no way to avoid the fact that there are people living immediately above, below, to the left, and to the right of the unit owner.

Adhering to the Bylaws, Rules, and Regulations is the responsibility of all unit owners. Violating the terms of the Rules and Regulations can lead to liens against the unit, lawsuits, and even eviction (forcible entry and detainer) actions. If a unit owner fails to pay the required assessments or otherwise violates the Rules, that unit owner can face lawsuits and can even be removed from possession of the unit owner's own condo.

It is also important to remember that Condominium Associations are a powerful form of democracy. It is the unit owners who control and elect the Board of Managers. In fact, the Board of Managers is made up of unit owners. Many unit owners think that disputes with the Association is a matter of "them against me," when really the unit owner is a part of "them." If there is a policy that a unit owner does not like or that affects the unit owner in particular, the unit owner can change the policy, if the unit owner can convince enough other unit owners to agree. For instance, if a unit owner wants to have a dog, but the condominium is a "no pet" complex, the unit owner can lead an effort to change the Bylaws (or Rules and Regulations) to allow pets. Condominium Associations are a form of direct participation democracy. The power is in the hands of the Board of Managers, but they derive the power from all of the unit owners.

4. Contract Provision

Paragraph 15 of the contract describes, in part, what the parties must do if the property is a condominium. It states:

15. **CONDOMINIUM/COMMON INTEREST ASSOCIATIONS:** (If applicable) The Parties agree that the terms contained in this paragraph, which may be contrary to other terms of this Contract, shall supersede any conflicting terms.

(a) Title when conveyed shall be good and merchantable, subject to terms, provisions, covenants and conditions of the Declaration of Condominium/ Covenants, Conditions and Restrictions ("Declarations/CCRs") and all amendments; public and utility easements including any easements established by or implied from the Declarations/CCRs or amendments thereto; party wall rights and agreements; limitations and conditions imposed by the Condominium Property Act; installments due after the date of Closing of general assessments established pursuant to the Declarations/CCRs.

(b) Seller shall be responsible for all regular assessments due and levied prior to Closing and for all special assessments confirmed prior to the Date of Acceptance.

(c) Seller shall notify Buyer of any proposed special assessment or increase in any regular assessment between the Date of Acceptance and Closing. The parties shall have three (3) Business Days to reach agreement relative to payment thereof. Absent such agreement, either party may declare the contract null and void.

(d) Seller shall, within five (5) Business Days from the Date of Acceptance, apply for those items of disclosure as described in the Illinois Condominium Property Act, and provide same in a timely manner, but no later than the time period provided by law. This contract is subject to the condition that Seller be able to procure and provide to Buyer a release or waiver of any option of first refusal or other pre-emptive rights of purchase created by the Declaration/CCRs. In the event the Condominium Association requires personal appearance of Buyer and/or additional documentation, Buyer agrees to comply with same.

(e) In the event the documents and information provided by Seller to Buyer disclose that the existing improvements are in violation of existing rules, regulations or other restrictions or that the terms and conditions contained within the documents would unreasonably restrict Buyer's use of the premises or would result in increased financial obligations unacceptable to Buyer in connection with owning the Real Estate, then Buyer may declare this Contract null and void by giving Seller written notice within five (5) Business Days after the receipt of the documents and information required by this Paragraph, listing those deficiencies which are unacceptable to Buyer. If Notice is not served within the time specified, Buyer shall be deemed to have waived this contingency, and this Contract shall remain in full force and effect.

(f) Seller shall not be obligated to provide a condominium survey.

(g) Seller shall provide a certificate of insurance showing Buyer and Buyer's mortgagee, if any as an insured.

As described above, the Seller is required to pay any assessments due up to the date of Closing, provide the condominium Declarations, and provide a certificate of insurance. In addition, the Association is required to provide a **22.1 Disclosure**, which includes a copy of the Bylaws, financial statements, any liens on the property, disclosures of proposed expenditures, the amount of the assessments, etc. The "22.1" refers to Section 22.1 of the Illinois Condominium Act.

(765 ILCS 605/22.1) (from Ch. 30, par. 322.1)

Sec. 22.1. (a) In the event of any resale of a condominium unit by a unit owner other than the developer such owner shall obtain from the Board of Managers and shall make available for inspection to the prospective purchaser, upon demand, the following:

(1) A copy of the Declaration, by laws, other condominium instruments and any rules and regulations.

(2) A statement of any liens, including a statement of the account of the unit setting forth the amounts of unpaid assessments and other charges due and owing as authorized and limited by the provisions of Section 9 of this Act or the condominium instruments.

(3) A statement of any capital expenditures anticipated by the unit owner's Association within the current or succeeding two fiscal years.

(4) A statement of the status and amount of any reserve for replacement fund and any portion of such fund earmarked for any specified project by the Board of Managers.

(5) A copy of the statement of financial condition of the unit owner's Association for the last fiscal year for which such statement is available.

(6) A statement of the status of any pending suits or judgments in which the unit owner's Association is a party.

(7) A statement setting forth what insurance coverage is provided for all unit owners by the unit owner's Association.

(8) A statement that any improvements or alterations made to the unit, or the limited common elements assigned thereto, by the prior unit owner are in good faith believed to be in compliance with the condominium instruments.

(9) The identity and mailing address of the principal officer of the unit owner's Association or of the other officer or agent as is specifically designated to receive notices.

(b) The principal officer of the unit owner's Association or such other officer as is specifically designated shall furnish the above information when requested to do so in writing and within 30 days of the request.

(c) Within 15 days of the recording of a mortgage or trust deed against a unit ownership given by the owner of that unit to secure a debt, the owner shall inform the Board of Managers of the unit owner's Association of the identity of the lender together with a mailing address at which the lender can receive notices from the Association. If a unit owner fails or refuses to inform the Board as required under subsection (c) then that unit owner shall be liable to the Association for all costs, expenses and reasonable attorneys fees and such other damages, if any, incurred by the Association as a result of such failure or refusal.

A reasonable fee covering the direct out of pocket cost of providing such information and copying may be charged by the Association or its Board of Managers to the unit Seller for providing such information.

A copy of a 22.1 Disclosure request letter is included at the end of this chapter.

5. Cooperatives

A cooperative is another form of shared ownership of a property. Unlike a condominium, where the individual unit owners own the units outright and own a shared interest in the common areas, a cooperative works in a very different manner. In a **cooperative**, the property is owned by a corporation and the residents are **shareholders** in the corporation. Thus, the residents do not "own" their units in Fee Simple, they are shareholders in the corporation. The fees that the shareholders pay go toward the payment of the corporation's loan on the property, as well as monthly upkeep and other charges. There are many types of cooperatives (for farming, business, social concerns, etc.), in addition to housing cooperatives.

In the Chicago metropolitan area, roughly 17,000 households live under the cooperative housing structure, with 11,700 (69%) of the units located in Chicago (Affordable Housing Cooperatives, Conditions and Prospects in Chicago, June 2004).

In cooperatives, the corporation secures the funding for the project. The corporation holds the mortgage for the project. If an individual buys into a cooperative, the shareholder pays an upfront fee to acquire the share and agrees to pay part of the costs, based upon the percentage of ownership represented by the shares in the corporation.

The cooperative's Bylaws and documents are initially established by the shareholders. The shareholders elect a Board of Directors, usually from among the shareholders, who are tasked with the primary responsibility of management for the development, and approving the annual budget. The Board of Directors determines the Rules and Regulations. Voting rights for the shareholders are usually connected to membership status, that is, one share, one vote, although proportional voting may be allowed by the cooperative association.

The cooperative members collectively share decision-making responsibilities and share the expenses of operating the cooperative, including: maintenance, repairs, and property taxes. The shareholders pay a monthly fee (often called Rent, Assessment, or **Carrying Charge**) to pay the costs of the cooperative. The shareholder has the right to occupy a particular unit. In addition, the shareholders also maintain some of the benefits of home ownership, such as real estate tax deductions and mortgage deductions (see Chapter 7).

The Board of Directors often hires a management company to run the day-to-day operations of the cooperative. The management company collects the carrying charges, pays the bills, prepares the annual budget, and works with the members on behalf of the cooperative. Like many non-profit corporations, the Board of Directors may hire an independent auditor to perform an annual financial audit of the cooperative.

When a shareholder wishes to move and sell the share, the sale generally has to be approved by the other shareholders or, at least, by the Board of Directors. This helps maintain the integrity of the cooperative. It also helps to ensure that the new shareholder will be able to contribute to the cooperative and pay the shareholder's fair share of the expenses.

Key Terms

Unit Owner
Condo Conversion
Declaration of Condominium
Condominium Association
Bylaws
Rules and Regulations
Board of Managers
Assessment
Special Assessment
Mortgagee Clause
ISAOA
ATIMA
Real Estate Taxes
Paid Assessment Letter
22.1 Disclosure
Right of First Refusal
Cooperative
Shareholder
Carrying Charge

Review Questions

1. What does somebody own when that person owns a condominium?
2. What is a condominium association?
3. Define assessments and special assessments.
4. What is a paid assessment letter?
5. What is a cooperative?

Materials included in the following chapter appendix include:

- 22.1 Disclosure for Purchase of Condominium
- Paid Assessment Letter Request
- Paid Assessment Letter
- *Gotham Lofts Condominium Association v. Donald Kaider*, 4 N.E.3d 92 (Ill, 1st, 2013)

Chapter 5 Appendix

Housing Cooperative Overview

Thinking of buying a cooperatively owned house or apartment? If you are, you may have noticed that housing co-ops are a bit different than other types of homeownership. This page offers a full complement of information on what's involved in buying into Housing Cooperatives.

What is a housing cooperative?

A housing cooperative is formed when people join with each other on a democratic basis to own or control the housing and/or related community facilities in which they live. Usually they do this by forming a not-for-profit cooperative corporation. Each month they simply pay an amount that covers their share of the operating expenses of their cooperative corporation. Personal income tax deductions, lower turnover rates, lower real estate tax assessments (in some local areas), controlled maintenance costs, and resident participation and control are some of the benefits of choosing cooperative homeownership.

What do you actually own?

The main distinction between a housing co-op and other forms of homeownership is that in a housing co-op you don't directly own real estate. But if you don't own real estate, what exactly are you buying? You are buying shares or a membership in a cooperative housing corporation. The corporation owns or leases all real estate. As part of your membership (being a shareholder) in the cooperative you have an exclusive right to live in a specific unit (this is established thorough a occupancy agreement or proprietary lease) for as long as you want, as long as you don't break any of the rules or regulations of the cooperative. As part of your membership, you also have a vote in the affairs of the corporation.

What does the share or membership purchase price involve?

When you buy a share or membership in a housing cooperative, you are paying for just that-a share of the cooperative housing corporation. The purchase price will vary depending on what kind of neighborhood it is in, how big the unit is, whether the co-op limits resale prices, and whether the co-op has an underlying mortgage for the entire property

What is a share loan?

Let's say you were going to buy a $100,000 home. Most likely you would not be able to pay the seller $100,000 in cash for the house. Instead, you would pay a down payment, and you would get a mortgage from a lender to cover the rest of the purchase price. In a co-op, since you are actually buying a share(s) in a corporation rather than real estate, you get a type of loan called a share loan from a lender. A share loan is like a mortgage. It provides you with borrowed funds to buy the share(s) from the seller. You then make monthly payments on the share loan to the lenders and monthly carrying charge (maintenance) payments to the co-op.

How do I accumulate equity?

Good question. It actually depends on what type of cooperative you are buying into. There are three different types of housing cooperatives as far as equity is concerned.

1. **Market-rate housing cooperatives**

   In a market-rate cooperative you can buy or sell a membership or shares at whatever price the market will bear. Purchase prices and equity accumulation are very similar to condominium or single-family ownership.

2. **Limited-equity housing cooperatives**

   In a limited-equity housing cooperative (LEC) there are restrictions on what outgoing members can get from sale of their shares. These are usually imposed because the co-op's members benefit from below-market interest rate mortgage loans, grants, real estate tax abatement, or other features that make the housing more "affordable" to both the initial and future residents for a specified period of time. In some co-ops these limitations are voluntarily imposed by the members. These restrictions are usually found in

NAHC National Association of Housing Cooperatives

the cooperative's bylaws. The documents may also establish maximum income limits for new members to further target the special benefits of the housing to families who need them the most.

3. **Leasing cooperatives (or zero-equity)**
   In a leasing cooperative, the cooperative corporation leases the property from an outside investor (often a nonprofit corporation that is set up specifically for this purpose). Since the cooperative corporation does not own any real estate, the cooperative is not in a position to build up any equity (just as a renter doesn't build any equity). However, as a corporation, the cooperative is often in a position to buy the property if it comes up for sale later and convert to a market rate or limited-equity cooperative. And some leasing cooperatives allow outgoing members to take with them at least part of their share of the cash reserves built up by the cooperative corporation while they were in occupancy.

What are the monthly charges for?
Almost all co-ops charge residents a monthly carrying charge (often called a monthly maintenance fee). The amount of the monthly charge varies from co-op to co-op. The charges cover your proportionate share of operating and maintaining the cooperative, which can include blanket mortgage payments, property taxes, management fees, maintenance costs, insurance premiums, utilities, and contributions to reserve funds.

Do I pay real estate taxes?
Taxes are assessed on the cooperative corporation, as owner of the property. Your monthly payments to the co-op are, in part, used by the co-op to pay the real estate taxes. Even thought you don't pay real estate taxes directly, federal tax law allows you to deduct your share of the co-op tax payments, as well as your mortgage interest payments, on your personal income tax return.

Are co-ops allowed to discriminate?
Like any other form of housing, cooperatives may not discriminate based on the protected classes listed in the Fair Housing Act, which includes race, color, religion, sex, familial status, national origin, or disability. Historically, the basic cooperative principles include both open membership without restriction as provided by law and non-partisan in politics and non-sectarian in religion. However, many co-ops are selective in approving memberships. As communities of people who share a financial obligation and responsibility for governing how they want to live together, it is important for co-ops to ensure that incoming members can meet their financial obligation and will abide by the rules of the community.

What do most housing cooperatives look like?
Co-ops can be almost any time of housing, and there is a wide variety in terms of what housing cooperatives look like. Housing cooperatives can be high-rise apartment buildings, garden-style apartments, townhouses, single-family homes, and senior housing.
There are other kinds of housing cooperatives. Mobile home park cooperatives usually own the land, utilities, and community facilities; their members own the individual "mobile homes." Some other housing cooperatives own land and community facilities and use legal documents including recorded covenants as the basis for maintaining the desired cooperative controls over functioning of the cooperative community.

What questions should I ask before buying into a cooperative?
Remember, since you are buying a share of a corporation that owns real estate, you will want to find out about the financial health of the corporation. You will also want a clear understanding of what your financial obligations to the cooperative will be. Be sure to find out what all the rules and regulations of the community are. Here are some sample questions to ask before making your investment:

- What is the share price?
- Where can I obtain share loan financing?

- How much are the monthly carrying charges?
- What is the underlying mortgage?
- What is your pet policy?
- What is your subletting policy?
- What is the policy for making alterations to my unit?
- Confused on any of these terms? Check out our glossary. Also, to understand your rights and responsibilities as a co-op resident, visit Living in a Housing Cooperative. If you have any legal questions about co-ops, you should be sure to consult an attorney.
- I'm interested in moving into a housing cooperative. How can I find a co-op in my area?

A local real estate professional may be able to offer assistance. You may also want to consult your local yellow pages. In many cities you can find co-ops listed under the apartments section.

Economic Advantages

- Affordable: Lower down payment, much lower closing costs, economies of scale, longer mortgage term all make co-ops more affordable than other ownership housing.
- Living in a Co-op Stays Affordable. Members have no reason to substantially increase monthly charges unless taxes or operating costs go up, so monthly charges remain reasonable.
- Tax Deductions. For income tax purposes, the co-op member is usually considered a homeowner and, as such, can deduct his or her share of the real estate taxes and mortgage interest paid by the cooperative. Equity. Co-ops can provide for accumulation of individual member equity. For market-rate co-ops, the accumulation of equity and resale prices are based on the market. Limited-equity co-ops establish limitations on the accumulation of equity to assure long-term affordability to new members.
- Limited Liability. Members have no personal liability on the co-op mortgage. The cooperative association is responsible for paying off any mortgage loans. This can often make it possible for persons whose income might not qualify them for an individual mortgage to buy a membership in a limited equity co-op.
- Consumer Action. Through their cooperative association, members can jointly exert influence in order to change tax rates and utility prices and obtain improved services from local governments. The co-op, as consumer advocate, can also join with other organizations.
- Savings. Co-op members can benefit from economy of scale in co-op operating costs as well as from not-for-profit operation. Also, when there are "transfers", only the out-going member's equity must be financed by the incoming member. Transfers of shares are subject to fewer settlement costs.

Social Advantages

- Elimination of Outside Landlord. Co-ops offer control of one's living environment and a security of tenure not available in rental housing.
- Community Control. As mutual owners, member residents participate at various levels in the decision-making process. This is not true of tenants who usually do not have the opportunity to exercise responsibility. Members own the cooperative together and have the security of being able to remain in their homes for as long as they wish, as long as they meet their monthly obligations, and abide by the co-op bylaws, rules, and regulations.
- Cultural Diversity. Many co-op members indicate that the possibility for interaction with people from different backgrounds, cultures, and income levels is a positive factor in their decision to become a member.
- Extended Services. By establishing cooperative procedures and working together, people are able to provide services for themselves that otherwise would be impossible to obtain. When one cooperatively organized venture is successful it often becomes clear that people can be successful in another area as well. As a result, the original effort often can be strengthened. Examples include athletic teams, co-op preschools, credit unions, tutoring, food-buying clubs, arts and crafts, and senior health care and support services.

Physical Benefits

- Shared Maintenance Responsibilities. Co-op members usually have limited direct maintenance responsibilities. The cooperative association is responsible for major repairs, insurance, replacement of worn-out equipment, and upkeep of common grounds and facilities.
- Vandalism and Security. Co-op members vigorously protect their association's property. An important benefit of converting rental properties to co-op ownership is reduction in vandalism and abuse of property and improved and shared security arrangements. And recent studies show that the co-ops presence in the neighborhood brings neighborhood crime down.

Standard Co-Op Practices

Members of the National Association of Housing Cooperatives agree that cooperative housing associations are most successful when operated in accordance with specific recommended practices, in addition to the general co-op principles.

The cooperative's board of directors should keep its members informed of all its actions. A regular communication system-a frequent newsletter, information bulletins, special meetings, solicitation of members for opinions and priorities-strengthens the relationship between the board of directors and the members. Leader accountability is central to the co-op concept. The board of directors should depend upon the two-way nature of communication to guide them in all decision-making.

The cooperative association must maintain adequate financial reserves to protect the cooperative and its members' interests. These usually include a general operating reserve and a reserve for replacing components of buildings as they deteriorate. Such reserves reduce the possibility of members having to pay unexpected special charges in emergencies. An annual audit should be conducted by professional accountants and made available to all members.

To protect the interests of the remaining residents, the co-op board must have the right to approve incoming members who take the place of those leaving the cooperative. A credit check and a visit with the membership committee are usually required. This process also helps orient the incoming member to their rights and responsibilities as co-op members.

Subleasing should be permitted only for the short-term absence of a member, if allowed at all. If permitted, the length of the sublease agreement and the amount of payment should be determined by the cooperative. To allow subleasing on any larger scale is seen as a return to absentee rental ownership.

More information may be available to you on a local or state level. Find out more about the nearest NAHC Member Association in your area at www.nahc.coop /Member Associations

1444 I Street, NW Suite 700 Washington, DC 20001 P: (202) 216-9646

(Reprinted from the National Association of Housing Cooperatives, available at: http://coophousing.org/wp-content/uploads/2014/09/Housing-Cooperative-Overview-General.pdf, last accessed, January 13, 2016)

Cooperative Principles

Cooperatives around the world generally operate according to a set of principles, adopted by the International Cooperative Alliance in 1995.

The principles, as stated by the National Cooperative Business Association, are:

1. Voluntary and Open Membership

Cooperatives are voluntary organizations, open to all people able to use its services and willing to accept the responsibility of membership, without gender, social, racial, political, or religious discrimination.

2. Democratic Member Control

Cooperatives are democratic organizations controlled by their members—those who buy the goods or use the services of the cooperative—who actively participate in setting policies and making decisions.

3. Members' Economic Participation

Members contribute equally to, and democratically control, the capital of the cooperative. This benefits members in proportion to the business they conduct with the cooperative rather than on the capital invested.

4. Autonomy and Independence

Cooperatives are autonomous, self-help organizations controlled by their members. If the co-op enters into agreements with other organizations or raises capital from external sources, it is done so based on terms that ensure democratic control by the members and maintains the cooperative's autonomy.

5. Education, Training, and Information

Cooperatives provide education and training for members, elected representatives, managers, and employees so they can contribute effectively to the development of their cooperative. Members also inform the general public about the nature and benefits of cooperatives.

6. Cooperation Among Cooperatives

Cooperatives serve their members most effectively and strengthen the cooperative movement by working together through local, national, regional, and international structures.

7. Concern for Community

While focusing on member needs, cooperatives work for the sustainable development of communities through policies and programs accepted by the members.

©2013 Illinois Cooperative Council | 1701 Towanda Ave., Bloomington, IL 61701 | Phone 309/557-3109

(Reprinted from Illinois Cooperative Council. Available at: http://illinois.coop/about-coops/cooperative-principles/. Last visited: January 18, 2016)

22.1 Disclosure

To: _____

_____

_____

_____

From: _____

Dated: _____

Subject: _____

The following documents and statements are provided as required by Section 22.1 of the Illinois Condominium Property Act:

a. A copy of the Declaration and Bylaws and any Rules and Regulations are attached hereto.

b. Copies of the latest financial statement, operating budget, and proposed budget of the Association are enclosed.

c. The Unit is subject to the following liens:

_____

_____

_____

d. The anticipated capital expenditures by the Association for the current or next two fiscal years that would require a special assessment or increase in the monthly assessment to the unit owners are as follows:

_____

_____

_____

e. The Association currently maintains the following reserves and/or any funds earmarked for specific projects:

_____

_____

_____

f. There are no pending lawsuits or judgments involving the Association.

g. The Association provides the following insurance coverage for all unit owners:

   1. Insurance Carrier: _____

   2. Policy No.: _____

   3. Type of Coverage: _____

   4. Policy Expiration Date: _____

   5. Amount of Insurance: _____

h. Any improvements or alterations in the Unit or in the limited common elements assigned to the Unit by the current and any prior owners are in good faith believed to be in compliance with the Condominium Declaration.

i. The amount of the monthly common expense assessment for the unit is $_____.

j. There are no unpaid common expenses or special assessments currently due and payable from the selling unit owner.

k. There are no other fees (other than monthly common expense assessment) payable by the unit owners.

_____

_____

By: _____

_____

PAID ASSESSMENT LETTER REQUEST

CHICAGO ILLINOIS MANAGEMENT COMPANY

Seller's Name: _____

Seller's Attorney: _____

Buyer's Name: _____

Buyer's Attorney: _____

Property Address: _____

Association: _____

Closing Date: _____

Addressee of Assessment Letter: _____

Fax Number: _____

Please attach a copy of the sales contract with your request.

The fee for the letter must accompany the request or it will not be processed.
The fee is $75.00 if this Request is received at least fourteen (14) days prior to Closing.
The fee is $150.00 if this Request is received less than fourteen (14) days prior to Closing.

Mail your request, contract, and check to:

CHICAGO ILLINOIS MANAGEMENT COMPANY
Attention: Closing Department
2501 W. Ashland Ave., Suite 312
Chicago, IL 60674
Phone: (312) 555-2341
Fax: (312) 555-2342

Paid Assessment Letter

CHICAGO ILLINOIS MANAGEMENT COMPANY

Illinois Poplar Creek Condominium Association

December 2, 2015

Mr. Adam Byron, Esq.
5452 S. Washington
Suite 23A
Chicago, IL 60631
(312) 555-3243
Fax: (312) 555-3244

RE: Illinois Poplar Creek Condominiums ("Association")
        876 N. Hyndman Street, Unit 232
        Chicago, IL 60698 ("Property")

Please be advised that the Monthly Assessments for the Property are **$230.00** per month. The current Assessments are paid through **December 31, 2012.**

There are **no** Special Assessments currently being assessed against the Property. However, CHICAGO ILLINOIS MANAGEMENT COMPANY cannot guarantee whether any Special Assessments will be assessed in the future.

The Association either has no or has waived any Right of First Refusal for the Property.

The Fee for this Paid Assessment Letter is **$75.00** and must be paid at Closing, by certified funds or Title Company check, payable to CHICAGO ILLINOIS MANAGEMENT COMPANY.

With regards,

CHICAGO ILLINOIS MANAGEMENT COMPANY

4 N.E.3d 92 (2013)

GOTHAM LOFTS CONDOMINIUM ASSOCIATION, Plaintiff-Appellant,

v.

Donald KAIDER, Defendants-Appellants.

No. 1-12-0400.

Appellate Court of Illinois, First District, Second Division.

February 5, 2013.

Andrew A. Girard and Bradley J. Rettig, Girard Law Group, P.C., Chicago, for appellant.

Marvin L. Husby III, Chicago, for appellee.

OPINION

Justice CONNORS delivered the judgment of the court, with opinion.

Plaintiff Gotham Lofts Condominium Association won a judgment of possession for defendant Donald Kaider's condominium property due to defendant's failure to pay assessments for common expenses. Defendant later filed a motion to vacate the judgment, asserting that his delinquent account had been satisfied because plaintiff leased the property to a tenant after the judgment. The circuit court agreed and, among other relief, ordered defendant to be reinstated into possession. We reverse and remand.

Taking possession of condominium property is one of the most powerful remedies that a condo association has available when owners fail to pay their assessments, but the process is under firm statutory control. See generally 765 ILCS 605/9.2 (West 2010) (remedies available for nonpayment of assessments); 735 ILCS 5/9-101 *et seq.* (West 2010) (forcible entry and detainer actions); see also generally *Knolls Condominium Ass'n v. Harms*, 202 Ill.2d 450, 269 Ill.Dec. 464, 781 N.E.2d 261 (2002) (discussing the contours of this type of action). When a condo association wins a judgment in a forcible entry and detainer action against a condo owner, the association is entitled to possession of the property until the property owner pays all current and back assessments as well as all costs and attorney fees associated with the forcible entry and detainer action. See 735 ILCS 5/9-111(a) (West 2010). After taking possession, the association has the option (but not the obligation) of leasing the property to a *bona fide* tenant for up to 13 months, which may be extended by order of court if the association is still entitled to possession at the end of the lease term. If the association chooses to lease the property, then it must apply all rental income to the owner's account. When all outstanding assessments, attorney fees, and court costs have been satisfied, the owner is entitled to any surplus in the rent received and may regain possession of the property at the end of the lease term. See 735 ILCS 5/9-111.1 (West 2010).

Plaintiff won a judgment of possession against defendant in September 2009, and it took possession of the property in March 2010. Plaintiff decided to lease the property in order to recoup defendant's delinquent account, which by that point was about

$5,800 and included all back assessments, attorney fees, and court costs associated with the forcible entry and detainer action. Plaintiff turned the property over to its property manager, Phoenix Rising Management Group, Ltd., which then located a tenant and negotiated a lease. Plaintiff entered into the lease with the tenant in April 2010, for a monthly rent of $1,450.

About six months later, however, plaintiff discovered some serious irregularities in its accounts, which led plaintiff to fire Phoenix Rising. Plaintiff hired a new company, Westward Property Management, Inc., and when Westward audited plaintiff's books it discovered that a number of plaintiff's accounts receivable were badly delinquent because Phoenix Rising had allegedly not been collecting payments from unit owners and lessees. Plaintiff hired a law firm to assist with collecting the overdue accounts, and the firm discovered that the tenant who was leasing defendant's property had apparently not paid any rent since she moved in. When pressed on the matter, the tenant refused to pay the alleged back rent and moved out.

By this point, over 13 months had passed since plaintiff had enforced the judgment of possession, so it returned to the trial court and asked for permission to lease the property to a tenant who would actually pay rent. Defendant did not appear at the hearing and the trial court granted plaintiff's motion. About a month later, defendant filed an emergency motion to vacate the leasing-extension order and restore him to possession. The trial court granted defendant's motion in July 2011, pending a final disposition of the issue. The trial court also ordered plaintiff to provide an accounting of all rent received from the tenant, or the absence thereof, but plaintiff was unable to provide any records whatsoever regarding the lease of the property because the relevant records were allegedly still in the exclusive possession of Phoenix Rising.

The trial court ultimately found that plaintiff had provided no evidence of a lease of the property to a tenant, much less any evidence that plaintiff had collected any rent from the alleged tenant. The court also found that, as a matter of law, plaintiff had a duty to exercise its right to lease out defendant's property in a reasonable manner, and that plaintiff was liable for the negligence of its agent Phoenix Rising in failing to collect rent from the tenant. Noting that plaintiff had, contrary to a court order, failed to provide the court with an accounting, the trial court ordered plaintiff to credit defendant's account over $20,000, which was the trial court's estimate of the amount of rental income that plaintiff should have been collecting from the tenant, along with some charges that the trial court found had been erroneously added to defendant's account. Plaintiff then appealed.

There are many problems with what happened in this case, but the crucial one is this: except for the original judgment of possession, none of the facts that we have just recited are actually facts at all. They are instead only allegations made by the parties' attorneys in their various postjudgment motions and at oral argument before the trial court during the hearing on defendant's motion. The dispositive issue in this case is whether the parties must submit evidence that supports their claims to the trial court, or whether mere allegations are sufficient.

Section 9-111 of the Code of Civil Procedure is the controlling law in postjudgment situations for forcible entry and detainer actions that involve condominium property,[1] and it provides:

> "If at any time, either during or after the period of stay, the defendant pays such expenses found due by the court, and costs, and reasonable attorney's fees as fixed by the court, and the defendant is not in arrears on his or her share of the common expenses for the period subsequent to that covered by the judgment, the defendant may file a motion to vacate the judgment in the court in which the judgment was entered, and, if the court, upon the hearing of such motion, is satisfied that the default in payment of the proportionate share of expenses has been cured, and if the court finds that the premises are not presently let by the board of managers as provided in Section 9-111.1 of this Act [(735 ILCS 5/9-111.1)], the judgment shall be vacated. If the premises are being let by the board of managers as provided in Section 9-111.1 of this Act [(735 ILCS 5/9-111.1)], when any judgment is sought to be vacated, the court shall vacate the judgment effective concurrent with the expiration of the lease term. Unless defendant files such motion to vacate in the court or the judgment is otherwise stayed, enforcement of the judgment may proceed immediately upon the expiration of the period of stay and all rights of the defendant to possession of his or her unit shall cease and determine until the date that the judgment may thereafter be vacated in accordance with the foregoing provisions * * *." 735 ILCS 5/9-111 (West 2010).

The meaning of a statute is a question of law that we review *de novo*. See *Mashal v. City of Chicago*, 2012 IL 112341, ¶ 21, 367 Ill.Dec. 223, 981 N.E.2d 951. "The primary goal of our review is to ascertain and give effect to the legislature's intent. [Citation.] In determining that intent, we may properly consider the language of the statute, the reason and necessity for the law, the evils sought to be remedied and the statute's ultimate aim." *Id.*

Under section 9-111(a), a condo association that prevails in a forcible entry and detainer action against an owner over unpaid assessments is entitled to possession of the owner's property until the owner files a motion to vacate the judgment of possession. As the statute states, the key issue that the court must decide in considering such a motion is whether "the default in payment of the proportionate share of expenses has been cured." 735 ILCS 5/9-111(a) (West 2010). Although not expressly stated in the statute, it is obvious under the plain language of section 9-111(a) that the hearing that the trial court is required to hold on the owner's motion to vacate the judgment is an evidentiary one because whether the default has been cured is a question of fact.

We ordinarily review the factual findings of the trial court only to determine whether they are against the manifest weight of the evidence (see, *e.g., Yellow Book Sales & Distribution Co. v. Feldman*, 2012 IL App (1st) 120069, ¶ 37, 367 Ill.Dec. 484, 982 N.E.2d 162), but the problem here is that no evidence was ever presented to the trial court and no evidentiary hearing ever occurred. Defendant's original motion asking to vacate the extension order and to restore him to possession and plaintiff's responses was neither verified nor included any affidavits, and neither side presented any witnesses, depositions, affidavits, or other evidence to the trial court during any of the postjudgment hearings conducted in this matter. Indeed, all that was presented at the final hearing was the arguments of the parties' attorneys, and the trial court lamented several times that it had been given no evidence regarding the crucial issues of the lease, payment of rent, receipt of rental income by plaintiff, or the balance of defendant's account.

Absent an evidentiary hearing, there is no basis in the record for any of the trial court's factual findings regarding the existence or nonexistence of the lease and any payments that the alleged tenant may or may not have made. The failure to conduct an evidentiary hearing on defendant's motion is fatal to the trial court's judgment in this case, so we must reverse on that ground alone. Before remanding this case, however, we think it important to discuss two other areas of concern so that they can be addressed by the trial court.

The first issue is the trial court's allocation of the relative burdens of the parties. Section 9-111(a) is silent as to the allocation of burdens, and the statute's only requirement is that the trial court be "satisfied" that the defendant's default in paying the assessments has been cured. So which party bears the burden of showing that the default has been cured? This is a crucial consideration in this case, given that defendant alleged that there was a lease to a tenant, and plaintiff denied that it ever received any rental income to satisfy the delinquent account. And although neither party ever produced any evidence of its claims, the trial court essentially presumed that the debt had been satisfied and required plaintiff to prove otherwise, placing the burden on plaintiff, not defendant, of introducing any and all evidence about the alleged lease and rental payments.

Although section 9-111 is silent on the burden question, the statute is analogous to sections 2-1203 and 2-1401 of the Code of Civil Procedure (735 ILCS 5/2-1202, 2-1203, 2-1401 (West 2010)). Like section 9-111, these sections also create procedures for attacking a judgment after trial. Importantly for our purposes, it is the party requesting relief from judgment that bears the burden of proof for motions under both of these sections. See *In re Haley D.*, 2011 IL 110886, ¶57, 355 Ill.Dec. 375, 959 N.E.2d 1108 (section 2-1401); *Espedido v. St. Joseph Hospital*, 172 Ill.App.3d 460, 467, 122 Ill.Dec. 405, 526 N.E.2d 664 (1988)(section 2-1203). Nowhere does section 9-111 indicate that plaintiff should bear the burden of showing that the debt has *not* been satisfied. Indeed, plaintiff won judgment at trial because it proved that defendant was delinquent in paying his assessments, and it is defendant, not plaintiff, who is now asking the trial court to vacate that judgment on the ground that his account is current. As is the case with sections 2-1203 and 2-1401, the party seeking to have the judgment vacated should bear the burden of proving any necessary supporting facts. The trial court's decision to place the burden of proof on plaintiff rather than defendant was therefore improper.

There is one important issue about this allocation of the burden that the trial court should be careful to consider in cases of this nature, however, and that is the parties' relative access to information regarding the satisfaction of the debt. In situations where an owner cures the default by paying the money owed directly to the association, the owner should have no trouble producing evidence proving that the debt has been paid. But in situations that involve a lease of the property under section 9-111.1, we can foresee problems arising when owners lack access to information about the lease and rental payments because that information is held by the condo association or its agents. That appears to be part of the problem in this case, given that all of the relevant documents were allegedly held by Phoenix Rising. We are confident, however, that the trial court has sufficient tools at its disposal to compel the production of relevant documents and, if necessary, impose sanctions for the failure to produce them, and the parties also have the ability to subpoena documents and witnesses for the purpose of an evidentiary hearing and to enforce those subpoenas through the trial court. But regardless of how the evidence is produced, defendant has the burden of proof under section 9-111 and must demonstrate to the trial court's satisfaction that the default has been cured before the judgment of possession can be vacated.

The second issue deals with the trial court's findings that plaintiff had a duty to exercise its right to possession of defendant's property reasonably, that Phoenix Rising was negligent in collecting rent from the tenant, and that plaintiff is liable for Phoenix Rising's negligence. Aside from the fundamental problem of the complete lack of any evidence supporting the second finding, these questions are collateral to the issue of possession and should not have been reached by the trial court. Section 9-106 mandates that, "[e]xcept as otherwise provided in Section 9-120 [which deals with leased premises involved in criminal activity], *no matters not germane to the distinctive purpose of the proceeding shall be introduced* by joinder, counterclaim or otherwise." (Emphasis added.) 735 ILCS 5/9-106 (West 2010). Although section 9-106 deals primarily with pleadings and evidence, there is nothing in the plain language of the section that excludes postjudgment proceedings from its requirements. Indeed, the term "distinctive purpose of the proceeding" refers to the limited nature of a forcible entry and detainer action, which is "to adjudicate the parties' rights to possession of the premises, and, therefore, such proceedings should not be burdened by matters not directly related to the issue of which party is entitled to possession." *Great American Federal Savings & Loan Ass'n v. Grivas*, 137 Ill.App.3d 267, 275, 91 Ill.Dec. 870, 484 N.E.2d 429 (1985). A motion under section 9-111 is designed for the sole purpose of determining whether the defendant is entitled to regain possession from the plaintiff after judgment, so section 9-106's germaneness requirement applies with equal force to postjudgment proceedings such as this one.

But the trial court did not confine its inquiry to the issue of possession, contrary to the mandate of section 9-106. The only purpose of a hearing on a motion to vacate the judgment of possession is to answer two factual questions: (1) whether "the default in the payment of the proportionate share of expenses has been cured," and (2) whether the premises are currently leased to a tenant. 735 ILCS 5/9-111 (West 2010). By considering the collateral question of whether plaintiff's agent had been negligent in leasing the property and whether plaintiff was liable for that negligence, the trial court allowed defendant to introduce issues that are not germane to the paramount issue of possession. See generally *Sawyier v. Young*, 198 Ill.App.3d 1047, 1054, 145 Ill.Dec. 141, 556 N.E.2d 759 (1990)(identifying germane issues).

Given the parties' allegations about the unusual circumstances of this case, we understand why the court felt that plaintiff's duties regarding the alleged lease and Phoenix Rising's alleged negligence should be addressed. But those issues are not germane to possession and therefore cannot be considered in the limited context of a forcible entry and detainer action, even after judgment. If defendant wishes to pursue his claim that plaintiff is liable for Phoenix Rising's alleged negligence, then he should test that claim in a collateral tort action, but he may not inject it into this particular proceeding.

Reversed and remanded.

Presiding Justice HARRIS and Justice SIMON concurred in the judgment and opinion.

[1] In its opening brief on appeal, plaintiff argued that the trial court lacked jurisdiction over defendant's motion to vacate because the motion did not satisfy the requirements of section 2-1401(a) of the Code of Civil Procedure (735 ILCS 5/2-1401(a) (West 2010)). This is incorrect, as the trial court's jurisdiction in this procedural context is grounded in section 9-111, which empowers the trial court to hear postjudgment motions to vacate a judgment of possession for condominium property due to failure to pay assessments.

MEMORANDUM

To: Student
From: Instructor
Re: Writing Assignment IV
Date: Today's Date

You are to research a set of the Condominium Declarations, Bylaws, or Rules and Regulations. They are commonly available through an Internet search.

Save an electronic copy of the documents to present to the Instructor.

You are to review the documents you choose and state which Association you will discuss. You are to type a **memorandum** (adapting this memorandum format) and answer the following five questions. You may copy and paste the material from the documents into your answer.

1) Is there a Pet Policy for the development? Where can it be found and what does it state?

2) What is the Rental Policy? That is, must the units be owner-occupied or can unit owners rent their units to tenants? Where can it be found and what does it state?

3) Is there a use restriction on the unit owners? That is, must the units be residential only or can the unit owners conduct business out of their units (and, if so, are there any restrictions on the types of business)? Also, is there a restriction on how many people can occupy the unit (hint, there usually is not, but it can happen)?

4) What are the remedies available for the Association if the unit owner fails to pay the Assessment or is in arrears? Where can it be found and what does it state?

5) What is the policy on insurance? Is the Association responsible for the insurance (and they usually are)? If so, what is the liability amount? Is the unit owner responsible for maintaining insurance as well?

Please print the memorandum and submit to the instructor.

Chapter 6

Deeds and Closing Documents

Learning Objectives

After studying Chapter 6, you will be able to:

- Identify the covenants of title
- Compare and contrast the different forms of deeds
- Explain the various closing documents

Chapter Summary

Topics covered:

- Warranty Deeds
- Quit Claim Deeds
- Closing Documents
- Recording Statutes

This chapter looks at the documents that are required to close a real estate transaction. The most important document in the conveyance of real property is the deed. The chapter begins by examining the various forms of deeds and interests that the various deeds convey. Present and future covenants are explained. The homestead right in the principal residence is described, as are the notary requirements for the deed. The rest of the chapter discusses the other documents that may be required in the real estate transaction, including bills of sale, affidavits of title, ALTA statements, and the various documents that may be required when purchasing transfer stamps. The chapter concludes with samples of the relevant documents.

1. Deeds

A **deed** is a document that transfers ownership of real estate. It contains the names of the current owner and new owner, as well as a legal description of the property, and is signed by the person transferring the property (the "**Grantor**") and that transfers the property to the Buyer (the "**Grantee**"). In order to transfer real estate there must be a deed in writing. There are several different types of deeds and each conveys different interests.

1. A **General Warranty Deed** conveys the property with all the protection of warranties of title. The Grantor "conveys and warrants" the property. There are many types of warranty deed, including: individual deeds, joint tenancy deeds, and tenancy by the entirety deeds.

2. A **Quit Claim Deed** conveys only the Grantor's interest in the property (if any) and the interest is conveyed without any warranty or representation on behalf of the Grantor. In addition to the deed itself, a "Grantor-Grantee" Clause must be signed and recorded with the deed at the recorder's office.

3. A **Special Warranty Deed** warrants title but only for the time period in which the Seller was in title. There are no assurances that cover title prior to the time the Seller was in title.

4. A **Trustee Deed** is drafted by a trust company and delivered when the property is held in trust. Remember, the actual owner of the property is the trust. As such, the trust company drafts the deed and the trustee signs the deed. A trustee's deed must be ordered well in advanced of Closing, so the trust company has sufficient time to draft the trustee's deed.

5. If the title is held by a corporation, the parties designated by the corporate resolution should execute the deed, typically the president or vice president and the corporate secretary.

6. If the title is held by a limited liability company, the member(s) or manager(s) listed in the articles of organization or operating agreement as the authorized signatories should execute the deed.

A Special Warranty Deed conveys the Grantor's title to the Grantee and promises to protect the Grantee against title defects or claims asserted by the Grantor and any persons whose right to assert a claim against the title arose *during the period in which the Grantor held title to the property.* In a special warranty deed, the Grantor guarantees to the Grantee that the Grantor has done nothing during the time he held title to the property that might in the future impair the Grantee's title.

The deed that provides the greatest protection for the Buyer is the General Warranty Deed, and it is the most preferred form of deed. The General Warranty Deed contains the six **Covenants of Title** (often a Special Warranty Deed will not contain all six covenants of title). A General Warranty Deed is a type of deed where the Grantor (Seller) guarantees to the Grantee (Buyer) that Seller holds "clear title" to the property and has the right to sell it.

The key point is that the warranties are not limited to the time the Seller owned the property — they extend back to the property's origins. A General Warranty

> **Ethics Alert:**
> **Remember:** The type of deed drafted can have very serious legal ramifications.
>
> - General Warranty Deed
> - Special Warranty Deed, and
> - Quit Claim Deed
>
> Each deed has different responsibilities and obligations. Paralegals must check with their supervising attorney prior to drafting a deed to make certain the correct deed is chosen.

Deed includes six Covenants of Title, also called Warranties of Title. The covenants of title can be broken down into two categories: present covenants and future covenants.

Present Covenants

Covenant of Seisin: Covenant that the Grantor has lawful title to the property.

Covenant of Right to Convey: Covenants the Grantor can validly grant or convey title to the Grantee.

Covenant Against Encumbrances: Covenant that the Grantor promises that there are no encumbrances, other than those that have been previously disclosed (like a mortgage).

Future Covenants

Covenant of Warranty: Covenant by which the Grantor assures, and is bound to defend, the security of the title.

Covenant of Quiet Enjoyment: A covenant whereby the Grantor promises to indemnify the Grantee against any defects in the title or any disturbances of the use and enjoyment of the land.

Covenant of Further Assurances: A covenant where the Grantor assures the Grantee that if the Grantor omitted something required to pass valid title, Seller promises to do whatever is necessary to pass title to Buyer.

The present covenants deal with the status of title at the time of conveyance. The future covenants deal with problems that may arise after the conveyance of the property, regardless of when the deficiency in the deed occurred. It may be prior to the Closing that the deficiency happened or, even, prior to contracting.

(765 ILCS 5/9) (from Ch. 30, par. 8)

Sec. 9. Deeds for the conveyance of land may be substantially in the following form:

The grantor (here insert name or names and place of residence), for and in consideration of (here insert consideration), conveys and warrants to (here insert the grantee's name or names) the following described real estate (here insert description), situated in the County of..., in the State of Illinois.

Dated (insert date).

(signature of grantor or grantors)

The names of the parties shall be typed or printed below the signatures. Such form shall have a blank space of 3 1/2 inches by 3 1/2 inches for use by the recorder. However, the failure to comply with the requirement that the names of the parties be typed or printed below the signatures and that the form have a blank space of 3 1/2 inches by 3 1/2 inches for use by the recorder shall not affect the validity and effect of such form.

Every deed in substance in the above form, when otherwise duly executed, shall be deemed and held a conveyance in fee simple, to the grantee, his heirs or assigns, with covenants on the part of the grantor, (1) that at the time of the making and delivery of such deed he was the lawful owner of an indefeasible estate in fee simple, in and to the premises therein described, and had good right and full power to convey the same; (2) that the same were then free from all encumbrances; and (3) that he warrants to the grantee, his heirs and assigns, the quiet and peaceable possession of such premises, and will defend the title thereto against all persons who may lawfully claim the same. Such covenants shall be obligatory upon any grantor, his heirs and personal representatives, as fully and with like effect as if written at length in such deed.

(765 ILCS 5/10) (from Ch. 30, par. 9)

Sec. 10. Quitclaim deeds may be, in substance, in the following form:

The grantor (here insert grantor's name or names and place of residence), for the consideration of (here insert consideration), convey and quit claim to (here insert grantee's name or names) all interest in the following described real estate (here insert description), situated in the County of..., in the State of Illinois.

Dated (insert date).

(signature of grantor or grantors)

The names of the parties shall be typed or printed below the signatures. Such form shall have a blank space of 3 1/2 inches by 3 1/2 inches for use by the recorder. However, the failure to comply with the requirement that the names of the parties be typed or printed below the signatures and that the form have a blank space of 3 1/2 inches by 3 1/2 inches for use by the recorder shall not affect the validity and effect of such form.

Every deed in substance in the form described in this Section, when otherwise duly executed, shall be deemed and held a good and sufficient conveyance, release and quit claim to the grantee, his heirs and assigns, in fee of all the then existing legal or equitable rights of the grantor, in the premises therein described, but shall not extend to after acquired title unless words are added expressing such intention.

Homestead Rights

Homestead rights are protected under Illinois statute (735 ILCS 5/12-901) to a spouse living or having lived on the premises, even if the spouse is not on title to the property. The limit of the homestead exemption is $15,000.00. This protects the homestead against creditors of the owners of the property.

To avoid title objections due to homestead rights, upon a conveyance of the property, a deed generally must be signed by both spouses (and must contain a clause specifically waiving such rights). A waiver of homestead must be in writing and signed by the owner and the owner's spouse. This is often the case when a property is being sold by a married person, but the title is in the name of only one of the spouses. In addition, virtually all mortgages on residential real property will require the mortgagor to waive their homestead rights, as this allows the mortgagee to potentially foreclosure on the entire property, even the portion normally covered by the homestead exemption.

(735 ILCS 5/12-901) (from Ch. 110, par. 12 901)

> Sec. 12 901. Amount. Every individual is entitled to an estate of homestead to the extent in value of $15,000 of his or her interest in a farm or lot of land and buildings thereon, a condominium, or personal property, owned or rightly possessed by lease or otherwise and occupied by him or her as a residence, or in a cooperative that owns property that the individual uses as a residence. That homestead and all right in and title to that homestead is exempt from attachment, judgment, levy, or judgment sale for the payment of his or her debts or other purposes and from the laws of conveyance, descent, and legacy, except as provided in this Code or in Section 20-6 of the Probate Act of 1975. This Section is not applicable between joint tenants or tenants in common but it is applicable as to any creditors of those persons. If 2 or more individuals own property that is exempt as a homestead, the value of the exemption of each individual may not exceed his or her proportionate share of $30,000 based upon percentage of ownership.

(765 ILCS 5/27) (from Ch. 30, par. 26)

> Sec. 27. No deed or other instrument shall be construed as releasing or waiving the right of homestead, unless the same shall contain a clause expressly releasing or waiving such right. And no release or waiver of the right of homestead by the husband or wife shall bind the other spouse unless such other spouse joins in such release or waiver.

Notary Clauses

In Illinois, all deeds must be signed by the Grantor (deeds are *not* signed by the Grantee) and all deeds must be notarized by an Illinois registered notary public. Deeds are *not* witnessed in Illinois. The purpose of the notary is to certify the identity of the person executing the deed. The notary does not guarantee the correctness of the deed.

There was a major change in the Illinois Notary Act (5 ILCS 312/), effective on June 1, 2009. Previously, the requirement was that the notary affirm the identity of the Grantor, affix the notary's signature, and stamp the document, and that was basically the extent of the notary's involvement. There were few requirements for record keeping or reporting. Other states require notaries to keep ledgers and report their actions as notaries.

In an effort to reduce fraud in the conveyance of real property in Cook County, Illinois, a recent law applies to every "notarial act in Illinois involving a document of conveyance that transfers or purports to transfer title to residential real property located in Cook County" (5 ILCS 312/3-102(a). **Please note: This is an Illinois Statute, but only applies to residential real estate in Cook County.**

In addition to verifying the identity of the Grantor,

> The notary public shall require the person signing the Document of Conveyance (including an agent acting on behalf of a principal under a duly executed power of attorney), whose signature is the subject of the notarial act, to place his or her right thumbprint on the Notarial Record. If the right thumbprint is not available, then the notary shall have the party use his or her left thumb, or any available finger, and shall so indicate on the Notarial Record. If the party signing the document is physically unable to provide a thumbprint or fingerprint, the notary shall so indicate on the Notarial Record and shall also provide an explanation of that physical condition. The notary may obtain the thumbprint by any means that reliably captures the image of the finger in a physical or electronic medium. (5 ILCS 312/3-102(c)(6))

The notary must also deliver a copy of the Notarial Record to the Cook County Recorder of Deeds Office within fourteen (14) days after the performance of the notarial act, for retention for a period of seven (7) years, along with a filing fee of $5.00.

This change in the law does not, in itself, prevent fraud. However, it is believed that it may help to reduce fraud that has occurred in the past.

Practice Tip:

It is generally a good idea for a paralegal to become a notary public. It is not difficult to become a notary public and may enhance a paralegal's employability.

Having notaries "in-house" is an invaluable service to the law office, especially in real estate law offices. However, it is vital that paralegals who become notaries learn and understand the notary act.

To become a notary, at minimum, an applicant must have resided in the state of Illinois for 30 days, be at least 18, be a US citizen or permanent legal resident, be able to read and write in English, never have been the holder of a notary public appointment that was revoked or suspended during the past 10 years, and not been convicted of a felony. (5 ILCS 312/2-102)

For more information, see the Illinois Secretary of State Notary Public Handbook, available at http://www.cyberdriveillinois.com/publications/pdf_publications/ipub16.pdf (last visited January 18, 2016).

---

2. Closing Documents

In addition to the deed, there are several additional documents that must be conveyed during the real estate transaction. These documents are generally drafted by the Seller's attorney and brought to the Closing for presentation to the Buyer. Some of the documents are recorded, some are executed by both the Seller and the Buyer, and some are presented to the Buyer directly.

Copies of all the documents described in this chapter are included at the end of this chapter.

Bill of Sale

The **bill of sale** conveys the personal property that is included with property to the Buyer, including, but not limited to, appliances, window treatments, tacked down carpeting, wall units, etc. Typically, these are the items that are listed on page one of the contract. The way to think of this is that the deed conveys the real property and the bill of sale conveys the personal property contained in the real property.

The Seller represents and warrants to Buyer that Seller is the absolute owner of said property, that the property is free and clear of all liens and the Seller has the authority to sell the personal property. What this means is that no one can come back to the property after Closing and attempt to repossess or otherwise remove the property. Previously (and still to this day with "rent to own" programs), a Seller of an item would take a security interest in the item and would have the ability to reclaim (repossess) the item in the event that the item was not paid for by the Buyer. In the vast majority of instances, this is no longer the case.

If someone buys something using a credit card (even most store credit cards), the agreement is that the credit card company agrees to lend the Buyer the money (that is, to extend the borrower the "credit") to buy the item. The credit card company is not the Seller. If the Buyer fails to pay, the credit card company's remedy is generally limited to suing the borrower (Buyer) for the debt. They have no ability to try to repossess the item, as they have no interest in the item.

Also note, the Seller of the property generally excludes any warranties of quality, fitness, and merchantability, except for those warranties which are incorporated into the contract (if any). There is usually an "as-is" provision in the bill of sale.

Affidavit of Title

The **Affidavit of Title** is the Seller's statement to the Buyer that the Seller has an interest in the premises, and that no labor or material has been furnished for premises within the last four months that is not fully paid for (or could cause a lien to be placed against the property). Also, that since the date of the title commitment nothing has been done to the property that could in any way affect the title to premises, and no proceedings have been filed by or against Seller, nor has any judgment or decree been rendered against Seller, nor is there any judgment note or other instrument that can result in a judgment or decree against Seller within five days from the date thereof.

Additionally, the Seller affirms that the Seller is in undisputed and peaceful possession of the premises and no other parties have any rights or claims to possession of the premises, unless specifically set forth in the Affidavit of Title. The Seller confirms that the water bill has been paid.

Finally, the Seller affirms that the covenants and warranties herein set forth are continuing covenants and warranties to and including the date of delivery of the deed to the above-identified Buyer, and shall have the same force and effect as if made on the date of such delivery of deed. The Seller, essentially, is affirming the covenants of title conveyed with a warranty deed discussed above.

ALTA Statement

The Affidavit of Title is the Seller's statement to the Buyer that the Seller has not done anything that would encumber title, and the **ALTA** (American Land Title Association) **Statement** is the Seller's and Buyer's statement to the Title Company that they have not done anything to encumber title. This is a general requirement for most title companies.

For the Seller, that includes not having tenants in the property who could have a property interest in the property, not having additional mortgages which have not been disclosed, not having additional contracts to sell the property, not having work done which could put a lien on the property, etc. These are similar to the statements made in the Affidavit of Title.

For the Buyer, signing the ALTA Statement means the Buyer did not borrow additional money against the property, did not contract for work on the property prior to Closing, or does not have a contract to sell the property prior to Closing the purchase. This helps assure the title company that the Buyer is the actual purchaser of the property.

This statement allows the title company to waive four of the five "General Exceptions":

1. Rights or claims of parties in possession not shown by the public records.

2. Encroachments, overlaps, boundary line disputes, or other matters which would be disclosed by an accurate survey and inspection of the premises.

3. Easements, or claims of easements, not shown by public record.

4. Any lien, or right to a lien, for services, labor, or material heretofore or hereafter furnished, imposed by law and not shown by public records.

5. Taxes or special assessments which are not shown as existing liens by public records.

Providing a survey allows the title company to waive the second General Exception. If something does happen after Closing (a second mortgage or a lien appears), and it was caused by the actions (or inactions) of the Buyer or Seller, the ALTA Statement essentially allows the title company to file suit against the offending party.

1099-S or Principal Place of Residence Certificate

Whenever a property is sold, taxes generally need to be paid on the proceeds. Like the sale of any asset, income is earned on the "profit" of the sale. It is somewhat the same for Sellers of homes. However, there is a very important exemption for Sellers of their principal place of residence.

In 1997, when President Bill Clinton executed the Taxpayer Relief Act of 1997, the way home sales were taxed changed dramatically. Prior to the change, the Seller of a home could delay paying tax on a home sale only if they "rolled-over" the gain and purchased a more expensive home within two (2) years of the sale. A separate rule applied to those over age 55 that gave them a single $125,000 exclusion. Under the new tax code, both the "rollover" provision and $125,000 exclusion are replaced with an exclusion that should allow most Sellers to sell the primary residence without tax.

Generally, when a Seller sells an asset for more than he/she paid, the Seller incurs a tax on the profit. This general rule applies to the sale of a home as well. However, under the current law, as long as this **profit** (also called the "gain") is less than $250,000 ($500,000 for joint filers) the gain will not be taxed. Any amount above these limits may be subject to capital gains taxes.

To determine if a property qualifies as a "principal place of residence," certain criteria must be satisfied. In order to qualify for the exclusion, the Seller must have owned and used the property as the Seller's principal residence for two (2) out of the five (5) years prior to the date of sale, that is, the Seller must have actual resided in the property for at least two (2) years of the previous five (5) years prior to the sale. Also, the Seller must not have sold another principal place of residence within the two-year period prior to the sale.

For married taxpayers who file a joint return, the exclusion is up to $500,000 of the gain. In this case, only one spouse need meet the two (2) out of the five (5) years ownership requirement, but both spouses must meet the two (2) out of the five (5) years use requirement. That is, if the wife has owned and used the house as her principal residence for two (2) out of the five (5) years, but her husband did not use the house as his principal residence for the required two (2) years, then the exclusion would only be $250,000.

For those who leave their home because of a disability, a special rule makes it easier to meet the two-year requirement. In such cases, if the Seller owned and used the home as a principal residence for at least one (1) of the five (5) years preceding the sale, then the Seller is treated as having used it as his/her principal residence while he/she is in a facility that is licensed to care for people in his/her condition. Other special use and ownership rules apply in the case of a deceased spouse and in the case of divorce.

These rules do not apply if part of the property was being used for any commercial purpose (such as a home office, where the Seller took a business tax deduction on the home office, although a business deduction is not required). It does not apply to investment property, rental property, or vacation property (there can only be one principal place of residence) and does not apply to vacant land.

If the exclusion applies, the Seller signs a Principal Place of Residence Certificate (please note: title companies call the form something slightly different). If the exclusion does not apply, the Seller(s) must sign a 1099-S form. The title company will then compute the gain realized on the sale and submit the form to the IRS accordingly.

Transfer Stamp Declarations

When a property is conveyed, taxes must be paid to various governmental taxing bodies (state, county, city, etc.). These are often called "**Transfer Stamps**," as the governmental entity will print a stamp to affix to the deed to prove the tax had been paid. In Illinois, the tax is $1.00 per $1,000.00 of the sale price (computed by $.50 per $500.00). In Cook County, the tax is $.50 per $1,000.00 (computed as $.25 per $500.00). Both the state and county stamps are paid by the Seller per statute.

For each municipality, the municipality determines the amount of the transfer tax (if any), the requirements to be met, and who is responsible for paying the tax. Every town has its own rate; some towns do not charge anything, some charge a very small amount, and a few (Chicago, Oak Park, Cicero) charge up to $11.00 per $1,000.00. In addition, every town has specific municipal requirements that must be satisfied prior to the issuance of the transfer stamp. It is critically important that the paralegal know and understand the municipal requirements of the town where the property is located. Failure to satisfy a requirement (failure to schedule an inspection, failure to request a reading for the final water bill, failure to obtain the transfer stamp, etc.) could cause severe delays for the Closing and result in tremendous expense and wasted time.

For example, in the City of Chicago, the tax is $10.50 per $1,000.00 (computed as $5.25 per $500.00) of the sales price. This is paid at a rate of $7.50 per $1,000.00 (computed at $3.75 per $500.00) paid by the Buyer and $3.00 per $1,000.00 (computed at $1.50 per $500.00) paid by the Seller. This is paid at Closing.

Please note, the transfer declaration forms are including in this textbook for the state of Illinois and Cook County, as well as the cities of Chicago, Naperville, and Peoria. Generally speaking, in many parts of the state these forms are no longer used, but have been replaced by an online form through the Illinois Department of Revenue. You can find what counties and cities use the online service on the Illinois Department of Revenue website. It is currently called MyDec.

Other Closing Documents

There are many other Closing documents that form part of a real estate Closing. There are payoffs of the Seller's loan(s), commission statements from the real estate broker, survey and other bills, **tax reproration agreements** (where appropriate), **FIRPTA** (Foreign Investment in Real Property Act) documents, and various escrow agreements.

Key Terms

Deed
Grantor
Grantee

General Warranty Deed
Quit Claim Deed
Special Warranty Deed
Trustee Deed
Covenant of Title
Covenant of Seisin
Covenant of Right to Convey
Covenant Against Encumbrances
Covenant of Warranty
Covenant of Further Assurances
Covenant of Quiet Enjoyment
Homestead Rights
Closing Document
Bill of Sale
Affidavit of Title
ALTA Statement
1099-S Form
Profit
Transfer Stamps
Tax Reproration Agreements
FIRPTA

Review Questions

1. What are three forms of deed?
2. What are the present and future covenants of title?
3. What is the "homestead exemption"?
4. What is a "bill of sale"?
5. Please explain the difference between an Affidavit of Title and an ALTA Statement.

Materials in the following chapter appendix include:

- Warranty Deed
- Quit Claim Deed
- Bill of Sale
- Affidavit of Title
- ALTA Loan and/or Owner's Policy Statement
- Certification for No Information Reporting on the Sale or Exchange of a Principal Residence
- Substitute 1099-S Form
- Illinois P-Tax Form
- Cook County Real Estate Transfer Declaration

- City of Chicago Real Property Transfer Tax Declaration
- Naperville Real Estate Transfer Declaration
- City of Peoria Real Estate Transfer Declaration
- City of Chicago Water Payment Declaration
- City of Chicago Zoning Certification Application
- Illinois Transfer on Death Instrument
- Notice of Death Affidavit and Acceptance of Transfer on Death Instrument
- *Chicago Title Insurance Company, as Subrogee of Waterside Partners, LLC, v. Aurora Loan Services, LLC,* 996 N.E.2d 44 (Ill. 1st, 2013)

Chapter 6 Appendix

WARRANTY DEED
Illinois Statutory
Mail to:
(**Name and address of grantee or attorney**)

Name & Address of Taxpayer:
(**Name and address of grantee**)

RECORDER'S STAMP

The GRANTOR(S): (**Name and marital status of grantor**) of the (**Type of town or city**) of (**Name of town**), County of (**Name of county**), State of Illinois for and in consideration of Ten Dollars ($10.00) and other good and valuable consideration in hand paid, CONVEY AND WARRANT to (**Name, marital status, and address of grantee**) all interest in the following described land in the County of (**Name of county**), State of Illinois; to wit:

LEGAL DESCRIPTION

Subject to:
Hereby releasing and waiving all rights under and by virtue of the Homestead Exemption Laws of the State of Illinois. TO HAVE AND TO HOLD said premises forever.
PIN: (**PIN**)

Property Address (**Street address of property**)

Dated (**Date**)

_____   _____
            Grantor   Grantor

STATE OF **ILLINOIS**   )
) ss
County of (**County**)   )

I, the undersigned, a Notary Public in and for said County, in the State of Illinois, DO HEREBY CERTIFY THAT (**Grantor's name**) personally known to me to be the same person(s) whose name(s) is/are subscribed to the foregoing instrument, appeared before me this day in person, and acknowledged that he/she/they signed, sealed, and delivered the said instrument as his/her/their free and voluntary act, for the uses and purposes therein set forth, including the release and waiver of the right of homestead.

Given under my hand and notarial seal, (**Date**).

WITNESS my hand and official seal.

Signature_____

My Commission Expires _____

(Seal)

Prepared By:

**This conveyance must contain the name and address of Grantee for tax billing purposes: Chap. 55 ILCS 5/3-5020) and name and address of the person preparing the instrument: (Chap. 55 ILCS 5/3-5022).

WARRANTY DEED
Tenancy by the Entirety
Illinois Statutory Deed
Mail To:
(Name and address of grantee)

Name & Address of Taxpayer:
(Name and address of grantee)

RECORDER'S STAMP

The GRANTOR(S): **(Name and marital status of grantor)** of the **(Type of town, city)** of **(Name of town, city)**, County of **(Name of county)**, State of Illinois for and in consideration of Ten Dollars ($10.00) and other good and valuable consideration in hand paid, CONVEY AND WARRANT to **(Names and marital status of grantees)** **Not** as Tenants in Common, **Nor** as Joint Tenants, but as **TENANTS BY THE ENTIRETY** all interest in the following described land in the County of (Name of county), State of Illinois; to wit:

LEGAL DESCRIPTION

Hereby releasing and waiving all rights under and by virtue of the Homestead Exemption Laws of the State of Illinois.
TO HAVE AND TO HOLD said premises Not as Tenants in Common, Not as Joint Tenants, but as **TENANTS BY THE ENTIRETY** forever.
PIN: **(PIN)**

Property Address **(Street address)**

Dated (Date)

_____   _____
            Grantor   Grantor

STATE OF **ILLINOIS**   )
) ss
County of **(County)**   )

I, the undersigned, a Notary Public in and for said County, in the State of Illinois, DO HEREBY CERTIFY THAT **(Name of grantor)** personally known to me to be the same person(s) whose name(s) is/are subscribed to the foregoing instrument, appeared before me this day in person, and acknowledged that he/she/they signed, sealed, and delivered the said instrument as his/her/their free and voluntary act, for the uses and purposes therein set forth, including the release and waiver of the right of homestead.

Given under my hand and notarial seal, **(Date)**.

WITNESS my hand and official seal.

Signature_____

(Seal)

Prepared By:

**This conveyance must contain the name and address of Grantee for tax billing purposes: Chap. 55 ILCS 5/3-5020) and name and address of the person preparing the instrument: (Chap. 55 ILCS 5/3-5022).

QUIT CLAIM DEED
Illinois Statutory
Mail To:
(Name and address of grantee)

Name & Address of Taxpayer:
(Name and address of grantee)

RECORDER'S STAMP

The GRANTOR(S): **(Name and marital status of grantor)** of **(City of residence)** County of **(County)**, State of Illinois for and in consideration of Ten Dollars ($10.00) and other good and valuable consideration in hand paid, CONVEY AND QUIT CLAIM to **(Name and marital status of grantee)** all interest in the following described land in the County of **(County)**, State of **Illinois**; to wit:

LEGAL DESCRIPTION

Subject to: **(Any restrictions)**

Hereby releasing and waiving all rights under and by virtue of the Homestead Exemption Laws of the State of Illinois. TO HAVE AND TO HOLD said premises forever.

PIN: **(PIN Number)**

Property Address **(Street address of property)**

Dated **(Date)**

_____(seal)_____(seal)

_____(seal)_____(seal)

STATE OF **ILLINOIS**   )
) ss
County of (**County**)   )

I, the undersigned, a Notary Public in and for said County, in the State of Illinois, DO HEREBY CERTIFY THAT (**Grantee's Name**) personally known to me to be the same person(s) whose name(s) is/are subscribed to the foregoing instrument, appeared before me this day in person, and acknowledged that he/she/they signed, sealed, and delivered the said instrument as his/her/their free and voluntary act, for the uses and purposes therein set forth, including the release and waiver of the right of homestead.

Given under my hand and notarial seal.

WITNESS my hand and official seal.

Signature_____

My Commission Expires_____

(Seal)

(Preparer of Document)

County—Illinois Transfer Stamps Exempt under provisions of paragraph _____ Section 31-45, Real Estate Transfer Tax Law Date:_____
_____ Buyer, Seller or Representative

**This conveyance must contain the name and address of Grantee for tax billing purposes: Chap. 55 ILCS 5/3-5020) and name and address of the person preparing the instrument: (Chap. 55 ILCS 5/3-5022).

(Required in Cook County, only)
STATEMENT BY GRANTOR AND GRANTEE

The Grantor or his or her agent affirms that, to the best of his or her knowledge, the name of the Grantee shown on the deed or assignment of beneficial interest in a land trust is either a natural person, an Illinois corporation, or foreign corporation authorized to do business or acquire and hold title to real estate in Illinois, a partnership authorized to do business or acquire and hold title to real estate in Illinois, or other entity recognized as a person and authorized to do business or acquire title to real estate under the laws of the State of Illinois.

Dated _____, 20_____ Signature:_____
Grantor or Agent

Subscribed and Sworn to before me by
the said_____
this ___ day of_____ 20____
NOTARY PUBLIC

The Grantee or his or her agent affirms and verifies that the name of the Grantor shown on the deed or assignment of beneficial interest in a land trust is either a natural person, an Illinois corporation, or foreign corporation authorized to do business or acquire and hold title to real estate in Illinois, a partnership authorized to do business or acquire and hold title to real estate in Illinois, or other entity recognized as a person and authorized to do business or acquire and hold title to real estate under the laws of the State of Illinois.

Dated _____, 20_____ Signature:_____
Grantor or Agent

Subscribed and Sworn to before me by
the said_____
this ___ day of_____ 20____
NOTARY PUBLIC

NOTE: Any person who knowingly submits a false statement concerning the identity of a Grantee shall be guilty of a Class C misdemeanor for the first offense and of a Class A misdemeanor for subsequent offenses.

(Attach to deed or ABI to be recorded in Cook County, Illinois, if exempt under the provisions of Section 4 of the Illinois Real Estate Transfer Tax Act.)

STATE OF ILLINOIS   )
)
COUNTY OF (**County**)   )

BILL OF SALE

Seller, _____, in consideration of Ten and No/100ths Dollars, do hereby sell, assign, transfer and set over to Buyer, _____, the following described personal property located at _____:

DESCRIPTION OF PROPERTY CONVEYED

Seller hereby represents and warrants to Buyer(s) that Seller is the absolute owner of said property, that said property is free and clear of all liens, charges, and encumbrances, and the Seller has full right, power, and authority to sell said personal property and to make this Bill of Sale. All warranties of quality, fitness, and merchantability are hereby excluded, other than those warranties, which are incorporated into the contract to purchase the real estate noted above.

If this Bill of Sale is signed by more than one person, all persons so signing shall be jointly and severally bound hereby.

IN WITNESS WHEREOF, Seller has signed and sealed this Bill of Sale at _____, IL, this ___ day of _____, 20__.

_____

Seller

_____

Seller

Subscribed and sworn to before me this ___ day of _____, 20__.

_____

Notary Public

STATE OF ILLINOIS   )
)
COUNTY OF (**County**))

AFFIDAVIT OF TITLE

The undersigned _____ (Sellers), being first duly sworn on oath, and also covenants with and warrants to the Grantee (Buyer) hereinafter named: _____;

That Seller has an interest in the premises described below or in the proceeds thereof or is the Grantor in the deed dated _____, 20__ to _____, Buyer, conveying the following described premises:

LEGAL DESCRIPTION

Common address: _____

That no labor or material has been furnished for premises within the last four months that is not fully paid for: **NONE**

That since the title date of _____, in the report on title issued by _____, Seller has not done or suffered to be done anything that could in any way affect the title to premises, and no proceedings have been filed by or against Seller, nor has any judgment or decree been rendered against Seller, nor is there any judgment note or other instrument that can result in a judgment or decree against Seller within five days from the date thereof.

That Seller is in undisputed and peaceful possession of the premises and no other parties have any rights or claims to possession of the premises, except as hereinafter set forth:

That all water taxes and sanitary sewer, except the current bill, have been paid. Any unpaid balance will be promptly paid within 30 days of receipt of outstanding bills.

Seller further states:

That the covenants and warranties herein set forth are continuing covenants and warranties to and including the date of delivery of the deed to the above-identified Buyer and shall have the same force and effect as if made on the date of such delivery of deed. That this instrument is made to induce, and in consideration of, the said Buyer's consummation of the purchase of the premises.

_____   _____

Grantor   Grantor

Subscribed and sworn to before me this _____ day of _____, 20__

_____

Notary Public

ALTA Loan and/or Owner's Policy Statement
Commitment File Number_____

The undersigned hereby certifies with respect to the land described in the above commitment:

That, to the best knowledge and belief of the undersigned, no contracts for the furnishing of any labor or material to the land or the improvements thereon, and no security agreements or leases in respect to any goods or chattels that have or are to become attached to the land or any improvements thereon as fixtures, have been given or are outstanding that have not been fully performed or satisfied; that there are no recorded or unrecorded: contracts to purchase the land, deeds of conveyance, mortgages, liens of any kind or leases to which the land is subject, except as shown in the above referenced title commitment, and except as listed below; and that if any leases are listed below: their term ends within 30 days of the date below, they contain no option to purchase, rights of renewal, or other unusual provisions, except as noted below. (If no leases, contracts, etc., state "none.")

_____

That, in the event the undersigned is a mortgagor in a mortgage to be insured under a loan policy to be issued pursuant to the above commitment, the mortgage and the principal obligations it secures are good and valid and free from all defenses; that any person purchasing the mortgage and the obligations it secures, or otherwise acquiring any interest therein, may do so in reliance upon the truth of the matters herein recited; and that this certification is made for the purpose of better enabling the holder or holders, from time to time, of the above mortgage and obligations to sell, pledge, or otherwise dispose of the same freely at any time, and to insure the purchasers or pledgees thereof against any defenses thereto by the mortgagor or the mortgagor's heirs, personal representative or assigns.

The undersigned make the above statements for the purpose of inducing _____, or its assigns to issue an owners and/or loan policy pursuant to the above commitment, and agree to indemnify said company against any false statement made herein.

Date: Date:

_____   _____
Seller: Buyer:

_____   _____
Seller: Buyer:

_____   _____
Corporations: **Corporations:**
IN WITNESS WHEREOF, _____   IN WITNESS WHEREOF, _____
_____has caused these presents to   _____has caused these presents to
be signed by _____ its   be signed by _____ its
President and attested by _____ its   President and attested by _____ its

Secretary under its corporate seal on the above date.

By:_____
　　　　　President

Attest:_____
　　　　　Secretary

Secretary under its corporate seal on the above date.

By:_____
　　　　　President

Attest:_____
　　　　　Secretary

If this statement is executed by a Trustee, the Beneficiary must also execute the statement

The above statements are made by
_____ not personally
but as Trustee under the Trust
Agreement known as Trust
No._____ on the
above date by virtue of the
written authority and direction
of the beneficiaries under the trust.

The above statements are made by
_____ not personally
but as Trustee under the Trust
Agreement known as Trust
No._____ on the
above date by virtue of the
written authority and direction
of the beneficiaries under the trust.

_____
Trust Officer

_____
Trust Officer

_____
Beneficiary (ies)

_____
Beneficiary (ies)

LENDER'S DISBURSEMENT STATEMENT

The undersigned hereby certifies that the proceeds of the loan secured by the mortgage to be insured under the loan policy to be issued pursuant to the above referenced title commitment were fully disbursed to or on the order of the mortgagor on _____; and to the best knowledge and belief of the undersigned, the proceeds are not to be used to finance the making of future repairs on the land. You are hereby authorized to date down the above commitment to cover the date of said disbursement.

_____
Signature   Date

CERTIFICATION FOR NO INFORMATION REPORTING ON THE SALE OR EXCHANGE OF A PRINCIPAL RESIDENCE

This form may be completed by the Seller of a principal residence. This information is necessary to determine whether the sale or exchange should be reported by the Seller, and to the Internal Revenue Service on Form 1099-S, Proceeds From Real Estate Transactions. If the Seller properly completes Parts I and III, and makes a "yes" response to assurances 1 through 4 in Part II, no information reporting to the Seller or to the Service will be required for that Seller. The term "Seller" includes each owner of the residence that is sold or exchanged. Thus, if a residence has more than one owner, a real estate reporting person must either obtain a certification from each owner (whether married or not) or file an information return and furnish a payee statement for any owner that does not make the certification.

Part I: Seller Information:

1. Name: _____

2. Address or legal description (including city, state, & zip code) of residence being sold/exchanged: _____

3. Taxpayer Identification Number (TIN): _____

4. Forwarding address:_____

Part II: Seller Assurances. Check "yes" or "no" for assurances 1 through 4:

YES   NO   1. I owned and used the residence as my principal residence for periods aggregating 2 years or more during the 5-year period ending on the date of the sale or exchange of the residence.

YES   NO   2. I have not sold or exchanged another principal residence during the 2-year period ending on the date of the sale or exchange of the residence (not taking into account any sale or exchange before May 7, 1997).

YES   NO   3. No portion of the residence has been used for business or rental purposes by me or my spouse if I am married (after May 6, 1997).

YES   NO   4. At least one of the following three statements applies:

The sale or exchange is of the entire residence for $250,000 or less; or

I am married, the sale or exchange is of the entire residence for $500,000 or less, and the gain on the sale or exchange of the entire residence is $250,000 or less; or

I am married, the sale or exchange is of the entire residence for $500,000 or less, and (a) I intend to file a joint return for the year of the sale or exchange, (b) my spouse also used the residence as his or her primary residence for periods aggregating 2 years or more during the 5-year period ending on the date of the sale or exchange of the residence (not taking into account any sale or exchange before May 7, 1997).

Part III: Seller Certification:

Under penalties of perjury, I certify that all of the above information is true and correct as of the end of the day of the sale or exchange.

_____

Signature of Seller   Date

Substitute 1099-S Form

Date: _____

Escrow No. _____

You are required by law to furnish your correct taxpayer identification number, and other information, to the "Settlement Agent" as defined in Section 6045(e) of the Internal Revenue Code, for purposes of 1099S information reporting on real estate transactions. Accordingly, information regarding this transaction will be sent to the Internal Revenue Service and State Franchise Tax Board. Failure to provide the settlement agent, _____, with your correct taxpayer identification number could result in civil or criminal penalties as imposed by law. Should you have any questions regarding the information reporting requirements of this section, you are advised to consult with your attorney, tax advisor, or the Internal Revenue Service.

SELLER'S NAME: (enter surname first)

_____

SELLER'S ADDRESS AFTER CLOSE:

_____

_____

TAXPAYER IDENTIFICATION NUMBER: (for the name shown at line (1) above)

Social Security Number: _____-___-_____

PROPERTY ADDRESS: _____

CERTIFICATION

Under penalties of perjury, I/we certify that the number shown on this form is my correct taxpayer identification number.

_____

(Seller)

Date: ___day of _____, 20__

PTAX-203
Illinois Real Estate
Transfer Declaration

Please read the instructions before completing this form.
This form can be completed electronically at **tax.illinois.gov/retd**.

Step 1: Identify the property and sale information.

1 _____
  Street address of property (or 911 address, if available)

  _____   _____
  City or village   ZIP

  Township
2 Write the total number of parcels to be transferred. _____
3 Write the parcel identifying numbers and lot sizes or acreage.

Property index number (PIN)	**Lot size or acreage**
a_____	_____
b_____	_____
c_____	_____
d_____	_____

Write additional property index numbers, lot sizes or acreage in Step 3.

4 Date of instrument: ____ ____ / ____ ____ ____ ____
                       Month   Year
5 Type of instrument (Mark with an "X.") :   _____ Warranty deed
   _____ Quit claim deed _____ Executor deed _____ Trustee deed
   _____ Beneficial interest _____ Other (specify): _____
6 _____ Yes _____ No Will the property be the buyer's principal residence?
7 _____ Yes _____ No Was the property advertised for sale?
              (i.e., media, sign, newspaper, realtor)
8 Identify the property's current and intended primary use.
   Current Intended   (Mark **only one item per column** with an "X.")
   a_____ _____ Land/lot only
   b_____ _____ Residence (single-family, condominium, townhome, or duplex)
   c_____ _____ Mobile home residence
   d_____ _____ Apartment building (6 units or less) No. of units: _____
   e_____ _____ Apartment building (over 6 units) No. of units: _____
   f _____ _____ Office
   g_____ _____ Retail establishment
   h_____ _____ Commercial building (specify): _____
   i _____ _____ Industrial building
   j _____ _____ Farm
   k_____ _____ Other (specify): _____

9 Identify any significant physical changes in the property since
  January 1 of the previous year and **write the date of the change.**
  Date of significant change: ____ ____ / ____ ____ ____ ____
                                        Month   Year
  (Mark with an "X.")
  _____ Demolition/damage _____ Additions _____ Major remodeling
  _____ New construction _____ Other (specify): _____
10 Identify only the items that apply to this sale. (Mark with an "X.")
   a _____ Fulfillment of installment contract —
           year contract initiated : ____ ____ ____ ____
   b _____ Sale between related individuals or corporate affiliates
   c _____ Transfer of less than 100 percent interest
   d _____ Court-ordered sale
   e _____ Sale in lieu of foreclosure
   f _____ Condemnation
   g _____ Short sale
   h _____ Bank REO (real estate owned)
   i _____ Auction sale
   j _____ Seller/buyer is a relocation company
   k _____ Seller/buyer is a financial institution or government agency
   l _____ Buyer is a real estate investment trust
   m _____ Buyer is a pension fund
   n _____ Buyer is an adjacent property owner
   o _____ Buyer is exercising an option to purchase
   p _____ Trade of property (simultaneous)
   q _____ Sale-leaseback
   r _____ Other (specify): _____
           _____
   s _____ Homestead exemptions on most recent tax bill:
           1 General/Alternative $_____
           2 Senior Citizens $_____
           3 Senior Citizens Assessment Freeze $_____

Step 2: Calculate the amount of transfer tax due.

Note: Round Lines 11 through 18 to the next highest whole dollar. If the amount on Line 11 is over $1 million and the property's current use on Line 8 above is marked "e," "f," "g," "h," "i," or "k," complete Form PTAX-203-A, Illinois Real Estate Transfer Declaration Supplemental Form A. If you are recording a beneficial interest transfer, do not complete this step. Complete Form PTAX-203-B, Illinois Real Estate Transfer Declaration Supplemental Form B.

11	Full actual consideration	11	$ _____
12a	Amount of personal property included in the purchase	12a	$ _____
12b	Was the value of a mobile home included on Line 12a?	12b	_____ Yes _____ No
13	Subtract Line 12a from Line 11. This is the net consideration for real property.	13	$ _____
14	Amount for other real property transferred to the seller (in a simultaneous exchange) as part of the full actual consideration on Line 11	14	$ _____
15	Outstanding mortgage amount to which the transferred real property remains subject	15	$ _____
16	If this transfer is exempt, use an "X" to identify the provision.	16	_____b _____k _____m
17	Subtract Lines 14 and 15 from Line 13. **This is the net consideration subject to transfer tax.**	17	$ _____
18	Divide Line 17 by 500. Round the result to the next highest whole number (e.g., 61,002 rounds to 62).	18	_____
19	Illinois tax stamps — multiply Line 18 by 0.50.	19	$ _____
20	County tax stamps — multiply Line 18 by 0.25.	20	$ _____
21	Add Lines 19 and 20. **This is the total amount of transfer tax due.**	21	$ _____

Step 3: Write the legal description from the deed. Write, type (minimum 10-point font required), or attach the legal description from the deed. If you prefer, submit an 8¹/₂" x 11" copy of the extended legal description with this form. You may also use the space below to write additional property index numbers, lots sizes or acreage from Step 1, Line 3.

Step 4: Complete the requested information.
The buyer and seller (or their agents) hereby verify that to the best of their knowledge and belief, the full actual consideration and facts stated in this declaration are true and correct. If this transaction involves any real estate located in Cook County, the buyer and seller (or their agents) hereby verify that to the best of their knowledge, the name of the buyer shown on the deed or assignment of beneficial interest in a land trust is either a natural person, an Illinois corporation or foreign corporation authorized to do business or acquire and hold title to real estate in Illinois, a partnership authorized to do business or acquire and hold title to real estate in Illinois, or other entity recognized as a person and authorized to do business or acquire and hold title to real estate under the laws of the State of Illinois. Any person who willfully falsifies or omits any information required in this declaration shall be guilty of a Class B misdemeanor for the first offense and a Class A misdemeanor for subsequent offenses. Any person who knowingly submits a false statement concerning the identity of a grantee shall be guilty of a Class C misdemeanor for the first offense and of a Class A misdemeanor for subsequent offenses.

Seller Information (Please print.)

Seller's or trustee's name   Seller's trust number (if applicable - **not** an SSN or FEIN)

Street address (after sale)   City   State   ZIP
                                               (   )
Seller's or agent's signature   Seller's daytime phone

Buyer Information (Please print.)

Buyer's or trustee's name   Buyer's trust number (if applicable - **not** an SSN or FEIN)

Street address (after sale)   City   State   ZIP
                                               (   )
Buyer's or agent's signature   Buyer's daytime phone
Mail tax bill to:

Name or company   Street address   City   State   ZIP

Preparer Information (Please print.)

Preparer's and company's name   Preparer's file number (if applicable)

Street address   City   State   ZIP
                                               (   )
Preparer's signature   Preparer's daytime phone

Preparer's e-mail address (if available)

Identify any required documents submitted with this form. (Mark with an "X.") ____ Extended legal description   ____Form PTAX-203-A
                                                                                   ____ Itemized list of personal property ____Form PTAX-203-B

To be completed by the Chief County Assessment Officer	
1 ___ ___ ___ ___ ___ ___ County Township Class Cook-Minor Code 1 Code 2	**3** Year prior to sale ___ ___ ___ ___
	4 Does the sale involve a mobile home assessed as
2 Board of Review's final assessed value for the assessment year prior to the year of sale.	real estate? ___ Yes ___ No
Land ___,___ ___ ___,___ ___ ___,___ ___ ___	**5** Comments
Buildings ___,___ ___ ___,___ ___ ___,___ ___ ___	
Total ___,___ ___ ___,___ ___ ___,___ ___ ___	
Illinois Department of Revenue Use	**Tab number**

COOK COUNTY

REAL ESTATE TRANSFER DECLARATION

The following is required by the Cook County Real Property Tax Ordinance effective September 1, 1993. Any transferor of transferee who fails to file with the Recorder a real property transfer declaration as required by Section 7 of this ordinance or a supplemental transfer declaration as required by Section 10 of this ordinance or willfully falsifies the value of transferred real estate, shall be subject to a penalty equal to the amount of the applicable tax; and shall be fined an amount not to exceed $1000.00 or imprisoned for a period not to exceed six months, or both.

Except as to Exempt Transactions, the Recorder is prohibited by law from accepting any deed, assignment or other instrument of transfer for recordation unless it is accompanied by a declaration containing all of the information requested therein.

Recorder's Validation

PROPERTY IDENTIFICATION:

Address of Property _____

Street or Rural Route   City   Zip Code

Permanent Real Estate Index No. _____ Township _____

Date of Deed _____ Type of Deed _____

TYPE OF PROPERTY:

☐ Single Family   ☐ Commercial

☐ Condo, co-op   ☐ Industrial

☐ 4 or more units (residential)   ☐ Vacant Land

☐ Mixed use (commer. & resid.)   ☐ Other (attach description)

INTEREST TRANSFERRED

☐ Fee title   ☐ Controlling interest in real estate entity (ord. Sec. 2)

☐ Beneficial Interest in a land trust

☐ Lessee interest in a ground lease   ☐ Other (attach description)

LEGAL DESCRIPTION:

Sec. _____ Twp. _____ Range _____

(Use additional sheet, if necessary)

COMPUTATION OF TAX:

Full actual consideration	$	_____
Less amount of personal property included in purchase	$	_____
Net consideration for real estate	$	_____
Less amount of mortgage to which property remains subject	$	_____
Net taxable consideration	$	_____
Amount of tax stamps ($.25 per $500 or part thereof)	$	_____

ATTESTATION OF PARTIES: We hereby declare the full actual consideration and above facts contained in this declaration to be true and correct.

Name and Address of Seller (Please Print)   Street or Rural Route   City   Zip Code

Signature: _____
     Seller or Agent

Name and Address of Buyer (Please Print)   Street or Rural Route   City   Zip Code

Signature: _____
     Buyer or Agent

Use space below for tax mailing address, if different from above.

EXEMPT TRANSFERS

(Check the Appropriate Box)

Exempt transfers are subject to the requirement contained in subsection 7(c) of this ordinance.

7(c)   "No transfer shall be exempt from the tax imposed by this ordinance unless the declaration describes the facts supporting the exemption and is accompanied by such supporting documentation as the Recorder may reasonably require."

☐ A.   Transfers of real property made prior to May 21, 1979 where the deed was recorded after that date or assignments of beneficial interest in real property dated prior to August 1, 1985, where the assignment was delivered on or after August 1, 1985;

☐ B.   Transfers involving real property acquired by or from any governmental body or acquired by any corporation, society, association, foundation or institution organized and operated exclusively for charitable, religious or educational purposes or acquired by any international organization not subject to local taxes under applicable law;
(Copy of IRS granting tax exempt status must be attached)

☐ C.   Transfers in which the deed, assignment or other instrument of transfer secures debt or other obligations;

☐ D.   Transfers in which the deed, assignment or other instrument of transfer, without additional consideration, confirms, corrects, modifies, or supplements a deed, assignment or other instrument of transfer previously recorded or delivered;

☐ E.   Transfers in which the transfer price is less than $100.00;

☐ F.   Transfers in which the deed is a tax deed;

☐ G.   Transfers in which the deed, assignment or other instrument of transfer releases property which secures debt or other obligations;

☐ H.   Transfers in which the deed is a deed of partition; provided, however, that if a party receives a share greater than its undivided interest in the real property, then such party shall be liable for tax computed upon any consideration paid for the excess;

☐ I.   Transfers between a subsidiary corporation and its parent or between subsidiary corporations of a common parent either pursuant to a plan of merger or consolidation or pursuant to an agreement providing for the sale of substantially all of the seller's assets;

☐ J.   Transfers from a subsidiary corporation to its parent for no consideration other than the cancellation or surrender of the subsidiary's stock and transfers from a parent corporation to its subsidiary for no consideration other than the issuance or delivery to the parent of the subsidiary's stock;

☐ K.   Transfers made pursuant to a confirmed plan of reorganization as provided under section 1146 (c) of Chapter 11 of the U.S. Bankruptcy Code of 1978, as amended;
Provide bankruptcy court docket number:_____;

☐ L.   Deeds representing transfers subject to the imposition of a documentary stamp tax imposed by the government of the United States, except that such deeds shall not be exempt from filing the declaration; and

☐ M.   Transfers in which the deed or other instrument of transfer is issued to the mortgagee or secured creditor pursuant to a mortgage or security interest foreclosure proceeding or sale or pursuant to a transfer in lieu of foreclosure.

CITY OF CHICAGO
DEPARTMENT OF FINANCE
REAL PROPERTY TRANSFER TAX DECLARATION
FORM - 7551
This form may also be filed on-line at *ezdecillinois.com/login*

STATUS [   ]
For office use only

ACCOUNT NUMBER ☐

Note: this form must be filled out completely for ALL real estate transfers, including transfers for which an exemption is claimed (see Municipal Code 3-33-070). If any information is omitted, this declaration form will be deemed incomplete and you may be assessed penalties and interest. Please use black or blue ink. You must complete all pages of this form.

Section 1. General Information about Property

For use by Cook County Recorder of Deeds
County document #

Street Number ☐   Direction ☐

Street Name ☐

Date ☐

Unit/Apt # ☐   Zip Code ☐

PIN ☐   PIN ☐

PIN ☐   PIN ☐

PIN ☐   PIN ☐

☐ Check here if an exempt transfer.

☐ Check here if this is an amended declaration.   ☐ Check here if supplemental declarations will be filed in the future.
Original Declaration filed on _____ .

☐ Check here if this is a supplemental Declaration (Open Transfer). ___monthly ____annually _____ other.

Type of property (check appropriate box below)

1. ☐ Detached single family Residence/Townhome
2. ☐ Condominium or Co-op
3. ☐ Parking Space
4. ☐ Multi-unit residential building/SRO
   # of units .. ☐

5. ☐ Mixed use (residential and commercial)
   # of residential .... ☐
   # of commercial .... ☐
6. ☐ Commercial: Place x in box
   ☐ Office   ☐ Shopping Center
   ☐ Retail   ☐ Hotel/Motel
   ☐ Parking Garage ☐ Bank
   ☐ Other

7. ☐ Industrial
8. ☐ Vacant Land
9. ☐ Other (you must attach a description)

Buildings with 4 or more residential units **MUST** attach to this form either (i) the original Multiple Dwelling Registration Statement or (ii) original receipt thereof, disclosing the Buyer/Transferee's registration information as required in Section 8 of this form.

Section 2. Interest Transferred (check appropriate box below)

1. ☐ Fee title
2. ☐ Beneficial interest in a land trust
3. ☐ "Lessee interest in a ground lease"

4. ☐ "Controlling interest" in a "real estate entity"
5. ☐ Interest in a real estate co-op
6. ☐ Other (you must attach a description)

7 ☐ Installment Sale

See Municipal Code 3-33-020 for definitions.

■ ACCOUNT NUMBER [   ]   REVISION NUMBER [   ]   ■

Section 3. Transfers exempt from tax (check appropriate box below)

Buyer Seller

A. ☐ ☐ Deleted

B. ☐ ☐ Transfer involving real property acquired by or from a governmental body; or acquired by a not-for-profit charitable, religious, or educational organization; or acquired by any international organization not subject to local taxes. (IRS notice granting 501(c)(3) exemption must be attached.) (NOTE: Transfers from Federal National Mortgage and Federal Home Mortgage Corporation are not exempt.)

C. ☐ ☐ Transfer in which the deed, assignment or other instrument of transfer secures debt or other obligations.

D. ☐ ☐ Transfer in which the deed, assignment or other instrument of transfer, without additional consideration, confirms, corrects, modifies, or supplements a deed, assignment, or other instrument of transfer previously recorded or delivered. Explain correction:_____

E. ☐ ☐ If claiming exemption under this section, you must check the relevant reason below and fully explain the reason. Attach additional sheet if necessary. Place x in box
    ☐ Transfer in which transfer price was less than $500. Was something given besides money? __ yes __ no. Were delinquent real property taxes paid? __ yes __ no.
    ☐ Transfer to trust by beneficiary (ies).
    ☐ Transfer to beneficiary (ies) by trust. (NOTE; if a beneficiary receives a greater share than the beneficiary's undivided share of the trust property, then the transfer is not exempt. If the beneficiary transfers any consideration to the trust or to the other beneficiaries in return of the beneficiary's excess distribution.)
    ☐ Gift or inheritance. What is the transferee's relationship to transferor? _____
    ☐ Other. Explain _____

    NOTE: Transfers pursuant to divorce or separation are not exempt (See Real Property Transfer Tax Ruling #3. Exchanges of real property for real property are not exempt. The debt includes any debt or obligation canceled or discharged as part of the transfer.)

F. ☐ ☐ Transfer in which the deed is a tax deed.

G. ☐ ☐ Transfer in which the deed, assignment or other instrument of transfer releases property which secures debt or other obligations.

H. ☐ ☐ Transfer in which the deed is a deed of partition. Note: If a party receives a share greater than its undivided interest in the real property, then it must pay tax on any consideration paid for the excess.

I. ☐ ☐ Transfer between a wholly owned subsidiary corporation and its parent or between wholly owned subsidiary corporations of common parent pursuant to a plan of merger or consolidation or pursuant to an agreement providing for the sale of substantially all of the seller's assets.

J. ☐ ☐ Transfer from a wholly owned subsidiary corporation to its parent for no consideration other than the cancellation or surrender of the subsidiary's stock, or transfer from a parent corporation to its wholly owned subsidiary for no consideration other than the issuance or delivery to the parent of the subsidiary's stock.

K. ☐ ☐ Transfer made pursuant to a confirmed plan of reorganization as provided under section 1146 (c) of Chapter 11 of the U. S. Bankruptcy Code of 1978, as amended.
    Provide bankruptcy court docket number: .... [| | | | | | | | |]

    State of Filing/Court District [| |] / [| |]

L. ☐ ☐ Transfer of the title to, or beneficial interest in, real property used primarily for commercial or industrial purposes located in a city enterprise zone. (Conversion from industrial/commercial to residential is not exempt. See Real Property Transfer Tax Ruling #2.)
    Provide enterprise zone number: .... [|]

M. ☐ ☐ Transfer in which the deed is issued to the mortgagee or secured creditor who initially filed the foreclosure proceeding or threaten to bring foreclosure proceeding (when the deed is transferred in lieu of foreclosure):
    Are you the only secured creditor __ yes __ no. (Note: A deed transferred to a junior lien holder is not exempt to the extent of the amount of the lien of the senior (prior) lien holder).
    Did you acquire your secured interest in the property after the foreclosure proceedings were started? ☐yes ☐no.

N. ☐ ☐ Transfer in which the purchaser has completed the State of Illinois' Home Ownership Made Easy Program (HOME).
    Date Completed __ / __ / ____

"Section 3-33-060 (O) includes an exemption for the CTA portion of tax for transferees who are age 65 years or older, who occupy purchased property as their personal dwelling for at least one year following the transfer, if the transfer price is $250,000 or less. This exemption is administered through a refund administered by the Chicago Tax Assistance Center of the city's Budget Office located at 121 N. LaSalle, City Hall, room 604. Application forms are also available online at www.cityofchicago.org/city/en/depts/fin.html"

■ Page 2   Rev 003 022508   **755101202** ■

ACCOUNT NUMBER [   ]   REVISION NUMBER [   ]

Section 4. Additional Transfer Information

1. Enter the earlier of (1) the date of delivery or (2) the date of recording of the instrument of transfer...

2. Does any part of the transfer price consist of consideration other than cash? If yes, attach separate sheet with description of consideration...   Yes ☐   No ☐

3. Is any part of the transfer price contingent upon the occurrence of a future event or the attainment of future levels of financial performance? If yes, explain. (attach additional sheet if necessary)   Yes ☐   No ☐

4. Will this property be converted from it's current use? ....   Yes ☐   No ☐
   If so, what type of use _____

5. If conversion will result in co-operative or condominium units, how many units are expected to result from the conversion? ....

ACCOUNT NUMBER   [   ]   REVISION NUMBER   [   ]

Section 5. Computation of tax stamps purchased (Transfer price must be included on line 4, even if transfer is exempt; if exempt, do not compute beyond line 4). NOTE: With the exception of line 5, you must round to the nearest whole number for the following amounts.

1. Total amount paid ....

2. Fair Market Value of personal property ....

3. Fair Market Value of other property (fully describe other property) ....

4. Transfer price (note: transfer price includes consideration in any form. Determined without any deduction for mortgages. (see Sec 3-33-020(H)) (Subtract line 2 & 3 from line 1) ...

5. Divide line 4 by $500.00 (note: you must round up to the nearest whole number)...........................

	A BUYER (CITY) $3.75	B SELLER (CTA) $1.50	A + B Total
6. Applicable tax stamp rate			
7. Total value of tax stamps purchased (If buyer, multiply line 5 by line 6A; If seller, multiply line 5 by line 6B..........			
8. Interest (see Section 3-4-190)			
9. Penalty (see Section 3-4-200 and 3-33-110)			
10. Total tax, penalty and interest due (add line 7, 8, and 9)			

Section 6. Title Company Information

[ ] Check this box if a title company is not utilized.

Title Company Name   [   ]

                     First Name   Last Name

Title Company Representative   [   ]   [   ]

Title Company Code # (applicable only if title company resells Chicago tax stamps)   [   ]

ACCOUNT NUMBER [＿＿＿＿＿＿＿]　　REVISION NUMBER [＿＿＿＿＿＿＿]

Section 7. Attestation of Parties　　　　**Seller/Transferor Statement**

Under penalty of perjury, I certify that I have examined this return and it is true, correct, and complete.

Name of Seller if individual

Name of Seller if not individual (include trust name and number if trust)

Mailing Address (after sale)　　　　　　　　　　　　　Daytime Phone Number

City　　　　　　　　　　　　　State　　Zip

Signature of Seller or Seller's agent (required)　　　　　Date

Name of Individual Signing Seller/Transferor Statement (if not the seller)

Title

Mailing Address　　　　　　　　　　　　　　　　　Daytime Phone Number

City　　　　　　　　　　　　　State　　Zip

Business or Firm Name

Buyer/Transferee Statement

Under penalty of perjury, I certify that I have examined this return and it is true, correct, and complete.

Name of Buyer if individual

Name of Buyer if not individual (include trust name and number if trust)

Mailing Address (after sale)　　　　　　　　　　　　　Daytime Phone Number

ACCOUNT NUMBER [   ]   REVISION NUMBER [   ]

City [   ]   State [   ]   Zip [   ]

Signature of Buyer or Buyer's Agent (required) [   ]   Date [| | |]

Name of Individual Signing Buyer/Transferee Statement (if not the buyer) [   ] [ ] [   ]

Title [   ]

Mailing Address [   ]   Daytime Phone Number [| | |]

City [   ]   State [   ]   Zip [   ]

Business or Firm Name [   ]

Section 8. Department Certifications

1. **Building Registration Certificate.** A Multiple Dwelling Registration Statement issued by the Department of Buildings disclosing the Buyer/Transferee's registration information is required for buildings containing either 4 or more family units or sleeping accommodations for 10 or more persons (except if the building is a condominium or a co-op) (Municipal Code 13-10-070). The Registration Statement may be obtained from the Department of Buildings at 120 N. Racine. Check the applicable box:

    ☐ Registration certificate submitted   ☐ Registration requirement is not applicable

2. **Zoning Compliance Certificate.** A certificate of zoning compliance is required for residential property zoned for, or occupied by, buildings having five or fewer units (except if the building is a condominium, a co-op, or a newly constructed dwelling sold to the initial occupant (Municipal Code 3-33-045)). The certificate may be obtained from the Department of Housing and Economic Development in room 905 of City Hall. Check the applicable box:

    ☐ Zoning certificate submitted   ☐ Zoning certificate is not required

3. **Water and Sewer Charge Full Payment Certification** (available at 333 South State Street, Room 330), is required for **ALL** real property transfers.

The Department of Finance certifies that all water and sewer charges rendered up to [| | |]

are paid in full for property located at [   ]

Account # [   ]   Application # [   ]

Certified by [   ]   Date [| | |]

ACCOUNT NUMBER [   ]   REVISION NUMBER [   ]

Section 9. Preparer Information (only preparer's name is required if other information about preparer is disclosed in Section 7 above.)

Name of Preparer

Business or Firm Name

Mailing Address   Daytime Phone Number

City   State   Zip Code   Date

Section 10. Where to File This Form and Purchase Transfer Stamps

1. If the deed or other instrument of transfer is recorded, then file this form with the Cook County Recorder of Deeds, County Building, 118 North Clark Street, Room 120, Chicago, IL 60602.

2. If the deed or other instrument of transfer is not recorded, then file this form with the Chicago Department of Finance, 121 North LaSalle Street, Room 107, Chicago, IL 60602.

3. Real Property Transfer Stamps may be purchased at the Chicago Department of Finance, 121 North LaSalle Street, Room 107, Chicago, IL 60602.

4. For additional information call 312-747-IRIS(4747) and for TTY 312-742-1974)

Place water validation stamp below line

Effective date: 04/01/2008

For DOF Use Only   Postmark Date   Receipt Number

 **Naperville**

REAL ESTATE TRANSFER DECLARATION

Permanent Real Estate Index No. (PIN) _____ Date of Deed _____

Address of Property _____
                    Street or Rural Route

Full Actual Consideration $ _____

Less Amount of Personal Property Included in Purchase $ _____

Net Consideration for Real Estate $ _____

Amount of Tax Stamps ($1.50 per $500 or part thereof of taxable consideration) $ _____

Closing Date _____   School District _____

   Residential Property ☐   Non-Residential Property ☐   Land/Lot ☐

**We hereby declare the full actual consideration and above facts contained in this declaration
to be true and correct. Signature required by seller, buyer or agent**

Name and Address of **Seller** (Please Print)   Street or Rural Route   City, State, ZIP Code

Signature _____
            Seller or Agent

Name and Address of **Buyer** (Please Print)   Street or Rural Route   City, State, ZIP Code

Signature _____
            Buyer or Agent

Check for Building Inspection Fees/Issues Prior to Purchase

** For information regarding the status of any outstanding building permits, building fees, or code enforcement actions and
   outstanding fines on property, you are considering buying in the City of Naperville:
      Please call 630-420-6100   •   For Building Department issues, enter Option # 2

Rev. 7/20/11 LMH

City of Naperville ⚓ 400 South Eagle Street ⚓ Naperville, IL ⚓ 60540 ⚓ Phone (630) 420-4116 ⚓ Fax (630) 305-6226

CITY OF
PEORIA

REAL ESTATE TRANSFER DECLARATION
CITY OF PEORIA, ILLINOIS

Permanent Real Estate Index No._____

Date of Deed_____

Address of Property_____

Closing Date_____

Full consideration	$_____	Amount of tax stamps
		$2.50 per $1,000.00 or
Less amount of personal		part thereof of taxable
Property included in		consideration:
Purchase	$_____	
		$_____
Net consideration		
For real estate	$_____	

We hereby declare the full actual consideration and above facts contained in this declaration to be true and correct.

_____

Name and Address of Seller/Grantor (Please Print)

Signature_____
        Seller/Grantor or Agent

_____

Name and Address of Buyer/Grantee (Please Print)

Signature_____
        Buyer/Grantee or Agent

Please check one:

☐ Property is/will be Owner Occupied

☐ Property is/will be Non-Owner Occupied

FULL PAYMENT CERTIFICATE APPLICATION City of Chicago Department of Finance 333 South State Street- Suite 330 Phone: (312) 744-4426 | Email: fpc@cityofchicago.org Monday-Friday 8:30 AM – 4:30 PM	CERTIFICATE #:	DATE:	A.K.A
	BOOK	Page	MC#(s)

APPLICATIONS ARE REQUIRED FOR ALL TRANSFERS OF PROPERTY. SEPARATE APPLICATIONS ARE REQUIRED FOR EACH PROPERTY TO BE TRANSFERRED.
FPC Fee $50 per account. The FPC fee is waived if the subject property is exempt from the City of Chicago Real Property Transfer Tax. APPLICATION # _____ OF _____ (Qty)
Failure to include all required documentation may result in delay or denial of your application

1. PREMISES INFORMATION
PREMISES ADDRESS(ES): _____
PROPERTY INDEX # (S): _____ WATER ACCOUNT # (S): _____
CHECK ALL APPLICABLE: □ SINGLE FAMILY HOME □ CONDO/TOWNHOUSE/CO-OP (INDIVIDUALLY BILLED) □ CONDO/TOWNHOUSE/CO-OP (ASSOCIATION BILLED) □ CONDO CONVERSION
□ APT BLDG < 6 UNITS # of units _____ □ APT BLDG ≥ 6 UNITS # of units _____ □ MIXED USE □ COMMERCIAL □ INDUSTRIAL □ NEW CONSTRUCTION □ RAILROAD □ REFINANCE ONLY
□ VACANT LOT □ CORNER PROPERTY □ MULTIPLE PINs □ FORECLOSURE □ TAX SALE □ RECEIVERSHIP □ TRANSFER TAX EXEMPT Exemption #_____
□ OTHER _____

2. SUPPORTING DOCUMENTATION REQUIRED
(CHECK TO CONFIRM THE ATTACHMENT OF SUPPORTING DOCUMENTS REQUIRED FOR PROCESSING.)

3. PROPERTY ACCESS CONTACT
SUPPLY INFORMATION FOR A LOCAL CONTACT PERSON WHO IS ABLE TO PROVIDE ACCESS TO THE PROPERTY FROM 7 AM - 3:30 PM, MON - FRI.
NAME: _____
PHONE: _____

DOCUMENT	REQUIRED FOR
□ LEGAL DESCRIPTION	- COMMERCIAL, MIXED USE, CORNER PROPERTY, CONDO CONVERSION, MULTIPLE PINs, APT BLDG ≥ 6 UNITS
□ PLAT OF SURVEY	- NEW CONSTRUCTION, INDUSTRIAL, VACANT LAND, RAILROAD, OTHER
□ PAID ASSESSMENT LETTER	- CONDO/TOWNHOUSE/CO-OP ASSOCIATION BILLED
□ COURT ORDER/DEED	- FORECLOSURE, TAX SALE, RECEIVERSHIP
□ DEED	- ALL TRANSACTIONS

4. BUYER/GRANTEE INFORMATION
NAME: _____ EMAIL: _____ PHONE: _____
BUYER REQUESTS FUTURE BILL TO BE MAILED TO:
NAME: _____ ADDRESS: _____

5. SELLER/GRANTOR INFORMATION
NAME: _____ EMAIL: _____ PHONE: _____

6. APPLICANT INFORMATION
COMPANY NAME: _____ EMAIL: _____ PHONE: _____

PRINT APPLICANT NAME _____   SIGNATURE OF APPLICANT (CIRCLE ONE) SELLER/BUYER/ATTORNEY/AGENT

ACKNOWLEDGMENT - Applicant, as named above, requests that the City of Chicago update its billing records to reflect the transfer or pending of the premises that is the subject of this Application. If new service charges accrue to the account prior to transfer of ownership of the subject property, the Department of Finance reserves the right to recalculate the balance owed. Under penalties provided by law pursuant to Section 1-109 of the Code of Civil Procedure, Applicant certifies that the statements set forth in this document are true and correct. Applicant acknowledges that persons who make material false statements may be fined not less than $500, nor more than $1,000, plus three times the City's damages, litigation costs, collection costs, and attorney's fees pursuant to Section 1-21-010 of the Municipal Code of Chicago.

Applicant, affirms that he, she or it acquired the property listed above pursuant to a judicial deed subsequent to a judicial foreclosure action. The Full Payment Certificate that transfers the above listed premises due to a Judicial Deed to the above named Grantee will reflect zero balance as of the execution date shown on the Judicial Deed. This Full Payment Certificate does not relieve the above listed Grantee of any service charges that have accrued or will accrue after the execution date of Judicial Deed.

_____ Initial here if property acquire pursuant to judicial deed

OFFICE USE ONLY
Water Acct#: _____   Water Charge $ _____   FPC Charge $: _____
Water Acct#: _____   Water Charge $ _____   FPC Charge $: _____
Water Acct#: _____   Water Charge $ _____   FPC Charge $: _____
Based Upon   FINAL METER READING TAKEN _____/_____/_____   NON-METERED _____/_____/_____
1. CLOSING BASED UPON A FINAL METER READING MUST OCCUR WITHIN 60 DAYS OF EITHER: (A) THE FINAL READING DATE, OR (B) THE AUTHORIZATION DATE, WHICHEVER IS EARLIER
2. CLOSING BASED UPON A NON-METERED TERM MUST OCCUR WITHIN 60 DAYS OF THE AUTHORIZATION DATE
3. ATTORNEYS ARE RESPONSIBLE FOR PRORATING FROM THE DATE ABOVE TO THE DATE OF CLOSING. CHARGES THAT ACCRUE AFTER THIS DATE WILL BE TRANSFERRED TO THE BUYER.
CERTIFICATION AUTHORIZED BY: _____   AUTHORIZATION DATE: _____/_____/_____   FPC COMPLETION DATE: _____/_____/_____

IMPORTANT INFORMATION AND INSTRUCTIONS FOR COMPLETING THIS APPLICATION ARE PROVIDED ON THE BACK OF THIS FORM.
White - Cashier's Copy   Yellow - Customer's Copy   Pink - Audit Units Copy   Gold - Data Processing's Copy

INFORMATION AND INSTRUCTIONS FOR COMPLETING THE FULL PAYMENT CERTIFICATE

1. PREMISES INFORMATION
Premises Addresses(s): List address(es) of property. For Condominium or Townhouse, include the precise unit number.
Property Index Number(s): Provide all the P.I.N.s that are identified with the property address(es) listed. P.I.N.s may be obtained from the property tax bill or the Cook County Assessor.
Water Account Number(s): Provide the City of Chicago Water Account numbers for the property address(es) listed if known.
CHECK ALL APPLICABLE: Check all categories which apply to the property. For example, if the property is a 5 unit Apartment Building on a corner, check both APT BLDG<6 UNITS and CORNER PROPERTY; if it is a single family dwelling for refinancing only, check SINGLE FAMILY HOME and REFINANCE ONLY; if it is a foreclosure property transaction, check FORECLOSURE and TRANSFER TAX EXEMPT, etc.
-CONDO/TOWNHOUSE/CO-OP, INDIVIDUALLY BILLED: Check box and circle the property type which applies if it has its own water service (not a member of an association).
-CONDO/TOWNHOUSE/CO-OP, ASSOCIATION BILLED: Check box and circle the property type which applies if a formal Homeowner's Association exists and members pay their water bill through the Association. Further: (a) If the Association's account reflects no past due balance, an FPC will be issued without additional documentation; (b) if the Association's account reflects a past due balance, a formal "Paid Assessment Letter" is required. The Association balance may be obtained by calling **(312) 744-4426**, selecting the "Billing and Payment" option, and entering the water account number.
-TRANSFER TAX EXEMPT: Check this box if the property transfer is exempt from the CITY OF CHICAGO Real Property Transfer Tax Stamp (Municipal Code 3-33-070) **and indicate in the blank the exact code letter found on Page 2 of the Real Property Transfer Tax (RPTT) Declaration (form 7551)** which describes the appropriate category for the property exemption. Contact the Department of Finance Tax division for more information concerning exemptions. The FPC fee is waived if the subject property is exempt from the City of Chicago Real Property Transfer Tax.

2. SUPPORTING DOCUMENTATION
Check the document category that corresponds to the property or transaction type listed and submit the required document(s) with the application.
-ALL TRANSACTIONS: The signed, notorized, and unrecorded deed must be provided. A signed sales contract or title commitment can be submitted if the deed has not been prepared. However, the deed must be provided if the application is marked Transfer Tax Exempt.
-NEW CONSTRUCTION, REHABS AND CONDO CONVERSIONS: a) All necessary plumbing permits must be obtained; (b) the Meter(s) must be set by a licensed, bonded plumbing contractor; (c) the Meter(s) must be "controlled" by the Meter Shop – necessary arrangements may be made by calling **(312) 747-2862.** A property that is in the hands of a developer is not treated as a condo until 75% of the units have been sold.
SPECIAL NOTE: In addition, it is possible that after field review, properties not listed in the documentation categories may still require additional documents, such as Legal descriptions and/or Plats of Survey to be submitted in order for the application to be processed.

3. PROPERTY ACCESS CONTACT
Name/ Local Daytime Phone: Provide the name and local phone of a contact person who can provide access to the property in case the property needs to be accessed for a meter reading, confirmation of accounts, etc. This person **must be available** to provide access on the scheduled reading date **between the hours of 7 AM and 3:30 PM.**

4. BUYER INFORMATION
Provide the name of the buyer, current contact phone and email address. Provide name of buyer's attorney and phone number. Under *BUYER REQUESTS FUTURE BILLS BE MAILED TO,* provide the exact address to which the buyer wishes the bills to be mailed. Clearly indicate if bills are to be sent in care of (c/o) a party or entity other than the buyer.

5. SELLER INFORMATION
Provide the name of the seller, current address, contact phone and email address. Provide the name of the seller's attorney and contact phone.

6. APPLICANT INFORMATION
Provide the name, address, contact phone and email address of the person who is submitting the application. Applicant must print name, sign and indicate the relationship to the transaction underneath the signature line (seller, buyer, preparer, or attorney). When the FPC is ready for payment and download, an email will be sent to the address provided.

FPC APPLICATIONS BY EMAIL: Email all applications to: fpc@cityofchicago.org.
Emailed applications must include all necessary documentation as specified on the application. When emailing a legal description, an address must be written on the legal document. Once the application is processed, an email will be sent to the address provided in Section Six. The email will contain a link and instructions for paying any remaining balance and downloading the certificate.

Certificate of Zoning Compliance

A Certificate of Zoning Compliance is required whenever residential property containing five or fewer dwelling units is transferred or sold in the City of Chicago. The requirement does not apply to the transfer or sale of condominiums or cooperative buildings.

A Certificate of Zoning Compliance certifies the number of residential dwelling units at the property that are legal under the Chicago Zoning Ordinance. Under the ordinance, a dwelling unit is "one or more rooms arranged, designed or used as independent living quarters for a single household. Buildings with more than one kitchen or more than one set of cooking facilities are deemed to contain multiple dwelling units unless the additional cooking facilities are clearly accessory and not intended to serve additional households."

The Department of Housing and Economic Development makes an initial decision within five business days after an application is received. When the number of legal dwelling units cannot be certified based on a review of the ordinance and city records, an inspection of the property is performed.

If certification is denied, the contact person listed on the application will be notified. Any person whose application is denied may request that the Zoning Administrator reconsider his or her determination. If such a request for reconsideration is made, the Zoning Administrator shall review any additional information presented and shall have an on-site inspection of the property conducted, even if an on-site inspection was previously made. No on-site inspection shall be conducted without the prior written consent of the owner or the owner's agent. Within five business days after the request for reconsideration is made, the Zoning Administrator shall render a final decision which shall consist of either issuance of the certificate or issuance of a written statement setting forth the reasons for denial. The failure of the Zoning Administrator to act within five business days of the request for reconsideration shall be considered a waiver of the requirement for the issuance of a certificate.

A certificate does not authorize a property owner to expand a dwelling unit that is a nonconforming use. A nonconforming use is a use that was lawfully established in accordance with the zoning regulations in effect at the time of its establishment but is no longer allowed by the use regulations of the zoning district in which it is now located. A nonconforming use cannot be expanded without an administrative adjustment from the Zoning Administrator or a variation from the Zoning Board of Appeals.

Applications are available at the Certification Window at City Hall, Room 905. The filing fee is $120.

The following information is required:

The property address
Property Index Number (PIN)
The number of dwelling units within the structure
The location of the dwelling units by floor
Owner applicant information
Contact/return mail information

Certificates, if approved, are issued within five business days (not including date of filing, weekends, or holidays) and held at the department's Certification Window. After seven days, certificates are mailed to the applicants.

http://www.cityofchicago.org/city/en/depts/dcd/supp_info/certificate_of_zoningcompliance.html   (last viewed July 31, 2012).

CERTIFICATE OF ZONING COMPLIANCE

Department of Housing and	Phone: 312-744-6317
Economic Development	TTY: 312-744-2950
City Hall, Room 905	No fax filing permitted
121 N. La Salle Street	Hours: 8:30 a.m.- 4:15 p.m.
Chicago, IL 60602-1211	

Date Received:

A Certificate of Zoning Compliance certifies the number of dwelling units at a property that are legal under the Chicago Zoning Ordinance (Title 17 of the Municipal Code of Chicago). This form is for use with buildings containing one to five dwelling units that are not condominiums or co-ops. Please read the instructions and disclaimers on both sides of this form before filling out this application.

This Certificate may be picked up on:

Part One: Application for Certificate of Zoning Compliance

INSTRUCTIONS: This section must be filled out completely, signed by the owner or the owner's agent, and presented in person or by mail to the Department of Housing and Economic Development. Payment of a $90.00 fee is required at the time this application is filed, payable to "City of Chicago Dept. of Revenue." **Please clearly print or type.**

After 7 days, this Certificate will be mailed to the Owner listed in Section 4.

1. Address of the Property:_____

2. PIN: _____ – _____ – _____ – _____ — 0000

3. Number of Dwelling Units at the Property	Main or Front Building	Rear or Other Building
Basement		
First Floor		
Second Floor		
Third Floor		
Other (specify)		
Total:		

4. **Owner Information:**

Name:_____

Address:_____

City:_____ State:____ Zip:_____

5. **Contact Person:**

Name:_____

Phone: _____

6. **I, the undersigned, certify that the information provided above is true, correct, and complete.**

Signature: _____ Date: _____

Print Name:_____ ☐ Owner ☐ Agent

DEPARTMENT OF HOUSING AND ECONOMIC DEVELOPMENT ONLY
DO NOT FILL IN BELOW THIS LINE.

Part Two: Certificate of Zoning Compliance

The application is: ☐ Approved   ☐ Denied

DISCLAIMER: This Certificate does not certify a dwelling unit's compliance with the Chicago Building Code or the permit requirements of the Chicago Building Code.

Certified as _____ total dwelling units

White Copy – Applicant • Yellow Copy – Department of Housing and Economic Development • Pink Copy – Department of Revenue • Goldenrod Copy – Mail-in/Receipt

ILLINOIS TRANSFER ON
DEATH INSTRUMENT

MAIL TO:

_____

_____

_____

NAME AND ADDRESS OF TAXPAYER:

_____

_____

Above reserved for official use only

On this date, _____, _____, (Owner) a _____ person (marital status) residing at _____, Illinois _____, (Address) executes this transfer on death instrument. _____ will transfer upon his/her death the following residential real estate in its entirety:

Street Name and #:   _____
City: _____
County :   _____
State: Illinois
Zip Code: _____
Property Identification Number ("PIN"): _____

(Legal Description)

SUBJECT to all easements, rights-of-way, protective covenants and mineral reservations of record, if any, to _____, residing at _____, and to _____, residing at _____, in equal shares as _____.

Upon my death, I transfer my interest in the above described property to the beneficiaries as designated above.

This instrument revokes any and all prior transfer on death instruments made by the above-mentioned owner for the above-mentioned residential real estate.

Before my death, I have the right to revoke this instrument.

This instrument is to be recorded prior to the aforesaid owner's death in the public records in the office of the recorder of the county in which any part of the residential real estate is located.

_____

Owner Signature

_____

Owner Printed Name

_____

Dated

I, _____, attest that _____, the owner of the above-mentioned property, executed this Illinois Transfer on Death Instrument in my presence on the ___ of _____, 20__. This instrument was executed as a free and voluntary act by the owner. At the time of the execution, I believe the owner to be of sound mind and memory.

WITNESS: ADDRESS OF WITNESS:

Signed: _____   _____

Printed: _____   _____

Dated: _____   _____

I, _____, attest that _____, the owner of the above-mentioned property, executed this Illinois Transfer on Death Instrument in my presence on the ___ of _____, 20__. This instrument was executed as a free and voluntary act by the owner. At the time of the execution, I believe the owner to be of sound mind and memory.

WITNESS: ADDRESS OF WITNESS:

Signed: _____   _____

Printed: _____   _____

Dated: _____   _____

STATE OF ILLINOIS   )
) SS.
COUNTY OF COOK   )

The undersigned, a notary public in and for the above County and State, HEREBY CERTIFIES THAT _____, known to me to be the same person whose name is subscribed as the owner of the residential real estate, appeared before me and the witnesses _____ and _____ in person and acknowledged signing the instrument as the free and voluntary act of the owner who was acting of sound mind and memory for the uses and purposes therein set forth.

_____
     Dated

_____
     Notary Public

My commission expires: _____

This document was prepared by:

NOTICE OF DEATH AFFIDAVIT AND
ACCEPTANCE OF TRANSFER
ON DEATH INSTRUMENT

MAIL TO:

_____

_____

NAME AND ADDRESS OF TAXPAYER:

_____

_____

Above reserved for official use only

The undersigned beneficiary or beneficiaries, being duly sworn on oath state as follows:

That _____, (Owner), a _____ person (marital status) died on _____, 20__, a resident of _____, Illinois, owning residential real estate legally described below:

That the street address of the residential real estate is _____, and the property identification number is _____,

That the Transfer on Death Instrument is dated _____and recorded as Document No. _____ in the Office of the Recorder for _____ County, Illinois.

That the undersigned whose names and addresses appear below are all beneficiaries entitled to receive under the Transfer on Death Instrument:

Name	Address	Share
Name	Address	Share

In witness whereof, the undersigned beneficiaries hereby accept the transfer of residential real estate under the Transfer on Death Instrument this _____ day of _____, 20____.

_____   _____
Signature   Signature

_____   _____
Printed Name   Printed Name

STATE OF ILLINOIS

COUNTY OF COOK

I, the undersigned, a Notary Public in and for the State aforesaid, DO HEREBY CERTIFY THAT _____personally known to me to be the same person or persons whose name or names are subscribed to the foregoing instrument, appeared before me this day in person and swore on oath to the above foregoing affidavit. Signed and sworn to before me this ___ day of _____, A.D. 20____.

_____ My commission expires on _____
         Notary Public

Example: Crystal is selling her house. One month before Crystal lists the home, she has a new roof installed. Crystal fails to pay the roofing contractor. The house sells very quickly, prior to the contractor noticing that Crystal failed to pay. At the Closing, Crystal executes a General Warranty Deed. Three days after Closing, the contractor files a mechanics' lien against the property. The Buyer receives a copy of the recorded lien (which often does not happen) and calls his lawyer. The lawyer calls Crystal's lawyer threatening to sue and the title company, to file a claim with the title insurance.

Crystal has violated the Covenant against Encumbrances, since she stated in the deed that there were no unknown encumbrances (she also violated the Affidavit of Title and ALTA statements). Under the Future Covenants, she has agreed to defend the title (Covenant of Warranty), she must indemnify the Buyer for any losses, such as the Buyer's attorney fee in straightening out the situation, and she must do whatever she can to solve the problem (Covenant of Further Assurances). If the Buyer files a claim with the Title Company, since the Title Company is providing insurance against loss of this type, Crystal must work with them to solve the problem, since she stated in the ALTA Statement that she did not do anything to encumber title. Of course, the easiest thing for Crystal to do would be to pay the contractor, receive a release of lien, and record the release.

996 N.E.2d 44 (2013)

CHICAGO TITLE INSURANCE COMPANY, as Subrogee of Waterside Partners, LLC, Plaintiff-Appellant,

v.

AURORA LOAN SERVICES, LLC, Defendant-Appellee.

Docket No. 1-12-3510.

Appellate Court of Illinois, First District, Third Division.

August 30, 2013.

Flamm Teibloom & Stanko, Ltd., of Chicago (John W. Stanko, Jr., of counsel), for appellant.

McGinnis Wutscher Beiramee LLP, of Chicago (Ralph T. Wutscher, F. John McGinnis, and Kevin M. Hudspeth, of counsel), for appellee.

Justice PIERCE delivered the judgment of the court, with opinion.

OPINION

1 Plaintiff, Chicago Title Insurance Company, appealed the circuit court's order granting defendant's motion to dismiss the complaint with prejudice pursuant to section 2-619 of the Code of Civil Procedure (Code). 735 ILCS 5/2-619 (West 2010). For the reasons that follow, we affirm the circuit court's order.

2 BACKGROUND

3 Plaintiff filed a one-count verified complaint on April 20, 2010, for breach of special warranty deed. According to plaintiff's complaint, Aurora Loan Services, LLC (Aurora), conveyed the subject property located at 201 N. Westshore Drive, Unit 2603, in Chicago, Illinois, to Waterside Partners, LLC (Waterside), by special warranty deed on February 23, 2010. The special warranty deed was recorded on March 11, 2010. Chicago Title Insurance Company (Chicago Title) issued an owner's policy of title insurance for the subject property on March 11, 2010. Plaintiff alleged that Aurora breached its special warranty that it did not do anything or suffer anything to be done to encumber the property when Aurora: (1) failed to redeem a tax sale that was held prior to Aurora's ownership of the subject property; and (2) did not notify Waterside of a pending tax deed proceeding that ultimately divested Waterside of its interest in the property.

4 The following facts are agreed to by the parties. Pursuant to a judicial sale resulting from a foreclosure action, Aurora Loan Services obtained title to the property from Intercounty Judicial Sales Corporation on September 9, 2008. Prior to Aurora receiving the deed, however, delinquent special assessment taxes were purchased by the Salta Group, Inc. (Salta), on June 22, 2007. Salta recorded a lis pendens notice against the property. On February 22, 2010, Salta filed a petition for a tax deed under the June 22, 2007, tax sale. On February 23, 2010, Aurora conveyed the property to Waterside by special warranty deed. The tax sale was redeemable until June 21, 2010. Aurora did not redeem the 2007 tax sale although it did pay the special assessment taxes in 2009 and 2010. Aurora did not notify Waterside of the 2007 tax sale.

5 On March 2, 2010, Salta served Aurora with notice of a petition for issuance of a tax deed. Aurora did not notify Waterside of the petition for a tax deed. On October 29, 2010, a tax deed issued and Salta obtained title to the property. The tax deed was recorded on November 17, 2010. Waterside was then divested of its interest in the property. On December 6, 2010, Chicago Title paid its insured, Waterside, the policy limit and appraised value of the property, $290,000. Chicago Title, as Waterside's subrogee, thereafter filed this lawsuit.

6 The special warranty deed executed by Aurora provided that Aurora "does covenant, promise and agree, to and with [Waterside], their heirs and assigns, that it has not done or suffered to be done anything whereby the said premises hereby granted are, or may be, in any manner encumbered or charged." Plaintiff alleged that the title insurance policy was issued without an exception for the 2007 tax sale and Waterside suffered a full title loss because of the issuance of the tax deed to Salta. Plaintiff alleged that defendant breached its special warranty in that it allowed the encumbrance of the lis pendens notice to remain on the property on the day the special warranty deed was delivered and recorded.

7 Defendant moved to dismiss the complaint pursuant to sections 2-603 and 2-619 of the Code. 735 ILCS 5/2-603, 2-619 (West 2010). Defendant argued that the complaint should be dismissed pursuant to section 2-619 of the Code because it cannot be held liable for Waterside's loss under the terms of the special warranty deed. Specifically, defendant argued that the plain language of the special warranty was limited to actions done or suffered to be done by Aurora which created an encumbrance. Defendant argued that the encumbrance predated Aurora's ownership of the property and, therefore, was not within the scope of the special warranty made to Waterside. Aurora argues that the property was sold for unpaid taxes on June 22, 2007, and it did not obtain title to the property until September 9, 2008. Thus, the prior owner of the property, and not Aurora, caused the tax sale to occur on June 22, 2007. Therefore, defendant argued, under the terms of the special warranty deed, Aurora did not "do or suffer to be done" anything to cause the tax sale encumbrance and it cannot be held liable for an encumbrance caused by the prior owner.

8 Plaintiff argued in response that under the special warranty deed, defendant had (1) a duty to notify Waterside of the existence of the tax sale; and (2) defendant breached the covenant against encumbrances by (a) failing to redeem the property from the tax sale; and (b) failing to notify Waterside of the petition for a tax deed. Plaintiff argued that defendant's inaction encumbered the property by creating a defect in title.

9 On October 25, 2012, after full briefing and a hearing on the motion, the circuit court granted the section 2-619 motion to dismiss with prejudice. The circuit court found that because the delinquent special assessment tax encumbrance predated Aurora's ownership of the property, the encumbrance did not occur while Aurora held title and Aurora did not cause the encumbrance, therefore, Aurora did not breach the special warranty deed. The circuit court also found that Aurora did not breach the special warranty deed for failing to notify Waterside of the existence of the tax deed petition.

10 ANALYSIS

11 Plaintiff argues that the circuit court erred in granting defendant's motion and dismissing the complaint with prejudice pursuant to section 2-619 of the Code. A section 2-619 motion for involuntary dismissal admits the legal sufficiency of the complaint, but raises defects, defenses, or other affirmative matter which avoids the legal effect or defeats a plaintiff's claim. 735 ILCS 5/2-619(a)(9) (West 2010); *Mauvais-Jarvis v. Wong*, 2013 IL App (1st) 120070, ¶ 64, 370 Ill.Dec. 98, 987 N.E.2d 864.

. . .

13 The gist of plaintiff's breach of special warranty theory is that, although defendant did not cause the encumbrance, defendant failed to remove the encumbrance when warranting that it did not do anything or suffer anything to be done to encumber the property. Plaintiff argues that defendant breached the special warranty in one or all of three ways: (1) it conveyed title subject only to taxes "not yet due or payable" even though there had been a prior sale for delinquent taxes; (2) it conveyed title even though there had been a prior sale for delinquent taxes with a lis pendens recorded against the property; and (3) after it was served with notice of the tax deed proceeding, Aurora (a) failed to redeem the property or (b) notify Waterside of Salta's tax deed petition. Plaintiff argues that the circuit court erred in finding that the encumbrance was caused by acts of the owner before Aurora, therefore, Aurora did not breach the special warranty deed, negating plaintiff's claim. We affirm, and find the circuit court did not err in dismissing plaintiff's complaint with prejudice.

14 The primary goal in construing a deed is to ascertain the intent of the parties. *Diaz v. Home Federal Savings & Loan Ass'n of Elgin*, 337 Ill.App.3d 722, 727, 272 Ill.Dec. 199, 786 N.E.2d 1033 (2002). "[I]f language contained in an instrument has a well known meaning and significance in law, it will be presumed such meaning was in the minds of the parties using it, unless a contrary intent is made manifest by other language in the deed." *Tallman v. Eastern Illinois & Peoria R.R. Co.*, 379 Ill. 441, 444, 41 N.E.2d 537 (1942).

15 "A warranty deed is a stipulation by the grantor in which he guarantees to the grantee that title to the property at issue will be good and that the grantor's possession is undisturbed." *Midfirst Bank v. Abney*, 365 Ill.App.3d 636, 644, 302 Ill.Dec. 936, 850 N.E.2d 373 (2006). A special warranty deed is "[a] deed in which the grantor covenants to defend the title against only those claims and demands of the grantor and those claiming by and under the grantor." *Black's Law Dictionary* 477 (9th ed. 2009). A special warranty is a limited form of warranty and recovery only available if the defect in title occurs because of an act of the grantor. 20 Am.Jur.2d Covenants, Conditions, & Restrictions § 62 (2005). This limited warranty "does not render the grantor liable for defects in the title based on events that transpired when the property was in the hands of a prior titleholder." Id. Professor Richard A. Powell notes:

> "If the grantor covenants to warrant and defend title to the property against all claims whatsoever, regardless of their source, the covenant is a general warranty. However, if the grantor covenants to warrant and defend the title

only against claims arising by, through or under the grantor, it is a special warranty. Under a special warranty, if the claim arose under, or due to the actions of, a prior owner of the land, the covenantor has no liability. However, under a general warranty, if a claim is validly asserted against the property, regardless of who is responsible for its existence, the covenantor is liable." 14 Richard R. Powell, *Powell on Real Property* § 81A.06(2)(d)(iii), at 81A-122-23 (Michael Allan Wolf ed., 2000).

16 In considering this appeal, we found no Illinois case law that provides insight into the nature of a special warranty deed. Jurisdictions that frequently employ special warranty deeds inform our analysis of the issues. Courts have found that the grantor of a special warranty deed, unlike a general warranty deed, "does not warrant against defects in the title that existed before grantor was deeded the property." (Internal quotation marks omitted.) *Morello v. Land Reutilization Comm'n*, 265 Neb. 735, 659 N.W.2d 310, 314 (2003). The Florida district court discussed the use of special warranty deeds, observing:

> "Special warranty deeds are used when the grantor is unwilling to warrant against possible defects arising before he acquired title. Frequently, tax title holders, particularly those claiming through an administrative tax deed, who have not prosecuted a quiet title action against the former owners, convey by special warranty deed. A special warranty deed is, of course, effective to convey all the title and estate of the grantor. The covenants as such have no operative effect; they simply define the scope of the liability of the grantor for breach of covenant if less than an indefeasible title is passed." (Internal quotation marks omitted.) *Harris v. Sklarew*, 166 So.2d 164, 166 (Fla.3d Dist.Ct. App.1964).

17 A special warranty against title or encumbrances "is breached only if the grantor's own conduct creates an encumbrance on the title." *ASK Realty II Corp. v. First American Title Insurance Co.*, No. Civ. CCB-04-1400, 2004 WL 1254005, at *18 (D. Md. June 7, 2004). The nature of a special warranty deed does not require a grantor to extinguish all encumbrances on a property in existence at the time the property is conveyed through a special warranty deed. *Woolf v. 1417 Spruce Associates, L.P.*, 68 F.Supp.2d 569, 572 (E.D.Pa.1999). This would render the distinction between a general warranty and a special warranty meaningless. Id. The superior court of Delaware observed:

> "A covenant of special warranty is one the operation of which is limited or restricted to certain persons or claims. As a general rule, where a vendee receives a special warranty or quitclaim conveyance, he takes the estate subject to all the disadvantages that it was liable to in the hands of the vendor, and the law will presume notice of all encumbrances, either legal or equitable. The fact that a vendor refuses to make a full and complete assurance of title is said to be sufficient to excite suspicion and put the party upon inquiry." *Indian Harbor, Inc. v. Sea & Pines, Inc.*, 1987 WL 12424, at *3 (Del.Super. Ct. June 10, 1987).

18 In view of the foregoing, we find the special warranty made by Aurora defined the scope of its liability and placed Waterside on notice that it warranted only against title defects that were caused or created by its own conduct and that it was not responsible for defects arising before it acquired title and it was not required to extinguish all encumbrances on the property at the time of conveyance through the use of a special warranty deed.

19 The special warranty deed at issue provides that Aurora "does covenant, promise and agree, to and with [Waterside], their heirs and assigns, that it has not done or suffered to be done anything whereby the said premises hereby granted are, or may be, in any manner encumbered or charged."

20 An encumbrance is "any right to, or interest in, land which may subsist in a third party to the diminution of the value of the estate, but consistent with the passing of the fee by conveyance." (Internal quotation marks omitted.) *Inland Real Estate Corp. v. Oak Park Trust & Savings Bank,* 127 Ill.App.3d 535, 541, 82 Ill.Dec. 670, 469 N.E.2d 204 (1983). In *Rhone v. First American Title Insurance Co.,* 401 Ill.App.3d 802, 808, 340 Ill.Dec. 588, 928 N.E.2d 1185 (2010), we discussed various aspects of encumbrances and noted:

> "It [an encumbrance] may include any right to, or interest in, land which may subsist in a third party to the diminution of the value of the estate, but consistent with the passing of the fee by conveyance. [citations.] Encumbrances include not merely liens such as mortgages, judgment liens, [or] taxes *** but also attachments, leases, inchoate dower rights, water rights, easements, restrictions on use, or any right in a third party which diminishes the value or limits the use of the land granted." (Internal quotation marks omitted.)

21 In construing the word "suffer," we find particularly instructive a treatise addressing its use in a special warranty deed where unpaid property taxes are at issue:

> "'Suffered' in this context doesn't mean 'tolerated.' It means 'caused to be placed.' Consider the case of a property owner not paying property taxes. Eventually, the state will assert a lien against the property for unpaid taxes. It would be incorrect to say that the grantor 'created' the lien; the state did. But the grantor 'suffered' it to be created by failing to pay. If, however, the present owner paid the taxes but the predecessor didn't, and that is why the lien arose, the owner has no implied obligation to cure it, or any other flaw in title the owner didn't create."

11 George Lefcoe, *Thompson on Real Property* § 94.07 (1994).

22 Under the plain meaning of the special warranty deed at issue, Aurora warranted that it did not do anything to cause the property to be encumbered. The scope of Aurora's special warranty includes only encumbrances Aurora caused and does not include any pre-existing encumbrances which remained against the property through the time of the conveyance to Waterside.

23 Here, plaintiff argues that, at the time of the conveyance to Waterside, the earlier tax sale encumbered the property and defendant, which chose the language

of the special warranty deed, did not except the tax sale from the special warranty. Rather, defendant only excluded from the special warranty "taxes due and owing" and, therefore, defendant is liable for the 2007 tax sale encumbrance. We find this argument unpersuasive.

24 It is clear from the record that Aurora did not do anything to cause the encumbrance: the tax sale. The tax sale was caused because a prior owner did not pay the special assessment tax. Contrary to plaintiff's assertion, the lis pendens notice is not an encumbrance: it is a recorded notice that there exists a proceeding that may affect good title to the property and, if conveyed, the grantee may be adversely affected by that proceeding. *Knodle v. Jeffrey*, 189 Ill.App.3d 877, 888, 137 Ill.Dec. 256, 545 N.E.2d 1017 (1989). Nothing in the record suggests Aurora knew about the tax sale before it conveyed the property to Waterside. Even assuming Aurora knew of this tax delinquency and knew the non-payment would result in a tax sale, the special warranty limited Aurora's exposure to only those encumbrances Aurora created or that existed because of something Aurora did. A tax sale occurs only because there are unpaid taxes. Thus, the tax lien, not the tax sale, is the encumbrance. Aurora did not permit or allow the tax sale to occur. Aurora did not receive title to the property until 2008. The 2007 tax sale occurred prior to Aurora's ownership and, therefore, was not warranted against by Aurora in the special warranty deed.

25 Plaintiff argues that Aurora's failure to redeem the tax sale after it received notice of Salta's petition for a tax deed, and/or its failure to notify Waterside of the Salta's petition constituted a breach of the special warranty deed. First, we note that plaintiff failed to provide this court with relevant legal authority to support its contention that defendant had a duty to either redeem the property or inform plaintiff of the petition for the tax deed as required by Illinois Supreme Court Rule 341(h)(7) (eff. July 1, 2008). The failure to cite relevant authority to support a legal argument can result in its waiver. *Midfirst Bank*, 365 Ill.App.3d 636 at 650, 302 Ill.Dec. 936, 850 N.E.2d 373. Illinois Supreme Court Rule 341 is not a limitation on the court's jurisdiction, however, and we may consider the issue in the interest of finding a just result. *Kic v. Bianucci*, 2011 IL App (1st) 100622, ¶ 23, 357 Ill.Dec. 170, 962 N.E.2d 1071. Acknowledging that there is a lack of precedent on the issue presented by plaintiff, we will address plaintiff's argument.

26 The circuit court rejected this argument, finding: (1) defendant did not breach the special warranty deed because at the time the warranty was made, defendant did not receive notice of the tax deed petition; (2) plaintiff failed to explain why the title examination did not discover the tax sale when performing its due diligence; and (3) case law from other jurisdictions has held that the conveyance of a property through a special warranty deed "puts the grantee on constructive notice of certain defects that may cloud title."

27 We affirm the circuit court's finding that plaintiff's allegation of breach arising from any action or inaction by Aurora after the conveyance is negated as a matter of law.

28 A covenant that land is free from encumbrances is a personal covenant not running with the land. *Firebaugh v. Wittenberg*, 309 Ill. 536, 543, 141 N.E. 379 (1923). A covenant against encumbrances is breached at the moment it is made, when the deed is delivered. Id.; *Inland Real Estate Corp. v. Oak Park Trust & Savings Bank*, 127 Ill.App.3d 535, 541, 82 Ill.Dec. 670, 469 N.E.2d 204 (1983). Therefore, any claim for breach of Aurora's warranty under its terms, must have existed at the time of the delivery of the deed. *Firebaugh v. Wittenberg*, 309 Ill. 536, 543, 141 N.E. 379 (1923). Plaintiff's argument for breach premised on any action or inaction after the conveyance cannot serve as a basis of breach of the special warranty deed. Aurora's covenant against encumbrances was made when the deed was delivered and the basis of any alleged breach of this warranty can only be supported by events occurring when it was warranted, not later in time. See *Firebaugh v. Wittenberg*, 309 Ill. 536, 543, 141 N.E. 379 (1923). Therefore, plaintiff's allegation that Aurora's failure to redeem or notify its grantee after the delivery of the deed cannot constitute a breach of the special warranty as a matter of law and negates plaintiff's claim.

29 Furthermore, the recordation of the lis pendens by Salta served as notice to any future purchasers that a deed received after its recording might be affected by the tax sale. *Knodle v. Jeffrey*, 189 Ill. App.3d 877, 888, 137 Ill.Dec. 256, 545 N.E.2d 1017 (1989). Therefore, the recorded certificate of sale, issued on June 22, 2007, before Aurora purchased the property, put subsequent purchasers, including Waterside, on notice of Salta's interest in the property. Id. Plaintiff has failed to provide us with substantive argument and citation to relevant legal authorities to support its contention that defendant had a duty after the conveyance to take any action regarding the tax sale or petition for the tax deed.

30 In addition, section 21-345 of the Illinois Property Tax Code (Tax Code) governs the right to redeem a property from a tax sale (*In re Application of the County Treasurer & ex officio County Collector*, 394 Ill.App.3d 111, 119, 333 Ill.Dec. 346, 914 N.E.2d 1158 (2009)) and provides that the right to redeem a property from a tax sale exists "in any owner or person interested in that property." 35 ILCS 200/21-345 (West 2006). A stranger to the property, with no interest in the property, has no right to redeem when the property is sold for delinquent taxes. *In re Application of DuPage County Collector*, 98 Ill. App.3d 950, 952, 54 Ill.Dec. 301, 424 N.E.2d 1204 (1981).

31 On February 23, 2010, Aurora conveyed its interest in the subject property to Waterside. Pursuant to section 21-345 of the Tax Code, after the February 23 conveyance only Waterside, and not Aurora, could redeem the property from the tax sale. Because Aurora could not legally redeem the property after the conveyance to Waterside, plaintiff's claim that Aurora breached the special warranty deed in failing to redeem the tax sale after the conveyance to Waterside fails. Therefore, on this basis we find the circuit court property dismissed with prejudice the complaint pursuant to section 2-619(a)(9).

32 Lastly, plaintiff argues that pursuant to the terms of the deed, defendant excepted from the special warranty deed, only the "taxes not yet due and payable" and, by implication, the unpaid taxes which resulted in the 2007 tax sale were covered by the

special warranty. Defendant responds arguing that plaintiff failed to raise this argument in the circuit court and, therefore, it is waived for the purposes of appeal. Plaintiff asserts the argument was raised in its response to the motion to dismiss. The response in pertinent part states:

> "The [d]efendant had a duty to redeem prior to conveying title to the Waterside. Defendant did nothing to cause this encumbrance but if [sic] failed to remove the encumbrance. It warranted that there was no such encumbrance when it stated that the [sic] by the language in the conveyance and that it was subject only to taxes not yet due and payable."

Plaintiff in its response to the motion to dismiss did not argue that the unpaid taxes which caused the tax sale were within the "taxes not yet due and payable" exception. Rather, plaintiff's argument below was that defendant had warranted there was no prior encumbrance that was excepted from the conveyance. This a different argument than presented by plaintiff on appeal. Therefore, plaintiff's argument that the exception to the conveyance clause for taxes not yet due and payable is waived because it was not asserted in the circuit court and was made for the first time on appeal. *Johnson Press of America, Inc. v. Northern Insurance Co. of New York*, 339 Ill.App.3d 864, 874, 274 Ill.Dec. 880, 791 N.E.2d 1291 (2003). In addition, we note that plaintiff failed to provide us with relevant legal authority to support its argument, which is made in a conclusory fashion. " 'The appellate court is not a depository in which the appellant may dump the burden of argument and research.' " *In re Marriage of Petrik*, 2012 IL App (2d) 110495, ¶ 38, 362 Ill.Dec. 374, 973 N.E.2d 474 (quoting *Kic v. Bianucci*, 2011 IL App (1st) 100622, ¶ 23, 357 Ill.Dec. 170, 962 N.E.2d 1071).

33 In any event, the argument is legally and logically untenable. First, the purpose of selling delinquent taxes is to obtain the tax due through the sale and distribute the sale proceeds to the relevant taxing bodies. When sold, the statutory tax lien shifts from the county to the tax purchaser. 35 ILCS 200/21-240 (West 2006). Effectively, the taxes have been paid, therefore, no taxes are due and owing for that tax period and an encumbrance in favor of the tax buyer remains until redeemed or until a tax deed issues. Second, property taxes are a prior and first lien against the property from January 1 in the year in which they are levied and the lien remains until the taxes are paid or sold. 35 ILCS 200/21-75 (West 2006). In Illinois, current year real estate taxes are billed and payable in the following year. By custom and practice, unless the parties agree otherwise, the land purchaser typically receives a credit at closing for unpaid prior years' taxes and the pro-rata share of current year estimated taxes through the date to closing. The exception for "taxes not yet due and payable" clearly applies to taxes levied during 2010 but not yet payable at the time of the conveyance from defendant to Waterside. The special assessment taxes that were sold at the 2007 tax sale took place because they were previously levied, due, payable and delinquent long before defendant conveyed the property to Waterside on February 23, 2010, and, therefore, were not within the special warranty deed exception.

34 CONCLUSION

35 For the foregoing reasons we affirm the circuit court's dismissal of plaintiff's complaint with prejudice.

36 Affirmed.

Presiding Justice NEVILLE and Justice HYMAN concurred in the judgment and opinion.

Chapter 7

Financing and Real Estate Taxes

Learning Objectives

After studying Chapter 7, you will be able to:

- Distinguish between a note and mortgage
- Discuss real estate taxes and the exemptions available
- Explain the foreclosure process

Chapter Summary

Topics covered:

- Notes and Mortgages
- Foreclosures
- Real Estate Taxes

Chapter 7 has three primary topics: Financing of the real estate transaction, real estate tax considerations, and the foreclosure process. Several key terms required to understanding real estate financing are defined, including: note, mortgage, private mortgage insurance, collateral, interest, and points. Real estate taxes are discussed, including how real estate taxes are paid, the exemptions that may be available, and what happens when someone fails to pay the real estate taxes. The third primary topic is the foreclosure process. The reasons for foreclosures and the steps involved in the foreclosure process are discussed in detail. Sample lending documents are included at the end of the chapter.

1. Notes and Mortgages

As described in Chapter 3, it is rare that someone pays for a house with cash, although some forms of home buying may require cash payments (such as buying from a real estate auction, HUD, or sheriff's sale). For most homeowners, a home loan, secured by a mortgage, will be required.

A **note** is a written promise to pay something. A note can be **secured** (that is, backed up by some asset "securing" the note) or **unsecured** (that is, the promise to

265

pay is not backed up by any asset, but is up to the Borrower to pay based upon the Borrower's promise to pay).

Note: A real estate mortgage note ("note" or "mortgage note") is the legal document signed by the Borrower (Buyer or owner, in a refinance) that obligates the Borrower to repay the loan per the terms of the note, including the stated interest rate (fixed or adjustable), for the duration of the loan. The note will contain the important loan elements, including loan amount (that is, amount financed), the interest rate, the date payments are due, where to make the payments, any late charges, and that the note is secured by the mortgage.

Mortgage: The mortgage is the lien that is recorded against the property to acknowledge the Lender's interest in the property and provides the security for the note. The note is secured by a **mortgage** (or, in some states, a **Deed of Trust** or a **Security Deed**). The Borrower (or **Obligor**) is the Mortgagor and the Lender (or **Obligee**) is the Mortgagee. This may seem backwards, but it is the Borrower who is "granting" the mortgage to the Lender, even though it is the Lender that drafts the mortgage.

Deed of Trust: A deed of trust is a security instrument wherein legal title in real property is transferred to a trustee. A deed of trust involves three parties: a Lender, a Borrower, and a Trustee. The Lender lends the Borrower money. In exchange, the Borrower gives the Lender the deed of trust. As security for the promissory notes, the Borrower transfers a real property interest to the Trustee, who is a third party. Should the Borrower default on the terms of the loan, the Trustee may take full control of the property to correct the Borrower's default. The Trustee holds it as security for a loan (debt) between a Borrower and Lender. The Lender is the beneficiary. The equitable title remains with the Borrower. Deeds of Trust often include a power-of-sale clause, which allows the Trustee to conduct a non-judicial foreclosure. A non-judicial foreclosure allows the Lender to sell the property without first getting a court order. Illinois generally does not use Deeds of Trust, but uses mortgages.

Security Deed: A Security Deed directly puts the house up as collateral for the loan. It is similar to a Deed of Trust, except that the Security Deed passes a portion of the title to the Lender as security for the loan. The main difference between a mortgage and a Security Deed is how each is enforced and foreclosed. In the event of a default, the Security Deed requires that notices be sent to the Borrower, along with a publication of the foreclosure notice. In general, Security Deeds do not require any judicial procedures, unless the Lender seeks a deficiency judgment after the foreclosure. Illinois generally does not use Security Deeds, but uses mortgages.

Adjustable Rate Note: A loan where the interest rate adjusts at regular intervals, as defined in the note and mortgage. An adjustable rate note will have an interest rate that is fixed for a certain period of time (1 year, 3 years, 5 years, etc.) and then will change periodically, depending on the terms of the note.

Private Mortgage Insurance: Insurance that a Borrower obtains to insure the Lender in the case of default on the loan. "PMI," as it is called, is generally required when a Borrower has less than a standard percentage (usually 20%) of the acquisition cost as a down payment. This insurance allows the Lender to be "made whole" if the property goes into foreclosure and the property sells at auction for less than the outstanding balance of the foreclosure judgment. If someone has PMI, the insurance will stay on the home until the outstanding balance of the mortgage shrinks to 80% of the home's value. This can happen through payments or through appreciation in the home's value. Certain other home loans such as Federal Housing Administration (FHA) loans and reverse mortgages, may also require mortgage insurance.

Collateral: The mortgage secures the loan; the house is the collateral for that loan. If the Borrower fails to repay the debt, the Lender has the right to sue to take the property and sell it to cover the debt. This is what is known as **foreclosure**. In a foreclosure, the Borrower loses the home and the foreclosure will likely damage the person's credit rating, affecting his or her ability to buy a new home in the future. If the house is sold for less than the outstanding balance, the Lender may receive a deficiency judgment for the unpaid amount.

Principal: The principal is simply the sum of money borrowed on the loan. To lower the principal amount upfront, the Buyer generally makes a down payment, a percentage of the home's purchase price paid at Closing. Most Lenders require a down payment equal to 20 percent of the home's purchase price to qualify for a "prime" mortgage, although private mortgage insurance may be available for Buyers with less than 20 percent down.

Interest is what the Lender charges the Buyer to borrow the money. This is generally on a percentage basis called the **interest rate**. In addition to the interest rate, the Lender could also charge **points** and additional loan costs. A point is one percent of the financed amount and is financed along with the principal.

Principal and interest comprise the bulk of the monthly payments in a process called **amortization** (see below), which reduces the principal gradually over the life of the loan. With amortization, your monthly payments largely go toward paying off the interest in the early years, and gradually reduce the principal later on in the process.

Points: A point is a fee equal to one percent of the loan amount. A 30-year, $175,000 mortgage might have a rate of 5 percent but comes with a charge of 1 point, or $1,750. Lenders may charge one point, two points, or more. Whether there are points or not should be a careful consideration when deciding on the overall cost of the loan.

There are two kinds of points: discount points and origination points.

Discount Points: Discount points are prepaid interest on the mortgage loan. The more points the Buyer pays, the lower the interest rate on the loan and vice versa. Borrowers typically can pay anywhere from zero to three points, depending on how much they want to lower their rates. Discount points may be also be tax deductible. Points as prepaid interest reduce the interest rate, an advantage if the owner plans to stay in the home for a long time. By paying a percentage in advance, it can lower the rate and, ultimately lower the overall cost of the loan through amortization.

Origination Fee: Origination fees are charged by the Lender to cover the costs of generating and making the loan.

A Lender might offer a 30-year fixed mortgage of $165,000.00 at 6 percent interest with no points. The monthly mortgage principal and interest payment would be $989.00. If you pay 2 points at Closing (that's $3,300.00) the interest rate may be reduced to 5.5 percent, with a monthly payment of $937.00. The savings difference would be about $52.0 per month. It would take 64 months to earn back the $3,300 spent upfront via lower payments. If the Buyer thinks he/she will own the house for more than 5 1/2 years, the Buyer save money by paying the points.

Insurance: Properties are generally insured against loss. This is homeowner's insurance. In general, a property that is being secured by a mortgage must have homeowner's insurance for at least the amount of the loan (although having insurance for the total replacement value of the property, including the contents, is preferred). Most lenders will not allow a sale of property to close without proof that the Buyer has adequate insurance. Homeowner's insurance covers the house, land, and personal property against losses from fire, theft, weather damage, and related causes. If the property is located in a federally designated "flood zone" within a flood plain, flood insurance may be required. Flood insurance is administered through the National Flood Insurance Program (NFIP).

2. Real Estate Taxes

Real estate taxes are the taxes paid, twice a year, on the property. Property taxes are paid a year in **arrears**, which means that the payment being made in one year is actually for the previous year's taxes. For example: the first installment of taxes paid in 2017 (generally paid in the spring of 2017) would be for the 2016 tax year. The second installment paid in 2017 (generally paid in the summer of 2017) would be for the rest of 2016 tax year.

Property taxes are based on a property's value. They are often called "*ad valorem*" tax, which means "according to value." Illinois does not have a state property tax. Real estate taxes are paid to the county where the property is located, and vary widely from county to county and from community to community. The property tax is a local tax imposed by local government taxing districts (e.g., counties, school districts, municipalities) and administered by local officials (e.g., township assessors, county assessment officers, county collectors). Property taxes are collected and spent at the county and local level. Real estate taxes are the largest provider of funding for Illinois schools.

Every person and business in Illinois is affected by property taxes, whether by paying the tax or receiving services or benefits that are paid for by property taxes. Owners of real property pay property taxes directly. Even people who do not own real property most likely pay the tax indirectly, as part of the rent paid to a landlord. Everyone benefits from the real estate tax system, since public schools, roads and streets, libraries, police and fire protection services, and county services, are paid for, at least in part, by property taxes.

The way real estate taxes are billed and collected depends on the county where the property is located. For most counties, tax bills are generally mailed by May 1 of the year after the assessment year. The tax bill is mailed to the property owner or the person in whose name the property is taxed.

Property taxes are usually paid in two equal installments. The first installment is usually due on June 1st and the second on September 1st. Cook County, and a few other counties, use an "accelerated" billing method. Under this system, the first installment of taxes is 55 percent of last year's tax bill. This installment is usually mailed in January and, in Cook County, the first installment is due by March 1st. The second installment is mailed in late spring or early summer and is for the balance of taxes due. The balance is calculated by subtracting the first installment from the total taxes due for the present year. The second installment is usually due in late summer.

Many people pay their taxes through the Lender, using what is called an **Escrow Account**. The escrow account is a fund set up by the Lender and the estimate for the taxes and, often, homeowner's insurance, are included in the monthly loan payment, along with the principal and interest. The full payment is sometimes called **Principal, Interest, Taxes, and Insurance (PITI)**. Then, when the tax bills (and insurance) are due, the Lender sends the payments from the fund directly to the tax collector (and insurance company). This relieves the homeowner from having to make the payments. Section 10 of **Real Estate Settlement Procedures Act (RESPA)** controls how much can be held in this type of escrow account. If the amount in the fund is too low, the Lender may increase the monthly payment to help replenish the fund. If the Lender is holding too much money, RESPA places the "cushion" limit at 1/6 of the total disbursements for the year (so, basically, a two-month cushion), the Lender must refund any surplus to the homeowner. Some lenders require escrow accounts, particularly with new homeowners, or with borrowers putting down smaller (less than 20%) down payments. If there is an escrow account, the homeowner should still verify that the payments have been made.

There are also a variety of ways for the homeowner to lower tax payments. These are called **homestead exemptions**. Article IX, Section 6 of the Illinois Constitution permits the legislature to grant certain exemptions. The property generally must be occupied as a principal residence in order to qualify for the exemptions. Here are a few of the more common exemptions that can lower a homeowner's tax bill:

Homeowner Exemption: Residential property qualifies for this exemption from equalized assessed value for people who actually live in the property as the primary residence.

Senior Citizen Exemption:
- Homeowner is at least 65 years old during the year taxes accrued/assessed;
- Homeowner owns and occupies the property as a primary residence; and
- Homeowner is required to pay the property taxes for the residence.

Senior Freeze Exemption:

- Homeowner is at least 65 years old during the year taxes accrued/assessed;
- Homeowner has total household income is $55,000 or less; and
- Homeowner meets certain other qualifications.

This exemption "freezes" the property's assessed value the year that the homeowner qualifies for the exemption. The property's equalized assessed value does not increase as long as the senior qualifies for the exemption.

Disabled Veterans Homeowner Exemption: This exemption may be up to $70,000 of the assessed value for housing owned and used by a disabled veteran, spouse, or unmarried surviving spouse. The Illinois Department of Veterans' Affairs determines the eligibility for this exemption, which must be reestablished annually.

Disabled Persons Homeowner Exemption: Exemption is an annual $2,000 reduction in equalized assessed value of the primary residence that is owned and occupied by a disabled person who is liable for the payment of property taxes. The applicant must provide proof of disability in order to qualify for the exemption.

Note: For a single tax year, the property cannot receive this exemption and the Disabled Veterans Homeowner Exemption. There may be additional exemptions in individual counties or for other purposes, such as making substantial improvements to the house or when natural disasters strike.

Failing to pay the real estate taxes has serious consequences. If someone fails to pay their taxes, the property may be sold for the "back taxes" and the homeowner can lose the property. Article IX, Section 8 of the Illinois Constitution sets the basic requirements for tax sales. Tax sales, redemption requirements, and tax deed issues are often complex and the rules can be confusing. It is a highly specialized area of real estate law.

Annual Tax Sale

If the homeowner does not pay the taxes due, and they are delinquent, the county tax collector (generally, the county assessor or treasurer) lists the delinquent parcels in the Annual Tax Judgment, Sale, Redemption, and Forfeiture Record. If judgment is entered, a lien on the property in the amount of unpaid taxes and other associated costs is offered for sale. The property itself is not sold at this point. The homeowners is mailed an advance notice of the intended collection action and the county collector also publishes an advertisement in a local newspaper before appearing in court.

The property owner or any lienholder may pay the taxes to the county collector any time before the sale in order to avoid the sale. Frequently, the Lender will step in and pay the back real estate taxes and charge the homeowner for doing so. This can also be cause for a foreclosure, as failure to pay the taxes is usually a breach of the mortgage.

At the sale, the tax purchasers receive a certificate of purchase upon completion. The certificate describes the property lien (the back taxes) sold and lists the sale date and amount of taxes and other associated costs paid by the tax purchaser.

The homeowner has the right to redeem the back taxes. The Illinois Constitution gives the homeowner two (2) years to redeem the back taxes. If the homeowner (or other person with an interest in the property, such as the Lender) does not redeem in the allotted time, the tax purchaser may petition in circuit court for a tax deed. The purchaser may also extend the redemption period for up to three years from the sale date.

Sale of Forfeited Taxes (Scavenger Sale)

If the lien for a parcel of delinquent property is not purchased at the annual tax sale, the county may offer the forfeited taxes for sale in the future. If the taxes are delinquent for two or more years, the county collector may offer the property tax lien at a scavenger sale. For example, in Cook County, the biennial Scavenger Sale offers taxes on properties that have delinquencies of three or more years that were not purchased at the annual tax sale. In Cook County, the sale has traditionally taken place in the fall or early winter months and is conducted in odd-numbered years.

Tax Deed Court Process

The tax purchaser may petition in circuit court for a tax deed if the property owner (or other person with an interest in the property) does not redeem in the allotted time. Again, the Illinois Constitution requires that owners, occupants, and interested parties must receive advance notice of the tax deed proceeding. The circuit court in the jurisdiction hears the case (which court actually hears the case depends on the county where the property is located) and enters judgment and provides a tax deed if the tax purchaser is in compliance with all of the requirements. The tax buyer becomes the legal title holder of the property.

3. Foreclosure

If a homeowner fails to pay the note, or breaches some other provision of the mortgage (such as failing to pay real estate taxes or lying on the loan application), the Lender can file a **foreclosure** action. Illinois is a **judicial foreclosure** state. This means that the Lender must go to court in order to foreclosure on the property. In about thirty (30) states and the District of Columbia there is **non-judicial foreclosure**, which does not require court action, but allows the Lender to sell the property at auction without a court order.

General Foreclosure Process

In Illinois, the foreclosure process is governed by the Illinois Mortgage Foreclosure Law (IMFL), 735 ILCS 5/15–1101 et seq. The IMFL provides the exclusive method for foreclosing on all mortgages.

Foreclosures in Illinois take a long time; nine (9) months or longer is common. If the homeowner has a valid legal defense to the court action it may defeat the foreclosure action. If the homeowner participates in the foreclosure, through filing an answer, defense, mediation, etc., this can greatly prolong the foreclosure procedure. Foreclosures have substantial consequences for homeowners and the communities where the property is located. Foreclosure can result in loss of a home, including any payments made to that point, and there is also risk of a personal judgment against them for the remaining debt. It can render a family homeless and ruin credit, since foreclosures appear on credit reports.

Steps in a Foreclosure

Default: A "default" refers to the Borrower failing to make payments or uphold the terms of the mortgage. For non-payment cases, the mortgage generally states that when a Borrower is more than thirty (30) days late, the loan servicer must send a notice advising the Borrower that he or she has thirty (30) days to bring the account current or contact a housing counselor, in which case the Borrower will receive a second thirty (30) day period prior to the Lender taking legal action. This is called the "grace period" and, in Illinois, is a right under law, 735 ILCS 5/15-1502.5. Once the Borrower misses the third payment, the Lender can send a letter of **acceleration**, in which the Lender calls the loan due. The Lender informs the Borrower it intends to foreclose.

Foreclosure Court Filing: In Illinois, the foreclosure must be handled through the court system and must commence with filing a complaint to foreclose. The complaint must include the name of the Lender (and servicer), the name of the Borrower, the mortgage information, copies of the mortgage and note attached, and a specific statement about what relief the plaintiff (Lender) is requesting.

Service of Complaint and Summons: Like in any other case, the defendant (homeowner) must be served the summons and complaint. Personal service must be attempted before publication service is allowed. A "Homeowner Notice" advising the homeowner of their rights, including reinstatement and redemption, must be attached to the summons.

Filing an Appearance and Answer: Defendant (Borrower) has 30 days after service to file an appearance. The defendant (Borrower) may also file an answer. Defendant (Borrower) may also allege defenses or other claims in an answer.

Reinstatement Period: The defendant (Borrower, called the "Mortgagor" in the relevant statute, 735 ILCS 5/15-1602) has the right to reinstate the mortgage within ninety (90) days from the date the Mortgagor was served with the summons or served by publication. It is important to note that "reinstatement" means that the Mortgagor brings the loan current by paying all past due amounts. These include any unpaid principal, interest, taxes, insurance, escrow, assessments, costs, and fees. If the Mortgagor reinstates, the foreclosure shall be dismissed. According to the statute, this remedy can only be used once every five years, if the court makes an express written finding that the Mortgagor has exercised his or her right to reinstate.

Foreclosure Judgment: If defendant (Borrower) fails to file an answer, the plaintiff (Lender) may file a motion for a default judgment. If the defendant (Borrower) files an answer, but there are no defenses raised, the plaintiff (Lender) may file a motion for summary judgment alleging there are no genuine issues of material fact and that they are entitled to judgment as a matter of law. If the plaintiff's (Lender's) motion for summary judgment is granted, a judgment of foreclosure will be entered. If the defendant (Borrower) files an answer and defenses, those defenses will be heard at a hearing. The plaintiff (Lender) has the right to respond, and the court will decide the matter. If the plaintiff (Lender) wins, a judgment of foreclosure is entered. If the defendant (Borrower) wins, the case is dismissed.

Redemption Period: The "owner of redemption" (the Mortgagor or other owner or co-owner of the mortgaged real estate) has the right to "redeem" the amount secured by the mortgage by paying the entire remaining balance, including accrued interest, costs, fees, and any other amount authorized by the court. Under 735 ILCS 5/15-1603, the redemption period is the later of (i) the date 7 months from the date the Mortgagor or, if more than one, all the Mortgagors (A) have been served with summons or by publication or (B) have otherwise submitted to the jurisdiction of the court, or (ii) the date 3 months from the date of entry of a judgment of foreclosure, if the foreclosure is of a mortgage of real estate which is residential real estate at the time the foreclosure is commenced.

Judicial Sale: After the plaintiff (Lender) obtains a judgment for foreclosure, and after the redemption period expires, the Lender may proceed to sell the home by a "judicial sale." Notice of the sale must be given to all parties in the action who have appeared and have not been found in default for failure to plead. Notice of sale must also be published in the newspaper prior to the sale.

Confirmation of Judicial Sale: After the judicial sale occurs, the plaintiff then files a motion with the court to confirm the judicial sale. The court will confirm the sale unless it finds that notice of the sale was not proper, the terms of the sale were unconscionable, the sale was conducted fraudulently, or that justice was otherwise not done. This is pretty rare. The order confirming sale is the final order in a foreclosure.

Order for Possession. An order of possession will also be entered and stayed for at least thirty (30) days. At the end of the thirty (30) day stay, the new owner of the property can evict the former owner of the property.

Deficiency Judgment. If the property sells for less than the outstanding judgment amount, the defendant (Borrower) may be liable for the difference, for the "deficiency." For instance, if the property only sells for $50,000 but the Borrower owes $120,000, the order confirming the sale will establish the defendant (Borrower) is liable for a

$70,000 deficiency judgment. This may be waived by the plaintiff (Lender) or discharged in a Chapter 7 bankruptcy. This is important as it is a personal judgment and the Lender may try to collect on this judgment separately through other collection means.

Key Terms

Mortgage Note
Mortgage
Deed of Trust
Security Deed
Obligor
Obligee
Private Mortgage Insurance
Adjustable Rate Mortgage
Collateral
Principal
Interest
Points
Discount Points
Amortization
Origination Fee
Real Estate Taxes
Insurance
Arrears
ad valorem
PITI
Escrow Account
RESPA
Homestead Exemptions
Annual Tax Sale
Scavenger Sale
Tax Deed
Foreclosure
Default
Foreclosure Judgment
Reinstatement Period
Redemption Period
Right to Possession
Deficiency Judgment

Review Questions

1. What is an adjustable rate note?
2. How are real estate taxes paid?
3. What does PITI mean?
4. What type of foreclosure state is Illinois?
5. What is a deficiency judgment?

Materials in the following chapter appendix include:

- Promissory Note
- Adjustable Rate Note
- Mortgages
- Adjustable Rate Rider
- Condominium Rider
- Planned Unit Development Rider
- 1-4 Family Rider (Assignment of Rents)
- Sample Truth in Lending Disclosure
- *Nationstar Mortgage LLC v. Wayne Canale*, 10 N.E.3d 229 (Ill, 2nd, 2014)

Chapter 7 Appendix

PROMISSORY NOTE

_____ , _____ , _____
[Date]   [City]   [State]

_____
[Property Address]

1.BORROWER'S PROMISE TO PAY

In return for a loan that I have received, I promise to pay U.S. $_____ (this amount is called "Principal"), plus interest, to the order of the Lender. The Lender is _____

_____
_____. I will make all payments under this Note in the form of cash, check or money order.

I understand that the Lender may transfer this Note. The Lender or anyone who takes this Note by transfer and who is entitled to receive payments under this Note is called the "Note Holder."

2.INTEREST

Interest will be charged on unpaid principal until the full amount of Principal has been paid. I will pay interest at a yearly rate of _____%.

The interest rate required by this Section 2 is the rate I will pay both before and after any default described in Section 6(B) of this Note.

3.PAYMENTS

(A)Time and Place of Payments

I will pay principal and interest by making a payment every month.

I will make my monthly payment on the _____ day of each month beginning on _____, _____. I will make these payments every month until I have paid all of the principal and interest and any other charges described below that I may owe under this Note. Each monthly payment will be applied as of its scheduled due date and will be applied to interest before Principal. If, on _____, 20_____, I still owe amounts under this Note, I will pay those amounts in full on that date, which is called the "Maturity Date."

I will make my monthly payments at _____ _____ or at a different place if required by the Note Holder.

(B)Amount of Monthly Payments

My monthly payment will be in the amount of U.S. $_____.

4.BORROWER'S RIGHT TO PREPAY

I have the right to make payments of Principal at any time before they are due. A payment of Principal only is known as a "Prepayment." When I make a Prepayment, I will tell the Note Holder in writing that I am doing so. I may not designate a payment as a Prepayment if I have not made all the monthly payments due under the Note.

I may make a full Prepayment or partial Prepayments without paying a Prepayment charge. The Note Holder will use my Prepayments to reduce the amount of Principal that I owe under this Note. However, the Note Holder may apply my Prepayment to the accrued and unpaid interest on the Prepayment amount, before applying my Prepayment to reduce the Principal amount of the Note. If I make a partial Prepayment, there will be no changes in the due date or in the amount of my monthly payment unless the Note Holder agrees in writing to those changes.

5.LOAN CHARGES

If a law, which applies to this loan and which sets maximum loan charges, is finally interpreted so that the interest or other loan charges collected or to be collected in connection with this loan exceed the permitted limits, then: (a) any such loan charge shall be reduced by the amount necessary to reduce the charge to the permitted limit; and (b) any sums already collected from me which exceeded permitted limits will be refunded to me. The Note Holder may choose to make this refund by reducing the Principal I owe under this Note or by making a direct payment to me. If a refund reduces Principal, the reduction will be treated as a partial Prepayment.

6.BORROWER'S FAILURE TO PAY AS REQUIRED

(A)Late Charge for Overdue Payments

If the Note Holder has not received the full amount of any monthly payment by the end of _____ calendar days after the date it is due, I will pay a late charge to the Note Holder. The amount of the charge will be _____% of my overdue payment of principal and interest. I will pay this late charge promptly but only once on each late payment.

(B)Default

If I do not pay the full amount of each monthly payment on the date it is due, I will be in default.

(C)Notice of Default

If I am in default, the Note Holder may send me a written notice telling me that if I do not pay the overdue amount by a certain date, the Note Holder may require me to pay immediately the full amount of Principal which has not been paid and all the interest that I owe on that amount. That date must be at least 30 days after the date on which the notice is mailed to me or delivered by other means.

(D)No Waiver by Note Holder

Even if, at a time when I am in default, the Note Holder does not require me to pay immediately in full as described above, the Note Holder will still have the right to do so if I am in default at a later time.

(E)Payment of Note Holder's Costs and Expenses

If the Note Holder has required me to pay immediately in full as described above, the Note Holder will have the right to be paid back by me for all of its costs and expenses in enforcing this Note to the extent not prohibited by applicable law. Those expenses include, for example, reasonable attorneys' fees.

7.GIVING OF NOTICES

Unless applicable law requires a different method, any notice that must be given to me under this Note will be given by delivering it or by mailing it by first class mail to me at the Property Address above or at a different address if I give the Note Holder a notice of my different address.

Any notice that must be given to the Note Holder under this Note will be given by delivering it or by mailing it by first class mail to the Note Holder at the address stated in Section 3(A) above or at a different address if I am given a notice of that different address.

8.OBLIGATIONS OF PERSONS UNDER THIS NOTE

If more than one person signs this Note, each person is fully and personally obligated to keep all of the promises made in this Note, including the promise to pay the full amount owed. Any person who is a guarantor, surety or endorser of this Note is also obligated to do these things. Any person who takes over these obligations, including the obligations of a guarantor, surety or endorser of this Note, is also obligated to keep all of the promises made in this Note. The Note Holder may enforce its rights under this Note against each person individually or against all of us together. This means that any one of us may be required to pay all of the amounts owed under this Note.

9.WAIVERS

I waive the rights of Presentment and Notice of Dishonor. "Presentment" means the right to require the Note Holder to demand payment of amounts due. "Notice of Dishonor" means the right to require the Note Holder to give notice to other persons that amounts due have not been paid.

10.UNIFORM SECURED NOTE

This Note is a uniform instrument with limited variations in some jurisdictions. In addition to the protections given to the Note Holder under this Note, a Mortgage, Deed of Trust, or Security Deed (the "Security Instrument"), dated the same date as this Note, protects the Note Holder from possible losses which might result if I do not keep the promises which I make in this Note. That Security Instrument describes how and under what conditions I may be required to make immediate payment in full of all amounts I owe under this Note. Some of those conditions are described as follows:

> If all or any part of the Property or any Interest in the Property is sold or transferred (or if Borrower is not a natural person and a beneficial interest in Borrower is sold or transferred) without Lender's prior written consent, Lender may require immediate payment in full of all sums secured by this Security Instrument. However, this option shall not be exercised by Lender if such exercise is prohibited by Applicable Law.

> If Lender exercises this option, Lender shall give Borrower notice of acceleration. The notice shall provide a period of not less than 30 days from the date the notice is given in accordance with Section 15 within which Borrower must pay all sums secured by this Security Instrument. If Borrower fails to pay these sums prior to the expiration of this period, Lender may invoke any remedies permitted by this Security Instrument without further notice or demand on Borrower.

WITNESS THE HAND(S) AND SEAL(S) OF THE UNDERSIGNED.

_____ (Seal)

Borrower

_____ (Seal)

Borrower

[Sign Original Only]

ADJUSTABLE RATE NOTE

(1 Year Treasury Index — Rate Caps)

THIS NOTE CONTAINS PROVISIONS ALLOWING FOR CHANGES IN MY INTEREST RATE AND MY MONTHLY PAYMENT. THIS NOTE LIMITS THE AMOUNT MY INTEREST RATE CAN CHANGE AT ANY ONE TIME AND THE MAXIMUM RATE I MUST PAY.

_____, _____, _____

[Date]   [City]   [State]

_____

[Property Address]

1.   BORROWER'S PROMISE TO PAY

In return for a loan that I have received, I promise to pay U.S. $_____ (this amount is called "Principal"), plus interest, to the order of the Lender. The Lender   is

_____.

I will make all payments under this Note in the form of cash, check or money order.

I understand that the Lender may transfer this Note. The Lender or anyone who takes this Note by transfer and who is entitled to receive payments under this Note is called the "Note Holder."

2.   INTEREST

Interest will be charged on unpaid principal until the full amount of Principal has been paid. I will pay interest at a yearly rate of _____%. The interest rate I will pay will change in accordance with Section 4 of this Note.

The interest rate required by this Section 2 and Section 4 of this Note is the rate I will pay both before and after any default described in Section 7(B) of this Note.

3.   PAYMENTS

(A) Time and Place of Payments

I will pay principal and interest by making a payment every month.

I will make my monthly payment on the first day of each month beginning on _____, _____. I will make these payments every month until I have paid all of the principal and interest and any other charges described below that I may owe under this Note. Each monthly payment will be applied as of its scheduled due date and will be applied to interest before Principal. If, on _____, 20____, I still owe amounts under this Note, I will pay those amounts in full on that date, which is called the "Maturity Date."

I will make my monthly payments at _____

_____

or at a different place if required by the Note Holder.

(B) Amount of My Initial Monthly Payments

Each of my initial monthly payments will be in the amount of U.S. $_____. This amount may change.

(C) Monthly Payment Changes

Changes in my monthly payment will reflect changes in the unpaid principal of my loan and in the interest rate that I must pay. The Note Holder will determine my new interest rate and the changed amount of my monthly payment in accordance with Section 4 of this Note.

4.   INTEREST RATE AND MONTHLY PAYMENT CHANGES

(A) Change Dates

The interest rate I will pay may change on the first day of _____, _____, and on that day every 12th month thereafter. Each date on which my interest rate could change is called a "Change Date."

(B) The Index

Beginning with the first Change Date, my interest rate will be based on an Index. The "Index" is the weekly average yield on United States Treasury securities adjusted to a constant maturity of one year, as made available by the Federal Reserve Board. The most recent Index figure available as of the date 45 days before each Change Date is called the "Current Index."

If the Index is no longer available, the Note Holder will choose a new index which is based upon comparable information. The Note Holder will give me notice of this choice.

(C) Calculation of Changes

Before each Change Date, the Note Holder will calculate my new interest rate by adding _____ _____ percentage points (_____%) to the Current Index. The Note Holder will then round the result of this addition to the nearest one-eighth of one percentage point (0.125%). Subject to the limits stated in Section 4(D) below, this rounded amount will be my new interest rate until the next Change Date.

The Note Holder will then determine the amount of the monthly payment that would be sufficient to repay the unpaid principal that I am expected to owe at the Change Date in full on the Maturity Date at my new interest rate in substantially equal payments. The result of this calculation will be the new amount of my monthly payment.

(D) Limits on Interest Rate Changes

The interest rate I am required to pay at the first Change Date will not be greater than _____% or less than _____%. Thereafter, my interest rate will never be increased or decreased on any single Change Date by more than one percentage point (1.0%) from the rate of interest I have been paying for the preceding 12 months. My interest rate will never be greater than _____%.

(E) Effective Date of Changes

My new interest rate will become effective on each Change Date. I will pay the amount of my new monthly payment beginning on the first monthly payment date after the Change Date until the amount of my monthly payment changes again.

(F) Notice of Changes

The Note Holder will deliver or mail to me a notice of any changes in my interest rate and the amount of my monthly payment before the effective date of any change. The notice will include information required by law to be given to me and also the title and telephone number of a person who will answer any question I may have regarding the notice.

5. BORROWER'S RIGHT TO PREPAY

I have the right to make payments of Principal at any time before they are due. A payment of Principal only is known as a "Prepayment." When I make a Prepayment, I will tell the Note Holder in writing that I am doing so. I may not designate a payment as a Prepayment if I have not made all the monthly payments due under the Note.

I may make a full Prepayment or partial Prepayments without paying a Prepayment charge. The Note Holder will use my prepayments to reduce the amount of Principal that I owe under this Note. However, the Note Holder may apply my Prepayment to the accrued and unpaid interest on the Prepayment amount, before applying my Prepayment to reduce the Principal amount of the Note. If I make a partial Prepayment, there will be no changes in the due dates of my monthly payment unless the Note Holder agrees in writing to those changes. My partial Prepayment may reduce the amount of my monthly payments after the first Change Date following my partial Prepayment. However, any reduction due to my partial Prepayment may be offset by an interest rate increase.

6. LOAN CHARGES

If a law, which applies to this loan and which sets maximum loan charges, is finally interpreted so that the interest or other loan charges collected or to be collected in connection with this loan exceed the permitted limits, then: (a) any such loan charge shall be reduced by the amount necessary to reduce the charge to the permitted limit; and (b) any sums already collected from me which exceeded permitted limits will be refunded to me. The Note Holder may choose to make this refund by reducing the Principal I owe under this Note or by making a direct payment to me. If a refund reduces Principal, the reduction will be treated as a partial Prepayment.

7. BORROWER'S FAILURE TO PAY AS REQUIRED

(A) Late Charges for Overdue Payments

If the Note Holder has not received the full amount of any monthly payment by the end of __ calendar days after the date it is due, I will pay a late charge to the Note Holder. The amount of the charge will be ___% of my overdue payment of principal and interest. I will pay this late charge promptly but only once on each late payment.

(B) Default

If I do not pay the full amount of each monthly payment on the date it is due, I will be in default.

(C) Notice of Default

If I am in default, the Note Holder may send me a written notice telling me that if I do not pay the overdue amount by a certain date, the Note Holder may require me to pay immediately the full amount of Principal which has not been paid and all the interest that I owe on that amount. That date must be at least 30 days after the date on which the notice is mailed to me or delivered by other means.

(D) No Waiver by Note Holder

Even if, at a time when I am in default, the Note Holder does not require me to pay immediately in full as described above, the Note Holder will still have the right to do so if I am in default at a later time.

(E) Payment of Note Holder's Costs and Expenses

If the Note Holder has required me to pay immediately in full as described above, the Note Holder will have the right to be paid back by me for all of its costs and expenses in enforcing this Note to the extent not prohibited by applicable law. Those expenses include, for example, reasonable attorneys' fees.

8.   GIVING OF NOTICES

Unless applicable law requires a different method, any notice that must be given to me under this Note will be given by delivering it or by mailing it by first class mail to me at the Property Address above or at a different address if I give the Note Holder a notice of my different address.

Any notice that must be given to the Note Holder under this Note will be given by delivering it or by mailing it by first class mail to the Note Holder at the address stated in Section 3(A) above or at a different address if I am given a notice of that different address.

9.   OBLIGATIONS OF PERSONS UNDER THIS NOTE

If more than one person signs this Note, each person is fully and personally obligated to keep all of the promises made in this Note, including the promise to pay the full amount owed. Any person who is a guarantor, surety or endorser of this Note is also obligated to do these things. Any person who takes over these obligations, including the obligations of a guarantor, surety or endorser of this Note, is also obligated to keep all of the promises made in this Note. The Note Holder may enforce its rights under this Note against each person individually or against all of us together. This means that any one of us may be required to pay all of the amounts owed under this Note.

10.   WAIVERS

I waive the rights of Presentment and Notice of Dishonor. "Presentment" means the right to require the Note Holder to demand payment of amounts due. "Notice of Dishonor" means the right to require the Note Holder to give notice to other persons that amounts due have not been paid.

11.   UNIFORM SECURED NOTE

This Note is a uniform instrument with limited variations in some jurisdictions. In addition to the protections given to the Note Holder under this Note, a Mortgage, Deed of Trust, or Security Deed (the "Security Instrument"), dated the same date as this Note, protects the Note Holder from possible losses which might result if I do not keep the promises which I make in this Note. That Security Instrument describes how and under what conditions I may be required to make immediate payment in full of all amounts I owe under this Note. Some of those conditions are described as follows:

If all or any part of the Property or any Interest in the Property is sold or transferred (or if Borrower is not a natural person and a beneficial interest in Borrower is sold or transferred) without Lender's prior written consent, Lender may require immediate payment in full of all sums secured by this Security Instrument. However, this option shall not be exercised by Lender if such exercise is prohibited by Applicable Law. Lender also shall not exercise this option if: (a) Borrower causes to be submitted to Lender information required by Lender to evaluate the intended transferee as if a new loan were being made to the transferee; and (b) Lender reasonably determines that Lender's security will not be impaired by the loan assumption and that the risk of a breach of any covenant or agreement in this Security Instrument is acceptable to Lender.

To the extent permitted by Applicable Law, Lender may charge a reasonable fee as a condition to Lender's consent to the loan assumption. Lender may also require the transferee to sign an assumption agreement that is acceptable to Lender and that obligates the transferee to keep all the promises and agreements made in the Note and in this Security Instrument. Borrower will continue to be obligated under the Note and this Security Instrument unless Lender releases Borrower in writing.

If Lender exercises the option to require immediate payment in full, Lender shall give Borrower notice of acceleration. The notice shall provide a period of not less than 30 days from the date the notice is given in accordance with Section 15 within which Borrower must pay all sums secured by this Security Instrument. If Borrower fails to pay these sums prior to the expiration of this period, Lender may invoke any remedies permitted by this Security Instrument without further notice or demand on Borrower.

WITNESS THE HAND(S) AND SEAL(S) OF THE UNDERSIGNED.

_____ (Seal)
                                                                    Borrower

_____(Seal)
                                                                    Borrower

_____(Seal)
                                                                    Borrower

[Sign Original Only]

After Recording Return To:

_____

_____

_____

_____

_____[Space Above This Line For Recording Data]_____

MORTGAGE

DEFINITIONS

Words used in multiple sections of this document are defined below and other words are defined in Sections 3, 11, 13, 18, 20 and 21. Certain rules regarding the usage of words used in this document are also provided in Section 16.

(A)   **"Security Instrument"** means this document, which is dated _____, _____, together with all Riders to this document.

(B)   **"Borrower"**   is _____. Borrower is the mortgagor under this Security Instrument.

(C)   **"Lender"**   is _____. Lender is a _____ organized and existing under the laws of _____. Lender's address is _____. Lender is the mortgagee under this Security Instrument.

(D)   **"Note"** means the promissory note signed by Borrower and dated _____, _____. The Note states that Borrower owes Lender _____ Dollars (U.S. $_____) plus interest. Borrower has promised to pay this debt in regular Periodic Payments and to pay the debt in full not later than _____.

(E)   **"Property"** means the property that is described below under the heading "Transfer of Rights in the Property."

(F)   **"Loan"** means the debt evidenced by the Note, plus interest, any prepayment charges and late charges due under the Note, and all sums due under this Security Instrument, plus interest.

(G)   **"Riders"** means all Riders to this Security Instrument that are executed by Borrower. The following Riders are to be executed by Borrower [check box as applicable]:

☐ Adjustable Rate Rider   ☐ Condominium Rider

☐ Second Home Rider   ☐ Balloon Rider

☐ Planned Unit Development Rider   ☐ Other(s) [specify] _____

☐ 1-4 Family Rider   ☐ Biweekly Payment Rider

(H)   **"Applicable Law"** means all controlling applicable federal, state and local statutes, regulations, ordinances and administrative rules and orders (that have the effect of law) as well as all applicable final, non-appealable judicial opinions.

(I)   **"Community Association Dues, Fees, and Assessments"** means all dues, fees, assessments and other charges that are imposed on Borrower or the Property by a condominium association, homeowner's association or similar organization.

(J)   **"Electronic Funds Transfer"** means any transfer of funds, other than a transaction originated by check, draft, or similar paper instrument, which is initiated through an electronic terminal, telephonic instrument, computer, or magnetic tape so as to order, instruct, or authorize a financial institution to debit or credit an account. Such term includes, but is not limited to, point-of-sale transfers, automated teller machine transactions, transfers initiated by telephone, wire transfers, and automated clearinghouse transfers.

(K)   **"Escrow Items"** means those items that are described in Section 3.

(L)   **"Miscellaneous Proceeds"** means any compensation, settlement, award of damages, or proceeds paid by any third party (other than insurance proceeds paid under the coverages described in Section 5) for: (i) damage to, or destruction of, the Property; (ii) condemnation or other taking of all or any part of the Property; (iii) conveyance in lieu of condemnation; or (iv) misrepresentations of, or omissions as to, the value and/or condition of the Property.

(M)   **"Mortgage Insurance"** means insurance protecting Lender against the nonpayment of, or default on, the Loan.

(N)   **"Periodic Payment"** means the regularly scheduled amount due for (i) principal and interest under the Note, plus (ii) any amounts under Section 3 of this Security Instrument.

(O)   **"RESPA"** means the Real Estate Settlement Procedures Act (12 U.S.C. § 2601 et seq.) and its implementing regulation, Regulation X (24 C.F.R. Part 3500), as they might be amended from time to time, or any additional or successor legislation or regulation that governs the same subject matter. As used in this Security Instrument, "RESPA" refers to all requirements and restrictions that are imposed in regard to a "federally related mortgage loan" even if the Loan does not qualify as a "federally related mortgage loan" under RESPA.

(P)   **"Successor in Interest of Borrower"** means any party that has taken title to the Property, whether or not that party has assumed Borrower's obligations under the Note and/or this Security Instrument.

TRANSFER OF RIGHTS IN THE PROPERTY

This Security Instrument secures to Lender: (i) the repayment of the Loan, and all renewals, extensions and modifications of the Note; and (ii) the performance of Borrower's covenants and agreements under this Security Instrument and the Note. For this purpose, Borrower does hereby mortgage, grant and convey to Lender and

Lender's successors and assigns the following described property located in the [Type of Recording Jurisdiction]

which currently has the address of _____
                                  [Street]

_____, Illinois _____ ("Property Address"):

[City]   [Zip Code]

TOGETHER WITH all the improvements now or hereafter erected on the property, and all easements, appurtenances, and fixtures now or hereafter a part of the property. All replacements and additions shall also be covered by this Security Instrument. All of the foregoing is referred to in this Security Instrument as the "Property."

BORROWER COVENANTS that Borrower is lawfully seised of the estate hereby conveyed and has the right to mortgage, grant and convey the Property and that the Property is unencumbered, except for encumbrances of record. Borrower warrants and will defend generally the title to the Property against all claims and demands, subject to any encumbrances of record.

THIS SECURITY INSTRUMENT combines uniform covenants for national use and non-uniform covenants with limited variations by jurisdiction to constitute a uniform security instrument covering real property.

UNIFORM COVENANTS. Borrower and Lender covenant and agree as follows:

1. Payment of Principal, Interest, Escrow Items, Prepayment Charges, and Late Charges. Borrower shall pay when due the principal of, and interest on, the debt evidenced by the Note and any prepayment charges and late charges due under the Note. Borrower shall also pay funds for Escrow Items pursuant to Section 3. Payments due under the Note and this Security Instrument shall be made in U.S. currency. However, if any check or other instrument received by Lender as payment under the Note or this Security Instrument is returned to Lender unpaid, Lender may require that any or all subsequent payments due under the Note and this Security Instrument be made in one or more of the following forms, as selected by Lender: (a) cash; (b) money order; (c) certified check, bank check, treasurer's check or cashier's check, provided any such check is drawn upon an institution whose deposits are insured by a federal agency, instrumentality, or entity; or (d) Electronic Funds Transfer.

Payments are deemed received by Lender when received at the location designated in the Note or at such other location as may be designated by Lender in accordance with the notice provisions in Section 15. Lender may return any payment or partial payment if the payment or partial payments are insufficient to bring the Loan current. Lender may accept any payment or partial payment insufficient to bring the Loan current, without waiver of any rights hereunder or prejudice to its rights to refuse such payment or partial payments in the future, but Lender is not obligated to apply such payments at the time such payments are accepted. If each Periodic Payment is applied as of its scheduled due date, then Lender need not pay interest on unapplied funds. Lender may hold such unapplied funds until Borrower makes payment to bring the Loan current. If Borrower does not do so within a reasonable period of time, Lender shall either apply such funds or return them to Borrower. If not applied earlier, such funds will be applied to the outstanding principal balance under the Note immediately prior to foreclosure. No offset or claim which Borrower might have now or in the future against Lender shall relieve Borrower from making payments due under the Note and this Security Instrument or performing the covenants and agreements secured by this Security Instrument.

2. Application of Payments or Proceeds. Except as otherwise described in this Section 2, all payments accepted and applied by Lender shall be applied in the following order of priority: (a) interest due under the Note; (b) principal due under the Note; (c) amounts due under Section 3. Such payments shall be applied to each Periodic Payment in the order in which it became due. Any remaining amounts shall be applied first to late charges, second to any other amounts due under this Security Instrument, and then to reduce the principal balance of the Note.

If Lender receives a payment from Borrower for a delinquent Periodic Payment which includes a sufficient amount to pay any late charge due, the payment may be applied to the delinquent payment and the late charge. If more than one Periodic Payment is outstanding, Lender may apply any payment received from Borrower to the repayment of the Periodic Payments if, and to the extent that, each payment can be paid in full. To the extent that any excess exists after the payment is applied to the full payment of one or more Periodic Payments, such excess may be applied to any late charges due. Voluntary prepayments shall be applied first to any prepayment charges and then as described in the Note.

Any application of payments, insurance proceeds, or Miscellaneous Proceeds to principal due under the Note shall not extend or postpone the due date, or change the amount, of the Periodic Payments.

3. Funds for Escrow Items. Borrower shall pay to Lender on the day Periodic Payments are due under the Note, until the Note is paid in full, a sum (the "Funds") to provide for payment of amounts due for: (a) taxes and assessments and other items which can attain priority over this Security Instrument as a lien or encumbrance on the Property; (b) leasehold payments or ground rents on the Property, if any; (c) premiums for any and all insurance required by Lender under Section 5; and (d) Mortgage Insurance premiums, if any, or any sums payable by Borrower to Lender in lieu of the payment of Mortgage Insurance premiums in accordance with the provisions of Section 10. These items are called "Escrow Items." At origination or at any time during the term of the Loan, Lender may require that Community Association Dues, Fees, and Assessments, if any, be escrowed by Borrower, and such dues, fees and assessments shall be an Escrow Item. Borrower shall promptly furnish to Lender all notices of amounts to be paid under this Section. Borrower shall pay Lender the Funds for Escrow Items unless Lender waives Borrower's obligation to pay the Funds for any or all Escrow Items. Lender may waive Borrower's obligation to pay to Lender Funds for any or all Escrow Items at any time. Any such waiver may only be in writing.

In the event of such waiver, Borrower shall pay directly, when and where payable, the amounts due for any Escrow Items for which payment of Funds has been waived by Lender and, if Lender requires, shall furnish to Lender receipts evidencing such payment within such time period as Lender may require. Borrower's obligation to make such payments and to provide receipts shall for all purposes be deemed to be a covenant and agreement contained in this Security Instrument, as the phrase "covenant and agreement" is used in Section 9. If Borrower is obligated to pay Escrow Items directly, pursuant to a waiver, and Borrower fails to pay the amount due for an Escrow Item, Lender may exercise its rights under Section 9 and pay such amount and Borrower shall then be obligated under Section 9 to repay to Lender any such amount. Lender may revoke the waiver as to any or all Escrow Items at any time by a notice given in accordance with Section 15 and, upon such revocation, Borrower shall pay to Lender all Funds, and in such amounts, that are then required under this Section 3.

Lender may, at any time, collect and hold Funds in an amount (a) sufficient to permit Lender to apply the Funds at the time specified under RESPA, and (b) not to exceed the maximum amount a lender can require under RESPA. Lender shall estimate the amount of Funds due on the basis of current data and reasonable estimates of expenditures of future Escrow Items or otherwise in accordance with Applicable Law.

The Funds shall be held in an institution whose deposits are insured by a federal agency, instrumentality, or entity (including Lender, if Lender is an institution whose deposits are so insured) or in any Federal Home Loan Bank. Lender shall apply the Funds to pay the Escrow Items no later than the time specified under RESPA. Lender shall not charge Borrower for holding and applying the Funds, annually analyzing the escrow account, or verifying the Escrow Items, unless Lender pays Borrower interest on the Funds and Applicable Law permits Lender to make such a charge. Unless an agreement is made in writing or Applicable Law requires interest to be paid on the Funds, Lender shall not be required to pay Borrower any interest or earnings on the Funds. Borrower and Lender can agree in writing, however, that interest shall be paid on the Funds. Lender shall give to Borrower, without charge, an annual accounting of the Funds as required by RESPA.

If there is a surplus of Funds held in escrow, as defined under RESPA, Lender shall account to Borrower for the excess funds in accordance with RESPA. If there is a shortage of Funds held in escrow, as defined under RESPA, Lender shall notify Borrower as required by RESPA, and Borrower shall pay to Lender the amount necessary to make up the shortage in accordance with RESPA, but in no more than 12 monthly payments. If there is a deficiency of Funds held in escrow, as defined under RESPA, Lender shall notify Borrower as required by RESPA, and Borrower shall pay to Lender the amount necessary to make up the deficiency in accordance with RESPA, but in no more than 12 monthly payments.

Upon payment in full of all sums secured by this Security Instrument, Lender shall promptly refund to Borrower any Funds held by Lender.

4. Charges; Liens. Borrower shall pay all taxes, assessments, charges, fines, and impositions attributable to the Property which can attain priority over this Security Instrument, leasehold payments or ground rents on the Property, if any, and Community Association Dues, Fees, and Assessments, if any. To the extent that these items are Escrow Items, Borrower shall pay them in the manner provided in Section 3.

Borrower shall promptly discharge any lien which has priority over this Security Instrument unless Borrower: (a) agrees in writing to the payment of the obligation secured by the lien in a manner acceptable to Lender, but only so long as Borrower is performing such agreement; (b) contests the lien in good faith by, or defends against enforcement of the lien in, legal proceedings which in Lender's opinion operate to prevent the enforcement of the lien while those proceedings are pending, but only until such proceedings are concluded; or (c) secures from the holder of the lien an agreement satisfactory to Lender subordinating the lien to this Security Instrument. If Lender determines that any part of the Property is subject to a lien which can attain priority over this Security Instrument, Lender may give Borrower a notice identifying the lien. Within 10 days of the date on which that notice is given, Borrower shall satisfy the lien or take one or more of the actions set forth above in Section 4.

Lender may require Borrower to pay a one-time charge for a real estate tax verification and/or reporting service used by Lender in connection with this Loan.

5. Property Insurance. Borrower shall keep the improvements now existing or hereafter erected on the Property insured against loss by fire, hazards included within the term "extended coverage," and any other hazards including, but not limited to, earthquakes and floods, for which Lender requires insurance. This insurance shall be maintained in the amounts (including deductible levels) and for the periods that Lender requires. What Lender requires pursuant to the preceding sentences can change during the term of the Loan. The insurance carrier providing the insurance shall be chosen by Borrower subject to Lender's right to disapprove Borrower's choice, which right shall not be exercised unreasonably. Lender may require Borrower to pay, in connection with this Loan, either: (a) a one-time charge for flood zone determination, certification and tracking services; or (b) a one-time charge for flood zone determination and certification services and subsequent charges each time remappings or similar changes occur which reasonably might affect such determination or certification. Borrower shall also be responsible for the payment of any fees imposed by the Federal Emergency Management Agency in connection with the review of any flood zone determination resulting from an objection by Borrower.

If Borrower fails to maintain any of the coverages described above, Lender may obtain insurance coverage, at Lender's option and Borrower's expense. Lender is under no obligation to purchase any particular type or amount of coverage. Therefore, such coverage shall cover Lender, but might or might not protect Borrower, Borrower's equity in the Property, or the contents of the Property, against any risk, hazard or liability and might provide greater or lesser coverage than was previously in effect. Borrower acknowledges that the cost of the insurance coverage so obtained might significantly exceed the cost of insurance that Borrower could have obtained. Any amounts disbursed by Lender under this Section 5 shall become additional debt of Borrower secured by this Security Instrument. These amounts shall bear interest at the Note rate from the date of disbursement and shall be payable, with such interest, upon notice from Lender to Borrower requesting payment.

All insurance policies required by Lender and renewals of such policies shall be subject to Lender's right to disapprove such policies, shall include a standard mortgage clause, and shall name Lender as mortgagee and/or as an additional loss payee. Lender shall have the right to hold the policies and renewal certificates. If Lender requires, Borrower shall promptly give to Lender all receipts of paid premiums and renewal notices. If Borrower obtains any form of insurance coverage, not otherwise required by Lender, for damage to, or destruction of, the Property, such policy shall include a standard mortgage clause and shall name Lender as mortgagee and/or as an additional loss payee.

In the event of loss, Borrower shall give prompt notice to the insurance carrier and Lender. Lender may make proof of loss if not made promptly by Borrower. Unless Lender and Borrower otherwise agree in writing, any insurance proceeds, whether or not the underlying insurance was required by Lender, shall be applied to restoration or repair of the Property, if the restoration or repair is economically feasible and Lender's security is not lessened. During such repair and restoration period, Lender shall have the right to hold such insurance proceeds until Lender has had an opportunity to inspect such Property to ensure the work has been completed to Lender's satisfaction, provided that such inspection shall be undertaken promptly. Lender may disburse proceeds for the repairs and restoration in a single payment or in a series of progress payments as the work is completed. Unless an agreement is made in writing or Applicable Law requires interest to be paid on such insurance proceeds, Lender shall not be required to pay Borrower any interest or earnings on such proceeds. Fees for public adjusters, or other third parties, retained by Borrower shall not be paid out of the insurance proceeds and shall be the sole obligation of Borrower. If the restoration or repair is not economically feasible or Lender's security would be lessened, the insurance proceeds shall be applied to the sums secured by this Security Instrument, whether or not then due, with the excess, if any, paid to Borrower. Such insurance proceeds shall be applied in the order provided for in Section 2.

If Borrower abandons the Property, Lender may file, negotiate and settle any available insurance claim and related matters. If Borrower does not respond within 30 days to a notice from Lender that the insurance carrier has offered to settle a claim, then Lender may negotiate and settle the claim. The 30-day period will begin when the notice is given. In either event, or if Lender acquires the Property under Section 22 or otherwise, Borrower hereby assigns to Lender (a) Borrower's rights to any insurance proceeds in an amount not to exceed the amounts unpaid under the Note or this Security Instrument, and (b) any other of Borrower's rights (other than the right to any refund of unearned premiums paid by Borrower) under all insurance policies covering the Property, insofar as such rights are applicable to the coverage of the Property. Lender may use the insurance proceeds either to repair or restore the Property or to pay amounts unpaid under the Note or this Security Instrument, whether or not then due.

6. Occupancy. Borrower shall occupy, establish, and use the Property as Borrower's principal residence within 60 days after the execution of this Security Instrument and shall continue to occupy the Property as Borrower's principal residence for at least one year after the date of occupancy, unless Lender otherwise agrees in writing, which consent shall not be unreasonably withheld, or unless extenuating circumstances exist which are beyond Borrower's control.

7. Preservation, Maintenance and Protection of the Property; Inspections. Borrower shall not destroy, damage or impair the Property, allow the Property to deteriorate or commit waste on the Property. Whether or not Borrower is residing in the Property, Borrower shall maintain the Property in order to prevent the Property from deteriorating or decreasing in value due to its condition. Unless it is determined pursuant to Section 5 that repair or restoration is not economically feasible, Borrower shall promptly repair the Property if damaged to avoid further deterioration or damage. If insurance or condemnation proceeds are paid in connection with damage to, or the taking of, the Property, Borrower shall be responsible for repairing or restoring the Property only if Lender has released proceeds for such purposes. Lender may disburse proceeds for the repairs and restoration in a single payment or in a series of progress payments as the work is completed. If the insurance or condemnation proceeds are not sufficient to repair or restore the Property, Borrower is not relieved of Borrower's obligation for the completion of such repair or restoration.

Lender or its agent may make reasonable entries upon and inspections of the Property. If it has reasonable cause, Lender may inspect the interior of the improvements on the Property. Lender shall give Borrower notice at the time of or prior to such an interior inspection specifying such reasonable cause.

8. Borrower's Loan Application. Borrower shall be in default if, during the Loan application process, Borrower or any persons or entities acting at the direction of Borrower or with Borrower's knowledge or consent gave materially false, misleading, or inaccurate information or statements to Lender (or failed to provide Lender with material information) in connection with the Loan. Material representations include, but are not limited to, representations concerning Borrower's occupancy of the Property as Borrower's principal residence.

9. Protection of Lender's Interest in the Property and Rights Under this Security Instrument. If (a) Borrower fails to perform the covenants and agreements contained in this Security Instrument, (b) there is a legal proceeding that might significantly affect Lender's interest in the Property and/or rights under this Security Instrument (such as a proceeding in bankruptcy, probate, for condemnation or forfeiture, for enforcement of a lien which may attain priority over this Security Instrument or to enforce laws or regulations), or (c) Borrower has abandoned the Property, then Lender may do and pay for whatever is reasonable or appropriate to protect Lender's interest in the Property and rights under this Security Instrument, including protecting and/or assessing the value of the Property, and securing and/or repairing the Property. Lender's actions can include, but are not limited to: (a) paying any sums secured by a lien which has priority over this Security Instrument; (b) appearing in court; and (c) paying reasonable attorneys' fees to protect its interest in the Property and/or rights under this Security Instrument, including its secured position in a bankruptcy proceeding. Securing the Property includes, but is not limited to, entering the Property to make repairs, change locks, replace or board up doors and windows, drain water from pipes, eliminate building or other code violations or dangerous conditions, and have utilities turned on or off. Although Lender may take action under this Section 9, Lender does not have to do so and is not under any duty or obligation to do so. It is agreed that Lender incurs no liability for not taking any or all actions authorized under this Section 9.

Any amounts disbursed by Lender under this Section 9 shall become additional debt of Borrower secured by this Security Instrument. These amounts shall bear interest at the Note rate from the date of disbursement and shall be payable, with such interest, upon notice from Lender to Borrower requesting payment.

If this Security Instrument is on a leasehold, Borrower shall comply with all the provisions of the lease. If Borrower acquires fee title to the Property, the leasehold and the fee title shall not merge unless Lender agrees to the merger in writing.

10. Mortgage Insurance. If Lender required Mortgage Insurance as a condition of making the Loan, Borrower shall pay the premiums required to maintain the Mortgage Insurance in effect. If, for any reason, the Mortgage Insurance coverage required by Lender ceases to be available from the mortgage insurer that previously provided such insurance and Borrower was required to make separately designated payments toward the premiums for Mortgage Insurance, Borrower shall pay the premiums required to obtain coverage substantially equivalent to the Mortgage Insurance previously in effect, at a cost substantially equivalent to the cost to Borrower of the Mortgage Insurance previously in effect, from an alternate mortgage insurer selected by Lender. If substantially equivalent Mortgage Insurance coverage is not available, Borrower shall continue to pay to Lender the amount of the separately designated payments that were due when the insurance coverage ceased to be in effect. Lender will accept, use and retain these payments as a non-refundable loss reserve in lieu of Mortgage Insurance. Such loss reserve shall be non-refundable, notwithstanding the fact that the Loan is ultimately paid in full, and Lender shall not be required to pay Borrower any interest or earnings on such loss reserve. Lender can no longer require loss reserve payments if Mortgage Insurance coverage (in the amount and for the period that Lender requires) provided by an insurer selected by Lender again becomes available, is obtained, and Lender requires separately designated payments toward the premiums for Mortgage Insurance. If Lender required Mortgage Insurance as a condition of making the Loan and Borrower was required to make separately designated payments toward the premiums for Mortgage Insurance, Borrower shall pay the premiums required to maintain Mortgage Insurance in effect, or to provide a non-refundable loss reserve, until Lender's requirement for Mortgage Insurance ends in accordance with any written agreement between Borrower and Lender providing for such termination or until termination is required by Applicable Law. Nothing in this Section 10 affects Borrower's obligation to pay interest at the rate provided in the Note.

Mortgage Insurance reimburses Lender (or any entity that purchases the Note) for certain losses it may incur if Borrower does not repay the Loan as agreed. Borrower is not a party to the Mortgage Insurance.

Mortgage insurers evaluate their total risk on all such insurance in force from time to time, and may enter into agreements with other parties that share or modify their risk, or reduce losses. These agreements are on terms and conditions that are satisfactory to the mortgage insurer and the other party (or parties) to these agreements. These agreements may require the mortgage insurer to make payments using any source of funds that the mortgage insurer may have available (which may include funds obtained from Mortgage Insurance premiums).

As a result of these agreements, Lender, any purchaser of the Note, another insurer, any reinsurer, any other entity, or any affiliate of any of the foregoing, may receive (directly or indirectly) amounts that derive from (or might be characterized as) a portion of Borrower's payments for Mortgage Insurance, in exchange for sharing or modifying the mortgage insurer's risk, or reducing losses. If such agreement provides that an affiliate of Lender takes a share of the insurer's risk in exchange for a share of the premiums paid to the insurer, the arrangement is often termed "captive reinsurance." Further:

> (a) **Any such agreements will not affect the amounts that Borrower has agreed to pay for Mortgage Insurance, or any other terms of the Loan. Such agreements will not increase the amount Borrower will owe for Mortgage Insurance, and they will not entitle Borrower to any refund.**

> (b) **Any such agreements will not affect the rights Borrower has—if any—with respect to the Mortgage Insurance under the Homeowners Protection Act of 1998 or any other law. These rights may include the right to receive certain disclosures, to request and obtain cancellation of the Mortgage Insurance, to have the Mortgage Insurance terminated automatically, and/or to receive a refund of any Mortgage Insurance premiums that were unearned at the time of such cancellation or termination.**

11. **Assignment of Miscellaneous Proceeds; Forfeiture.** All Miscellaneous Proceeds are hereby assigned to and shall be paid to Lender.

If the Property is damaged, such Miscellaneous Proceeds shall be applied to restoration or repair of the Property, if the restoration or repair is economically feasible and Lender's security is not lessened. During such repair and restoration period, Lender shall have the right to hold such Miscellaneous Proceeds until Lender has had an opportunity to inspect such Property to ensure the work has been completed to Lender's satisfaction, provided that such inspection shall be undertaken promptly. Lender may pay for the repairs and restoration in a single disbursement or in a series of progress payments as the work is completed. Unless an agreement is made in writing or Applicable Law requires interest to be paid on such Miscellaneous Proceeds, Lender shall not be required to pay Borrower any interest or earnings on such Miscellaneous Proceeds. If the restoration or repair is not economically feasible or Lender's security would be lessened, the Miscellaneous Proceeds shall be applied to the sums secured by this Security Instrument, whether or not then due, with the excess, if any, paid to Borrower. Such Miscellaneous Proceeds shall be applied in the order provided for in Section 2.

In the event of a total taking, destruction, or loss in value of the Property, the Miscellaneous Proceeds shall be applied to the sums secured by this Security Instrument, whether or not then due, with the excess, if any, paid to Borrower.

In the event of a partial taking, destruction, or loss in value of the Property in which the fair market value of the Property immediately before the partial taking, destruction, or loss in value is equal to or greater than the amount of the sums secured by this Security Instrument immediately before the partial taking, destruction, or loss in value, unless Borrower and Lender otherwise agree in writing, the sums secured by this Security Instrument shall be reduced by the amount of the Miscellaneous Proceeds multiplied by the following fraction: (a) the total amount of the sums secured immediately before the partial taking, destruction, or loss in value divided by (b) the fair market value of the Property immediately before the partial taking, destruction, or loss in value. Any balance shall be paid to Borrower.

In the event of a partial taking, destruction, or loss in value of the Property in which the fair market value of the Property immediately before the partial taking, destruction, or loss in value is less than the amount of the sums secured immediately before the partial taking, destruction, or loss in value, unless Borrower and Lender otherwise agree in writing, the Miscellaneous Proceeds shall be applied to the sums secured by this Security Instrument whether or not the sums are then due.

If the Property is abandoned by Borrower, or if, after notice by Lender to Borrower that the Opposing Party (as defined in the next sentence) offers to make an award to settle a claim for damages, Borrower fails to respond to Lender within 30 days after the date the notice is given, Lender is authorized to collect and apply the Miscellaneous Proceeds either to restoration or repair of the Property or to the sums secured by this Security Instrument, whether or not then due. "Opposing Party" means the third party that owes Borrower Miscellaneous Proceeds or the party against whom Borrower has a right of action in regard to Miscellaneous Proceeds.

Borrower shall be in default if any action or proceeding, whether civil or criminal, is begun that, in Lender's judgment, could result in forfeiture of the Property or other material impairment of Lender's interest in the Property or rights under this Security Instrument. Borrower can cure such a default and, if acceleration has occurred, reinstate as provided in Section 19, by causing the action or proceeding to be dismissed with a ruling that, in Lender's judgment, precludes forfeiture of the Property or other material impairment of Lender's interest in the Property or rights under this Security Instrument. The proceeds of any award or claim for damages that are attributable to the impairment of Lender's interest in the Property are hereby assigned and shall be paid to Lender.

All Miscellaneous Proceeds that are not applied to restoration or repair of the Property shall be applied in the order provided for in Section 2.

12. Borrower Not Released; Forbearance by Lender Not a Waiver. Extension of the time for payment or modification of amortization of the sums secured by this Security Instrument granted by Lender to Borrower or any Successor in Interest of Borrower shall not operate to release the liability of Borrower or any Successors in Interest of Borrower. Lender shall not be required to commence proceedings against any Successor in Interest of Borrower or to refuse to extend time for payment or otherwise modify amortization of the sums secured by this Security Instrument by reason of any demand made by the original Borrower or any Successors in Interest of Borrower. Any forbearance by Lender in exercising any right or remedy including, without limitation, Lender's acceptance of payments from third persons, entities or Successors in Interest of Borrower or in amounts less than the amount then due, shall not be a waiver of or preclude the exercise of any right or remedy.

13. Joint and Several Liability; Co-signers; Successors and Assigns Bound. Borrower covenants and agrees that Borrower's obligations and liability shall be joint and several. However, any Borrower who co-signs this Security Instrument but does not execute the Note (a "co-signer"): (a) is co-signing this Security Instrument only to mortgage, grant and convey the co-signer's interest in the Property under the terms of this Security Instrument; (b) is not personally obligated to pay the sums secured by this Security Instrument; and (c) agrees that Lender and any other Borrower can agree to extend, modify, forbear or make any accommodations with regard to the terms of this Security Instrument or the Note without the co-signer's consent.

Subject to the provisions of Section 18, any Successor in Interest of Borrower who assumes Borrower's obligations under this Security Instrument in writing, and is approved by Lender, shall obtain all of Borrower's rights and benefits under this Security Instrument. Borrower shall not be released from Borrower's obligations and liability under this Security Instrument unless Lender agrees to such release in writing. The covenants and agreements of this Security Instrument shall bind (except as provided in Section 20) and benefit the successors and assigns of Lender.

14. Loan Charges. Lender may charge Borrower fees for services performed in connection with Borrower's default, for the purpose of protecting Lender's interest in the Property and rights under this Security Instrument, including, but not limited to, attorneys' fees, property inspection and valuation fees. In regard to any other fees, the absence of express authority in this Security Instrument to charge a specific fee to Borrower shall not be construed as a prohibition on the charging of such fee. Lender may not charge fees that are expressly prohibited by this Security Instrument or by Applicable Law.

If the Loan is subject to a law which sets maximum loan charges, and that law is finally interpreted so that the interest or other loan charges collected or to be collected in connection with the Loan exceed the permitted limits, then: (a) any such loan charge shall be reduced by the amount necessary to reduce the charge to the permitted limit; and (b) any sums already collected from Borrower which exceeded permitted limits will be refunded to Borrower. Lender may choose to make this refund by reducing the principal owed under the Note or by making a direct payment to Borrower. If a refund reduces principal, the reduction will be treated as a partial prepayment without any prepayment charge (whether or not a prepayment charge is provided for under the Note). Borrower's acceptance of any such refund made by direct payment to Borrower will constitute a waiver of any right of action Borrower might have arising out of such overcharge.

15. **Notices.** All notices given by Borrower or Lender in connection with this Security Instrument must be in writing. Any notice to Borrower in connection with this Security Instrument shall be deemed to have been given to Borrower when mailed by first class mail or when actually delivered to Borrower's notice address if sent by other means. Notice to any one Borrower shall constitute notice to all Borrowers unless Applicable Law expressly requires otherwise. The notice address shall be the Property Address unless Borrower has designated a substitute notice address by notice to Lender. Borrower shall promptly notify Lender of Borrower's change of address. If Lender specifies a procedure for reporting Borrower's change of address, then Borrower shall only report a change of address through that specified procedure. There may be only one designated notice address under this Security Instrument at any one time. Any notice to Lender shall be given by delivering it or by mailing it by first class mail to Lender's address stated herein unless Lender has designated another address by notice to Borrower. Any notice in connection with this Security Instrument shall not be deemed to have been given to Lender until actually received by Lender. If any notice required by this Security Instrument is also required under Applicable Law, the Applicable Law requirement will satisfy the corresponding requirement under this Security Instrument.

16. **Governing Law; Severability; Rules of Construction.** This Security Instrument shall be governed by federal law and the law of the jurisdiction in which the Property is located. All rights and obligations contained in this Security Instrument are subject to any requirements and limitations of Applicable Law. Applicable Law might explicitly or implicitly allow the parties to agree by contract or it might be silent, but such silence shall not be construed as a prohibition against agreement by contract. In the event that any provision or clause of this Security Instrument or the Note conflicts with Applicable Law, such conflict shall not affect other provisions of this Security Instrument or the Note which can be given effect without the conflicting provision.

As used in this Security Instrument: (a) words of the masculine gender shall mean and include corresponding neuter words or words of the feminine gender; (b) words in the singular shall mean and include the plural and vice versa; and (c) the word "may" gives sole discretion without any obligation to take any action.

17. **Borrower's Copy.** Borrower shall be given one copy of the Note and of this Security Instrument.

18. Transfer of the Property or a Beneficial Interest in Borrower. As used in this Section 18, "Interest in the Property" means any legal or beneficial interest in the Property, including, but not limited to, those beneficial interests transferred in a bond for deed, contract for deed, installment sales contract or escrow agreement, the intent of which is the transfer of title by Borrower at a future date to a purchaser.

If all or any part of the Property or any Interest in the Property is sold or transferred (or if Borrower is not a natural person and a beneficial interest in Borrower is sold or transferred) without Lender's prior written consent, Lender may require immediate payment in full of all sums secured by this Security Instrument. However, this option shall not be exercised by Lender if such exercise is prohibited by Applicable Law.

If Lender exercises this option, Lender shall give Borrower notice of acceleration. The notice shall provide a period of not less than 30 days from the date the notice is given in accordance with Section 15 within which Borrower must pay all sums secured by this Security Instrument. If Borrower fails to pay these sums prior to the expiration of this period, Lender may invoke any remedies permitted by this Security Instrument without further notice or demand on Borrower.

19. Borrower's Right to Reinstate After Acceleration. If Borrower meets certain conditions, Borrower shall have the right to have enforcement of this Security Instrument discontinued at any time prior to the earliest of: (a) five days before sale of the Property pursuant to Section 22 of this Security Instrument; (b) such other period as Applicable Law might specify for the termination of Borrower's right to reinstate; or (c) entry of a judgment enforcing this Security Instrument. Those conditions are that Borrower: (a) pays Lender all sums which then would be due under this Security Instrument and the Note as if no acceleration had occurred; (b) cures any default of any other covenants or agreements; (c) pays all expenses incurred in enforcing this Security Instrument, including, but not limited to, reasonable attorneys' fees, property inspection and valuation fees, and other fees incurred for the purpose of protecting Lender's interest in the Property and rights under this Security Instrument; and (d) takes such action as Lender may reasonably require to assure that Lender's interest in the Property and rights under this Security Instrument, and Borrower's obligation to pay the sums secured by this Security Instrument, shall continue unchanged unless as otherwise provided under Applicable Law. Lender may require that Borrower pay such reinstatement sums and expenses in one or more of the following forms, as selected by Lender: (a) cash; (b) money order; (c) certified check, bank check, treasurer's check or cashier's check, provided any such check is drawn upon an institution whose deposits are insured by a federal agency, instrumentality or entity; or (d) Electronic Funds Transfer. Upon reinstatement by Borrower, this Security Instrument and obligations secured hereby shall remain fully effective as if no acceleration had occurred. However, this right to reinstate shall not apply in the case of acceleration under Section 18.

20. Sale of Note; Change of Loan Servicer; Notice of Grievance. The Note or a partial interest in the Note (together with this Security Instrument) can be sold one or more times without prior notice to Borrower. A sale might result in a change in the entity (known as the "Loan Servicer") that collects Periodic Payments due under the Note and this Security Instrument and performs other mortgage loan servicing obligations under the Note, this Security Instrument, and Applicable Law. There also might be one or more changes of the Loan Servicer unrelated to a sale of the Note. If there is a change of the Loan Servicer, Borrower will be given written notice of the change which will state the name and address of the new Loan Servicer, the address to which payments should be made and any other information RESPA requires in connection with a notice of transfer of servicing. If the Note is sold and thereafter the Loan is serviced by a Loan Servicer other than the purchaser of the Note, the mortgage loan servicing obligations to Borrower will remain with the Loan Servicer or be transferred to a successor Loan Servicer and are not assumed by the Note purchaser unless otherwise provided by the Note purchaser.

Neither Borrower nor Lender may commence, join, or be joined to any judicial action (as either an individual litigant or the member of a class) that arises from the other party's actions pursuant to this Security Instrument or that alleges that the other party has breached any provision of, or any duty owed by reason of, this Security Instrument, until such Borrower or Lender has notified the other party (with such notice given in compliance with the requirements of Section 15) of such alleged breach and afforded the other party hereto a reasonable period after the giving of such notice to take corrective action. If Applicable Law provides a time period which must elapse before certain action can be taken, that time period will be deemed to be reasonable for purposes of this paragraph. The notice of acceleration and opportunity to cure given to Borrower pursuant to Section 22 and the notice of acceleration given to Borrower pursuant to Section 18 shall be deemed to satisfy the notice and opportunity to take corrective action provisions of this Section 20.

21. Hazardous Substances. As used in this Section 21: (a) "Hazardous Substances" are those substances defined as toxic or hazardous substances, pollutants, or wastes by Environmental Law and the following substances: gasoline, kerosene, other flammable or toxic petroleum products, toxic pesticides and herbicides, volatile solvents, materials containing asbestos or formaldehyde, and radioactive materials; (b) "Environmental Law" means federal laws and laws of the jurisdiction where the Property is located that relate to health, safety or environmental protection; (c) "Environmental Cleanup" includes any response action, remedial action, or removal action, as defined in Environmental Law; and (d) an "Environmental Condition" means a condition that can cause, contribute to, or otherwise trigger an Environmental Cleanup.

Borrower shall not cause or permit the presence, use, disposal, storage, or release of any Hazardous Substances, or threaten to release any Hazardous Substances, on or in the Property. Borrower shall not do, nor allow anyone else to do, anything affecting the Property (a) that is in violation of any Environmental Law, (b) which creates an Environmental Condition, or (c) which, due to the presence, use, or release of a Hazardous Substance, creates a condition that adversely affects the value of the Property. The preceding two sentences shall not apply to the presence, use, or storage on the Property of small quantities of Hazardous Substances that are generally recognized to be appropriate to normal residential uses and to maintenance of the Property (including, but not limited to, hazardous substances in consumer products).

Borrower shall promptly give Lender written notice of (a) any investigation, claim, demand, lawsuit or other action by any governmental or regulatory agency or private party involving the Property and any Hazardous Substance or Environmental Law of which Borrower has actual knowledge, (b) any Environmental Condition, including but not limited to, any spilling, leaking, discharge, release or threat of release of any Hazardous Substance, and (c) any condition caused by the presence, use or release of a Hazardous Substance which adversely affects the value of the Property. If Borrower learns, or is notified by any governmental or regulatory authority, or any private party, that any removal or other remediation of any Hazardous Substance affecting the Property is necessary, Borrower shall promptly take all necessary remedial actions in accordance with Environmental Law. Nothing herein shall create any obligation on Lender for an Environmental Cleanup.

NON-UNIFORM COVENANTS. Borrower and Lender further covenant and agree as follows:

22. Acceleration; Remedies. Lender shall give notice to Borrower prior to acceleration following Borrower's breach of any covenant or agreement in this Security Instrument (but not prior to acceleration under Section 18 unless Applicable Law provides otherwise). The notice shall specify: (a) the default; (b) the action required to cure the default; (c) a date, not less than 30 days from the date the notice is given to Borrower, by which the default must be cured; and (d) that failure to cure the default on or before the date specified in the notice may result in acceleration of the sums secured by this Security Instrument, foreclosure by judicial proceeding and sale of the Property. The notice shall further inform Borrower of the right to reinstate after acceleration and the right to assert in the foreclosure proceeding the non-existence of a default or any other defense of Borrower to acceleration and foreclosure. If the default is not cured on or before the date specified in the notice, Lender at its option may require immediate payment in full of all sums secured by this Security Instrument without further demand and may foreclose this Security Instrument by judicial proceeding. Lender shall be entitled to collect all expenses incurred in pursuing the remedies provided in this Section 22, including, but not limited to, reasonable attorneys' fees and costs of title evidence.

23. Release. Upon payment of all sums secured by this Security Instrument, Lender shall release this Security Instrument. Borrower shall pay any recordation costs. Lender may charge Borrower a fee for releasing this Security Instrument, but only if the fee is paid to a third party for services rendered and the charging of the fee is permitted under Applicable Law.

24. Waiver of Homestead. In accordance with Illinois law, the Borrower hereby releases and waives all rights under and by virtue of the Illinois homestead exemption laws.

25. Placement of Collateral Protection Insurance. Unless Borrower provides Lender with evidence of the insurance coverage required by Borrower's agreement with Lender, Lender may purchase insurance at Borrower's expense to protect Lender's interests in Borrower's collateral. This insurance may, but need not, protect Borrower's interests. The coverage that Lender purchases may not pay any claim that Borrower makes or any claim that is made against Borrower in connection with the collateral. Borrower may later cancel any insurance purchased by Lender, but only after providing Lender with evidence that Borrower has obtained insurance as required by Borrower's and Lender's agreement. If Lender purchases insurance for the collateral, Borrower will be responsible for the costs of that insurance, including interest and any other charges Lender may impose in connection with the placement of the insurance, until the effective date of the cancellation or expiration of the insurance. The costs of the insurance may be added to Borrower's total outstanding balance or obligation. The costs of the insurance may be more than the cost of insurance Borrower may be able to obtain on its own.

BY SIGNING BELOW, Borrower accepts and agrees to the terms and covenants contained in this Security Instrument and in any Rider executed by Borrower and recorded with it.

Witnesses:

_____   _____(Seal)
                                                                    Borrower

_____   _____(Seal)
                                                                    Borrower

_____[Space Below This Line for Acknowledgment]_____

ADJUSTABLE RATE RIDER
(1 Year Treasury Index—Rate Caps)

THIS ADJUSTABLE RATE RIDER is made this _____ day of _____, _____, and is incorporated into and shall be deemed to amend and supplement the Mortgage, Deed of Trust, or Security Deed (the "Security Instrument") of the same date given by the undersigned (the "Borrower") to secure Borrower's Adjustable Rate Note (the "Note") to _____ _____ (the "Lender") of the same date and covering the property described in the Security Instrument and located at:

_____

[Property Address]

THE NOTE CONTAINS PROVISIONS ALLOWING FOR CHANGES IN THE INTEREST RATE AND THE MONTHLY PAYMENT. THE NOTE LIMITS THE AMOUNT THE BORROWER'S INTEREST RATE CAN CHANGE AT ANY ONE TIME AND THE MAXIMUM RATE THE BORROWER MUST PAY.

ADDITIONAL COVENANTS. In addition to the covenants and agreements made in the Security Instrument, Borrower and Lender further covenant and agree as follows:

A. INTEREST RATE AND MONTHLY PAYMENT CHANGES

The Note provides for an initial interest rate of _____%. The Note provides for changes in the interest rate and the monthly payments as follows:

4. INTEREST RATE AND MONTHLY PAYMENT CHANGES

(A) Change Dates

The interest rate I will pay may change on the first day of _____, _____, and on that day every 12th month thereafter. Each date on which my interest rate could change is called a "Change Date."

(B) The Index

Beginning with the first Change Date, my interest rate will be based on an Index. The "Index" is the weekly average yield on United States Treasury securities adjusted to a constant maturity of one year, as made available by the Federal Reserve Board. The most recent Index figure available as of the date 45 days before each Change Date is called the "Current Index."

If the Index is no longer available, the Note Holder will choose a new index which is based upon comparable information. The Note Holder will give me notice of this choice.

(C) Calculation of Changes

Before each Change Date, the Note Holder will calculate my new interest rate by adding _____ percentage points (_____%) to the Current Index. The Note Holder will then round the result of this addition to the nearest one-eighth of one percentage point (0.125%). Subject to the limits stated in Section 4(D) below, this rounded amount will be my new interest rate until the next Change Date.

The Note Holder will then determine the amount of the monthly payment that would be sufficient to repay the unpaid principal that I am expected to owe at the Change Date in full on the maturity date at my new interest rate in substantially equal payments. The result of this calculation will be the new amount of my monthly payment.

(D) Limits on Interest Rate Changes

The interest rate I am required to pay at the first Change Date will not be greater than_____% or less than _____%. Thereafter, my interest rate will never be increased or decreased on any single Change Date by more than one percentage point (1.0%) from the rate of interest I have been paying for the preceding 12 months. My interest rate will never be greater than _____%.

(E) Effective Date of Changes

My new interest rate will become effective on each Change Date. I will pay the amount of my new monthly payment beginning on the first monthly payment date after the Change Date until the amount of my monthly payment changes again.

(F) Notice of Changes

The Note Holder will deliver or mail to me a notice of any changes in my interest rate and the amount of my monthly payment before the effective date of any change. The notice will include information required by law to be given to me and also the title and telephone number of a person who will answer any question I may have regarding the notice.

B. TRANSFER OF THE PROPERTY OR A BENEFICIAL INTEREST IN BORROWER

Section 18 of the Security Instrument is amended to read as follows:

Transfer of the Property or a Beneficial Interest in Borrower. As used in this Section 18, "Interest in the Property" means any legal or beneficial interest in the Property, including, but not limited to, those beneficial interests transferred in a bond for deed, contract for deed, installment sales contract or escrow agreement, the intent of which is the transfer of title by Borrower at a future date to a purchaser.

If all or any part of the Property or any Interest in the Property is sold or transferred (or if Borrower is not a natural person and a beneficial interest in Borrower is sold or transferred) without Lender's prior written consent, Lender may require immediate payment in full of all sums secured by this Security Instrument. However, this option shall not be exercised by Lender if such exercise is prohibited by Applicable Law. Lender also shall not exercise this option if: (a) Borrower causes to be submitted to Lender information required by Lender to evaluate the intended transferee as if a new loan were being made to the transferee; and (b) Lender reasonably determines that Lender's security will not be impaired by the loan assumption and that the risk of a breach of any covenant or agreement in this Security Instrument is acceptable to Lender.

To the extent permitted by Applicable Law, Lender may charge a reasonable fee as a condition to Lender's consent to the loan assumption. Lender may also require the transferee to sign an assumption agreement that is acceptable to Lender and that obligates the transferee to keep all the promises and agreements made in the Note and in this Security Instrument. Borrower will continue to be obligated under the Note and this Security Instrument unless Lender releases Borrower in writing

If Lender exercises the option to require immediate payment in full, Lender shall give Borrower notice of acceleration. The notice shall provide a period of not less than 30 days from the date the notice is given in accordance with Section 15 within which Borrower must pay all sums secured by this Security Instrument. If Borrower fails to pay these sums prior to the expiration of this period, Lender may invoke any remedies permitted by this Security Instrument without further notice or demand on Borrower.

BY SIGNING BELOW, Borrower accepts and agrees to the terms and covenants contained in this Adjustable Rate Rider.

_____(Seal)
Borrower

_____(Seal)
Borrower

CONDOMINIUM RIDER

THIS CONDOMINIUM RIDER is made this _____ day of _____, _____, and is incorporated into and shall be deemed to amend and supplement the Mortgage, Deed of Trust, or Security Deed (the "Security Instrument") of the same date given by the undersigned (the "Borrower") to secure Borrower's Note to

_____

(the "Lender") of the same date and covering the Property described in the Security Instrument and located at:

_____

[Property Address]

The Property includes a unit in, together with an undivided interest in the common elements of, a condominium project known as:

_____

[Name of Condominium Project]

(the "Condominium Project"). If the owners association or other entity which acts for the Condominium Project (the "Owners Association") holds title to property for the benefit or use of its members or shareholders, the Property also includes Borrower's interest in the Owners Association and the uses, proceeds and benefits of Borrower's interest.

CONDOMINIUM COVENANTS. In addition to the covenants and agreements made in the Security Instrument, Borrower and Lender further covenant and agree as follows:

A. **Condominium Obligations.** Borrower shall perform all of Borrower's obligations under the Condominium Project's Constituent Documents. The "Constituent Documents" are the: (i) Declaration or any other document which creates the Condominium Project; (ii) by-laws; (iii) code of regulations; and (iv) other equivalent documents. Borrower shall promptly pay, when due, all dues and assessments imposed pursuant to the Constituent Documents.

B. **Property Insurance.** So long as the Owners Association maintains, with a generally accepted insurance carrier, a "master" or "blanket" policy on the Condominium Project which is satisfactory to Lender and which provides insurance coverage in the amounts (including deductible levels), for the periods, and against loss by fire, hazards included within the term "extended coverage," and any other hazards, including, but not limited to, earthquakes and floods, from which Lender requires insurance, then: (i) Lender waives the provision in Section 3 for the Periodic Payment to Lender of the yearly premium installments for property insurance on the Property; and (ii) Borrower's obligation under Section 5 to maintain property insurance coverage on the Property is deemed satisfied to the extent that the required coverage is provided by the Owners Association policy.

What Lender requires as a condition of this waiver can change during the term of the loan.

Borrower shall give Lender prompt notice of any lapse in required property insurance coverage provided by the master or blanket policy.

In the event of a distribution of property insurance proceeds in lieu of restoration or repair following a loss to the Property, whether to the unit or to common elements, any proceeds payable to Borrower are hereby assigned and shall be paid to Lender for application to the sums secured by the Security Instrument, whether or not then due, with the excess, if any, paid to Borrower.

C.   **Public Liability Insurance.** Borrower shall take such actions as may be reasonable to insure that the Owners Association maintains a public liability insurance policy acceptable in form, amount, and extent of coverage to Lender.

D.   **Condemnation.** The proceeds of any award or claim for damages, direct or consequential, payable to Borrower in connection with any condemnation or other taking of all or any part of the Property, whether of the unit or of the common elements, or for any conveyance in lieu of condemnation, are hereby assigned and shall be paid to Lender. Such proceeds shall be applied by Lender to the sums secured by the Security Instrument as provided in Section 11.

E.   **Lender's Prior Consent.** Borrower shall not, except after notice to Lender and with Lender's prior written consent, either partition or subdivide the Property or consent to: (i) the abandonment or termination of the Condominium Project, except for abandonment or termination required by law in the case of substantial destruction by fire or other casualty or in the case of a taking by condemnation or eminent domain; (ii) any amendment to any provision of the Constituent Documents if the provision is for the express benefit of Lender; (iii) termination of professional management and assumption of self-management of the Owners Association; or (iv) any action which would have the effect of rendering the public liability insurance coverage maintained by the Owners Association unacceptable to Lender.

F.   **Remedies.** If Borrower does not pay condominium dues and assessments when due, then Lender may pay them. Any amounts disbursed by Lender under this paragraph F shall become additional debt of Borrower secured by the Security Instrument. Unless Borrower and Lender agree to other terms of payment, these amounts shall bear interest from the date of disbursement at the Note rate and shall be payable, with interest, upon notice from Lender to Borrower requesting payment.

BY SIGNING BELOW, Borrower accepts and agrees to the terms and covenants contained in this Condominium Rider.

_____(Seal)
Borrower

_____(Seal)
Borrower

PLANNED UNIT DEVELOPMENT RIDER

THIS PLANNED UNIT DEVELOPMENT RIDER is made this _____ day of _____, _____, and is incorporated into and shall be deemed to amend and supplement the Mortgage, Deed of Trust, or Security Deed (the "Security Instrument") of the same date, given by the undersigned (the "Borrower") to secure Borrower's Note to _____ _____ (the "Lender") of the same date and covering the Property described in the Security Instrument and located at:

_____

[Property Address]

The Property includes, but is not limited to, a parcel of land improved with a dwelling, together with other such parcels and certain common areas and facilities, as described in _____

_____ (the "Declaration"). The Property is a part of a planned unit development known as _____ [Name of Planned Unit Development] (the "PUD"). The Property also includes Borrower's interest in the homeowners' association or equivalent entity owning or managing the common areas and facilities of the PUD (the "Owners Association") and the uses, benefits and proceeds of Borrower's interest.

PUD COVENANTS. In addition to the covenants and agreements made in the Security Instrument, Borrower and Lender further covenant and agree as follows:

   A.   **PUD Obligations.** Borrower shall perform all of Borrower's obligations under the PUD's Constituent Documents. The "Constituent Documents" are the (i) Declaration; (ii) articles of incorporation, trust instrument or any equivalent document which creates the Owners Association; and (iii) any by-laws or other rules or regulations of the Owners Association. Borrower shall promptly pay, when due, all dues and assessments imposed pursuant to the Constituent Documents.

   B.   **Property Insurance.** So long as the Owners Association maintains, with a generally accepted insurance carrier, a "master" or "blanket" policy insuring the Property which is satisfactory to Lender and which provides insurance coverage in the amounts (including deductible levels), for the periods, and against loss by fire, hazards included within the term "extended coverage," and any other hazards, including, but not limited to, earthquakes and floods, for which Lender requires insurance, then: (i) Lender waives the provision in Section 3 for the Periodic Payment to Lender of the yearly premium installments for property insurance on the Property; and (ii) Borrower's obligation under Section 5 to maintain property insurance coverage on the Property is deemed satisfied to the extent that the required coverage is provided by the Owners Association policy.

   What Lender requires as a condition of this waiver can change during the term of the loan.

Borrower shall give Lender prompt notice of any lapse in required property insurance coverage provided by the master or blanket policy.

In the event of a distribution of property insurance proceeds in lieu of restoration or repair following a loss to the Property, or to common areas and facilities of the PUD, any proceeds payable to Borrower are hereby assigned and shall be paid to Lender. Lender shall apply the proceeds to the sums secured by the Security Instrument, whether or not then due, with the excess, if any, paid to Borrower.

C.   **Public Liability Insurance.** Borrower shall take such actions as may be reasonable to ensure that the Owners Association maintains a public liability insurance policy acceptable in form, amount, and extent of coverage to Lender.

D.   **Condemnation.** The proceeds of any award or claim for damages, direct or consequential, payable to Borrower in connection with any condemnation or other taking of all or any part of the Property or the common areas and facilities of the PUD, or for any conveyance in lieu of condemnation, are hereby assigned and shall be paid to Lender. Such proceeds shall be applied by Lender to the sums secured by the Security Instrument as provided in Section 11.

E.   **Lender's Prior Consent.** Borrower shall not, except after notice to Lender and with Lender's prior written consent, either partition or subdivide the Property or consent to: (i) the abandonment or termination of the PUD, except for abandonment or termination required by law in the case of substantial destruction by fire or other casualty or in the case of a taking by condemnation or eminent domain; (ii) any amendment to any provision of the "Constituent Documents" if the provision is for the express benefit of Lender; (iii) termination of professional management and assumption of self-management of the Owners Association; or (iv) any action which would have the effect of rendering the public liability insurance coverage maintained by the Owners Association unacceptable to Lender.

F.   **Remedies.** If Borrower does not pay PUD dues and assessments when due, then Lender may pay them. Any amounts disbursed by Lender under this paragraph F shall become additional debt of Borrower secured by the Security Instrument. Unless Borrower and Lender agree to other terms of payment, these amounts shall bear interest from the date of disbursement at the Note rate and shall be payable, with interest, upon notice from Lender to Borrower requesting payment.

BY SIGNING BELOW, Borrower accepts and agrees to the terms and covenants contained in this PUD Rider.

_____(Seal)
                                                           Borrower
_____(Seal)
                                                           Borrower

1-4 FAMILY RIDER
(Assignment of Rents)

THIS 1-4 FAMILY RIDER is made this _____ day of _____, _____, and is incorporated into and shall be deemed to amend and supplement the Mortgage, Deed of Trust, or Security Deed (the "Security Instrument") of the same date given by the undersigned (the "Borrower") to secure Borrower's Note to _____ _____ (the "Lender") of the same date and covering the Property described in the Security Instrument and located at:

_____

[Property Address]

1-4 FAMILY COVENANTS. In addition to the covenants and agreements made in the Security Instrument, Borrower and Lender further covenant and agree as follows:

A.   **ADDITIONAL PROPERTY SUBJECT TO THE SECURITY INSTRUMENT.** In addition to the Property described in Security Instrument, the following items now or hereafter attached to the Property to the extent they are fixtures are added to the Property description, and shall also constitute the Property covered by the Security Instrument: building materials, appliances and goods of every nature whatsoever now or hereafter located in, on, or used, or intended to be used in connection with the Property, including, but not limited to, those for the purposes of supplying or distributing heating, cooling, electricity, gas, water, air and light, fire prevention and extinguishing apparatus, security and access control apparatus, plumbing, bath tubs, water heaters, water closets, sinks, ranges, stoves, refrigerators, dishwashers, disposals, washers, dryers, awnings, storm windows, storm doors, screens, blinds, shades, curtains and curtain rods, attached mirrors, cabinets, paneling and attached floor coverings, all of which, including replacements and additions thereto, shall be deemed to be and remain a part of the Property covered by the Security Instrument. All of the foregoing together with the Property described in the Security Instrument (or the leasehold estate if the Security Instrument is on a leasehold) are referred to in this 1-4 Family Rider and the Security Instrument as the "Property."

B.   **USE OF PROPERTY; COMPLIANCE WITH LAW.** Borrower shall not seek, agree to or make a change in the use of the Property or its zoning classification, unless Lender has agreed in writing to the change. Borrower shall comply with all laws, ordinances, regulations and requirements of any governmental body applicable to the Property.

C.   **SUBORDINATE LIENS.** Except as permitted by federal law, Borrower shall not allow any lien inferior to the Security Instrument to be perfected against the Property without Lender's prior written permission.

D.   **RENT LOSS INSURANCE.** Borrower shall maintain insurance against rent loss in addition to the other hazards for which insurance is required by Section 5.

E.   **"BORROWER'S RIGHT TO REINSTATE" DELETED.** Section 19 is deleted.

F.   **BORROWER'S OCCUPANCY.** Unless Lender and Borrower otherwise agree in writing, Section 6 concerning Borrower's occupancy of the Property is deleted.

G.   **ASSIGNMENT OF LEASES.** Upon Lender's request after default, Borrower shall assign to Lender all leases of the Property and all security deposits made in connection with leases of the Property. Upon the assignment, Lender shall have the right to modify, extend or terminate the existing leases and to execute new leases, in Lender's sole discretion. As used in this paragraph G, the word "lease" shall mean "sublease" if the Security Instrument is on a leasehold.

H.   **ASSIGNMENT OF RENTS; APPOINTMENT OF RECEIVER; LENDER IN POSSESSION.** Borrower absolutely and unconditionally assigns and transfers to Lender all the rents and revenues ("Rents") of the Property, regardless of to whom the Rents of the Property are payable. Borrower authorizes Lender or Lender's agents to collect the Rents, and agrees that each tenant of the Property shall pay the Rents to Lender or Lender's agents. However, Borrower shall receive the Rents until (i) Lender has given Borrower notice of default pursuant to Section 22 of the Security Instrument and (ii) Lender has given notice to the tenant(s) that the Rents are to be paid to Lender or Lender's agent. This assignment of Rents constitutes an absolute assignment and not an assignment for additional security only.

If Lender gives notice of default to Borrower: (i) all Rents received by Borrower shall be held by Borrower as trustee for the benefit of Lender only, to be applied to the sums secured by the Security Instrument; (ii) Lender shall be entitled to collect and receive all of the Rents of the Property; (iii) Borrower agrees that each tenant of the Property shall pay all Rents due and unpaid to Lender or Lender's agents upon Lender's written demand to the tenant; (iv) unless applicable law provides otherwise, all Rents collected by Lender or Lender's agents shall be applied first to the costs of taking control of and managing the Property and collecting the Rents, including, but not limited to, attorney's fees, receiver's fees, premiums on receiver's bonds, repair and maintenance costs, insurance premiums, taxes, assessments and other charges on the Property, and then to the sums secured by the Security Instrument; (v) Lender, Lender's agents or any judicially appointed receiver shall be liable to account for only those Rents actually received; and (vi) Lender shall be entitled to have a receiver appointed to take possession of and manage the Property and collect the Rents and profits derived from the Property without any showing as to the inadequacy of the Property as security.

If the Rents of the Property are not sufficient to cover the costs of taking control of and managing the Property and of collecting the Rents any funds expended by Lender for such purposes shall become indebtedness of Borrower to Lender secured by the Security Instrument pursuant to Section 9.

Borrower represents and warrants that Borrower has not executed any prior assignment of the Rents and has not performed, and will not perform, any act that would prevent Lender from exercising its rights under this paragraph.

Lender, or Lender's agents or a judicially appointed receiver, shall not be required to enter upon, take control of or maintain the Property before or after giving notice of default to Borrower. However, Lender, or Lender's agents or a judicially appointed receiver, may do so at any time when a default occurs. Any application of Rents shall not cure or waive any default or invalidate any other right or remedy of Lender. This assignment of Rents of the Property shall terminate when all the sums secured by the Security Instrument are paid in full.

I.   **CROSS-DEFAULT PROVISION.** Borrower's default or breach under any note or agreement in which Lender has an interest shall be a breach under the Security Instrument and Lender may invoke any of the remedies permitted by the Security Instrument.

BY SIGNING BELOW, Borrower accepts and agrees to the terms and covenants contained in this 1-4 Family Rider.

_____(Seal)
Borrower

_____(Seal)
Borrower

The Truth-in-Lending Act is aimed at promoting the informed use of consumer credit by requiring disclosures about terms and costs.

SAMPLE TRUTH-IN-LENDING DISCLOSURE STATEMENT
(THIS IS NEITHER A CONTRACT NOR A COMMITMENT TO LEND)

Applicants:　　　　　　　*Because you may be paying points and other fees, the APR disclosed is often higher than the interest rate on your loan. The APR can be compared to other loans to give you a fair method of comparing prices.*

Prepared By:

Property Address:

Application No:

Date Prepared:

The mortgage amount minus prepaid finance charges (loan origination fees, points, adjusted interest and initial mortgage insurance premium) and any required balance. It represents a net figure to allow you to accurately assess the amount of credit actually provided.

ANNUAL PERCENTAGE RATE	FINANCE CHARGE	AMOUNT FINANCED	TOTAL OF PAYMENTS	
The cost of your credit as a yearly rate	The dollar amount the credit will cost you	The amount of credit provided to you or on your behalf	The amount you will have paid after making all payments as scheduled	*The estimated total amount you will have paid, including principal, interest, prepaid finance charges and mortgage insurance, if you make minimum payments for the entire loan term.*
%	$	$	$	

REQUIRED DEPOSIT:　The annual percentage rate does not take into account your required deposit

PAYMENTS:　Your payment schedule will be:

Number of Payments	Amount of Payments**	When Payments Are Due	Number of Payments	Amount of Payments**	When Payments Are Due	Number of Payments	Amount of Payments**	When Payments Are Due
		Monthly Beginning:			Monthly Beginning:			Monthly Beginning:

Principal, Interest and mortgage insurance if applicable.

The estimated total amount of interest payments for the term of the loan, the amount of interest paid at closing, origination fee and any other charges paid to the lender.

Defines circumstances under which the remaining principal and interest amount of the loan is due and payable on demand.

DEMAND FEATURE:　This obligation has a demand feature.

VARIABLE RATE FEATURE:　This loan has a variable rate feature.　A variable rate disclosure has been provided earlier.

CREDIT LIFE/CREDIT DISABILITY: Credit life insurance and credit disability insurance are not required to obtain credit, and will not be provided unless you sign and agree to pay the additional cost.

Type	Premium	Signature	
Credit Life		I want credit life insurance.	Signature:
Credit Disability		I want credit disability insurance.	Signature:
Credit Life and Disability		I want credit life and disability insurance.	Signature:

INSURANCE:　The following insurance is required to obtain credit:

　Credit life insurance　　　Credit disability　　　Property insurance　　　Flood insurance

You may obtain the insurance from anyone you want that is acceptable to creditor

　If you purchase　　property　　flood insurance from creditor you will pay $　　　for a one year term.

SECURITY:　You are giving a security interest in:

　The goods or property being purchased　　　　Real property you already own

FILING FEES: $　　　*An estimate of the cost of recording the legal documents (mortgage or deed of trust) connected with the transaction, which will be charged at closing.*

LATE CHARGE:　If a payment is more than　　days late, you will be charged　　% of the payment

Defines whether a fee will be charged and if you would be eligible for a refund if you wish to repay part or all of the loan in advance of the regular schedule. If you are not entitled to a refund, you will be charged interest for the period of time you used the money loaned to you. Your prepaid finance charges and any interest already paid are generally not refundable. If you pay the loan off early, you should not have to pay the full amount of the finance charges shown on the disclosure.

PREPAYMENT:　If you pay off early, you

　may　　　will not　　have to pay a penalty.

　may　　　will not　　be entitled to a refund of part of the finance charge.

Defines whether or not the loan can be passed on from a seller of a home to another buyer, where the buyer "assumes" all outstanding payments.

ASSUMPTION: Someone buying your property

　may　　　may, subject to condition　　　may not　　assume the remainder of your loan on the original terms.

See your contract documents for any additional information about nonpayment, default, any required repayment in full before the scheduled date and prepayment refunds and penalties.

** NOTE: The Payments shown above include reserve deposits for mortgage insurance (if applicable), but exclude property taxes and insurance.

THE UNDERSIGNED ACKNOWLEDGES RECEIVING A COMPLETED COPY OF THIS DISCLOURE.

_____
(Applicant)　　　　　　(Date)

_____
(Lender)　　　　　　　(Date)

Lenders are required by law to provide the information on this statement in a timely manner. Your signature merely indicates that you received this information and does not obligate you or the lender in any way.

The Real Estate Settlement Procedures Act (RESPA) is designed to inform consumers when shopping for a mortgage loan by disclosing the estimated costs associated with obtaining the loan.

SAMPLE GOOD FAITH ESTIMATE

Applicants: Application No:
Property Address: Date Prepared:
Prepared By: Loan Program:

The information provided below reflects estimates of the charges that you are likely to incur at the settlement of your loan. The fees listed are estimates - actual charges may be more or less. Your transaction may not involve a fee for every item listed. The numbers listed beside the estimates generally correspond to the numbered lines contained in the HUD-1 settlement statement, which you will be receiving at settlement. The HUD-1 settlement statement will show you the actual cost for items paid at settlement.

Total Loan Amount $ Interest Rate: % Term: mths

			PFC S F POC
800	ITEMS PAYABLE IN CONNECTION WITH LOAN:		
801	Loan Origination Fee	$	
802	Loan Discount		
803	Appraisal Fee		
804	Credit Report		
805	Lender's Inspection Fee		
808	Mortgage Broker Fee		
809	Tax Related Service Fee		
810	Processing Fee		
811	Underwriting Fee		
812	Wire Transfer Fee		

PFC= Prepaid Finance Charge (fees that affect the APR)
S= Seller Paid
F= FHA Allowable Fees
POC= Paid Outside of Closing

			PFC S F POC
1100	TITLE CHARGES:		
1101	Closing or Escrow Fee:	$	
1105	Document Preparation Fee		
1106	Notary Fees		
1107	Attorney Fees		
1108	Title Insurance:		
1200	GOVERNMENT RECORDING & TRANSFER CHARGES:		PFC S F POC
1201	Recording Fees:	$	
1202	City/County Tax/Stamps:		
1203	State Tax/Stamps:		
1300	ADDITIONAL SETTLEMENT CHARGES:		PFC S F POC
1302	Pest Inspection	$	

Estimated Closing Costs

			PFC S F POC
900	ITEMS REQUIRED BY LENDER TO BE PAID IN ADVANCE:		
901	Interest for days @ $ per day	$	
902	Mortgage Insurance Premium		
903	Hazard Insurance Premium		
904			
905	VA Funding Fee		

Elements of your projected loan payments (interest, taxes and insurance) that must be prepaid to establish the escrow account and the loan schedule.

				PFC S F POC
1000	RESERVES DEPOSITED WITH LENDER:			
1001	Hazard Insurance Premium	months @ $ per month	$	
1002	Mortgage Ins. Premium Reserves	months @ $ per month		
1003	School Tax	months @ $ per month		
1004	Taxes and Assessment Reserves	months @ $ per month		
1005	Flood Insurance Reserves	months @ $ per month		

Estimated Prepaid Items/Reserves

TOTAL ESTIMATED SETTLEMENT CHARGES $

TOTAL ESTIMATED FUNDS NEEDED TO CLOSE:		TOTAL ESTIMATED MONTLY PAYMENT:	
Purchase Price/Payoff (+)		New First Mortgage (-)	Principal & Interest
Loan Amount (-)		Sub Financing (-)	Other Financing (P & I)
Est. Closing Costs (+)		New 2nd Mtg Closing Costs (+)	Hazard Insurance
Est. Prepaid Items/Reserves (+)			Real Estate Taxes
Amount Paid by Seller (-)			Mortgage Insurance
			Homeowner Assn. Dues
			Other
Total Est. Funds needed to close			**Total Monthly Payment**

These estimates are provided pursuant to the Real Estate Settlement Procedures Act of 1974, as amended (RESPA). Additional information can be found in the HUD Special Information Booklet, which is to be provided to you by your mortgage broker or lender, if your application is to purchase residential real estate property and the lender will take a first lien on the property. The undersigned acknowledges receipt of the booklet "Settlement Costs," and if applicable the Consumer Handbook on ARM Mortgages.

_____ _____ _____ _____
Applicant Date Applicant Date

(735 ILCS 5/15-1504) (from Ch. 110, par. 15-1504)

Sec. 15-1504. Pleadings and service.

(a) Form of Complaint. A foreclosure complaint may be in substantially the following form:

(1) Plaintiff files this complaint to foreclose the mortgage (or other conveyance in the nature of a mortgage) (hereinafter called "mortgage") hereinafter described and joins the following person as defendants: (here insert names of all defendants).

(2) Attached as Exhibit "A" is a copy of the mortgage and as Exhibit "B" is a copy of the note secured thereby.

(3) Information concerning mortgage:

(A) Nature of instrument: (here insert whether a mortgage, trust deed or other instrument in the nature of a mortgage, etc.)

(B) Date of mortgage:

(C) Name of mortgagor:

(D) Name of mortgagee:

(E) Date and place of recording:

(F) Identification of recording: (here insert book and page number or document number)

(G) Interest subject to the mortgage: (here insert whether fee simple, estate for years, undivided interest, etc.)

(H) Amount of original indebtedness, including subsequent advances made under the mortgage:

(I) Both the legal description of the mortgaged real estate and the common address or other information sufficient to identify it with reasonable certainty:

(J) Statement as to defaults, including, but not necessarily limited to, date of default, current unpaid principal balance, per diem interest accruing, and any further information concerning the default:

(K) Name of present owner of the real estate:

(L) Names of other persons who are joined as defendants and whose interest in or lien on the mortgaged real estate is sought to be terminated:

(M) Names of defendants claimed to be personally liable for deficiency, if any:

(N) Capacity in which plaintiff brings this foreclosure (here indicate whether plaintiff is the legal holder of the indebtedness, a pledgee, an agent, the trustee under a trust deed or otherwise, as appropriate):

(O) Facts in support of redemption period shorter than the longer of (i) 7 months from the date the mortgagor or, if more than one, all the mortgagors (I) have been served with summons or by publication or (II) have otherwise submitted to the jurisdiction of the court, or (ii) 3 months from the entry of the judgment of foreclosure, if sought (here indicate whether based upon the real estate not being residential or real estate value less than 90% of amount owed, etc.):

(P) Statement that the right of redemption has been waived by all owners of redemption, if applicable:

(Q) Facts in support of request for attorneys' fees and of costs and expenses, if applicable:

(R) Facts in support of a request for appointment of mortgagee in possession or for appointment of receiver, and identity of such receiver, if sought:

(S) Offer to mortgagor in accordance with Section 15-1402 to accept title to the real estate in satisfaction of all indebtedness and obligations secured by the mortgage without judicial sale, if sought:

(T) Name or names of defendants whose right to possess the mortgaged real estate, after the confirmation of a foreclosure sale, is sought to be terminated and, if not elsewhere stated, the facts in support thereof:

REQUEST FOR RELIEF

Plaintiff requests:

(i) A judgment of foreclosure and sale.

(ii) An order granting a shortened redemption period, if sought.

(iii) A personal judgment for a deficiency, if sought.

(iv) An order granting possession, if sought.

(v) An order placing the mortgagee in possession or appointing a receiver, if sought.

(vi) A judgment for attorneys' fees, costs and expenses, if sought.

(b) Required Information. A foreclosure complaint need contain only such statements and requests called for by the form set forth in subsection (a) of Section 15-1504 as may be appropriate for the relief sought. Such complaint may be filed as a counterclaim, may be joined with other counts or may include in the same count additional matters or a request for any additional relief permitted by Article II of the Code of Civil Procedure.

(c) Allegations. The statements contained in a complaint in the form set forth in subsection (a) of Section 15-1504 are deemed and construed to include allegations as follows:

(1) that, on the date indicated, the obligor of the indebtedness or other obligations secured by the mortgage was justly indebted in the amount of the indicated original indebtedness to the original mortgagee or payee of the mortgage note;

(2) that the exhibits attached are true and correct copies of the mortgage and note and are incorporated and made a part of the complaint by express reference;

(3) that the mortgagor was at the date indicated an owner of the interest in the real estate described in the complaint and that as of that date made, executed and delivered the mortgage as security for the note or other obligations;

(4) that the mortgage was recorded in the county in which the mortgaged real estate is located, on the date indicated, in the book and page or as the document number indicated;

(5) that defaults occurred as indicated;

(6) that at the time of the filing of the complaint the persons named as present owners are the owners of the indicated interests in and to the real estate described;

(7) that the mortgage constitutes a valid, prior and paramount lien upon the indicated interest in the mortgaged real estate, which lien is prior and superior to the right, title, interest, claim or lien of all parties and nonrecord claimants whose interests in the mortgaged real estate are sought to be terminated;

(8) that by reason of the defaults alleged, if the indebtedness has not matured by its terms, the same has become due by the exercise, by the plaintiff or other persons having such power, of a right or power to declare immediately due and payable the whole of all indebtedness secured by the mortgage;

(9) that any and all notices of default or election to declare the indebtedness due and payable or other notices required to be given have been duly and properly given;

(10) that any and all periods of grace or other period of time allowed for the performance of the covenants or conditions claimed to be breached or for the curing of any breaches have expired;

(11) that the amounts indicated in the statement in the complaint are correctly stated and if such statement indicates any advances made or to be made by the plaintiff or owner of the mortgage indebtedness, that such advances were, in fact, made or will be required to be made,

and under and by virtue of the mortgage the same constitute additional indebtedness secured by the mortgage; and

(12) that, upon confirmation of the sale, the holder of the certificate of sale or deed issued pursuant to that certificate or, if no certificate or deed was issued, the purchaser at the sale will be entitled to full possession of the mortgaged real estate against the parties named in clause (T) of paragraph (3) of subsection (a) of Section 15-1504 or elsewhere to the same effect; the omission of any party indicates that plaintiff will not seek a possessory order in the order confirming sale unless the request is subsequently made under subsection (h) of Section 15-1701 or by separate action under Article 9 of this Code.

(d) Request for Fees and Costs. A statement in the complaint that plaintiff seeks the inclusion of attorneys' fees and of costs and expenses shall be deemed and construed to include allegations that:

(1) plaintiff has been compelled to employ and retain attorneys to prepare and file the complaint and to represent and advise the plaintiff in the foreclosure of the mortgage and the plaintiff will thereby become liable for the usual, reasonable and customary fees of the attorneys in that behalf;

(2) the plaintiff has been compelled to advance or will be compelled to advance, various sums of money in payment of costs, fees, expenses and disbursements incurred in connection with the foreclosure, including, without limiting the generality of the foregoing, filing fees, stenographer's fees, witness fees, costs of publication, costs of procuring and preparing documentary evidence and costs of procuring abstracts of title, Torrens certificates, foreclosure minutes and a title insurance policy;

(3) under the terms of the mortgage, all such advances, costs, attorneys' fees and other fees, expenses and disbursements are made a lien upon the mortgaged real estate and the plaintiff is entitled to recover all such advances, costs, attorneys' fees, expenses and disbursements, together with interest on all advances at the rate provided in the mortgage, or, if no rate is provided therein, at the statutory judgment rate, from the date on which such advances are made;

(4) in order to protect the lien of the mortgage, it may become necessary for plaintiff to pay taxes and assessments which have been or may be levied upon the mortgaged real estate;

(5) in order to protect and preserve the mortgaged real estate, it may also become necessary for the plaintiff to pay liability (protecting mortgagor and mortgagee), fire and other hazard insurance premiums on the mortgaged real estate, make such repairs to the mortgaged real estate as may reasonably be deemed necessary for the proper preservation

thereof, advance for costs to inspect the mortgaged real estate or to appraise it, or both, and advance for premiums for pre-existing private or governmental mortgage insurance to the extent required after a fore-closure is commenced in order to keep such insurance in force; and

(6) under the terms of the mortgage, any money so paid or expended will become an additional indebtedness secured by the mortgage and will bear interest from the date such monies are advanced at the rate provided in the mortgage, or, if no rate is provided, at the statutory judgment rate.

(e) Request for Foreclosure. The request for foreclosure is deemed and con-strued to mean that the plaintiff requests that:

(1) an accounting may be taken under the direction of the court of the amounts due and owing to the plaintiff;

(2) the defendants be ordered to pay to the plaintiff before expiration of any redemption period (or, if no redemption period, before a short date fixed by the court) whatever sums may appear to be due upon the taking of such account, together with attorneys' fees and costs of the proceedings (to the extent provided in the mortgage or by law);

(3) in default of such payment in accordance with the judgment, the mortgaged real estate be sold as directed by the court, to satisfy the amount due to the plaintiff as set forth in the judgment, together with the interest thereon at the statutory judgment rate from the date of the judgment;

(4) in the event the plaintiff is a purchaser of the mortgaged real estate at such sale, the plaintiff may offset against the purchase price of such real estate the amounts due under the judgment of foreclosure and order confirming the sale;

(5) in the event of such sale and the failure of any person entitled thereto to redeem prior to such sale pursuant to this Article, the defendants made parties to the foreclosure in accordance with this Article, and all nonrecord claimants given notice of the foreclosure in accordance with this Article, and all persons claiming by, through or under them, and each and any and all of them, may be forever barred and fore-closed of any right, title, interest, claim, lien, or right to redeem in and to the mortgaged real estate; and

(6) if no redemption is made prior to such sale, a deed may be issued to the purchaser thereat according to law and such purchaser be let into possession of the mortgaged real estate in accordance with Part 17 of this Article.

(f) Request for Deficiency Judgment. A request for a personal judgment for a deficiency in a foreclosure complaint if the sale of the mortgaged real estate fails to produce a sufficient amount to pay the amount found due, the plaintiff may have a personal judgment against any party in the foreclosure indicated as being personally liable therefor and the enforcement thereof be had as provided by law.

(g) Request for Possession or Receiver. A request for possession or appointment of a receiver has the meaning as stated in subsection (b) of Section 15-1706.

(h) Answers by Parties. Any party may assert its interest by counterclaim and such counterclaim may at the option of that party stand in lieu of answer to the complaint for foreclosure and all counter complaints previously or thereafter filed in the foreclosure. Any such counterclaim shall be deemed to constitute a statement that the counter claimant does not have sufficient knowledge to form a belief as to the truth or falsity of the allegations of the complaint and all other counterclaims, except to the extent that the counterclaim admits or specifically denies such allegations.

(735 ILCS 5/15-1602) (from Ch. 110, par. 15-1602)

Sec. 15-1602. Reinstatement. In any foreclosure of a mortgage executed after July 21, 1959, which has become due prior to the maturity date fixed in the mortgage, or in any instrument or obligation secured by the mortgage, through acceleration because of a default under the mortgage, a mortgagor may reinstate the mortgage as provided herein. Reinstatement is effected by curing all defaults then existing, other than payment of such portion of the principal which would not have been due had no acceleration occurred, and by paying all costs and expenses required by the mortgage to be paid in the event of such defaults, provided that such cure and payment are made prior to the expiration of 90 days from the date the mortgagor or, if more than one, all the mortgagors (i) have been served with summons or by publication or (ii) have otherwise submitted to the jurisdiction of the court. When service is made by publication, the first date of publication shall be used for the calculation. Upon such reinstatement of the mortgage, the foreclosure and any other proceedings for the collection or enforcement of the obligation secured by the mortgage shall be dismissed and the mortgage documents shall remain in full force and effect as if no acceleration or default had occurred. The relief granted by this Section shall not be exhausted by a single use thereof, but if the court has made an express written finding that the mortgagor has exercised its right to reinstate pursuant to this Section, such relief shall not be again available to the mortgagor under the same mortgage for a period of five years from the date of the dismissal of such foreclosure. The provisions of Section 9-110 of the Code of Civil Procedure shall be inapplicable with respect to any instrument which is deemed a mortgage under this Article. The court may enter a judgment of foreclosure prior to the expiration of the reinstatement period, subject to the right of the mortgagor to reinstate the mortgage under this Section.

NATIONSTAR MORTGAGE, LLC, Plaintiff-Appellee,

v.

WAYNE CANALE, a/k/a Wayne F. Canale, Defendant-Appellant, (RBS Citizens, N.A., SBM Charter One Bank, N.A., Unknown Owners, and Nonrecord Claimants, Defendants).

No. 2-13-0676.

Appellate Court of Illinois, Second District.

Opinion filed April 9, 2014.

JUSTICE JORGENSEN delivered the judgment of the court, with opinion.

Justices McLaren and Hudson concurred in the judgment and opinion.

OPINION

1 Defendant, Wayne Canale, the property owner in a foreclosure action, appeals after the trial court confirmed the judicial sale of the property at issue. He asserts that, because plaintiff, Nationstar Mortgage, LLC, failed to comply with the statutory pleading requirements for a foreclosure action (see 735 ILCS 5/15-1504(a) (West 2010)), the trial court lacked subject matter jurisdiction to enter a foreclosure judgment for plaintiff. We disagree, and thus we affirm.

2 I. BACKGROUND

3 Plaintiff filed a foreclosure complaint relating to the property at 5S365 Vest Avenue, Naperville, on September 8, 2011. It made defendant a defendant as the property owner and borrower and alleged that he was in default on the note at issue. It also named two banks—RBS Citizens, N.A. (RBS), and SBM Charter One Bank, N.A. (SBM)—and unknown owners and nonrecord claimants. The complaint stated that the "mortgagee, trustee or grantee in the Mortgage" was Mortgage Electronic Registration Systems, Inc., as nominee for Silver Mortgage Bancorp, Inc. The attached mortgage was consistent with that allegation. Plaintiff stated that the capacity in which it brought the action was "mortgagee and holder of the note." However, the attached note showed a single endorsement, from Silver Mortgage Bancorp, Inc., to Ohio Savings Bank (OSB), "ITS SUCCESSORS AND/OR ASSIGNS." Also part of the record is a mortgage modification agreement between defendant and Amtrust Bank (Amtrust).

4 RBS and SBM appeared and answered. Defendant did neither. Plaintiff moved for summary judgment against the banks and default judgment against defendant.

5 On June 5, 2012, the court entered a judgment of foreclosure in favor of plaintiff, i.e., it entered judgment for $107,466.04 in favor of plaintiff and ordered the sale of the property to satisfy that judgment. The judgment also described the mortgage lien as plaintiff's. The sale took place on October 11, 2012. Plaintiff bid the judgment indebtedness and was the winning bidder.

6 Plaintiff moved to confirm the sale. Defendant appeared pro se and filed an objection. His objection included the assertions that he had been present at the sale and that no public offering of the property had occurred. The court confirmed the sale

on April 4, 2013. On May 3, 2013, defendant moved to vacate the confirmation, arguing that a slight delay in his arrival in the courtroom resulted in his inability to argue his objection. However, for the first time, he also asserted, on information and belief, that the original mortgagee had never properly assigned the note and mortgage to plaintiff and that plaintiff was asserting rights "without showing whether any proper assignment occurred between [the known earlier owners of the note and mortgage] over time." He described this as an issue of standing.

7 The court denied the motion, ruling that defendant had forfeited the standing issue by failing to file an answer. Defendant timely appealed.

8 II. ANALYSIS

9 On appeal, defendant concedes that, in *Lebron v. Gottlieb Memorial Hospital*, 237 Ill. 2d 217, 252–53 (2010), the supreme court held that a lack of standing is an affirmative defense, which the defendant forfeits if he does not timely plead. However, defendant asserts that, in a foreclosure action, standing must be pleaded by the plaintiff. Specifically, under the Illinois Mortgage Foreclosure Law (735 ILCS 5/15-1101 et seq. (West 2010)), the plaintiff must allege the "[c]apacity in which [the] plaintiff brings this foreclosure," i.e., "the legal holder of the indebtedness, a pledgee, an agent, the trustee under a trust deed or otherwise." 735 ILCS 5/15-1504(a)(3)(N) (West 2010). Noting that plaintiff's allegation that it was the "mortgagee and holder of the note" was unsupported (if not refuted) by the attached mortgage and note, defendant concludes that plaintiff failed to plead its standing and that the resulting judgment was void for lack of subject matter jurisdiction, a defect that cannot be forfeited (Lebron, 237 Ill. 2d at 252).

10 *In Deutsche Bank National Trust Co. v. Gilbert*, 2012 IL App (2d) 120164, ¶ 16, the defendant likewise argued that the Illinois Mortgage Foreclosure Law shifted to the plaintiff the burden to plead and prove standing. We were not required to resolve that issue, "because even if [the defendant] bore the burden of showing that [the plaintiff] lacked standing, he met that burden." Id. We need not resolve the issue here either. Here, even if plaintiff had the burden to plead its standing, and even if it failed to do so, its failure to do so did not deprive the trial court of subject matter jurisdiction.

11 Defendant relies almost exclusively on *City National Bank of Hoopeston v. Langley*, 161 Ill. App. 3d 266 (1987), which does tend to support his contention. There, sua sponte, the appellate court deemed it "necessary to address the trial court's subject-matter jurisdiction based upon the short form statutory complaint for foreclosure." Id. at 275. The court observed that the plaintiff was statutorily required to "attach a copy of the mortgage and a copy of the note secured thereby." Id. at 276 (citing Ill. Rev. Stat. 1983, ch. 110, ¶ 15-108(2) (now 735 ILCS 5/15-1504(a)(2) (West 2010))). Noting that the plaintiff, in violation of that requirement, had "fail[ed] to match up documentation," the court deemed the judgment void. Id. at 277.

12 The difficulty is that *Langley* rests on a defunct view of subject matter jurisdiction. In *Belleville Toyota, Inc. v. Toyota Motor Sales, U.S.A., Inc.*, 199 Ill. 2d 325 (2002), the supreme court explained that, under the Illinois Constitution of 1870, "in cases

involving purely statutory causes of action, *** unless the statutory requirements were satisfied, a court lacked jurisdiction to grant the relief requested." Id. at 336–37. However, under our present constitution, "[w]ith the exception of the circuit court's power to review administrative action, which is conferred by statute, a circuit court's subject matter jurisdiction is conferred entirely by our state constitution." Id. at 334. That jurisdiction extends to all " 'justiciable matters.' " Id. (quoting Ill. Const. 1970, art. VI, § 9). "Thus, in order to invoke the subject matter jurisdiction of the circuit court, a plaintiff's case, as framed by the complaint or petition, must [merely] present a justiciable matter." Id. Although the plaintiff's pleadings thus are pertinent, "[s]ubject matter jurisdiction does not depend upon the legal sufficiency of the pleadings." Id. at 340. "Indeed, even a defectively stated claim is sufficient to invoke the court's subject matter jurisdiction ***." *In re Luis R.,* 239 Ill. 2d 295, 301 (2010). "[T]he only consideration is whether the alleged claim falls within the general class of cases that the court has the inherent power to hear and determine. If it does, then subject matter jurisdiction is present." (Emphasis in original.) Id.

13 In *Belleville Toyota,* the supreme court went on the explain the practical importance of this broad view of subject matter jurisdiction:

> "Our conclusion, while firmly rooted in our constitution, is also consistent with the trend of modern authority favoring finality of judgments over alleged defects in validity. [Citations.] Labeling the requirements in statutory causes of action 'jurisdictional' would permit an unwarranted and dangerous expansion of the situations where a final judgment may be set aside on a collateral attack. [Citation.] Even if the statutory requirement is considered a nonwaivable condition, the same concern over the finality of judgments arises. Once a statutory requirement is deemed 'nonwaivable,' it is on equal footing with the only other nonwaivable conditions that would cause a judgment to be void, and thus subject to collateral attack—a lack of subject matter jurisdiction, or a lack of personal jurisdiction. [Citation.] As our appellate court has observed, '[b]ecause of the disastrous consequences which follow when orders and judgments are allowed to be collaterally attacked, orders should be characterized as void only when no other alternative is possible.' [Citations.]" *Belleville Toyota,* 199 Ill. 2d at 341.

14 In *Langley,* the appellate court equated the plaintiff's violation of the statutory requirements for a foreclosure action with the trial court's lack of subject matter jurisdiction. See also *Mortgage Electronic Registration Systems, Inc. v. Barnes,* 406 Ill. App. 3d 1, 6 (2010) (suggesting that trial court had jurisdiction of foreclosure action because complaint "was legally and factually sufficient and included allegations relative to standing"). This equation is error. Those requirements might go to the complaint's legal sufficiency, but they do not pertain to the court's subject matter jurisdiction. The latter turns only on whether the claim, even if defectively stated, presents a "justiciable matter," i.e., "falls within the general class of cases that the court has the inherent power to hear and determine." *Luis R.,* 239 Ill. 2d at 301. There is no doubt that courts have the inherent power to hear and determine foreclosure cases. Cf.

Belleville Toyota, 199 Ill. 2d at 340 (claim under statute was justiciable matter). Thus, here, plaintiff's claim, even if defectively stated, presented a justiciable matter, invoking the trial court's subject matter jurisdiction.

15 A different outcome is not required by the fact that the purported defect in plaintiff's claim was plaintiff's failure to plead its standing. To be sure, the supreme court has stated that standing is "an element of justiciability." *People v. Greco*, 204 Ill. 2d 400, 409 (2003). This is not to say, however, that a plaintiff who lacks standing cannot assert a "justiciable matter." Indeed, if such were the case, the plaintiff's lack of standing would itself defeat the trial court's subject matter jurisdiction, and the defendant could not forfeit the lack of standing. Cf. *Lebron*, 237 Ill. 2d at 252–53. Thus, though standing might be "an element of justiciability" (*Greco*, 204 Ill. 2d at 409), it is not a requirement for a "justiciable matter."

16 An Ohio appellate court has explored this nuance. In *Deutsche Bank National Trust Co. v. Finney*, 2013-Ohio-4884, appeal allowed, 2014-Ohio-1182, on facts substantially identical to these, the defendants asserted that "the trial court lacked subject-matter jurisdiction to enter the default judgment because [the plaintiff] did not demonstrate that it had standing as the real party in interest at the time it filed the foreclosure action." Id. ¶ 12. The appellate court observed that, like in Illinois, the Ohio Constitution grants trial courts jurisdiction " 'over all justiciable matters.' " Id. ¶ 22 (quoting OH Const. art. IV, § 4(B)). The court further noted that, as the defendants argued, "a legal action filed by a party who lacks standing is not justiciable." Id. ¶ 23. However, the court rejected the defendants' conclusion that the lack of this "justiciability" resulted in a lack of subject matter jurisdiction:

> "Rather, we recognize that subject-matter jurisdiction is not dependent upon the justiciability of any particular case. *** [A] court may have jurisdiction over the subject-matter of a case and yet not be empowered to adjudicate it to final judgment for reasons particular to that case, including the lack of standing of the plaintiff. Where an action is brought by a plaintiff who lacks standing, the action is not justiciable because it fails to present a case or controversy between the parties before it. [Citation.] But the court's lack of 'jurisdiction,' i.e., its ability to properly resolve a particular action due to the lack of a real case or controversy between the parties, does not mean that the court lacked subject-matter jurisdiction over the case." Id. ¶ 24.

Thus, the court accepted the plaintiff's argument that, whereas subject matter jurisdiction exists as long as "the matter alleged is within the class of cases in which a particular court has been empowered to act" (id. ¶ 18), "justiciability" implicates only a different type of jurisdiction, " 'the trial court's authority to determine a specific case within that class of cases that is within its subject matter jurisdiction. It is only when the trial court lacks subject matter jurisdiction that its judgment is void; lack of jurisdiction over the particular case merely renders the judgment voidable' " (emphasis omitted) (id. ¶ 17 (quoting *Pratts v. Hurley*, 102 Ohio St. 3d 81, 2004-Ohio-1980, 806 N.E.2d 992, at ¶ 12)). The court agreed with the plaintiff that, because "its foreclosure complaint alleged [a] cognizable cause of action within the subject-matter jurisdiction of the [trial court], i.e., foreclosure" (id. ¶ 19), the trial court had subject matter jurisdiction despite the nonjusticiability of the particular case, and the judgment was not void (id. ¶ 26).

17 Although Ohio's view of jurisdiction might not be a perfect analogue of our own, *Finney* strongly supports our conclusion that a plaintiff's standing, though "an element of justiciability" (*Greco*, 204 Ill. 2d at 409), is not an element of the trial court's subject matter jurisdiction. Again, the latter requires only a "justiciable matter," which a foreclosure clearly is. Thus, here, the trial court's judgment was not void.

18 In sum, we reject the precise argument that defendant raises: that plaintiff's failure to plead its standing, assuming that it had the burden to do so, deprived the trial court of subject matter jurisdiction and thus rendered the foreclosure judgment void. Again, even if plaintiff lacked standing, it presented a "justiciable matter," as a foreclosure case "falls within the general class of cases that the court has the inherent power to hear and determine" (*Luis R.*, 239 Ill. 2d at 301). Thus, the trial court had subject matter jurisdiction. We note, however, that we do not hold that plaintiff had standing. Indeed, in light of the apparent discrepancy between plaintiff's complaint and the attached documents, plaintiff's standing is much in doubt. See *Gilbert*, 2012 IL App (2d) 120164, ¶ 17 ("[The plaintiff's] name does not appear on either of these documents. Thus, the documents attached to the complaint contradict [the plaintiff's] allegation that it was 'the mortgagee' and support [the defendant's] argument that [the plaintiff] did not have an interest in the mortgage that would confer standing."). Nevertheless, as noted, defendant conditions our reaching the merits of that issue on his assertion that plaintiff's lack of standing deprived the trial court of subject matter jurisdiction. Because that assertion is not correct, we do not reach the merits of the standing issue.

19 Defendant does not provide a convincing alternative argument as to why we should reach the merits of that issue. He says only that, "should this court not find the judgment(s) below void, [he] respectfully request[s that] this Court address the issue of standing of Plaintiff pursuant to considerations of substantial justice, plain error and/or public importance." He cites two cases for the boilerplate proposition that we may ignore a forfeiture as necessary to ensure a just result. See, e.g., *In re Marriage of Rodriguez*, 131 Ill. 2d 273, 279 (1989). In this context, however, that proposition is not applicable. Although after a judicial sale a court may vacate a default judgment of foreclosure if "justice was otherwise not done" (735 ILCS 5/15-1508(b)(iv) (West 2010)), that provision "merely codif[ied] the long-standing discretion of the courts of equity to refuse to confirm a judicial sale" (*Wells Fargo Bank, N.A. v. Mc-Cluskey*, 2013 IL 115469, ¶ 19). That discretion is " 'not a mere arbitrary discretion but must be exercised in accordance with established principles of law.' " Id. (quoting *Shultz v. Milburn*, 366 Ill. 400, 403 (1937)). Specifically, it may not be invoked "merely to protect an interested party 'against the result of his own negligence.' " Id. (quoting *Shultz*, 366 Ill. at 405). Thus, once the plaintiff moves to confirm the sale:

> "To vacate both the sale and the underlying default judgment of foreclosure, the [defendant] must not only have a meritorious defense to the underlying

judgment, but must establish under section 15-1508(b)(iv) that justice was not otherwise done because either the [plaintiff], through fraud or misrepresentation, prevented the [defendant] from raising his meritorious defenses to the complaint at an earlier time in the proceedings, or the [defendant] has equitable defenses that reveal he was otherwise prevented from protecting his property interests. *** See, e.g., *** *Deutsche Bank National Trust Co. v. Snick*, 2011 IL App (3d) 100436, ¶ 9 (court held it was far too late to assert the defense of standing where the plaintiff had already moved for confirmation of the judicial sale). This interpretation is consistent with the legislative policy of balancing the competing objectives of efficiency and stability in the sale process and fairness in protecting the [defendant's] equity in the property and preserving the integrity of the sale." Id. ¶ 26.

Thus, here, we may not reach defendant's standing issue merely in the interest of achieving a just result. Rather, defendant must satisfy the standard of "justice" under section 15-1508(b)(iv). He has not attempted to do so.

20 III. CONCLUSION

21. For the reasons stated, the judgment of the circuit court of Du Page County is affirmed.

22. Affirmed.

Chapter 8

Landlord-Tenant Law

Learning Objectives

- Interpret the provisions of a lease
- Understand the uses of a security deposit
- Identify a late fee and limits on a late fee

Chapter Summary

Topics covered:

- Leases and Rentals

Chapter 8 shifts to an entirely different topic. Landlord-tenant law is something that almost every real estate professional deals with at one time or another. The basics of landlord-tenant law are discussed. The chapter looks at leasing, security deposits, and security deposit returns, and the various laws that concern landlord-tenant issues. Several related topics, including late fees and habitability, are discussed.

1. Leases and Rentals

Landlord-tenant law is a combination of state statues, local ordinances, and case law. Leasing is covered by contract law, see *Towne Realty, Inc. v. Shaffer*, 331 Ill.App.3d 531, 773 N.E.2d 47, 51, 265 Ill.Dec. 685 (4th Dist. 2002). Leases may be oral or written. Under the Statute of Frauds, there is no requirement that leases be in writing, unless the lease is for more than one (1) year. It is, however, highly recommended that all tenancies be in writing. There are many form leases commercially available. Not all leases address all issues that may arise and if a landlord wishes to utilize a form lease, the landlord must thoroughly review the lease to determine if it covers all the contingencies that may arise. In addition, tenants must read the lease carefully in order to understand their rights and responsibilities.

In Illinois, 765 ILCS 700 is the Landlord Tenant Section of the Illinois Compiled Statutes. Among the statues are:

765 ILCS 705/ Landlord and Tenant Act.

765 ILCS 710/ Security Deposit Return Act.

765 ILCS 715/ Security Deposit Interest Act.

765 ILCS 720/ Retaliatory Eviction Act.

765 ILCS 725/ Property Taxes of Alien Landlords Act.

765 ILCS 730/ Rent Concession Act.

765 ILCS 735/ Rental Property Utility Service Act.

765 ILCS 740/ Tenant Utility Payment Disclosure Act.

765 ILCS 742/ Residential Tenants' Right to Repair Act.

765 ILCS 745/ Mobile Home Landlord and Tenant Rights Act.

765 ILCS 750/ Safe Homes Act.

Copies of 765 ILCS 705, 765 ILCS 710, 765 ILCS 715, and 765 ILCS 720 are included at the end of this chapter. Another very important statute related to landlord and tenant law is the Forcible Entry and Detainer Act, 735 ILCS 5/9. The Forcible Entry and Detainer Act will be discussed in this chapter.

In addition to state statutes, many municipalities also have promulgated ordinances. Among the most comprehensive is the Chicago Residential Landlord Tenant Ordinance (**RLTO**). A copy of the RLTO is included at the end of this chapter. For the purposes of this chapter, the RLTO shall be examined.

The RLTO supersedes any conflicting provision in the Forcible Act. See *City of Evanston v. Create, Inc.*, 85 Ill. 2d 101, 111, 421 N.E.2d 196, 199–201 (1981); *Reed v. Burns*, 238 Ill. App. 3d 148, 153, 606 N.E.2d 152, 155 (1st Dist. 1992).

Federal Law

In addition to state and local laws, federal laws and regulations govern the process of evicting tenants from public housing and other federally subsidized housing. In addition, there are federal laws that touch on housing issues, such as the Americans With Disabilities Act, especially 42 U.S. Code § 12183, and the Fair Housing Act, especially 42 U.S. Code § 3604.

Leases

What is a lease? As mentioned above, a **lease** is a contract between a landlord and a tenant. In residential tenancies, the tenant is usually presented with a preprinted form and told to sign it. There is generally little negotiation and the tenant is not in a favorable bargaining position. Tenant applicants can always try to negotiate the terms of form leases presented to them with prospective landlords, but due to the difference in bargaining position, most landlords are not willing to negotiate very much, especially when using a preprinted lease. As such, the RLTO is written to be somewhat favorable to the tenant.

Duration

Where no lease term is specified in an oral or written lease, courts imply renewable lease terms for the periods for which rental payments are paid, e.g., a month-to-month tenancy where rent is paid every month, a week-to-week tenancy where rent is paid every week. If the lease is oral, and the rent is paid monthly, that would be a month-to-month lease. This is the most common form of oral lease.

Many form leases provide for renewal of the tenancy on a periodic basis (e.g. month to month) after the expiration of the first lease term. Tenants must review these provisions carefully. Under the RLTO, §5-12-130(i) and (j) set the rules for renewals.

> (i) Notice Of Renewal Of Rental Agreement. No tenant shall be required to renew a rental agreement more than 90 days prior to the termination date of the rental agreement. If the landlord violates this subsection, the tenant shall recover one month's rent or actual damages, whichever is greater.

> (j) Notice Of Refusal To Renew Rental Agreement. Provided that the landlord has not exercised, or is not in the process of exercising, any of its rights under Section 5-12-130 (a)—(h) hereof, the landlord shall notify the tenant in writing at least 30 days prior to the stated termination date of the rental agreement of the landlord's intent either to terminate a month to month tenancy or not to renew an existing rental agreement. If the landlord fails to give the required written notice, the tenant may remain in the dwelling unit for up to 60 days after the date on which such required written notice is given to the tenant, regardless of the termination date specified in the existing rental agreement. During such occupancy, the terms and conditions of the tenancy (including, without limitation, the rental rate) shall be the same as the terms and conditions during the month of tenancy immediately preceding the notice; provided, however, that if rent was waived or abated in the preceding month or months as part of the original rental agreement, the rental amount during such 60 day period shall be at the rate established on the last date that a full rent payment was made.

Thus, the rule is, a landlord must inform the tenant of the renewal between 30 and 90 days of the expiration of the lease. If the landlord fails to inform the tenant in writing of the landlord's intent not to renew at least 30 days prior to the termination date, the tenant may remain for 60 days after the notice date, but must continue to pay rent and any other required fees.

Construction of Leases

As mentioned above, the rules of contract law apply to leases. *Midland Management Co. v. Helgason*, 158 Ill.2d 97, 630 N.E.2d 836 (1994). Ambiguities are construed against the drafter. *Rose v. Chicago Housing Authority*, 148 Ill Dec. 534, 560 N.E. 2d 1131 (1990), *American Apartment Mngmnt Co. v. Phillips*, 210 Ill Dec. 639, 653 N.E. 2d 834 (1995).

Security Deposits

The Security Deposit Return Act, 765 ILCS 710 (a copy of which is included at the end of this chapter) governs the return of security deposits, unless there is a municipal ordinance, like the RLTO.

Normally, a **security deposit** is held by the landlord as security against the tenant damaging the property during the tenancy (ordinary wear and tear notwithstanding) or for failure to pay rent. The security deposit is *not* to be used for the last month's rent and no landlord should ever allow the tenant to use the security deposit as the last month's rent. In fact, many landlords are now requiring the tenant to tender the first month's rent, last month's rent, and a security deposit at the beginning of the tenancy. If a residential property contains five or more units, a landlord who has received a security deposit from a tenant *must* provide the tenant with a written statement of any damage to the property before deducting repair costs from the security deposit.

In other words, the landlord may not withhold any part of the deposit as compensation for property damage unless the landlord has, within 30 days of the date the tenant vacates, sent the tenant a *written itemized statement* of the damages caused by the tenant to the premises, along with a written estimate of the costs of repair and/or paid receipts for the repairs. The landlord may perform the work himself and charge the tenant for the reasonable cost of labor, although this is not commonly done in practice. If an estimate is provided, the landlord must follow-up by providing receipts of the actual costs within 30 days.

Thus, the default rule is that the landlord must return the security deposit within 45 days of the tenant vacating, unless the landlord furnishes the tenant with the statement and receipts.

Please note, the Security Deposit Return Act does not require a landlord to send any statement to the tenant if the landlord withheld the security deposit because of unpaid rent and not because of property damage.

If the landlord fails to return the security deposit, the tenant may file an action in circuit court if the landlord violates the Security Deposit Return Act. If a circuit court finds that the landlord has refused to supply the itemized statement required by this section, or has supplied such statement in bad faith, and has failed or refused to return the amount of the security deposit due within the time limits provided, the landlord shall be liable for an *amount equal to twice the amount of the security deposit due, together with court costs and reasonable attorney's fees.*

The RLTO, § 5-12-080 provides a tenant with protections as to return of a security deposit.

> (d) The landlord shall, within 45 days after the date that the tenant vacates the dwelling unit or within 7 days after the date that the tenant provides notice of termination of the rental agreement pursuant to Section 5-12-110(g), return to the tenant the security deposit or any balance thereof and the required interest thereon; provided, however, that the landlord may deduct from such security deposit or interest due thereon for the following:
>
> (1) any unpaid rent which has not been validly withheld or deducted pursuant to state or federal law or local ordinance; and
>
> (2) a reasonable amount necessary to repair any damage caused to the premises by the tenant or any person under the tenant's control or on the premises with the tenant's consent, reasonable wear and tear excluded. In case of such damage, the landlord shall deliver or mail to the last known address of the tenant within 30 days an itemized statement of the damages allegedly caused to the premises and the estimated or actual cost for repairing or replacing each item on that statement, attaching copies of the paid re-

ceipts for the repair or replacement. If estimated cost is given, the landlord shall furnish the tenant with copies of paid receipts or a certification of actual costs of repairs of damage if the work was performed by the landlord's employees within 30 days from the date the statement showing estimated cost was furnished to the tenant.

Under the RLTO, a landlord must return a security deposit within 45 days after the date the tenant vacates the dwelling unit. However, the landlord may deduct from the security deposit (1) any unpaid rent which has not been validly withheld or deducted pursuant to state or federal law or local ordinance, and (2) a reasonable amount necessary to repair any damage caused to the premises by the tenant or any person under the tenant's control. The landlord may not deduct for damage based only on reasonable wear and tear.

In the case of damage, the landlord must deliver or mail to the last known address of the tenant within 30 days an itemized statement of damages and the estimated or actual cost for repairing or replacing each item. The landlord must attach copies of paid receipts for the repair or replacement to the statement. If an estimated cost is given, the landlord must furnish the tenant with copies of paid receipts within 30 days from the date the damage statement was furnished to the tenant.

If the landlord or landlord's agent fails to comply with section 5-12-080 of the ordinance, the tenant shall be awarded damages of two times the security deposit plus court costs and reasonable attorney's fees.

Security Deposit Interest

The Security Deposit Interest Act, 765 ILCS 715

The act applies to buildings or complexes with 25 or more residential units. The landlord must have held the security deposit for more than six months. The landlord must pay interest on security deposits computed from the date of the tenant's deposit with the landlord. Interest must be paid at a rate equal to the minimum passbook savings account interest rate paid by the largest Illinois commercial bank as of December 31 of the year prior to the beginning of the lease. Landlord must make the interest payment by cash or by credit against rent due within 30 days of the end of each 12-month rental period, unless the tenant is in default under the lease.

A tenant may bring an action against a landlord who violates the act. A landlord who willfully fails or refuses to pay the interest due is liable for the entire security deposit, together with court costs and reasonable attorney's fees.

For tenancies governed by the Chicago ordinance, all non-exempt landlords who hold a security deposit for more than six months must pay interest on the deposit. The rate is determined by the city comptroller based on a formula contained in RLTO section 5-12-081. The interest rate is published in January of each year. The published rate applies to rental agreements that are entered into that calendar year. The landlord must pay interest within thirty (30) days after the end of each twelve (12) month rental period to the tenant by cash or credit to be applied to the rent due. In addition, the landlord must pay interest on the deposit within forty-five (45) days after the tenant moves out of the dwelling unit.

The ordinance also requires a landlord to hold all security deposits in a federally insured interest-bearing account in a bank, savings and loan association, or other financial institution located in Illinois. The landlord may not commingle a security deposit with the landlord's assets. The security deposit continues to be the property of the tenant.

If the landlord or landlord's agent fails to comply with the interest requirements under section 5-12-080, the tenant shall be awarded *damages of two times the security deposit plus court costs and reasonable attorney's fees.*

Late Fees

The RLTO sets limits on how much a landlord can charge for a **late fee**. RLTO § 5-12-140 states:

> (h) ... that a tenant shall pay a charge, fee or penalty in excess of $10.00 per month for the first $500.00 in monthly rent plus 5% per month for any amount in excess of $500.00 in monthly rent for the late payment of rent.

Warranty of Habitability

A **warranty of habitability** is implied in every residential lease. *Jack Spring v. Little*, 50 Ill.2d 351, 280 N.E. 2d 208 (1972); *Glasoe v. Trinkle*, 107 Ill.2d 1, 479 N.E.2d 915, 88 Ill Dec. 895 (1985). Tenants may enforce this warranty in affirmative lawsuits, or in defense to eviction actions based on non-payment of rent. RLTO § 5-12-100 states that the landlord must disclose any building code violations or any intent to terminate utility services to the unit.

Covenant of Quiet Enjoyment

Every tenant is entitled to the **covenant of quiet enjoyment**. A landlord is prohibited from interfering with the tenant's use of the premises. For instance, the landlord may not enter the premises without the tenant's permission or as provided in the parties' lease. *Chapman v. Brokaw*, 588 N.E.2d 462, 167 Ill. Dec. 821 (3rd 1992). RLTO § 5-12-050 permits the landlord to enter the premises, but prescribes specific written notification (at least two (2) days, unless the entry is an emergency).

(765 ILCS 710/) Security Deposit Return Act.

> (765 ILCS 710/0.01) (from Ch. 80, par. 100)

> Sec. 0.01. Short title. This Act may be cited as the Security Deposit Return Act.

> (765 ILCS 710/1) (from Ch. 80, par. 101)

> Sec. 1. A landlord of residential real property, containing 5 or more units, who has received a security deposit from a tenant to secure the payment of rent or to compensate for damage to the leased property may not withhold any part of that deposit as compensation for property damage unless he has, within 30 days of the date that the tenant vacated the premises, furnished to the tenant, delivered in person or by mail directed

to his last known address, an itemized statement of the damage allegedly caused to the premises and the estimated or actual cost for repairing or replacing each item on that statement, attaching the paid receipts, or copies thereof, for the repair or replacement. If the landlord utilizes his or her own labor to repair any damage caused by the tenant, the landlord may include the reasonable cost of his or her labor to repair such damage. If estimated cost is given, the landlord shall furnish the tenant with paid receipts, or copies thereof, within 30 days from the date the statement showing estimated cost was furnished to the tenant, as required by this Section. If no such statement and receipts, or copies thereof, are furnished to the tenant as required by this Section, the landlord shall return the security deposit in full within 45 days of the date that the tenant vacated the premises.

Upon a finding by a circuit court that a landlord has refused to supply the itemized statement required by this Section, or has supplied such statement in bad faith, and has failed or refused to return the amount of the security deposit due within the time limits provided, the landlord shall be liable for an amount equal to twice the amount of the security deposit due, together with court costs and reasonable attorney's fees.

(765 ILCS 710/1.1) (from Ch. 80, par. 101.1)

Sec. 1.1. In the event of a sale, lease, transfer or other direct or indirect disposition of residential real property, other than to the holder of a lien interest in such property, by a landlord who has received a security deposit or prepaid rent from a tenant, the transferee of such property shall be liable to that tenant for any security deposit, including statutory interest, or prepaid rent which the tenant has paid to the transferor. Transferor shall remain jointly and severally liable with the transferee to the tenant for such security deposit or prepaid rent.

(765 ILCS 710/2) (from Ch. 80, par. 102)

Sec. 2.

This Act takes effect January 1, 1974, and applies to leases executed on or after that date.

(765 ILCS 715/) Security Deposit Interest Act.

(765 ILCS 715/0.01) (from Ch. 80, par. 120)

Sec. 0.01. Short title. This Act may be cited as the Security Deposit Interest Act.

(765 ILCS 715/1) (from Ch. 80, par. 121)

Sec. 1. A landlord of residential real property, containing 25 or more units in either a single building or a complex of buildings located on contiguous parcels of real property, who receives a security deposit from a tenant to secure the payment of rent or compensation for damage to property shall pay interest to the tenant computed from the date of the deposit at a rate equal to the interest paid by the largest commercial bank, as measured by total assets, having its main banking premises in this State on minimum deposit passbook savings accounts as of December 31 of the calendar year immediately preceding the inception of the rental agreement on any deposit held by the landlord for more than 6 months.

(765 ILCS 715/2) (from Ch. 80, par. 122)

Sec. 2. The landlord shall, within 30 days after the end of each 12 month rental period, pay to the tenant any interest, by cash or credit to be applied to rent due, except when the tenant is in default under the terms of the lease.

A landlord who willfully fails or refuses to pay the interest required by this Act shall, upon a finding by a circuit court that he has willfully failed or refused to pay, be liable for an amount equal to the amount of the security deposit, together with court costs and reasonable attorneys fees.

(765 ILCS 715/3) (from Ch. 80, par. 123)

Sec. 3. This Act does not apply to any deposit made with respect to public housing.

Historical and Current Interest Rates under Illinois and Chicago Security Deposit Law

Time Period	Chicago	Illinois
Interest rate Jan 1, 2017 to Dec 31, 2017	0.01%	0.01%
Interest rate Jan 1, 2016 to Dec 31, 2016	0.01%	0.05%
Interest rate Jan 1, 2015 to Dec 31, 2015	0.01%	0.005%
Interest rate Jan 1, 2014 to Dec 31, 2014	0.013%	0.005%
Interest rate Jan 1, 2013 to Dec 31, 2013	0.023%	0.005%
Interest rate Jan 1, 2012 to Dec 31, 2012	0.057%	0.005%
Interest rate Jan 1, 2011 to Dec 31, 2011	0.073%	0.195%
Interest rate Jan 1, 2010 to Dec 31, 2010	0.073%	0.095%
Interest rate Jan 1, 2009 to Dec 31, 2009	0.12%	0.25%
Interest rate Jan 1, 2008 to Dec 31, 2008	1.26%	0.35%
Interest rate Jan 1, 2007 to Dec 31, 2007	1.68%	0.50%
Interest rate Jan 1, 2006 to Dec 31, 2006	1.71%	0.55%
Interest rate Jan 1, 2005 to Dec 31, 2005	1.01%	0.40%
Interest rate Jan 1, 2004 to Dec 31, 2004	0.42%	0.30%
Interest rate Jan 1, 2003 to Dec 31, 2003	0.52%	0.40%
Interest rate Jan 1, 2002 to Dec 31, 2002	0.83%	0.45%
Interest rate Jan 1, 2001 to Dec 31, 2001	3.10%	1.73%
Interest rate Jan 1, 2000 to Dec 31, 2000	2.71%	1.73%
Interest rate Jan 1, 1999 to Dec 31, 1999	2.63%	1.88%
Interest rate Jan 1, 1998 to Dec 31, 1998	3.38%	2.50%
Interest rate Jan 1, 1997 to Dec 31, 1997	3.42%	2.50%
Interest rate Jan 1, 1996 to Dec 31, 1996	5.00%	2.50%
Interest rate Jan 1, 1995 to Dec 31, 1995	5.00%	2.50%
Interest rate Jan 1, 1994 to Dec 31, 1994	5.00%	2.50%
1993 and prior	5.00%	5.00%

Key Terms

Leases
Security Deposit
RLTO
Security Deposit Interest
Late Fee
Warranty of Habitability
Covenant of Quiet Enjoyment

Review Questions

1.   What is a lease?
2.   What is a security deposit?
3.   What is a late fee?
4.   What is the covenant of quiet enjoyment?
5.   What is the warranty of habitability?

Materials in the following chapter appendix include:

- Sample Chicago Lease
- Sample Chicago Residential Landlord Tenant Ordinance Summary
- *Aurelia Lawrence v. Regent Realty Group, Inc., et al.*, 754 N.E.2d 334, 197 Ill.2d 1, 257 Ill. Dec. 676 (2001)

Chapter 8 Appendix

SAMPLE CHICAGO LEASE

CHICAGO APARTMENT LEASE

DATE OF LEASE	TERM OF LEASE	MONTHLY RENT
	SECURITY DEPOSIT*	
	BEGINNING ENDING	

* if none enter none

LESSEE:

NAME:
ADDRESS:
STREET
APT #
CITY
STATE
ZIP

LESSOR:

NAME:
ADDRESS:
STREET
SUITE #
CITY
STATE
ZIP
TELEPHONE

NAME:
ADDRESS:
STREET
SUITE #
CITY
STATE
ZIP
TELEPHONE

NAME:
ADDRESS:
STREET
SUITE #
CITY
STATE
ZIP
TELEPHONE

APPLICATION AND OCCUPANCY NOTICE TO TENANT

LESSEE ACKNOWLEDGES THAT THIS LEASE HAS BEEN EXTENDED TO LESSEE PURSUANT TO AN APPLICATION THEREFOR SUBMITTED BY LESSEE. THE ACCURACY OF THE INFORMATION THEREIN CONTAINED IS A MATERIAL CONDITION OF LESSOR IN EXTENDING THIS LEASE TO LESSEE. LESSEE WARRANTS THAT ALL THE INFORMATION GIVEN BY LESSEE IN APPLYING FOR THIS LEASE IS TRUE AND ACKNOWLEDGES THAT PROVIDING FALSE INFORMATION IS A MATERIAL BREACH OF THIS LEASE. OCCUPANCY BY MORE PERSONS AS SET FORTH IN THIS LEASE OR APPLICATION SHALL CONSTITUTE A MATERIAL BREACH OF THIS LEASE.

NOTICE OF CONDITIONS AFFECTING HABITABILITY

I hereby acknowledge that Lessor has disclosed any code violations, code enforcement litigation, and/or compliance board proceedings during the previous 12 months for the apartment and common area and any notice of intent to terminate utility service, copies of which, if any, are attached to this lease.

_____
Initials of Lessee

FURTHER ACKNOWLEDGEMENTS BY LESSEE

Lessee hereby acknowledges that on _____, 20___, he/she/they received from _____, (Lessor or representative) in connection with the rental of the dwelling located at _____ _____, (address of premises) the following documents:

☐   Security Deposit Receipt   _____
                                                     (Acknowledgement by Lessee)

☐   Heating Cost Disclosure Statement   _____
                                                     (Acknowledgement by Lessee)

☐   Protect Your Family from Lead in
      Your Home Brochure   _____
                                                      (Acknowledgement by Lessee)

In consideration of the mutual agreements and covenants herein set forth, and in further consideration of the statements made by Lessee in the Application for Lease and all supporting documents thereto, the truth and accuracy thereof being attested to by Lessee, and the information therein contained being incorporated into this lease as if set forth herein in full, Lessor hereby leases to Lessee, and Lessee hereby leases from Lessor, for use as a private dwelling unit only, the above noted premises, together with the fixtures and appliances belonging thereto, for the above Term:

_____   _____
           DATE   DATE

_____   _____
           DATE   DATE

LEASE COVENANTS AND AGREEMENTS:

1. RENT: Lessee shall pay to Lessor or Lessor's authorized agent, at the address set forth above, or as hereafter changed by written notice to lessee, as rent for the Premises, the sum stated above. Rent is due and payable on the first day of each calendar month, in advance. The timely payment of each installment of rent is deemed to be of the essence of this Lease.

2. LATE CHARGES: Rent received by Lessor later than the 5th day of the month on which such payment is due shall bear a late charge of $10.00 plus 5% of any rent due in excess of $500.00. If Lessee mails rent to Lessor, the late charge will apply if the rent is received later than the 5th day of the month, regardless of the date Lessee mailed such rent payment. If a payment of rent is made by personal check which is later dishonored by the Lessee's bank, the tenant shall be assessed any bank charges incurred by Lessor as a result of such dishonored check, in addition to the rent and late charge due on the payment of rent.

3. SECURITY DEPOSIT: Lessee has deposited with Lessor, the sum set forth above as a security deposit to be held by the Lessor in accordance with State or local law or ordinance to secure the faithful performance by the Lessee of all of the provisions contained in this lease. If Lessee performs all of the obligations as provided in this lease and pays all sums due Lessor, then Lessor, after the Lessee has surrendered possession of the premises and delivered the keys thereto to Lessor, shall refund said deposit to Lessee, including interest as provided by law. If Lessee has failed to perform or comply with any of the provisions of the lease, then Lessor may apply all or any part of the security deposit in payment of any sums due from Lessee to Lessor, or to pay for repair of any damages caused by Lessee, Lessee's co-occupants, or guests. The security deposit shall not be treated as advance payment of rent, and the Lessee shall not apply the security deposit as rent during the term of the lease unless Lessee obtains written permission from Lessor to do so.

4. POSSESSION: If Lessor cannot deliver possession of the premises at the commencement of the lease term, the rent shall be abated until the premises are available for occupancy by Lessee, or at Lessee's option, the Lessee may terminate this lease upon written notice to Lessor. Lessor shall not be liable to Lessee for any consequential damages to Lessee arising as a result of Lessor's inability to give Lessee possession of the premises at the commencement of the lease term.

5. CONDITION OF PREMISES: Lessee has examined the premises prior to accepting the same and prior to the execution of this lease, and is satisfied with the physical condition thereof, including but not limited to the heating, plumbing, and smoke detectors. Lessee's acceptance of possession shall constitute conclusive evidence of Lessee's receipt of the premises in good order and repair as of the commencement of the lease term. Lessor or his agent has made no promises as to condition or repair to Lessee, unless they are expressed in this lease or a rider hereto signed by Lessee and Lessor or his agent, and no promises to decorate, alter, or repair the premises have been made by Lessor or his agent, unless expressed herein.

6. LIMITATION OF LIABILITY: Except as provided by state or local law or ordinance, Lessor shall not be liable for any damage (a) occasioned by failure to keep Premises in repair; (b) for any loss or damage of or to Lessee's property wherever located in or about the building or premises, or (c) acts or neglect of other tenants, occupants, or others at the building.

7. LESSEE TO MAINTAIN: Lessee shall keep the premises and the fixtures and appliances therein in a clean and healthy condition, and in good working order, and in accordance with any and all ordinances applicable to the tenancy, at Lessee's own expense, and upon the termination of this lease, for any reason, Lessee shall return the premises to Lessor in as good a condition of cleanliness and repair as at the commencement of this lease, reasonable wear and tear excepted. Lessee shall make all necessary repairs to the premises whenever damage has occurred or repairs are required due to Lessee's conduct or neglect. Lessee shall replace all broken glass and fixtures and shall maintain all smoke and carbon monoxide detectors in good condition at all times, including replacing spent batteries as necessary. Upon Lessee vacating the premises, if the premises are not clean and in good repair, Lessor or his agent may replace the premises in the same condition of repair and cleanliness as existed at the commencement of the lease term. Lessee agrees to pay Lessor for all expenses incurred by Lessor in replacing the premises in that condition. Lessee shall not cause or permit any waste, misuse, or neglect to occur to the water, gas, utilities, or any other portion of the premises.

8. USE OF PREMISES: The premises shall be occupied for residential purposes only, and only by the persons disclosed in this lease and on the Application for Lease submitted by Lessee in connection with the renting of the premises. Lessee shall not engage in any activity, which will increase the rate of insurance on the property. Lessee shall not allow trash to accumulate in the common areas of the premises or allow objects to be thrown from windows. Lessee shall not hang objects out of windows or place objects on windowsills or ledges, which may fall and injure persons below. Lessee shall not keep any pet in the premises without written permission being first obtained from Lessor. Lessee shall not use porches for cooking, sleeping or storage of furniture, bicycles or other items of personal property. In no case shall Lessee allow porches or decks to be overloaded or occupied by more people than would be reasonably safe based on the condition of such porch or deck.

9. APPLIANCES: Lessee shall not install any air conditioning, heating, or cooling equipment or dishwashers or clothes washers or dryers or other appliances in any portion of the building or premises occupied by Lessee without first obtaining Lessor's written permission to do so. All such appliances installed by Lessee shall be maintained in good working order by Lessee and removed by Lessee at the expiration of the term of the lease. Any damage caused by appliances installed by Lessee shall be the responsibility of Lessee and Lessee shall reimburse Lessor for the cost of repair of any damage caused by such appliances.

10. HEAT AND HOT WATER: Lessor agrees to provide Lessee with heat and hot water in sufficient quantities as may be required by law or ordinance during the term of the lease. If the Premises contains separate heating and/or hot water fixtures, then Lessor's sole obligation shall be to provide Lessee such fixtures in good operating condition at the commencement of the lease, and Lessee shall be responsibility for the utility costs for the operation thereof.

11. DISTURBANCE: Lessee agrees not to play televisions, radios, or musical instruments or musical playback equipment in a manner which disturbs other tenants, and shall maintain the volume of such equipment at reasonable levels. In addition, Lessee agrees to limit playing of such equipment between the hours of 10:00 p.m. and 7:00 a.m. to a volume that cannot be heard by persons outside of the premises.

12. ACCESS TO PREMISES: Lessee shall permit the Lessor access to the premises at all reasonable times, subject to the notice requirements of applicable law or ordinance, to inspect the premises and/or to make any necessary repairs, maintenance, or improvements or supply necessary or agreed upon services, or to determine Lessor's compliance with the provisions of this Lease. In the event of an emergency or where repairs in the building require access to Lessee's premises, Lessor may enter without prior notice to Lessee, without the same being considered a forcible entry by Lessor. Lessee's failure to provide such access shall be a breach of this lease, and Lessor shall be entitled to terminate this lease in the event such access is denied by Lessee.

13. SUBLET OR ASSIGNMENT: Lessee shall not sublet the premises or any part thereof, nor assign this lease, without obtaining Lessor's prior written permission to sublet or assign. Lessor shall not unreasonably withhold permission and will accept a reasonable sublease as provided by ordinance.

14. HOLDING OVER: If the Lessee remains in possession of the premises or any part thereof after the termination of the lease by lapse of time or otherwise, then the Lessor may, at Lessor's option, consider such holding over as constituting a month-to-month tenancy, upon the terms of this lease except at double the monthly rental specified above. Lessee shall also pay to Lessor all damages sustained by Lessor resulting from Lessee's retaining possession of the premises. In the event Lessor accepts a payment of rent for a period after the expiration of this lease in the absence of any specific written agreement, continued occupancy shall be deemed a month-to-month tenancy, on the same terms and conditions as herein provided, except for the double rent provision, to the extent permitted by state or local law or ordinance.

15. FORCIBLE DETAINER: If Lessee defaults in the payment of rent or any part thereof, Lessor may distrain for rent and shall have a lien on Lessee's property for all monies due Lessor, or if Lessee defaults in the performance of any of the covenants or agreements herein contained, Lessor or his agents, at Lessor's option, may terminate this Lease and, if abandoned or vacated, may re-enter the premises. Non-performance of any of Lessee's obligations shall constitute a default and forfeiture of this lease, and Lessor's failure to take action on account of Lessee's default shall not constitute a waiver of said default.

16. LIABILITY FOR RENT: Lessee shall continue paying rent and all other charges for the Premises to the end of the term of this lease, whether or not the Premises becomes vacant by reason of abandonment, breach of the lease by Lessee, wrongful termination by Lessee, or if the Lessee has been evicted for breach of this lease, to the extent said obligation for rent has not been mitigated, abated, or discharged, in whole or in part, by any law or ordinance. Notwithstanding any of the provisions contained in this section, the Landlord shall make a good faith effort to re-let the Premises (but not in priority to other vacancies) and if the Premises is re-let, Lessee shall be responsible for the balance of the rent, costs, advertising costs, and attorney's fees in connection therewith.

17. BINDING EFFECT: If Lessee shall violate any covenant or provision of this lease, Lessor shall have the right to terminate this lease or Lessee's right to possession pursuant to the lease upon appropriate legal notice to Lessee. If Lessee assigns this lease, whether with or without Lessor's permission as required herein, the covenants and conditions contained in the Lease shall nonetheless be binding on the assignee as if assignee had signed the lease. Nothing contained in this paragraph 17 shall preclude Lessor from commencing legal proceedings against any assignee of this lease who obtained possession from the party named as Lessee in this Lease without Lessor's written permission as required in paragraph 13 above.

18. ATTORNEY'S FEES: If Lessor commences legal proceedings to enforce the covenants of this lease due to Lessee's breach thereof, Lessee shall pay Lessor's reasonable attorney's fees incurred to enforce Lessee's compliance with the terms of this Lease.

19. CONTINUOUS OCCUPANCY: Lessee shall maintain continuous occupancy of the premises, and not allow the same to remain vacant for any period in excess of ten days without notifying the Lessor of such vacancy. Lessee shall not allow persons other than those authorized by the Lease to occupy the premises as guests for periods exceeding seven consecutive days during the term of the Lease for any reason.

20. REMEDIES CUMULATIVE: Lessor's remedies contained in this Lease are cumulative and are in addition to, and not in lieu of, any other remedies granted to Lessor pursuant to this Lease or applicable State or Local Law or Ordinance.

21. FIRE OR CASUALTY: If the Premises, Building, or any part thereof shall become uninhabitable as a result of fire, explosion, or other casualty, Lessor and Lessee shall have all of the rights provided by state or local law or ordinance. For purposes of this paragraph, Lessor's good faith effort to obtain insurance adjustments, settlements, or awards to obtain sufficient funds to perform repairs made necessary due to fire, explosion, or other casualty shall be deemed diligent efforts to repair the Building within a reasonable time.

22. SECURITY GATES OR BARS: The installation by Lessee of any metal gate or bars on doors or windows is dangerous and strictly prohibited. Lessee shall immediately remove same upon notice by Lessor to Lessee to do so and Lessor shall have the right to immediately remove any such installation at Lessee's expense if Lessee shall fail to do so upon notice. Lessee hereby grants Lessor access to the leased premises at all reasonable times for the purpose of removing such gates or bars. The cost of repairing any damage to the leased premises caused by the installation and/or removal or such gates or bars shall be paid by Lessee upon demand by Lessor therefore, in addition to all costs of enforcement of this paragraph 22, including reasonable attorney's fees incurred by Lessor in enforcing this provision. In addition to the foregoing, the installation of such gates or bars shall constitute a breach of this lease, entitling Lessor, at Lessor's sole option, to terminate Lessee's right to possession of the premises pursuant to this lease and commence proceedings to dispossess Lessee from the premises.

23. MECHANIC'S LIENS: Lessee shall not place or allow to be placed on the Premises, the building, or elsewhere on the real property, any mechanic's lien or any other claim for lien for any repairs, maintenance, alterations, or modifications performed by, or ordered or contradicted by, the Lessee, whether or not same were rightfully performed or ordered by the Lessee. The placement of any such lien shall constitute a breach of this lease and upon ten days' notice to cure said lien or lien claim, Lessor may terminate Lessee's tenancy or right to possession. In addition, Lessor shall have the right to satisfy and remove said lien without regard to the merits thereof and Lessee shall be responsible for the damages incurred in removing the lien, along with other damages, costs, and attorney's fees incurred by Lessor in connection therewith.

24. RULES AND REGULATIONS: Lessee agrees to obey the Rules and Regulations contained in this Lease, and any attachments and inclusions hereto as well as any further reasonable Rules and Regulations established by the Lessor during the pendency of this lease. The Rules and Regulations are hereby incorporated into and made a part of this lease. Failure to observe the Rules and Regulations shall be deemed to be a material breach of this lease, and in event of such breach, Lessor shall be entitled to terminate Lessee's right to possession under the Lease upon ten days' notice, and shall further be entitled to such rights and remedies as provided by applicable state or local law or ordinance.

25. SUBORDINATION OF LEASE: This lease is subordinate to all mortgages which may now or hereafter affect the real property of which the Premises forms a part. The recordation of this lease, or any memorandum thereof by Lessee shall constitute a material breach of this lease.

26. SEVERABILITY: If any clause, phrase, provision, or portion of this lease, or the application thereof to any person or circumstance, shall be determined to be an invalid or unenforceable under applicable law or ordinance, such event shall not affect, impair, or render invalid or unenforceable the remainder of this lease or any other clause, phrase, provision, or portion hereof, nor shall it affect the applicability of any clause, provision, or portion hereof to other persons or circumstances, and the lease shall be interpreted in accordance with said ordinance.

1. No dogs, cats, or other animals shall be kept in the premises except with the Lessor's prior consent, and subject to the conditions set forth in any such consent. No animals are permitted without a leash in any public areas of the premises.
2. No additional locks or other similar devices shall be attached to any door without Lessor's written consent.

3. Lessee shall not install or operate any machinery, refrigeration, or heating devices or use or permit onto the premises any inflammable fluids or materials which may be hazardous to life or property.

4. Hallways, stairways, and elevators shall not be obstructed or used for any purpose other than ingress and egress from the building. Children are not permitted to play in the common areas. Lessee may not store any items in the hallways or common areas of the building.

5. Operation of electrical appliances or other devices which interfere with radio or television reception is not permitted.

6. Deliveries and moving of furniture must be conducted through the rear entrance of the building at times permitted by Lessor.

7. Lessee may not barbeque or operate cooking equipment on porches or balconies.

8. Lessee shall not dispose of rubbish, rags, or other items which might clog toilets or sink drains into toilets or sink drains.

9. Lessee shall not place any signs or advertisements on the windows or within the apartment or otherwise upon the Building, if such signs are visible from the street.

10. Lessee shall dispose of garbage and refuse by securely bagging or wrapping same and disposing of it in designated garbage containers or incinerators. Lessee shall not allow garbage containers to overflow and shall see to it that garbage container lids are fully closed and secure at all times.

11. Lessee shall not install a waterbed or any other unusually heavy item of furniture without prior written permission from Lessor.

12. Lessee shall not interfere in any manner with the heating or lighting or other fixtures in the building nor run extension cords or electrical appliances in violation of the Building Code.

13. Lessor may bar individuals from the building and/or Lessee's premises. All guests and invitees of Lessee shall observe all rules and regulations of the building. If these provisions are violated by guests, they may be barred and/or arrested for criminal trespass, after they have received a barred notice and then have been placed on a barred list by Lessor. Violation of this rule are grounds for termination of your tenancy.

In consideration of One Dollar to the undersigned in hand paid, and of other good and valuable consideration, the receipt of which is hereby acknowledged, Lessor hereby transfers, assigns and sets over to _____ all right, title and interest in and to the above Lease and the rent thereby reserved, except rent due and payable prior to _____ 20____.

                                                    Dated _____, 20_____.

_____(SEAL)

_____(SEAL)

In consideration of One Dollar and other good and valuable consideration, the receipt of which is hereby acknowledged, the undersigned Guarantor hereby guarantees the payment of rent and performance by Lessee. Lessee's heirs, executors, administrators, successors, or assigns of all covenants and agreements of the above Lease.

                                                    Dated _____ 20____.

_____(SEAL)

_____(SEAL)

CITY OF CHICAGO
RESIDENTIAL LANDLORD AND
TENANT ORDINANCE SUMMARY

The Department of
HOUSING and
ECONOMIC
DEVELOPMENT

City of Chicago
Rahm Emanuel
Mayor

At initial offering, this Summary of the ordinance must be attached to every written rental agreement and also upon initial offering for renewal. The Summary must also be given to a tenant at initial offering of an oral agreement, whether the agreement is new or a renewal. Unless otherwise noted, all provisions are effective as of November 6, 1986. {Mun. Code Ch. 5-12-170}

IMPORTANT: IF YOU SEEK TO EXERCISE RIGHTS UNDER THE ORDINANCE, OBTAIN A COPY OF THE ENTIRE ORDINANCE TO DETERMINE APPROPRIATE REMEDIES AND PROCEDURES. CONSULTING AN ATTORNEY WOULD ALSO BE ADVISABLE. FOR A COPY OF THE ORDINANCE, VISIT THE CITY CLERK'S OFFICE ROOM 107, CITY HALL, 121 N. LASALLE, CHICAGO, ILLINOIS.

IMPORTANT NOTICE
A message about porch safety: The porch or deck of this building should be designed for a live load of up to 100 lbs. per square foot, and is safe only for its intended use. Protect your safety. Do not overload the porch or deck. If you have questions about porch or deck safety, call the City of Chicago non-emergency number, 3-1-1.

WHAT RENTAL UNITS ARE COVERED BY THE ORDINANCE? {MUN. CODE CH. 5-12-010 & 5-12-020}
- Rental units with written or oral leases (including all subsidized units such as CHA, IHDA, Section 8 Housing Choice Vouchers, etc.)
EXCEPT
- Units in owner occupied buildings with six or fewer units.
- Units in hotels, motels, rooming houses, unless rent is paid on a monthly basis and unit is occupied for more than 32 days.
- School dormitory rooms, shelters, employee's quarters, non-residential rental properties.
- Owner occupied co-ops and condominiums.

WHAT ARE THE TENANT'S GENERAL DUTIES UNDER THE ORDINANCE? {MUN. CODE CH. 5-12-040}
The tenant, the tenant's family and invited guests must comply with all obligations imposed specifically upon tenants by the Municipal Code, including:
- Buying and installing working batteries in smoke and carbon monoxide detectors within tenant's apartment.
- Keeping the unit safe and clean.
- Using all equipment and facilities in a reasonable manner.
- Not deliberately or negligently damaging the unit.
- Not disturbing other residents.

LANDLORD'S RIGHT OF ACCESS {MUN. CODE CH. 5-12-050}
- A tenant shall permit reasonable access to a landlord upon receiving two days notice by mail, telephone, written notice or other means designed in good faith to provide notice.
- A general notice to all affected tenants may be given in the event repair work on common areas or other units may require such access.
- In the event of emergency or where repairs elsewhere unexpectedly require access, the landlord must provide notice within two days after entry.

SECURITY DEPOSITS AND PREPAID RENT {MUN. CODE CH. 5-12-080 AND 5-12-081}
- A landlord must give a tenant a receipt for a security deposit including the owner's name, the date it was received and a description of the dwelling unit. The receipt must be signed by the person accepting the security deposit.
- However, if the security deposit is paid by means of an electronic funds transfer, the landlord has the option to give an electronic receipt. The electronic receipt must describe the dwelling unit, state the amount and date of the deposit, and have an electronic or digital signature. (eff. 10-8-10)
- However, the landlord may accept the payment of the first month's rent and the security deposit in one check or one electronic funds transfer and deposit such rent and security deposit into one account, if the landlord within 5 days of such acceptance transfers the security deposit into a separate account. (eff. 10-8-10)
- A landlord must hold all security deposits in a federally insured interest-bearing account in a financial institution located in Illinois. Security deposits and interest thereon shall not be commingled with the assets of the landlord.
- A written rental agreement must specify the financial institution where the security deposit will be deposited. If there is no written rental agreement, the landlord must in writing provide such information to the tenant within 14 days of the receipt of the security deposit. If the security deposit is transferred to another financial institution, the landlord must notify the tenant within 14 days of the transfer the name and address of the new financial institution. (eff. 10-8-10)

SECURITY DEPOSITS AND PREPAID RENT {MUN. CODE CH. 5-12-080 AND 5-12-081} (cont.)

- A landlord must pay interest each year on security deposits and prepaid rent held more than six months. (eff. 1-1-92)
- The rate of interest a landlord must pay is set each year by the City Comptroller. (eff. 7-1-97)
- Before expenses for damages can be deducted from the security deposit, the landlord must provide the tenant with an itemized statement of the damages within 30 days of the date the tenant vacates the dwelling unit.
- A landlord must return all security deposits and required interest, if any, minus unpaid rent and expenses for damages, within 45 days from the date the tenant vacates the unit.
- In the event of a fire, a landlord must return all security deposit and required interest, if any, minus unpaid rent and expenses for damages, within seven days from the date that the tenant provides notice of termination of the rental agreement. (eff. 1-1-92)
- In the event of a sale or any other disposition of residential real property by a landlord, the successor landlord is liable to the tenant for any security deposit or prepaid rent paid to the original landlord. The successor landlord must notify the tenant, in writing, within 14 days from the disposition that the deposit or prepaid rent was transferred to the successor landlord. The original landlord remains liable for the deposit or prepaid rent until the original landlord transfers the deposit or prepaid rent to the successor landlord and provides proper notice of such transfer to the tenant. (Mun. Code Ch. 5-12-080 (e) eff. 5-18-10)
- Subject to correcting a deficient amount of interest paid to a tenant on a security deposit if a landlord fails to comply with specified security deposit requirements the tenant shall be awarded damages in an amount equal to two times the security deposit plus interest. (eff. 10-8-10)

WHAT ARE THE LANDLORD'S GENERAL DUTIES UNDER THE ORDINANCE?

- To give tenant written notice of the owner's or manager's name, address and telephone number. {Mun. Code Ch. 5-12-090}
- Within seven (7) days of being served a foreclosure complaint an owner or landlord of a premises that is the subject of the foreclosure complaint shall disclose, in writing, to all tenants of the premises that a foreclosure action has been filed. The owner or landlord shall also notify of a foreclosure suit, in writing, before a tenant signs a lease.
  {Mun. Code Ch. 5-12-095 eff.11-05-08}
- To give new or renewing tenants notice of:
  1) Code citations issued by the City in the previous 12 months;
  2) Pending Housing Court or administrative hearing actions;
  3) Water, electrical or gas service shut-offs to the building during entire occupancy. {Mun. Code Ch. 5-12-100}
- To maintain the property in compliance with all applicable provisions of the Municipal Code. {Mun. Code Ch. 5-12-070}
- To not require a tenant to renew an agreement more than 90 days before the existing agreement terminates. (eff. 1-1-92) {Mun. Code Ch. 5-12-130 (i)}
- To provide a tenant with at least 30 days written notice if the rental agreement will not be renewed. If the landlord fails to give the required written notice, the tenant may remain in the dwelling unit for 60 days under the same terms and conditions as the last month of the existing agreement. (eff. 1-1-92) {Mun. Code Ch. 5-12-130 (j)}
- To not enforce prohibited lease provisions. {Mun Code Ch. 5-12-140}

TENANT REMEDIES {MUN. CODE CH. 5-12-110}

Minor Defects
- If the landlord fails to maintain the property in compliance with the Code and the tenant or the tenant's family or guests are not responsible for the failure, the tenant may:
  1) Request in writing that the landlord make repairs within 14 days, and if the landlord fails to do so the tenant may withhold an amount of rent that reasonably reflects the reduced value of the unit. Rent withholding begins from the fifteenth day until repairs are made; OR
  2) Request in writing that the landlord make repairs within 14 days and if the landlord fails to do so the tenant may have the repairs made and deduct up to $500 or 1/2 of the month's rent, whichever is more, but not to exceed one month's rent. Repairs must be done in compliance with the Code. Receipt for the repairs must be given to the landlord and no more than the cost of the repairs can be deducted from the rent; and also
  3) File suit against the landlord for damages and injunctive relief.

Major Defects
- If the landlord fails to maintain the property in compliance with the Code, and the failure renders the premises not reasonably fit and habitable, the tenant may request in writing that the landlord make repairs within 14 days. If after 14 days repairs are not made, the tenant may immediately terminate the lease. Tenant must deliver possession and move out in 30 days or tenant's notice is considered withdrawn. (eff. 1-1-92)

FAILURE TO PROVIDE ESSENTIAL SERVICES (HEAT, RUNNING OR HOT WATER, ELECTRICITY, GAS OR PLUMBING) {MUN. CODE CH. 5-12-110(f)}

- If, contrary to the lease, an essential service is not provided, or if the landlord fails to maintain the building in material compliance with the Code to such an extent that such failure constitutes an immediate danger to the health and safety of the tenant, and the tenant or tenant's family or guests are not responsible for such failure, after giving written notice, the tenant may do ONE of the following:
  1) Procure substitute service, and upon presenting paid receipts to the landlord, deduct the cost from the rent; OR
  2) File suit against the landlord and recover damages based on the reduced value of the dwelling unit; OR
  3) Procure substitute housing and be excused from paying rent for that period. The tenant may also recover from the landlord the cost of substitute housing up to an amount equal to the monthly rent for each month or portion thereof; OR
  4) Request that the landlord correct the failure within 24 hours and if the landlord fails to do so, withhold the monthly rent an amount that reasonably reflects the reduced value of its premises. Rent withholding cannot start until after the 24 hours expires and applies only to days past the 24-hour waiting period; OR (eff. 1-1-92)

5) Request that the landlord correct the failure within 72 hours and if the landlord fails to do so, terminate the rental agreement. If the rental agreement is terminated, the tenant must deliver possession and move out within 30 days or the notice of termination is considered withdrawn. (eff. 1-1-92)

Note: Remedies 4) and 5) may not be used if the failure is due to the utility provider's failure to provide service. For the purposes of this section only, the notice a tenant provides must be in writing, delivered to the address the landlord has given the tenant as an address to which notices should be sent. If the landlord does not inform the tenant of an address, the tenant may deliver written notice to the last known address of the landlord or by any other reasonable means designed in good faith to provide written notice to the landlord. (eff.1-1-92)

FIRE OR CASUALTY DAMAGE {MUN. CODE CH. 5-12-110 (g)}

• If a fire damages the unit to an extent that it is in material noncompliance with the Code and the tenant, tenant's family or guests are not responsible for the fire or accident, the tenant may:

1) Move out immediately, but if this is done, the tenant must provide written notice to the landlord of the intention to terminate within 14 days after moving out.

2) The tenant may stay in the unit, if it is legal, but if the tenant stays and cannot use a portion of the unit because of damage, the rent may be reduced to reflect the reduced value of the unit.

3) If the tenant stays, and the landlord fails to diligently carry out the work, the tenant may notify the landlord, in writing, within 14 days after the tenant becomes aware that the work is not being diligently carried out, of the tenant's intention to terminate the rental agreement and move out.

SUBLEASES {MUN. CODE CH. 5-12-120}

• The landlord must accept a reasonable subtenant offered by the tenant without charging additional fees.
• If a tenant moves prior to the end of the rental agreement, the landlord must make a good faith effort to find a new tenant at a fair rent.
• If the landlord is unsuccessful in re-renting the unit, the tenant remains liable for the rent under the rental agreement, as well as the landlord's cost of advertising.

WHAT HAPPENS IF A TENANT PAYS RENT LATE? {MUN. CODE CH. 5-12-140 (h)}

• If the tenant fails to pay rent on time, the landlord may charge a late fee of $10.00 per month on rents under $500 plus 5 percent per month on that part of the rent that exceeds $500.00 (i.e., for a $450.00 monthly rent the late fee is $10.00, for a $700 monthly rent the late fee is $10 plus 5% of $200.00 or $20.00 total) (eff. 1-1-92)

WHAT HAPPENS IF A TENANT PAYS RENT DUE AFTER THE EXPIRATION OF THE TIME PERIOD SET FORTH IN A TERMINATION NOTICE? {MUN. CODE CH. 5-12-140 (g) CH. 5-12-130 (g)}

• If the landlord accepts the rent due knowing that there is a default in payment, the tenant may stay.

LANDLORD REMEDIES {MUN. CODE CH. 5-12-130}

• If the tenant fails to pay rent, the landlord, after giving five days written notice to the tenant, may terminate the rental agreement.
• If the tenant fails to comply with the Code or the rental agreement, the landlord, after giving 10 days written notice to the tenant, may terminate the rental agreement if tenant fails to correct the violation.
• If the tenant fails to comply with the Code or the rental agreement, the landlord may request in writing that the tenant comply as promptly as conditions permit in the case of emergency, or within 14 days. If the breach is not corrected in the time period specified, the landlord may enter the dwelling unit and have the necessary work done. In this case, the tenant shall be responsible for all costs of repairs.

LOCKOUTS {MUN. CODE CH. 5-12-160}

This section applies to every residential rental unit in Chicago. There are no exceptions.

• It is illegal for a landlord to lock out a tenant, or change locks, or remove doors of a rental unit, or cut off heat, utility or water service, or to do anything which interferes with the tenant's use of the apartment.
• All lockouts are illegal and the Police Department is responsible for enforcement against such illegal activity. (eff. 1-1-92) (Police Special Order 93-12)
• The landlord shall be fined $200 to $500 for each day the lockout occurs or continues.
• The tenant may sue the landlord to recover possession of the unit and twice the actual damages sustained or two months' rent, whichever is greater.

PROHIBITION ON RETALIATORY CONDUCT BY LANDLORD {MUN. CODE CH. 5-12-150}

• A tenant has the right to complain or testify in good faith about their tenancy to governmental agencies or officials, police, media, community groups, tenant unions or the landlord. A landlord is prohibited from retaliating by terminating or threatening to terminate a tenancy, increasing rent, decreasing services, bringing or threatening to bring an eviction action, or refusing to renew a lease agreement.

ATTORNEY'S FEES {MUN. CODE CH. 5-12-180}

• Except in eviction actions, the prevailing plaintiff in any action arising from the application of this Ordinance shall be entitled to recover all court costs and reasonable attorney's fees. (eff. 1-1-92)

WHERE CAN I GET A COPY OF THE ORDINANCE?

• For a copy of the Ordinance, visit the Office of the City Clerk, Room 107, City Hall, 121 North LaSalle Street, Chicago, Illinois or view it at the Municipal Reference Library, Harold Washington Library, 5th Floor, 400 S. State Street, Chicago, Illinois.

Approved by the City of Chicago, July 2010

Chicago Rents Right

Good Tenants, Good Landlords, Great Neighborhoods!

For more information, please call 312-742-RENT (7368)

754 N.E.2d 334 (2001)

197 Ill.2d 1

257 Ill.Dec. 676

Aurelia LAWRENCE, Appellee,

v.

REGENT REALTY GROUP, INC., et al., Appellants.

No. 88237.

Supreme Court of Illinois.

July 26, 2001.

Sanford Kahn, Ltd., Chicago (Richard W. Christoff, of counsel), for appellants.

Sorling, Nothrup, Hanna, Cullen & Cochran, Ltd., Springfield (Stephen J. Bochenek and James G. Fahey, of counsel), for amicus curiae Illinois Association of Realtors.

Holland & Knight LLP, Chicago (Steven M. Elrod, Peter M. Friedman and Naomi F. Katz, of counsel), for amicus curiae Chicago Association of Realtors.

Daniel A. Edelman, Cathleen M. Combs, James O. Latturner and Tara Goodwin, of Edelman, Combs & Latturner, Chicago, for amicus curiae Illinois Consumer Justice Council, Inc.

Lawrence D. Wood, Chicago for amicus curiae Legal Assistance Foundation of Chicago.

Chief Justice HARRISON delivered the opinion of the court:

Aurelia Lawrence (Lawrence) brought an action in the circuit court of Cook County to recover damages from her landlord, Regent Realty Group (Regent), for failure to make annual interest payments on her security deposit as required by section 5-12-080(c) of Chicago's Residential Landlord and Tenant Ordinance (RLTO) (Chicago Municipal Code § 5-12-080(c) (amended November 6, 1991)). The matter was tried before the court, sitting without a jury, which entered judgment in favor of Regent. The court denied Lawrence's claim for double damages as authorized by the section 5-12-080(f) of the RLTO (Chicago Municipal Code § 5-12-080(f) (amended November 6, 1991)) and refused to entertain her claim for costs and attorney fees (see Chicago Municipal Code § 5-12-180 (amended November 6, 1991)), but ordered Regent to refund to Lawrence the amount of her security deposit with accrued interest.

Lawrence moved for a new trial or reconsideration. When that motion was denied, she appealed. The appellate court reversed and remanded. It held that Lawrence was entitled to judgment for double the amount of her deposit plus interest, as specified by the Chicago Municipal Code. It further held that Lawrence should be given a hearing on her fee petition and that she was entitled to an award of her reasonable attorney fees. 307 Ill.App.3d 155, 160–61, 240 Ill.Dec. 350, 717 N.E.2d443. We granted Regent's petition for leave to appeal (177 Ill.2d R. 315) and subsequently allowed the Chicago Association of Realtors and the Illinois Association of Realtors to file amicus curiae briefs in support of Regent. We also allowed the Illinois Consumer Justice Council, Inc., and the Legal Assistance Foundation of Chicago to file amicus curiae briefs in support of Lawrence. 155 Ill.2d R. 346. For the reasons that follow, we now affirm the judgment of the appellate court.

The facts, which come to us through a bystanders' report, are straightforward. Lawrence rented an apartment in a building managed by Regent. The apartment was located in the City of Chicago in a building containing more than six residential dwelling units and was subject to the provisions of the RLTO. Lawrence lived there from October 1, 1990, to November 1, 1996. During the term of her occupancy, she received and executed a series of leases. Pursuant to the provisions of those leases, Lawrence paid Regent security deposits, including deposits to cover damage by pets. The security deposits, including the pet deposits, were each held for a period in excess of six months.

During Lawrence's first year in the apartment, Regent paid her interest on the total amount of her security deposit, including the amount designated as a pet deposit. In subsequent years, however, it only paid her interest on the basic security deposit. No interest was paid on the portion of the security deposit designated as the pet deposit. The specifics of each lease follow.

During the first year, which commenced October 1, 1990, and ended September 30, 1991, Lawrence paid Regent a basic security deposit of $435, which was equivalent to one month's rent. She also paid Regent an additional $100 as her pet deposit.

The next year, October 1, 1991, through September 30, 1992, Regent increased Lawrence's monthly rent to $455. Regent carried over her $435 basic security deposit and $100 pet deposit. At the same time, it credited Lawrence for $26.75. That sum represented interest earned on the full amount of the $535 security deposit held by Regent during the previous year, calculated at an annual rate of 5%, the amount fixed by law. Regent did not pay this money directly to Lawrence. Instead, it held it as an additional security deposit. Including the interest credit, Lawrence's total security deposit for 1991–92 was $561.75.

In 1992–93, Regent increased Lawrence's monthly rent to $460. It carried over her prior security deposit of $561.75. It also credited Lawrence for an additional $23.09 in interest, which it applied to increase Lawrence's total security deposit to $584.84. The $23.09 was computed by applying the statutory interest rate of 5% to $461.75 of Lawrence's security deposit. For purposes of determining the interest due, Lawrence's $100 pet deposit was not included.

By letter dated December 30, 1992, Lawrence advised Regent that the $100 had not been included in its interest calculation. Lawrence asked that any corrections or explanations regarding the interest calculation be in writing. Regent did not respond. Instead, it continued to exclude that portion of the security deposit attributable to the pet deposit when computing the interest it owed.

During the 1993–94 lease term, Regent increased Lawrence's monthly rent to $465. The $584.84 security deposit was carried over. In addition, Regent credited Lawrence for $24.24 in interest. As in 1992–93, that credit was computed by multiplying the

5% interest rate by the amount of the security deposit less the $100 attributable to the pet deposit. Regent retained this credit and added it to Lawrence's security deposit, increasing the amount of the deposit to $609.08.

For 1994–95, Lawrence's monthly rent was raised to $475. The $609.08 security deposit was carried over, and Regent credited Lawrence for $25.45 in interest, representing 5% of $509.08, the amount of the prior security deposit excluding the $100 pet deposit. That credit was retained by Regent and added to Lawrence's security deposit, increasing the amount of the deposit to $634.53.

Finally, in 1995–96, Lawrence paid rent of $495 per month. The $634.53 security deposit was carried over, and Regent credited Lawrence for $26.73 in interest, representing 5% of $534.53, the amount of the prior security deposit excluding the $100 pet deposit. As before, that credit was retained by Regent and added to Lawrence's security deposit, increasing the amount of the deposit to $661.26.

The 1995–96 lease was the final agreement between the parties. Under the lease, Lawrence's tenancy was month to month. She terminated her tenancy effective November 1, 1996. Shortly before moving out, she initiated these proceedings in the circuit court of Cook County. As indicated above, Lawrence premised her complaint on Chicago's Residential Landlord and Tenant Ordinance (RLTO). Section 5-12-080 of that ordinance provides:

"(c) A landlord who holds a security deposit or prepaid rent pursuant to this section, after the effective date of this chapter shall pay interest to the tenant accruing from the beginning date of the rental term specified in the rental agreement at the rate [of five percent per year]. The landlord shall, within 30 days after the end of each 12 month rental period, pay to the tenant any interest, by cash or credit to be applied to the rent due.

* * *

(f) If the landlord or landlord's agent fails to comply with any provision of Section 5-12-080(a)(e), the tenant shall be awarded damages in an amount equal to two times the security deposit plus interest at [five percent]. This subsection does not preclude the tenant from recovering other damages to which he may be entitled under this chapter."

Chicago Municipal Code §§ 5-12-080(c), (f) (amended November 6, 1991).

In addition, section 5-12-180 of the ordinance states:

"Except in cases of forcible entry and detainer actions, the prevailing plaintiff in any action arising out of a landlord's or tenant's application of the rights or remedies made available in this ordinance shall be entitled to all court costs and reasonable attorney's fees * * *." Chicago Municipal Code § 5-12-180 (amended November 6, 1991).

In her complaint, Lawrence alleged that the $100 pet deposit was part of the security deposit paid to Regent and that Regent had failed to pay interest on the pet deposit in violation of the ordinance. Based on that violation, Lawrence sought damages, as authorized by the ordinance, in an amount equal to two times the amount of the security deposit, including the pet deposit, plus interest. She also sought the costs of the action and reasonable attorney fees.

At trial, there was no dispute that the apartment leased by Lawrence was subject to the provisions of the RLTO, nor was there any dispute that Regent stopped paying Lawrence interest on the pet deposit portion of her security deposit after the first year of her tenancy. The company's defense was that it did not regard the pet deposit as a security deposit within the meaning of the RLTO's interest requirements and that any violation of the law on its part was unintentional.

In support of its defense, Regent presented the testimony of Jay Strauss, who was the only witness to testify at trial on behalf of the company. Strauss was Regent's chairman and was personally responsible for keeping track of Lawrence's security deposit and calculating the interest Regent was obligated to pay on that deposit. Although Lawrence's $100 pet deposit was specifically included in each lease under the section designated for the security deposit, Strauss claimed that he did not pay interest on that amount for the years 1991 through 1995 because he viewed the pet deposit as a pet "fee" or "charge" and not as a security deposit. Strauss did not explain how he reached that conclusion, nor did he account for why he had credited Lawrence for interest earned on her pet deposit in 1990.

The circuit court rejected Strauss' characterization of the pet deposit, concluding that it did constitute a security deposit for purposes of Chicago's Residential Landlord and Tenant Ordinance. The court nevertheless ruled that Regent's failure to pay interest on the pet deposit was not sufficient to trigger relief under the ordinance. The circuit court accepted Regent's contention that the right to collect double the amount of the security deposit plus interest under the ordinance applied only where the landlord's failure to pay was willful. The court did not believe that condition had been met here. It characterized Regent's failure to pay the full amount of interest due as nothing more than an error of judgment. Accordingly, it entered judgment for Regent, dismissed Lawrence's complaint and denied her request to submit a petition for attorney fees. At the same time, however, it ordered the company to refund Lawrence's security deposit and the interest on that deposit, including the interest attributable to the pet deposit.

Lawrence moved for a new trial or, in the alternative, for reconsideration of the judgment. When that motion was denied, Lawrence appealed. The appellate court rejected the circuit court's interpretation of the RLTO, holding that a showing of willfulness is not required to subject a landlord to the remedies provided under the ordinance. As noted above, the appellate court therefore reversed and remanded with directions to vacate the judgment in favor of Regent, to enter judgment for Lawrence for double the amount of the deposit plus interest, and to conduct a hearing on Lawrence's petition for attorney fees. 307 Ill.App.3d at 160–61, 240 Ill.Dec. 350, 717 N.E.2d 443.

We granted Regent's petition for leave to appeal, and the matter is before us for review. The sole issue presented for our consideration is whether the trial court was correct in concluding that the RLTO requires a landlord's violation of the interest payment provisions to have been willful before the tenant is entitled to recover the damages, attorney fees and costs provided by the ordinance. Because that determination turns on the construction and legal effect of the RLTO, our review is de novo. See *Plambeck v. Greystone Management & Columbia National Trust Co.*, 281 Ill.App.3d 260, 266, 217 Ill.Dec. 1, 666 N.E.2d 670 (1996).

The terms of the pertinent provisions of the RLTO have been set forth above. As we have indicated, the trial court in this case specifically found that the pet deposit given by Lawrence to Regent constituted a security deposit within the meaning of section 5-12-080(c) and that Regent had failed to pay Lawrence any interest on that deposit after the first year of the lease. The trial court's findings are undisputed. Under the clear and unambiguous terms of section 5-12-080(f) of the RLTO, Lawrence was therefore entitled to an award of "damages in an amount equal to two times the security deposit plus interest at [five percent]."

Regent cannot deny that it was fully aware of the law. Under the express provisions of the RLTO, it was required to attach to the lease agreements a copy of a summary of the law, including a summary of the provisions governing the payment of interest. Chicago Municipal Code § 5-12-170 (amended November 6, 1991). That Regent's violation of the ordinance's interest requirements may have been the product of poor judgment, as the trial court believed, is of no consequence. Nothing in section 5-12-080(f) requires proof that the landlord's actions were knowing or willful. A landlord's duty to comply with the statute is absolute. If a landlord requires a security deposit, the landlord is required to pay the tenant interest on that deposit. If he fails to do so, he is liable to the tenant for the damages specified in the ordinance. There are no exceptions. Where a statute is clear and unambiguous, as this one is, the court should not look to extrinsic aids for construction. *Board of Education of Rockford School District No. 205 v. Illinois Educational Labor Relations Board*, 165 Ill.2d 80, 87, 208 Ill.Dec. 313, 649 N.E.2d 369 (1995). The statute must be enforced as written, and a court may not depart from its plain language by reading into it exceptions, limitations, or conditions not expressed by the legislature. *People v. Wright*, 194 Ill.2d 1, 29, 251 Ill.Dec. 469, 740 N.E.2d 755 (2000).

Regent argues that a willfulness requirement is necessary to avoid unjust results. That contention is untenable. The purpose of the law is to help protect the rights of tenants with respect to their security deposits, including the right to receive interest. In most cases, the amount of interest landlords owe for security deposits is small, too small to warrant litigation against a landlord who refuses to abide by the law. Without the prospect of liability for significant additional damages, landlords would therefore have little incentive to meet their statutory obligations. They could withhold the interest payments with impunity. And many do. A study cited by plaintiff and presented to the circuit court showed that failure of landlords to pay interest on security deposits is a pervasive problem in the City of Chicago.

The city council has elected to address this problem by imposing an absolute duty on landlords to pay the interest they owe and conferring on tenants the right to recover double the amount of their security deposits when that duty is breached. While one may personally disagree with the wisdom of this choice, it is not this court's function to second-guess the city council's judgment in such matters. As our decisions have made clear, responsibility for the wisdom or justice of legislation rests with the legislature. Under our system of government, courts may not rewrite statutes to make them consistent with their own ideas of orderliness and public policy. *Wright*, 194 Ill.2d at 29, 251 Ill.Dec. 469, 740 N.E.2d 755.

The body of law concerned with the implication of mental states in criminal cases does not support a contrary result. Absolute liability and the implication of mental states in criminal cases have been specifically addressed by the General Assembly. See 720 ILCS 5/4-3(b), 4-9 (West 1998); *People v. Anderson*, 148 Ill.2d 15, 23–24, 169 Ill.Dec. 288, 591 N.E.2d 461 (1992). The matter before us, however, is not a criminal case. We deal here with a municipal ordinance. In contrast to matters arising under the Unified Code of Corrections, neither the General Assembly nor the Chicago city council have promulgated rules allowing implication of mental states for ordinance violations where no mental state has been expressly provided.

That willfulness is not required to recover double damages under section 5-12-080(f) of the RLTO is further supported by a comparison between that ordinance and this state's Security Deposit Interest Act (765 ILCS 715/0.01 et seq. (West 1998)). In contrast to section 5-12-080(f), the Security Deposit Interest Act imposes statutory penalties for a lessor's failure or refusal to pay interest on security deposits as required by the Act only where such failure or refusal is willful. 765 ILCS 715/2 (West 1998). The willfulness requirement is specifically set forth in the Act, which predates the RLTO. The Chicago city council was presumably aware of that statute when it enacted the ordinance at issue here, but chose not to include the statute's willfulness requirement in its own version of the law. There is no valid basis for regarding that omission as anything but informed and deliberate. Narrowing the ordinance to situations where the landlord acted willfully would, in fact, run directly counter to the city council's command that the ordinance "shall be liberally construed * * * to promote its purposes and policies." Chicago Municipal Code § 5-12-010 (amended November 6, 1991).

Szpila v. Burke, 279 Ill.App.3d 964, 216 Ill.Dec. 297, 665 N.E.2d 357 (1996), cited by Regent, was properly distinguished by the appellate court. To the extent it might be construed as supporting the circuit court's judgment in the case before us, it is hereby overruled.

For the foregoing reasons, the judgment of the appellate court is affirmed.

Affirmed.

Justice FREEMAN, dissenting:

There are two issues that must be resolved in this case. The first issue is whether the Chicago Residential Landlords and Tenants Ordinance (the Ordinance) (Chicago Municipal Code § 5-12-010 et seq. (amended November 6, 1991)) is a remedial ordinance or a penal ordinance. The second issue is what, if any, scienter must be shown in an action under the Ordinance. The appellate court found that the Ordinance is remedial and, consequently, a showing of willfulness is not required to subject a landlord to the penalties provided in the Ordinance. 307 Ill.App.3d 155, 156, 240 Ill.Dec.

350, 717 N.E.2d 443. The majority affirms. It imposes absolute liability upon landlords for violations of the Ordinance, even though it recognizes that, under the terms of the Ordinance, landlords are subject to "significant additional damages." 197 Ill.2d at 10, 257 Ill.Dec. at 681, 754 N.E.2d at 339. In a case involving a one-year lease and interest of 5% per annum, the "significant additional damages" amount to 40 times the actual damages suffered by the tenant, together with interest, court costs, and attorney fees.

It is exactly because landlords are subject to significant penalties for violations of the Ordinance that I cannot join the majority opinion. I believe that the Ordinance, while remedial in purpose, is also penal. Furthermore, because the provisions of the Ordinance at issue in this appeal are penal, I believe this court may not impose absolute liability upon Regent absent either a clear indication that the legislature intended to impose absolute liability, or an important public policy favoring absolute liability. Instead, I would require that Regent have acted with knowledge, as opposed to either intent or recklessness, to be subject to liability for the violations of the Ordinance.

I do not believe that the Chicago city council intended to punish landlords for inadvertent mistakes and violations of the Ordinance. I do not believe that the Chicago city council intended to force smaller landlords out of business by imposing "significant additional damages" upon these landlords. As expressly stated in section 5-12-010 of the Ordinance, the Chicago city council intended to "establish the rights and obligations of the landlord and the tenant in the rental of dwelling units, and to encourage the landlord and the tenant to maintain and improve the quality of housing." To impose "significant additional damages" upon landlords without a requirement of scienter is to effectively decrease the number of dwelling units that are available for rental in the City of Chicago. The decision of this court does not further the policies of the Ordinance. Accordingly, I dissent.

ANALYSIS

A. Nature of Ordinance

The first issue that must be addressed in this case is whether the Ordinance is remedial or penal. If a statute is penal in nature, this court will not impose absolute liability absent either a clear indication that the legislature intended to impose absolute liability or an important public policy favoring absolute liability. See *People v. Gean*, 143 Ill.2d 281, 287, 158 Ill.Dec. 5, 573 N.E.2d 818 (1991). Instead, this court will impose a scienter requirement, whether that be intent, knowledge or recklessness. See *People v. Anderson*, 148 Ill.2d 15, 23, 169 Ill.Dec. 288, 591 N.E.2d 461 (1992).

Both the circuit court and the appellate court addressed this issue. The majority, however, does not feel constrained to do so. In the absence of any discussion in the majority opinion, I outline my thoughts on the nature of the Ordinance, and the intention of the Chicago city council in enacting the Ordinance.

As noted in the bystanders' report, the circuit court found that Regent's "mistake of judgment" in characterizing the pet deposit as a "fee" or "charge" and not as a "security deposit" did not rise to the level of willfulness, as discussed in *Szpila*, which would support an award of twice the amount of the security deposit.

In *Szpila*, the tenant entered into a one-year lease from May 1, 1989, to May 1, 1990, and paid $975 as a security deposit. At the expiration of the lease term, the parties orally agreed to renew the lease. The building owners deposited rent money they received into the same account in which they held the tenant's security deposit. The tenant vacated the premises on September 30, 1993. The owners claimed that the tenant had admitted breaking a key off in a lock and had requested that the owners deduct the cost of the repair from the security deposit. By October 11, 1993, the owners refunded the tenant $926 of his security deposit. They had deducted $49 from the deposit for the repair, but failed to send the tenant a receipt for the repair. Further, at no time during the tenancy did the owners pay the tenant interest on his security deposit or provide him with a summary of the Ordinance.

In a complaint against the owners, the tenant alleged that the owners had violated: section 5-12-080(a) of the Ordinance, which requires that a landlord keep a tenant's security deposit in a different account from that used for rent collected; section 5-12-080(c) of the Ordinance, which required a landlord to pay his tenant 5% interest on a security deposit; section 5-12-080(d) of the Ordinance, which requires that a landlord provide the tenant with a receipt for all repair costs deducted from the security deposit; and section 5-12-170 of the Ordinance, which requires that a landlord provide the tenant with a summary of the Ordinance. The tenant claimed a separate violation of section 5-12-080(c) of the Ordinance for each year that the owners failed to pay interest on the security deposit. For each violation of section 5-12-080, the tenant requested two times the security deposit as a penalty under the Ordinance. The tenant also requested the yearly interest payments on the security deposit, and $100 as a penalty under section 5-12-170. In all, the tenant requested $12,044 for the owners' failure to pay him a total of $195 in interest over a four-year period, for the owners' failure to provide him with a summary of the Ordinance, for the owners' failure to send him a receipt for the repair of the lock and for the owners' failure to keep the security deposit in a separate account.

The trial court awarded the tenant the $100 penalty for the owners' failure to give the tenant a summary of the Ordinance, attorney fees and court costs. The trial court also awarded the tenant twice the amount of the security deposit for one of the violations of section 5-12-080. However, the trial court determined that the tenant was not entitled to separate penalties for each violation of section 5-12-080. The appellate court affirmed. Initially, the appellate court noted that section 5-12-080 of the Ordinance does not contain a "willfulness" requirement. The appellate court also noted the rule of statutory construction that when necessary to effectuate the intent of the legislature a court may alter, supply or modify words and obvious mistakes. The appellate court then stated:

"We judge, therefore, that to avoid the absurd and unjust result urged upon us by the [tenant], the city council intended that violations under the ordinance, in order to be subject to the penalty provisions, must have been willful. At the very least, the [tenant] should have made some requests for the summary, the receipt and the interest payments. * * *

For these reasons, the trial judge's holding that the [tenant] was not entitled to separate penalties is affirmed. We note parenthetically, although the [owners] do not cross-appeal, that under our holding the [tenant] should not have received a payment of a sum double the amount of the security deposit under any count." *Szpila v. Burke,* 279 Ill.App.3d 964, 972–73, 216 Ill.Dec. 297, 665 N.E.2d 357 (1996).

In *Szpila,* the appellate court did not refer to the Ordinance as being remedial or penal. However, noting the court's reference to willfulness, other panels of the appellate court have stated that *Szpila* found the Ordinance to be penal. See *Namur v. Habitat Co.,* 294 Ill.App.3d 1007, 1011, 229 Ill.Dec. 309, 691 N.E.2d 782 (1998); 307 Ill.App.3d at 156, 240 Ill.Dec. 350, 717 N.E.2d 443 ("a willfulness requirement can only stand if the ordinance is penal").

In *Namur,* the court held that sections 5-12-080(f) and 5-12-170 of the Ordinance are penal. Initially, the court observed that:

"A statute is penal if it imposes automatic liability for a violation of its terms and if the amount of liability is predetermined by the statute and imposed without actual damages suffered by the plaintiff. [Citation.] A statute is remedial where it imposes liability only for actual damages resulting from a violation." *Namur,* 294 Ill.App.3d at 1010–11, 229 Ill.Dec. 309, 691 N.E.2d 782.

The court stated that sections 5-12-080(f) and 5-12-170 of the Ordinance are penal because they specify either the amount of damages that can be awarded for violations or the formula by which the amount of damages is to be calculated. *Namur,* 294 Ill.App.3d at 1011, 229 Ill.Dec. 309, 691 N.E.2d 782. The court also recognized that some portions of the Ordinance are remedial because they permit recovery of actual damages. *Namur,* 294 Ill.App.3d at 1011, 229 Ill.Dec. 309, 691 N.E.2d 782.

Other panels of the appellate court have distinguished *Szpila,* or simply refused to follow its reasoning. Thus, in *Friedman v. Krupp Corp.,* 282 Ill.App.3d 436, 217 Ill.Dec. 957, 668 N.E.2d 142 (1996), a panel of the appellate court found that the Ordinance is remedial, not penal. The court looked to the statement of purpose contained in section 5-12-010 of the Ordinance to support its finding that the Ordinance is remedial:

"It is the purpose of this chapter and the policy of the city, in order to protect and promote the public health, safety and welfare of its citizens, to establish the rights and obligations of the landlord and the tenant in the rental of dwelling units, and to encourage the landlord and the tenant to maintain and improve the quality of housing." Chicago Municipal Code § 5-12-010 (amended November 6, 1991).

The court employed a rule of liberal construction to give effect to the Ordinance's stated purpose. *Friedman,* 282 Ill.App.3d at 443, 217 Ill.Dec. 957, 668 N.E.2d 142.

Likewise, in the case at bar, the appellate court stated that the clear intent of the Ordinance is to protect tenants and hold landlords to a high standard of conduct when entrusted with a tenant's money. 307 Ill.App.3d at 159, 240 Ill.Dec. 350, 717 N.E.2d 443. The court reasoned:

"The primary role of statutory construction is to give effect to the legislative purpose, and an inquiry into the legislative intent must begin with the language of the statute.

[Citation.] One clear purpose of the ordinance is to protect tenants. This purpose is rooted in the public policy that recognizes that tenants are in a disadvantageous position with respect to landlords. Viewing section 5-12-080(f) as penal, with respect to the single-count violation, would defeat its remedial purpose." 307 Ill.App.3d at 160, 240 Ill.Dec. 350, 717 N.E.2d 443.

See also *Plambeck v. Greystone Management & Columbia National Trust Co.*, 281Ill.App.3d 260, 217 Ill.Dec. 1, 666 N.E.2d 670 (1996) (directing that the trial court award the tenant damages in an amount equal to two times the security deposit plus interest for the landlord's failure to keep two small increases in the security deposit in a separate account from that used for rent monies, and that the trial court award the tenant an identical sum for the landlord's failure to pay interest on the security deposit).

In *Friedman*, and in the case at bar, the appellate court focused on the statement of purpose to find the Ordinance remedial. I am no less conscious of the purpose of the Ordinance. I am also aware that certain sections of the Ordinance provide damages which are remedial in nature. See Chicago Municipal Code § 5-12-060 (landlord's remedies for improper denial of access to premises); § 5-12-110 (tenant's remedies for landlord's failure to maintain premises); § 5-12-120 (landlord's remedies for early termination of rental agreement); § 5-12-130 (landlord's remedies for tenant's failure to pay rent and failure to maintain premises). However, I cannot agree that the Ordinance is purely remedial.

A remedial statute contemplates recovery of direct damages sustained by reason of the omission or failure of which complaint is made. Compensation for injuries inflicted, not punishment, is the ground of recovery. *Odin Coal Co. v. Denman*, 185 Ill. 413, 417-18, 57 N.E. 192 (1900). By contrast, as we explained in *Bell v. Farwell*, 176 Ill. 489, 52 N.E. 346 (1898):

""A penal statute is one which imposes a forfeiture or penalty for transgressing its provisions or for doing a thing prohibited." It is the effect — not the form — of the statute that is to be considered, and when its object is clearly to inflict a punishment on a party for violating it, — i.e., doing what is prohibited or failing to do what is commanded to be done, — it is penal in its character.'" *Bell*, 176 Ill. at 496, 52 N.E. 346, quoting *Diversey v. Smith*, 103 Ill. 378, 390, 1882 WL 10327 (1882).

See also *Hoffmann v. Clark*, 69 Ill.2d 402, 429, 14 Ill.Dec. 269, 372 N.E.2d 74 (1977).

A review of the Ordinance shows that it must be construed as both remedial and penal. For example, section 5-12-080, at issue in this case, provides that the tenant shall be awarded damages in an amount equal to two times the security deposit plus interest. Section 5-12-150 prohibits retaliatory conduct by the landlord and provides that the tenant shall recover an amount equal to not more than two months' rent or twice the damages sustained by him, whichever is greater, and reasonable attorney fees. Section 5-12-160 prohibits an interruption of the tenant's occupancy and provides that a tenant shall recover an amount equal to not more than two months' rent or twice the actual damages sustained by him, whichever is greater. In addition, section 5-12-160 provides that the Chicago police department shall investigate and determine whether a violation of the section has occurred. Any person found guilty of violating the section shall be fined not less than $200 or more than $500, and each day that such violation shall occur or continue shall constitute a separate and distinct offense for which a fine shall be imposed. These damage provisions give a tenant an incentive to enforce the Ordinance. Concurrently, the provisions serve to discourage future violations of the Ordinance by landlords. I, therefore, conclude that the Ordinance is both remedial and penal.

That a statute may be both remedial and penal is well supported in our jurisprudence. See *Harris v. Manor Healthcare Corp.*, 111 Ill.2d 350, 361, 95 Ill.Dec. 510, 489 N.E.2d 1374 (1986) ("Although we believe that section 3-602 [of the Nursing Home Care Reform Act of 1979] was enacted primarily to encourage private enforcement of the Act and to compensate residents for violations of their rights, we agree that the section also must be construed as being punitive"); *Acme Fireworks Corp. v. Bibb*, 6 Ill.2d 112, 126 N.E.2d 688 (1955); *Cedar Park Cemetery Ass'n v. Cooper*, 408 Ill. 79, 96 N.E.2d 482 (1951); *Howlett v. Doglio*, 402 Ill. 311, 318, 83 N.E.2d 708 (1949) ("Although the Dram Shop Act is penal in character and should be strictly construed, [citations] the legislation is, at the same time, remedial and should be so construed as to suppress the mischief and advance the remedy"); *Bell*, 176 Ill. at 496, 52 N.E. 346, quoting *Diversey*, 103 Ill. at 390 ("' "A penal law may also be remedial, and a statute may be remedial in one part and penal in another"'"). See also 73 Am.Jur.2d Statutes §§ 13, 292 (1974); 3 N. Singer, Sutherland on Statutory Construction § 60.04 (5th ed. 1992).

I believe that a balanced approach, which recognizes that certain portions of the Ordinance are remedial and certain portions are penal, furthers the goal of the Ordinance to promote the public health, safety and welfare of the citizens of Chicago by establishing the rights and obligations of the landlord and the tenant in the rental of dwelling units, and encouraging the landlord and the tenant to maintain and improve the quality of housing.

The majority rejects such a balanced approach. Instead, the majority states "[t]he purpose of the law is to help protect the rights of tenants with respect to their security deposits, including the right to receive interest." 197 Ill.2d at 10, 257 Ill.Dec. at 681, 754 N.E.2d at 339. The majority nowhere acknowledges the Chicago city council's intention to establish the rights of landlords, and to protect both landlords and tenants in order to promote the goal of quality housing. In my view, the majority's approach to the Ordinance is unbalanced, serving as it does the interests of only one of the two constituencies the Chicago city council intended to protect.

B. Scienter Requirement

The second issue that must be addressed is the scienter requirement for a violation of the Ordinance. Turning to section 5-12-080 of the Ordinance, I note that it provides the tenant shall be awarded damages in an amount equal to two times the security deposit, together with interest, court costs and attorney fees for a violation of the section. Thus, section 5-12-080 is penal in nature.

As noted in the bystanders' report, the circuit court concluded that a finding of will-fulness was required in order for Lawrence to recover damages pursuant to section 5-12-080. In this appeal, Lawrence maintains that the circuit court erred in holding that a finding of willfulness was required in order for Lawrence to recover damages pursuant to section 5-12-080 of the Ordinance. Pointing to the lack of express language describing a mental state, Lawrence explains that the Chicago city council intended to impose strict and certain liability for violations of section 5-12-080. Lawrence con-cludes that a finding of willfulness, or any other scienter requirement, is not necessary for recovery under section 5-12-080. The majority agrees.

In considering whether a statute imposes absolute liability for certain conduct, the fact that the statute does not contain express language calling for a mental state does not, of itself, lead to a conclusion that no mental state is required. *People v. Farmer*, 165 Ill.2d 194, 202–03, 209 Ill.Dec. 33, 650 N.E.2d 1006 (1995); *People v. Whitlow*, 89 Ill.2d 322, 332, 60 Ill.Dec. 587, 433 N.E.2d 629 (1982); *People v. Nunn*, 77 Ill.2d 243, 250, 32 Ill.Dec. 914, 396 N.E.2d 27 (1979). This court looks, instead, to sources beyond the statutory language to ascertain the intent of the legislature and determine whether the conclusion that the statute imposes absolute liability is warranted. *Farmer*, 165 Ill.2d at 205–06, 209 Ill.Dec. 33, 650 N.E.2d 1006; *People v. Sevilla*, 132 Ill.2d 113, 118–19, 138 Ill.Dec. 148, 547 N.E.2d 117 (1989). This court has heretofore rec-ognized that the penalty for a violation of a statute is an important factor in deter-mining whether the legislature intended to impose absolute liability. *Gean*, 143 Ill.2d at 287, 158 Ill.Dec. 5, 573 N.E.2d 818; *Sevilla*, 132 Ill.2d at 122, 138 Ill.Dec. 148, 547 N.E.2d 117. Where the penalty for a violation of a statute is great, it is less likely that the legislature intended to create an absolute liability offense. *Farmer*, 165 Ill.2d at 206, 209 Ill.Dec. 33, 650 N.E.2d 1006; *People v. Valley Steel Products Co.*, 71 Ill.2d 408, 425, 17 Ill.Dec. 13, 375 N.E.2d 1297 (1978). Absent either a clear indication that the legislature intended to impose absolute liability, or an important public policy favoring absolute liability, this court has generally not been willing to interpret a statute as imposing absolute liability. See *Gean*, 143 Ill.2d at 286, 158 Ill.Dec. 5, 573 N.E.2d 818 (and cases cited therein).

As Lawrence notes, section 5-12-080 does not contain a mental state element. More-over, the balance of the Ordinance does not contain a clear indication that the Chicago city council intended to impose absolute liability for violations of the section. The penalty imposed under section 5-12-080 (twice the amount of the security deposit plus interest, court costs, and attorney fees) can be substantial. And, with respect to a landlord's failure to pay interest on the security deposit, as well as the landlord's failure to segregate the security deposit from other assets, the damages recovered by the tenant will be totally disproportionate to the loss he suffers. Given the lack of clear legislative intent and the implications to the landlord for failure to pay interest on the security deposit, I am of the opinion that the Chicago city council did not in-tend to impose absolute liability for violations of section 5-12-080.

The majority disagrees. It finds that the Ordinance is "clear and unambiguous." From there, it concludes that the Ordinance must be enforced as written, without resort to extrinsic aids for construction. See 197 Ill.2d at 10, 257 Ill.Dec. at 681, 754 N.E.2d at 339. The majority fails to recognize, however, that in considering whether a statute imposes absolute liability for certain conduct, the fact that the statute does not contain express language calling for a mental state does not, of itself, lead to a conclusion that no mental state is required. By limiting its analysis to the "clear and unambiguous" language of the Ordinance, the majority fails to determine the actual intent of the Chicago city council in enacting the Ordinance.

When a statute neither prescribes a particular mental state nor creates an absolute liability offense, either intent, knowledge or recklessness applies. *Anderson*, 148 Ill.2d at 23, 169 Ill.Dec. 288, 591 N.E.2d 461; *Gean*, 143 Ill.2d at 288, 158 Ill.Dec. 5, 573 N.E.2d 818. In determining the appropriate mental state, this court looks to other provisions in the statute, or to the language of any parallel statute. *Sevilla*, 132 Ill.2d at 123–24, 138 Ill.Dec. 148, 547 N.E.2d 117.

Three other provisions of the Ordinance are instructive. Section 5-12-150 provides that a landlord may not knowingly terminate a tenancy or refuse to renew a lease because the tenant has complained of code violations, sought assistance to remedy a code violation or requested that the landlord make repairs to the premises. A tenant shall recover an amount equal to two months' rent or twice the damages sustained by him, whichever is greater, for a violation of this provision. Section 5-12-160 provides that it is unlawful for any landlord knowingly to oust or dispossess or threaten or attempt to oust or dispossess a tenant from a dwelling unit without authority of law. A tenant shall recover an amount equal to two months' rent or twice the damages sustained by him, whichever is greater, for a violation of this provision. Lastly, section 5-12-110 provides that if a person's failure to deliver possession of a dwelling unit is willful, an aggrieved person may recover from the person withholding possession an amount not more than two months' rent or twice the actual damages sustained, whichever is greater. All three provisions thus require that the landlord have acted with knowledge in committing the particular infraction. See 720 ILCS 5/4-5 (West 1998) (conduct performed knowingly or with knowledge is performed willfully, within the meaning of a statute using the term "wilfully," unless the statute clearly requires another meaning).

I also find instructive the language of the Security Deposit Interest Act (765 ILCS 715/1 et seq. (West 1998)). Section 1 of the Security Deposit Interest Act provides that, with respect to buildings or complexes containing at least 25 units, a landlord who receives a security deposit from a tenant shall pay interest to the tenant if the landlord holds the deposit for more than six months. 765 ILCS 715/1 (West 1998). A landlord who willfully fails or refuses to pay the interest required by the act shall, upon a finding by a circuit court that the landlord has willfully failed or refused to pay, be liable for an amount equal to the amount of the security deposit together with court costs and reasonable attorney fees. 765 ILCS 715/2 (West 1998); see also *Gittleman v. Create, Inc.*, 189 Ill.App.3d 199, 136 Ill.Dec. 713, 545 N.E.2d 237 (1989) (finding a violation of the Security Deposit Interest Act where the landlord was fully aware of its legal obligation to pay interest on the security deposits but attempted to circumvent the statute by claiming, contrary to a lease provision setting the rent at $300, that the gross rent was actually $301.25; that the tenant paid only $300 per month; and that $1.25 was credited each month to the tenant's account as interest on the security deposit).

Many of our sister states have adopted legislation regulating payment of interest on security deposits and the return of the security deposits. The enactments fall into four categories: (1) those imposing absolute liability for any retention of the security deposits in violation of the statute; (2) those prohibiting unreasonable retention of the security deposits, that is a retention without reasonable justification or basis as determined by a fact finder; (3) those prohibiting wrongful and willful retention of the security deposits; and (4) those prohibiting bad-faith retention of the security deposits. See Annot., 63 A.L.R.4th 901, 1988 WL 546546 (1988). Within the enactments proscribing wrongful and willful retention, certain statutes have been interpreted as requiring only deliberate or intentional conduct (see *Martinez v. Steinbaum*, 623 P.2d 49 (Colo. 1981)), while others have been interpreted as requiring bad-faith retention (see *Karantza v. Salamone*, 435 A.2d 1384 (Me. 1981)) or an arbitrary and unjustified withholding (see *Calix v. Whitson*, 306 So.2d 62 (La.App.1974)).

My review of the other portions of the Ordinance, the Security Deposit Interest Act, and parallel enactments in our sister states convinces me that knowledge, as opposed to either intent or recklessness, is the appropriate mental state for a violation of section 5-12-080 of the Ordinance. Knowledge generally refers to an awareness of the existence of the facts which make an individual's conduct unlawful. See *Sevilla*, 132 Ill.2d at 125, 138 Ill.Dec. 148, 547 N.E.2d 117. In arriving at this conclusion, I am keenly aware that the Ordinance is both penal and remedial. I believe that a requirement that the landlord have acted intentionally or with bad faith is not in keeping with the remedial purpose of the Ordinance. Such a holding would set too high a bar to recovery under section 5-12-080 of the Ordinance. On the other hand, I believe that knowledge is required for a violation of the section. Such a requirement furthers the remedial purpose of the Ordinance while appropriately restricting the penal consequences of the section by excluding violations which are merely inadvertent.

The majority rejects my conclusion. The majority states that: "The body of law concerned with the implication of mental states in criminal cases does not support a contrary result." 197 Ill.2d at 11, 257 Ill.Dec. at 682, 754 N.E.2d at 340. Further, the Chicago city council has not "promulgated rules allowing implication of mental states for ordinance violations where no mental state has been expressly provided." 197 Ill.2d at 11, 257 Ill.Dec. at 682, 754 N.E.2d at 340. Thus, the majority concludes that the law regarding scienter does not apply to a municipal ordinance.

The majority's reasoning is based on the premise that the title of a statute is more important than its substance, a premise this court has heretofore rejected. See *Bell*, 176 Ill. at 496, 52 N.E. 346 ("It is the effect—not the form—of the statute that is to be considered, and when its object is clearly to inflict a punishment on a party for violating it,—i.e., doing what is prohibited or failing to do what is commanded to be done,—it is penal in its character"). What matters that the Ordinance is a municipal ordinance if the relevant provisions are penal in nature? If the provisions are intended to impose "significant" penalties upon a landlord, and, if the Ordinance does not contain a clear indication that the Chicago city council intended to impose absolute liability for violations of the Ordinance, this court must impose a scienter requirement.

I note that in *People v. O'Brien*, 197 Ill.2d 88, 257 Ill.Dec. 669, 754 N.E.2d 327 (2001), a case filed concurrently with the case at bar, this court rejects the narrow approach to the application of scienter the majority here advances. Instead, in *O'Brien*, this court recognizes that the scienter requirement of section 4-9 of the Criminal Code of 1961 (720 ILCS 5/4-9 (West 1998)): "applies to all criminal penalty provisions, including those outside the Criminal Code of 1961." *O'Brien*, 197 Ill.2d at 91, 257 Ill.Dec. 671, 754 N.E.2d 329. Thus, the *O'Brien* court applies "[t]he body of law concerned with the implication of mental states in criminal cases" (197 Ill.2d at 11, 257 Ill.Dec. at 682, 754 N.E.2d at 340 (supra)) in determining whether section 3-707 of the Illinois Vehicle Code (625 ILCS 5/3-707 (West 1998)) creates an absolute liability offense.

The *O'Brien* court recognizes that the substance of a statute and the nature of the penalties imposed by the statute are to be taken into account in determining whether the legislative body intended to create an absolute liability statute.

CONCLUSION

Today, the majority imposes absolute liability upon a landlord for a violation of the Ordinance. The majority does so because it believes that "failure of landlords to pay interest on security deposits is a pervasive problem in the City of Chicago." 197 Ill.2dat 10, 257 Ill.Dec. at 681–82, 754 N.E.2d at 339–40. This belief rests largely upon a 1995 study that Lawrence cited to the circuit court. I agree that certain landlords are lax in the payment of interest on their tenants' security deposits, and should be held accountable under the Ordinance. I cannot agree, however, that a study performed several years after the Ordinance was adopted is instructive on the intent of the Chicago city council in enacting the Ordinance.

Further, I cannot agree that punishing landlords for inadvertent infractions of the Ordinance best serves the interests of tenants and the City of Chicago in quality housing. The penalties imposed by the Ordinance are substantial. They apply to landlords who own large buildings as well as the landlord whose building contains only six apartments. If the penalties accumulate over the length of a long-term lease, or are multiplied by a number of tenants, they may devastate the smaller landlord. I do not believe that the Chicago city council intended to force smaller landlords out of business. Instead, I believe that the Chicago city council intended to punish landlords only for knowing violations of the Ordinance. Where a landlord inadvertently violates the Ordinance, for example by entering the wrong number on a calculator, the landlord should not be liable for "significant additional damages." Accordingly, I dissent.

Justice McMORROW joins in this dissent.

[1] There are no records of Chicago city council proceedings regarding the Ordinance. Thus, this court does not have a source of "legislative history" from which it could infer the intent of the Chicago city council.

[2] Although the majority states that it is not relying on "extrinsic aids for construction," the majority cites to a 1995 study for the proposition that "failure of landlords to pay interest on security deposits is a pervasive problem in the City of Chicago." See 197 Ill.2d at 10, 257 Ill.Dec. at 681, 754 N.E.2d at 339. The majority also looks to the Security Deposit Interest Act (765 ILCS 715/0.01 et seq. (West 1998)) as an aid in construing the Ordinance. See 197 Ill.2d at 11, 257 Ill.Dec. at 682, 754 N.E.2d at 340 ("The Chicago city council was presumably aware of that statute when it enacted the ordinance at issue here, but chose not to include the statute's willfulness requirement in its own version of the law.").

Chapter 9

The Eviction Process

Learning Objectives

After studying Chapter 9, you will be able to:

- Identify breaches of a lease and the notices required
- Explain the remedies available for a breach of the lease
- Summarize the eviction process

Chapter Summary

Topic covered:

- Eviction Proceedings

This chapter examines the eviction process. **Eviction** is the process through which a landlord can forcibly eject a tenant from an apartment or other living arrangement. The notices required for different breaches of the lease are discussed. The chapter looks at the eviction court process, the court orders, and the requirements on how a sheriff can remove the tenant. The statutes involved in landlord-tenant law are included at the end of the chapter.

1. The Eviction Process

Eviction

The eviction process is delineated in the Forcible Entry and Detainer Act (735 ILCS 5) and also in the RLTO § 5-12-130. There are four main steps to an eviction:

1) Notice of the breach (or notice of non-renewal, as applicable)

2) Filing of the action

3) Trial

4) Sheriff's eviction

Note, at no time may a landlord change the locks, threaten the tenant with the police, or otherwise intimidate a tenant into leaving. The landlord *must* comply with the statute. Far more forcible entry and detainer actions are defeated through procedural errors than through defenses on the part of the tenant. The procedures must be followed strictly in order for the action to be successful.

Also, if the property is owned by a corporation, limited liability company, or other legal entity, the plaintiff must be represented by an attorney. The landlord in these instances is the entity and only a licensed attorney may represent another legal "person" in court. The manager of the building, a member of the LLC, or officer of the corporation is not allowed to file an action on behalf of the entity or represent the entity in court.

Notice of Breach (or Notice of Non-Renewal)

Service of Notices

Service of notices is governed by 735 ILCS 5/9-211. Notices can be served in one of four ways in most cases:

1) Personal service on the tenant;

2) Personal service on someone at the tenant's home who is 13 years old or older;

3) Mailing the notice to the tenant by certified or registered mail, with a return receipt from the tenant; or

4) If no one is living at the tenant's house, the landlord may post the notice.

> 735 ILCS 5/9-211. Service of demand or notice. Any demand may be made or notice served by delivering a written or printed, or partly written and printed, copy thereof to the tenant, or by leaving the same with some person of the age of 13 years or upwards, residing on or in possession of the premises; or by sending a copy of the notice to the tenant by certified or registered mail, with a returned receipt from the addressee; and in case no one is in the actual possession of the premises, then by posting the same on the premises.

If the tenant gets the notice, improper service may be waived, *Prairie Management Corp. v. Bell*, 289 Ill. App.3d 746, 682 N.E.2d 141 (1st Dist. 1997). Proof of nonreceipt can be difficult if the service of notice is proper on its face. Occasionally, the landlord deliberately provides improper service, for example, by posting the notice when the tenant is in possession.

Failure to Pay Rent

A tenant's failure to pay the rent when due is grounds for an eviction. In this case, the landlord must give the tenant a five (5) day notice of intent to terminate. This is called a **Five Day Notice**. Note, this time period may be longer for certain subsidized housing. A copy of a five-day notice is included at the end of this chapter.

> RLTO § 5-12-130(a) Failure To Pay Rent. If all or any portion of rent is unpaid when due and the tenant fails to pay the unpaid rent within five days after written notice by the landlord of his intention to terminate the rental agreement if rent is not so paid, the landlord may terminate the rental agreement. Nothing in this subsection shall affect

a landlord's obligation to provide notice of termination of tenancy in subsidized housing as required under federal law or regulations. A landlord may also maintain an action for rent and/or damages without terminating the rental agreement.

If the tenant pays the back amount due in full prior to the expiration of the notice period, the Landlord must accept the rent due and may not continue with the eviction. However, if the tenant tenders only partial payment, the landlord generally may still terminate the lease, unless the landlord states in writing that the partial payment is being accepted to reinstate the tenancy (or to cure the notice).

Breach of a Material Term in the Lease

If the tenant breaches a material term in the lease, the landlord may serve the tenant with a **Ten Day Notice**, which must specifically state the nature of the breach.

> (b) Noncompliance By Tenant. If there is material noncompliance by a tenant with a rental agreement or with Section 5-12-040, the landlord of such tenant's dwelling unit may deliver written notice to the tenant specifying the acts and/or omissions constituting the breach and that the rental agreement will terminate upon a date not less than 10 days after receipt of the notice, unless the breach is remedied by the tenant within that period of time. If the breach is not remedied within the 10 day period, the residential rental agreement shall terminate as provided in the notice. The landlord may recover damages and obtain injunctive relief for any material non-compliance by the tenant with the rental agreement or with Section 5-12-040. If the tenant's noncompliance is wilful, the landlord may also recover reasonable attorney's fees. § 5-12-130(b)

This notice is used when the tenant has breached a material provision of the lease (such as having a dog in the unit when the lease states "no pets"). Once again, in Chicago, under the RLTO, the tenant has the right to cure. A copy of a ten (10) day notice is included at the end of this chapter.

Non-Renewal of Tenancy

If the tenancy is not being renewed (for instance, with a month-to-month oral lease, or at the end of lease which is not being renewed), the landlord must provide a **Thirty Day Notice**. There is no cure provision in a 30-day notice, the tenancy just ends.

> Notice of Refusal To Renew Rental Agreement. Provided that the landlord has not ex-ercised, or is not in the process of exercising, any of its rights under Section 5-12-130 (a)–(h) hereof, the landlord shall notify the tenant in writing at least 30 days prior to the stated termination date of the rental agreement of the landlord's intent either to terminate a month to month tenancy or not to renew an existing rental agreement. If the landlord fails to give the required written notice, the tenant may remain in the dwelling unit for up to 60 days after the date on which such required written notice is given to the tenant, regardless of the termination date specified in the existing rental agreement. During such occupancy, the terms and conditions of the tenancy (including, without limitation, the rental rate) shall be the same as the terms and conditions during the month of tenancy immediately preceding the notice; provided, however, that if

rent was waived or abated in the preceding month or months as part of the original rental agreement, the rental amount during such 60 day period shall be at the rate established on the last date that a full rent payment was made. RLTO § 5-12-130(j)

In this case, the tenancy ends and the tenant must vacate. The problem is determining when the 30 days begins. For a lease, it is simple; it is the month prior to the end of the lease. If the lease ends May 31, then the notice must be served on or before May 1. If the lease ends February 28, the notice must be served on or before January 29, to provide for a full 30-day period. With a month-to-month lease, the same rule applies. If the lease is month to month, the notice must be 30 days prior to the end of the next month. If the tenancy ends June 30, the notice must be served prior to May 31. It is always a good idea to serve the notice just prior to the beginning of the last full month of the tenancy.

A copy of a thirty (30) day notice is included at the end of this chapter.

How to Calculate the Notice Period

The notice period begins with the day *after* the notice is served. If the last day of the notice period falls on a Saturday, Sunday, or holiday, then that day is excluded. If the landlord serves the tenant by certified mail, the notice period starts from the day after the tenant actually received the notice. This can be very difficult to prove, since there will be a delay in receiving the notice card back from the post office. For example, if the landlord mails a five-day notice to the tenant on June 1, and the tenant receives the notice on June 4, the five-day notice period starts from June 5 and the tenant must pay the rent amount by June 9.

If the tenant refuses to accept the notice, the landlord can inform the tenant what the notice is and leave it in front of the tenant's apartment. If there is no one living at the tenant's house (that is, they abandoned the premises), the landlord can post the notice on the door of the premises.

Filing the Action

The next (and very important) step is to wait until the notice period expires. If the tenant fails to comply, the landlord can file a forcible entry and detainer action in the civil court (and pay the required filing fee). In Chicago, that would be at the Daley Center. A copy of a sample complaint and summons are included at the end of this chapter.

After the complaint and summons are filed with the clerk, the landlord must then have the complaint and summons served by the sheriff's office (and pay a fee to the sheriff). The complaint and summons must be served on each tenant on the lease. Typically, the notice, complaint and summons also name unknown occupants.

There will be a return date on the summons and the landlord is required to appear. The Sheriff must have served the tenants at least three days prior to the court hearing date.

If the tenant was not served, the landlord may ask for a continuance and file a motion for an "alias summons" to be served by a process server. If the tenant appears and claims to have a defense, the case is held over for a trial. The landlord must prove that they have a right to the premises, and that the defendant did not pay rent/breached/held over. The defendant may raise any defenses that are germane.

Like the plaintiff in any action, the landlord bears the burden of proof. The landlord, or landlord's attorney, should produce the following at court:

- The original notice and affidavit of service (signed by a notary public);
- The complaint and summons, with proof of service;
- A copy of the lease;
- Any witnesses to support the landlord's case; and
- Any receipts or exhibits for the court to consider prior to rendering a decision.

If there is a judgment in the favor of the landlord, there is a written **Order for Possession** drafted by the plaintiff. Typically, the court will allow the tenant a certain amount of time to vacate the premises, often 7–14 days. This is referred to as a **Stay of Enforcement** of the order. If the tenant does not vacate in that time, the landlord may then take the order to the Sheriff and have the Sheriff evict the tenant. Typically, this can take another two (2) or three (3) weeks.

Only the tenant or the Sheriff may remove the tenant's belongings; the landlord can never remove the tenant's belongings on his own. The Sheriff will supervise the removal of the belongings, with the landlord hiring movers to remove the belongings. If the tenant has abandoned the property, the landlord may remove the belongings, but must store the belongings, if they have value, for a reasonable time period.

(e) Abandonment. Abandonment of the dwelling unit shall be deemed to have occurred when:

(1) actual notice has been provided to the landlord by the tenant indicating the tenant's intention not to return to the dwelling unit, or

(2) all persons entitled under a rental agreement to occupy the dwelling unit have been absent from the unit for a period of 21 days or for one rental period when the rental agreement is for less than a month, and such persons have removed their personal property from the premises, and rent for that period is unpaid; or

(3) all persons entitled under a rental agreement to occupy the dwelling unit have been absent from the unit for a period of 32 days, and rent for that period is unpaid. Notwithstanding the above, abandonment of the dwelling unit shall not be deemed to have occurred if any person entitled to occupancy has provided the landlord a written notice indicating that he still intends to occupy the unit and makes full payment of all amounts due to the landlord.

If the tenant abandons the dwelling unit, the landlord shall make a good faith effort to re-rent it at a fair rental, which shall be the rent charged for comparable dwelling units in the premises or in the same neighborhood. If the landlord succeeds in re-renting the dwelling unit at a fair rental, the tenant shall be liable for the amount by which the rent due from the date of abandonment to the termination of the initial rental agreement exceeds the fair rental subsequently received by the landlord from the date of abandonment to the termination of the initial rental agreement. If the landlord makes a good faith effort to re-rent the dwelling unit at a fair rental and is unsuccessful, the tenant shall be liable for the rent due for the period of the rental agreement. The tenant shall also be liable for the reasonable advertising expenses and reasonable redecoration costs incurred by the landlord pursuant to this subsection. RLTO § 5-12-130(e)

(f) Disposition Of Abandoned Property. If the tenant abandons the dwelling unit as described in subsection (e) hereof, or fails to remove his personal property from the premises after termination of a rental agreement, the landlord shall leave the property in the dwelling unit or remove and store all abandoned property from the dwelling unit and may dispose of the property after seven days. Notwithstanding the foregoing, if the landlord reasonably believes such abandoned property to be valueless or of such little value that the cost of storage would exceed the amount that would be realized from sale, or if such property is subject to spoilage, the landlord may immediately dispose of such property. RLTO § 5-12-130(f)

(765 ILCS 705/) Landlord and Tenant Act.

765 ILCS 705/0.01) (from Ch. 80, par. 90)

Sec. 0.01. Short title. This Act may be cited as the Landlord and Tenant Act.

(765 ILCS 705/1) (from Ch. 80, par. 91)

Sec. 1. Liability exemptions.

(a) Except as otherwise provided in subsection (b), every covenant, agreement, or understanding in or in connection with or collateral to any lease of real property, exempting the lessor from liability for damages for injuries to person or property caused by or resulting from the negligence of the lessor, his or her agents, servants or employees, in the operation or maintenance of the demised premises or the real property containing the demised premises shall be deemed to be void as against public policy and wholly unenforceable.

(b) Subsection (a) does not apply to a provision in a non-residential lease that exempts the lessor from liability for property damage.

(765 ILCS 705/3)

Sec. 3. Rent payments at business office; cross-reference. Leases and other rental agreements may be subject to Section 9-218 of the Code of Civil Procedure (735 ILCS 5/9-218).

(765 ILCS 705/5)

Sec. 5. Class X felony by lessee or occupant.

(a) If, after the effective date of this amendatory Act of 1995, any lessee or occupant is charged during his or her lease or contract term with having committed an offense on the premises constituting a Class X felony under the laws of this State, upon a judicial finding of probable cause at a preliminary hearing or indictment by a grand jury, the lease or contract for letting the premises shall, at the option of the lessor or the lessor's assignee, become void, and the owner or the owner's assignee may notify the lessee or occupant by posting a written notice at the premises requiring the lessee or occupant to vacate the leased premises on or before a date 5 days after the giving of the notice. The notice shall state the basis for its issuance on forms provided by the circuit court clerk of the county in which the real property is located. The owner or owner's assignee may have the same remedy to recover possession of the premises as against a tenant holding over after the expiration of his or her term. The owner or lessor may bring a forcible entry and detainer action.

(b) A person does not forfeit his or her security deposit or any part of the security deposit due solely to an eviction under the provisions of this Section.

(c) If a lessor or the lessor's assignee voids a contract under the provisions of this Section, and a tenant or occupant has not vacated the premises within 5 days after receipt of a written notice to vacate the premises, the lessor or the lessor's assignee may seek relief under Article IX of the Code of Civil Procedure. Notwithstanding Sections 9-112, 9-113, and 9-114 of the Code of Civil Procedure, judgment for costs against the plaintiff seeking possession of the premises under this Section shall not be awarded to the defendant unless the action was brought by the plaintiff in bad faith. An action to possess premises under this Section shall not be deemed to be in bad faith if the plaintiff based his or her cause of action on information provided to him or her by a law enforcement agency or the State's Attorney.

(d) The provisions of this Section are enforceable only if the lessee or occupant and the owner or owner's assignee have executed a lease addendum for drug free housing as promulgated by the United States Department of Housing and Urban Development or a substantially similar document.

(765 ILCS 705/10)

Sec. 10. Failure to inform lessor who is a child sex offender and who resides in the same building in which the lessee resides or intends to reside that the lessee is a parent or guardian of a child under 18 years of age. If a lessor of residential real estate resides at such real estate and is a child sex offender as defined in Section 11-9.4 of the Criminal Code of 1961 and rents such real estate to a person who does not inform the lessor that the person is a parent or guardian of a child or children under 18 years of age and subsequent to such lease, the lessee discovers that the landlord is a child sex offender, then the lessee may not terminate the lease based upon such discovery that the lessor is a child sex offender and such lease shall be in full force and effect. This subsection shall apply only to leases or other rental arrangements entered into after the effective date of this amendatory Act of the 95th General Assembly.

(765 ILCS 720/) Retaliatory Eviction Act.

(765 ILCS 720/0.01) (from Ch. 80, par. 70)

Sec. 0.01. Short title. This Act may be cited as the Retaliatory Eviction Act.

(765 ILCS 720/1) (from Ch. 80, par. 71)

Sec. 1. It is declared to be against the public policy of the State for a landlord to terminate or refuse to renew a lease or tenancy of property used as a residence on the ground that the tenant has complained to any governmental authority of a bona fide violation of any applicable building code, health ordinance, or similar regulation. Any provision in any lease, or any agreement or understanding, purporting to permit the landlord to terminate or refuse to renew a lease or tenancy for such reason is void.

Chicago Residential Landlord and Tenant Ordinance

Chapter 5-12.

Residential Landlords And Tenants.

Sections:

5-12-010 Title, Purpose And Scope.

This chapter shall be known and may be cited as the "Residential Landlord and Tenant Ordinance," and shall be liberally construed and applied to promote its purposes and policies.

It is the purpose of this chapter and the policy of the city, in order to protect and promote the public health, safety and welfare of its citizens, to establish the rights and obligations of the landlord and the tenant in the rental of dwelling units, and to encourage the landlord and the tenant to maintain and improve the quality of housing.

This chapter applies to, regulates and determines rights, obligations and remedies under every rental agreement for a dwelling unit located within the City of Chicago, regardless of where the agreement is made, subject only to the limitations contained in Section 5-12-020 This chapter applies specifically to rental agreements for dwelling units operated under subsidy programs of agencies of the United States and/or the State of Illinois, including specifically, programs operated or subsidized by the Chicago Housing Authority and/or the Illinois Housing Development Authority to the extent that this chapter is not in direct conflict with statutory or regulatory provisions governing such programs. (Prior code § 193.1-1; Added Council Journal of Proceedings, September 8, 1986, page 33771; Amend. Council Journal of Proceedings, November

6, 1991, page 7198; Amend. Council Journal of Proceedings, March 31, 2004, page 20938);

5-12-020 Exclusions.

Rental of the following dwelling units shall not be governed by this chapter, unless the rental agreement thereof is created to avoid the application of this chapter:

(a) dwelling units in owner-occupied buildings containing six units or less; provided, however, that the provisions of Section 5-12-160 shall apply to every rented dwelling unit in such buildings within the City of Chicago;

(b) dwelling units in hotels, motels, inns, bed-and-breakfast establishments, rooming houses and boardinghouses, but only until such time as the dwelling unit has been occupied by a tenant for 32 or more continuous days and tenant pays a monthly rent, exclusive of any period of wrongful occupancy contrary to agreement with an owner. Notwithstanding the above, the prohibition against interruption of tenant occupancy set forth in Section 5-12-160 shall apply to every rented dwelling unit in such buildings within the City of Chicago. No landlord shall bring an action to recover possession of such unit, or avoid renting monthly in order to avoid the application of this chapter. Any willful attempt to avoid application of this chapter by an owner may be punishable by criminal or civil action;

(c) housing accommodations in any hospital, convent, monastery, extended care facility, asylum or not-for-profit home for the aged, temporary overnight shelter, transitional shelter, or in a dormitory owned and operated by an elementary school, high school or institution of higher learning;

(d) a dwelling unit that is occupied by a purchaser pursuant to a real estate purchase contract prior to the transfer of title to such property to such purchaser, or by a seller of property pursuant to a real estate purchase contract subsequent to the transfer of title from such seller;

(e) a dwelling unit occupied by an employee of a landlord whose right to occupancy is conditional upon employment in or about the premises; and

(f) a dwelling unit in a cooperative occupied by a holder of a proprietary lease. (Prior code § 193.1-2; Added Council Journal of Proceedings, September 8, 1986, page 33771; Amend. Council Journal of Proceedings, November 6, 1991, pages 7198–7199; Amend. Council Journal of Proceedings, September 4, 2003, page 7130)

5-12-030 Definitions.

Whenever used in this chapter, the following words and phrases shall have the following meanings:

(a) "Dwelling unit" means a structure or the part of a structure that is used as a home, residence or sleeping place by one or more persons who maintain a household, together with the common areas, land and appurtenant buildings thereto, and all housing services, privileges, furnishings and facilities supplied in connection with the use or occupancy thereof, including garage and parking facilities.

(b) "Landlord" means the owner, agent, landlord or sublandlord, or the successor in interest of any of them, of a dwelling unit or the building of which it is part.

(c) "Owner" means one or more persons, jointly or severally, in whom is vested all or part of the legal title to property, or all or part of the beneficial ownership and a right to present use and enjoyment of the premises, including a mortgagee in possession.

(d) "Person" means an individual, corporation, government, governmental subdivision or agency, business trust, estate, trust, partnership or association or any other legal or commercial entity.

(e) "Premises" means the dwelling unit and the structure of which it is a part, and facilities and appurtenances therein, and grounds, areas and facilities held out for the use of tenants.

(f) "Rent" means any consideration, including any payment, bonus, benefits or gratuity, demanded or received by a landlord for or in connection with the use or occupancy of a dwelling unit.

(g) "Rental agreement" means all written or oral agreements embodying the terms and conditions concerning the use and occupancy of a dwelling unit.

(h) "Tenant" means a person entitled by written or oral agreement, subtenancy approved by the landlord or by sufferance, to occupy a dwelling unit to the exclusion of others. (Prior code § 193.1-3; Added Council Journal of Proceedings, September 8, 1986, page 33771; Amend. Council Journal of Proceedings November 6, 1991, page 7199)

5-12-040 Tenant Responsibilities.

Every tenant must:

(a) comply with all obligations imposed specifically upon tenants by provisions of the municipal code applicable to dwelling units;

(b) keep that part of the premises that he occupies and uses as safe as the condition of the premises permits;

(c) dispose of all ashes, rubbish, garbage and other waste from his dwelling unit in a clean and safe manner;

(d) keep all plumbing fixtures in the dwelling unit or used by the tenants as clean as their condition permits;

(e) use in a reasonable manner all electrical, plumbing, sanitary, heating, ventilating, air-conditioning and other facilities and appliances, including elevators, in the premises;

(f) not deliberately or negligently destroy, deface, damage, impair or remove any part of the premises or knowingly permit any person on the premises with his consent to do so; and

(g) conduct himself and require other persons on the premises with his consent to conduct themselves in a manner that will not disturb his neighbors' peaceful enjoyment of the premises. (Prior code § 193.1-4; Added Council Journal of Proceedings, September 8, 1986, page 33771)

5-12-050 Landlord's Right Of Access.

A tenant shall not unreasonably withhold consent to the landlord to enter the dwelling unit:

(a) to make necessary or agreed repairs, decorations, alterations or improvements;

(b) to supply necessary or agreed services;

(c) to conduct inspections authorized or required by any government agency;

(d) to exhibit the dwelling unit to prospective or actual purchasers, mortgagees, workmen or contractors;

(e) to exhibit the dwelling unit to prospective tenants 60 days or less prior to the expiration of the existing rental agreement;

(f) for practical necessity where repairs or maintenance elsewhere in the building unexpectedly require such access;

(g) to determine a tenant's compliance with provisions in the rental agreement; and

(h) in case of emergency.

The landlord shall not abuse the right of access or use it to harass the tenant except in cases where access is authorized by subsection (f) or (h) of this section, the landlord shall give the tenant notice of the landlord's intent to enter of no less than two days. Such notice shall be provided directly to each dwelling unit by mail, telephone, written notice to the dwelling unit, or by other reasonable means designed in good faith to provide notice to the tenant. If access is required because of repair work or common facilities or other apartments, a general notice may be given by the landlord to all potentially affected tenants that entry may be required. In cases where access is authorized by subsection (f) or (h) of this section, the landlord may enter the dwelling unit without notice or consent of the tenant. The landlord shall give the tenant notice of such entry within two days after such entry.

The landlord may enter only at reasonable times except in case of an emergency. An entry between 8:00 A.M. and 8:00 P.M. or at any other time expressly requested by the tenant shall be presumed reasonable. (Prior code § 193.1-5; Added Council Journal of Proceedings, September 8, 1986, page 33771)

5-12-060 Remedies For Improper Denial Of Access.

If the tenant refuses to allow lawful access, the landlord may obtain injunctive relief to compel access or terminate the rental agreement pursuant to Section 5-12-130(b) of this chapter. In either case, the landlord may recover damages. If the landlord makes an unlawful entry or a lawful entry in an unreasonable manner or makes repeated unreasonable demands for entry otherwise lawful, but which have the effect of harassing the tenant, the tenant may obtain injunctive relief to prevent the recurrence of the conduct, or terminate the rental agreement pursuant to the notice provisions of Section 5-12-110(a). In each case, the tenant may recover an amount equal to not more than one month's rent or twice the damage sustained by him, whichever is greater. (Prior code § 193.1-6; Added Council Journal of Proceedings, September 8, 1986, page 33771; Amend. Council Journal of Proceedings, November 6, 1991, page 7202)

5-12-070 Landlord's Responsibility To Maintain.

The landlord shall maintain the premises in compliance with all applicable provisions of the municipal code and shall promptly make any and all repairs necessary to fulfill this obligation. (Prior code § 193.1-7; Added Council Journal of Proceedings, September 8, 1986, page 33771)

5-12-080 Security Deposits.

(a) A landlord shall hold all security deposits received by him in a federally insured interest-bearing account in a bank, savings and loan association or other financial institution located in the State of Illinois. A security deposit and interest due thereon shall continue to be the property of the tenant making such deposit, shall not be commingled with the assets of the landlord, and shall not be subject to the claims of any creditor of the landlord or of the landlord's successors in interest, including a foreclosing mortgagee or trustee in bankruptcy.

(b) Any landlord or landlord's agent who receives a security deposit from a tenant or prospective tenant shall give said tenant or prospective tenant at the time of receiving such security deposit a receipt indicating the amount of such security deposit, the name of the person receiving it and, in the case of the agent, the name of the landlord for whom such security deposit is received, the date on which it is received, and a description of the dwelling unit. The receipt shall be signed by the person receiving the security deposit. Failure to comply with this subsection shall entitle the tenant to immediate return of security deposit.

(c) A landlord who holds a security deposit or prepaid rent pursuant to this section shall pay interest to the tenant accruing from the beginning date of the rental term specified in the rental agreement at the rate determined in accordance with Section 5-12-081. The landlord shall, within 30 days after the end of each 12-month rental period, pay to the tenant any interest, by cash or credit to be applied to the rent due. (Amend. Council Journal of Proceedings, November 6, 1991, page 7203; Added Council Journal of Proceedings, May 14, 1997, page 4516; Amend. Council Journal of Proceedings, March 31, 2004, page 20939)

(d) The landlord shall, within 45 days after the date that the tenant vacates the dwelling unit or within 7 days after the date that the tenant provides notice of termination of the rental agreement pursuant to Section 5-12-110(g), return to the tenant the security deposit or any balance thereof and the required interest thereon; provided, however, that the landlord may deduct from such security deposit or interest due thereon for the following:

(1) any unpaid rent which has not been validly withheld or deducted pursuant to state or federal law or local ordinance; and

(2) a reasonable amount necessary to repair any damage caused to the premises by the tenant or any person under the tenant's control or on the premises with the tenant's consent, reasonable wear and tear excluded. In case of such damage, the landlord shall deliver or mail to the last known address of the tenant within 30 days an itemized statement of the damages allegedly caused to the premises and the estimated or actual cost for repairing or replacing each item on that statement, attaching copies of the paid receipts for the repair or replacement. If estimated cost is given, the landlord shall furnish the tenant with copies of paid receipts or a certification of actual costs of repairs of damage if the work was performed by the landlord's employees within 30 days from the date the statement showing estimated cost was furnished to the tenant.

(e) In the event of a sale, lease, transfer or other direct or indirect disposition of residential real property, other than to the holder of a lien interest in such property, a landlord who has received a security deposit or prepaid rent from a tenant, the successor landlord of such property shall be liable to that tenant for any security deposit, including statutory interest, or prepaid rent which the tenant has paid to the transferor.

The successor landlord shall, within 10 days from the date of such transfer, notify the tenant who made such security deposit by delivering or mailing to the tenant's last known address that such security deposit was transferred to the successor landlord and that the successor landlord is holding said security deposit Such notice shall also contain the successor landlord's name, business address, and business telephone number of the successor landlord's agent, if any. The notice shall be in writing.

The transferor shall remain jointly and severally liable with the successor landlord to the tenant for such security deposit or prepaid rent, unless and until such transferor transfers said security deposit or prepaid rent to the successor landlord and provides notice, in writing, to the tenant of such transfer of said security deposit or prepaid rent, specifying the name, business address and business telephone number of the successor landlord or his agent within 10 days of said transfer.

If the landlord or landlord's agent fails to comply with any provision of Section 5-12-080 (a)–(e), the tenant shall be awarded damages in an amount equal to two times the security deposit plus interest at a rate determined in accordance with Section 5-12-081. This subsection does not preclude the tenant from recovering other damages to which he may be entitled under this chapter. (Prior code § 193.1-8; Added Council Journal of Proceedings, September 8, 1986, page 33771; Amend. Council Journal of Proceedings, November 6, 1991, page 7204; Added Council Journal of Proceedings, May 14, 1997, page 45168)

5-12-081 Interest Rate On Security Deposits.

During June of 1997 and thereafter during December of each year, the city comptroller shall review the status of banks within the city and interest rates on passbook savings accounts, insured money market accounts and six-month certificates of deposit at commercial banks located within the city. On the first business day of July of 1997, and thereafter on the first business day of each year, the city comptroller shall announce the rates of interest, as of the last business day of the prior month, on passbook savings accounts, insured money market accounts and six-month certificates of deposit at the commercial bank having its main branch located in the city and having the largest total asset value. The rates for money market accounts shall be based on the minimum deposits for such investments. The rates for certificates of deposit shall be based on a deposit of $1,000. The city comptroller shall calculate and announce the average of the three rates.

The average of these rates so announced by the city comptroller shall be the rate of interest on security deposits under rental agreements governed by this chapter and made or renewed after the most recent announcement.[1] (Added Council Journal of Proceedings, May 14, 1997, page 45168)

5-12-082 Interest Rate Notification.

The city comptroller, after computing the rate of interest on security deposit governed by this chapter, shall cause the new rate of security deposit interest to be published for five consecutive business days in two or more newspapers of general circulation in the city. The mayor shall direct the appropriate city department to prepare and publish for free public distribution at government offices, libraries, schools and community organizations, a pamphlet or brochure describing the respective rights, obligations and remedies of landlords and tenants with respect to security deposits, including the new interest rate as well as the interest rate for each of the prior two years. The commissioner shall also distribute the new rate of security deposit interest, as well as the interest rate for each of the prior two years, through public service announcements to all radio and television outlets broadcasting in the city. (Added Council Journal of Proceedings, May 7, 1997, page 45169)

5-12-090 Identification Of Owner And Agents.

A landlord or any person authorized to enter into an oral or written rental agreement on the landlord's behalf shall disclose to the tenant in writing at or before the commencement of the tenancy the name, address, and telephone number of:

---

1. Current rate–January 1, 2008 through December 31, 2013: 0.023%.

(a) the owner or person authorized to manage the premises; and

(b) a person authorized to act for and on behalf of the owner for the purpose of service of process and for the purpose of receiving and receipting for notices and demands.

A person who enters into a rental agreement and fails to comply with the requirements of this section becomes an agent of the landlord for the purpose of (i) service of process and receiving and receipting for notices and demands and (ii) performing the obligations of the landlord under this chapter under the rental agreement.

The information required to be furnished by this section shall be kept current and this section extends to and is enforceable against any successor landlord, owner or manager.

If the landlord fails to comply with this section, the tenant may terminate the rental agreement pursuant to the notice provisions of Section 5-12-110(a). If the landlord fails to comply with the requirements of this section after receipt of written notice pursuant to Section 5-12-110(a), the tenant shall recover one month's rent or actual damages, whichever is greater. (Prior code § 193.1-9; Added Council Journal of Proceedings, September 8, 1986, page 33771; Amend. Council Journal of Proceedings, November 6, 1991, page 7205)

5-12-100 Notice Of Conditions Affecting Habitability.

Before a tenant initially enters into or renews a rental agreement for a dwelling unit, the landlord or any person authorized to enter into a rental agreement on his behalf shall disclose to the tenant in writing:

(a) Any code violations which have been cited by the City of Chicago during the previous 12 months for the dwelling unit and common areas and provide notice of the pendency of any code enforcement litigation or compliance board proceeding pursuant to Chapter 13-8-070 of the municipal code affecting the dwelling unit or common area. The notice shall provide the case number of the litigation and/or the identification number of the compliance board proceeding and a listing of any code violations cited. (Amend. Council Journal of Proceedings, November 6, 1991, page 7205)

(b) Any notice of intent by the City of Chicago or any utility provider to terminate water, gas, electrical or other utility service to the dwelling unit or common areas. The disclosure shall state the type of service to be terminated, the intended date of termination, and whether the termination will affect the dwelling unit, the common areas or both. A landlord shall be under a continuing obligation to provide disclosure of the information described in this subsection (b) throughout a tenancy. If a landlord violates this section, the tenant or prospective tenant shall be entitled to remedies described in Section 5-12-090. (Prior code § 193.1-10, Added Council Journal of Proceedings, September 8, 1986, page 33771; Amend. Council Journal of Proceedings, November 6, 1991, page 7206)

5-12-110 Tenant Remedies.

In addition to any remedies provided under federal law, a tenant shall have the remedies specified in this section under the circumstances herein set forth. For purposes of this section, material noncompliance with Section 5-12-070 shall include, but is not limited to, any of the following circumstances:

failure to maintain the structural integrity of the building or structure or parts thereof;

failure to maintain floors in compliance with the safe load-bearing requirements of the municipal code;

failure to comply with applicable requirements of the municipal code for the number, width, construction, location or accessibility of exits;

failure to maintain exit, stairway, fire escape or directional signs where required by the municipal code;

failure to provide smoke detectors, sprinkler systems, standpipe systems, fire alarm systems, automatic fire detectors or fire extinguishers where required by the municipal code;

failure to maintain elevators in compliance with applicable provisions of the municipal code;

failure to provide and maintain in good working order a flush water closet, lavatory basin, bathtub or shower or kitchen sink;

failure to maintain heating facilities or gas-fired appliances in compliance with the requirements of the municipal code;

failure to provide heat or hot water in such amounts and at such levels and times as required by the municipal code;

failure to provide hot and cold running water as required by the municipal code;

failure to provide adequate hall or stairway lighting as required by the municipal code;

failure to maintain the foundation, exterior walls or exterior roof in sound condition and repair, substantially watertight and protected against rodents;

failure to maintain floors, interior walls or ceilings in sound condition and good repair;

failure to maintain windows, exterior doors or basement hatchways in sound condition and repair and substantially tight and to provide locks or security devices as required by the municipal code, including deadlatch locks, deadbolt locks, sash or ventilation locks, and front door windows or peep holes;

failure to supply screens where required by the municipal code;

failure to maintain stairways or porches in safe condition and sound repair;

failure to maintain the basement or cellar in a safe and sanitary condition;

failure to maintain facilities, equipment or chimneys in safe and sound working conditions;

failure to prevent the accumulation of stagnant water;

failure to exterminate insects, rodents or other pests;

failure to supply or maintain facilities for refuse disposal;

failure to prevent the accumulation of garbage, trash, refuse or debris as required by the municipal code;

failure to provide adequate light or ventilation as required by the municipal code;

failure to maintain plumbing facilities, piping, fixtures, appurtenances and appliances in good operating condition and repair;

failure to provide or maintain electrical systems, circuits, receptacles and devices as required by the municipal code;

failure to maintain and repair any equipment which the landlord supplies or is required to supply; or

failure to maintain the dwelling unit and common areas in a fit and habitable condition.

(a) Noncompliance By Landlord. If there is material noncompliance by the landlord with a rental agreement or with Section 5-12-070 either of which renders the premises not reasonably fit and habitable, the tenant under the rental agreement may deliver a written notice to the landlord specifying the acts and/or omissions constituting the material noncompliance and specifying that the rental agreement will terminate on a date not less than 14 days after receipt of the notice by the landlord, unless the material noncompliance is remedied by the landlord within the time period specified in the notice. If the material noncompliance is not remedied within the time period so specified in the notice, the rental agreement shall terminate, and the tenant shall deliver possession of the dwelling unit to the landlord within 30 days after the expiration of the time period specified in the notice. If possession shall not be so delivered, then the tenant's notice shall be deemed withdrawn and the lease shall remain in full force and effect. If the rental agreement is terminated, the landlord shall return all prepaid rent, security and interest recoverable by the tenant under Section 5-12-080.

(b) Failure To Deliver Possession. If the landlord fails to deliver possession of the dwelling unit to the tenant in compliance with the residential rental agreement or Section 5-12-070, rent for the dwelling unit shall abate until possession is delivered, and the tenant may:

(1) upon written notice to the landlord, terminate the rental agreement and upon termination the landlord shall return all prepaid rent and security; or

(2) demand performance of the rental agreement by the landlord and, if the tenant elects, maintain an action for possession of the dwelling unit against the landlord or any person wrongfully in possession and recover the damages sustained by him.

If a person's failure to deliver possession is wilful, an aggrieved person may recover from the person withholding possession an amount not more than two months' rent or twice the actual damages sustained by him, whichever is greater.

(c) Minor Defects. If there is material noncompliance by the landlord with the rental agreement or with Section 5-12-070, and the reasonable cost of compliance does not exceed the greater of $500.00 or one-half of the monthly rent, the tenant may recover damages for the material noncompliance or may notify the landlord in writing of his intention to correct the condition at the landlord's expense; provided, however, that this subsection shall not be applicable if the reasonable cost of compliance exceeds one month's rent. If the landlord fails to correct the defect within 14 days after being notified by the tenant in writing or as promptly as conditions require in case of emergency, the tenant may have the work done in a workmanlike manner and in compliance with existing law and building regulations and, after submitting to the landlord a paid bill from an appropriate tradesman or supplier, deduct from his or her rent the amount thereof, not to exceed the limits specified by this subsection and not to exceed the reasonable price then customarily charged for such work. A tenant shall not repair at the landlord's expense if the condition was caused by the deliberate or negligent act or omission of the tenant, a member of the tenant's family, or other person on the premises with the tenant's consent.

Before correcting a condition affecting facilities shared by more than one dwelling unit, the tenant shall notify all other affected tenants and shall cause the work to be done so as to create the least practical inconvenience to the other tenants. Nothing herein shall be deemed to grant any tenant any right to repair any common element or dwelling unit in a building subject to a condominium regime other than in accordance with the declaration and bylaws of such condominium building; provided, that the declaration and bylaws have not been created to avoid the application of this chapter.

For purposes of mechanics' lien laws, repairs performed or materials furnished pursuant to this subsection shall not be construed as having been performed or furnished pursuant to authority of or with permission of the landlord.

(d) Failure To Maintain. If there is material noncompliance by the landlord with the rental agreement or with Section 5-12-070, the tenant may notify the landlord in writing of the tenant's intention to withhold from the monthly rent an amount which reasonably reflects the reduced value of the premises due to the material noncompliance. If the landlord fails to correct the condition within 14 days after being notified by the tenant in writing, the tenant may, during the time such failure continues, deduct from the rent the stated amount. A tenant shall not withhold rent under this subsection if the condition was caused by the deliberate or negligent act or omission of the tenant, a member of the tenant's family, or other person on the premises with the tenant's consent.

(e) Damages And Injunctive Relief. If there is material noncompliance by the landlord with the rental agreement or with Section 5-12-070, the tenant may obtain injunctive relief, and/or recover damages by claim or defense. This subsection does not preclude the tenant from obtaining other relief to which he may be entitled under this chapter.

(f) Failure To Provide Essential Services. If there is material noncompliance by the landlord with the rental agreement or with Section 5-12-070, either of which constitutes an immediate danger to the health and safety of the tenant or if, contrary to the rental agreement or Section 5-12-070, the landlord fails to supply heat, running water, hot water, electricity, gas or plumbing, the tenant may give written notice to the landlord specifying the material noncompliance or failure. If the landlord has, pursuant to this ordinance or in the rental agreement, informed the tenant of an address at which notices to the landlord are to be received, the tenant shall mail or deliver the written notice required in this section to such address. If the landlord has not informed the tenant of an address at which notices to the landlord are to be received, the written notice required in this section shall be delivered by mail to the last known address of the landlord or by other reasonable means designed in good faith to provide written notice to the landlord. After such notice, the tenant may during the period of the landlord's noncompliance or failure:

(1) procure reasonable amounts of heat, running water, hot water, electricity, gas or plumbing service, as the case may be and upon presentation to the landlord of paid receipts deduct their cost from the rent; or

(2) recover damages based on the reduction in the fair rental value of the dwelling unit; or

(3) procure substitute housing, in which case the tenant is excused from paying rent for the period of the landlord's noncompliance. The tenant may recover the cost of the reasonable value of the substitute housing up to an amount equal to the monthly rent for each month or portion thereof of noncompliance as prorated.

In addition to the remedies set forth in Section 5-12-110 (1) (1) –(3), the tenant may:

(4) withhold from the monthly rent an amount that reasonably reflects the reduced value of the premises due to the material noncompliance or failure if the landlord fails to correct the condition within 24 hours after being notified by the tenant; provided, however, that no rent shall be withheld if the failure is due to the inability of the utility provider to provide service; or

(5) terminate the rental agreement by written notice to the landlord if the material noncompliance or failure persists for more than 72 hours after the tenant has notified the landlord of the material noncompliance or failure; provided, however, that no termination shall be allowed if the failure is due to the inability of the utility provider to provide service. If the rental agreement is terminated, the landlord shall return all prepaid rent, security deposits and interest thereon in accordance with Section 5-12-080 and tenant shall deliver possession of the dwelling unit to the landlord within 30 days after the expiration of the 72-hour time period specified in the notice. If possession shall not be so delivered, then the tenant's notice shall be deemed withdrawn and the lease shall remain in full force and effect.

If the tenant proceeds under this subsection (f), he may not proceed under subsection (c) or (d). The tenant may not exercise his rights under this subsection if the condition was caused by the deliberate or negligent act or omission of the tenant, a member of his family, or other person on the premises with his consent. Before correcting a condition, the repair of which will affect more than his own dwelling unit, the tenant shall notify all other tenants affected and shall cause the work to be done so as to result in the least practical inconvenience to other tenants.

(g) Fire Or Casualty Damage. If the dwelling unit or common area is damaged or destroyed by fire or casualty to an extent that the dwelling unit is in material noncompliance with the rental agreement or with Section 5-12-070, the tenant may:

(1) immediately vacate the premises and notify the landlord in writing within 14 days thereafter of the tenant's intention to terminate the rental agreement, in which case the rental agreement terminates as of the date of the fire or casualty; or

(2) if continued occupancy is lawful, vacate any part of the dwelling unit rendered unusable by the fire or casualty, in which case the tenant's liability for rent is reduced in proportion to the reduction in the fair rental value of the dwelling unit; or

(3) if the tenant desires to continue the tenancy, and if the landlord has promised or begun work to repair the damage or destruction but fails to carry out the work to restore the dwelling unit or common area diligently and within a reasonable time, notify the landlord in writing within 14 days after the tenant becomes aware that the work is not being carried out diligently or within a reasonable time of the tenant's intention to terminate the rental agreement, in which case the rental agreement terminates as of the date of the fire or casualty.

If the rental agreement is terminated under this subsection (g), the landlord shall return all security and all prepaid rent in accordance with Section 5-12-080(d). Accounting for rent in the event of termination or apportionment shall be made as of the date of the fire or casualty. A tenant may not exercise remedies in this subsection if the fire or casualty damage was caused by the deliberate or negligent act or omission of the tenant, a member of his family or a person on the premises with his consent. (Prior code § 193. 1-1 1; Added Council Journal of Proceedings, September 8, 1986, page 33771; Amend. Council Journal of Proceedings, November 6, 1991, pages 7206–7212)

5-12-120 Subleases.

If the tenant terminates the rental agreement prior to its expiration date, except for cause authorized by this chapter, the landlord shall make a good faith effort to re-rent the tenant's dwelling unit at a fair rental, which shall be the rent charged for comparable dwelling units in the premises or in the same neighborhood. The landlord shall accept a reasonable sublease proposed by the tenant without an assessment of additional fees or charges.

If the landlord succeeds in re-renting the dwelling unit at a fair rental, the tenant shall be liable for the amount by which the rent due from the date of premature termination to the termination of the initial rental agreement exceeds the fair rental subsequently received by the landlord from the date of premature termination to the termination of the initial rental agreement.

If the landlord makes a good faith effort to re-rent the dwelling unit at a fair rental and is unsuccessful, the tenant shall be liable for the rent due for the period of the rental agreement. The tenant shall also be liable for the reasonable advertising costs incurred by the landlord in seeking to re-rent the dwelling unit. (Prior code § 193.1-12; Added Council Journal of Proceedings, September 8, 1986, page 33771)

5-12-130 Landlord Remedies.

Every landlord shall have the remedies specified in this section for the following circumstances:

(a) Failure To Pay Rent. If all or any portion of rent is unpaid when due and the tenant fails to pay the unpaid rent within five days after written notice by the landlord of his intention to terminate the rental agreement if rent is not so paid, the landlord may terminate the rental agreement. Nothing in this subsection shall affect a landlord's obligation to provide notice of termination of tenancy in subsidized housing as required under federal law or regulations. A landlord may also maintain an action for rent and/or damages without terminating the rental agreement.

(b) Noncompliance By Tenant. If there is material noncompliance by a tenant with a rental agreement or with Section 5-12-040, the landlord of such tenant's dwelling unit may deliver written notice to the tenant specifying the acts and/or omissions constituting the breach and that the rental agreement will terminate upon a date not less than 10 days after receipt of the notice, unless the breach is remedied by the tenant within that period of time. If the breach is not remedied within the 10 day period, the residential rental agreement shall terminate as provided in the notice. The landlord may recover damages and obtain injunctive relief for any material noncompliance by the tenant with the rental agreement or with Section 5-12-040. If the tenant's noncompliance is wilful, the landlord may also recover reasonable attorney's fees.

(c) Failure To Maintain. If there is material noncompliance by the tenant with Section 5-12-040 (other than subsection (g) thereof), and the tenant fails to comply as promptly as conditions permit in case of emergency or in cases other than emergencies within 14 days of receipt of written notice by the landlord specifying the breach and requesting that the tenant remedy it within that period of time, the landlord may enter the dwelling unit and have the necessary work done in the manner required by law. The landlord shall be entitled to reimbursement from the tenant of the costs of repairs under this section.

(d) Disturbance Of Others. If the tenant violates Section 5-12-040(g) within 60 days after receipt of a written notice as provided in subsection (b), the landlord may obtain injunctive relief against the conduct constituting the violation, or may terminate the rental agreement on 10 days written notice to the tenant.

(e) Abandonment. Abandonment of the dwelling unit shall be deemed to have occurred when:

(1) actual notice has been provided to the landlord by the tenant indicating the tenant's intention not to return to the dwelling unit, or

(2) all persons entitled under a rental agreement to occupy the dwelling unit have been absent from the unit or a period of 21 days or for one rental period when the rental agreement is for less than a month, and such persons have removed their personal property from the premises, and rent for that period is unpaid; or

(3) all persons entitled under a rental agreement to occupy the dwelling unit have been absent from the unit for a period of 32 days, and rent for that period is unpaid. Notwithstanding the above, abandonment of the dwelling unit shall not be deemed to have occurred if any person entitled to occupancy has provided the landlord a written notice indicating that he still intends to occupy the unit and makes full payment of all amounts due to the landlord.

If the tenant abandons the dwelling unit, the landlord shall make a good faith effort to re-rent it at a fair rental, which shall be the rent charged for comparable dwelling units in the premises or in the same neighborhood. If the landlord succeeds in re-renting the dwelling unit at a fair rental, the tenant shall be liable for the amount by which the rent due from the date of abandonment to the termination of the initial rental agreement exceeds the fair rental subsequently received by the landlord from the date of abandonment to the termination of the initial rental agreement. If the landlord makes a good faith effort to re-rent the dwelling unit at a fair rental and is unsuccessful, the tenant shall be liable for the rent due for the period of the rental agreement. The tenant shall also be liable for the reasonable advertising expenses and reasonable redecoration costs incurred by the landlord pursuant to this subsection.

(f) Disposition Of Abandoned Property. If the tenant abandons the dwelling unit as described in subsection (e) hereof, or fails to remove his personal property from the premises after termination of a rental agreement, the landlord shall leave the property in the dwelling unit or remove and store all abandoned property from the dwelling unit and may dispose of the property after seven days. Notwithstanding the foregoing, if the landlord reasonably believes such abandoned property to be valueless or of such little value that the cost of storage would exceed the amount that would be realized from sale, or if such property is subject to spoilage, the landlord may immediately dispose of such property.

(g) Waiver Of Landlord's Right To Terminate. If the landlord accepts the rent due knowing that there is a default in payment of rent by the tenant, he thereby waives his right to terminate the rental agreement for that breach.

(h) Remedy After Termination. If the rental agreement is terminated, the landlord shall have a claim for possession and/or for rent.

(i) Notice Of Renewal Of Rental Agreement. No tenant shall be required to renew a rental agreement more than 90 days prior to the termination date of the rental agreement. If the landlord violates this subsection, the tenant shall recover one month's rent or actual damages, whichever is greater.

(j) Notice Of Refusal To Renew Rental Agreement. Provided that the landlord has not exercised, or is not in the process of exercising, any of its rights under Section 5-12-130 (a)–(h) hereof, the landlord shall notify the tenant in writing at least 30 days prior to the stated termination date of the rental agreement of the landlord's intent either to terminate a month to month tenancy or not to renew an existing rental agreement. If the landlord fails to give the required written notice, the tenant may remain in the dwelling unit for up to 60 days after the date on which such required written notice is given to the tenant, regardless of the termination date specified in the existing rental agreement. During such occupancy, the terms and conditions of the tenancy (including, without limitation, the rental rate) shall be the same as the terms and conditions during the month of tenancy immediately preceding the notice; provided, however, that if rent was waived or abated in the preceding month or months as part of the original rental agreement, the rental amount during such 60 day period shall be at the rate established on the last date that a full rent payment was made. (Prior Code § 193.1-13; Added Council Journal of Proceedings, September 8, 1986, page 33771; Amend. Council Journal of Proceedings, November 6, 1991, page 7215)

5-12-140 Rental Agreement.

Except as otherwise specifically provided by this chapter, no rental agreement may provide that the landlord or tenant:

(a) agrees to waive or forego rights, remedies or obligations provided under this chapter;

(b) authorizes any person to confess judgment on a claim arising out of the rental agreement;

(c) agrees to the limitation of any liability of the landlord or tenant arising under law;

(d) agrees to waive any written termination of tenancy notice or manner of service thereof provided under state law or this chapter;

(e) agrees to waive the right of any party to a trial by jury;

(f) agrees that in the event of a lawsuit arising out of the tenancy the tenant will pay the landlord's attorney's fees except as provided for by court rules, statute, or ordinance;

(g) agrees that either party may cancel or terminate a rental agreement at a different time or within a shorter time period than the other party, unless such provision is disclosed in a separate written notice;

(h) agrees that a tenant shall pay a charge, fee or penalty in excess of $10.00 per month for the first $500.00 in monthly rent plus 5% per month for any amount in excess of $500.00 in monthly rent for the late payment of rent; and

(i) agrees that, if a tenant pays rent before a specified date or within a specified time period in the month, the tenant shall receive a discount or reduction in the rental amount in excess of $10.00 per month for the first $500.00 in monthly rent plus 5% per month for any amount in excess of $500.00 in monthly rent.

A provision prohibited by this section included in a rental agreement is unenforceable. The tenant may recover actual damages sustained by the tenant because of the enforcement of a prohibited provision. If the landlord attempts to enforce a provision in a rental agreement prohibited by this section the tenant may recover two months' rent. Prior code § 193.1-14; Added Council Journal of Proceedings, September 8, 1986, page 33771; Amend. Council Journal of Proceedings, November 6, 1991, pages 7215–7216))

5-12-150 Prohibition On Retaliatory Conduct By Landlord.

It is declared to be against public policy of the City of Chicago for a landlord to take retaliatory action against a tenant, except for violation of a rental agreement or violation of a law or ordinance. A landlord may not knowingly terminate a tenancy, increase rent, decrease services, bring or threaten to bring a lawsuit against a tenant for possession or refuse to renew a lease or tenancy because the tenant has in good faith:

(a) complained of code violations applicable to the premises to a competent governmental agency, elected representative or public official charged with responsibility for enforcement of a building, housing, health or similar code; or

(b) complained of a building, housing, health or similar code violation or an illegal landlord practice to a community organization or the news media; or

(c) sought the assistance of a community organization or the news media to remedy a code violation or illegal landlord practice; or

(d) requested the landlord to make repairs to the premises as required by a building code, health ordinance, other regulation, or the residential rental agreement; or

(e) becomes a member of a tenant's union or similar organization; or

(f) testified in any court or administrative proceeding concerning the condition of the premises; or

(g) exercised any right or remedy provided by law.

If the landlord acts in violation of this section, the tenant has a defense in any retaliatory action against him for possession and is entitled to the following remedies: he shall recover possession or terminate the rental agreement and, in either case, recover an amount equal to and not more than two months' rent or twice the damages sustained by him, whichever is greater, and reasonable attorney's fees. If the rental agreement is terminated, the landlord shall return all security and interest recoverable under Section 5-12-080 and all prepaid rent. In an action by or against the tenant, if there is evidence of tenant conduct protected herein within one year prior to the alleged act of retaliation, that evidence shall create a rebuttable presumption that the landlord's conduct was retaliatory. The presumption shall not arise if the protected tenant activity was initiated after the alleged act of retaliation. (Prior code § 193.1-15, Added. Council Journal of Proceedings, September 8, 1986. page 33771)

5-12-160 Prohibition On Interruption Of Tenant Occupancy By Landlord.

It is unlawful for any landlord or any person acting at his direction knowingly to oust or dispossess or threaten or attempt to oust or dispossess any tenant from a dwelling unit without authority of law, by plugging, changing, adding or removing any lock or latching device; or by blocking any entrance into said unit; or by removing any door or window from said unit; or by interfering with the services to said unit; including but not limited to electricity, gas, hot or cold water, plumbing, heat or telephone service; or by removing a tenant's personal property from said unit; or by the removal or incapacitating of appliances or fixtures, except for the purpose of making necessary repairs; or by the use or threat of force, violence or injury to a tenant's person or property; or by any act rendering a dwelling unit or any part thereof or any personal property located therein inaccessible or uninhabitable. The foregoing shall not apply where:

(a) a landlord acts in compliance with the laws of Illinois pertaining to forcible entry and detainer and engages the sheriff of Cook County to forcibly evict a tenant or his personal property; or

(b) a landlord acts in compliance with the laws of Illinois pertaining to distress for rent; or

(c) a landlord interferes temporarily with possession only as necessary to make needed repairs or inspection and only as provided by law; or

(d) the tenant has abandoned the dwelling unit, as defined in Section 5-12-130(e).

Whenever a complaint of violation of this provision is received by the Chicago Police Department, the department shall investigate and determine whether a violation has occurred. Any person found guilty of violating this section shall be fined not less than $200.00 nor more than $500.00, and each day that such violation shall occur or continue shall constitute a separate and distinct offense for which a fine as herein provided shall be imposed. If a tenant in a civil legal proceeding against his landlord establishes that a violation of this section has occurred he shall be entitled to recover possession of his dwelling unit or personal property and shall recover an amount equal to not more than two months' rent or twice the actual damages sustained by him, whichever is greater. A tenant may pursue any civil remedy for violation of this section regardless of whether a fine has been entered against the landlord pursuant to this section. (Prior code § 193.1-16; Added Council Journal of Proceedings, September 8, 1986, page 33771; Amend. Council Journal of Proceedings, November 6, 1991, page 7218)

5-12-170 Summary Of Ordinance Attached To Rental Agreement.

The commissioner of the department of housing shall prepare a summary of this chapter, describing the respective rights, obligations and remedies of landlords and tenants hereunder, and shall make such summary available for public inspection and copying. The commissioner shall also, after the city comptroller has announced the rate of interest on security deposits on the first business day of the year, prepare a separate summary describing the respective rights, obligations and remedies of landlords and tenants with respect to security deposits, including the new interest rate as well as the rate for each of the prior two years. The commissioner shall also distribute the new rate of security deposit interest, as well as the rate for each of the prior two years, through public service announcements to all radio and television outlets broadcasting in the city. A copy of such summary shall be attached to each written rental agreement when any such agreement is initially offered to any tenant or prospective tenant by or on behalf of a landlord and whether such agreement is for a new rental or a renewal thereof. Where there is an oral agreement, the landlord shall give to the tenant a copy of the summary.

The summary shall include the following language:

"The porch or deck of this building should be designed for a live load of up to 100 pounds, per square foot and is safe only for its intended use. Protect your safety. Do not overload the porch or deck. If you have questions about porch or deck safety, call the City of Chicago non-emergency Number 3-1-1."

If the landlord acts in violation of this section, the tenant may terminate the rental agreement by written notice. The written notice shall specify the date of termination no later than 30 days from the date of the written notice. If a tenant in a civil legal proceeding against his landlord establishes that a violation of this section has occurred, he shall be entitled to recover $100.00 in damages. (Prior code § 193.1-17; Added Council Journal of Proceedings, September 8, 1986, page 33771; Amend. Council Journal of Proceedings, May 14, 1997, page 45167; Amend. Council Journal of Proceedings, October 1, 2003, page 9191)

5-12-180 Attorney's Fees.

Except in cases of forcible entry and detainer actions, the prevailing plaintiff in any action arising out of a landlord's or tenant's application of the rights or remedies made available in this ordinance shall be entitled to all court costs and reasonable attorney's fees; provided, however, that nothing herein shall be deemed or interpreted as precluding the awarding of attorney's fees in forcible entry and detainer actions in accordance with applicable law or as expressly provided in this ordinance. (Added Council Journal of Proceedings, November 6, 1991, page 7219)

5-12-190 Rights And Remedies Under Other Laws.

To the extent that this chapter provides no right or remedy in a circumstance, the rights and remedies available to landlords and tenants under the laws of the State of Illinois or other local ordinances shall remain applicable. (Prior code § 193.1-18; Added Council Journal of Proceedings, September 8, 1986, page 33771; Amend. Council Journal of Proceedings, November 6, 1991, page 7219)

5-12-200 Severability.

If any provision, clause, sentence, paragraph, section, or part of this chapter or application thereof to any person or circumstance, shall for any reason be adjudged by a court of competent jurisdiction to be unconstitutional or invalid, said judgment shall not affect, impair or invalidate the remainder of this chapter and the application of such provision to other persons or circumstances, but shall be confined in its operation to the provision, clause, sentence, paragraph, section, or part thereof directly involved in the controversy in which such judgment shall have been rendered and to the person and circumstances affected thereby. (Prior code § 193.1-19; Added Council Journal of Proceedings, September8, 1986, page 33771; Amend. Council Journal of Proceedings, November 6, 1991, page 7220)

Key Terms

Eviction
Five Day Notice
Ten Day Notice
Thirty Day Notice
Non-Renewal of Tenancy
Order for Possession
Stay of Enforcement
Abandonment

Review Questions

- When is a Five Day Notice used?
- Must the tenant be in breach to use a Thirty Day Notice?
- What are the forms of service for a notice?
- What are three steps in an eviction?
- What does "Stay of Enforcement" mean in an eviction?

Materials in the following chapter appendix include:

- Five Day Notices
- Ten Day Notice
- Thirty Day Notice
- Sample Complaint
- Sample Summons for Trial
- *Midland Management Company v. Ronald Helgason*, 630 N.E.2d 836, 158 Ill.2d 98, 196 Ill. Dec. 671 (1994)

Chapter 9 Appendix

LANDLORD'S FIVE DAY NOTICE

State of Illinois)

) ss.

County of Cook)

To:

_____

_____

YOU ARE HEREBY NOTIFIED that there is now due the undersigned Landlord, the sum of _____, being rent for the premises situated in the City of _____ and County of _____, State of Illinois and described as follows, to wit:

The property at _____ Unit Number _____, City of _____, Illinois _____ together with all buildings, sheds, closets, out-buildings, garages and other structures used in connection with said premises.

YOU ARE FURTHER NOTIFIED that payment of said sum so due has been and is hereby demanded of you and that UNLESS PAYMENT THEREOF IS MADE ON OR BEFORE THE EXPIRATION OF FIVE DAYS AFTER THE SERVICE OF THIS NOTICE, YOUR LEASE OF SAID PREMISES WILL BE TERMINATED FIVE DAYS AFTER SERVICE OF THIS NOTICE.

ONLY FULL PAYMENT of the rent due in this notice will waive the Landlord's right to terminate the lease under this Notice, unless the Landlord agrees in writing to continue the lease in exchange for receiving partial payment.

Dated this _____ day of _____, 20__.

_____

LANDLORD

AFFIDAVIT OF SERVICE

I, _____, being duly sworn, on oath deposes and says that on the _____ day of _____, 20__(s)he served the within Notice on the tenant named therein by delivering a copy thereof to _____

(signature of person delivering notice)

SUBSCRIBED and SWORN to before me this.............. day of ....

.... , 20__

NOTARY PUBLIC

5 DAY NOTICE

TO: [Tenant's Name and Address]

YOU ARE HEREBY NOTIFIED THAT there is now due and owing the undersigned landlord in the sum of $[Amount landlord claims is due], being rent for the premises situated in the City of [Tenant's City], County of [Tenant's County], and State of Illinois, being described as follows [Tenant's Street Address].

And you are further notified that payment of said sum has been and is demanded of you, and that unless payment thereof is made on or before [DATE], your possession of the premises will be terminated.

ONLY FULL PAYMENT OF THE RENT DEMANDED IN THIS NOTICE, WITHIN FIVE DAYS OF THE DATE OF SERVICE OF THIS NOTICE, WILL WAIVE THE LANDLORD'S RIGHT TO TERMINATE THE LEASE UNDER THIS NOTICE, UNLESS THE LANDLORD AGREES IN WRITING TO CONTINUE THE LEASE IN EXCHANGE FOR RECEIVING PARTIAL PAYMENT.

Dated this [Day] of [Month], [Year]

By: [Signature]

STATE OF ILLINOIS)

) SS

COUNTY OF _____)

[Server's name], being duly sworn, on oath deposes and says that on the [Day] of [Month], [Year], he served the above notice on the tenant named above as follows:

_____1) by delivering a copy thereof to the above-named tenant;

_____2) by delivering a copy thereof to a person above the age of 13 years, residing on or in charge of the above described premises

_____3) by sending a copy thereof to said tenant by certified mail, with request for return of receipt from the addressee

_____4) by posting a copy thereof on the main door of the above described premises, no one being in actual possession thereof.

Subscribed and sworn to me this [Day] of [Month], [Year].

[Signature and Seal of Notary Public]

10 DAY NOTICE

TO: [Tenant's Name and Address]

YOU ARE HEREBY NOTIFIED THAT you have violated the terms of the lease for the premises situated in the City of [Tenant's City], County of [Tenant's County], and State of Illinois, being described as follows: [Tenant's Street Address]. You have violated the lease by [List of lease violations].

And you are further notified that your lease is terminated as of [DATE].

Demand is hereby made that you vacate the said premises and deliver up possession thereof to the undersigned at that time. No further demand shall be necessary before bringing legal proceedings to recover the premises.

Dated this [Day] of [Month], [Year].

By: [Signature]_____

State of Illinois   )

)

County of Cook   )

[Server's name], being duly sworn, on oath deposes and says that on the [Day] of [Month], [Year], he served the above notice on the tenant named above as follows:

_____ 1) by delivering a copy thereof to the above-named tenant;

_____ 2) by delivering a copy thereof to a person above the age of 13 years, residing on or in charge of the above described premises;

_____ 3) by sending a copy thereof to said tenant by certified mail, with request for return of receipt from the addressee; or

_____ 4) by posting a copy thereof on the main door of the above described premises, no one being in actual possession thereof.

Subscribed and sworn to me this [Day] of [Month], [Year].

[Signature and Seal of Notary Public]

30 DAY NOTICE

TO: [Tenant's Name and Address]

YOU ARE HEREBY NOTIFIED THAT your tenancy in the premises situated in the City of [Tenant's City], County of [Tenant's County], and State of Illinois, being described as follows: [Tenant's Street Address] shall be terminated as of [Date].

Demand is hereby made that you vacate the said premises and deliver up possession thereof to the undersigned at that time. No further demand shall be necessary before bringing legal proceedings to recover the premises.

Dated this [Day] of [Month], [Year].

By: [Signature]_____

STATE OF ILLINOIS   )

) SS

COUNTY OF _____   )

[Server's name], being duly sworn, on oath deposes and says that on the [Day] of [Month], [Year], he served the above notice on the tenant named above as follows:

_____ 1) by delivering a copy thereof to the above-named tenant;

_____2) by delivering a copy thereof to a person above the age of 13 years, residing on or in charge of the above described premises;

_____3) by sending a copy thereof to said tenant by certified mail, with request for return of receipt from the addressee; or

_____4) by posting a copy thereof on the main door of the above described premises, no one being in actual possession thereof.

Subscribed and sworn to me this [Day] of [Month], [Year].

[Signature and Seal of Notary Public]

This form replaces CCMD-81, & 81 A, CCM1-81 & 81A   (2/24/09) CCM N081

IMPORTANT INFORMATION FOR DEFENDANTS

THIS IS AN EVICTION SUMMONS

On the date and at the time shown on the other side, the court will decide whether you will have to move or whether you can continue to stay. **YOU MUST BE ON TIME FOR COURT. HAVING TO GO TO WORK, BEING ILL, OR DOING SOMETHING ELSE DOES NOT MEAN YOU CAN MISS COURT.**

APPEARANCE FEES INCLUDE A COUNTY LAW LIBRARY FEE OF $13.00, THE COURT AUTOMATION FEE OF $15.00, A DOCUMENT STORAGE FEE OF $15.00, THE COURT SERVICES FEE OF $25.00, CHILDREN'S WAITING ROOM FEE OF $10.00 AND THE MANDATORY ARBITRATION FEE OF $10.00 WHERE APPLICABLE.

JURY FEES ARE AS FOLLOWS:

APPEARANCE FEES (BASED ON AMOUNT OF CLAIM)
(ALL CASES; NO DISPUTE RESOLUTION CHARGED)

FORCIBLE DETAINER (POSSESSION ONLY)	$168.00
$1,500.00 OR LESS	$168.00
$1,500.00 TO $15,000.00	$178.00
MORE THAN $15,000.00	$198.00

CLAIMS FOR DAMAGES NOT IN EXCESS OF $10,000.00
*SIX-PERSON $12.50
*TWELVE-PERSON JURY $25.00 or
$12.50 if another party paid for a jury of six

CLAIMS FOR DAMAGES NOT IN EXCESS OF $15,000.00
*SIX-PERSON $115.00
*TWELVE-PERSON JURY $230.00 or
$115.00 if another party paid for a jury of six

*THESE FEES MAY BE WAIVED BY APPROPRIATE COURT ORDER.
YOU HAVE THE RIGHT TO FILE A PETITION SEEKING SUCH
AN ORDER.

CLAIMS FOR DAMAGES IN EXCESS OF $15,000.00
*TWELVE-PERSON JURY $230.00

IF YOU DON'T COME TO COURT

The court may order you to move within a short period of time. **IF YOU DON'T MOVE**, your landlord can have the **SHERIFF** move you and all of your belongings out. The sheriff will put your property outside and you will have to make arrangements to move it somewhere else.

YOU HAVE RIGHTS

1. You have the right to come to court and tell your side of the case.

2. You have a right to a trial by jury. A request for a jury trial must be in writing and filed with the Clerk of the Circuit Court prior to your hearing. You must request the jury trial immediately when your case is called, before your trial actually starts.

3. You may come to court and speak for yourself, or you may have a lawyer represent you. If you want a lawyer, you must get one right away. If you are unable to come to court for any reason, you should talk to a lawyer.

4. If you do not have a lawyer, and are not able to afford one, you may call one of the following Lawyer Referral Services and ask them to recommend a lawyer for you:

   - CARPLS (Cook County's Legal Aid Hotline), Telephone (312) 738-9200
   - Chicago Bar Association Lawyer Referral Service, 321 S. Plymouth Ct., Chicago, IL 60604, Telephone (312) 554-2001
   - Illinois Tenants Union Eviction Hotline, Telephone (773) 478-1133
   - Cook County Bar Association Lawyer Referral Service, 188 W. Randolph St., Suite 720, Chicago, IL 60601, Telephone (312) 630-1157
   - Other Lawyer Referral Services are listed in your telephone directory.

5. If you cannot afford a lawyer, you may call one of the following agencies that may be able to provide you with free legal help:

   - Cabrini-Green Legal Aid; 206 W. Division Chicago, IL 60610, Telephone (312) 266-1345   (Initial $20 Fee)
   - Chicago Volunteer Legal Services, Telephone (312) 332-1624
   - Legal Assistance Foundation of Metropolitan Chicago; 111 W. Jackson Blvd., 3rd Floor; Chicago, IL 60604, Telephone (312) 341-1070 Fax (312) 341-1041
   - Law Offices of Kent College of Law Advice Desk, Room 602 Daley Center, Telephone (312) 603-3579
   - Lawyer's Committee for Better Housing, Inc.; 220 S. State, Suite 1700; Chicago, IL 60604, Telephone (312) 347-7600 Fax (312) 347-7604

Participating agencies of the Housing Advocacy Consortium: Cabrini-Green Legal Aid; CARPLS; Chicago Lawyer's Committee for Civil Rights; Lawyers' Committee for Better Housing, Inc.; Legal Assistance Foundation of Metropolitan Chicago; Metropolitan Tenants Organization and National Center on Poverty Law.

DOROTHY BROWN, CLERK OF THE CIRCUIT COURT OF COOK COUNTY, ILLINOIS

0005
0006
Complaint (Joint Action) Forcible Detainer-Rent/Damage Claims   CCM N020-60M-3/02/05 (   )

IN THE CIRCUIT COURT OF COOK COUNTY, ILLINOIS
MUNICIPAL DEPARTMENT/DISTRICT __FIRST__

PRINT NAME OF PERSON OR PARTY SUING
_____
                                    Plaintiff(s)   No. __CLERK WILL ASSIGN YOUR CASE NUMBER__
                v.   __PRINT AMOUNT__
                                                     Rent or Damage Claimed $ __PLUS COURT COSTS__
                                                                 CHECK BLACKBOARD FOR RETURN DATE
PRINT NAME OF PERSON OR PARTY BEING SUED
_____   Return Date ____PRINT RETURN DATE____
                                    Defendant(s)

COMPLAINT

The Plaintiff(s) claim as follows:

1. The Plaintiff(s) is/are entitled to the possession of the following described premises in the City or Village of:

_____
                    PRINT THE COMPLETE ADDRESS OF
                    THE PERSON OR PARTY BEING SUED
_____
                    INCLUDING CITY AND ZIP CODE
_____

_____

_____

2. The Defendant(s) unlawfully withhold possession thereof from the Plaintiff(s) _____
_____ PRINT NAME OF PERSON OR PARTY SUING _____.

3. There is due to Plaintiff(s) from the Defendant(s) for rent or for damages for withholding possession of said
premises from _____PRINT FIRST DATE OF UNPAID RENT_____, to _____PRINT CURRENT DATE_____, _____
after allowing the Defendant(s) all just credits, deductions and set-offs, the sum of $ _____PRINT AMOUNT_____.

The Plaintiff(s) claim(s) possession of the property and $ _____PRINT AMOUNT_____ as
rent or damages.

Atty. Code: PRINT "PRO SE-99500" IF NO ATTORNEY   _____
                                                          Attorney for Plaintiff(s)
Name: _____PRINT YOUR NAME_____

Attorney for: ____IF NO ATTORNEY, LEAVE BLANK____

Address: _____PRINT YOUR ADDRESS_____

City/State/Zip: ___PRINT YOUR CITY, STATE AND ZIP CODE___

Telephone: ___PRINT YOUR COMPLETE TELEPHONE NUMBER___

I/We, _____PRINT NAME OF PERSON OR PARTY SUING_____, on oath state that I/we am/are the
Plaintiff(s) in the above entitled action. The allegations in this complaint are true.

                              PLEASE SIGN YOUR NAME
                              _____
                        [x] Under penalties as provided by law pursuant to 735 ILCS 5/1-109
                            the abovesigned certifies that the statements set forth herein are
                            true and correct.

DOROTHY BROWN, CLERK OF THE CIRCUIT COURT OF COOK COUNTY, ILLINOIS
                    ORIGINAL COURT FILE

2120 - Served	2220 - Not Served	2620 - Sec. of State	
2121 - Alias Served	2221 - Alias Not Served	2621 - Alias Sec. of State	(2/24/09) CCM N081

IN THE CIRCUIT COURT OF COOK COUNTY, ILLINOIS
MUNICIPAL DEPARTMENT, _First_ DISTRICT

Print Name or Person or Party Suing

_____
Plaintiff(s)

v.

Print Name of Person or Party Being Sued

_____
Defendant(s)

Case No. _Please See Clerk for Case Number_

Rent Amount Claimed: $ _Print Amount Plus Court Cost_

* Trial Date: _Print trial date_ **Time:** _Print_

Court Location: _Richard J. Daley Center_
50 W Washington, Chicago

SUMMONS FOR TRIAL
BEFORE YOU GO TO COURT, YOU MUST PAY YOUR APPEARANCE FEE.

You are hereby SUMMONED to Court, however, you must file your appearance and pay the required fee with the Clerk of the Circuit Court's Office at the court location on this form, on or before the date and before the time of the trial. IF YOU DO NOT FILE AN APPEARANCE and contest the claim, a JUDGMENT BY DEFAULT may be entered for the relief requested in the complaint, ordering that you be evicted. If judgment is entered against you, the SHERIFF may evict you. A money judgment may also be entered against you if requested in the complaint.

The Plaintiff(s), named above, has/have filed a complaint in this Court to have you evicted. A true and correct copy of the complaint is attached.

THEREFORE, you, the Defendant(s), after you have filed an appearance, are hereby summoned to appear in person before
Check Blackboard for Court Date, Time and Room Number

this Court on* _Print Court Date_ _____, at _Print Time_ (a.m.)(p.m.) in Courtroom _Print Rm #_

at _Richard J. Daley Center, 50 W. Washington, Chicago, IL_ _____, at which time and place a
(Court location)

TRIAL will be held on the complaint. (See top of this form if blanks not filled in.)

*Not less than 7 days nor more than 40 days after issuance of summons.

SEE FEES ON THE REVERSE SIDE OF THIS FORM.

INSTRUCTIONS TO SHERIFF

This summons must be returned by the officer or other person to whom it was given for service, with endorsement of service and fees, if any, immediately after service and not less than seven (7) days before the day for appearance. If service cannot be made, this summons shall be returned so endorsed.

This summons may not be served later than seven (7) days before the trial date.

Atty. No.: _Print "Pro Se - 99500" If No Attorney_

Name: _Print Your Name_

Atty. for: _If No Attorney, Leave Blank_

Address: _Print Your Address_

City/State/Zip: _Print Your City, State and Zip Code_

Telephone: _Print Your complete Telephone Number_

WITNESS _Upon Payment of Filing Fee_ , _____

Clerk Will Sign and Seal

_____
DOROTHY BROWN, Clerk of Court

DATE OF SERVICE _____, _____
(To be inserted by officer on copy left with Defendant or other person)

DOROTHY BROWN, CLERK OF THE CIRCUIT COURT OF COOK COUNTY, ILLINOIS

This form replaces CCMD-81, & 81 A, CCM1-81 & 81A   (OVER)

ORIGINAL – COURT FILE

630 N.E.2d 836 (1994)

158 Ill.2d 98

196 Ill.Dec. 671

MIDLAND MANAGEMENT COMPANY, Appellant,

v.

Ronald HELGASON, Appellee.

No. 75195.

Supreme Court of Illinois.

January 20, 1994.

Sanford Kahn, Ltd., Chicago (Richard W. Christoff, of counsel), for appellant.

Terrence McKeown and Sarah Megan, St. Charles, and Gerald Brask, Jr., Rockford, all of Prairie State Legal Services, Inc., St. Charles, for appellee.

Justice FREEMAN delivered the opinion of the court:

Plaintiff, Midland Management Company (Midland), as landlord, appeals from the appellate court's affirmance of the circuit court of Kane County's determination that Midland waived its right to assert a forcible entry and detainer action by accepting Federal housing assistance payments, made on behalf of defendant, Ronald Helgason.

FACTS

Defendant entered into a written lease agreement with Midland for the lease of a residential unit at Harbor Village Apartments in Aurora. Defendant's tenancy was subsidized under section 8 of the United States Housing Act of 1937 (Section 8) (42 U.S.C. § 1437f (1991)). As a result of the subsidy, defendant was required to pay a total monthly rent amount of $6. The remainder of the fair market rent value for the unit was to be paid under Section 8 in the form of a housing assistance payment.

Pursuant to the lease agreement, defendant, as tenant, agreed to pay the costs of repairs for damage to the property resulting from his carelessness, misuse or neglect. On April 3, 1991, Midland served defendant with a demand for reimbursement for the repair of defendant's water-damaged floor. Defendant refused the demand and, subsequently, tendered his $6 monthly rental payment to Midland.

On May 15, 1991, Midland served defendant with notice of termination of the tenancy for failure to reimburse for the water-damage repair and also returned defendant's rent. Midland, however, continued to receive Section 8 housing assistance payments through August 1991.

When defendant failed to vacate the leasehold pursuant to the termination notice, Midland brought an action in forcible entry and detainer. (Ill.Rev.Stat.1991, ch. 110, par. 9-101 et seq.) The trial court entered judgment for Midland, and awarded it possession, damages, and costs. Subsequently, however, the trial court granted defendant's motion to vacate the judgment, ruling that, inter alia, Midland's continued acceptance of the housing assistance payments subsequent to serving notice of termination of the tenancy constituted waiver of the breach of the lease as a matter of law.

The appellate court affirmed (241 Ill. App.3d 899, 181 Ill.Dec. 570, 608 N.E.2d 643), and we granted Midland's petition for leave to appeal (134 Ill.2d R. 315(a)). We now reverse that decision.

Section 8

Prior to our discussion, we deem it necessary to discuss the nature of the Section 8 rent subsidy program and housing assistance payments. Section 8 is a Federal housing subsidy program administered by the United States Department of Housing and Urban Development (HUD). (42 U.S.C. § 1437f (1991).) Section 1437f(a) provides, in pertinent part:

> "For the purpose of aiding low-income families in obtaining a decent place to live and of promoting economically mixed housing, assistance payments may be made with respect to existing housing * * *." (42 U.S.C. § 1437f(a) (1991).)

To that end, HUD is authorized to enter into housing assistance payment contracts with owners of housing in which some or all of the units shall be available for occupancy by low-income families. See 42 U.S.C. § 1437f(b) (1991).

Housing assistance payment contracts establish the maximum monthly rent which the owner is "entitled" to receive for each dwelling unit with respect to which such "*housing assistance payments*" are to be made. (Emphasis added.) (42 U.S.C. § 1437f(c)(1) (1991).) Pursuant to the Code, the assistance contract shall provide that assistance payments may be made only with respect to a dwelling unit under lease for occupancy by a family found to be a low-income family at the time it initially occupied such dwelling unit. However, vacancy payments may be made with respect to unoccupied units for a period not exceeding 60 days in the event that a family vacates a dwelling unit before the expiration date of the lease for occupancy or where a good-faith effort is being made to fill an unoccupied unit. 42 U.S.C. § 1437f(c)(4) (1991).

For Section 8 purposes, HUD utilizes a formula to determine the rental value of a housing unit based upon a fair market rental value in the nonsubsidized housing market. (42 U.S.C. § 1437f(c)(1) (1991).) A tenant eligible to participate in the Section 8 program pays a portion of the market rental value, or rent, based upon his income. (See 42 U.S.C. § 1437a(a)(1) (1991); *East Lake Management & Development Corp. v. Irvin* (1990), 195 Ill.App.3d 196, 199, 141 Ill.Dec. 279, 551 N.E.2d 272. The amount of the monthly assistance payment is the difference between the maximum monthly rent which the contract provides that the owner is to receive for the unit and the rent the family is required to pay under section 1437a(a). 42 U.S.C. § 1437f(c)(3)(A) (1991); *East Lake Management*, 195 Ill.App.3d at 199, 141 Ill. Dec. 279, 551 N.E.2d 272.

DISCUSSION

The singular issue which we decide is whether Midland's acceptance of Section 8 housing assistance payments resulted in a waiver of its right to forfeiture of the lease.

It has long been established that any act of a landlord which affirms the existence of a lease and recognizes a tenant as his lessee after the landlord has knowledge of a breach of lease results in the landlord's waiving his right to forfeiture of the lease. (*Vintaloro v. Pappas* (1923), 310 Ill. 115, 117, 141 N.E. 377.) Simply put, evidence of acts inconsistent with a declaration of a termination of the lease may prove waiver of the breach, which operates to reinstate the lease. (See *Simmons v. Berryman* (1930), 342 Ill. 274, 278, 174 N.E. 410.) Acceptance of rent accruing subsequent to a breach is one such inconsistent act. (See *Weiss v. Johnson* (1963), 28 Ill.2d 259, 261, 190 N.E.2d 834.) It is immaterial by whom the rent is paid if it is received as rent and on behalf of the lessee. 51C C.J.S. Landlord & Tenant § 117(4) (1968).

Defendant contends that the appellate court correctly held that Section 8 housing assistance payments constitute rent, the continued acceptance of which resulted in a waiver of Midland's right to forfeiture. We note that our appellate court, sitting in the first district, has held otherwise. See *East Lake Management & Development Corp. v. Irvin* (1990), 195 Ill.App.3d 196, 141 Ill.Dec. 279, 551 N.E.2d 272.

We agree, for various reasons, with the decision in *East Lake Management* that the assistance payments do not constitute rent. The most compelling of these reasons is our construction of the lease agreement between Midland and defendant. (Cf. *National Corp. for Housing Partnerships v. Chapman* (1984), 18 Ohio App.3d 104, 18 OBR 468, 481 N.E.2d 654 (in determining that housing assistance payment was not rent, court examined terms of landlord/tenant agreement and also determined that because assistance was not personal to tenant, it was not rent).) Significantly, HUD is not a party to the lease agreement, and, incidentally, there is no contention that defendant is a party to the housing assistance payment contract between HUD and Midland.

A lease is an agreement which gives rise to the relationship of landlord and tenant. (24 Ill. L. & Prac. Landlord & Tenant § 2 (1980).) It is essentially a type of contract (*Illinois Central R.R. Co. v. Michigan Central R.R. Co.* (1958), 18 Ill.App.2d 462, 484, 152 N.E.2d 627), and, as such, it is governed by the rules which govern contracts generally (*Design Studio International Inc. v. Chicago Title & Trust Co.* (1989), 185 Ill.App.3d 797, 802, 133 Ill.Dec. 728, 541 N.E.2d 1166; 51C C.J.S. Landlord & Tenant § 202(2) (1969)). "[W]herever there is a contract its terms must control the rights of the parties." (*Fichter v. Milk Wagon Drivers' Union, Local 753* (1943), 382 Ill. 91, 100, 46 N.E.2d 921.) Thus, we believe that regardless of our characterization of the housing assistance payment, the rights and obligations of defendant and Midland are controlled by the terms of their agreement. Conceivably, even if such payments constitute rent, parties entering into a lease agreement would, nonetheless, be free to agree on the effect of the landlord's acceptance of such payments after a tenant's breach.

The principal function of the court in construing a lease is to give effect to the intention of the parties as expressed in the language of the document when read as a whole. (See *Dix Mutual Insurance Co. v. LaFramboise* (1992), 149 Ill.2d 314, 320, 173 Ill.Dec. 648, 597 N.E.2d 622.) Relevant to disposition of the issue now before us is whether the parties intended that housing assistance payments constitute rent.

We note that the lease agreement included in the record recites neither the most current term of the lease nor the most current rent amount. However, the agreement was admitted, without objection, into evidence as representative of the agreement between the parties.

The clause in the lease concerning rent provides that defendant, as the tenant, agrees to pay a sum certain amount for rent per month. The clause also provides:

> "The Tenant understands that his monthly rent is less than the market (un-subsidized) rent due on this unit. This lower rent is available either because the mortgage on this project is subsidized by the Department of Housing and Urban Development (HUD) and/or because HUD makes monthly pay-ments to the Landlord on behalf of the Tenant. The amount, if any, that HUD makes available monthly on behalf of the Tenant is called the tenant assistance payment and is shown on the ' "Assistance Payment" ' line of the Certification and Recertification of Tenant Eligibility Form which is Attach-ment No. 1 to this Agreement."

The lease further provides that the landlord may terminate the agreement for non-payment of rent. In that regard, we note that no similar remedy is available to Midland in the event of nonreceipt of the housing assistance payment.

Nowhere in the lease agreement is the housing assistance payment defined or referred to as rent. It is simply characterized as a separate payment made on behalf of the tenant in the form of a tenant assistance payment. Under the terms of the agreement between defendant and Midland, rent is the monthly dollar amount tendered by de-fendant to Midland in consideration of the lease. Under the terms of the lease, the housing assistance payment was not received as rent. Thus, Midland's acceptance of such payments did not operate to waive forfeiture of breach.

Our conclusion with respect to the assistance payments may be supported on yet an-other basis. Rent is given in consideration of a lease. As we have already stated, a lease gives rise to the landlord-tenant relationship. In order to establish the relation of land-lord and tenant, the possession and control or the right thereto of the property must pass to the tenant. (24 Ill. L. & Prac. Landlord & Tenant § 3 (1980); 51C C.J.S. Landlord & Tenant § 2(2) (1968).) No such relationship is created between HUD and the owner of property. Significantly, HUD is not a party to the lease agreement, and it does not appear from the lease that HUD acquired any possessory interest in the property.

The housing assistance payment contract has not been provided as part of the record. However, based upon our review of the statutory provisions concerning such contracts, we believe that such contracts have as their purpose to make non-low-income housing available to low-income families, thereby achieving HUD's goal of economically mixed housing. Although the housing assistance payment is equal to some portion of the fair market rent to which the landlord is entitled, that fact does not define the nature of the payment as rent. In the most traditional sense, "[r]ent is the return made to the lessor by the lessee for his *use* of the land." (Emphasis added.) (*Automobile Supply Co. v. Scene-In-Action Corp.* (1930), 340 Ill. 196, 200, 172 N.E. 35; *Cottrell v. Gerson* (1939), 371 Ill. 174, 181, 20 N.E.2d 74.) It is the tenant, not HUD, who has the use of the land.

Further, we believe it significant that when a subsidized housing unit becomes vacant following the owner's eviction of an eligible tenant, under the terms of the housing assistance payment contract, the landlord is entitled to continue to receive vacancy payments for a period of 60 days or more upon a showing that he is actively seeking to fill the vacancy with another Section 8 eligible tenant. (See 42 U.S.C. § 1437f(c)(4) (1991).) This suggests to us that the housing assistance payment flows with the rental unit, and not the Section 8 tenant. Thus, the housing assistance payment contract, unlike a lease, survives the landlord-tenant relationship.

Finally, we do not believe that HUD intended that housing assistance payments be considered rent. To characterize the assistance as such would effectively defeat HUD's interest in the development and availability of economically mixed housing for low-income families. As a practical matter, landlords confronted with the possibility of forfeiture of breach for the acceptance of housing assistance payments would be less apt to open their doors to low-income families and would seek to fill their vacancies with non-rent-assisted families. But see *Greenwich Gardens Associates v. Pitt* (1984), 126 Misc.2d 947, 484 N.Y.S.2d 439 (holding that intent of legislature was that assistance be considered rent because, inter alia, contract rent, as defined in 24 C.F.R. § 880.201 (1993), is the total amount of rent specified in the contract as payable by HUD and the tenant to the owner for an assisted unit).

We conclude that under the terms of the lease agreement, Section 8 housing assistance payments did not constitute rent. Thus, Midland's continued acceptance of such payments did not effect a waiver of breach of the lease.

We note that defendant raises two arguments: (1) whether Midland failed to meet its burden of proof as required under Federal housing regulations and the terms of the lease, and (2) whether Midland established sufficient cause to terminate the tenancy.

These issues were presented in the appellate court and resolved in favor of Midland. Reconsideration by this court would yield no different result. We therefore, decline further review.

CONCLUSION

For all the forgoing reasons, we reverse the judgments of the appellate and circuit courts and remand the cause to the circuit court for further proceedings.

Judgments reversed; cause remanded.

Justice HEIPLE, dissenting:

This case illustrates the resourcefulness of the judicial mind when confronted with the application of a rule of law which produces a result deemed to be undesirable. The straightforward approach to such a dilemma offers but two possibilities. The first option is to apply the law to the case and let the painful result occur. The second option, available to a court of last resort at least, is to change the rule of law. Make a new one. However, if neither of these two options is attractive, the resourceful judicial mind has yet a third option. It can redefine the terms so that the rule does not apply to the case at hand. This approach was chosen by the majority in the instant case.

The application of this technique is well illustrated and perhaps reached its zenith in the Canadian case of *Regina v. Ojibway*, 8 *Criminal Law Quarterly* 137 (Toronto, 1965) in an opinion rendered by Blue, J. The case was an appeal by the Crown by way of a stated case from a decision of the magistrate acquitting the accused of a charge under the Small Birds Act, R.S.O. 1960, c. 724, § 2. The facts were not in dispute. The opinion is set out here in haec verba:

"Fred Ojibway, an Indian, was riding his pony through Queen's Park on January 2, 1965. Being impoverished, and having been forced to pledge his saddle, he substituted a downy pillow in lieu of the said saddle. On this particular day the accused's misfortune was further heightened by the circumstance of his pony breaking its right foreleg. In accord with Indian custom, the accused then shot the pony to relieve it of its awkwardness.

The accused was then charged with having breached the Small Birds Act, s. 2 of which states:

'Anyone maiming, injuring or killing small birds is guilty of an offense and subject to a fine not in excess of two hundred dollars.'

The learned magistrate acquitted the accused, holding in fact, that he had killed his horse and not a small bird. With respect I cannot agree.

In Light of the definition section my course is quite clear. Section 1 defines 'bird' as a 'two legged animal covered with feathers.' There can be no doubt that this case is covered by this section.

Counsel for the accused made several ingenious arguments to which, in fairness, I must address myself. He submitted that the evidence of the expert clearly concluded that the animal in question was a pony and not a bird, but this is not the issue. We are not interested in whether the animal in question is a bird or not, in fact, but whether it is one in law. Statutory interpretation has forced many a horse to eat birdseed for the rest of its life.

Counsel also contended that the neighing noise emitted by the animal could not possibly be produced by a bird. With respect the sounds emitted by an animal are irrelevant to its nature, for a bird is no less a bird because it is silent.

Counsel for the accused also argued that since there was evidence to show accused had ridden the animal, this pointed to the fact that it could not be a bird but was actually a pony. Obviously, this avoids the issue. The issue is not whether the animal was ridden or not, but whether it was shot or not, for to ride a pony or a bird is no offense at all. I believe that counsel now sees his mistake.

Counsel contends that the iron shoes found on the animal decisively disqualify it from being a bird. I must inform counsel, however, that how an animal dresses is of no concern to this Court.

Counsel relied on the decision in *Re Chicadee*, where he contends that in similar circumstances the accused was acquitted. However, this is a horse of a different color. A close reading of that case indictes [sic] that the animal in question there was not a small bird, but, in fact, a midget of a much larger species. Therefore, that case is inapplicable to our facts.

Counsel finally submits that the word 'small' in the title Small Birds Act refers not to 'Birds' but to 'Act,' making it the Small Act relating to Birds. With respect, counsel did not do his homework very well, for the Large Birds Act * * * is just as small. If pressed, I need only refer to the Small Loans Act * * * which is twice as large as the Large Birds Act.

It remains then to state my reason for judgment which, simply, is as follows: Different things may take on the same meaning for different purposes. For the purpose of the Small Birds Act, all two-legged, feather-covered animals are birds. This, of course, does not imply that only two-legged animals qualify, for the legislative intent is to make two legs merely the minimum requirement. The statute therefore contemplated multilegged animals with feathers as well. Counsel submits that having regard to the purpose of the statute only small animals 'naturally covered' with feathers could have been contemplated. However, had this been the intention of the legislature I am certain that the phrase 'naturally covered' would have been expressly inserted just as 'Long' was inserted in the Longshoreman's Act.

Therefore, a horse with feathers on its back must be deemed for the purposes of this Act to be a bird, and a fortiori, a pony with feathers on its back is a small bird.

Counsel posed the following rhetorical question: If the pillow had been removed prior to the shooting, would the animal still be a bird? To this, let me answer rhetorically: Is a bird any less of a bird without its feathers?"

To return to the case before the court, the relevant facts are that the tenant occupied a privately owned apartment under Section 8 of the United States Housing Act of 1937, a Federal welfare program which provides subsidized rent to qualified tenants. (42 U.S.C. § 1427f (1991) (Section 8).) Total rent for the apartment was approximately $573 per month, of which the tenant paid $6 and the Federal government paid approximately $567. At some point, the landlord determined that the tenant was abusing the premises and was therefore in breach of the lease. A notice to quit was served which was followed up by an eviction suit at law. Subsequent to the filing of the forcible entry and detainer suit, the landlord refused to accept the tenant's $6 share of the monthly rent but continued to accept the monthly government checks of approximately $567.

The applicable law is clear cut, simple, and conceded by the majority. Acceptance of rental payments which have accrued subsequent to a breach amounts to a waiver of the breach. Also, it is immaterial by whom the rent is paid if it is received as rent on behalf of tenant. 158 Ill.2d at 104, 196 Ill.Dec. at 674, 630 N.E.2d at 839.

Both the trial court and the appellate court below ruled that acceptance of the rent money from the government amounted to a waiver of the breach. The landlord appealed and a majority of this court reverses. Its rationale? The monies which the landlord received from the government are not rent. Rather, they are housing assistance payments. Thus, since the landlord accepted housing assistance payments but not rent, there was no waiver of the tenant's breach by the landlord.

The majority cites both the lease agreement between the parties and Section 8 of the United States Housing Act of 1937 (the Act) (42 U.S.C. § 1427f (1991), which authorizes the HUD payments, in support of its conclusion. To begin, it is important to note that we should read the lease and the legislation in a light disfavoring forfeiture. "The forfeiture of leases is not favored and courts will readily adopt any circumstances that indicate an intent to waive a forfeiture." (*Housing Authority for La Salle County v. Little* (1978), 64 Ill.App.3d 149, 150, 21 Ill. Dec. 25, 380 N.E.2d 1201.) It is also significant that plaintiff drafted the lease. Thus, any ambiguities in the lease should be construed against plaintiff, i.e., in favor of finding waiver. *Duldulao v. St. Mary of Nazareth Hospital* (1987), 115 Ill.2d 482, 493, 106 Ill.Dec. 8, 505 N.E.2d 314.

The majority first examines the lease to determine whether the HUD payments were intended as rent. It focuses on one clause which states that the tenant will pay a certain amount for "rent," and that HUD will "make[] monthly payments to the Landlord on behalf of the Tenant * * * called the tenant assistance payment[s]." To the majority, the different semantics of "rent" and "tenant assistance payments" demonstrate that HUD's payments are not rent.

I would first point out that, had the plaintiff referred to both the tenant's payments and the HUD payments as "rent," the result would have been confusing. Since plaintiff drafted the lease, instead of construing its attempt at clarity as creating two classes of payment with only one relevant in a waiver of forfeiture claim, the onus should be placed on plaintiff to specifically state that acceptance of the HUD payments is not tantamount to acceptance of rent.

Further, there are two other sections of the lease which indicate that the HUD payments were part of the total rent. Paragraph 4 is entitled "Changes in the Tenant's *Share* of the Rent" (emphasis added), which implies that HUD is paying the balance of the rent. Paragraph 4b again refers to the tenant's "share of the rent." Paragraph 7a indicates that the heat, cooking and water utilities are included in the "Tenant Rent." Since it is unreasonable to believe that $6 per month could cover these utilities, the "Tenant Rent" must include the HUD payments.

Again, we should construe the lease against the drafter and against forfeiture. These rules of construction, applied to the terms of the lease, counsel a ruling that plaintiff waived its right of forfeiture by accepting the HUD payments.

The majority also comments upon the lack of a landlord/tenant relationship between plaintiff and HUD. They note that while plaintiff could terminate the agreement for nonpayment of rent, there was no similar remedy for nonreceipt of the housing assistance payment. (158 Ill.2d at 105, 196 Ill. Dec. at 675, 630 N.E.2d at 840.) In addition, the majority makes the general observation that "HUD is not a party to the lease agreement and, it does not appear from the lease that HUD acquired any possessory interest in the property." (158 Ill.2d at 105, 196 Ill.Dec. at 675, 630 N.E.2d at 840.) These observations lead the majority to conclude that, whatever HUD was doing, it was not paying rent.

Regarding the ramification of nonreceipt of the so-called housing assistance payment, if HUD were to conclude that the tenant was not entitled to the assistance payments and would stop making payments, the lease provides that the tenant is obligated to pay the entire rent.

The majority's conclusion that HUD is not a party to the lease agreement is likewise erroneous. Although it is true that HUD gains no proprietary interest, the lease is replete with conditions precedent requiring HUD approval. The rent may only increase with HUD approval; additional utility charges may be imposed on the tenant with HUD approval; assistance payments will only be made so long as HUD determines that the tenant is maintaining the dwelling in habitable condition; the tenant must supply HUD with income and family information before the lease agreement can be renewed; HUD sets the minimum size of the dwelling, based on a consideration of the size of the household and the ages and genders of its members; conditions of the lease may only be changed with HUD approval; termination of tenancy must be carried out in accordance with HUD regulations; and notices of termination must be given in advance, the time of which is set by HUD. HUD appears in 25 paragraphs or subparagraphs of the lease. It is an integral part of the agreement.

The majority then turns to the Act to determine whether Congress intended the assistance payments to serve as rent. They initially note that, following the owner's eviction of a tenant, the owner is entitled to vacancy payments for 60 days. "This suggests to us that the housing assistance payment flows with the rental unit, and not the Section 8 tenant." 158 Ill.2d at 106, 196 Ill.Dec. at 675, 630 N.E.2d at 840.

I disagree. This suggests to me only the commonsense recognition that landlords might be unwilling to take on low-income tenants without a guarantee of rent. Congress tempered this caution with this two month guarantee. This is entirely in accord with the Act's purpose of "aiding low-income families in obtaining a decent place to live and of promoting economically mixed housing." (42 U.S.C. § 1437f(a) (1991).) Further, to suggest that the payment flows with the rental unit and not the tenant ignores the fact that receipt of payment depends entirely on the tenant. Sixty days after he leaves, payment stops. New payments do not begin until there is a new tenant. Moreover, this rental guarantee is not designed to alter fundamental landlord/tenant law. It merely exists to protect the landlord in the event the tenant vacates the premises. It does not purport to exonerate a landlord who wishes to evict a tenant for a breach of a lease. The landlord in this situation has the option to either evict the tenant for a breach and eschew continuing rental payments or to waive the breach and allow the occupancy to continue.

The majority finally states that "we do not believe that HUD intended that housing assistance payments be considered rent. To characterize the assistance as such would effectively defeat HUD's interest in the development and availability of economically mixed housing for low-income families. As a practical matter, landlords confronted with the possibility of forfeiture of breach for the acceptance of housing assistance payments would be less apt to open their doors to low-income families and would seek to fill their vacancies with non-rent-assisted families." 158 Ill.2d at 106, 196 Ill.Dec. at 676, 630 N.E.2d at 841.

The majority offers nothing to indicate how it comes to believe that HUD did not intend the assistance payments be considered rent. Indeed, an examination of the statute and the Federal regulations demonstrates the opposite intent. The statute provides:

> "The amount of the monthly assistance payment with respect to any dwelling unit shall be the difference between the maximum monthly rent which the contract provides that the owner is to receive for the unit and the rent the family is required to pay under [42 U.S.C. § 1437a(a) (1991)]." (42 U.S.C. § 1437f(c)(3)(A) (1991).)

The Federal regulations implementing the statute define contract rent as "[t]he total amount of rent specified in the Housing Assistance Payments (HAP) Contract as payable to the owner by the Family, and by HUD or the PHA on the Family's behalf (24 C.F.R. § 813.102), and again as "the rent payable to the owner under the contract, including the portion of the rent payable by the family." 24 C.F.R. § 886.302.

The regulations define the housing assistance payment as "the payment made by the contract administrator to the Owner of an assisted unit as provided in the Contract. Where the unit is leased to an eligible Family, the payment is the different between the Contract Rent and the Tenant Rent." (24 C.F.R. § 886.302.) The regulations further provide that the "Housing Assistance Payments will cover the difference between the Contract Rent and the Tenant Rent." 24 C.F.R. § 886.309.

These sections demonstrate that the rent is divided into two categories: the amount to be paid by the tenant and the amount to be paid by HUD. Acceptance of either of these subparts of the rent is an acceptance of rent.

Webster's Dictionary generally defines rent as income from a piece of property. (*Webster's Third International Dictionary* 1923 (1986).) *Black's Law Dictionary* defines rent as "[c]onsideration paid for use or occupation of property. In a broader sense, it is the compensation or fee paid, usually periodically, for the use of any property, land, buildings, equipment, etc." (*Black's Law Dictionary* 1166 (5th ed. 1979).) And, as stated by the appellate court below, "[i]t is difficult to imagine what the assistance payments are if they are not rent. The government sets the monthly rent for the unit. The family is required to pay a percentage of their income as part of the rental payment. The remainder is provided by HUD. It is unlikely that Congress intended for the tenant portion of the rent to be considered rent and the HUD portion to be considered nonrent." 241 Ill. App.3d at 908, 181 Ill.Dec. 570, 608 N.E.2d 643.

Accordingly, I respectfully dissent from the majority's conclusion to the contrary.

HARRISON J., joins in this dissent.

24 N.E.3d 851 (2014)

2014 IL App (1st) 132073

DRAPER AND KRAMER, INC., as Managing Agent for Island Terrance,
Plaintiff-Appellee,

v.

Nicole KING, Defendant-Appellant.

No. 1-13-2073.

Appellate Court of Illinois, First District, Fifth Division.

December 19, 2014.

Rehearing Denied January 28, 2015.

LAF, of Chicago (Lawrence D. Wood, Miriam Hallbauer, and Meghan P. Carter, of
counsel), for appellant.

Sanford Kahn, Ltd., of Chicago (Richard W. Christoff, of counsel), for appellee.

OPINION

Presiding Justice PALMER delivered the judgment of the court, with opinion.

1 Defendant Nicole King resides with her two minor children in an apartment at
Island Terrace in the City of Chicago, a section 8 housing unit for which she paid a
reduced amount of rent based on a percentage of her income. [1] Plaintiff, Draper
& Kramer, Inc., as representative of Island Terrace, filed a forcible entry and detainer
action for possession against defendant on April 3, 2013, for nonpayment of rent.
The complaint alleged that defendant owed the sum of $189 in rent. The matter was
set for proceedings before the circuit court on April 18, 2013.

2 On April 18, 2013, defendant appeared in court without the assistance of an attorney.
The circuit court entered an order granting possession and recovery of $198.09, plus
costs, to plaintiff. The order provided that enforcement of the judgment was stayed
until May 15, 2013. Written at the top of the typed order was the word "Agreed" next
to the title of the order. At the bottom, the word "Agreed" was again written in, with
defendant's signature next to it.

3 On May 7, 2013, defendant's attorney filed an appearance and demand for a jury
trial, along with a motion to vacate the April 18 agreed order pursuant to section 2-
1301(e) of the Illinois Code of Civil Procedure (the Code) (735 ILCS 5/2-1301(e)
(West 2012)). Defendant argued that the April 18 order should be vacated because
she did not understand that she was agreeing to pay the amount due and also surrender
possession of the apartment; she believed she was agreeing to pay the amount demanded and remain in the apartment. She urged that the order should be vacated
because of the gross disparity in the parties' capacities and bargaining positions as
defendant was not represented by counsel, was unsophisticated and unfamiliar with
the law and courtroom procedures, the order was unreasonably favorable to plaintiff,
and she had a meritorious defense to the eviction action.

4 In defendant's affidavit attached to her motion, she averred that she currently paid
"$17 or $9" per month in rent[2] and her federally subsidized rental assistance runs

with the premises, so she would lose it if forced to leave. She averred that she receives $526 per month in food stamps and has no other source of income. She previously received a "Temporary Assistance to Needy Families" cash grant (TANF) in the amount of $437, but her TANF benefits stopped in February 2013 and she last received TANF money in January 2013. Her rent in December 2012 was $5, and in January 2013, it increased to $77 because her TANF benefits had been increased. She averred that she paid her January rent on January 18, 2013. She then received a "Notice of Change" from the Illinois Department of Human Services (DHS) around January or February 2013 (TANF notice) advising her that the TANF benefits would stop. She averred that she received the TANF notice on a Friday after 5 p.m., and she brought it to the property manager's office on the following Monday and gave it to "Sandy" at the front desk. However, Sandy would not take the TANF notice and instructed her to return after lunch. Defendant averred that she was unable return that afternoon because of childcare duties, but that evening, defendant made a copy of the TANF notice and placed the copy in the management office's drop box attached to the office door because it was afterhours. She averred that plaintiff accepts rent and other letters through the drop box. She did not hear from plaintiff and assumed that the letter was received and she would be informed when to come to the office. However, on approximately March 9, 2013, defendant received a five-day notice from plaintiff informing her that she owed $189.09 in unpaid rent. She did not receive a notice in February regarding February's rent. The notice was placed under her door.

5 Defendant averred that the Monday following receipt of the five-day notice, she spoke with plaintiff's property manager, Antoinette Moton, who informed her that defendant never paid February or March rent. Defendant averred that she told Moton that she placed the TANF notice regarding her change of income in the drop box, but Moton indicated that she never received it. Defendant told Moton she would obtain another copy of the TANF notice for Moton. Defendant had misplaced her copy and she went to the DHS office to get another copy on March 12, 2013. However, her caseworker was on vacation, so defendant had to return a week later and she was able to obtain a copy of the letter at that point. Defendant averred that she gave Moton a copy of the TANF notice on March 21, 2013. On that same day, she received a letter from Moton. Defendant also averred that she went to speak with Moton that day, and Moton told her that she owed the rent because she did not put the TANF notice "in her hand," and told defendant to pay the rent and fees. When defendant stated that she could not afford to, Moton indicated that there was nothing she could do because "it was already in court." Defendant averred that she also received court papers instructing her to go to court on April 18, 2013.

6 Defendant further averred that she went to court on April 18, without an attorney, but was unfamiliar with the procedure and did not know she "could ask for a continuance to get a free lawyer." While she was looking for her line number outside the courtroom, the attorney for plaintiff, Eileen Kahn, asked if she wanted to discuss the case. Defendant averred that Kahn asked if she had the money, and defendant stated that she did. She asked if defendant had the fees, but defendant indicated that she

did "not have them all" and did not know how much they were. Defendant averred that Kahn indicated that she also did not know. Kahn told defendant, "it was no deals if I did not have the money." She confirmed that she had the $189. They then went into the courtroom and sat in different areas. Defendant averred that Kahn summoned her and stated that she "would give me time to pay" and said defendant had until April 30, 2013. Defendant asked for more time, and Kahn gave her until May 15, 2013. Kahn then "wrote 'agreed' on an order" but defendant did not sign anything at the time.

7 Defendant further averred that when her case was called, the judge asked whether they had come to an agreement, and Kahn affirmed that they agreed defendant would pay $189 plus fees by May 15, 2013. The judge asked defendant if she agreed, and defendant said "yes." Kahn stated that defendant "needed to sign the paper," so defendant signed it, but she did not read it. Defendant then raised her hand and the judge allowed her to ask a question, and she asked how much she had to pay in attorney fees. The judge responded that she only had to pay court costs, which were approximately $375. The judge stamped the paper and the clerk gave defendant a copy. Defendant averred that she thought she was agreeing to pay the money by May 15, 2013, but she did not know that she had also agreed to surrender possession in the order.

8 Defendant further averred that her property manager was on vacation around that time, but she called Moton on Monday, April 22, 2013, to tell her that she had the money and to ask if she had talked to Kahn about the agreed order. However, Moton stated that she [Moton] would not accept defendant's money because the "judge had given her [Moton] possession of the property, and she [Moton] just wants me [defendant] out." Defendant responded that no one told her that she had agreed to move. Defendant went to Moton's office to explain what happened in court. Moton explained "that what she [Moton] meant by 'no deals' was she just wanted me [defendant] out period, no deals, no money."

9 Defendant averred that she had meritorious defenses to the eviction action and she would not be able to afford other safe and decent housing for her children based on her limited income. Defendant testified that she did not pay within the five days of the five-day notice because she also received a paper regarding the matter going to court and because Moton told her that she was sending the matter to plaintiff's attorney.

10 In addition to her affidavit, defendant also attached to her motion to vacate the TANF notice, which was dated January 31, 2013; plaintiff's five-day notice dated March 9, 2013; and plaintiff's March 21, 2013, letter. The TANF noticed stated that her cash benefits would stop as of February 17, 2013. The five-day notice stated that defendant owed $189.09 in rent, and unless payment was made within five days after service of the notice, her right of possession of the apartment would be terminated. It indicated that it was served on defendant "by delivering a true copy to" defendant. The March 21, 2013, letter from Moton stated that the five-day notice period had expired and defendant owed $189.09, and that her account "will be forwarded to the

attorney on Friday, March 22, 2013, NO EXCEPTIONS. Once your account goes to the attorney your account could be billed up to $600 for legal fees."

11 At the hearing on defendant's motion to vacate on May 28, 2013, defendant's counsel argued that the April 18 agreed order should be vacated because defendant thought she was agreeing to "pay and stay" and because of the disparity in bargaining power as defendant was not represented by counsel at the time. Plaintiff's counsel, Kahn, stated that she never promises anyone that they can "pay and stay" and she never told defendant that she could "pay and stay." She argued that her file indicated "no deals" and "no promise." Counsel asserted that plaintiff did not wish to accept the money even though defendant had the money in court that day.

12 Defendant's testimony at the May 28 hearing was similar to her statements in her affidavit. She reiterated that she believed she was agreeing to "pay the money to stay, which was all that me [sic] and Ms. Antoinette [Moton] talked about face to face." Defendant testified that she asked Moton if she could pay the money, and Moton told her, "yeah, plus fees. No deal. If I have all the money, then she was going to take the money." She testified that Moton never told her that she had to move out, and Kahn never told defendant at the April 18 court date that the May 15 date was a "move-out date." Defendant testified that it was her understanding based on her conversations with Moton that when she came to court on April 18, she would be allowed to pay the money demanded and remain in the unit. She testified that she had two conversations with Moton regarding paying the rent, but Moton never told her "I had to get out." Defendant testified that Moton informed her that the case "went to go [sic] to the court. It's nothing [sic] she can do about it. Because I was telling her that I didn't have a whole $700. She said, well, if you don't have all your money, then you can't stay. She said she want all of the money." She testified that she did not pay within the five-day notice period because she also received a paper instructing her to go to court and Moton told her that she "was sending it to the attorneys."

13 Regarding the April 18 court proceeding, defendant testified that Kahn "said something about no deals. I said does that mean having all my money. She said, yeah." Defendant testified that after they entered the courtroom and again discussed her case, defendant showed Kahn the TANF notice and counsel responded, "okay. That's fine. And something about she was going to give me until April 30 to pay the money. She asked me did I need a little more time. She said, okay. I'll give you to May the 15th to pay the money and that I had to sign the paper." Defendant testified that she did not intend to agree to pay and leave the apartment; she "would have never said that. I don't have any income so why would I pay money and still leave and have to go? * * * I got [sic] two small children. * * * Every time I talked to Antoinette [Moton], she never told me I had to go until that paper." Defendant testified that Kahn informed her that she could request a continuance to hire an attorney; however, defendant agreed to the April 18 order because defendant "thought I [defendant] was staying and paying the money."

14 Moton also testified at the May 28, 2013, hearing. She testified that on March 9, 2013, she sent a notice to defendant regarding the amount due of $189.09, and defendant then called her regarding her reduced income and the TANF notice. Moton testified that she never received the TANF notice despite defendant's assertion that she tried to give it to Moton's assistant and put it in the dropbox. Moton explained that when a tenant provides information regarding a reduction in income, the new rental amount is effective the following month and a tenant must sign off on the changes to the rental amount, but defendant never followed up to make sure an adjustment was made. Moton testified that she received the TANF notice from defendant on March 21, and Moton reduced the rent to $17 per month effective April 2013. Moton admitted that she told defendant that she "can pay before the actual account went to the attorney. And once it went to the attorney, I told her that * * * the attorney wasn't going to make any deals." She also conceded that she gave defendant a second opportunity to pay after the five-day notice expired. Moton admitted that she had previously told defendant that she would accept the past due rent and court costs before the case went to court. When defense counsel asked, "So you sent her a letter telling her you would accept past-due rent and the court costs and allow her to stay there, but then you told her no deals?" Moton responded, "Uh-huh."

15 During the hearing, plaintiff's attorney and the court questioned Moton regarding other alleged problems with defendant's tenancy. Moton testified that she was no longer willing to accept defendant's money because of other complaints she had received about defendant. Moton testified that incidents occurred before and after the five-day notice was sent to defendant. Over defense counsel's objection based on relevance, Moton testified:

"It started with like lots of noise complaints and, you know, asking Ms. King to, you know, turn her music down and so forth. And a lot of times when we went to the unit, Ms. King wasn't even at home. There was somebody else in her unit playing the loud music.

And, then, other incidents where one of her cousins got into it with someone else in the building. He got really, really upset and came to the office telling me how he was going to kill somebody, and I'm like we can't have this type of activity on the property. * * *

And, then, tenant complaints about the guests that's [sic] coming to her unit. People afraid for their kids, their daughters because it's different men going in and out of the property."[3]

16 Moton testified that the complaints regarding defendant's cousin occurred after the five-day notice was sent. Moton indicated that after the cousin was barred from the building, he continued to enter the building anyway.

17 With regard to these complaints, defendant admitted that she had played loud music occasionally, but she denied that she had guests at night. She also explained that in January, her cousin and someone else (who either lived in the building or

was related to someone who lived in the building) got into a fight at someone's house around the corner from the apartment building. Defendant was at the store at the time, but she then saw her cousin running around the corner. She brought her cousin into the apartment building to speak with Moton about it. Moton stated that her cousin had to leave and could not return. However, regarding the other incidents where Moton alleged that the cousin had entered the apartment complex, defendant testified that she did not know he came into the building, she did not let him in, and Moton never informed her that he had tried to reenter the building on other occasions.

18 The circuit court noted that plaintiff did not initially file the eviction proceeding based any problems with the tenancy other than nonpayment of rent. The court observed that defendant admitted to playing loud music in her apartment, but there was conflicting testimony regarding her cousin. The court held that "[t]he problem here simply is that there are problems with the unit and if not for that, this would have been a case I would have voided my usual rule and just vacated the judgment." However, given the problems with loud music and people in the unit, the court denied the motion to vacate the April 18, 2013, order of possession.

19 On June 4, 2013, defendant filed a motion to reconsider, which she later withdrew. Defendant filed a notice of appeal on June 27, 2013, from the April 18 and May 28, 2013, orders. Defendant also moved to stay enforcement of the order of possession pending appeal. The circuit court granted a stay until August 15, 2013, at which point it entered an order denying without prejudice defendant's motion to stay pending appeal on grounds that the motion should be presented to this court instead. On September 5, 2013, this court granted defendant's emergency motion to stay enforcement of the order of possession and granted defendant's motion for use and occupancy pending appeal on condition that she pay monthly rent during the pendency of this appeal.

20 ANALYSIS

21 Initially, plaintiff asserts that defendant failed to provide a sufficient record to enable review of her claims because she did not provide a transcript of the court proceeding on April 18, 2013. "[T]he appellant is required to provide the reviewing court with a record sufficient to support his or her claims of error * * *." *In re Marriage of Abu-Hashim*, 2014 IL App (1st) 122997, 15, 383 Ill.Dec. 241, 14 N.E.3d 524. While the record does not contain a transcript of the April 18, 2013, proceeding, the record does contain the transcript of the May 28, 2013, hearing on defendant's motion to vacate, which is the subject of her appeal. That hearing contains the testimony of defendant and Moton, along with statements from the trial judge and plaintiff's counsel regarding the April 18 proceeding. In addition, the record contains defendant's affidavit regarding what occurred at the April 18 proceeding, along with other documents involved in this case such as the five-day notice and the TANF letter. The transcript of April 18 was not provided to the trial court in reviewing defendant's motion to vacate. We find that the April 18 transcript is not needed to review defendant's claims and the record is sufficient to permit review. *Id.* However, any "doubts

and deficiencies arising from an insufficient record will be construed against" defendant. *Id.*

22 On appeal, defendant contends that the April 18, 2013, order should be vacated because there was no "meeting of the minds" by the parties as defendant believed she was agreeing to pay the overdue amounts and retain possession. She asserts that she diligently attempted to inform plaintiff of her reduction in income and then subsequently diligently challenged the April 18 order upon realizing that it did not reflect the bargain she thought she had struck. She emphasizes the disparity in the parties' respective bargaining positions given that she represented herself at the April 18, 2013, court proceeding while plaintiff had an attorney. She maintains that she has meritorious defenses to eviction because she did not owe the amounts claimed in the five-day notice and because the notice was defective. Defendant argues that she would suffer a severe penalty if the eviction order was carried out as she would lose her federal housing assistance and this would likely result in homelessness. As such, defendant asserts that the order was unconscionable considering the disparity of bargaining power, the fact that the order was wholly one-sided, and her meritorious defenses to eviction.

23 Defendant moved to vacate the agreed order pursuant to section 2-1301 of the Code, which provides in pertinent part that a court "may on motion filed within 30 days after entry thereof set aside any final order or judgment upon any terms and conditions that shall be reasonable." 735 ILCS 5/2-1301(e) (West 2012). Under section 2-1301(e), "the litigant need not necessarily show the existence of a meritorious defense and a reasonable excuse for not having timely asserted such defense. [Citation.] Rather, the overriding consideration is simply whether or not substantial justice is being done between the litigants and whether it is reasonable, under the circumstances, to compel the other party to go to trial on the merits." *In re Haley D.,* 2011 IL 110886, 57, 355 Ill.Dec. 375, 959 N.E.2d 1108. "In making this assessment, a court should consider all events leading up to the judgment. 'What is just and proper must be determined by the facts of each case, not by a hard and fast rule applicable to all situations regardless of the outcome. [Citation.]'" *Id.* 69 (quoting *Mann v. The Upjohn Co.,* 324 Ill.App.3d 367, 377, 257 Ill.Dec. 257, 753 N.E.2d 452 (2001)). "Whether substantial justice is being achieved by vacating a judgment or order is not subject to precise definition, but relevant considerations include diligence or the lack thereof, the existence of a meritorious defense, the severity of the penalty resulting from the order or judgment, and the relative hardships on the parties from granting or denying vacatur." *Jackson v. Bailey,* 384 Ill.App.3d 546, 549, 323 Ill.Dec. 266, 893 N.E.2d 280 (2008) (citing *Mann,* 324 Ill.App.3d at 377, 257 Ill.Dec. 257, 753 N.E.2d 452).

24 We note that, while defendant discusses and relies on section 2-1401 and *In re Marriage of Rolseth,* 389 Ill. App.3d 969, 330 Ill.Dec. 84, 907 N.E.2d 897 (2009) and the cases cited therein on appeal, her motion to vacate was made under section 2-1301 in the circuit court, which governs vacatur of default orders and final orders less than 30 days old. It is correct that agreed orders may be modified or vacated pursuant to section 2-1401 of the Code (735 ILCS 5/2-1401 (West 2012)), which allows

for relief from final orders after 30 days but less than two years after entry. *In re Marriage of Rolseth*, 389 Ill.App.3d at 972, 330 Ill.Dec. 84, 907 N.E.2d 897; *Thompson v. IFA, Inc.*, 181 Ill.App.3d 293, 297, 129 Ill.Dec. 919, 536 N.E.2d 969 (1989). The Second District in *In re Marriage of Rolseth* observed that the precise nature of the exceptions to vacating or modifying agreed orders has been subject to some dispute in the case law and that, with the enactment of section 72 of the Civil Practice Act (Ill.Rev.Stat. 1969, ch. 110, 72), which is currently section 2-1401 of the Code, "challenges to agreed orders were to be judged 'by the broad equitable considerations which govern all Section 72 petitions.'" *In re Marriage of Rolseth*, 389 Ill.App.3d at 972, 330 Ill.Dec. 84, 907 N.E.2d 897 (quoting *City of Des Plaines v. Scientific Machinery Movers, Inc.*, 9 Ill.App.3d 438, 443, 292 N.E.2d 154 (1972)). As such, a successful section 2-1401 petition will "affirmatively set forth specific factual allegations supporting each of the following elements: (1) a meritorious claim or defense; (2) due diligence in presenting the claim in the original action; and, (3) due diligence in filing the section 2-1401 petition for relief." *Thompson*, 181 Ill.App.3d at 298-99, 129 Ill.Dec. 919, 536 N.E.2d 969.

25 However, in the present case, defendant filed the motion to vacate within 30 days of the entry of the April 18 agreed order. We note that *In re Marriage of Rolseth* relied on cases such as *Thompson*, which involved circumstances where a motion to vacate an agreed order was made after 30 days had passed, and therefore is distinguishable from the present circumstances. *Thompson*, 181 Ill. App.3d at 295, 129 Ill.Dec. 919, 536 N.E.2d 969. See also *City of Des Plaines*, 9 Ill. App.3d at 441, 292 N.E.2d 154 (petition to vacate filed almost one year after consent decree was entered). As *Rolseth* relied on cases involving petitions brought after the passing of 30 days, we respectfully disagree that it necessarily follows that motions to vacate an agreed order brought within 30 days must be judged pursuant to a rule intended to govern motions brought after 30 days. Section 2-1301, as described above, presents a much lower hurdle for the movant to overcome, that being a showing that substantial justice was not achieved. This is the movant's "reward" for filing the motion in a more timely manner than if it was brought under section 2-1401. It is well recognized that motions to vacate under section 2-1301 are routinely granted in order to achieve substantial justice. We find that this is the standard that should apply to motions to vacate agreed orders brought within 30 days. As a result, we respectfully decline to follow *Rolseth*. Put another way, we see no reason to impose the stricter section 2-1401 standard upon a movant who has filed a timely motion to vacate pursuant to section 2-1301 simply because the subject of the motion is an agreed order. We find that the case law upon which *Rolseth* is based does not support such a conclusion. Nevertheless, as noted above, the question of whether substantial justice was achieved still requires an analysis of several considerations, including "diligence or the lack thereof, the existence of a meritorious defense, the severity of the penalty resulting from the order or judgment, and the relative hardships on the parties from granting or denying vacatur." *Jackson*, 384 Ill.App.3d at 549, 323 Ill.Dec. 266, 893 N.E.2d 280.

26 As a decision whether to grant a motion under section 2-1301 is discretionary (*In re Haley D.*, 2011 IL 110886, 69, 355 Ill.Dec. 375, 959 N.E.2d 1108), we review a circuit court's ruling on a motion under this section for an abuse of discretion (*Standard Bank & Trust Co. v. Madonia*, 2011 IL App (1st) 103516, 8, 357 Ill.Dec. 755, 964 N.E.2d 118). An abuse of discretion occurs when the circuit court "'acts arbitrarily without the employment of conscientious judgment or if its decision exceeds the bounds of reason and ignores principles of law such that substantial prejudice has resulted.'" *Aurora Loan Services, LLC, v. Kmiecik*, 2013 IL App (1st) 121700, 26, 372 Ill.Dec. 586, 992 N.E.2d 125 (quoting *Marren Builders, Inc. v. Lampert*, 307 Ill.App.3d 937, 941, 241 Ill.Dec. 256, 719 N.E.2d 117 (1999)).

27 With respect to defendant's assertion that the April 18 order should be vacated because there was no "meeting of the minds," we note that as an agreed order is considered to be a contract between the parties, "its construction is governed by principles of contract law." *Elliott v. LRSL Enterprises, Inc.*, 226 Ill. App.3d 724, 728-29, 168 Ill.Dec. 674, 589 N.E.2d 1074 (1992). The primary purpose of contract interpretation is to effectuate the intent of the parties. *Id.* at 729, 168 Ill.Dec. 674, 589 N.E.2d 1074. "[T]he order must be interpreted in its entirety, considering all facts and circumstances surrounding its execution, as well as all pleadings and motions from which it emanates." *Id.* We review *de novo* the construction, interpretation, and effect of a contract. *Avery v. State Farm Mutual Automobile Insurance Co.*, 216 Ill.2d 100, 129, 296 Ill.Dec. 448, 835 N.E.2d 801 (2005).

28 As agreed orders are effectively the parties' private contractual agreement, they are "generally binding on the parties and cannot be amended or varied without the consent of each party." *In re Marriage of Rolseth*, 389 Ill.App.3d at 971, 330 Ill.Dec. 84, 907 N.E.2d 897. However, exceptions arise where one party shows "fraudulent misrepresentation or coercion in the making of the agreement, the incompetence of one of the parties, gross disparity in the position or capacity of the parties, errors of law apparent on the face of the record, or newly discovered evidence." *City of Marseilles v. Radke*, 287 Ill.App.3d 757, 760, 223 Ill.Dec. 181, 679 N.E.2d 125 (1997). See also *In re Marriage of Rolseth*, 389 Ill.App.3d at 971-72, 330 Ill.Dec. 84, 907 N.E.2d 897 (same); *Thompson*, 181 Ill.App.3d at 296, 129 Ill.Dec. 919, 536 N.E.2d 969 (same). "Settlement agreements are binding only if there is an offer, an acceptance, and a meeting of the minds as to the terms of the agreement." *Sementa v. Tylman*, 230 Ill.App.3d 701, 705, 172 Ill.Dec. 327, 595 N.E.2d 688 (1992). Further, "'[i]n order to be unconscionable, a contract provision must be both procedurally and substantively unconscionable.'" *Aliaga Medical Center, S.C. v. Harris Bank N.A.*, 2014 IL App (1st) 133645, 27, 387 Ill.Dec. 32, 21 N.E.3d 1203 (quoting *Kinkel v. Cingular Wireless, LLC*, 357 Ill.App.3d 556, 562, 293 Ill.Dec. 502, 828 N.E.2d 812 (2005)). A contract is considered procedurally unconscionable "'if some impropriety in the formation of the contract leaves a party with no meaningful choice in the matter'" and it is substantively unconscionable "'if it is overly harsh or one-sided.'" *Aliaga Medical Center*, 2014 IL App (1st) 133645, 27, 387 Ill.Dec. 32, 21 N.E.3d 1203 (quoting *Kinkel*, 357 Ill.App.3d at 562, 293 Ill.Dec. 502, 828 N.E.2d 812).

29 Plaintiff maintains that an agreed order in a forcible detainer action may be vacated based only on fraud. Plaintiff primarily relies on two cases: *Sitelis v. Mouhelis*, 13 Ill.App.2d 131, 141 N.E.2d 92 (1957), and *Watson v. Kenores*, 338 Ill.App. 202, 86 N.E.2d 875 (1949). However, these cases were decided over 50 years ago and are abstract opinions. We do not agree that these cases are precedential. See *Schusse v. Pace Suburban Bus Division of the Regional Transportation Authority*, 334 Ill.App.3d 960, 968 n. 1, 268 Ill.Dec. 645, 779 N.E.2d 259 (2002) (noting that the defendant improperly cited an abstract opinion as precedent, a practice "consistently * * * condemned by courts of review," and finding that "an abstract cannot be relied upon as precedent").

30 On the other hand, defendant urges this court to look to a case from the New Jersey Supreme Court, *Community Realty Management, Inc. v. Harris*, 155 N.J. 212, 714 A.2d 282 (1998). The defendant in *Harris* lived in federally subsidized housing and faced eviction proceedings for nonpayment of rent, and she was not represented by counsel when she entered into a consent agreement in which she paid the back rent and agreed to vacate the apartment. *Harris*, 714 A.2d at 285–86. Upon realizing that she would be forced to leave, defendant obtained counsel and sought to vacate the consent judgment for possession. *Id.* at 286. The defendant testified that she told the plaintiff's attorney at the initial court date that she did not have the money and he gave her 11 days to pay it; when she returned to pay it, she then signed the consent order after speaking with a paralegal employed by plaintiff's attorney. *Id.* at 286-87. The defendant testified that based on the conversation with the paralegal, she believed she would be able to remain in the apartment if she met certain conditions after a six-month stay period, but the paralegal's testimony contradicted this. *Id.* at 287. Although the plaintiff conceded that the defendant's expectation that paying the amounts demanded would avoid eviction were consistent with general practices, it nonetheless sought enforcement of the warrant for removal "because of an undefined problem with defendant's son." *Id.* at 292. On appeal, the court held that the defendant was entitled to relief from the agreed order for possession given the evidence that the defendant did not have a "knowing and intelligent understanding of what transpired" as the defendant reasonably believed she would remain in possession if she paid the amounts demanded by a certain deadline, and she did not understand what a "hardship stay," "judgment for possession," and a "warrant for removal" were. *Id.* at 290-92.

31 "Although the decisions of foreign courts are not binding, 'the use of foreign decisions as persuasive authority is appropriate where Illinois authority on point is lacking or absent.'" *Rhone v. First American Title Insurance Co.*, 401 Ill.App.3d 802, 812, 340 Ill.Dec. 588, 928 N.E.2d 1185 (2010) (quoting *Carroll v. Curry*, 392 Ill.App.3d 511, 517, 332 Ill.Dec. 86, 912 N.E.2d 272 (2009)). Although *Harris* is not precedential, it bears obvious similarities to the instant case. Like in *Harris*, defendant in the present case lives in federally subsidized housing and faces eviction for nonpayment of rent, and she appeared at the court hearing regarding the eviction complaint without the assistance of an attorney. Like the defendant in *Harris*, the defendant reasonably believed, based on the evidence presented at the hearing on her motion to vacate the

agreed order, that she was agreeing to pay the amounts demanded while retaining possession of the apartment. The record reflects that Moton admitted in her testimony that before the April 18 court date, she told defendant that she could pay the amounts due and remain in the apartment. According to defendant, when she came to court and spoke with plaintiff's attorney, she informed the attorney that she had "worked it out with the manager already." Although defendant indicated that the attorney told her there were "no deals," when defendant asked the attorney whether this meant that she must present all of the money owed, the attorney responded, "yeah." There is nothing in this exchange which further clarified that defendant was also agreeing to surrender possession of the apartment. It also does not appear from the record available that when her case was called and discussed before the court, she was informed that she was agreeing to vacate the premises in addition to paying the rent and costs. She indicated that she did not think she needed an attorney because she believed she was agreeing to pay the amounts due and remain in the apartment. Considering both defendant's testimony, Moton's testimony, and the statements of plaintiff's attorney, it is understandable that defendant was under the impression that she had agreed she could remain in the apartment by paying the amounts demanded. Whether defendant was agreeing to pay the rent and costs while retaining her tenancy was a material feature of the parties' agreed order. See *John Burns Construction Co. v. Interlake, Inc.,* 105 Ill.App.3d 19, 25, 60 Ill.Dec. 888, 433 N.E.2d 1126 (1982) (a contract may be rescinded based on mistake where there it is shown that the mistake related to a "material feature of the contract," the mistake would entail "such grave consequence that enforcement of the contract would be unconscionable," that the mistake occurred despite exercising reasonable care, and that "the other party can be placed in *statu[s] quo*").

32 The record also supports that defendant exercised diligence in attempting to inform plaintiff of her change in income and in challenging the April 18 order. *Jackson,* 384 Ill.App.3d at 549, 323 Ill.Dec. 266, 893 N.E.2d 280. According to defendant's affidavit and testimony, she attempted to inform plaintiff of her change of income promptly after she received the TANF notice in late January or early February of 2013. Sandy did not take the notice when defendant presented it to her. And for reasons not clear in the record, Moton apparently did not receive the copy of the TANF notice that defendant placed in the office dropbox later that same day. Defendant then obtained another copy of the TANF notice and provided it to Moton. The record also reflects that when defendant spoke with Moton a few days after the April 18 court date and realized that the April 18 order had actually given plaintiff possession of the apartment in addition to ordering her to pay the overdue rent and costs, defendant diligently attempted to timely challenge the order by obtaining counsel and filing the motion to vacate within 30 days.

33 Moreover, we also consider the relative hardships of the parties and the severity of the penalty if the agreed order is allowed to stand. *Jackson,* 384 Ill.App.3d at 549, 323 Ill.Dec. 266, 893 N.E.2d 280. Defendant argues that her federal housing subsidy is tied to the particular apartment and she would lose it if evicted, and eviction would have grave consequences for her. On the other hand, if the motion to vacate were

granted, plaintiff would continue to receive rent at the applicable rate based on a percentage of defendant's income while proceeding to a trial on the merits in this case. Defendant was ready and able to pay the amounts demanded by plaintiff. In light of the severity of the penalty that would result from affirming the trial court's order denying defendant's motion to vacate, we find that the relative hardships in this case favor defendant. *Id.*

34 In addition, defendant asserts on appeal that she has two viable defenses to the eviction action. Defendant argues (1) that she did not owe the amounts claimed in the notice because of the change in income she experienced, and (2) that the five-day notice was defective because service was made only by delivering it to her personally. We disagree with plaintiff's argument that by agreeing to the order, defendant waived any defenses to it, as defendant is challenging the validity of the very same order.

35 Section 886.124(b) of the federal regulations governing Section 8 Housing Assistance Payments provides that a family receiving housing assistance "must comply with provisions in its lease regarding interim reporting of changes in income. If the owner receives information concerning a change in the family's income * * * between regularly scheduled reexaminations, the owner must consult with the family and make any adjustments determined to be appropriate." 24 C.F.R. §886.124(b) (2012). That the regulations required plaintiff to adjust defendant's rent when her income was reduced was also supported by Moton's testimony when she is notified that a tenant's income changes, the rent is adjusted in the month following the notice. As previously stated, defendant testified that she attempted to give the TANF notice to plaintiff shortly after she received it in January or February of 2013, but Sandy would not accept it and defendant then placed it in the dropbox. Moton claimed she never received the letter until defendant obtained a second copy and brought it to her on March 21, but this does not necessarily negate defendant's testimony that she provided the letter much earlier. Although plaintiff asserts that defendant's testimony was vague regarding the exact date she first provided notice, we note that section 2-1301 of the Code does not require defendant to affirmatively prove a defense. Rather, whether meritorious defenses exist is one of several relevant considerations in determining whether substantial justice would be achieved by vacating the order. *Jackson,* 384 Ill.App.3d at 549, 323 Ill.Dec. 266, 893 N.E.2d 280.

36 Defendant also asserts that plaintiff's personal service of the five-day notice failed to satisfy the service requirements under the applicable federal regulations. Section 886.128 (24 C.F.R. §886.128 (2012)) provides that section 247.1 (24 C.F.R. §247.1 *et seq.* (2012)) applies to the termination and eviction of a tenant receiving assistance under this section. Section 247.4(a) provides that a decision to terminate a tenancy: "shall: (1) State that the tenancy is terminated on a date specified therein; (2) state the reasons for the landlord's action with enough specificity so as to enable the tenant to prepare a defense; (3) advise the tenant that if he or she remains in the leased unit on the date specified for termination, the landlord may seek to enforce the termination only by bringing a judicial action, at which time the tenant may present a defense;

and (4) be served on the tenant in the manner prescribed by paragraph (b) of this section." 24 C.F.R. §247.4(a) (2012).

37 Further, this section provides that the notice required under paragraph (a):

"shall be accomplished by: (1) Sending a letter by first class mail, properly stamped and addressed, to the tenant at his or her address at the project, with a proper return address, and (2) serving a copy of the notice on any adult person answering the door at the leased dwelling unit, or if no adult responds, by placing the notice under or through the door, if possible, or else by affixing the notice to the door. *Service shall not be deemed effective until both notices provided for herein have been accomplished.* The date on which the notice shall be deemed to be received by the tenant shall be the date on which the first class letter provided for in this paragraph is mailed, or the date on which the notice provided for in this paragraph is properly given, whichever is later." (Emphasis added.) 24 C.F.R. §247.4(b) (2012).

38 Defendant asserts that plaintiff failed to properly effectuate service as it only slipped the five-day notice under her door. The regulations make clear that service must be effectuated by first-class mail *and* personally served on an adult in the unit or slipped under the door if no adult answered the door. Plaintiff maintains that defendant has waived her notice argument as it was not presented in the trial court and she admitted that she received notice. However, section 247.4(f) directs that "[t]he failure of the tenant to object to the termination notice shall not constitute a waiver of his rights to thereafter contest the landlord's action in any judicial proceeding." 24 C.F.R. §247.4(f) (2012).

39 While we are mindful that the standard of review in this case is an abuse discretion, all defendant seeks in this case is a trial on the merits. Given the facts of this case, we believe that substantial justice is best accomplished by vacating the April 18 order. *In re Haley D.,* 2011 IL 110886, 69, 355 Ill.Dec. 375, 959 N.E.2d 1108; *Jackson,* 384 Ill.App.3d at 549, 323 Ill.Dec. 266, 893 N.E.2d 280. The record supports that defendant misunderstood the terms of the order that she signed and that this misunderstanding was reasonable given Moton's statements before the court proceeding and what transpired during the proceeding. The record also supports that defendant diligently attempted to notify plaintiff of her change in income and later diligently attempted to contest the April 18 order upon realizing that the order granted plaintiff possession. Also of significance is the disparity in the parties' bargaining power given that defendant was not represented by an attorney and did not believe she needed one as she thought she was agreeing to "pay and stay." As noted, we are mindful of the relative hardships at stake. Moreover, under the law, there is a clear preference for disposing of issues based on the merits. *In re Application of the County Collector of Lake County,* 343 Ill.App.3d 363, 373, 278 Ill.Dec. 204, 797 N.E.2d 1122 (2003). "The law prefers that controversies be determined according to the substantive rights of the parties" and the Code should be "liberally construed toward that end." *In re Haley D.,* 2011 IL 110886, 69, 355 Ill.Dec. 375, 959 N.E.2d 1108. Accordingly, we find that the circuit court abused its discretion in denying defendant's motion to vacate.

40 Defendant also raises a constitutional claim on appeal in arguing that her due process rights were violated because the circuit court based its decision on allegations which plaintiff failed to include in the five-day notice of termination or the complaint. Plaintiff makes no reply to this argument in its response brief.

41 "[D]ue process principles require that one cannot be deprived of property without adequate notice and an opportunity to defend." *In re Possession of Control of the Commissioner of Banks & Real Estate of Independent Trust Corp.*, 327 Ill.App.3d 441, 466-67, 261 Ill.Dec. 775, 764 N.E.2d 66 (2001). Where an individual has a statutory entitlement to welfare benefits, he is entitled to adequate notice and an opportunity to be heard before those benefits are suspended. *Goldberg v. Kelly*, 397 U.S. 254, 267-68, 90 S.Ct. 1011, 25 L.Ed.2d 287 (1970). The notice must be "reasonably calculated * * * to apprise interested parties of the pendency of the action and afford them an opportunity to present their objections" and it must also "reasonably * * * convey the required information." *Mullane v. Central Hanover Bank & Trust Co.*, 339 U.S. 306, 314, 70 S.Ct. 652, 94 L.Ed. 865 (1950). In the context of federally assisted housing, courts have held that

"state-created, federally-funded, locally administered housing authority had to provide the following before evicting a tenant:

(1) timely and adequate notice detailing the reasons for a proposed termination, (2) an opportunity on the part of the tenant to confront and cross-examine adverse witnesses, (3) the right of a tenant to be represented by counsel, provided by him to delineate the issues, present the factual contentions in an orderly manner, conduct cross-examination and generally to safeguard his interests, (4) a decision, based on evidence adduced at the hearing, in which the reasons for decision and the evidence relied on are set forth, and (5) an impartial decision maker." (Internal quotation marks omitted.) *Johnson v. Illinois Department of Public Aid*, 467 F.2d 1269, 1272 (7th Cir.1972).

42 In *Johnson*, the court disagreed with the defendants' assertion "that tenancy in public housing is a privilege, not a right, and as such can be terminated at the will of the Authority, without regard to the tenants' constitutional rights." *Johnson*, 467 F.2d at 1273.[4]

43 As defendant notes, section 247.3 required plaintiff to provide notice of the reasons for termination of tenancy in accordance with section 247.4. 24 C.F.R. §247.3(a), (c) (2012). A tenant's conduct "cannot be deemed other good cause under §247.3(a)(4) unless the landlord has given the tenant prior notice that said conduct shall henceforth constitute a basis for termination of occupancy," and the notice must be served as set forth in section 247.4(b). 24 C.F.R. §247.3(b) (2012). In turn, section 247.4(a) requires that the termination notice be in writing and state with sufficient specificity "the reasons for the landlord's action * * * so as to enable the tenant to prepare a defense." 24 C.F.R. §247.4(a) (2012).

44 Although defendant raises this issue as a separate justification for vacating the April 18 order, we have already determined that vacatur of the order is appropriate.

We further observe, however, that we are troubled by the trial court's reliance on allegations that were not set forth in the initial five-day notice to defendant or in the complaint. The five-day notice and complaint only included the nonpayment of rent allegation. The other allegations involving noise complaints, defendant's cousin, and inappropriate guests in her apartment at night were not included. Plaintiff did not file a response to defendant's motion to vacate, but brought these allegations up at the hearing on defendant's motion. As such, defendant was not provided with advance notice that these allegations would serve as a basis for eviction and, consequently, she was not provided an opportunity to prepare a defense to these accusations before the hearing. Her attorney repeatedly objected to this evidence at the hearing and informed the court that she had not received a copy of any notices sent to defendant regarding the incidents.[5] In deciding to deny defendant's motion to vacate, the circuit court stated:

"Ordinarily what we do in these cases is if there's an agreement, ordinarily—again, that's in the ordinary case—we just accept it and that's it.

The reason I wanted to hear more here was to see really the reasoning why the money isn't accepted, and I realize they didn't proceed originally on the count of, you know, problems with the unit. But, you know, the reality is is that when someone plays loud music, you know, people are entitled to a night's sleep, and no one should be forced to listen late at night to people's music. I think the defendant was very candid that she did do that.

* * *

The problem here simply is that there are problems with the unit and if not for that, this would have been a case I would have voided my usual rule and just vacated the judgment. But I think here given the fact that there are obviously problems with loud music, with certain people in the unit, I think I'm going to deny the motion to vacate the possession order."

45 Thus, it is clear that the circuit court based its decision on these other allegations, which were not contained in the notice or the complaint and about which defendant had no prior notice or opportunity to prepare a defense. This issue provides additional support for our conclusion that the decision to deny defendant's motion to vacate did not accomplish substantial justice in this case and was an abuse of discretion.

46 CONCLUSION

47 For the reasons stated above, we reverse the circuit court's order denying defendant's motion to vacate the April 18 order.

48 Reversed and remanded.

Justices GORDON and REYES concurred in the judgment and opinion.

[1] "Section 8 is a Federal housing subsidy program administered by the United States Department of Housing and Urban Development (HUD)" which assists low-income families to find decent and affordable housing. *Midland Management Co. v. Helgason,* 158 Ill.2d 98, 101, 196 Ill.Dec. 671, 630 N.E.2d 836 (1994) (citing 42 U.S.C. § 1437f

(Supp. III 1991)). HUD enters into contracts with housing owners which makes units available to low-income families, and the rental amount is determined by a formula based on income. *Id.* at 101-01, 196 Ill.Dec. 671, 630 N.E.2d 836.

[2] The complaint stated that her monthly rental rate was $9, effective on April 1, 2013. Defendant averred that her "recertification paperwork says $17" per month.

[3] Moton provided two incident reports dated March 1, 2013. Defense counsel objected based on relevance as the case only involved nonpayment of rent and because she had never seen the reports before. The circuit court overruled the objection and indicated that the reports were relevant.

[4] See also *Thorpe v. Housing Authority of the City of Durham,* 393 U.S. 268, 89 S.Ct. 518, 21 L.Ed.2d 474 (1969) (finding that a HUD circular regarding eviction of a tenant requiring notice of the reasons for the eviction and an opportunity to reply must be followed by public housing project); *Glover v. Housing Authority of the City of Bessemer,* 444 F.2d 158, 161 (5th Cir.1971) (observing that a HUD regulation requiring a hearing before an impartial official or panel was based on *Goldberg v. Kelly*); *Chicago Housing Authority v. Harris,* 49 Ill.2d 274, 275 N.E.2d 353 (1971) (concluding that HUD circulars were valid and applicable and that housing authorities are required to comply with them).

[5] The circuit court indicated that evidence of these other complaints was relevant and would be allowed under Illinois Supreme Court Rule 286(b) (eff. Aug. 1, 1992), which provides that in "any small claims case, the court may * * * adjudicate the dispute at an informal hearing" and that "all relevant evidence shall be admissible." However, "'small claim[s]'" are defined in Rule 281 "only as including 'civil action[s] based on either tort or contract for money not in excess of $10,000, exclusive of interest and costs, or for the collection of taxes not in excess of that amount.'" *Stone Street Partners, LLC v. City of Chicago Department of Administrative Hearings,* 2014 IL App (1st) 123654, 20, 382 Ill.Dec. 412, 12 N.E.3d 691 (quoting Ill. S.Ct. R. 281 (eff. Jan. 1, 2006)). The instant case involved a forcible detainer action for possession.

Chapter 10

The Transaction

Learning Objectives

After studying Chapter 10, you will be able to:

- Assemble and draft a deed and related closing documents
- Complete a Seller's Closing Statement
- Inspect and interpret a HUD-1 Settlement Statement

Chapter Summary

Topics covered:

- Conducting a Mock Closing from Start to Finish

This chapter is the culmination of the entire text. In this chapter, the hypothetical begun in Chapter 2 is concluded. The documents for the Closing, including the deed, bill of sale, affidavit of title, and others, are prepared. The Seller's loan payoff and real estate broker's statement are examined. A Closing statement is completed and the final "reconciliation" document, a HUD-1 Settlement Statement, also called the "RESPA" or "ALTA SETTLEMENT STATEMENT," is prepared. The documents that are prepared in this chapter constitute the primary documents required to close a real estate transaction.

Building upon the assignment from the previous weeks, you will be taking the contract reviewed earlier in this text for the attorney review assignment and will work on an entire transaction, picking up the transaction from the point of the home inspection through to Closing.

As a reminder, the student may assume that the contract has been signed by both parties on the dates of the contract. The Seller owns the property outright (subject to any liens on the property) and has the right to convey. Also, the Buyer is married to Brett Buyer, but please note that only Roberta has signed the contract (students may decide whether Roberta and Brett Buyer are going to live in the property as their permanent residence—remember, it may affect how they can take title).

The Buyer has had an inspection done by Home Wright Inspection, owned by Willie Wright (see Chapter 3). The fee for the inspection was $300.00, which was paid outside of Closing. As a result of the home inspection, the Seller agreed to a $1,000.00 closing credit for the home inspection issues.

As stated in the contract, the mortgage broker is Hi-Interest Mortgage. The "End Lender" (the lender who is actually supplying the loan) is Ninth Illinois State Bank Mortgage. The loan amount is $240,000.00. The Seller's attorney fee is $500.00 (find the Buyer's attorney fee). The appraisal, performed by Appraise the World and costing $400.00, will be paid at Closing.

The Lender's fees include the appraisal,

origination fee of $1,000.00,

processing fee of $500.00,

broker's fee of $600.00,

credit fee of $35.00,

flood determination fee of $95.00,

escrow fee of $95.00, and tax service fee of $50.00.

The Lender is requiring an escrow account to be set up for taxes and insurance (2 months of taxes, $460.57, and insurance, $87.00) and prepaid interest of $224.32.

Students will be working through the Closing documents and will also be completing the HUD-/RESPA/Settlement Statement. Although that would normally be completed by a title company, it is important to understand what the numbers are, what they mean, and where they go in order to explain the statement to the client.

Review Questions

1.   Which Closing documents generally need to be notarized?
2.   What is a Lender Payoff Statement?
3.   What is a Certification for No Information Reporting on the Sale or Exchange of a Principal Residence?
4.   What is a broker's commission statement?
5.   What does HUD mean?

Materials in the following appendix include:

- Warranty Deed
- Bill of Sale
- Affidavit of Title
- ALTA Loan and/or Owner's Policy Statement
- Certification for No Information Reporting on the Sale or Exchange of a Principal Residence
- Sample Lender Payoff Statement
- Sample Survey Invoice

- Sample Real Estate Broker's Commission Statement
- Illinois P-Tax Form
- Cook County Real Estate Transfer Declaration
- City of Chicago Real Property Transfer Tax Declaration
- Closing Statement
- HUD-1 Settlement Statement

Chapter 10 Appendix

WARRANTY DEED
Statutory (Illinois)

Mail to:

Name & address of taxpayer:

THE   GRANTOR(S)
_____, for and in con-
sideration of TEN and NO/100ths DOLLARS and other good and valuable considerations in hand paid.

CONVEY AND WARRANT to _____ (address),
all interest in the following described real estate situated in the County of Cook, in
the State of Illinois, to wit:

*Subject to general real estate taxes not due and payable at time of Closing, covenants,
conditions and restrictions of record, building lines, and easements, if any, so long as they
do not interfere with the current use and enjoyment of the property.*

Hereby releasing and waiving all rights under and by virtue of the Homestead Exemption Laws of the State of Illinois. TO HAVE AND HOLD said premises in Fee
Simple forever.

Permanent index number(s)
Property address:
DATED this _____ day of _____, 20__.

_____   _____

Grantor   Grantor

WARRANTY DEED

Statutory (Illinois)

State of ILLINOIS,   )

ss.   )

County of Cook   )

I, the undersigned, a Notary Public in and for said County, in the State aforesaid, DO HEREBY CERTIFY that _____ personally known to me to be the same person(s) whose names are subscribed to the foregoing instrument, appeared before me this day in person, and the person(s) acknowledged that the persons signed, sealed, and delivered the instrument as their free and voluntary act, for the uses and purposes therein set forth.

Given under my hand and official seal this ___ day of _____, 20__.

_____

      Notary Public

Commission expires: _____

NAME AND ADDRESS OF PREPARER:

STATE OF ILLINOIS   )

)

COUNTY OF COOK   )

BILL OF SALE

Sellers, _____, in consideration of Ten and No/100ths Dollars, do hereby sell, assign, transfer and set over to Buyer, _____, the following described personal property located at _____:

Seller hereby represents and warrants to Buyer(s) that Seller is the absolute owner of said property, that said property is free and clear of all liens, charges, and encumbrances, and the Seller has full right, power, and authority to sell said personal property and to make this Bill of Sale. All warranties of quality, fitness, and merchantability are hereby excluded, other than those warranties, which are incorporated into the contract to purchase the real estate noted above.

If this Bill of Sale is signed by more than one person, all persons so signing shall be jointly and severally bound hereby.

IN WITNESS WHEREOF, Seller has signed and sealed this Bill of Sale at Chicago, IL, this ___ day of _____, 20__.

_____   _____

Grantor   Grantor

Subscribed and sworn to before me this ___ day of _____, 20__.

_____

Notary Public

STATE OF ILLINOIS   )

)

COUNTY OF COOK   )

AFFIDAVIT OF TITLE

The undersigned _____ (Sellers), being first duly sworn on oath, and also covenants with and warrants to the Grantee (Buyer) hereinafter named: _____;

That Seller has an interest in the premises described below or in the proceeds thereof or is the Grantor in the deed dated _____, 20__ to _____, Buyer, conveying the following described premises:

Common address:

_____

That no labor or material has been furnished for premises within the last four months that is not fully paid for:

That since the title date of _____, in the report on title issued by _____, Seller has not done or suffered to be done anything that could in any way affect the title to premises, and no proceedings have been filed by or against Seller, nor has any judgment or decree been rendered against Seller, nor is there any judgment note or other instrument that can result in a judgment or decree against Seller within five days from the date thereof.

That Seller is in undisputed and peaceful possession of the premises and no other parties have any rights or claims to possession of the premises, except as hereinafter set forth:

That all water taxes and sanitary sewer, except the current bill, have been paid. Any unpaid balance will be promptly paid within 30 days of receipt of outstanding bills.

Seller further states:

That the covenants and warranties herein set forth are continuing covenants and warranties to and including the date of delivery of the deed to the above-identified Buyer and shall have the same force and effect as if made on the date of such delivery of deed. That this instrument is made to induce, and in consideration of, the said Buyer's consummation of the purchase of the premises.

_____   _____

Grantor   Grantor

Subscribed and sworn to before me this _____ day of _____, 20__

_____

Notary Public

ALTA Loan and/or Owner's Policy Statement

Commitment File Number_____

The undersigned hereby certifies with respect to the land described in the above commitment:

That, to the best knowledge and belief of the undersigned, no contracts for the furnishing of any labor or material to the land or the improvements thereon, and no security agreements or leases in respect to any goods or chattels that have or are to become attached to the land or any improvements thereon as fixtures, have been given or are outstanding that have not been fully performed or satisfied; that there are no recorded or unrecorded: contracts to purchase the land, deeds of conveyance, mortgages, liens of any kind or leases to which the land is subject, except as shown in the above referenced title commitment, and except as listed below; and that if any leases are listed below: their term ends within 30 days of the date below, they contain no option to purchase, rights of renewal, or other unusual provisions, except as noted below. (If no leases, contracts, etc., state "none.")

That, in the event the undersigned is a mortgagor in a mortgage to be insured under a loan policy to be issued pursuant to the above commitment, the mortgage and the principal obligations it secures are good and valid and free from all defenses; that any person purchasing the mortgage and the obligations it secures, or otherwise acquiring any interest therein, may do so in reliance upon the truth of the matters herein recited; and that this certification is made for the purpose of better enabling the holder or holders, from time to time, of the above mortgage and obligations to sell, pledge, or otherwise dispose of the same freely at any time, and to insure the purchasers or pledgees thereof against any defenses thereto by the mortgagor or the mortgagor's heirs, personal representative, or assigns.

The undersigned make the above statements for the purpose of inducing _____, or its assigns to issue an owners and/or loan policy pursuant to the above commitment, and agree to indemnify said company against any false statement made herein.

Date:

_____   _____

Seller: Buyer:

Corporations:

IN WITNESS WHEREOF, _____

has caused these presents to be signed by _____ its President and attested by its _____Secretary under its corporate seal on the above date.

Corporations:

IN WITNESS WHEREOF, _____

has caused these presents to be signed by _____ its President and attested by its _____Secretary under its corporate seal on the above date.

By:_____   By:_____
        President   President

Attest:_____   Attest:_____
        Secretary   Secretary

If this statement is executed by a Trustee, the Beneficiary must also execute the statement

The above statements are made by _____ not personally but as Trustee under the Trust agreement known as Trust No._____ on the above date by virtue of the written authority and direction of the beneficiaries under the trust.

The above statements are made by _____ not personally but as Trustee under the Trust agreement known as Trust No._____ on the above date by virtue of the written authority and direction of the beneficiaries under the trust.

_____
      Trust Officer

_____
      Trust Officer

_____
    Beneficiary (ies)

_____
    Beneficiary (ies)

LENDER'S DISBURSEMENT STATEMENT

The undersigned hereby certifies that the proceeds of the loan secured by the mortgage to be insured under the loan policy to be issued pursuant to the above referenced title commitment were fully disbursed to or on the order of the mortgagor on _____; and to the best knowledge and belief of the undersigned, the proceeds are not to be used to finance the making of future repairs on the land. You are hereby authorized to date down the above commitment to cover the date of said disbursement.

_____
Signature   Date

CERTIFICATION FOR NO INFORMATION REPORTING ON THE SALE OR EXCHANGE OF A PRINCIPAL RESIDENCE

This form may be completed by the Seller of a principal residence. This information is necessary to determine whether the sale or exchange should be reported by the Seller, and to the Internal Revenue Service on Form 1099-S, Proceeds From Real Estate Transactions. If the Seller properly completes Parts I and III, and makes a "yes" response to assurances 1 through 4 in Part II, no information reporting to the Seller or to the Service will be required for that Seller. The term "Seller" includes each owner of the residence that is sold or exchanged. Thus, if a residence has more than one owner, a real estate reporting person must either obtain a certification from each owner (whether married or not) or file an information return and furnish a payee statement for any owner that does not make the certification.

Part I: Seller Information:

1.   Name: _____

2.   Address or legal description (including city, state, & zip code) of residence being sold/exchanged:

3.   Taxpayer Identification Number (TIN): _____

4.   Forwarding address: _____

Part II: Seller Assurances. Check "yes" or "no" for assurances 1 through 4:

YES NO   1. I owned and used the residence as my principal residence for periods aggregating 2 years or more during the 5-year period ending on the date of the sale or exchange of the residence.

YES NO   2. I have not sold or exchanged another principal residence during the 2-year period ending on the date of the sale or exchange of the residence (not taking into account any sale or exchange before May 7, 1997).

YES NO   3. No portion of the residence has been used for business or rental purposes by me or my spouse if I am married (after May 6, 1997).

YES NO   4. At least one of the following three statements applies:

The sale or exchange is of the entire residence for $250,000 or less; or

I am married, the sale or exchange is of the entire residence for $500,000 or less, and the gain on the sale or exchange of the entire residence is $250,000 or less; or

I am married, the sale or exchange is of the entire residence for $500,000 or less, and (a) I intend to file a joint return for the year of the sale or exchange, (b) my spouse also used the residence as his or her primary residence for periods aggregating 2 years or more during the 5-year period ending on the date of the sale or exchange of the residence (not taking into account any sale or exchange before May 7, 1997).

Part III: Seller Certification:

Under penalties of perjury, I certify that all of the above information is true and correct as of the end of the day of the sale or exchange.

_____

Seller   Date

State Bank of Nowhere

120 N. LaSalle Street
Chicago, IL 60603
(312) 555-9865
Fax: (312) 555-9866

Payoff Statement

Borrower: Jonathan Seller
                   4802 W. Wellington
                   Chicago, IL 60641

Taxpayer Identification Number: XXX-XX-9824

Loan Number: XXXXXXXXXXXXX5874

Loan Amount Due: $175,500.00 as of July 23, 2015.

Per Diem: $45.22/day after July 23, 2015.

Check must be made via certified funds and sent to:

Payoffs
678 King Dr.
Louisville, KY 48574-4562

This statement expires on July 30, 2015. Any payments made after that date will not be accepted and a new payoff statement must be ordered.

Lurvey Survey

7894 W. Belmont, Suite 212 Chicago, IL 60641

July 16, 2015

Invoice

Quantity	Description	Date Ordered	Date Delivered	Price
1	Plat of Survey 4802 W. Wellington Chicago, IL 60641	7/1/12	7/15/12	$300.00

All items are due net at Closing, or within 30 days from date of date of delivery, if survey is not performed in connection with a real estate Closing.

Sales Max of Nowhere

The Finest in Property Sales and Management

Broker's Commission Statement

Purchase Price: $285,000.00
Commission: 6%
Broker's Commission: 3% + $295.00 listing fee
Co-Broker's Commission 3%—$295.00 listing fee

Total Commission: $17,100.00

Seller's Broker: John Attack, Sales Max of Nowhere
$8,550.00 + $295.00 = $8,845.00
Seller's Broker holds $5,000.00 Earnest Money
Due at Closing: $3,845.00

Buyer's Broker: Jane Coldheart, Buywell Banker of Nowhere

$8,550.00—$295.00 = $8,255.00

PTAX-203
Illinois Real Estate
Transfer Declaration

Please read the instructions before completing this form.
This form can be completed electronically at **tax.illinois.gov/retd.**

Step 1: Identify the property and sale information.

1 _____
Street address of property (or 911 address, if available)

_____
City or village   ZIP

_____
Township

2 Write the total number of parcels to be transferred. _____

3 Write the parcel identifying numbers and lot sizes or acreage.

Property index number (PIN)	Lot size or acreage
a_____	_____
b_____	_____
c_____	_____
d_____	_____

Write additional property index numbers, lot sizes or acreage in Step 3.

4 Date of instrument: ____ ____ / ____ ____ ____ ____
                        Month   Year

5 Type of instrument (Mark with an "X."):   ____ Warranty deed
____ Quit claim deed ____ Executor deed ____ Trustee deed
____ Beneficial interest ____ Other (specify): _____

6 ____ Yes ____ No Will the property be the buyer's principal residence?

7 ____ Yes ____ No Was the property advertised for sale?
                      (i.e., media, sign, newspaper, realtor)

8 Identify the property's current and intended primary use.
   Current Intended   (Mark **only one item per column** with an "X.")
a____ ____ Land/lot only
b____ ____ Residence (single-family, condominium, townhome, or duplex)
c____ ____ Mobile home residence
d____ ____ Apartment building (6 units or less) No. of units: _____
e____ ____ Apartment building (over 6 units) No. of units: _____
f____ ____ Office
g____ ____ Retail establishment
h____ ____ Commercial building (specify): _____
i____ ____ Industrial building
j____ ____ Farm
k____ ____ Other (specify): _____

9 Identify any significant physical changes in the property since January 1 of the previous year and **write the date of the change.**
   Date of significant change: ____ ____ / ____ ____ ____ ____
   (Mark with an "X.")   Month   Year
   ____ Demolition/damage ____ Additions ____ Major remodeling
   ____ New construction   ____ Other (specify): _____

10 Identify only the items that apply to this sale. (Mark with an "X.")
a ____ Fulfillment of installment contract —
         year contract initiated : ____ ____ ____ ____
b ____ Sale between related individuals or corporate affiliates
c ____ Transfer of less than 100 percent interest
d ____ Court-ordered sale
e ____ Sale in lieu of foreclosure
f ____ Condemnation
g ____ Short sale
h ____ Bank REO (real estate owned)
i ____ Auction sale
j ____ Seller/buyer is a relocation company
k ____ Seller/buyer is a financial institution or government agency
l ____ Buyer is a real estate investment trust
m ____ Buyer is a pension fund
n ____ Buyer is an adjacent property owner
o ____ Buyer is exercising an option to purchase
p ____ Trade of property (simultaneous)
q ____ Sale-leaseback
r ____ Other (specify): _____

s ____ Homestead exemptions on most recent tax bill:
         1 General/Alternative $_____
         2 Senior Citizens $_____
         3 Senior Citizens Assessment Freeze $_____

Step 2: Calculate the amount of transfer tax due.

Note: Round Lines 11 through 18 to the next highest whole dollar. If the amount on Line 11 is over $1 million and the property's current use on Line 8 above is marked "e," "f," "g," "h," "i," or "k," complete Form PTAX-203-A, Illinois Real Estate Transfer Declaration Supplemental Form A. If you are recording a beneficial interest transfer, do not complete this step. Complete Form PTAX-203-B, Illinois Real Estate Transfer Declaration Supplemental Form B.

11	Full actual consideration	11	$ _____
12a	Amount of personal property included in the purchase	12a	$ _____
12b	Was the value of a mobile home included on Line 12a?	12b	____ Yes ____ No
13	Subtract Line 12a from Line 11. This is the net consideration for real property.	13	$ _____
14	Amount for other real property transferred to the seller (in a simultaneous exchange) as part of the full actual consideration on Line 11	14	$ _____
15	Outstanding mortgage amount to which the transferred real property remains subject	15	$ _____
16	If this transfer is exempt, use an "X" to identify the provision.	16	___b ___k ___m
17	Subtract Lines 14 and 15 from Line 13. **This is the net consideration subject to transfer tax.**	17	$ _____
18	Divide Line 17 by 500. Round the result to the next highest whole number (e.g., 61.002 rounds to 62).	18	_____
19	Illinois tax stamps — multiply Line 18 by 0.50.	19	$ _____
20	County tax stamps — multiply Line 18 by 0.25.	20	$ _____
21	Add Lines 19 and 20. **This is the total amount of transfer tax due.**	21	$ _____

This form is authorized in accordance with 35 ILCS 200/31-1 et seq. Disclosure of this information is REQUIRED. This form has been approved by the Forms Management Center.   IL-492-0227

Step 3: Write the legal description from the deed. Write, type (minimum 10-point font required), or attach the legal description from the deed. If you prefer, submit an 8¹/₂" x 11" copy of the extended legal description with this form. You may also use the space below to write additional property index numbers, lots sizes or acreage from Step 1, Line 3.

Step 4: Complete the requested information.

The buyer and seller (or their agents) hereby verify that to the best of their knowledge and belief, the full actual consideration and facts stated in this declaration are true and correct. If this transaction involves any real estate located in Cook County, the buyer and seller (or their agents) hereby verify that to the best of their knowledge, the name of the buyer shown on the deed or assignment of beneficial interest in a land trust is either a natural person, an Illinois corporation or foreign corporation authorized to do business or acquire and hold title to real estate in Illinois, a partnership authorized to do business or acquire and hold title to real estate in Illinois, or other entity recognized as a person and authorized to do business or acquire and hold title to real estate under the laws of the State of Illinois. Any person who willfully falsifies or omits any information required in this declaration shall be guilty of a Class B misdemeanor for the first offense and a Class A misdemeanor for subsequent offenses. Any person who knowingly submits a false statement concerning the identity of a grantee shall be guilty of a Class C misdemeanor for the first offense and of a Class A misdemeanor for subsequent offenses.

Seller Information (Please print.)

Seller's or trustee's name	Seller's trust number (if applicable - **not** an SSN or FEIN)
Street address (after sale)	City State ZIP
Seller's or agent's signature	( ) Seller's daytime phone

Buyer Information (Please print.)

Buyer's or trustee's name	Buyer's trust number (if applicable - **not** an SSN or FEIN)
Street address (after sale)	City State ZIP
Buyer's or agent's signature	( ) Buyer's daytime phone

Mail tax bill to:

Name or company Street address	City	State ZIP

Preparer Information (Please print.)

Preparer's and company's name	Preparer's file number (if applicable)
Street address	City State ZIP
Preparer's signature	( ) Preparer's daytime phone

Preparer's e-mail address (if available)

Identify any required documents submitted with this form. (Mark with an "X.") ____ Extended legal description   ____Form PTAX-203-A
   ____ Itemized list of personal property   ____Form PTAX-203-B

To be completed by the Chief County Assessment Officer

1 ___ ___ ___ ___ ___ ___ ___ ___ ___ ___ ___
  County   Township   Class   Cook-Minor   Code 1   Code 2

3 Year prior to sale ___ ___ ___ ___
4 Does the sale involve a mobile home assessed as real estate? ___ Yes ___ No

2 Board of Review's final assessed value for the assessment year prior to the year of sale.
  Land   ___ , ___ ___ ___ , ___ ___ ___ , ___ ___ ___
  Buildings   ___ , ___ ___ ___ , ___ ___ ___ , ___ ___ ___
  Total   ___ , ___ ___ ___ , ___ ___ ___ , ___ ___ ___

5 Comments

Illinois Department of Revenue Use	Tab number

Page 2 of 4   PTAX-203 (R-10/10)

Instructions for Form PTAX-203, Illinois Real Estate Transfer Declaration

General Information

The information requested on this form is required by the Real Estate Transfer Tax Law (35 ILCS 200/31-1 *et seq*.). All parties involved in the transaction must answer each question completely and truthfully.

What is the purpose of this form?

County offices and the Illinois Department of Revenue use this form to collect sales data and to determine if a sale can be used in assessment ratio studies. This information is used to compute equalization factors. Equalization factors are used to help achieve a state-wide uniform valuation of properties based on their fair market value.

Must I file Form PTAX-203?

You must file either (1) Form PTAX-203 and any required documents with the deed or trust document **or** (2) an exemption notation on the original deed or trust document at the County Recorder's office within the county where the property is located. File Form PTAX-203 for all real estate transfers except those qualifying for exempt status under (a), (c), (d), (e), (f), (g), (h), (i), (j), or (l) listed below.

Which property transfers are exempt from real estate transfer tax?

The following transactions are exempt from the transfer tax under 35 ILCS 200/31-45.

(a) Deeds representing real estate transfers made before January 1, 1968, but recorded after that date and trust documents executed before January 1, 1986, but recorded after that date.

(b) Deeds to or trust documents relating to (1) property acquired by any governmental body or from any governmental body, (2) property or interests transferred between governmental bodies, or (3) property acquired by or from any corporation, society, association, foundation or institution organized and operated exclusively for charitable, religious or educational purposes. However, deeds or trust documents, other than those in which the Administrator of Veterans' Affairs of the United States is the grantee pursuant to a foreclosure proceeding, shall not be exempt from filing the declaration.

(c) Deeds or trust documents that secure debt or other obligation.

(d) Deeds or trust documents that, without additional consideration, confirm, correct, modify, or supplement a deed or trust document previously recorded.

(e) Deeds or trust documents where the actual consideration is less than $100.

(f) Tax deeds.

(g) Deeds or trust documents that release property that is security for a debt or other obligation.

(h) Deeds of partition.

(i) Deeds or trust documents made pursuant to mergers, consolidations or transfers or sales of substantially all of the assets of corporations under plans of reorganization under the Federal Internal Revenue Code (26 USC 368) or Title 11 of the Federal Bankruptcy Act.

(j) Deeds or trust documents made by a subsidiary corporation to its parent corporation for no consideration other than the cancellation or surrender of the subsidiary's stock.

(k) Deeds when there is an actual exchange of real estate and trust documents when there is an actual exchange of beneficial interests, except that money difference or money's worth paid from one to the other is not exempt from the tax. These deeds or trust documents, however, shall not be exempt from filing the declaration.

(l) Deeds issued to a holder of a mortgage, as defined in Section 15-103 (now Section 15-1207) of the Code of Civil Procedure, pursuant to a mortgage foreclosure proceeding or pursuant to a transfer in lieu of foreclosure.

(m) A deed or trust document related to the purchase of a principal residence by a participant in the program authorized by the Home Ownership Made Easy Act, except that those deeds and trust documents shall not be exempt from filing the declaration.

PTAX-203 (R-10/10)

Can criminal penalties be imposed?

Anyone who willfully falsifies or omits any required information on Form PTAX-203 is guilty of a Class B misdemeanor for the first offense and a Class A misdemeanor for subsequent offenses. Anyone who knowingly submits a false statement concerning the identity of a grantee of property in Cook County is guilty of a Class C misdemeanor for the first offense and a Class A misdemeanor for subsequent offenses. The penalties that could be imposed for each type of misdemeanor are listed below (35 ILCS 200/31-50 and 730 ILCS 5/5-8-3 and 5/5-9-1).

Misdemeanor	Prison Term	Maximum Fines
Class A	less than 1 year	$2,500
Class B	not more than 6 months	$1,500
Class C	not more than 30 days	$1,500

Line-by-line Instructions

The sellers and buyers or their agents must complete Steps 1 through 4 of this form. For transfers of a land trust, complete the form substituting the words "assignor" for "seller" and "assignee" for "buyer."

Step 1: Identify the property and sale information.

Line 1 — Write the property's street address (or 911 address, if available), city or village, zip code, and township in which the property is located.

Line 3 — Write all the parcel identifying numbers and the properties' lot sizes (*e.g.*, 80' x 100') or acreage. If only the combined lot size or acreage is available for multiple parcels, write the total on Line 3a under the "lot size or acreage" column. If transferring only a part of the parcel, write the letters "PT" before the parcel identifying number and write the lot size or acreage of the split parcel. If transferring a condominium, write the parcel identifying number and the square feet of the condominium unit. If surface rights are not being transferred, indicate the rights being transferred (*e.g.*, "minerals only"). If transferring right-of-way (ROW) property that does not have a parcel identifying number, write "ROW only." If five or more parcels are involved, use the space provided on Page 2, Step 3. The parcel identifying number is printed on the real estate tax bill and assessment notice. The chief county assessment officer can assist you with this information.

Line 4 — Write the month and year from the instrument.

Line 5 — Use an "X" to identify the type of instrument (*i.e.*, deed, trust document, or facsimile) to be recorded with this form. For a deed-in-trust, limited warranty, special warranty, trust deed, or other deed types not listed on this form, select "Other" and write the deed type. "Joint tenancy" and "tenants-in-common" identify ownership rights and **cannot** be used as a deed type.

Line 6 — Select "Yes" if the property will be used as the buyer's principal dwelling place and legal residence.

Line 7 — Select "Yes" if the property was sold using a real estate agent or advertised for sale by newspaper, trade publication, radio/electronic media, or sign.

Line 8 — Use an "X" to select **one** item under each of the column headings "Current" and "Intended." "Current" identifies the current or most recent use of the property. "Intended" identifies the intended or expected use of the property after the sale. If the property has more than one use, identify the **primary** use only.

Line 8h, Commercial building — Write the type of business (bank, hotel/motel, parking garage, gas station, theater, golf course, bowling alley, supermarket, shopping center, *etc.*).

Line 8k, Other — Choose this item only if the primary use is not listed and write the primary use of the property.

Note: For Lines 8h and 8k, if the current and intended categories are the same but the specific use will change, (*i.e.*, from bank to theater), write the **current** use on the line provided and write the **intended** use **directly below** the line provided.

Page 3 of 4

Line 9 — Use an "X" to identify any significant physical changes in the property since January 1 of the previous year. Write the date the change was completed or the property was damaged.

Line 10 — Select only the items that apply to this sale. A definition is provided below for all items marked with an asterisk.

Line 10a, Fulfillment of installment contract — The installment contract for deed is initiated in a calendar year prior to the calendar year in which the deed is recorded. Write the year the contract was initiated between the seller and buyer. Do **not** select this item if the installment contract for deed was initiated and the property was transferred within the same calendar year.

Line 10c, Transfer of less than 100 percent interest — The seller transfers a portion of the total interest in the property. Other owners will keep an interest in the property. Do **not** consider severed mineral rights when answering this question.

Line 10d, Court-ordered sale — The property's sale was ordered by a court (*e.g.*, bankruptcy, foreclosure, probate).

Line 10g, Short sale — The property was sold for less than the amount owed to the mortgage lender or mortgagor, if the mortgagor has agreed to the sale.

Line 10h, Bank REO (real estate owned) — The first sale of the property owned by a financial institution as a result of a judgment of foreclosure, transfer pursuant to a deed in lieu of foreclosure, or consent judgment occurring after the foreclosure proceeding is complete.

Line 10k, Seller/buyer is a financial institution — "Financial institution" includes a bank, savings and loan, credit union, Resolution Trust Company, and any entity with "mortgage company" or "mortgage corporation" as part of the business name.

Line 10o, Buyer is exercising an option to purchase — The sale price was predicated upon the exercise of an option to purchase at a predetermined price.

Line 10p, Trade of property (simultaneous) — Buyer trades or exchanges with the seller one or more items of real estate for part or all of the full actual consideration (sale price) on Line 11.

Line 10r, Other — Explain any special facts or circumstances involving this transaction that may have affected the sale price or sale agreement or forced the sale of the property. This includes property that is subject to an existing lease or property that is part of an IRC §1031 Exchange.

Line 10s, Homestead exemptions on most recent tax bill — Write the dollar amount for any homestead exemption reflected on the most recent annual tax bill.

Step 2:   Calculate the amount of transfer tax due.

Round Lines 11 through 18 to the next highest whole dollar.

Note: File PTAX-203-B, Illinois Real Estate Transfer Declaration Supplemental Form B, when filing instruments other than deeds, or trust documents. (Do **not** complete Step 2, of the PTAX-203 when filing the PTAX-203-B).

Line 11 — Write the full actual consideration (sale price). Full actual consideration is the amount actually paid, excluding any amount credited against the purchase price or refunded to the buyer for improvements or repairs to the property. Include the amount for other real estate transferred in a simultaneous exchange from the buyer to the seller, even if the transfer involves an even exchange. Also include the amount of outstanding mortgages to which the property remains subject at the time of the transfer.

Note: File PTAX-203-A, Illinois Real Estate Transfer Declaration Supplemental Form A, if the amount on Line 11 is over $1 million and the property's current use on Line 8 is marked "Apartment building (over 6 units)," "Office," "Retail establishment," "Commercial building," "Industrial building," or "Other."

Line 12a — Write the amount of personal property items included in the sale price on Line 11. Do **not** include the value of a beneficial interest of a land trust. Personal property items are generally listed on the "bill of sale." If you are uncertain as to whether an item is real estate or personal property, consult your attorney, tax advisor, or the chief county assessment officer.

On 8¹/₂" x 11" paper, submit an itemized list of personal property (include values) transferred from the seller to the buyer if this sale meets either of the following conditions:

- residential property — if the amount of personal property (not including the value of a mobile home) on Line 12a is greater than 5 percent of the sale price on Line 11, **or**
- non-residential property — if the amount of personal property on Line 12a is greater than 25 percent of the sale price on Line 11.

Residential personal property — Generally, "personal property" includes items that are **not** attached (built-in) to the home and that are normally removed by the seller when vacating the property. Examples include artwork, automobiles and boats, draperies, furniture, free-standing appliances (*e.g.*, refrigerators, stoves, washers and dryers, but **not** built-in appliances), lawn mowers, tractors, snow blowers, rugs (excludes wall-to-wall carpets), and window air-conditioners (excludes central air). Include the value of a mobile home as personal property on Line 12a if it meets **all** of the following conditions:

- The value of the mobile home was included on Line 11.
- The value of the mobile home was not included on the real estate tax bill.

Commercial/industrial personal property — Generally, "personal property" is any item that is **not** a permanent improvement to the land and includes, but is not limited to, intangibles such as goodwill, licenses, patents, franchises, business or enterprise value; and certain tangibles such as inventories, cash registers and shopping carts, free-standing shelving and displays, furniture, office equipment and supplies, vehicles, and machinery and equipment not assessed as real estate.

Generally, "personal property" does **not** include building components (*e.g.*, wiring and lighting, heating, air-conditioning, plumbing, fire protection); foundations, pits and other building components for specialized or heavy machinery; permanent fixtures including, but not limited to, machinery and equipment and cranes assessed as real estate, craneways, and non-portable tanks; and site improvements such as paving and fencing.

Line 14 — Write the amount of other real estate transferred from the buyer to the seller that was included in the sale price on Line 11. This value only applies to a **simultaneous** exchange between the parties involved in this transaction. Do **not** include the value of property involved in a deferred exchange under IRC §1031.

Line 15 — Write an amount **only** if the deed or trust document states that the transferred property remains subject to a mortgage at the time of the transfer.

Line 16 — Use an "X" to identify the letter of the provision for the exemption from the transfer tax (*i.e.*, (b), (k), or (m)) that applies to this transfer. See "Which property transfers are exempt from real estate transfer tax?" in these instructions.

Step 3:   Write the legal description from the deed.

Write the legal description from the deed. Use a minimum 10-point font if the legal description is typed. If the legal description will **not** fit in the space provided, submit an 8¹/₂" x 11" copy of the extended legal description from the deed with this form.

Step 4:   Complete the requested information.

Write the requested information for the seller, buyer, and preparer.

Write the addresses and daytime phone numbers where the seller and buyer can be contacted **after** the sale.

The seller and buyer (or their agents) and preparer **must** sign this form. By signing the form, the parties involved in the real estate transfer verify that

- they have examined the completed Form PTAX-203,
- the information provided on this form is true and correct, and
- they are aware of the criminal penalties of law associated with falsifying or omitting any information on this form.

Use an "X" to identify any required documents submitted with this form.

COOK COUNTY

REAL ESTATE TRANSFER DECLARATION

The following is required by the Cook County Real Property Tax Ordinance effective September 1, 1993. Any transferor of transferee who fails to file with the Recorder a real property transfer declaration as required by Section 7 of this ordinance or a supplemental transfer declaration as required by Section 10 of this ordinance or willfully falsifies the value of transferred real estate, shall be subject to a penalty equal to the amount of the applicable tax; and shall be fined an amount not to exceed $1000.00 or imprisoned for a period not to exceed six months, or both.

Except as to Exempt Transactions, the Recorder is prohibited by law from accepting any deed, assignment or other instrument of transfer for recordation unless it is accompanied by a declaration containing all of the information requested therein.

Recorder's Validation

PROPERTY IDENTIFICATION:

Address of Property _____
                          Street or Rural Route   City   Zip Code

Permanent Real Estate Index No. _____ Township _____

Date of Deed _____ Type of Deed _____

TYPE OF PROPERTY:		**INTEREST TRANSFERRED**	
☐ Single Family	☐ Commercial	☐ Fee title	☐ Controlling interest in real estate entity (ord. Sec. 2)
☐ Condo, co-op	☐ Industrial	☐ Beneficial Interest in a land trust	
☐ 4 or more units (residential)	☐ Vacant Land	☐ Lessee interest in a ground lease	☐ Other (attach description)
☐ Mixed use (commer. & resid.)	☐ Other (attach description)		

LEGAL DESCRIPTION:

Sec. _____ Twp. _____ Range _____

(Use additional sheet, if necessary)

COMPUTATION OF TAX:

Full actual consideration	$ _____
Less amount of personal property included in purchase	$ _____
Net consideration for real estate	$ _____
Less amount of mortgage to which property remains subject	$ _____
Net taxable consideration	$ _____
Amount of tax stamps ($.25 per $500 or part thereof)	$ _____

ATTESTATION OF PARTIES: We hereby declare the full actual consideration and above facts contained in this declaration to be true and correct.

Name and Address of Seller (Please Print)   Street or Rural Route   City   Zip Code

Signature: _____
                 Seller or Agent

Name and Address of Buyer (Please Print)   Street or Rural Route   City   Zip Code

Signature: _____
                 Buyer or Agent

Use space below for tax mailing address, if different from above.

EXEMPT TRANSFERS

(Check the Appropriate Box)

Exempt transfers are subject to the requirement contained in subsection 7(c) of this ordinance.

7(c)   "No transfer shall be exempt from the tax imposed by this ordinance unless the declaration describes the facts supporting the exemption and is accompanied by such supporting documentation as the Recorder may reasonably require."

☐ A.   Transfers of real property made prior to May 21, 1979 where the deed was recorded after that date or assignments of beneficial interest in real property dated prior to August 1, 1985, where the assignment was delivered on or after August 1, 1985;

☐ B.   Transfers involving real property acquired by or from any governmental body or acquired by any corporation, society, association, foundation or institution organized and operated exclusively for charitable, religious or educational purposes or acquired by any international organization not subject to local taxes under applicable law; (Copy of IRS granting tax exempt status must be attached)

☐ C.   Transfers in which the deed, assignment or other instrument of transfer secures debt or other obligations;

☐ D.   Transfers in which the deed, assignment or other instrument of transfer, without additional consideration, confirms, corrects, modifies, or supplements a deed, assignment or other instrument of transfer previously recorded or delivered;

☐ E.   Transfers in which the transfer price is less than $100.00;

☐ F.   Transfers in which the deed is a tax deed;

☐ G.   Transfers in which the deed, assignment or other instrument of transfer releases property which secures debt or other obligations;

☐ H.   Transfers in which the deed is a deed of partition; provided, however, that if a party receives a share greater than its undivided interest in the real property, then such party shall be liable for tax computed upon any consideration paid for the excess;

☐ I.   Transfers between a subsidiary corporation and its parent or between subsidiary corporations of a common parent either pursuant to a plan of merger or consolidation or pursuant to an agreement providing for the sale of substantially all of the seller's assets;

☐ J.   Transfers from a subsidiary corporation to its parent for no consideration other than the cancellation or surrender of the subsidiary's stock and transfers from a parent corporation to its subsidiary for no consideration other than the issuance or delivery to the parent of the subsidiary's stock;

☐ K.   Transfers made pursuant to a confirmed plan of reorganization as provided under section 1146 (c) of Chapter 11 of the U.S. Bankruptcy Code of 1978, as amended; Provide bankruptcy court docket number:_____;

☐ L.   Deeds representing transfers subject to the imposition of a documentary stamp tax imposed by the government of the United States, except that such deeds shall not be exempt from filing the declaration; and

☐ M.   Transfers in which the deed or other instrument of transfer is issued to the mortgagee or secured creditor pursuant to a mortgage or security interest foreclosure proceeding or sale or pursuant to a transfer in lieu of foreclosure.

CITY OF CHICAGO
DEPARTMENT OF FINANCE
REAL PROPERTY TRANSFER TAX DECLARATION
FORM - 7551
This form may also be filed on-line at *ezdecillinois.com/login*

STATUS [   ]
For office use only

ACCOUNT NUMBER

Note: this form must be filled out completely for ALL real estate transfers, including transfers for which an exemption is claimed (see Municipal Code 3-33-070). If any information is omitted, this declaration form will be deemed incomplete and you may be assessed penalties and interest. Please use black or blue ink. You must complete all pages of this form.

Section 1. General Information about Property

For use by Cook County Recorder of Deeds
County document #

Street Number   Direction

Street Name

Date

Unit/Apt #   Zip Code

PIN   PIN

PIN   PIN

PIN   PIN

☐ Check here if an exempt transfer.

☐ Check here if this is an amended declaration.   ☐ Check here if supplemental declarations will be filed in the future.
Original Declaration filed on _____ .

☐ Check here if this is a supplemental Declaration (Open Transfer). ___monthly ____annually _____ other.

Type of property (check appropriate box below)

1. ☐ Detached single family Residence/Townhome
2. ☐ Condominium or Co-op
3. ☐ Parking Space
4. ☐ Multi-unit residential building/SRO
   # of units ..

5. ☐ Mixed use (residential and commercial)
   # of residential ....
   # of commercial ....
6. ☐ Commercial: Place x in box
   ☐ Office   ☐ Shopping Center
   ☐ Retail   ☐ Hotel/Motel
   ☐ Parking Garage ☐ Bank
   ☐ Other

7. ☐ Industrial
8. ☐ Vacant Land
9. ☐ Other (you must attach a description)

Buildings with 4 or more residential units **MUST** attach to this form either (i) the original Multiple Dwelling Registration Statement or (ii) original receipt thereof, disclosing the Buyer/Transferee's registration information as required in Section 8 of this form.

Section 2. Interest Transferred (check appropriate box below)

1. ☐ Fee title
2. ☐ Beneficial interest in a land trust
3. ☐ "Lessee interest in a ground lease"

4. ☐ "Controlling interest" in a "real estate entity"
5. ☐ Interest in a real estate co-op
6. ☐ Other (you must attach a description)

7 ☐ Installment Sale

See Municipal Code 3-33-020 for definitions.

Page 1   Rev 003 022508   **755101102**

■ ACCOUNT NUMBER [_____]   REVISION NUMBER [_____]   ■

Section 3. Transfers exempt from tax (check appropriate box below)

Buyer Seller

A. ☐ ☐   Deleted

B. ☐ ☐   Transfer involving real property acquired by or from a governmental body; or acquired by a not-for-profit charitable, religious, or educational organization; or acquired by any international organization not subject to local taxes. (IRS notice granting 501(c)(3) exemption must be attached.) (NOTE: Transfers from Federal National Mortgage and Federal Home Mortgage Corporation are not exempt.)

C. ☐ ☐   Transfer in which the deed, assignment or other instrument of transfer secures debt or other obligations.

D. ☐ ☐   Transfer in which the deed, assignment or other instrument of transfer, without additional consideration, confirms, corrects, modifies, or supplements a deed, assignment, or other instrument of transfer previously recorded or delivered. Explain correction:_____

E. ☐ ☐   If claiming exemption under this section, you must check the relevant reason below and fully explain the reason. Attach additional sheet if necessary. Place x in box
☐ Transfer in which transfer price was less than $500. Was something given besides money? __ yes __ no.
   Were delinquent real property taxes paid? __ yes __ no.
☐ Transfer to trust by beneficiary (ies).
☐ Transfer to beneficiary (ies) by trust. (NOTE: if a beneficiary receives a greater share than the beneficiary's undivided share of the trust property, then the transfer is not exempt. If the beneficiary transfers any consideration to the trust or to the other beneficiaries in return of the beneficiary's excess distribution.)
☐ Gift or inheritance. What is the transferee's relationship to transferor? _____
☐ Other. Explain _____

NOTE: Transfers pursuant to divorce or separation are not exempt (See Real Property Transfer Tax Ruling #3. Exchanges of real property for real property are not exempt. The debt includes any debt or obligation canceled or discharged as part of the transfer.)

F. ☐ ☐   Transfer in which the deed is a tax deed.

G. ☐ ☐   Transfer in which the deed, assignment or other instrument of transfer releases property which secures debt or other obligations.

H. ☐ ☐   Transfer in which the deed is a deed of partition. Note: If a party receives a share greater than its undivided interest in the real property, then it must pay tax on any consideration paid for the excess.

I. ☐ ☐   Transfer between a wholly owned subsidiary corporation and its parent or between wholly owned subsidiary corporations of common parent pursuant to a plan of merger or consolidation or pursuant to an agreement providing for the sale of substantially all of the seller's assets.

J. ☐ ☐   Transfer from a wholly owned subsidiary corporation to its parent for no consideration other than the cancellation or surrender of the subsidiary's stock, or transfer from a parent corporation to its wholly owned subsidiary for no consideration other than the issuance or delivery to the parent of the subsidiary's stock.

K. ☐ ☐   Transfer made pursuant to a confirmed plan of reorganization as provided under section 1146 (c) of Chapter 11 of the U. S. Bankruptcy Code of 1978, as amended.
Provide bankruptcy court docket number: .... [ ][ ][ ][ ][ ][ ][ ][ ][ ][ ]

State of Filing/Court District   [ ][ ] / [ ][ ]

L. ☐ ☐   Transfer of the title to, or beneficial interest in, real property used primarily for commercial or industrial purposes located in a city enterprise zone. (Conversion from industrial/commercial to residential is not exempt. See Real Property Transfer Tax Ruling #2.)
Provide enterprise zone number: ....   [ ][ ]

M. ☐ ☐   Transfer in which the deed is issued to the mortgagee or secured creditor who initially filed the foreclosure proceeding or threaten to bring foreclosure proceeding (when the deed is transferred in lieu of foreclosure):
Are you the only secured creditor __ yes __ no. (Note: A deed transferred to a junior lien holder is not exempt to the extent of the amount of the lien of the senior (prior) lien holder.)
Did you acquire your secured interest in the property after the foreclosure proceedings were started? ☐yes ☐no.

N. ☐ ☐   Transfer in which the purchaser has completed the State of Illinois' Home Ownership Made Easy Program (HOME).
Date Completed __ / __ / ____

"Section 3-33-060 (O) includes an exemption for the CTA portion of tax for transferees who are age 65 years or older, who occupy purchased property as their personal dwelling for at least one year following the transfer, if the transfer price is $250,000 or less. This exemption is administered through a refund administered by the Chicago Tax Assistance Center of the city's Budget Office located at 121 N. LaSalle, City Hall, room 604. Application forms are also available online at www.cityofchicago.org/city/en/depts/fin.html"

ACCOUNT NUMBER [   ]   REVISION NUMBER [   ]

Section 4. Additional Transfer Information

1. Enter the earlier of (1) the date of delivery or (2) the date of recording of the instrument of
transfer..   [| / | / | |]

2. Does any part of the transfer price consist of consideration other than cash? If yes, attach
separate sheet with description of consideration...   Yes ☐   No ☐

3. Is any part of the transfer price contingent upon the occurrence of a future event or the
attainment of future levels of financial performance? If yes, explain. (attach additional ....
sheet if necessary)   Yes ☐   No ☐

4. Will this property be converted from it's current use? ....   Yes ☐   No ☐
If so, what type of use _____

5. If conversion will result in co-operative or condominium units, how many units are expected
to result from the conversion? ....   [| | |]

Rev 003 022506   **755101302**

ACCOUNT NUMBER [　　　　　]   REVISION NUMBER [　　　　　]

Section 5. Computation of tax stamps purchased (Transfer price must be included on line 4, even if transfer is exempt; if exempt, do not compute beyond line 4). NOTE: With the exception of line 5, you must round to the nearest whole number for the following amounts.

1. Total amount paid .... [　　　　　　　] . [0][0]

2. Fair Market Value of personal property .... [　　　　　　　] . [0][0]

3. Fair Market Value of other property (fully describe other property) .... [　　　　　　　] . [0][0]

4. Transfer price (note: transfer price includes consideration in any form. Determined
    without any deduction for mortgages). (see Sec 3-33-020(H)) (Subtract line 2 & 3 from line 1) ... [　　　　　　　] . [0][0]

5. Divide line 4 by $500.00 (note: you must round <u>up</u> to the nearest whole number)................ [　　　　　　　] . [0][0]

	A BUYER (CITY) $3.75	B SELLER (CTA) $1.50	A + B Total
6. Applicable tax stamp rate			
7. Total value of tax stamps purchased (If buyer, multiply line 5 by line 6A; If seller, multiply line 5 by line 6B............	[　　　　]	[　　　　]	[　　　　]
8. Interest (see Section 3-4-190)	[　　　　]	[　　　　]	[　　　　]
9. Penalty (see Section 3-4-200 and 3-33-110)	[　　　　]	[　　　　]	[　　　　]
10. Total tax, penalty and interest due (add line 7, 8, and 9)	[　　　　]	[　　　　]	[　　　　]

Section 6. Title Company Information

[ ] Check this box if a title company is not utilized.

Title Company Name   [　　　　　　　　　　　　　　　　]

Title Company Representative   First Name [　　　　　]   Last Name [　　　　　]

Title Company Code # (applicable only if title company resells Chicago tax stamps)   [　　　　　　]

ACCOUNT NUMBER [ ] REVISION NUMBER [ ]

Section 7. Attestation of Parties   **Seller/Transferor Statement**

Under penalty of perjury, I certify that I have examined this return and it is true, correct, and complete.

Name of Seller if individual

[ ] [ ]

Name of Seller if not individual (include trust name and number if trust)

[ ]

Mailing Address (after sale)   Daytime Phone Number

[ ] [ ]

City   State   Zip

[ ]

Signature of Seller or Seller's agent (required)   Date

[ ] [ ]

Name of Individual Signing Seller/Transferor Statement (if not the seller)

[ ] [ ]

Title

[ ]

Mailing Address   Daytime Phone Number

[ ] [ ]

City   State   Zip

[ ]

Business or Firm Name

[ ]

Buyer/Transferee Statement

Under penalty of perjury, I certify that I have examined this return and it is true, correct, and complete.

Name of Buyer if individual

[ ] [ ]

Name of Buyer if not individual (include trust name and number if trust)

[ ]

Mailing Address (after sale)   Daytime Phone Number

[ ] [ ]

ACCOUNT NUMBER [   ]   REVISION NUMBER [   ]

City   State   Zip

Signature of Buyer or Buyer's Agent (required)   Date

Name of Individual Signing Buyer/Transferee Statement (if not the buyer)

Title

Mailing Address   Daytime Phone Number

City   State   Zip

Business or Firm Name

Section 8. Department Certifications

1. **Building Registration Certificate.** A Multiple Dwelling Registration Statement issued by the Department of Buildings disclosing the Buyer/Transferee's registration information is required for buildings containing either 4 or more family units or sleeping accommodations for 10 or more persons (except if the building is a condominium or a co-op) (Municipal Code 13-10-070). The Registration Statement may be obtained from the Department of Buildings at 120 N. Racine. Check the applicable box:

   ☐ Registration certificate submitted   ☐ Registration requirement is not applicable

2. **Zoning Compliance Certificate.** A certificate of zoning compliance is required for residential property zoned for, or occupied by, buildings having five or fewer units (except if the building is a condominium, a co-op, or a newly constructed dwelling sold to the initial occupant (Municipal Code 3-33-045)). The certificate may be obtained from the Department of Housing and Economic Development in room 905 of City Hall. Check the applicable box:

   ☐ Zoning certificate submitted   ☐ Zoning certificate is not required

3. **Water and Sewer Charge Full Payment Certification** (available at 333 South State Street, Room 330), is required for **ALL** real property transfers.

The Department of Finance certifies that all water and sewer charges rendered up to

are paid in full for property located at

Account # [   ]   Application # [   ]

Certified by [   ]   Date [   ]

ACCOUNT NUMBER [   ]   REVISION NUMBER [   ]

Section 9. Preparer Information (only preparer's name is required if other information about preparer is disclosed in Section 7 above.)

Name of Preparer

[ ][ ][ ][ ][ ][ ][ ] [ ] [ ][ ][ ][ ][ ][ ][ ][ ][ ][ ][ ][ ][ ][ ][ ][ ]

Business or Firm Name

[ ]

Mailing Address   Daytime Phone Number

[ ][ ][ ][ ][ ][ ][ ][ ][ ][ ][ ][ ][ ][ ][ ][ ][ ][ ] [ ][ ][ ]+[ ][ ][ ]+[ ][ ][ ][ ]

City   State Zip Code   Date

[ ][ ][ ][ ][ ][ ][ ][ ][ ][ ][ ][ ][ ][ ] [ ][ ] [ ][ ][ ][ ][ ] [ ][ ]+[ ][ ]+[ ][ ][ ]

Section 10. Where to File This Form and Purchase Transfer Stamps

1. If the deed or other instrument of transfer is recorded, then file this form with the Cook County Recorder of Deeds, County Building, 118 North Clark Street, Room 120, Chicago, IL 60602.

2. If the deed or other instrument of transfer is not recorded, then file this form with the Chicago Department of Finance, 121 North LaSalle Street, Room 107, Chicago, IL 60602.

3. Real Property Transfer Stamps may be purchased at the Chicago Department of Finance, 121 North LaSalle Street, Room 107, Chicago, IL 60602.

4. For additional information call 312-747-IRIS(4747) and for TTY 312-742-1974)

Place water validation stamp below line

Effective date: 04/01/2008

For DOF Use Only   Postmark Date   Receipt Number

CLOSING STATEMENT

Sellers: Buyer:
Property Address:

Seller's Attorney: Buyer's Attorney:

Closing Date:
File:
Closing Location:

<u>Purchase Price</u>

1.   Purchase Price $

Seller's Expenses

2.   Real Estate Commission $
3.   Loan Payoff $
      Second Loan Payoff $
4.   Earnest Money $
5.   Attorney's Fees $
6.   Real Estate Tax Credit
      2014 $
      2014 (Second Install) $
      2015 $
7.   Association Dues $
8.   Association/Assessment Letter $
9.   Special Assessment $
10.   State Transfer Stamp $
11.   County Transfer Stamp $
12.   City Transfer Stamp $
13.   Title Insurance $
14.   Survey $
15.   Credit $

                    Total Expenses $

                    <u>Cash to Seller</u>
                                        $

OMB Approval No. 2502-0265

 A. **Settlement Statement (HUD-1)**

B. Type of Loan

1. ☐ FHA 2. ☐ RHS 3. ☐ Conv. Unins.	6. File Number:	7. Loan Number:	8. Mortgage Insurance Case Number:
4. ☐ VA 5. ☐ Conv. Ins.			

C. Note: This form is furnished to give you a statement of actual settlement costs. Amounts paid to and by the settlement agent are shown. Items marked "(p.o.c.)" were paid outside the closing; they are shown here for informational purposes and are not included in the totals.

D. Name & Address of Borrower:	E. Name & Address of Seller:	F. Name & Address of Lender:

G. Property Location:	H. Settlement Agent:	I. Settlement Date:
	Place of Settlement:	

J. Summary of Borrower's Transaction		**K. Summary of Seller's Transaction**	
100. Gross Amount Due from Borrower		**400. Gross Amount Due to Seller**	
101. Contract sales price		401. Contract sales price	
102. Personal property		402. Personal property	
103. Settlement charges to borrower (line 1400)		403.	
104.		404.	
105.		405.	
Adjustment for items paid by seller in advance		Adjustment for items paid by seller in advance	
106. City/town taxes to		406. City/town taxes to	
107. County taxes to		407. County taxes to	
108. Assessments to		408. Assessments to	
109.		409.	
110.		410.	
111.		411.	
112.		412.	
120. Gross Amount Due from Borrower		**420. Gross Amount Due to Seller**	
200. Amount Paid by or in Behalf of Borrower		**500. Reductions In Amount Due to seller**	
201. Deposit or earnest money		501. Excess deposit (see instructions)	
202. Principal amount of new loan(s)		502. Settlement charges to seller (line 1400)	
203. Existing loan(s) taken subject to		503. Existing loan(s) taken subject to	
204.		504. Payoff of first mortgage loan	
205.		505. Payoff of second mortgage loan	
206.		506.	
207.		507.	
208.		508.	
209.		509.	
Adjustments for items unpaid by seller		Adjustments for items unpaid by seller	
210. City/town taxes to		510. City/town taxes to	
211. County taxes to		511. County taxes to	
212. Assessments to		512. Assessments to	
213.		513.	
214.		514.	
215.		515.	
216.		516.	
217.		517.	
218.		518.	
219.		519.	
220. Total Paid by/for Borrower		**520. Total Reduction Amount Due Seller**	
300. Cash at Settlement from/to Borrower		**600. Cash at Settlement to/from Seller**	
301. Gross amount due from borrower (line 120)		601. Gross amount due to seller (line 420)	
302. Less amounts paid by/for borrower (line 220)	( )	602. Less reductions in amounts due seller (line 520)	( )
303. Cash ☐ From ☐ To Borrower		**603. Cash** ☐ To ☐ From Seller	

The Public Reporting Burden for this collection of information is estimated at 35 minutes per response for collecting, reviewing, and reporting the data. This agency may not collect this information, and you are not required to complete this form, unless it displays a currently valid OMB control number. No confidentiality is assured; this disclosure is mandatory. This is designed to provide the parties to a RESPA covered transaction with information during the settlement process.

L. Settlement Charges

	Paid From Borrower's Funds at Settlement	Paid From Seller's Funds at Settlement
700. Total Real Estate Broker Fees		
Division of commission (line 700) as follows :		
701. $ to		
702. $ to		
703. Commission paid at settlement		
704.		
800. Items Payable in Connection with Loan		
801. Our origination charge $ (from GFE #1)		
802. Your credit or charge (points) for the specific interest rate chosen $ (from GFE #2)		
803. Your adjusted origination charges (from GFE #A)		
804. Appraisal fee to (from GFE #3)		
805. Credit report to (from GFE #3)		
806. Tax service to (from GFE #3)		
807. Flood certification to (from GFE #3)		
808.		
809.		
810.		
811.		
900. Items Required by Lender to be Paid in Advance		
901. Daily interest charges from to @ $ /day (from GFE #10)		
902. Mortgage insurance premium for months to (from GFE #3)		
903. Homeowner's insurance for years to (from GFE #11)		
904.		
1000. Reserves Deposited with Lender		
1001. Initial deposit for your escrow account (from GFE #9)		
1002. Homeowner's insurance months @ $ per month $		
1003. Mortgage insurance months @ $ per month $		
1004. Property Taxes months @ $ per month $		
1005. months @ $ per month $		
1006. months @ $ per month $		
1007. Aggregate Adjustment -$		
1100. Title Charges		
1101. Title services and lender's title insurance (from GFE #4)		
1102. Settlement or closing fee $		
1103. Owner's title insurance (from GFE #5)		
1104. Lender's title insurance $		
1105. Lender's title policy limit $		
1106. Owner's title policy limit $		
1107. Agent's portion of the total title insurance premium to $		
1108. Underwriter's portion of the total title insurance premium to $		
1109.		
1110.		
1111.		
1200. Government Recording and Transfer Charges		
1201. Government recording charges (from GFE #7)		
1202. Deed $ Mortgage $ Release $		
1203. Transfer taxes (from GFE #8)		
1204. City/County tax/stamps Deed $ Mortgage $		
1205. State tax/stamps Deed $ Mortgage $		
1206.		
1300. Additional Settlement Charges		
1301. Required services that you can shop for (from GFE #6)		
1302. $		
1303. $		
1304.		
1305.		
1400. Total Settlement Charges (enter on lines 103, Section J and 502, Section K)		

Comparison of Good Faith Estimate (GFE) and HUD-1 Charrges		Good Faith Estimate	HUD-1
Charges That Cannot Increase	**HUD-1 Line Number**		
Our origination charge	# 801		
Your credit or charge (points) for the specific interest rate chosen	# 802		
Your adjusted origination charges	# 803		
Transfer taxes	# 1203		

Charges That In Total Cannot Increase More Than 10%		Good Faith Estimate	HUD-1
Government recording charges	# 1201		
	#		
	#		
	#		
	#		
	#		
	#		
	#		
	Total		
	Increase between GFE and HUD-1 Charges	$ or	%

Charges That Can Change		Good Faith Estimate	HUD-1
Initial deposit for your escrow account	# 1001		
Daily interest charges $ /day	# 901		
Homeowner's insurance	# 903		
	#		
	#		
	#		

Loan Terms

Your initial loan amount is	$
Your loan term is	years
Your initial interest rate is	%
Your initial monthly amount owed for principal, interest, and any mortgage insurance is	$ includes ☐ Principal ☐ Interest ☐ Mortgage Insurance
Can your interest rate rise?	☐ No ☐ Yes, it can rise to a maximum of %. The first change will be on and can change again every after . Every change date, your interest rate can increase or decrease by %. Over the life of the loan, your interest rate is guaranteed to never be **lower** than % or **higher** than %.
Even if you make payments on time, can your loan balance rise?	☐ No ☐ Yes, it can rise to a maximum of $
Even if you make payments on time, can your monthly amount owed for principal, interest, and mortgage insurance rise?	☐ No ☐ Yes, the first increase can be on and the monthly amount owed can rise to $. The maximum it can ever rise to is $
Does your loan have a prepayment penalty?	☐ No ☐ Yes, your maximum prepayment penalty is $
Does your loan have a balloon payment?	☐ No ☐ Yes, you have a balloon payment of $ due in years on .
Total monthly amount owed including escrow account payments	☐ You do not have a monthly escrow payment for items, such as property taxes and homeowner's insurance. You must pay these items directly yourself. ☐ You have an additional monthly escrow payment of $ that results in a total initial monthly amount owed of $. This includes principal, interest, any mortgage insurance and any items checked below: ☐ Property taxes ☐ Homeowner's insurance ☐ Flood insurance ☐ ☐

Note: If you have any questions about the Settlement Charges and Loan Terms listed on this form, please contact your lender.

Index